REFERENCE GRAMMAR OF THE
⁂ GERMAN LANGUAGE

THE SCRIBNER GERMAN SERIES

General Editor, Harold von Hofe
UNIVERSITY OF SOUTHERN CALIFORNIA

American Edition by **Herbert Lederer**

UNIVERSITY OF CONNECTICUT

NEW YORK

REFERENCE
GRAMMAR
OF THE
German
LANGUAGE

Based on

GRAMMATIK DER DEUTSCHEN SPRACHE

by **Dora Schulz** GOETHE INSTITUTE, MUNICH

and **Heinz Griesbach** BAD REICHENHALL

CHARLES SCRIBNER'S SONS

To the Students

of my course in Advanced German Grammar
and Composition at Queens College, who,
although they did not know it, acted as
guinea pigs during the formulations of
many concepts contained in this book.

H.L.

❧ Preface to the German Edition

This grammar of the German language is a reference source and a workbook for Germans and for those who possess a fundamental knowledge of German. It presents a survey of the various linguistic forms which exist in the language today, explains the use of these forms, and then leads into German syntax in a modern approach. In its structure and its systematic sequence this book, for methodological reasons, follows the traditional manner of presentation, but also goes beyond it to present more recent methods of linguistic analysis of the German language. Thus the reader obtains a deeper insight into the nature of the language than was possible by the methods of presentation formerly used for foreign language teaching.

The source material for the many selections of linguistic forms and expressions was taken from cultivated colloquial usage which has also found its way into modern German literature. Only material of general validity was used; works of those modern authors whose language is either highly individualistic in style and coinage or contains regionalisms and dialect forms were not used as examples. In the case of many linguistic phenomena which as yet have not been fully analyzed, the authors had to rely on their own intuitive feeling for the language. The scope of the subject matter did not make it possible to treat and clarify in complete detail all the many questions which arose from the new functional and structural approach to German.

The present grammar arose from practical teaching experience and from material which the authors have been collecting for years. Many valuable hints and suggestions, however, were also gained from the following works: Hans Glinz, *Die innere Form des Deutschen* (BERN, 1952); Hans Glinz, *Der deutsche Satz* (DÜSSELDORF, 1957); Johannes Erben, *Abriß der deutschen Grammatik* (BERLIN, 1959) and Duden, *Grammatik der deutschen Gegenwartssprache* (MANNHEIM, 1959).

BAD REICHENHALL and MUNICH, July 1960   H.G.
D.S.

⤳ Preface to the American Edition

The *Grammatik der deutschen Sprache* by Dora Schulz and Heinz Griesbach has become a widely known, highly respected, and immensely valuable reference tool in the analysis, understanding, and teaching of contemporary German. The present edition represents a revision and adaptation of that book from an American perspective, stressing the parallels and contrasts between English and German. While adhering to the basic structure and format of the original, it is nevertheless far more than a translation: there have been many changes in terminology, manner, and sequence of presentation, and a great deal of original material has been added in order to make this text more useful for American undergraduate students majoring in German, graduate students, German teachers, scholars, and writers.

Much that is obvious to a native speaker of German needed elaboration from an English point of view; on the other hand, some material which would strike English-speaking readers as self-evident was omitted or shortened. Many illustrative examples had to be changed, others added. Although the paragraph-numbering pattern of the original edition was maintained wherever possible, many changes, rearrangements, and additions were unavoidable.

Whole sections, such as the treatment of adverbs, limiting and descriptive adjectives, or that of intensifiers, were rewritten in the light of American linguistic research on the subject. Other new material includes a discussion of interjections, a presentation of primary and secondary objects, a functional analysis of conditional and subjunctive forms, a review of extended modifier

ix

constructions, and other topics. In addition, there are various appendices, a comprehensive English-German, German-English glossary of grammatical terms, and a full index, combining vocabulary and topical references in a single alphabetical listing. This edition thus represents the first complete analysis of the German language in English since Curme's *Grammar of the German Language* (New York, 1922; 3rd ed. 1952), and the first one using the methods and concepts of modern descriptive linguistics.

Among the many standard works consulted, the following should be especially mentioned, in addition to the ones listed in the German preface:

Otto Behagel, *Die deutsche Sprache* (HALLE, 1953).
Hans Brinkmann, *Die deutsche Sprache: Gestalt und Leistung* (DÜSSELDORF, 1962).
Duden, *Hauptschwierigkeiten der deutschen Sprache* (MANNHEIM, 1965).
————, *Stilwörterbuch der deutschen Sprache* (MANNHEIM, 1962).
Herbert L. Kufner, *The Grammatical Structures of English and German* (CHICAGO, 1962).
William G. Moulton, *A Linguistic Guide to Language Learning* (NEW YORK, 1966).
————, *The Sounds of English and German* (CHICAGO, 1962).
Theodor Siebs, *Deutsche Hochsprache* (18th ed., BERLIN, 1961).
Gerhard Wahrig, *Das große deutsche Wörterbuch* (GÜTERSLOH, 1967).
Leo Weisgerber, *Vom Weltbild der deutschen Sprache* (2 vols., DÜSSELDORF, 1953/4).

I wish to express my appreciation for the encouragement and guidance received by the staff of Charles Scribner's Sons; to the General Editor of the Scribner German Series, Professor Harold von Hofe, for his invaluable advice and counsel; to the Max Hueber Verlag in Munich — Mr. Ernst Hueber himself, the authors of the original German edition, and the general manager Dr. Roland Schäpers — for their cooperation, helpfulness, and many corrections; and last, but by no means least, to my wife Eva for her patient understanding, her insights, her help in the formulation of many passages, and for her general assistance in all aspects of manuscript preparations.

FLUSHING, N.Y.   *Herbert Lederer*
September 1968

☙ Table of Contents

C. THE NOUN

D. PRONOUNS AND PRONOMINAL ADJECTIVES

E. ADJECTIVES AND ADVERBS

REFERENCE GRAMMAR OF THE
✣ ✣ ✣ ✣ GERMAN LANGUAGE

⚡ Introduction

I. Principles of Organization

The logical sequence by which this book proceeds runs from the letter to the
sound, from there to the syllable, further to the word, the phrase, the clause,
and the sentence, and finally to the connected utterance. Each chapter in the
text is identified by a letter of the alphabet at the head of the chapter (A–K),
which also precedes each paragraph number. Each new grammatical concept
is contained in a paragraph, identified by the chapter letter and by an arabic
number, e.g. G 345. Cross references and references in the index use these
paragraph numbers. Some paragraphs are subdivided into decimal units,
e.g. E 802.1. Numbers run consecutively within a given contextual unit.
When a new subject matter is introduced, a new numbering sequence begins.
Minor subdivisions may be indicated by the omission of one or two numbers;
larger ones are grouped in units of fives, tens, and hundreds.

Within each chapter, the subject matter is presented in a logical and
methodical topical sequence, to the extent that this is possible in a systematic
grammar. Where reference to as yet unexplained material is inevitable, a
cross-reference number indicates the paragraph where this subject will be more
fully explained.

The reader is advised to read a chapter over quickly at first, in order to
gain a general orientation, before he delves more deeply into a specific point
of grammar.

Almost every chapter begins with an introduction, which is intended to

1

present a general survey. Chapter A deals with sounds and word components. In the treatment of the various parts of speech, morphological problems are discussed first, in order to present the various forms of the different parts of speech and review special inflectional problems. Following the analysis of forms, there are detailed discussions and rules concerning the use of the part of speech involved, which often lead into questions of syntax and style. The sequence within the treatment of parts of speech is guided by the extent of inflectional forms. Here the verb occupies the first position (Chapter B), since it exhibits the greatest variety of forms and also plays the most important role in the sentence. It is followed by the noun (Chapter C), which indicates the beings, things, or concepts the statement deals with. Next, Chapter D deals with pronouns and pronominal (limiting) adjectives which can replace nouns in a sentence and often accompany them. Chapter D also contains a brief discussion on the use of cases. A chapter on descriptive adjectives (Chapter E) concludes the treatment of inflected parts of speech. These are followed by uninflected words, first the adverbs (also Chapter E), then the prepositions (Chapter F) and conjunctions (Chapter G), both of which perform purely functional tasks within the sentence. Chapter G concludes with a survey of interjections.

After the parts of speech, the structure of the German sentence is investigated in Chapter H. After a discussion of types and forms of sentences, especially the concept of the sentence field, there follows an analysis of the parts of the sentence, the sentence units (subject, object, predicate complements, predicate modifiers). The investigation of the position of sentence units leads into a treatment of various types of clauses and questions of style. Subsequently, the inner form of sentence units and their parts is investigated in Chapter J. Finally, in Chapter K, the reader will find some remarks concerning German sentence intonation in isolation and in connected utterances.

The following practical suggestions are recommended to the user of this book: In order to understand the characteristic essence and peculiarity of the German language, it is first necessary to gain an overall view of the structure of the German sentence. A valuable aid for this comprehension will be found in the grammatical summary beginning on page 4 of this introduction. When looking up a particular problem (the extensive index should facilitate this task), it is recommended to check the cross-references indicated in the various sections, so that the overall perspective is maintained. A further task for the user would then be to analyze textual samples with reference to sentence structure and style. If possible, one should not begin with literary selections for this purpose, since such texts often contain personal idiosyncrasies of the author which one can only recognize and appreciate after he has mastered the basic structure of the language, from which literary texts may sometimes deviate. In the investigation of the structure of a sentence, it is best to proceed in the sequence indicated by the following questions:

1. What are the parts of the predicate? Where are they located? How is the predicate formed?
2. What sentence units does the sentence contain? What sentence units are replaced by pronouns, which ones by dependent clauses, infinitive clauses, or participial clauses? What is the sequence of the sentence units within the sentence field?
3. How does the sentence fit into the total linguistic context? Which sentence unit occupies the prefield? Does the sentence unit in the prefield introduce a new idea, or does it represent a connection to what has previously been stated?
4. How are the sentence units composed (attributes, attributive clauses)?
5. What sentence units do the dependent clauses and attributive clauses contain?

At the end of such an investigation, the reader may wish to draw up a schematic sentence diagram, such as illustrated on pages 599–602. By means of such a diagram, it is possible to obtain a clear concept of the forms of the German sentence.

The basic texts which introduce the student into the approach to language which is used in this grammar are, for the beginner, *Basic German* (in English) and (in German) *Deutsche Sprachlehre für Amerikaner* (American edition) or *Deutsche Sprachlehre für Ausländer, Grundstufe I* (German edition); at the intermediate level, *Deutsche Sprachlehre für Ausländer, Grundstufe II*, and for a more advanced student, *Moderner deutscher Sprachgebrauch, Mittelstufe*. *Basic German* is a general introduction for the English-speaking student. The *Grundstufe* texts, in the progression of presentation, follow German morphology and thus lay the foundation for German sentence structure. The *Mittelstufe* text analyzes the syntax of the German sentence in connection with linguistic content and its manners of expression. Furthermore, it deepens and broadens the understanding of, and the ability to apply, the various German word forms.

In the presentation of grammar in the present book, the traditional and internationally used Latin grammatical terms were used wherever possible, even though modern linguistic concepts of analyzing the structure of present-day German underlie the basic method of presentation. This terminology was chosen, since these terms are presumed to be familiar to the reader from his previous study of English, German, and other foreign languages. Since the learning and the mastery of a foreign language depends to a large extent on conscious or unconscious comparisons between the target language and one's native tongue, this task is made easier if identical terms are used to designate and describe identical or similar phenomena. There seemed little point in forcing the student to learn German grammatical terminology. (These terms are listed in the glossary, however.)

3

A certain caution must be observed in the use of the traditional Latin designations, since they must be understood to apply *only* to the grammatical forms and functions to which they specifically refer in this text. To use them in the specific sense applicable to other languages would often be misleading, since this may not apply to the German language at all, or not in the same way. Exact definitions and explanations of the specific meaning in which these grammatical terms are being used within the context of this book are to be found in the glossary on page 655. This glossary also contains the German equivalents for these terms.

In many instances, however, the traditional labels were found to be inadequate since modern linguistic research has discovered (or in some cases created) new grammatical categories or new ways of approaching old problems. Where it was considered necessary, the terminology of descriptive and structural linguistics as applied to the analysis and teaching of foreign languages has been used. Some terms traditionally applied to German grammatical concepts have been preserved, even where they are not completely satisfactory from a strictly descriptive viewpoint, if their use nevertheless fulfilled a need and a purpose (e.g. weak and strong verbs); others (e.g. weak, strong, and mixed adjective endings) have been abandoned if they served no useful function and have been replaced by an approach which facilitates understanding of the actual linguistic phenomenon involved (in the example above, primary and secondary endings). In the process, it has at times been necessary to coin new descriptive terms, dictated by a new method of analyzing and solving a problem, or by the fact that comparable phenomena do not occur in English. Most of these, it is hoped, should be self-explanatory within the context in which they are used and from the examples which were chosen to illustrate their application. Again, they are all defined in the appendix.

In addition, traditional sequences in the presentation of a given topic and especially in the construction of paradigms have often been discarded in line with current linguistic practices. Again, it should be emphasized that these are not changes for the sake of changes, but have only been undertaken in order to facilitate learning. Thus, the gender sequence — masculine, neuter, feminine — and the case sequence — nominative, accusative, dative, genitive — have been adopted, since these sequences make possible the construction of tables which give a far clearer picture of internal similarities and parallels.

II. Grammatical Summary

1. Every linguistic utterance is an attempt to recreate reality. To be sure, reality cannot be imitated or described in its entirety. Each individual utterance, however, has a linguistic context which corresponds to a certain con-

figuration of elements within reality. Such configurations contain several recognizable situational components simultaneously. It is the task of a speaker or writer to define this reality by making a description of the situational components comprehensible to the reader or listener. The general inadequacy of language for this purpose represents a tremendous difficulty, not only in terms of vocabulary but also (and even predominantly) in terms of grammatical structure. It is not enough to indicate individual items and details of a situation by naming them — they have to be brought into a meaningful relationship to one another. The naive assumption, however, that the grammatical relationship of the various words in a sentence corresponds directly to the relationships exhibited by the situation in reality is simply not supported by facts.

The basic problem which the language must solve by means of grammar results from the fact that in reality many situational components coexist simultaneously, whereas their linguistic description by means of words must necessarily be performed by means of a consecutive arrangement (in contrast, for example, to a picture which is capable of presenting a certain aspect of reality simultaneously in its entirety). From the continuous and consecutive description of individual aspects of reality, made up partly of content components which describe a specific detail and partly of functional components which indicate the relationship between these details, the reader or listener must reconstitute the image of reality in its proper context.

He is capable of doing so, because he is by linguistic habit accustomed to a certain sequential pattern in which he expects to receive bits and pieces of information, in order to rearrange them mentally into the desired total picture. Any marked deviation from the traditional sequence to which he is used would tend to confuse him and thus to render the original statement incomprehensible.

It must be borne in mind, however, that the principles of sequence which any language uses to accomplish this purpose are strictly arbitrary and have validity for this particular language only. The most important task confronting the student of a foreign language, therefore, is to familiarize himself with and to accept the sequential organization, i.e. the principles of syntax, which govern this language, and by means of which it expresses its view of reality [→ Chapter H].

2. According to the function of the linguistic utterance we distinguish between
   a. the statement: it describes, reports, or explains an aspect of a situation.
   b. the question: it inquires after a certain aspect of a situation and requests a statement in reply.
   c. the command: it requests a certain action and thus aims to change a certain aspect of the situation.
   d. the exclamation: it constitutes a spontaneous emotional reaction to a certain aspect of the situation.

5

In their structural form, question, command, and exclamation largely coincide with the statement.

3. A statement is made in the form of an utterance, if we translate its content into the structural concepts of language. An utterance is thus the grammatical form in which the content of a statement is expressed.

CONTENT:	GRAMMATICAL FORM:
Statement	Utterance

4. If the content of a statement is divided into its constituent parts, we arrive at various aspects of the situation (cf. 1). The grammatical form in which a situation is expressed is called a sentence. A sentence is part of an utterance and describes a given situation.

CONTENT:	GRAMMATICAL FORM:
Situation	Sentence

5. A situation is composed of
   a. an event or a state of being, and
   b. agents, i.e. beings, things, or concepts which participate in the event or state of being.
No situation can be described without the constituent parts a and b.
   An event (action or process) or a state of being is described in the sentence by the predicate, either alone or with a predicate complement. Agents appear in the sentence in the functions of subject and object.

CONTENT:	GRAMMATICAL FUNCTION:
Event State of Being	Predicate with or without Complement
Agents	Subject Objects

6. A situation can be further characterized by a closer description of the

6

circumstances under which it takes place. These circumstances describe place, time, manner, reason, etc. They appear in the sentence as modifiers.

CONTENT:	GRAMMATICAL FUNCTION:
Circumstances	Modifiers

7. The description of the event or the state of being forms the sentence core. Agents and circumstances are added to the sentence core as sentence units. Such sentence units, if they consist of more than one word, are made up of a unit core and one or more attributes. The function of the attributes is to describe and identify the unit core, which by itself fulfills the function of the sentence unit.

CONTENT:	GRAMMATICAL FUNCTION:
Conceptual Unit	Sentence Unit

8. If within a sentence an entire situation is used as a sentence unit, then this sentence unit is given the form of a dependent or subordinate clause.

CONTENT:	GRAMMATICAL FUNCTION:	FORM:
Situation	Sentence Unit	Dependent Clause

9. If within a sentence unit, an entire situation is used to describe or characterize the unit core, the attribute which contains this situation is also given the form of a dependent clause. Such dependent clauses are called attributive clauses. The most frequent form of an attributive clause is a relative clause.

CONTENT:	GRAMMATICAL FUNCTION:	FORM:
Situation	Attribute	Attributive Clause

10. Summary:

Content: Situation (Event or State of Being + Agents) + Circumstances

Form and Function: Basic Sentence Core (Predicate with or without Complements + Subject and Objects) + Predicate Modifiers

Conceptual Unit: Sentence Unit (Unit Core + Attributes)[1]

FUNCTION INDICATORS

11. The various functions of sentence units within a sentence structure can be identified by means of certain indicators:

    a. morphological indicators, i.e. inflectional changes

    b. syntactic indicators, i.e. the position in the sentence.

Missing declensional forms are replaced by prepositions (for sentence units and attributes) or by conjunctions (for dependent clauses and attributes).

FUNCTION	INDICATOR
Subject	Nominative, Conjunction
Object	Accusative, Dative, Genitive, Preposition, Conjunction
Predicate Complement	Nominative, Accusative, Genitive, Preposition, Conjunction
Modifier	Accusative, Dative, Genitive, Preposition, Conjunction
Attribute	All Declensional Forms, Prepositions, Conjunctions, Relative Pronouns, Relative Adverbs

PARTS of SPEECH

12. As sentences are the structural components of an utterance and sentence units the structural components of a sentence, so words are the structural components of a sentence unit. They thus form the smallest independent conceptual unit of a language. (Components below the level of the word, i.e. syllable and sound, do not have independent meanings of their own.) The parts of speech existing in German are classified according to the typical meaning or conceptual content to which they refer, and according to their ability for inflection. Thus, we distinguish the following categories:

---

[1] A sentence unit may be a single word or a phrase.

PART OF SPEECH	REFERENTIAL CONTENT	FUNCTION	FORM
Verb	Event (Action or Process) or State of Being	Predicate	Personal forms Tense forms Past participle Infinitive
		Subject and Object	Infinitive Present participle Past participle
		Modifier	Present participle Past participle
		Predicate complement	Infinitive Present participle Past participle
		Attribute	Present participle Past participle
Noun	Beings, Things, Places, Concepts	Subject and Object Predicate complement Attribute	Singular and Plural, Case forms
Pronoun	Beings, Things, Places, Concepts	Subject and Object Predicate complement Attribute	Singular and Plural, Case forms
Adjective	Quantity or Quality	Subject and Object Modifier Predicate complement Attribute	Declensional forms
Adverb	Quantity or Quality, Time or Place, Subjective attitude	Modifier Predicate complement Attribute	No inflectional forms

9

Prepositions and conjunctions have no referential content. They are merely function indicators, and have no inflectional forms, although they influence the inflection of words to which they refer. Articles do not form a separate part of speech, but may occur either as pronouns or as limiting adjectives, serving as functional indicators for the nouns which they modify. Interjections are not properly speaking parts of speech, since they do not perform any function within the sentence structure. They are, in effect, miniature sentences of their own, expressing a reaction toward an aspect of reality.

The ATTITUDE of the SPEAKER toward his utterance

13. If we investigate the types of linguistic utterances, we can differentiate the following two categories, which can be recognized by the sentence melody and by the selection of linguistic devices.

a. *The objective description of a situation.* In an objective description, the speaker does not show any personal attitude towards the situation. He merely reports the facts and avoids any judgments.

The speaker describes the action or the condition of the subject, or the behavior or relationship of the subject with respect to the objects. Furthermore, he may describe the relationships among the objects, or the relationship of the subject and/or the objects with other persons, things, or concepts mentioned in the sentence. All sentence units or parts of sentence units used in such a sentence can be inquired after by means of informational questions (who?, what?, where?, when?, how?, why?, etc.).

b. *The subjective description of a situation.* Here the speaker does not limit himself to a simple description or explanation of a situation, but he also explicitly or implicitly states his own relationship with, attitude toward, or opinion of that which he describes. For this purpose, he has various grammatical devices at his disposal: these are the future tense [B 564], the future perfect tense [B 582–4], modal verbs [B 630 ff.], the subjunctive [B 700 ff.], particles [H 600 ff.], and attributes of intensification [J 180 ff.]. None of the sentence units or parts of sentence units used for a subjective description can be inquired after by means of informational questions.

A

❧ Letter — Sound — Syllable — Word

LETTERS OF THE ALPHABET

The German alphabet has 26 letters. The table below identifies these letters by their German names: A 001

a	*ah*	j	*jot* or *jeh* [1]	s	*ess*
b	*beh*	k	*kah*	t	*teh*
c	*tseh*	l	*ell*	u	*uh*
d	*deh*	m	*emm*	v	*fau*
e	*eh*	n	*enn*	w	*weh*
f	*eff*	o	*oh*	x	*iks*
g	*geh*	p	*peh*	y	*üppsilon*
h	*hah*	q	*kuh* or *kweh* [1]	z	*tsett*
i	*ih*	r	*err*		

[1] Primarily in Austria.

A 002   Six of these letters designate vowels:

a   e   i   o   u   y

The others designate consonants.[1]

A 003   The three vowels **a**, **o**, and **u** may be modified by a so-called UMLAUT (sound modification) into the vowels **ä**, **ö**, and **ü**. These symbols were originally composites of **a**, **o**, and **u** with **e**.[2] In Gothic script,[3] the **e** was written above the vowels. The two dashes or dots of the *Umlaut* symbols are derived from this letter **e**.

A 005   The symbol **ß** (*ess-tset* or *scharfes ess*) originated from the combination of **s** and **z** in Gothic script.[3] [→ A 040.5]

A 006   Most consonants can be doubled, except for **c**, **h**, **j**, **q**, **v**, and **x**. In German words, **kk** becomes **ck**, but reverts to **k-k** when the syllables are separated; **zz** in German words becomes **tz**, which is maintained even in syllabication [→ A 060.2]:

> *Stock, backen, meckern (mek-kern)* — but *Mokka, Akkusativ*
> *Hitze, Schutz, Katze (Kat-ze)* — but *Bajazzo, Skizze*

SOUNDS

A 020   Letters are written symbols; they represent certain sounds. Most letters, such as **j**, **m**, **n**, **k**, **l**, **r**, **t**, etc., are symbols designating ONE PARTICULAR SOUND. The letters **x** and **z** represent SOUND COMBINATIONS: $x = ks$, $z = ts$; the letters **qu** represent the German sound combination kw.

A 021   Some sounds are represented by a SET OF LETTERS: **sch**, **ch**, **ng**.[4]

A 022   Some letters or sets of letters may represent VARIOUS SOUNDS:[5]

> **c** = *z: Celsius*   or = *k: Café*   or = ***tsch**: Cello*
> **ch** = *ç: Becher*   or = *χ: Buch*   or = *k: Christ*   or = ***sch**: Chef*
> **g** = *g: gut*   or = *ʒ: Genie*
> **t** = *t: Tür*   or = *z: Nation*
> **v** = *f: vier*   or = *w: November*

---

[1] The letter **j**, corresponding to the English semi-vowel y, is considered a consonant in German. [→ A 040.8]

[2] In proper names, the spelling **ae**, **oe**, and **ue** sometimes survives: *Goethe, Mueller*.

[3] See Appendix.

[4] The letters **ng** represent a single sound in German, that of the English word *singer*, never two separate sounds as in the English word *finger*.

[5] See also allophonic variations of **b**, **d**, **g**, and **s**: A 040.1–040.3.

12

Different letters or sets of letters may also represent IDENTICAL SOUNDS: A 023

> *ph* = *f* = *v: Philosoph, fünf, viel*
> *chs* = *x* = *ks: Achse, Hexe, Knicks*
> *ä* = *e: älter, Eltern*
> *ei* = *ai* = *ey* = *ay: mein, Mai, Meyer, Mayer*
> *y* = *ü: Lyrik, Bühne*
> *v* = *w: Klavier, wir*

Occasionally, some letters do not designate any sound; they are SILENT A 025
and only serve to designate the length of the preceding vowel [→ A 031,
032, 040.4]:

> *Tier — Bahn — stiehlt — Paar — Flüsse — immer*

Vowels

The six available letters used to designate vowels do not suffice to A 030
identify the German vowels unequivocally, since the same letter is used
to represent long or short, open or closed, stressed or unstressed vowels:

> *Graf, scharf — Brot, Topf — es regnet, gestern — Blume, Ulme — Fibel,*
> *sicher — Bär, färben — Öl, fördern — grün, fünf*

A German vowel is LONG under any of the following circumstances: A 031

1. The vowel occurs at the end of a syllable within a word (i.e. before a
single consonant):

> *Sa-me, Re-gen, Fi-bel, Kro-ne, Blu-me, Rä-der, mö-gen, lü-gen, ly-risch*

2. The vowel is followed by a silent **h**:

> *Bahn, sehr, ihm, Kohle, Stuhl, ähnlich, versöhnen, Bühne*

3. The vowel is doubled (possible only for **a**, **e**, and **o**):

> *Saal, Meer, Boot*

4. The vowel occurs before **ß** followed by another vowel [→ A 040.5]:

> *Straße, rußig, mäßig, Blöße*

5. The vowel **i** is lengthened by a silent **e** following it:

> *Ziel, viel, die, Schiene*

13

Sometimes the lengthening of the **i** is indicated by **-eh**:

Vieh, stiehlt, zieht

A 032   A German vowel is always SHORT when it occurs before a double consonant:

alle, hemmen, immer, offen, Suppe, kämmen, öffnen, Schlüssel, Idyll

A 033   The letter **e** in the final syllables **-e**, **-el**, **-en**, **-er** and in inseparable prefixes like **be-**, **emp-**, **ent-**, **er-**, **ge-**, **ver-**, **zer-** is always short and unstressed, but must be audible [ə]:

Fahne, Vogel, haben, Vater
bekommen, Empfang, entführen, erzählen, Gesicht, verwandt, zerstört

Diphthongs

A 035   A DIPHTHONG is a combination of two vowel sounds; there are three common diphthongs in German:

ei (ai, ey, ay), eu (äu), au;

in these vowel combinations only the first vowel carries stress.

A 036   The combination **ui** also occurs occasionally: *pfui*.

A 037   German diphthongs are always short:

mein, Mai, heute, Häute, aus

A 038   The combination **ie** is not a diphthong, but represents a long **i**: *viel* [→ A 031.5].[1]

Consonants

A 040   The following important principles must be observed in the pronunciation of German consonants:

1. At the end of a syllable and before consonants, **b**, **d**, and **g** become voiceless and are pronounced like **p**, **t**, and **k**:

loben, er lobt — Rinde, Rind — Tage, Tag

---

[1] In a few loan words, mostly of French origin, the combination ie represents two separate sounds: *Familie (fa-mil-je)*.

14

2. In final position and before consonants, the suffix **-ig** is pronounced like **-ich**: *König, Ewigkeit*. The **g** is pronounced like an initial **g-**, however, when the suffix **-ig** is followed by a vowel (*Könige, Königin*), before the suffix **-lich** (*königlich*), and in the word *Königreich*.

3. The letter **s** is VOICED:

> initially before vowels (*sagen, Silber, sein, selbst*);
> medially between vowels (*Reise, Besen, Nase*);
> when it is preceded by **r, l, m**, or **n** and followed by a vowel (*Ursula, Else, Amsel, Linse*).

In all other occurrences, **s** is VOICELESS.

4. DOUBLE CONSONANTS are pronounced like a single consonant:

> *hoffen, Kamm, bitten, Mappe*

If two identical or similar consonants coincide at the juncture of two words or syllables, the consonant sound is slightly lengthened:

> *Grassamen, Schlafwagen, zahllos*

In the case of stops (**b, d, g, p, t, k**), the sound becomes markedly plosive:

> *Erbprinz, Handtuch, Dickkopf*

If a double consonant coincides with another identical consonant at the juncture of two words or syllables, only two symbols are used:

> *Schiffahrt, Schwimmeister*[1]

5. The symbol **ss** can occur between two vowels only if the first vowel is short. In no case is **ss** found at the end of a word or syllable, or before consonants; in these instances it is replaced by **ß**:

> *müssen, ich muß, du mußt*
> *essen, ich esse, du ißt, eßbar*
> *Fluß, Flüsse, Flüßchen*

When **ß** occurs between two vowels, the first vowel is always long:

> *Füße, Maße* (as against *Masse*), *Größe, Grüße*

---

[1] If syllabication occurs at the end of a line, all three consonants are restored: *Schiff-fahrt, Schwimm-meister.*

The following possibilities exist for the pronunciation of a vowel before ß:

Final position (word or syllable):

long vowel + ß: *Fuß, Großstadt*
short vowel + ß: *muß, Rußland*

Medial position (word or syllable):

long vowel + ß + consonant: *er grüßt*
short vowel + ß + consonant: *du mußt*
long vowel + ß + vowel: *grüßen*
but: short vowel + ss + vowel: *müssen*

6. In German words, **st** and **sp** are pronounced **scht** and **schp** initially and after most prefixes; otherwise they are pronounced **s-t** and **s-p**. In foreign words they remain **s-t** and **s-p** initially or medially:

Stern, Stufe, verstehen — Kasten
Spiel, spalten, besprechen — Wespe
Institut, Inspiration

7. **ch** is a palatal fricative [ç] after front vowels and consonants, a velar fricative [χ] after back vowels:[1]

echt, ich, Teich, Bäche, euch, Löcher, Bücher, Milch;
ach, noch, suchen, auch

8. **j** is considered a consonant in German, pronounced like the semi-vowel y in English "yes":

ja, jetzt, jung

SYLLABLES

A 050   A word consists of one or more sound groups. These sound groups are called SYLLABLES. We have to distinguish between PHONETIC syllables and MORPHEMIC syllables, which may or may not coincide. By dividing a word into PHONETIC SYLLABLES we separate the sound groups which as a rule are pronounced as a unit:

Rech-nung, kom-men, nie-mand

[1] This difference is merely allophonic rather than phonemic. German speakers make it automatically, without being aware of it. In the suffix **-chen**, the palatal fricative is always used, even after back vowels: *das Schuhchen, mein Frauchen.*

16

MORPHEMIC SYLLABLES, on the other hand, are the component parts of A 051
a word which divide the word into prefix, stem, and suffix:

be-komm-en, er be-komm-t; ab-fahr-en; Rechn-ung

The recognition of morphemic syllables is necessary for the under- A 052
standing of the word. Phonetic syllables are important for spelling, since
at the end of a line German words are divided according to phonetic
syllables. The following principles apply to phonetic syllables.

SYLLABICATION AT THE END OF A LINE

Each phonetic syllable must contain a VOWEL; a word therefore has as A 055
many syllables as it has vowels or diphthongs [→ A 001–2, A 031.5,
A 035–6]:

>   one syllable: *Durst, Kleid*
>   two syllables: *A-bend, Vor-trag*
>   three syllables: *Be-am-ter, Ra-di-o*
>   four syllables: *be-ein-flus-sen*
>   five syllables: *Wie-der-ein-rei-se*
>   six syllables: *un-vor-her-ge-se-hen*

The following rules apply to syllabication:

Vowels
A 056

1. Single vowels, although they constitute a phonetic syllable, are NOT
separated: *Ebe-ne*, not *E-be-ne*; *Fa-mi-lie*, not *Fa-mi-li-e*. Diphthongs
are treated like a single vowel: *Kleie*, not *Klei-e*; Eier, not *Ei-er*.
2. Two vowels or two diphthongs are separated, if they are pronounced
separately: *Be-am-ter, Fei-er-tag, Trau-ung, Drei-einig-keit*; *be-in-hal-ten*
(not *bein-hal-ten*!).

Consonants
A 060

1. A SINGLE consonant appears at the beginning of the next syllable
(but → A 065):

ge-ben, Ha-se, je-der, Stie-fel, be-we-gen

In this context, **ch**, **ph**, **ß**, **sch**, **x**, and **z** are considered single consonants:

la-chen, Phi-lo-so-phie, Fü-ße, Wä-sche, He-xe, schneu-zen

17

2. In the case of MULTIPLE consonants, the last one begins the next syllable (but → A 065); **ck** is divided as **k-k**:

> *Tisch-ler, Gas-se, im-mer, Kat-ze, emp-fan-gen, Ver-wechs-lung; bak-ken*

Medial **ng** and **sp** are considered as two consonants:

> *Fin-ger, Hun-ger, Knos-pe;* but *auf-sprin-gen*

st is never separated; both consonants come at the beginning of the next syllable:

> *be-ste, er-ste, Fen-ster, ge-stern*

A 065   COMPOUND WORDS are divided according to their basic components:

> *Wand-schrank, ent-er-ben, be-gra-ben, be-ob-ach-ten, hier-in, dar-auf, war-um*

A 070   In the case of foreign words, syllabication often follows the rules of the language from which the word is borrowed; the syllabication is indicated in any good dictionary: *Mi-kro-skop.*

STRESS

In multisyllabic words, one syllable carried the primary stress ('); in words of three or more syllables, some other syllable may carry a secondary stress ( ). In general, German words carry the MAIN STRESS on the FIRST SYLLABLE. This is true for simple words, compound words, and verbs with **separable prefixes** [→ A 250 ff., B 300 ff.]:

> *Stíefel, Ántwort, Vórsicht, Háustür, Éisenbahnwàgen, Áufgabe, ánkòmmen, tótschlàgen*

A 081   Verbs with **inseparable prefixes** [→ A 285 ff., B 330 ff.] and words derived from them, as well as nouns and adjectives with the prefixes **be-** and **ge-**, carry the MAIN STRESS on the FIRST SYLLABLE of the STEM:

> *besúchen, der Besúch; verkáufen, der Verkáuf, der Verkäufer; Gebírge, Bestéck, gedúldig*

A 085   Words which begin with the prefixes **da-, dar-, durch-, her-, hin-, in-, miß-, ob-, über-, um-, un-, unter-, voll-, vor-, wider-, wieder-,** and **zu-** may carry the primary stress on the first syllable of the prefix or on the first syllable of the stem [→ A 255, B 340]. Sometimes two pronunciations are possible for the same word: normal stress on the stem or, for the sake of emphasis, primary stress on the first syllable and a strong secondary stress on the stem (Normal: *unmŏglich*; emphatic: *únmŏglich*).

dúrchschneiden or *durchschnéiden*	*úndankbar*, but *undénkbar*;
[→ B 340];	*vollénden*, but *Vóllmacht*;
das Míßtrauen, but *ich mißtráue*;	*Zúkunft*, but *zusámmen*;
Ínhaber, but *infólge*;	*Wíedersehen*, but *Wiederhólung*

Exceptions

Other than foreign words, which often follow the rules of the language from which they are borrowed,[1] only a few German words (or word compounds) and loan words deviate from the general principles of accentuation: A 090

1. Some German words like:

   alléin, abschéulich (but *der Ábscheu*), *Forélle, Hermelín, Holúnder, lebéndig, Posáune, Trompéte*

2. Words ending in **-ei, -ie,** and **-ieren** (or **-ierer**) carry the primary stress on the first syllable of the ending:

   Bäckeréi, Partéi, Spieleréi, Prophezéiung, Magíe, Theoríe, rasíeren, studíeren, Hausíerer

3. Some geographic names like:

   Französe, Afrikáner, Európäer, Asiáte, Berlín

4. Abbreviations, the letters of which are fully pronounced, carry the primary stress on the last syllable:

   das Abc (A-be-cé), die USA (U-Es-Á), die UdSSR (U-de-Es-Es-Ér)

---

[1] Many foreign words are stressed on the last syllable: *Universitä̈t, Konzért, Physík*. In general, however, it is recommended to look up the pronunciation of foreign words in a good dictionary.

If the abbreviation is pronounced as a single word, however, stress reverts to the first syllable:

NATO (Náto)

5. Word groups linked by hyphen often carry the stress on the last word; numbers above one hundred stress the unit numeral:

schwarz-rot-góld, das Auf-und-Áb, das Einmaléins, dreitausendachthundert-fünfzehn, neunzehnhundertvíerundachtzig

6. Some adverbial compounds are also stressed on the last syllable:

tagéin, tagáus; stromáb, stromáuf; himmelán, nachdém

A 095 Most other compound words carry the primary stress on the first word:

Wándschrank, Rótkèhlchen, Versícherungsgesèllschaft, Éisenbahnbeàmter

A 096 A few of the most important exceptions from this rule are:

Jahrzéhnt, Jahrhúndert, Jahrtáusend; Muttergóttes, Vaterúnser; as well as almost all holidays (except *Wéihnachten*): *Allerhéiligen, Allerséelen, Karfréitag, Ostersónntag, Aschermíttwoch,* etc.

WORDS

WORD CATEGORIES

A 100 Words are the smallest independent units of a language. They can be divided into two categories: words which carry referential MEANING (content words), such as

geben, Mann, Hoffnung, schön, ich, etwas

and words which do not carry independent meaning of their own, but only indicate the RELATIONSHIP between various parts of the sentence (function words or operators), such as

an, der, und, als

A 105 It is also possible to divide words into PARTS OF SPEECH, some of which can change their form and some of which can not. Parts of speech which

20

CAN HAVE INFLECTIONAL ENDINGS include **verbs** [→ B], **nouns** [→ C], **pronouns** [→ D], and **adjectives** [→ E]:[1]

> *kommen, er kommt; Baum, Bäume; ich, mir; alt, altes*

Parts of speech which REMAIN UNINFLECTED are **adverbs** [→ E], **prepositions** [→ F], and **conjunctions** [→ G]:

> *für, ohne, und, denn, nachdem, noch, nur, doch*

Interjections are not parts of speech in the strict sense of the word [→ G 800 ff.].

CAPITALIZATION

In German, words can also be divided into those which are capitalized   A 110
and those which are not. The rules for capitalization are not very simple; in case of doubt, it is generally advisable to use a small initial. The basic principles are given below.

The following words are always CAPITALIZED in German: A 111

1. The first word of a sentence, i.e. at the beginning of a paragraph, after a period, a question mark, an exclamation point, or (for direct discourse) after a colon.
2. All proper names.
3. All functional nouns, i.e. all common nouns and all other parts of speech used as nouns:

> *das Haus, das Kind, der Arme, das Beste, der Reisende, das Bekannte, das Du, das Nichts, die Acht, mein Lieber, das Wenn und Aber, das Lesen und das Schreiben, das A und das O*

To this group also belong all adjectives after indefinite pronouns [→ D 750 ff.] such as *alles, etwas, nichts, viel,* etc.:

> *alles Gute, etwas Besonderes, nichts Wichtiges, viele Blinde*

4. Pronouns for the familiar form of address, second person (*du* and *ihr*) as well as the possessive forms *dein* and *euer* are capitalized in letters,

---

[1] Articles are treated under the heading of limiting adjectives.

and written in small letters elsewhere. The polite form of address *Sie* and its possessive *Ihr* are always capitalized.[1]

5. Adjectives ending in **-er** which are derived from the names of cities, towns, and countries:

> *Münchener Zeitung, Emmentaler Käse, Frankfurter Würstchen*

6. Adjectives derived from proper names, when they denote a personal attribute (answering the question *whose?*):

> *Schillersche Balladen, Grimmsche Märchen, Kantsche Philosophie*

but not, when they denote a characteristic (answering the question *what kind of?*):

> *die lutherische Religion, eine homerische Landschaft*

7. Adjectives as parts of titles and proper names:

> *der Große Bär, die Neue Zeitung, die Dresdner Bank, Friedrich der Große, Otto der Erste, das Staatliche Konservatorium*

A 112   For titles of books, plays, articles, etc., the general capitalization rules apply, e.g. only those words are capitalized which are always written with a capital.

WORD FORMATION

A 120   The stem syllable indicates the basic meaning of the word:

> *schließ-:* **schließ**-*en, zu-***schließ**-*en, ver-***schließ**-*bar*
> *Mann:* **männ**-*lich, sich er-***mann**-*en,* **mann**-*haft,* **Mann**-*schaft*
> *groß:* *ver-***größ**-*ern,* **Größ**-*e*

The German vocabulary contains a great many words which are expanded from simple stems. Such words are called **derivatives** and **compounds**. Compound words are formed from two or more independent words, or by the addition of prefixes. All parts of speech are subject to compounding; words formed by derivation or compounding often constitute a different part of speech than the original stem.

---

[1] Forms of the pronoun *ich* are **not** capitalized.

DERIVATION

A derivation changes, contracts, or expands the meaning of a word by altering its sound structure (usually the stem vowel) or by adding syllables which do not have any meaning by themselves. The stem word is usually changed to a different part of speech. $\qquad$ A 130

Verb: *trinken*; noun: *Trank*; adjective: *trinkbar*

Sometimes, the part of speech remains the same: $\qquad$ A 131

fallen — fällen [→ A 147]

Derivation without Suffix

A. Nominal Derivation

Derivation by CHANGING THE STEM VOWEL is limited to strong verbs as stems: $\qquad$ A 135

werfen — der Wurf; reißen — der Riß

Only nouns are derived from verbs in this fashion; the derivatives themselves may form other parts of speech by adding suffixes.

Derivatives formed from the INFINITIVE of strong and weak verbs (mostly masculine nouns): $\qquad$ A 136

> *der Fall, der Fang, der Rat, der Ruf, der Schein, der Schlaf, der Schlag, der Schreck, der Schrei, der Kauf, der Dank, der Gruß; das Grab, das Leid, das Siegel; die Klingel, die Trommel*

Derivations with the PRESENT TENSE VOWEL: $\qquad$ A 137

> *der Stich, der Tritt*

Derivations with the PAST TENSE VOWEL: $\qquad$ A 138

> *der Band, der Drang, der Griff, der Klang, der Riß, der Ritt, der Schnitt, der Schritt, der Schwur, der Sang, der Trank, der Wuchs; das Schloß, das Maß, das Band*

Derivations with the VOWEL of the PAST PARTICIPLE (**o** often becomes **u**) $\qquad$ A 139

> *der Bund, der Bruch, der Fund, der Flug, der Fluß, der Guß, der Hang, der Schub, der Schwund, der Sprung, der Trunk*

23

B. Verbal Derivatives

A 140   Verbs may be derived from nouns, adjectives, or other verbs, without suffix (other than the infinitive ending -en).

A 145   Derivations from NOUNS are very frequent, especially in technical language; they sometimes show *Umlaut*:

> *pflügen, drahten, kabeln, landen; frühstücken, antworten* [→ B 350]

A 146   Derivations from ADJECTIVES also frequently show *Umlaut*:

> *lauten, läuten, heilen, sichern, grünen, röten*

A 147   Weak verbs may be derived from STRONG VERBS, using mostly the vowel of the past tense (often with *Umlaut*), sometimes that of the infinitive. These verbs are called factitive or causative verbs:

> *führen* (from *fuhr*), *legen* (from *lag, ä > e*), *setzen* (from *saß*),
> *fällen, bücken* (from *biegen*, with unvoicing of final consonant)

Derivation by Means of Suffixes

A 150   By means of suffixes, the stem can be changed into a different part of speech. The basic meaning of the word stem does not change:

> *fragen, die Frage, fraglich; glauben, der Glaube, glaubhaft; die*
> *Sünde, sündig, sündigen; das Glück, glücklich, glücklicherweise*

A 151   If the derivation is the same part of speech as the original stem word, the intensity of meaning is usually altered:

> *das Kind, das Kindchen; der Baum, das Bäumlein; spotten, spötteln;*
> *lachen, lächeln; rot, rötlich; krank, kränklich; schwach, schwächlich*

A 152   Most suffixes form definite parts of speech:

1. Suffixes which form NOUNS are -el, -er, -ling, and -s for masculine, -chen, -lein, and -sel for neuter, and -ei, -heit, -keit, -in, -schaft, -t, and -ung for feminine nouns. The suffixes -de, -e, -nis, -sal, -st, and -tum form nouns of different genders:

> *die Freude, das Gemälde; die Treue, der Glaube; das Gefängnis,*
> *die Finsternis; das Schicksal, die Trübsal; die Kunst, das Gespinst;*
> *das Fürstentum, der Reichtum*

24

2. Suffixes which form ADJECTIVES are *-bar*, *-en*, *-ern*, *-haft*, *-ig*, *-isch*, *-lich*, and *-sam*.

3. Suffixes which form VERBS are *-eln*, *-ern*, *-igen*, *-ieren*, and *-eien*.

4. Suffixes which form ADVERBS are *-e*, *-s*, *-weise*, and *-lich*.

The Most Important Suffixes

-bar: forms adjectives from nouns and other parts of speech: A 153

> *sichtbar, fruchtbar, tragbar, offenbar*

When derived from verbs, such adjectives express the possibility of something being done, and exhibit the character of a process [→ B 620]:

> *erfüllbar* (can be fulfilled), *unbezahlbar* (can not be paid)

-chen, -lein:[1] form neuter diminutives from nouns, usually with *Umlaut*; A 154
-chen is the more common diminutive form today; the endings **-e** and **-en** of the stem word are usually left out:

> *das Kindchen, das Fläschchen, das Städtchen, das Mädchen; das Schneiderlein, das Brüderlein, das Fräulein; das Häschen, das Gärtchen*

-de: forms feminine and neuter nouns from verbs; no new formations A 155
possible in modern German:

> *die Freude, die Zierde, die Schande* (from *schämen*), *die Gemeinde; das Gebäude, das Gelübde* (from *geloben*), *das Getreide* (from *tragen*)

-e: forms nouns from verbs or adjectives, often with *Umlaut* or vowel A 156
change:

> *die Hilfe, die Bitte, die Sprache, die Liebe; der Wille, der Glaube; die Größe, die Breite, die Ebene, die Höhe, die Röte*

Often such nouns designate tools or instruments:

> *die Säge, die Schraube, die Winde, die Stütze, die Leuchte*

For prefix **Ge-** and suffix **-e**, → A 321.

-e also forms adverbs from adjectives; most of these derivations today

---

[1] Diminutive suffixes *-el*, *-erl*, *-le* occur mostly in dialect forms; only a few, such as *Mädel*, have been accepted into standard speech.

25

are either obsolescent or have become colloquial, but still frequently occur in poetic usage:

lange, stille, balde

A 157   **-ei:** Originally a foreign suffix, it is now considered completely German, but still shifts the primary stress to the last syllable (*Bäckeréi* → A 090.2); forms feminine nouns from verbs and nouns. These nouns indicate

1. an intensive activity, sometimes with a derogatory connotation:

    die Zauberei, die Schmeichelei, die Schreiberei, die Klingelei

2. a place of business, occupation, or activity:

    die Molkerei, die Druckerei, die Bücherei, die Schneiderei, die Abtei, die Einsiedelei

A 158   **-el:** forms mostly masculine, occasionally feminine nouns from verbs; these nouns often indicate tools or instruments:

    der Deckel, der Hebel, der Schlüssel, der Flügel; die Schüssel

A 159   **-eln, -ern:** form verbs from verbs or other parts of speech, expressing the repetition of a process or an activity, usually in a diminishing sense[1]; verbs in **-ern** are often derived from onomatopoetic words:

    lächeln, witzeln, spötteln, frösteln; wiehern, meckern

A 160   **-en, -ern:** form adjectives from nouns to designate a material:

    golden, seiden, wollen, silbern; by analogy to *silbern: hölzern, gläsern, eisern* [→ A 166]

A 161   **-er:** forms masculine nouns from verbs (and occasionally other parts of speech) to designate occupations (*Umlaut*):

    der Bäcker, der Verkäufer, der Lehrer; der Schreiner, der Tischler, der Schüler, der Schäfer

---

[1] This does not include verbs in *-eln* or *-ern* which are derived from words ending in *-el* and *-er: fesseln, betteln, handeln, schaufeln, schaukeln; ändern, erwidern.*

26

Such nouns also characterize persons by a particular attribute or by place of origin:

> *der Schwindler, der Bettler, der Sammler, der Betrüger; der Berliner, der Holländer, der Italiener*

The derivations can also designate instruments:

> *der Bohrer, der Empfänger, der Sender* (radio), *der Kocher, der Wecker, der Schalter*

Sometimes nouns ending in **-er** can not be derived from the stem verb itself, but only from a compound verb form:

> *der Überbringer* (not *der Bringer*), *der Absender* (not *der Sender*),[1] *der Nachfolger* (not *der Folger*)

-haft: forms adjectives from nouns and other adjectives to designate the type of quality: $\qquad$ A 163

> *krank**haft**, mädchen**haft**, laien**haft**, sünd**haft***

Some adjectives have the additional suffix **-ig**:

> *wahr**haftig**, leib**haftig***

-heit (-keit): forms nouns designating a condition or a characteristic from nouns, adjectives, or participles (always feminine): $\qquad$ A 165

> *die Schön**heit**, die Bos**heit**, die Schlau**heit**, die Mensch**heit**, die Gott**heit**, die Christen**heit**, die Gelegen**heit**, die Verschwiegen**heit**, die Vergangen**heit***

-keit is used after the suffixes **-bar, -ig, -lich, -sam**, and usually after **-el** and **-er**:

> *die Dank**barkeit**, die Süßig**keit**, die Freund**lichkeit**, die Einsam**keit**, die Heiter**keit**, die Tapfer**keit**, die Eitel**keit**;*
> but: *die Sicher**heit**, die Dunkel**heit***

-ig: forms adjectives which show a condition or a similarity; some of these derivations have *Umlaut*: $\qquad$ A 166

> *freud**ig**, traur**ig**, gefäll**ig**, anmut**ig**, schläfr**ig**, schaur**ig**, dein**ig**, hies**ig**, dort**ig***

---

[1] Except in the sense of a radio transmission.

27

Compare *silbern* (made of silver) and *silbrig* (like silver); *hölzern* (made of wood) and *holzig* (like wood).

A 167 Factitive or causative verbs may be formed from some of these adjectives:

> *sündigen, mäßigen, entschuldigen*

There are also analogous formations like

> *reinigen, besänftigen, beleidigen*

A 168 **-in** (plural **-innen**): forms feminine nouns from masculines to indicate the female counterpart; an **-e** ending on the stem is omitted:

> *die Lehrerin, die Studentin, die Schülerin, die Ärztin, die Münchnerin, die Sekretärin, die Königin, die Freundin; die Löwin, die Zeugin, die Beamtin*

Extended to **-essin** for *die Prinzessin*, to **-issin** for *die Äbtissin*.

A 169 **-isch**: forms adjectives designating origin, property or characteristic (often negative [→ A 174]) from nouns and pronouns, occasionally from verbs:

> *französisch, arabisch, münchnerisch, irdisch, himmlisch; geographisch, chemisch, alkoholisch, photographisch; diebisch, kindisch, weibisch, launisch, gespenstisch; malerisch, zeichnerisch*

A 170 **-keit** → **-heit** [A 165].

A 171 **-lein** → **-chen** [A 154].

A 172 **-lich**: forms adjectives denoting characteristic qualities from all parts of speech. The syllable **-lich** was originally a noun meaning "body." If the stem ends in **-n**, a linking **-d-** or **-t-** occurs before the ending:

> *freundlich, herzlich, ängstlich, zerbrechlich, erfreulich; wissentlich, wesentlich, namentlich* (not the same as *nämlich*); by analogy with *ärgerlich: lächerlich*

Umlaut is found only occasionally:

> *empfänglich, gebräuchlich, verläßlich, sächlich* (not to be confused with *sachlich*)

Notice the difference between **-ig** and **-lich**: A 173

> *halbjährlich:* every half year; *halbjährig:* lasting half a year (or half
> a year old); similarly: *stündlich* and (*ein*)*stündig*
> *geschäftlich:* commercial; *geschäftig:* busy
> *geistlich:* clerical, religious; *geistig:* intellectual, spiritual
> *mündlich:* oral; *mündig:* of age
> *vorzeitlich:* prehistoric; *vorzeitig:* premature
> *verständlich:* comprehensible; *verständig:* reasonable
> *fremdsprachlich:* dealing with a foreign language; *fremdsprachig:* in
> a foreign language

Notice the difference between **-lich** and **-isch**: A 174

> *weiblich:* feminine; *weibisch:* effeminate
> *kindlich:* childlike; *kindisch:* childish
> *herrlich:* magnificent; *herrisch:* domineering

Without pejorative connotation in the suffix **-isch**:

> *höflich:* courteous; *höfisch:* courtly
> *nördlich:* northern; *nordisch:* Norse
> *heimlich:* secret; *heimisch:* domestic

-ling: forms masculine nouns from verbs, adjectives, or other nouns. A 175
The derivatives describe a person by means of the condition or activity
in which he finds himself; they usually carry *Umlaut*:

> *der Flüchtling, der Lehrling, der Säugling,*
> *der Sträfling, der Jüngling, der Liebling*

Often they have a diminutive or strongly pejorative connotation:

> *der Dichterling, der Schwächling, der Feigling*

Some formations with **-ling** are impersonal:

> *der Frühling, der Silberling*

-nis (plural **-nisse**): forms neuter or feminine nouns designating actions, A 176
conditions, or things from verbs, adjectives, or nouns:

> *das Gefängnis, das Verzeichnis, das Hindernis, das Bündnis; die Bitternis,*
> *die Wildnis, die Finsternis*

29

A 177 **-s** or **-ens:** forms adverbs from nouns and adjectives:[1]

tags, flugs, rechts, meistens, erstens

A 178 **-s:** forms masculine nouns from verbs:

der Knicks, der Klaps, der Schnaps, der Schwips

A 179 **-sal, -sel:** forms mostly neuter nouns, mainly from verbs:

das Schicksal, das Scheusal, das Labsal; die Trübsal; das Rätsel, das Mitbringsel, das Überbleibsel; der Stöpsel

A 180 **-sam:** forms adjectives from abstract nouns, verbs, and other adjectives:

arbeitsam, biegsam, lenksam, langsam

A 181 **-schaft:** forms feminine collective nouns designating territory, a group, a condition, or a property, usually from other nouns, sometimes from adjectives and participles:

die Grafschaft, die Herrschaft, die Landschaft;
die Bürgerschaft, die Lehrerschaft, die Arbeiterschaft;
die Freundschaft, die Bruderschaft;
die Eigenschaft, die Gemeinschaft, die Gefangenschaft, die Verwandtschaft

A 182 **-st:** forms abstract nouns from verbs; no new formations possible any more:

der Gewinst, das Gespinst, die Kunst (from *können*)

A 183 **-t:** forms feminine nouns from verbs; no new formations possible any more:

die Fahrt, die Wacht, die Tracht, die Furt

A 184 **-tum:** forms nouns, mostly neuter, which (like *-schaft*) can designate territory or group, but may also show abstract qualities:

das Fürstentum, das Königtum (not identical with *Königreich!*),
das Bauerntum, das Bürgertum, das Altertum;
der Reichtum, der Irrtum

---

[1] This **-s** is originally the genitive ending of masculine or neuter nouns; by analogy it also occurs with feminine nouns today: *nachts.*

-ung: forms feminine nouns from verbs, often verbs with prefixes: A 185

> *die Hoffnung, die Haltung, die Scheidung, die Schilderung, die Verbeugung,*
> *die Bekanntmachung, die Voraussetzung, die Beerdigung, die Genugtuung,*
> *die Mitteilung*

-weise: forms adverbs, which can occasionally be used as adjectives, A 186
from nouns and adjectives; since **weise** was originally a noun, a linking
-s- is often used after nouns, a linking **-er-** after adjectives:

> *zwangsweise, ausnahmsweise, meterweise;*
> *glücklicherweise, dummerweise, klugerweise*

Foreign Suffixes

In addition to the suffixes listed above, foreign suffixes can also be used A 190
to derive words. They are often affixed to German stems.

Masculine nouns [→ C 020.9] are formed with the suffixes **-ismus:** A 191

> *Sozialismus, Kapitalismus, Realismus, Expressionismus* (but: *die Klassik,*
> *die Romantik*)[1]

-and, -ant, -är, -ast, -eur (feminine: **-euse**), **-ier, -ist, -or** (all except **-ast**
and **-or** designate only persons):

> *Konfirmand, Spekulant, Volontär, Enthusiast, Friseur (Friseuse), Bankier,*
> *Humanist, Professor; Kontrast, Motor, Faktor, Sektor*

Feminine nouns [→ C 040.6] are formed with the suffixes A 192
-ion, -ur, -age (often from verbs ending in *-ieren*):

> *Rebellion, Politur, Natur, Blamage*

-tät, -enz, -ie, -ik:

> *Universität, Pestilenz, Melodie, Drogerie, Philosophie, Politik, Physik*

-itis (medical terms):

> *Bronchitis, Rachitis*

Neuter nouns [→ C 030.0] are formed with the suffixes **-ett, -il, -in,** A 193
-ium, -ma, -ment, -um:

> *Sonett, Fossil, Benzin, Ministerium, Plasma, Parlament, Album*

---

[1] The suffix **-zismus** carries imitative or pejorative connotations: *der Klassizismus.*

31

A 195   Adjectives (rarely from German stems) are formed with the suffixes **-abel, -al, -an (-än), -ant, -är, -at, -ell, -ent, -esk, -ett, -ibel, -id, -il, -iv, -os (-ös)**:

> *blamabel, radikal, human, souverän, markant, revolutionär, obligat, materiell, eminent, grotesk, honett, flexibel, morbid, senil, negativ, rigoros, generös*

A 196   Verbs can be derived with the suffixes **-ieren** and **-eien**; **-ieren** also occurs with words of German origin:

> *rasieren, addieren, amtieren, halbieren, hofieren;*
> *prophezeien, benedeien*

Causative or factitive verbs often expand the suffix **-ieren** to **-isieren** or **-fizieren**:

> *nationalisieren, glorifizieren*

Note: *elektrisieren:* to charge with electricity;
elektrifizieren: to provide with electricity

COMPOUNDS

COMPOUNDS OF SEPARATE WORDS

A 200   The ability to form new words by the compounding of two or more words is a characteristic feature of the German language which considerably expands the vocabulary. One or more modifying words may be placed before the stem word:

Modifying Word	Stem Word
Auf-	*seher*
Ober-auf-	*seher*
Gefängnis-ober-auf-	*seher*

A 201   The STEM WORD determines the FORM of the compound; i.e. gender, number, and case endings of nouns:

> *das Tischtuch, die Tischtücher, mit den Tischtüchern*

endings of adjective declension:

> *der Schwerkranke, ein Leichtkranker*

32

and conjugational forms of verbs:

> *freimachen, freigemacht; vorübergehen, vorübergehend;*
> *übertreiben, übertrieben; unterlassen, unterläßt*

The MODIFYING WORD determines the precise MEANING of the compound: A 202

> *das Tischtuch, das Halstuch, das Handtuch;*
> *maschineschreiben, aufschreiben, abschreiben, unterschreiben;*
> *dunkelrot, blutrot, kupferrot;*
> *dahin, dorthin;*
> *einmal, hundertmal;*

The modifying word may completely change the meaning of the stem   A 203
[→ A 260]:

> *fangen, anfangen*

The modifying word may be any part of speech (except a conjunction);   A 205
the stem is usually a noun, a verb, or an adjective.

Modifier	Stem		
	NOUN	VERB	ADJECTIVE
VERB	*Strick-**garn***	*sitzen-**bleiben***	*lese-**freudig***
NOUN	*Haus-**schuh***	*rad-**fahren***	*blut-**rot***
ADJECTIVE	*Roh-**eisen***	*lieb-**haben***	*bitter-**böse***
NUMERAL	*Vier-**füßler***	*vier-**teilen***	*zweit-**beste***
PRONOUN	*Ich-**sucht***	*du-**sagen***	*selbst-**sicher***
PREPOSITION	*Vor-**ort***	*an-**kommen***	*auf-**recht***
ADVERB	*Jetzt-**zeit***	*vorwärts-**bringen***	*nicht-**deutsch***

ADVERBS and PREPOSITIONS as stem words are combined mostly with   A 206
other adverbs or prepositions as modifiers:

> *wo*-**von**, *dort*-**hin**

The PRIMARY STRESS lies on the modifying word; if the compound con-   A 207
sists of more than two words, there may be a secondary stress on the
first syllable of the stem:

> *Schútz-scheibe*   *Wínd-schutz-schèibe*

33

A 208   In a few cases, the stem word indicates the actual meaning of the compound; in these instances, the primary stress lies on the stem word:

Jahr-húndert, Lebe-wóhl, berg-áb, fluß-áuf [→ A 096]

The Modifier

A 210   A **noun** as modifier can appear before the stem unchanged:

Eisbahn, Eisenbahn, wasserfest, luftgekühlt

A 211   Feminine nouns may lose the **-e** at the end of the word:

sorglos, Schulzimmer, Kirchturm

A 212   Between a noun as a modifier and the stem word, there may be a LINKING SOUND or a linking syllable. These linkages originally indicated a declensional ending (genitive singular, plural); today there have been so many analogous formations, that the declension of the noun can no longer be recognized from the linking letter.

A 213   The modifier is often a plural. Plural endings of nouns [→ C 100 ff.] therefore frequently appear as linking letters. According to its meaning, however, the modifier should often be a singular:

Pferdestall (even for one horse); *Hühnerei* (of one chicken); *Rinderbrust* (of one steer); *Ohrenschmerzen* (in one ear)

A 214   On the other hand, the modifier sometimes appears in the singular, although its meaning is plural:

Baumschule, Wortspiel, Bischofskonferenz

A 215   In many cases, however, the modifier is either singular or plural according to its meaning:

das Rindfleisch, die Rinderherde
der Hausverwalter, der Häusermakler
der Landtag, die Länderversammlung
mausgrau, Mäusegift
Tageszeit, Tagebuch

34

Various Linking Letters:

-(e)n, other than as a plural ending, may indicate a former genitive   A 218
ending of masculine or feminine nouns:

> *Sonnenschirm, Lindenblatt, Wochentag, Bühnendeutsch*

-(e)s, **-(e)ns** is derived from masculine or neuter genitive endings, but   A 220
is also found with some feminine nouns:

> *Königskrone, Glaubensgenosse, Schweinsleder; Liebeslied, Geburtstag,
> Hochzeitsreise*

-s as a linking letter always appears after the suffixes *-heit, -ing, -ion,*   A 221
-keit, -ling, -schaft, -tät, -tum, -ung:

> *Freiheitskrieg, Faschingsprinz, traditionsgebunden, Säuglingspflege,
> Freundschaftsdienst, Universitätsprofessor, Altertumskunde, Zei-
> tungsstand* (but: *Stellungnahme*)

It also often appears after a verb as modifier: A 222

> *empfehlenswert, sehenswürdig*

Some nouns may appear with or without a linking **-s**:   A 223

> *Königskrone, Königreich; Liebesbrief, liebevoll; Schiffbruch, Schiffs-
> junge; Tag(e)werk, Tageszeit; Kalbfleisch, Kalbsleder; Rathaus,
> Ratsherr; Herzenslust, Herzblut; Landsmann* (fellow-countryman),
> *Landmann* (farmer); *Wassernot* (shortage of water), *Wassersnot*
> (inundation)

If the modifier is itself a compound, it may contain a linking **-s**, even if   A 224
a one-word modifier would not have any linking letter:

> *Durchfahrtserlaubnis, Fahrterlaubnis; Kirchhofstor, Hoftor; Oberlandes-
> gericht, Landgericht* [1]

A **verb** as a modifier can remain unchanged only if the stem word is   A 230
also a verb:

> *sitzenbleiben, spazierengehen*

---

[1] The form *Landesgericht* occurs primarily in Austria.

A 231 If the stem word is some other part of speech, the verb loses the infinitive ending, and may insert the linking vowel -e-:

Heizrohr, Spaziergang, Trinkgeld, Kaufkraft; Werbebrief, Lesezimmer

A 232 Some verbs ending in -nen lose the first -n-, if a consonant precedes:

zeichnen, der Zeichenblock; rechnen, das Rechenbuch;
but: *sehnen, die Sehnsucht*

A 240 **Adjectives**, **adverbs**, and **prepositions** as modifiers are placed unchanged directly before the stem word. No linking letter occurs between modifier and stem:

Starkbier, Kleinwohnung, Hinterhaus, minderwertig, Aufstand

A 241 The only exceptions are compounds like *der Hohepriester*. Here the adjective is declined: *den Hohenpriester*.
In the case of *Langeweile*, the adjective may either be inflected or uninflected: *aus Langerweile, aus Langeweile*.

A 242 Prepositions may change the meaning of the stem word in a variety of ways [→ Use of prepositions, F 100 ff.].

Verbs as Stem Words

A 250 If the stem word is a verb, it enters into a different relationship with its modifier than other parts of speech. In most instances, there is no inseparable connection with the stem word. Only in the infinitive, the present participle, and in dependent clause positions of conjugated verbs is the modifier directly connected with the verb:

heimfahren; heimfahrend; . . . als er heimfuhr; . . . weil er heimfährt

A 251 In the past participle, the modifier stands before the prefix (here actually an infix) **ge-**: *heimgefahren*. In all other forms, the modifier is not connected with the verb [→ B 310 ff.].

A 252 The modifier, however, does not constitute a sentence unit of its own, but is the second (non-verbal) part of the predicate [→ H 113]. It is called the VERB COMPLEMENT:

Er fährt jeden Sonntag heim. Fahre bald heim!

gef· prefix

In most instances, the verb complement is a PREPOSITION (*ab, an, aus,*   A 253
durch, in,[1] *gegenüber, vor, zu,* etc.); it can also be an ADVERB (*zurück,*
vorwärts), a VERB (*sitzen, spazieren, stehen*), or a NOUN (*Kopf, Maschine*).

The verb complement always carries stress: A 254

ánkommen, **zurück**gehen, *vórwärtsschreiten,* **sítzen**bleiben, **rádfahren,**
maschíneschreiben, **kópfstehen**

Some prepositions can be combined with the verb either separably or   A 255
inseparably. Inseparable compounds act like verbs with prefixes
[→ A 280 ff.] and are stressed on the stem syllable [→ B 340]:

Wir **brachen** *den Ast* **dúrch**. *Der Fluß* **durchbrách** *den Damm.*

If the verb complement is not a preposition, it does not enter into an   A 256
inseparable compound with the verb:

Er schreibt **maschine**. *Sie gehen* **vorwärts**, *Er blieb* **stehen**.

For derivations from nouns → B 350.   A 257

In contrast to the other parts of speech, prepositions as verb comple-   A 260
ments can change the meaning of the verb in various ways. For example:

1. The verb complement is identical with the preposition which governs
   the use of the stem verb:

ein Tischtuch **auf**legen (*ein Tuch* **auf** *den Tisch legen*)
eine Wand **an**streichen (*Farbe* **an** *eine Wand streichen*)
jemanden **ein**sperren (*jemanden* **ins** *Gefängnis sperren*)[1]

2. The stem word uses the object with a different preposition:

Gott **an**beten (**zu** *Gott beten*)
jemanden **aus**lachen (**über** *jemanden lachen*)

3. The verb complement can produce a perfective verb [→ B 461],
   showing a change of condition:

ausruhen, **auf**blühen, **auf**wachen, **ein**schlafen

---

[1] The preposition **in** is replaced by the verb complement **ein-**: *eintreten, einreisen, einatmen.*

4. The verb complement may give a completely different meaning to the verb:

fangen — anfangen; hören — aufhören; kommen — vorkommen.

COMPOUNDING WITH PREFIXES

A 280 In contrast to modifying words, PREFIXES today are not words any longer. Like the suffixes [→ A 150 ff.], they are syllables which can not stand by themselves and carry independent meaning. They are always inseparably connected with the verb in all its forms.

A 281 Prefixes change the meaning of the stem word; they may also change verb constructions with prepositional phrases into verbs with various case objects:

Treue — Untreue; Gunst — Mißgunst; recht — gerecht;
halten — behalten; kommen — verkommen;

Er bewohnt ein altes Haus. Er wohnt in einem alten Haus.
Wir gedenken der Toten. Wir denken an die Toten.

A 282 With prefixes, VERBS may be formed from nouns, adjectives, or adverbs. This may be done simply by adding the infinitive ending, often with *Umlaut*:

bemannen, verfeinden, verfilmen;
erneuern, ergänzen, erwidern, entfremden;
vernichten, verneinen

A 283 Sometimes, a DERIVATIVE SUFFIX must be added [→ A 167, A 172]:

sich befleißigen, befriedigen, verstaatlichen

A 284 The prefixes *aber-* (*after-*), *erz-*, *un-*, *ur-*, and foreign prefixes such as *a-*, *anti-*, *super-*, *vize-* occur only before NOUNS and ADJECTIVES. All these prefixes, including the foreign ones, carry the primary stress:

Áberglaube, Áftermieter, érzdumm, úntreu, úralt, ásozial, ántialkohòlisch, súperfein, Vízepräsidènt

A 285 The prefixes *be-*, *ent-*, (*emp-*), *er-*, *hinter-*,[1] *ob-*, *ver-*, *zer-* [→ B 332], as

[1] For *hinter-* → B 333, footnote.

well as foreign prefixes such as *ad-, de-* (*des-*), *es-* (*ex-*), *in-* (*im-*), *kon-*, *pre-, re-* occur only before VERBS, or parts of speech derived from verbs.

The prefixes *ge-, miß-*, and foreign prefixes such as *dis-, es-, pro-, trans-*   A 286
occur before NOUNS, ADJECTIVES, and VERBS.

The prefixes listed in A 285 and A 286 are unstressed, if they are of   A 287
German origin. The accentuation of foreign prefixes can be found in
any good dictionary. The prefix **miß-** may be stressed or unstressed
[→ A 325 ff., B 334]:

> *bekómmen,* *entdécken,* *empfángen,* *ergánzen,* *verwálten,* *zerstóren;*
> *gerécht, mißáchten, Míßtrauen; Proféssor, Transpórt*

For many of these compounds, the stem no longer occurs by itself in   A 288
modern German:

> *geschehen, gebären, gesund, verlieren, entbehren*

The Most Important Prefixes

aber- (after-) is not very frequent, can no longer be used for new   A 300
formations, and indicates the opposite of the stem word, something
false, or something subordinate. It is not used with verbs:

> *Aberglaube, **abermals**, Aberwitz*
> *Aftermieter* (today mostly *Untermieter*), *Afterlehre, Afterkönigin*

be- is a VERB PREFIX which can make an intransitive verb transitive;   A 301
sometimes the compound has a perfective function:

> *eine Straße **befahren**, ein Haus **bewohnen**; jemanden **belügen**, **belauschen**,*
> ***bestaunen**, **beweinen**; **beheben**, **bereichern***

The prefix *be-* can also be used to form verbs from other parts of speech:[1]   A 302

> *beleidigen, bevorschussen, bemitleiden, beurlauben, befreunden*

ent- is a VERB PREFIX, a shortened form of *entgegen*, which usually   A 305
indicates separation or the opposite:

> *entfliehen, entnehmen, entführen, enthaupten;*
> *entdecken, entehren, entschädigen, entwaffnen;*

---

[1] But note that *begegnen* takes a dative object: *Er begegnet **mir**.*

39

A 306 *ent-* may also show the beginning of an activity or have a causative meaning; it may also form verbs from other parts of speech:

> *entflammen, entzünden, entleeren, entfremden*

A 307 In some words, *ent-* has become **emp-** or **em-**:

> *empfangen, empfehlen, empfinden; empören*

A 310 **er-** is a VERB PREFIX which corresponds to the noun prefix *ur-* [→ A 340]. It can indicate the beginning of a new state of being or the achievement of an end by means of the stem verb. Occasionally, *er-* forms verbs from other parts of speech:

> *erwachen, erscheinen;*
> *erreichen, erschlagen, ersteigen, erraten, erkämpfen;*
> *erhitzen* (to make hot, to become hot), *erwidern* (also *entgegnen*)

A 315 **erz-** is a NOUN PREFIX, developed from *archi-*, which indicates an intensification of meaning, usually with pejorative connotation:

> *Erzgauner, Erzschwindler, erzdumm, erzfaul*

A 316 It is still found in a few words with positive meaning:

> *Erzbischof, Erzengel, Erzherzog, Erzvater*

A 320 **ge-** can occur before NOUNS, ADJECTIVES, and VERBS [→ A 081]; verbs obtain a perfective meaning (*ge-* as prefix of the past participle), although the stem verb often no longer exists by itself, or has changed in meaning:

> *die Gefahr, die Geduld;*
> *gesund, gehässig, gerade;* shortened in *gleich*
> *gelingen, gereichen, geschehen, gewöhnen, gestehen, gehören, genießen,*
> *gebären, geloben;* shortened in *glauben*

A 321 Today, new formations of nouns with the prefix **Ge-** and the suffix **-e** are still possible [→ A 156]; the suffix sometimes is lost again later. These nouns designate neuter collective concepts:

> *das Gebirge, das Gemüse, das Gerippe, das Getreide;*
> *das Gebäck, das Gefieder, das Gebiß, das Gewissen, das Gespräch;*
> plural only: *die Geschwister, die Gebrüder*

Ge- may also be used to derive neuter nouns from verbs to indicate a repeated activity, usually one which has become undesirable through repetition:

A 322

>   *das Geschrei, das Geklimper, das Getue*

Sometimes, neuter nouns of a different meaning are formed, indicating the object produced:

A 323

>   *das Gedicht, das Gefühl, das Genick, das Geschäft*

Derivations from past participles may include masculine and feminine nouns, as well as neuters:

A 324

>   *das Gebot, das Gelächter, das Geschoß;*
>   *der Gebrauch, der Genosse, der Gefährte, der Gehalt* (also *das Gehalt*)*;*
>   *die Geduld, die Geschichte*

miß- occupies a special place among these prefixes, because it may be either STRESSED or UNSTRESSED.

A 325

It can occur before VERBS, before NOUNS which designate concepts, and before ADJECTIVES. It is usually stressed before nouns and adjectives, usually unstressed before verbs, although there usage varies.[1] It indicates the opposite of the stem word, usually in a negative sense:

A 326

>   *mißáchten, mißbráuchen, mißhándeln, mißlíngen;*
>   *mißfarbig, mißliebig, mißtrauisch;*
>   *die Mißernte, der Mißstand, das Mißgeschick*

Notice the difference in accentuation:

>   *mißbráuchen — der Mißbrauch; mißtráuen, das Mißtrauen*

By analogy to the nouns:

>   *mißverstehen*

As a verb prefix, **miß-** is inseparable. There is a fluctuation of usage,

---

[1] For example, *mißdeuten* or *mißdéuten.*

41

however, in the position of the *ge-* in past participles, and the *zu* in infinitives:

> *miȷ́áchtet* as well as *miȷ́geachtet;*
> *miȷ́bráucht,* but *miȷ́gebildet, miȷ́gelaunt;*
> zu *miȷ́áchten,* but *miȷ́zuverstehen*

A 330   **ob-**, shortened from *oben* or *ober*, has formed only a few verbs, with which it is inseparably connected:

> *obliegen, obsiegen, obwalten*

The separation of the prefix (*es liegt mir ob*) is not recommended.

A 335   **un-** is a NOUN or ADJECTIVE PREFIX and forms words which indicate the opposite or the negation of the stem. It usually designates concepts:

> *Untreue, Unglaube, Undank, Unsicherheit;*
> *unlesbar, unbezahlbar, unweigerlich, unfern;*
> *Unmensch, Unhold, Unkraut*

A 336   There are differences between the compound with *un-* and the opposite of the stem word or its negation with *nicht:*

1. The compound with *un-* is slightly less strong than the opposite:

> *fern — unfern — nahe*   *schön — unschön — häßlich*

2. The compounding with *un-* may contain a value judgment, similar to but stronger than the foreign prefix **a-**:

> *unmoralisch:* immoral; *amoralisch:* amoral
> *unsozial:* antisocial; *asozial:* unsociable

A 338   The compound with *un-* may sometimes intensify the meaning of the stem word:

> *Unwetter, Unkosten, Unmenge, Unzahl, Untier, ungeheuer, Untiefe*[1]

A 340   **ur-** is a NOUN or ADJECTIVE PREFIX and corresponds to the verb prefix *-er* [→ A 310]. It indicates the first or primitive state, the origin of things, concepts, and beings:

> *Urzustand, Urwald, Urmensch, Ursache, ursprünglich, urchristlich, Uraufführung, Urgroßvater (Vater des Großvaters)*

---

[1] *Untiefe* may have two meanings: shallowness (*not* deep) and abyss (*very* deep).

It may also indicate an intensification of the base word (never in a negative sense, as with *erz-*):

*uralt, **ur**gemütlich, **ur**plötzlich, Urgewalt*

The prefix *ur-* with nouns may replace the prefix *er-* with verbs:

erlauben — Urlaub; erteilen — Urteil

ver- is a VERB PREFIX making compound verbs from other verbs, occasionally from other parts of speech. These verbs can have causative or factitive meaning (often from comparatives):

verwirklichen, vernichten, verbauern;
verbessern, verschönern, versichern

Verbs with the prefix *ver-* also indicate intensification or completion of an action, sometimes in a negative sense:

verstecken, verhungern, verdienen, verbrennen, verbrauchen, versinken, versuchen, verschließen, vergehen, versprechen

The prefix *ver-* may also indicate the conversion into a different state, mostly from nouns:

verfilmen, vergolden, versilbern

Sometimes it may indicate a negative opposite of the stem word, often in a sense of doing something wrong or incorrectly (mostly reflexive verbs):

sich verlaufen, sich verirren, sich versprechen,[1]
verkennen, verträumen, verachten, verraten

Occasionally, the prefix **ver-** indicates the counter-aspect of the stem verb, i.e. the same action seen from a different perspective:

kaufen — verkaufen; mieten — vermieten

zer- is a VERB PREFIX which makes compounds from other verbs, sometimes other parts of speech. It indicates the forceful breaking up into parts to the point of destruction:

zerbrechen, zerschneiden, zerfallen, zerstören

---

[1] Notice the difference between **etwas versprechen** and **sich versprechen**.

B

⤳ The Verb

I. FORMS OF THE VERB

⤳ *Introduction*

B 010   Verbs form a class of words whose function it is to describe an ACTION (*ich schreibe*), a PROCESS (*das Auto fährt, es regnet*) or a STATE OF BEING (*er schläft, die Blume blüht*). Within the sentence, verbs perform the function of the predicate [→ H 110].

B 011   Verb inflections are called **conjugations**. The FORM of the verb, through its morphological changes, can express the following:

1. The person or thing to which the verb refers (PERSONAL ENDINGS);
2. The time to which the action, process, or state of being refers (TENSE);
3. Whether the statement indicates reality, potentiality, or a command (MOOD);
4. Whether the statement is active or passive (VOICE).[1]

[1] German verbs show passive voice only in compound forms.

44

There are three PERSONS for both singular and plural: B 012

	1ST PERSON	2ND PERSON[1]	3RD PERSON
SINGULAR	ich gehe	du schreibst	der Zug hält
PLURAL	wir gehen	ihr schreibt	die Züge halten

TENSES are either formed directly from the verb stem (simple tenses) or   B 013
with auxiliary verbs (compound tenses).

Simple Tense Forms:

PRESENT:	*ich schreibe*
(SIMPLE) PAST (IMPERFECT, PRETERITE):	*ich schrieb*

Compound Tense Forms:

Perfekt— bin gek...
Imperfekt kam

(PRESENT) PERFECT:	*ich habe geschrieben* *Präsens komme*
PAST PERFECT (PLUPERFECT):	*ich hatte geschrieben* *Plusquamperfekt*
FUTURE:	*ich werde schreiben* *Futur I*
FUTURE PERFECT:	*ich werde geschrieben haben* *Futur II*

Futur II

German verbs occur in three MOODS: (*Aussageweise*)   B 014

1.	INDICATIVE:	*er **kommt**; er war*
2.	SUBJUNCTIVE (*Konjunktiv*):	*Wenn er nur **käme**! Er sagte, er **sei** krank.*
3.	IMPERATIVE:	***Komm** her! **Seien** Sie so freundlich!*

German verbs also have two VOICE forms to indicate whether the event   B 015
is described as an action (**active**) or as a process (**passive**) [→ B 590 ff.]:

Verhaltensrichtung

ACTIVE:	*Er **schrieb** den Brief.*
PASSIVE:	*Der Brief **wurde geschrieben**.*

NON-FINITE VERB FORMS

German verbs have certain forms which do not indicate any relation to   B 020
persons or things and which by themselves do not express time (nonfinite forms) [→ H 112–113]. These forms are:

INFINITIVE:	*lesen*[2]
PRESENT PARTICIPLE:	*lesend*
PAST PARTICIPLE:	*gelesen*

[1] For **Sie**, → D 025.

[2] The form *lesen* is called the **active infinitive**. There are also other forms: the **passive
infinitive** (*gelesen werden*), the **past infinitive** (*gelesen haben*), and the **past passive infinitive**
(*gelesen worden sein*). For a discussion of these forms and their use → B 451 ff.

B 021　These forms are uninflected as long as they are used as verbs. If they function as other parts of speech, however, they will have inflectional endings:

Die Zeit des Lernens; ein Reisender; gesammelte Werke

B 030　The STEM of the verb expresses its MEANING:

ich **kauf-**te　　　er **geh-**t

kauf-en　　　**geh-**en

ge-**kauf-**t　　　**geh-**end

B 040　We distinguish between two types of verb conjugations: WEAK (or regular) and STRONG (or irregular) verbs.[1]

B 041　Weak verbs do not change their stem:

sag-en:　er sag-t, er sag-te, ge-sag-t

B 042　Strong verbs change their stem:

nehm-en:　er nimm-t, er nahm, ge-nomm-en

THE FORMS OF WEAK VERBS

Present Indicative

B 100　The following endings are added to the verb stem in the PRESENT TENSE:

SINGULAR	1st person	-e	ich sag-**e**
	2nd person	-st	du sag-**st**
	3rd person	-t	er[2] sag-**t**
PLURAL	1st person	-en	wir sag-**en**
	2nd person	-t	ihr sag-**t**
	3rd person	-en	sie sag-**en**[3]

[1] The terms "weak" and "strong," although linguistically nondescriptive, are being used here partly for traditional reasons and partly because the terms "regular" and "irregular" are equally inadequate: The so-called weak verbs have certain irregularities, and there are regularities among the so-called strong verbs.

[2] For the sake of simplicity, all verb paradigms list only the masculine **er** for the third person singular. The same ending pattern, to be sure, also applies to the feminine **sie** (singular) and the neuter **es**: *sie sag-t, es sag-t.*

[3] The polite (formal, conventional) form of address **Sie** (used for both singular and plural) always follows the ending pattern of the third person plural: *Sie sag-en* [→ D 025].

46

If the stem of the verb ends in **-d** or **-t**, or if it ends in **-m** or **-n** preceded   B 101
by another consonant (except **-l-** or **-r-**), a linking **-e-** is inserted before
the ending of the second and third person singular and the second person plural, for the sake of ease of pronunciation:[1]

-e	ich arbeit -e	bad -e	atm -e	rechn -e
-e-st	du arbeit-e-st	bad-e-st	atm-e-st	rechn-e-st
-e-t	er arbeit-e-t	bad-e-t	atm-e-t	rechn-e-t
-en	wir arbeit -en	bad -en	atm -en	rechn -en
e-t	ihr arbeit-e-t	bad-e-t	atm-e-t	rechn-e-t
-en	sie arbeit -en	bad -en	atm -en	rechn -en

But: *er erbarmt sich, er lernt, er qualmt, er filmt*

If the stem of the verb ends in **-s**, **-ß**,[2] **-x**, or **-z**, modern German usage   B 102
omits the **-s-** in the ending of the 2nd person singular, so that 2nd and
3rd person coincide, both using a **-t** ending:

modern: *du grüß-t*   *du mix-t*   *du kratz-t*   *du ras-t*
           er grüß-t   *er mix-t*   *er kratz-t*   *er ras-t*

obsolete (or poetic):
           du grüß-e-st   (no form)   *du kratz-e-st*   *du ras-e-st*

If the infinitive of the verb ends in **-eln**, the stem loses the **-e-** in the first   B 103
person singular:

       klingel-n: ich klingl-e,   but   *du klingelst*, etc.

If the infinitive ends in **-ern**, the **-e-** is usually maintained:

         änder-n: ich ändere, du änderst, etc.

However, the **-e-** may occasionally be omitted in the 1st person:

         ich ändre

If the infinitive of the verb ends in **-eln** or **-ern**, the ending for the 1st and   B 104

---

[1] If the stem ends in **-sch**, modern German no longer uses the linking **-e-**, except in poetic
usage: *der Wind rauscht, du fischst, ihr wascht.* But poetic: *"Es rauschet der Wind."*

[2] Verb stems ending in **-ss** change to **-ß** before the **-t** ending of the 2nd and 3rd person
singular and the 2nd person plural [→ A 040.5]: *hassen — ich hasse, du haßt, er haßt, wir
hassen, ihr haßt, sie hassen.*

3rd person plural is only **-n**; these personal forms thus correspond to the infinitive:

klingeln	*ändern*	*verbessern*
wir klingel-n	*wir änder-n*	*wir verbesser-n*
sie klingel-n	*sie änder-n*	*sie verbesser-n*

B 105   If the infinitive ends in **-ien**, the **-e-** is considered part of the stem, although it is pronounced like an infinitive ending. The **-e-** is pronounced when it acts as an ending:

ich kni-e, du knie-st, er knie-t, wir kni-en, ihr knie-t, sie kni-en

B 106   The omission of the **-e-** in the plural after an **-h-** occurs only in poetic or in substandard colloquial use: *gehn, ziehn, ruhn.*

B 107   The verbs **haben** and **wissen** show irregularities in the singular [→ B 194]; the plural is regular:

haben — ich habe, du hast, er hat; wir haben, ihr habt, sie haben
wissen — ich weiß, du weißt, er weiß; wir wissen, ihr wißt, sie wissen

Past Indicative (Preterite, Imperfect)

B 110   In the past tense, weak verbs add the past tense indicator **-te** to the stem (similar to English *-ed*). There are no further endings in the 1st and 3rd person singular; in the 2nd person singular and in the plural, the conjugational endings of the present tense are added, except that the **-en** ending is shortened to **-n**:

-te	ich sag-**te**
-te-st	du sag-**te**-st
-te	er sag-**te**
-te-n	wir sag-**te**-n
-te-t	ihr sag-**te**-t
-te-n	sie sag-**te**-n

B 111   If the stem of the verb ends in **-d** or **-t**, or in **-m** or **-n** preceded by another

48

consonant (except for **-l-** and **-r-**), the linking vowel **-e-** is inserted between the stem and the past tense indicator [→ B 101]:

> *ich bad-e-te*   *du arbeit-e-test*   *er antwort-e-te*
> *wir atm-e-ten*   *ihr öffn-e-tet*   *sie rechn-e-ten*

But: *er erbarm-te sich, du lern-test, ich qualm-te, wir film-ten.*

Imperative

In the IMPERATIVE (command) form, the following endings are added to the stem:

                                                  B 120

du:	-, -e	sag! sag-e!	rechn-e!
ihr:	-t, -et	sag-t!	rechn-et!
Sie:	-en Sie	sag-en Sie!	rechn-en Sie!

The imperative of the 2ND PERSON SINGULAR (*du*) is formed from the   B 121
infinitive stem by omitting the **-n** ending of the infinitive. This form is
used WITHOUT the pronoun **du**:

> *kaufe(n):*   *Kaufe mir ein Buch!*
> *rede(n):*   *Rede nicht so laut!*

In many verbs, the **-e** ending may be omitted, particularly in colloquial   B 122
usage, using the stem only:

> *kauf(en):*   *Kauf mir ein Buch!*
> *rauch(en):*   *Rauch nicht so viel!*
> *mach(en):*   *Mach deine Aufgaben!*

If the stem of the verb ends in **-d**, **-t**, or **-ig**, or in **-m** or **-n** preceded by   B 123
a consonant other than **-l-** and **-r-** [→ B 101 and 111], the **-e** ending of
the imperative may not be omitted in written German:

> *antworte(n):*   *Antworte mir sofort!*
> *bade(n):*   *Bade nicht so heiß!*
> *entschuldige(n):*   *Entschuldige bitte!*
> *atme(n):*   *Atme tief!*
> *öffne(n):*   *Öffne die Tür!*

But: *lern(en):*   *Lern deine Aufgabe!* or
                                    Lerne deine Aufgabe!

B 124 If the infinitive of the verb ends in **-eln** [→ B 104], the **-e-** in the last syllable of the stem is usually dropped, but the imperative ending **-e** must be maintained; verbs ending in **-ern** also often omit the **-e-** in the stem:[1]

klingeln: *Klingle laut!*
ändern: *Ändre (or ändere) deine Meinung!*

B 126 The imperative of the SECOND PERSON PLURAL corresponds to the conjugational forms of the 2nd person plural present indicative, without the pronoun **ihr**:

hören — ihr hört: **Hört** *auf eure Eltern!*
öffnen — ihr öffnet: **Öffnet** *die Tür!*

B 127 For rules regarding the use of the linking **-e-**, → B 101.

B 128 The imperative for the formal or CONVENTIONAL FORM of ADDRESS corresponds to the conjugational form of the 3rd person plural present indicative, and has both singular and plural meaning [→ D 025]; the personal pronoun **Sie** is used after the verb:

kaufen — Sie kaufen: **Kaufen Sie** *das Buch!*
atmen — Sie atmen: **Atmen Sie** *tief!*

B 129 A command in the FIRST PERSON PLURAL may be considered an imperative or a subjunctive [→ B 706][2]; it corresponds to the conjugational form of the first person plural present indicative, with the personal pronoun **wir** following the verb:

reden — wir reden: **Reden wir** *nicht mehr davon!*
öffnen — wir öffnen: **Öffnen wir** *die Tür!*

Subjunctive

B 130 German has two subjunctive forms; they are designated here merely as subjunctive I and subjunctive II. Terms like "present" and "past" subjunctive are misleading, since the form and the tense to which the form refers often do not coincide [→ B 716]. "Primary" and "secondary"

---

[1] For these verbs, the omission of the **-e** ending in the imperative is considered a substandard colloquialism.

[2] The command form in the 3rd person singular is clearly a subjunctive [→ B 706].

subjunctive, on the other hand, may be interpreted as implying levels of importance or frequency of occurrence; this is patently untrue, since in modern German subjunctive II occurs far more frequently in writing, and almost exclusively in spoken utterances. [→ B 700 ff.]

The FORM of SUBJUNCTIVE I is derived from the form of the 1st person plural PRESENT indicative; the FORM of SUBJUNCTIVE II is derived from the form of the 1st person plural PAST indicative. Both subjunctive forms have the same personal endings: **B 131**

	SUBJUNCTIVE I *(wir sag-en)*	SUBJUNCTIVE II *(wir sagt-en)*
-e	ich sag-**e**	ich sagt-**e**
-est	du sag-**est**	du sagt-**est**
-e	er sag-**e**	er sagt-**e**
-en	wir sag-**en**	wir sagt-**en**
-et	ihr sag-**et**	ihr sagt-**et**
-en	sie sag-**en**	sie sagt-**en**

Note that for weak verbs, only the following subjunctive I forms differ from the forms of the present indicative: **B 132**

> 3rd person singular for all verbs: *er sagt — er sage.*
> 2nd person singular and plural only for those verbs which do not insert a linking -e- between stem and ending [→ B 100–101]:

> > *du sagst — du sagest;   ihr sagt — ihr saget*
> But: *du öffnest, ihr öffnet* (both indicative and subjunctive)

Verbs ending in **-eln** or **-ern** do not insert an **-e-** in the 2nd person singular or plural subjunctive; **B 133**

> *du klingelst, ihr klingelt* (both indicative and subjunctive)
> *du änderst, ihr ändert*   (both indicative and subjunctive)

The verbs *haben* and *wissen* are irregular in the singular present indicative [→ B 107, B 194]; they are regular in the formation of subjunctive I: **B 134**

> *ich habe, du habest, er habe, wir haben, ihr habet, sie haben*
> *ich wisse, du wissest, er wisse, wir wissen, ihr wisset, sie wissen*

B 135   All other forms of subjunctive I correspond to the forms of the present indicative [→ B 103–105].

B 140   For weak verbs, the forms of subjunctive II coincide with the forms of the past tense [→ B 110–111]. For exceptions → B 196.

Infinitive

B 150   The INFINITIVE adds the following endings to the verb stem:

> **-en**:   *sag-**en**, lach-**en**, arbeit-**en***
> **-n**:[1]   *klingel-**n**, änder-**n***

B 151   The infinitive can be used in the formation of compound tense forms [→ B 451].

Participle

B 160   We distinguish two types of participles: PRESENT PARTICIPLE and PAST PARTICIPLE (or perfect participle). The following forms are used:

PRESENT PARTICIPLE: **-end, -nd**	*sag-**end**, lächel-**nd***
PAST PARTICIPLE: **ge — t, ge — et**	*ge-sag-**t**, ge-arbeit-**et***

B 170   The PRESENT PARTICIPLE is formed by adding the ending **-d** to the infinitive:

> *sagen-**d***   *klingeln-**d***   *ändern-**d***

B 180   The PAST PARTICIPLE is formed by placing the prefix **ge-** before the stem and adding the **-t** or **-et**. [For verbs using the linking **-e-** → B 101]:

> *sagen — **ge**-sag-**t***   *antworten — **ge**-antwort-**et***

B 181   Compound verbs with separable prefixes place the **-ge-** between the verb modifier and the stem [→ A 250 ff.]:

> *einkaufen — ein-**ge**-kauft*   *aussagen — aus-**ge**-sagt*

---

[1] The omission of the -e- in the infinitive after an -h- occurs only in poetic or in substandard colloquial usage: *gehn, ziehn, ruhn*, etc.

For compounds with **miß-** → A 327. For prefixes which can be separable or inseparable → B 340.

The following verbs form their past participle without the prefix **ge-**: B 182
a) All compound verbs with inseparable prefixes [→ B 331 f.]:

> *verkaufen — verkauft*   *beantworten — beantwortet*

b) Verbs which are not stressed on the stem syllable. These are mostly B 183
words of foreign origin, all of them conjugated as weak verbs, above all
verbs with the endings **-ieren** and **-eien**:

> *rasíeren — rasiert*   *trompéten — trompetet*
> *studíeren — studiert*   *kredénzen — kredenzt*
> *frisíeren — frisiert*   *rumóren — rumort*
> *prophezéien — prophezeit*   *áusposáunen — ausposaunt*

There are a few exceptions from this principle: B 184

> *benedéien — gebenedeit*
> *frohlócken — frohlockt* or *gefrohlockt*
> *liebkósen — liebkost* or *geliebkost*
> *offenbáren — offenbart* or *geoffenbart*

Special Problems

The following verbs CHANGE THEIR STEM, but use the endings of the B 190
weak conjugation:

| | 3rd Person Singular | | |
INFINITIVE	PRESENT	PAST	PAST PARTICIPLE
brennen	er brenn-t	er brann-te	ge-brann-t
kennen	er kenn-t	er kann-te	ge-kann-t
nennen	er nenn-t	er nann-te	ge-nann-t
rennen	er renn-t	er rann-te	ge-rann-t
senden	er send-et	er sand-te	ge-sand-t
wenden	er wend-et	er wand-te	ge-wand-t
bringen	er bring-t	er brach-te	ge-brach-t
denken	er denk-t	er dach-te	ge-dach-t

B 191   The verb *dünken — deuchte — gedeucht* also belongs into this group; these conjugational forms, however, are obsolete. Today, the accepted forms are **dünken — dünkte — gedünkt.**

B 192   The verbs *senden* and *wenden* also have regular past tense and past participle forms:[1]

> *senden:*   *er send-et, er send-ete, ge-send-et*
> *wenden:*   *er wend-et, er wend-ete, ge-wend-et*

B 193   The verbs *senden* and *wenden* form their subjunctive II according to the regular weak conjugation:

> *er sendete, er wendete*

B 194   The verbs *haben* and *wissen* are irregular in the singular present indicative and change their stem in the past tense; *wissen* also changes its stem vowel in the past participle:

> *haben:*   *ich habe, du hast, er hat*   *wir haben,* etc.
>   *ich hatte,* etc.   *gehabt*
> *wissen:*   *ich weiß, du weißt, er weiß*   *wir wissen,* etc.
>   *ich wußte,* etc.   *gewußt*

Both verbs form the imperative from the regular infinitive stem:

> *habe!*   *wisse!*

Subjunctive I forms are also regular:

> *er habe*   *er wisse*

B 195   The verbs *brennen, kennen, nennen,* and *rennen* are irregular in forming subjunctive II: they substitute an **-e-** for the **-a-** of the past tense. (Subjunctive I forms are regular):

INFINITIVE	PAST TENSE	SUBJUNCTIVE II
brennen	wir brannten	wir brennten
kennen	wir kannten	wir kennten
nennen	wir nannten	wir nennten
rennen	wir rannten	wir rennten

---

[1] These forms have a special meaning: *Der Münchner Rundfunk sendete früher um diese Zeit die Nachrichten. Der alte Mantel ist gewendet worden.*

The verbs *haben, denken, bringen,* and *wissen* form their subjunctive II   B 196
with an *Umlaut*:

INFINITIVE	PAST TENSE	SUBJUNCTIVE II
haben	wir hatten	wir hätten
denken	wir dachten	wir dächten
bringen	wir brachten	wir brächten
wissen	wir wußten	wir wüßten

The verbs *mahlen* and *salzen* form their past participles according to the   B 197
strong conjugational pattern [→ B 290]:

mahlen — mahlte — gemahlen[1]
salzen — salzte — gesalzen

The verb *spalten* may have either a weak or a strong past participle:

Er hat Holz gespaltet. Das Holz ist gespalten.

For other verbs with mixed or dual forms, → B 290 ff.

MODAL AUXILIARIES have a special conjugational pattern. [→ B 420 ff.]   B 198

THE FORMS OF STRONG VERBS

STRONG VERBS change their stem vowel in the past tense and in the past   B 200
participle (often also in the 2nd and 3rd person singular present indicative) according to seven basic patterns, the so-called *Ablaut* classes
[→ B 280 ff.]. In a number of strong verbs, the consonants at the end
of the stem also change.

Present Indicative

The ending pattern for the present tense of strong verbs follows the   B 210
same basic rules as the weak verbs [→ B 100]. The linking -e- in the
2nd and 3rd person singular and in the 2nd person plural is added after

---

[1] Do not confuse **mahlen** (to grind) with **malen** (to paint), which is a regular weak verb:
malen, malte, gemalt.

the same consonants or consonant clusters [→ B 101]. The linking -e- is omitted, however, if the stem vowel carries an *Umlaut*:

> *ich komme, du kommst, er kommt*
> *ich binde, du bindest, er bindet*
> *ich reite, du reitest, er reitet*

but: *ich rate, du rätst, er rät*
ich lade, du lädst, er lädt[1]

B 211   Strong verbs with the stem vowels -e-, -a-, and -au- (and one with the vowel -o-) change their stem vowel (*nehmen* also the consonants) in the 2nd and 3rd person singular: the vowel -e- changes to -i- or -ie-, -a- to -ä-,[2] and -au- to -äu-. The verb *stoßen* changes to -ö-. All plural forms follow the pattern of weak verbs:

	geben	*sehen*	*nehmen*	*fahren*	*laufen*	*stoßen*
ich	gebe	sehe	nehme	fahre	laufe	stoße
du	gibst	siehst	nimmst	fährst	läufst	stößt
er	gibt	sieht	nimmt	fährt	läuft	stößt
wir	geben	sehen	nehmen	fahren	laufen	stoßen
ihr	gebt	seht	nehmt	fahrt	lauft	stoßt
sie	geben	sehen	nehmen	fahren	laufen	stoßen

B 212   The verbs *gehen, stehen,* and *heben* do not change their stem vowel:

> *ich gehe, er geht; ich stehe, du stehst,* etc.

The same also applies to verbs which may be conjugated either weak or strong [→ B 294 ff.]: *er bewegt, er pflegt, er schafft, er haut,* etc. The *Umlaut* form *er kömmt* no longer exists in modern German.

B 213   The verbs *erlöschen* and *verlöschen* change their stem vowel to -i-:

> *es erlischt*

Note, however, that the basic verb *löschen* follows the weak conjugation and is used transitively:

[1] *Umlaut* is sometimes omitted and a linking -e- inserted in poetic or colloquial usage: *Er ladet mich ein.*
[2] By analogy, an ä also sometimes appears on weak verbs: *er frägt.* This, however, is *not* accepted as standard German.

56

> *Er löscht das Licht.*　　but:　*Das Licht erlischt.*
> *Er löschte das Licht.*　　　　*Das Licht erlosch.*

The verb *tun* formerly had the ending **-en** in the 1st and 3rd person　B 214
plural present indicative. These forms are no longer used today. Modern
German uses the regular ending pattern throughout the present tense:

> *ich tue, du tust, er tut, wir tun, ihr tut, sie tun*

The verbs **sein** and **werden** have irregular forms in all tenses　B 215
[→ B 410 ff.].

Past Indicative (Preterite, Imperfect)

The strong verbs CHANGE their STEM in the past tense and add the fol-　B 220
lowing endings:[1]

	kommen	*fahren*	*gehen*
—	ich kam	ich fuhr	ich **ging**
-st	du kam-st	du fuhr-st	du **ging**-st
—	er kam	er fuhr	er **ging**
-en	wir kam-en	wir fuhr-en	wir **ging**-en
-t	ihr kam-t	ihr fuhr-t	ihr **ging**-t
-en	sie kam-en	sie fuhr-en	sie **ging**-en

The vowels change according to definite patterns, the so-called ABLAUT　B 221
CLASSES [→ B 280 ff.]. The consonants at the end of the stem change
according to VERNER'S LAW (*Grammatischer Wechsel*) regarding the
unvoicing or transformation of final consonants, e.g. **d** > **tt**: *leiden,
litt*; **h** > **g**: *ziehen, zog*; **s** > **r**: *erkiesen, erkor*. Other possible CON-
SONANTAL CHANGES are doubling to indicate a short vowel (*reiten, ritt*;
pfeifen, pfiff), loss of a double consonant to indicate a long vowel
treffen, traf; *kommen, kam*), a change from **tz** to **ß** (*sitzen, saß*), addition
or substitution of consonants (*hauen, hieb*; *gehen, ging*; *stehen, stand*;
tun, tat), or the substitution of a different stem (*sein, war*).

---

[1] Note that the personal endings are identical with those which weak verbs add to the past
tense indicator **-te** [→ B 110].

57

B 222   If the stem of the verb ends in **-t**, **-d**, **-ss** (**-ß**), or **-chs**, a linking **-e-** is inserted between the stem and the ending of the 2nd person singular or plural, to facilitate pronunciation [→ B 101]. In colloquial usage, this linking **-e-** may be omitted, except in the 2nd person plural after **-d-** or **-t-**:

		bieten	*laden*	*essen*	*wachsen*
—	*ich*	bot	lud	aß	wuchs
-e-st	*du*	bot-e-st	lud-e-st	aß-e-st	wuchs-e-st
—	*er*	bot	lud	aß	wuchs
-en	*wir*	bot-en	lud-en	aß-en	wuchs-en
-e-t	*ihr*	bot-e-t	lud-e-t	aß-e-t	wuchs-e-t
-en	*sie*	bot-en	lud-en	aß-en	wuchs-en

B 223   If the stem of the verb ends in **-ie** in the past tense, the **-e-** of the ending is omitted in the 1st and 3rd person plural. The **-e** of the stem is then pronounced as if it were part of the ending:

   ich schrie, wir schri-en, sie schri-en   [→ B 105]

Imperative

B 230   The IMPERATIVE of strong verbs has the following forms:

du:	-, -e	komm! komme!	nimm!	biete!
ihr:	-t, -et[1]	kommt!	nehmt!	bietet!
Sie:	-en Sie	kommen Sie!	nehmen Sie!	bieten Sie!

B 231   The Imperative in the 2nd Person Singular:

Verbs which do *not* change their stem vowel to **-i-** or **-ie-** in the 2nd and

---

[1] For rules regarding the linking **-e-**, → B 101. The verb *tun* also uses the **-et** ending in the 2nd person plural: *Tuet recht!* This ending also occurs with other verbs in poetic usage: *Fanget an!*

3rd person singular present indicative, form the imperative of the 2nd person singular like the weak verbs [→ B 121 ff.]:

> *kommen: Komme morgen zu mir!   Komm schnell her!*
> *fahren: Fahre mit der Bahn!   Fahr vorsichtig!*
> *tun: Tue recht und scheue niemand!   Tu mir den Gefallen!*

Verbs which change their stem vowel to **-i-** or **-ie-** in the present tense form their imperative for the 2nd person singular from the 2nd person singular present indicative, always omitting the conjugational ending: {B 232}

> *nehmen, du nimmst: Nimm deinen Hut!*
> *helfen, du hilfst: Hilf deinem Freund!*
> *essen, du ißt: Iß mehr Obst!*
> *lesen, du liest: Lies dieses Buch!*

For bibliographic references, the form **siehe** is customary as the imperative of *sehen*: *Siehe Seite 8. Siehe auch Müller, ,,Klima und Wettervoraussage.''* The exclamation *sieh da!* is also often replaced by **siehe da!**, especially if it does not come at the beginning of the sentence: {B 233}

> *Gestern habe ich an ihn gedacht, und* **siehe da**, *heute hat er geschrieben!*

The verb *werden* forms the imperative for the 2nd person singular from the infinitive stem: {B 234}

> *werden, du wirst: Werde glücklich!*[1]

The imperative of the 2nd person plural (*ihr*) and the conventional form of address (*Sie*) is formed exactly as for the weak verbs [→ B 126 ff.]: {B 237}

> *Geht jetzt nach Hause!   Fahrt mit der Straßenbahn!   Haltet an!*
> *Essen Sie viel Obst!   Helfen Sie Ihren Freunden!*

For a command in the first person plural, → B 129 and B 706: {B 238}

> *gehen, wir gehen: Gehen wir nach Hause!*[2]

Subjunctive

As in the case of the weak verb, we distinguish between two subjunctive forms [→ B 130]. The form of subjunctive I is obtained from the form {B 240}

---

[1] See also *wissen* and its imperative for the 2nd person singular: *wisse!* [→ B 194].

[2] For the verb *sein*, such a command is clearly subjunctive: *Seien wir froh, daß alles gut vorüber ist!*

of the 1st person plural present indicative, that of subjunctive II from the form of the first person plural past indicative. Strong verbs with the vowels **a**, **o**, and **u** in the past tense use *Umlaut* in subjunctive II. Both subjunctive forms have the same personal endings, identical with those for weak verbs [→ B 131]:

	SUBJUNCTIVE I (*wir fahr-en*)	SUBJUNCTIVE II (*wir fuhr-en*)
-e	ich fahr-**e**	ich führ-**e**
-est	du fahr-**est**	du führ-**est**
-e	er fahr-**e**	er führ-**e**
-en	wir fahr-**en**	wir führ-**en**
-et	ihr fahr-**et**	ihr führ-**et**
-en	sie fahr-**en**	sie führ-**en**

B 241 Note that for strong verbs only the following forms of subjunctive I differ from the present indicative:

	IND.	SUBJ.
2nd and 3rd person singular:	*du fährst* —	*du fahrest*
	er fährt —	*er fahre*
2nd person plural:	*ihr fahrt* —	*ihr fahret*

B 242 The difference in the 2nd person singular disappears for verbs without a vowel change in the present indicative, if they add a linking **-e-** to the stem:

> *du findest* (both indicative and subjunctive)
> but: *du rätst* (ind.) — *du ratest* (subj.)

The difference in the 2nd person plural disappears for all verbs which add a linking **-e-** to the stem:

> *ihr findet* (both indicative and subjunctive)
> *ihr ratet* (both indicative and subjunctive)

B 243 The verbs *sein* and *werden* use subjunctive I forms which differ from the present indicative [→ B 410]:

60

IND.	SUBJ.	IND.	SUBJ.
ich bin	ich sei	ich werde	ich werde
du bist	du seiest	du wirst	du werdest
er ist	er sei	er wird	er werde
	etc.		etc.

All other verb forms are identical in the present indicative and in subjunctive I. [For modals → B 421.]   B 244

For SUBJUNCTIVE II, all forms differ from the past indicative for verbs with an **a**, **o**, or **u** in the past indicative stem, since these take *Umlaut* in the subjunctive: B 245

> *wir fuhren — wir führen;   du fuhrst — du führest*

If the stem vowel does not have an *Umlaut*, the forms of the 1st and 3rd person plural are identical for the past indicative and subjunctive II: B 246

> *wir blieben, sie blieben* (both indicative and subjunctive)

A few strong verbs have IRREGULAR FORMS for subjunctive II, involving a vowel change to -**ü**-:   B 250

	PAST INDICATIVE	SUBJUNCTIVE II
wir	starben	stürben
wir	halfen	hülfen
wir	warfen	würfen
wir	standen	stünden
wir	verdarben	verdürben
wir	warben	würben

Other irregular subjunctive forms are obsolete today and are replaced by regular forms in modern German: B 252

	PAST INDICATIVE	FORMER SUBJUNCTIVE	CURRENT USAGE
wir	empfahlen	empföhlen	empfählen
wir	begannen	begönnen	begännen
wir	sannen	sönnen	sännen

61

Infinitive

B 260   The INFINITIVE of strong verbs always has the ending **-en**:

*komm-**en**   nehm-**en**   biet-**en***

B 261   The only exception is the verb **tun**; the 1st and 3rd person plural present indicative follow the infinitive: *wir tun, sie tun* [→ B 214].

B 262   The strong verbs follow the same principles for the use of compound tenses as the weak verbs [→ B 451].

Participles

B 265   Just as with weak verbs, we distinguish between PRESENT and PAST participles [→ B 160]:

> PRESENT PARTICIPLE: **-en-d**: *komm-en-**d**, geb-en-**d**, biet-en-**d***
> PAST PARTICIPLE: **ge- — -en**: ***ge**-komm-**en**, **ge**-geb-**en**, **ge**-bot-**en***

B 266   The PRESENT PARTICIPLE is formed, as with the weak verbs, by adding the ending **-d** to the infinitive: *kommen-**d**, spechen-**d*** [→ B 170].

B 267   For the verb *tun*, an **-e-** is inserted (mainly in compounds):

wohltuend

B 270   The PAST PARTICIPLE is formed with the prefix **ge-** before the stem and the ending **-en** after it. As for the past tense, strong verbs change the stem vowel for the past participle. The resulting vowel may be the same as that of the past tense, that of the infinitive, or a different vowel [→ B 280 ff.]:

INFINITIVE		PAST TENSE		PAST PARTICIPLE
schreiben	—	schrieb	—	geschrieben
biegen	—	bog	—	gebogen
fahren	—	fuhr	—	gefahren
kommen	—	kam	—	gekommen
werfen	—	warf	—	geworfen
singen	—	sang	—	gesungen

The prefix **ge-** is omitted in the past participle if the verb begins with an   B 271
inseparable prefix [→ B 182, 330 ff., 340]:

> *entwerfen — entworfen*   *widersprechen — widersprochen*
> *zerspringen — zersprungen*   *vollbringen — vollbracht*

For some of these verbs, the infinitive and the past participle may be   B 272
identical:

> *bekommen — bekam — bekommen*
> *geschehen — geschah — geschehen*
> *empfangen — empfing — empfangen*

The verb *tun* has the ending **-n** for the past participle [→ B 261]:   B 275

> *tun — tat — getan*

The verb *essen* inserts the infix **-g-** in the past participle between the   B 276
prefix **ge-** and the stem:

> *essen — aß — gegessen*

Conjugational Patterns

According to the changes in the stem vowel of strong verbs, we can   B 280
distinguish seven major CONJUGATIONAL PATTERNS or *Ablaut* series:

I

a)	ei — ie — ie:	schreiben	—	schrieb	—	geschrieben	B 281
b)	ei — i — i:	leiden	—	litt	—	gelitten	
		pfeifen	—	pfiff	—	gepfiffen	
		reißen	—	riß	—	gerissen	
		reiten	—	ritt	—	geritten	

a) Stem vowel **long** in past tense and past participle.
b) Stem vowel **short** in past tense and past participle. Stem vowel followed by **d, f, ß,** and **t**. (Note change to **ff** and **tt** in past tense and past
   participle, **ss** in past participle and past tense plural [→ B 221].)

II

a) ie	— o — o:	biegen	— bog	— gebogen
		ziehen [→ B 221]	— zog	— gezogen

Variations:

e	— o — o:	heben	— hob	— gehoben
au	— o — o:	saugen	— sog	— gesogen
ä	— o — o:	gären	— gor	— gegoren
ö	— o — o:	schwören	— schwor	— geschworen
ü	— o — o:	lügen	— log	— gelogen

b) ie	— o — o:	schießen	— schoß	— geschossen

Variations:

e (i)[1]	— o — o:	schmelzen, schmilzt	— schmolz	— geschmolzen
au (äu)	— o — o:	saufen, säuft	— soff	— gesoffen

Stem vowel usually **ie**, sometimes **e**; other variations rare.

a) Stem vowel **long** in past tense and past participle.
b) Stem vowel **short** in past tense and past participle. (Note consonant changes [→ B 221].)

III

a) i — a — u:	finden	— fand	— gefunden
	singen	— sang	— gesungen
	stinken	— stank	— gestunken
b) i — a — o:	schwimmen	— schwamm	— geschwommen
	beginnen	— begann	— begonnen

a) Stem vowel **i** followed by **nd**, **ng**, or **nk**.
b) Stem vowel **i** followed by **mm** or **nn**.

---

[1] Vowels in parentheses indicate 2nd and 3rd person singular present.

IV

a) e (ie) — a — o:	stehlen, stiehlt — stahl — gestohlen	B 284
Variation:		
ä — a — o:	gebären — gebar — geboren	
b) e (i) — a — o:	brechen, bricht — brach — gebrochen	
	treffen, trifft — traf — getroffen [→ B 221]	
	nehmen, nimmt — nahm — genommen [→ B 221]	
Variation:		
o — a — o:	kommen — kam — gekommen	
c) e (i) — a — o:	werfen, wirft — warf — geworfen	
	helfen, hilft — half — geholfen	

Stem vowel usually **e**, followed by **l**, **m**, **n**, or **r** (**r** may occur *before* the stem vowel).

a) Stem vowel **long** in past tense and past participle.

b) Stem vowel **long** in past tense, **short** in past participle.

c) Stem vowel **short** in past tense and past participle.

V

a)	e (ie) — a — e:	lesen, liest — las — gelesen	B 285
	e (i) — a — e:	geben, gibt — gab — gegeben	
	Variations:		
	i — a — e:	bitten — bat — gebeten	
	ie — a — e:	liegen — lag — gelegen	
b)	e (i) — a — e:	messen, mißt — maß — gemessen	
	Variation:		
	i — a — e:	sitzen [→ B 221] — saß — gesessen	

Stem vowel usually **e**, followed by consonant other than **l**, **m**, **n**, or **r**.

a) Stem vowel **long** in past tense and past participle.

b) Stem vowel **long** in past tense, **short** in past participle.

65

VI

B 286

a (ä) — u — a:	fahren, fährt	—	fuhr	— gefahren

Variations:

e — a — a:	stehen [→ B 221]	—	stand	— gestanden
e — i — a:	gehen [→ B 221]	—	ging	— gegangen

Stem vowel usually **a**.

VII

B 287

a)
a (ä) — ie — a:	schlafen, schläft	— schlief	— geschlafen
a (ä) — i — a:	fangen, fängt	— fing	— gefangen

b)
au (äu) — ie — au:	laufen, läuft	— lief	— gelaufen
au — ie — au:	hauen [→ B 221]	— hieb	— gehauen

Variations:

o (ö) — ie — o:	stoßen, stößt	— stieß	— gestoßen
u — ie — u:	rufen	— rief	— gerufen
ei — ie — ei:	heißen	— hieß	— geheißen

Stem vowel usually **a** or **au**. Stem vowel of infinitive repeated in past participle.

Irregular Conjugational Patterns and Mixed Forms

B 290 There are a number of verbs in German for which both weak and strong forms exist, where alternate forms occur, or where past tense and past participle no longer follow the same conjugational pattern. The most important of these verbs are:[1]

INFINITIVE	PAST TENSE	PAST PARTICIPLE
backen, bäckt	backte/buk	gebacken
dingen	dingte/dang	gedungen/gedingt
dünken	dünkte/deuchte	gedünkt/gedeucht
fragen	fragte/frug	gefragt
gären	gor/gärte	gegoren/gegärt
glimmen	glimmte/glomm	geglommen/geglimmt
hauen	haute/hieb	gehaut/gehauen
klimmen	klomm/klimmte	geklommen/geklimmt

[1] Unless there are special explanations indicated by cross reference numbers, the first form is in more frequent use in modern German.

INFINITIVE	PAST TENSE	PAST PARTICIPLE
mahlen [→ B 197]	mahlte	gemahlen
melken	melkte, molk	gemolken, gemelkt
salzen [→ B 197]	salzte	gesalzen
saugen	saugte/sog	gesaugt/gesogen
schallen	schallte/scholl	geschallt/geschollen
scheren	schor/scherte	geschoren/geschert
schnauben	schnaubte/schnob	geschnaubt/geschnoben
schwören	schwor/schwörte	geschworen/geschwört
senden [→ B 190]	sandte/sendete	gesandt/gesendet
sieden	siedete/sott	gesotten/gesiedet
spalten [→ B 197]	spaltete	gespalten/gespaltet
triefen	triefte/troff	getrieft
verderben, verdirbt	verdarb	verdorben/verderbt [1]
weben	webte/wob	gewebt/gewoben
wenden [→ B 190]	wandte/wendete	gewandt/gewendet
werden, wird	wurde/ward	geworden

Other verbs follow the weak conjugation when they are transitive and the strong conjugation when they are used intransitively; the infinitive is the same in both uses. Such verbs are mostly causative verbs; some of them are:

B 295

erschrecken {erschrak — erschrocken [→ B 467] / erschreckte — erschreckt}
Das laute Geschrei hat ihn **erschreckt**.
Er ist vor dem Hund **erschrocken**.

hängen {hing — gehangen / hängte — gehängt}
Der Mantel **hing** *am Haken*.
Ich habe den Mantel an den Haken **gehängt**.

stecken {stak / steckte} gesteckt (only weak form)
Er **steckte** *den Pfahl in die Erde*.
Der Pfahl **stak** *(steckte) in der Erde*.[2]

schmelzen {schmolz — geschmolzen / schmelzte — geschmelzt}
Der Schnee **schmilzt** — **schmolz** — *in der Sonne*.
Die Sonne **schmelzt** *(schmilzt)* — **schmelzte** *(schmolz)* — *den Schnee*.[3]

---

[1] *Verderbt* is used mainly in a moral sense: corrupt, depraved.

[2] Weak form often used.

[3] Strong form often used; intransitive past participle: *ist geschmolzen*.

$$\textit{pflegen} \quad \begin{cases} \textit{pflog} & \textit{gepflogen} \\ \textit{pflegte} & \textit{gepflegt} \end{cases}$$

Er **pflog** (*pflegte*) *der Ruhe.*[1]
Sie **pflegte** *den Kranken.*

B 296 Other verbs follow the weak conjugation as simple verbs, while strong forms are still preserved in compounds. Some of these verbs are:

bleichen   *bleichte*   *gebleicht*

$$\textit{erbleichen} \quad \begin{cases} \textit{erblich} & \textit{erblichen}[2] \\ \textit{erbleichte} & \textit{erbleicht} \end{cases}$$

Die Sonne hat die Wäsche **gebleicht**.
Als er das hörte, **erblich** (*erbleichte*) er.

löschen   *löschte*   *gelöscht*   [→ B 213]
erlöschen   *erlosch*   *erloschen*
    Ich habe das Feuer **gelöscht**.
    Das Feuer flammte noch einmal auf und **erlosch**.

B 297 Some verbs have a different meaning when they follow either the weak or the strong conjugation. Some of these verbs are:

backen (*bäckt*)   *backte/buk*   *gebacken*   to bake
backen (*backt*)   *backte*   *gebackt*   to cling, adhere, cake
    Das Brot wird im Backofen **gebacken**.
    Der Schnee ist an meinem Ski fest**gebackt**.

schleifen   *schliff*   *geschliffen*   to sharpen, grind
schleifen   *schleifte*   *geschleift*   to drag, trail
    Das Messer ist **geschliffen**.
    Das Pferd **schleifte** den Reiter am Boden.

bewegen   *bewog*   *bewogen*   to induce
bewegen   *bewegte*   *bewegt*   to move
    Er hat mich **bewogen**, ihm zu helfen.
    Er **bewegte** die Arme hin und her.

schaffen   *schuf*   *geschaffen*   to create
schaffen   *schaffte*   *geschafft*   to work hard; to manage
    Am Anfang **schuf** Gott Himmel und Erde.
    Der Künstler hat ein großes Werk **geschaffen**.
    Er **schaffte** Tag und Nacht.
    Jetzt hat er es **geschafft**!

---

[1] Weak form often used; weak form must be used in the sense of "to be accustomed to":
Ich pflegte früh aufzustehen.

[2] The form *verblichen* survives only as a past participle.

68

wiegen	wog	gewogen	to weigh
wiegen	wiegte	gewiegt	to rock, to cradle

*Das Kind **wog** bei der Geburt 8 Pfund.*
*Sie **wiegte** das Kind in ihren Armen.*

Summary of Conjugational Endings

PRESENT INDICATIVE (*weak and strong*)		PAST INDICATIVE		SUBJUNCTIVE I & II *weak and strong*	B 299
		weak	*strong*		
ich	-e	-(e)te	—	-e	
du	-(e)st	-(e)te-st	-(e)st	-est	
er	-(e)t	-(e)te	—	-e	
wir	-en	-(e)te-n	-en	-en	
ihr	-(e)t	-(e)te-t	-(e)t	-et	
sie	-en	-(e)te-n	-en	-en	

PRESENT PARTICIPLE *weak and strong*	PAST PARTICIPLE	
	weak	*strong*
-en-d	ge—t	ge—en

COMPOUND VERBS

Many verbs can be compounded by combining them with other words   B 300
or syllables as prefixes. These prefixes and verb complements change the
meaning of the stem. They stand before the infinitive, and form a single
word:

fangen	**an**fangen	**auf**fangen	**ver**fangen
kommen	**be**kommen	**unter**kommen	**vorwärts**kommen
schlagen	**ab**schlagen	**tot**schlagen	**entzwei**schlagen
bleiben	**ver**bleiben	**stehen**bleiben	**unter**bleiben
schreiben	**be**schreiben	**maschine**schreiben	**auf**schreiben
gehen	**spazieren**gehen	**unter**gehen	**entlang**gehen

In conjugated verb forms, the SYLLABIC PREFIX (inseparable prefix,   B 301
bound morpheme) is always connected with the verb stem [→ B 330],
whereas the VERB COMPLEMENT (separable prefix, free morpheme) may
also occupy a different position in the sentence [→ B 310, H 113].

69

B 302   The conjugated forms of compound verbs follow the conjugational pattern of the verb stem. [For exceptions → B 296 and B 352.]

kommen — kam — gekommen: bekommen — bekam — bekommen
                                     ankommen — kam . . . an — angekommen

raten (rät) — riet — geraten: verraten (verrät) — verriet — verraten
                                     abraten (rät . . . ab) — riet . . . ab —
                                         abgeraten

B 310   The VERB COMPLEMENT, which carries the main STRESS, stands at the end of the sentence or main clause for conjugated verb forms (**separable verbs**):

*ábfahren: Ich **fahre** . . . . **ab**.*
          *Ich **fahre** morgen vormittag um 9 Uhr mit dem Zug **ab**.*

B 311   In the past participle [→ B 180, 270] and for infinitives using **zu** [→ B 453, 900 ff.], **ge-** and **zu** act as INFIXES, occurring between the verb complement and the stem and forming a single word with them:

ábfahren: abgefahren, abzufahren

B 312   The **-ge-** infix of the past participle is omitted, if the first syllable of the stem verb is unstressed [→ B 182, 271]. The infix **-zu-**, however, is used for these verbs as well:

ábstèllen, abgestellt, abzustellen

BUT: *ábbestèllen, abbestellt, abzubestellen*
      vórberèiten, vorbereitet, vorzubereiten
      aúsradièren, ausradiert, auszuradieren
      héimbeglèiten, heimbegleitet, heimzubegleiten
      míßverstèhen, mißverstanden, mißzuverstehen [but → A 327, B 334]

B 320   In a DEPENDENT CLAUSE, where the conjugated verb must come at the end [→ H 125], the verb is again united with the verb complement:

*Ich kann dich leider nicht besuchen, weil ich morgen vormittag um 9 Uhr mit dem Zug **abfahre**.*

B 330   PREFIXES which are UNSTRESSED (*bound morphemes*) remain connected with the verb in all conjugated forms (**inseparable verbs**). These prefixes do not have independent meaning and existence as words by themselves:

besuchen: Mein Freund besucht mich morgen.
erklären: Erklären Sie mir die Regel!

These verbs are conjugated like the simple verbs from which they are   B 331
derived. They do not, however, use the prefix **ge-** in the past participle
[→ B 182, 271]:

> *Mein Freund hat mich gestern besucht.*
> *Ich habe die Erklärung nicht verstanden.*

Note that verbs with the prefix **ge-** have the same past participle as the   B 332
simple verbs from which they are derived. The past participle may also
coincide with the infinitive [→ B 272]:

simple verb:	*hören*	*hörte*	*gehört*
compound verb:	*gehören*	*gehörte*	*gehört*
simple verb:	*fallen*	*fiel*	*gefallen*
compound verb:	*gefallen*	*gefiel*	*gefallen*

Verbs with the prefixes **be-**, **ent-** (or **emp-** before **-f-**), **er-**, **ge-**, **hinter-**,[1]   B 333
ob-, **ver-**, and **zer-** are always inseparable, since these prefixes are always
unstressed:

> *besúchen, entschúldigen, empfángen, erklären, gehören, hinterlássen,*
> *oblíegen, verstéhen, zerréißen*

Verbs with the prefix **miß-** are always inseparable, whether the prefix is   B 334
stressed or not: *míßdeuten* or *mißdéuten*. Usage fluctuates, however,
with the infixes **-ge-** and **-zu-** [→ A 325, B 312]:

> *mißachtet, mißgeachtet; zu mißachten, mißzuverstehen*

If an inseparable prefix is followed by a verb complement which would   B 335
normally be separable, the entire compound is inseparable:

abreden: *ich rede . . . ab*;	**verab**reden: *ich verabrede*
auftragen: *ich trage . . . auf*;	**beauf**tragen: *ich beauftrage*

If, on the other hand, an inseparable prefix follows a verb complement   B 336
which is normally separable, only the verb complement is separable
[→ B 352]:

behalten: *ich behalte*;	**beibe**halten: *ich behalte . . . bei*
vertrauen: *ich vertraue*;	**anver**trauen: *ich vertraue . . . an*

If a compound verb begins with a PREPOSITION (*an-, auf-, vor-, zu-,* etc.),   B 337
an ADVERB (*vorbei-, vorwärts-, zurück-,* etc.), an ADJECTIVE (*tot-, frei-,*

---

[1] The prefix **hinter-** is sometimes separable in colloquial language: *Die Frau geht hinter.*
This is not considered correct German and should be replaced by: *Die Frau geht nach hinten.*

etc.), another VERB (*spazieren-*, *stehen-*, etc.), or a NOUN (*maschine-*, *rad-*, etc.), the verb complement is almost always stressed. These verbs are separable [→ A 253]:

> *ich komme . . . an*, *er fährt . . . vor*; *wir gehen . . . zurück*, *er läuft . . . vorbei*; *er schlägt die Fliege tot*; *er blieb auf der Treppe stehen*; *sie schreibt maschine.*

B 340 Verbs with the complement **durch-**, **über-**, **um-**, **unter-**, **voll-**, **wider-**, and **wieder-** may be separable or inseparable.[1] The meaning of the verbs differ in the two forms. The inseparable verbs often have an abstract or figurative meaning, and the prefix is always unstressed [→ A 255]:

dúrchschneiden:	*Die Mutter schneidet den Apfel durch.*
durchschnéiden:	*Das Schiff durchschneidet die Wellen.*
übersetzen:	*Er hat die Leute mit seinem Boot übergesetzt.*
übersétzen:	*Ich habe den Brief ins Deutsche übersetzt.*
úmfahren:	*Das Auto fuhr den Mann um.*
umfáhren:	*Wir umfuhren die Stadt.*
únterhalten:	*Er hält die Hand unter.*
unterhálten:	*Er unterhält seine Familie.* (Two meanings)
vóllmachen:	*Machen Sie das Glas nicht so voll!*
vollbríngen:	*Er vollbrachte ein großes Werk.*
wíderspiegeln:[2]	*Sein Gesicht spiegelte sich im Wasser wider.*
widerspréchen:	*Widersprich mir nicht immer!*
wíederkommen:	*Er kommt heute abend wieder.*
wiederhólen:	*Der Lehrer wiederholt die Regel.*

B 345 Note the difference between a verb complement and a preposition:

> *Wir durchreísten Frankreich:* We traveled all over France.
> *Wir reisten durch Frankreich:* We traveled through France (i.e. on our way from Germany to Spain).
>
> *Ich übergéhe das nächste Kapitel:* I'm going to skip the next chapter. (I shall *not* discuss it.)
> *Ich gehe zum nächsten Kapitel über:* I now come to the next chapter. (I *will* discuss it.)
> *Ich gehe über die Straße:* I am crossing the street.[3]

---

[1] When used separably, these verbs use the infix **-ge-** in the past participle: *durchgeschnitten*. When used inseparably, there is no **-ge-**: *durchschnitten*.

[2] The verb *widerhallen* may be used either as a separable or an inseparable verb.

[3] Similarly also *Er übertritt das Gesetz; er tritt zu einer anderen Partei über; er tritt über den Stein.*

Apparent Compound Verbs

Many verbs look like compound verbs, but are in reality derived from NOUNS or ADJECTIVES and their compounds. These verbs are always *inseparable*, even though they are stressed on the first syllable, the apparent verb complement: **B 350**

das Frühstück: frühstücken, ich frühstücke, ich habe gefrühstückt
die Antwort: antworten, ich antworte, ich habe geantwortet
der Wetteifer: wetteifern, ich wetteifere, ich habe gewetteifert

Note the difference between compound verbs and verbs derived from nouns: Noun derivations are weak, and the prefix is inseparable: **B 352**

	tragen, er trägt	*— trug*	*— getragen*
	auftragen, er trägt . . . auf	*— trug . . . auf*	*— aufgetragen*
der Auftrag:	**beauftragen, er beauftragt**	**— beauftragte**	**— beauftragt**
	antragen, er trägt . . . an	*— trug . . . an*	*— angetragen*
der Antrag:	**beantragen, er beantragt**	**— beantragte**	**— beantragt**
	leiden	*— litt*	*— gelitten*
das Mitleid:	**bemitleiden**	**— bemitleidete**	**— bemitleidet**
	haben	*— hatte*	*— gehabt*
die Handhabe:	**handhaben**	**— handhabte**	**— gehandhabt**
	schlagen	*— schlug*	*— geschlagen*
der Ratschlag:	**beratschlagen**	**— beratschlagte**	**— beratschlagt**
	fahren	*— fuhr*	*— gefahren*
die Wallfahrt:	**wallfahrten**	**— wallfahrtete**	**— gewallfahrtet**
Similarly:	*brechen*	*— brach*	*— gebrochen*
	radebrechen	**— radebrechte**	**— geradebrecht**

Defective Forms of Compound Verbs

There are some verbs which, when they appear in a main clause, exist only in the INFINITIVE and the PAST PARTICIPLE, such as: **B 360**

kunststopfen — kunstgestopft   uraufführen — uraufgeführt
nottaufen   — notgetauft   notlanden — notgelandet
nachtwandeln — nachtgewandelt   auferstehen — auferstanden

Most compounds with **wett-** occur only in the infinitive:[1] **B 361**

wettlaufen, wettrennen, wettschwimmen, wettrüsten

---

[1] The verb *wetteifern*, however, has inseparable tense forms: *Er wetteifert mit mir.* The verb *wettmachen*, on the other hand, has separable tense forms: *Wie mache ich das wett?*

B 362   Some compound verbs are used only in the past participle:

preisgekrönt, totgeboren

B 363   For all verbs of this type, present and past tense forms as well as the imperative must be paraphrased:

Der Intendant bereitete eine Uraufführung vor.
Der Pfarrer mußte das Kind nottaufen.
Der Pilot konnte notlanden.
Laufen wir um die Wette!

B 365   If the verbs, however, occur in a dependent clause, where verb complement and verb stem are reunited at the end of the clause, present and past tense forms are possible:

*Wer **fernsieht**, weiß, was auf der Welt geschieht.*
*Es war ein großes Ereignis, als das Stadttheater dieses Werk **uraufführte**.*
*Obwohl das Flugzeug **notlandete**, waren die Passagiere unverletzt.*

AUXILIARY VERBS

B 400   There are only two SIMPLE TENSES in German, i.e. tenses which the verb can form by itself. Each of these occurs in two moods, the indicative and the subjunctive.[1] They are present and past indicative, and subjunctive I and II. All other verb tenses are formed with the auxiliary verbs **haben**, **sein**, or **werden** and either the past participle or the infinitive. These are called COMPOUND TENSES.[2]

B 401   The **perfect** (present perfect) [→ B 455 ff., B 540 ff.] and the **past perfect** (pluperfect) [→ B 470, B 550] are formed with the auxiliary verbs **haben** or **sein** and the PAST PARTICIPLE:

$$Present \text{ tense of } \begin{cases} haben \\ sein \end{cases} + \text{Past Participle} \quad = Present \text{ Perfect}$$

$$Past \text{ tense of } \begin{cases} haben \\ sein \end{cases} + \text{Past Participle} \quad = Past \text{ Perfect}$$

B 402   The **future** [→ B 473, B 560 ff.] and the **future perfect** [→ B 475, B 580 ff.] are formed with the auxiliary verb **werden** and the INFINITIVE or PERFECT INFINITIVE [→ B 451–2] respectively:

$$\text{Present tense of } werden + \begin{cases} \text{Infinitive} & = \text{Future} \\ \text{Perfect Infinitive} & = \text{Future Perfect} \end{cases}$$

---

[1] The imperative is also a simple verb form, occurring only in the present tense.

[2] Compound tenses of the subjunctive are formed by using the corresponding subjunctive I or II forms of the auxiliaries *haben, sein,* and *werden* in the respective constructions.

74

The **passive** [→ B 480 ff., 590 ff.] is formed with **werden** and the PAST   B 403
PARTICIPLE:

> Any tense of   *werden* +   Past Participle   = Passive

The Forms of the Auxiliary Verbs   B 410

INFINITIVE		*haben*	*sein*	*werden*
PRESENT INDICATIVE	*ich*	habe	bin	werde
	du	hast	bist	wirst
	er	hat	ist	wird
	wir	haben	sind	werden
	ihr	habt	seid	werdet
	sie	haben	sind	werden
PAST INDICATIVE	*ich*	hatte	war	wurde
	du	hattest	warst	wurdest
	er	hatte	war	wurde
	wir	hatten	waren	wurden
	ihr	hattet	wart	wurdet
	sie	hatten	waren	wurden
SUBJUNCTIVE I	*ich*	habe	sei	werde
	du	habest	seiest	werdest
	er	habe	sei	werde
	wir	haben	seien	werden
	ihr	habet	seiet	werdet
	sie	haben	seien	werden
SUBJUNCTIVE II	*ich*	hätte	wäre	würde
	du	hättest	wärest	würdest
	er	hätte	wäre	würde
	wir	hätten	wären	würden
	ihr	hättet	wäret	würdet
	sie	hätten	wären	würden
PRESENT PARTICIPLE		habend	seiend	werdend
PAST PARTICIPLE		gehabt	gewesen	worden

The verbs **haben, sein,** and **werden** have meanings of their own as in-   B 415
dependent verbs which, in turn, are capable of forming all tenses, using
themselves and one another as auxiliaries:

> *ich habe gehabt, ich bin gewesen, ich bin geworden:*[1]
> *ich werde haben, ich werde sein, ich werde werden*

[1] Note that **werden** uses the past participle **worden** as an auxiliary verb [→ B 410] and the
past participle **geworden** as an independent verb.

75

B 416 As independent verbs, **haben**, **sein**, and **werden** can also form an imperative:

du:	*habe! hab!*	*sei!*	*werde!*
ihr:	*habt!*	*seid!*	*werdet!*
Sie:	*haben Sie!*	*seien Sie!*	*werden Sie!*

B 417 In solemn or poetic usage, the old past tense form **ward** still occurs in the singular only:

> *Gott sprach: „Es werde Licht!" und es **ward** Licht.*
> *Er **ward** nie mehr gesehen.*

MODAL VERBS

B 420 Modal verbs usually occur together with the infinitive of another verb. They indicate a certain attitude towards the events described.

For meaning and use of modals, → B 630 ff.

Forms of Modal Auxiliaries

B 421

INFINITIVE:		*dürfen*	*können*	*mögen*	*müssen*	*sollen*	*wollen*
PRESENT:	*ich*	darf	kann	mag	muß	soll	will
	du	darfst	kannst	magst	mußt	sollst	willst
	er	darf	kann	mag	muß	soll	will
	wir	dürfen	können	mögen	müssen	sollen	wollen
	ihr	dürft	könnt	mögt	müßt	sollt	wollt
	sie	dürfen	können	mögen	müssen	sollen	wollen
PAST:	*ich*	durfte etc.	konnte	mochte	mußte	sollte	wollte
SUBJUNCTIVE I:	*ich*	dürfe etc.	könne	möge	müsse	solle	wolle
SUBJUNCTIVE II:	*ich*	dürfte etc.	könnte	möchte	müßte	sollte	wollte
PRESENT PARTICIPLE:[1]		dürfend	könnend	mögend	müssend	sollend	wollend
SUBSTITUTE INFINITIVE:[2]		dürfen	können	mögen	müssen	sollen	wollen

[1] The present participle of modals occurs very rarely, mostly in compounds or with some other expression: *wohlwollend, vermögend, nicht enden wollend.*

[2] The substitute infinitive replaces the past participle [→ B 422, B 468, B 996].

76

The modal verbs can also exist by themselves, and then form their past B 422
participle regularly [→ B 469]:

gedurft gekonnt gemocht gemußt gesollt gewollt

As a rule, modal verbs can not form an imperative. Some such forms, B 423
however, occasionally exist in literary language:

Wolle! Wollet!

Within a sentence, the modal auxiliary is conjugated; the main verb, in B 430
the infinitive, comes at the end of the sentence or main clause:[1]

*Er **muß** einen Brief **schreiben**. Ich **will** in Berlin **studieren**.*

COMPOUND VERB FORMS

⅋ *Introduction*

The German verb has only five SIMPLE finite forms; they are statements B 450
of reality (indicative) in the PRESENT and PAST tense, statements of potentiality in SUBJUNCTIVE I and II, and commands in the IMPERATIVE. All
other verb forms are constructed with auxiliary verbs and the past participle or the infinitive of the main verb. The main verb is then placed at
the end of the main clause. The COMPOUND FORMS are: the PRESENT
PERFECT, the PAST PERFECT, the FUTURE, the FUTURE PERFECT, PAST SUB-
JUNCTIVE I and II, and all tenses of the PASSIVE. The infinitive itself may
also occur in compound forms.

Infinitive

The INFINITIVE exists in the following forms: B 451

(*Active*) *Infinitive*	sagen	fahren
Past Infinitive[2]	gesagt haben	gefahren sein
Passive Infinitive	gesagt werden	gefahren werden
Past Passive Infinitive[2]	gesagt worden sein	gefahren worden sein

---

1 Only rarely, in poetic or philosophic usage, a modal infinitive occurs together with another
(or the same) modal in conjugated form:

> *Kein Mensch **muß müssen**.*
> *Man **kann wollen**, soviel man will, man kann die*
> *Dinge doch nicht ändern.*

2 Also called perfect infinitive and perfect passive infinitive, respectively.

77

B 452   In a sentence, the infinitive is often used with the preposition **zu**. This preposition occupies the following positions:

(*Active*) *Infinitive*	zu sagen	zu fahren
Past Infinitive[1]	gesagt zu haben	gefahren zu sein
Passive Infinitive	gesagt zu werden	gefahren zu werden
Past Passive Infinitive[1]	gesagt worden zu sein	gefahren worden zu sein

B 453   For separable verbs, the preposition **zu** forms an infix between the verb complement and the stem [→ B 311–312]:

auszukommen — teilzunehmen — radzufahren — spazierenzugehen

Present Perfect

B 455   The PRESENT PERFECT, often merely called perfect tense, is formed with the PRESENT tense of the auxiliary verbs **haben** or **sein** [→ B 410] and the PAST PARTICIPLE of the main verb [→ B 180 ff., 270 ff.]. The past participle always remains uninflected and occurs at the end of the sentence or main clause:

> Ich **habe** gestern einen Brief **geschrieben**.
> Du **hast** gestern einen Brief **geschrieben**.
> etc.

> Ich **bin** spät nach Hause **gekommen**.
> Du **bist** spät nach Hause **gekommen**.
> etc.

B 456   Most German verbs form the perfect tenses with the auxiliary **haben**. This includes the following verbs:

1. All TRANSITIVE verbs, i.e. all verbs which are capable of taking a direct object in the accusative:

> Mein Freund **hat** mich gestern **besucht**.
> Ich **habe** das Heft **gefunden**.
> Er **hat** das Buch **gekauft**.

---

[1] Also called perfect infinitive and perfect passive infinitive, respectively.

78

2. All REFLEXIVE verbs, regardless of whether the reflexive pronoun occurs in the dative or the accusative:

> *Der Mann **hat** sich nach dem Weg **erkundigt.***
> *Ich **habe** mich **gewaschen.***
> *Ich **habe** mir die Hände **gewaschen.***
> *Du **hast** dich **geweigert.***
> *Du **hast** dir nur **geschadet.***

3. Many INTRANSITIVE verbs, above all those which show a continuing state or action:

> *Die Männer **haben** auf der Bank **gesessen.**[1]*
> *Das Buch **hat** auf dem Tisch **gelegen.**[1]*
> *Ich **habe** vor dem Haus **gestanden.**[1]*
> *Wir **haben** gut **geschlafen.***
> *Ich **habe** dem armen Mann **geholfen.***
> *Hast du an mich **gedacht**?*

4. Most IMPERSONAL verbs:

> *Gestern **hat es geregnet.***
> *Es **hat** mir gut **gefallen.***
> *Es **hat gedonnert** und **geblitzt.***
> *Heute **hat es** ein gutes Essen **gegeben.***

Exceptions: **geschehen, gelingen, passieren, vorkommen, bekommen** (in the impersonal sense):

> *Es **ist** bei diesem Unfall nicht viel **geschehen.***
> *Es **ist** mir **gelungen,** ihn zu überzeugen.*
> *Was **ist** denn hier **passiert**?*
> *So etwas **ist** mir noch nie **vorgekommen**!*
> *Das fette Essen **ist** mir nicht **bekommen.***

5. All MODAL verbs:

> *Mein Vater **hat** ins Büro gehen **müssen.***
> *Er **hat** die Rechnung nicht bezahlen **können.***
> *Das Kind **hat** nicht zu Bett gehen **wollen.***

---

[1] In southern Germany, Austria, and Switzerland, the verbs **sitzen, liegen,** and **stehen** are usually conjugated with **sein** in the perfect tense: *Die Männer **sind** auf der Bank gesessen. Das Buch **ist** auf dem Tisch gelegen. Ich **bin** vor dem Haus gestanden.*

B 460   The following verbs form the perfect tense with the auxiliary **sein**:

1. INTRANSITIVE verbs which indicate a CHANGE OF CONDITION [→ B 461]:

> *Er ist gestern spät **eingeschlafen**.*
> *Der Kranke ist heute nacht **gestorben**.*
> *Der See ist noch nicht **zugefroren**.*
> *Der Autoreifen ist **geplatzt**.*
> *Über Nacht ist es plötzlich kalt **geworden**.*

2. This group especially includes all verbs which indicate a CHANGE OF POSITION, i.e. a motion from one place to another [but → B 465]:

> *Heute **sind** meine Freunde **gekommen**.*
> *Er ist am Nachmittag **spazierengegangen**.*
> *Wir **sind** nach Deutschland **gefahren**.*

3. The verbs **sein** and **bleiben**:

> *Karl **ist** im letzen Jahr in Köln **gewesen**.*
> *Dort ist er drei Monate **geblieben**.*

4. A few impersonal verbs [→ B 456.4].

B 461   Verbs which indicate a change of condition by showing a transition from one state of being to another, such as **einschlafen, aufwachen, sterben, verschwinden, werden,** etc. are called "perfective verbs." These verbs are conjugated with **sein** [→ B 460].

First state of being	*Transition*	*New state of being*
ich bin wach	ich **schlafe ein**	ich schlafe
er schläft	er **wacht auf**	er ist wach
sie lebt	sie **stirbt**	sie ist tot
es ist hier	es **verschwindet**	es ist fort
es ist warm	es **wird** kalt	es ist kalt

B 462   Some verbs can form their perfect tense with either **haben** or **sein**.

These verbs may either indicate an ACTION or a PROCESS; if they indicate an action, they are transitive and form their perfect tense with **haben**; if they indicate a process, they are intransitive (i.e. they can not have an

accusative object), and form their present perfect with **sein**.[1] Some of
these verbs are:

	PRESENT	PERFECT
brechen:	Er bricht sein Wort.	Er **hat** sein Wort gebrochen.
	Das Eis bricht.	Das Eis **ist** gebrochen.
zerbrechen:	Sie zerbricht das Glas.	Sie **hat** das Glas zerbrochen.
	Das Glas zerbricht.	Das Glas **ist** zerbrochen.
heilen:	Der Arzt heilt die Wunde.	Der Arzt **hat** die Wunde geheilt.
	Die Wunde heilt gut.	Die Wunde **ist** gut geheilt.
schmelzen:	Die Sonne schmilzt den Schnee.	Die Sonne **hat** den Schnee geschmolzen.
	Der Schnee schmilzt.	Der Schnee **ist** geschmolzen.
spritzen:	Er spritzt den Garten.	Er **hat** den Garten gespritzt.
	Das Wasser spritzt auf die Straße.	Das Wasser **ist** auf die Straße gespritzt.
stoßen:	Er stößt ihn.	Er **hat** ihn gestoßen.
	Er stößt auf einen Bekannten.	Er **ist** auf einen Bekannten gestoßen.
trocknen:	Ich trockne die Wäsche.	Ich **habe** die Wäsche getrocknet.
	Die Wäsche trocknet in der Sonne.	Die Wäsche **ist** in der Sonne getrocknet.
verderben:	Schlechte Filme verderben die Jugend.	Schlechte Filme **haben** die Jugend verdorben.
	Das Fleisch verdirbt bei der Hitze.	Das Fleisch **ist** bei der Hitze verdorben.

The verb **folgen** forms its perfect tense with **haben** in the sense of "to
obey"; it uses **sein** in the sense of "to follow": B 463

> *Das Kind folgt seiner Mutter* (i.e. does what his mother wants).
> *Das Kind hat seiner Mutter gefolgt.*
>
> *Das Kind folgt seiner Mutter* (i.e. walks behind his mother).
> *Das Kind ist seiner Mutter gefolgt.*

[1] In many cases, these verbs have identical forms for the present perfect indicative and the so-called "apparent passive" or "passive of being" which is a description of a condition in the present tense [→ B 610]: *Das Eis ist gebrochen* may either mean "the ice **has** broken" (process) or "the ice **is** broken" (condition).

B 464 Some verbs may either express a CONTINUOUS CONDITION or a PROCESS. If they indicate a condition, they form their perfect with **haben**. If they indicate a process, they use **sein**. For instance:

	PRESENT	PERFECT
irren:	Hier irrt der Autor.	Hier **hat** der Autor geirrt.
	Er irrt durch die Straßen.	Er **ist** durch die Straßen geirrt.
tropfen:	Der Wasserhahn tropft.	Der Wasserhahn **hat** getropft.
	Das Wasser tropft auf den Boden.	Das Wasser **ist** auf den Boden getropft.

B 465 Some verbs of motion form their perfect tense with **haben**, if they are used transitively to indicate the action of motion itself, but not the goal of the motion. For instance:

	PRESENT	PERFECT
tanzen:	Er tanzt jeden Tanz.	Er **hat** jeden Tanz getanzt.
	Wir tanzen durch den Saal.	Wir **sind** durch den Saal getanzt.
fahren:	Ich fahre den Wagen selbst.	Ich **habe** den Wagen selbst gefahren.
	Ich fahre nach Frankfurt.	Ich **bin** nach Frankfurt gefahren.
schwimmen:	Er schwimmt eine Stunde.	Er **hat** eine Stunde geschwommen.
	Er schwimmt über den Fluß	Er **ist** über den Fluß geschwommen.
laufen:	Er läuft die Meile in vier Minuten.	Er **hat** die Meile in vier Minuten gelaufen.
	Er läuft schnell.	Er **ist** schnell gelaufen.
ziehen:	Das Pferd zieht den Wagen.	Das Pferd **hat** den Wagen gezogen.
	Wir ziehen nach Berlin.	Wir **sind** nach Berlin gezogen.

B 466 COMPOUND VERBS often do not use the same auxiliary in the perfect tense as the basic verb from which they are derived. For instance:

82

kommen: *Ich **bin** gekommen; ich **habe** bekommen; es **ist** vorgekommen.*
kochen: *Ich **habe** die Suppe gekocht; das Fleisch **ist** verkocht.*
gehen: *Er **ist** nach Hause gegangen; er **hat** eine schlechte Tat begangen.*
reisen: *Ich **bin** durch Frankreich gereist; ich **habe** Frankreich bereist.*

The verb **erschrecken** follows the weak conjugation when it expresses an action, and then forms its perfect tense with *haben*; when **erschrecken** expresses a process, it follows the strong conjugation and forms its perfect tense with *sein* [→ B 295]:   B 467

Der Hund erschreckt das Kind. —   *Der Hund **hat** das Kind erschreckt.*
*Das Kind erschrickt vor dem Hund. — Das Kind **ist** erschrocken.*

1. MODAL AUXILIARIES form their perfect tense with the infinitive (substitute infinitive) [→ B 996] instead of the past participle, when they are used together with another verb [→ B 421, H 113]. These forms are called DOUBLE INFINITIVES:[1]   B 468

> *Ich habe in die Schule **gehen müssen.***
> *Er hat nicht ins Kino **kommen dürfen.***
> *Er hat die Arbeit gut **machen können.***
> *Er hat Fleisch **kaufen sollen.***
> *Er hat die Suppe nicht **essen mögen.***
> *Das Kind hat nicht **einschlafen wollen.***

2. This principle also applies to a few other verbs, when they are used together with an infinitive:[2]

> *Ich habe ihn **kommen** sehen.*
> *Ich habe mir einen Anzug **machen** lassen.*
> *Ich habe ihn **singen** hören.*
> *Er hat mir die Koffer **tragen** helfen.*
> *Wir haben unsere Gäste **willkommen** heißen.*
> *Er hat uns Deutsch **sprechen** lehren.*
> *Er hat viel von sich **reden** machen.*
> *Er hatte sie in Berlin **kennen**lernen.*

[1] Multiple infinitives may occasionally occur, but are considered inelegant: *Sie sagten, daß sie uns haben spazierengehen sehen können.*

[2] With the verbs **sehen** and **lassen**, past participles occur in colloquial speech, but are considered inelegant: *Ich habe ihn kommen **gesehen**. Er hat das Buch fallen **gelassen**.* [→ B 492] With **hören**, both the infinitive and the past participle are commonly used: *Ich habe ihn singen **gehört**.* With **helfen, heißen, lehren, lernen,** and **machen**, the corresponding past participle forms are preferred today: *Er hat mir die Koffer tragen **geholfen**. Er hatte sie in Berlin **kennengelernt**. Wir haben die Gäste willkommen **geheißen**. Er hat uns Deutsch sprechen **gelehrt**,* etc.

3. This construction is also used when **brauchen** occurs together with **zu** and an infinitive [→ B 654.3]:

> *Er hat den Brief nicht **zu schreiben brauchen**.*

B 469 When modals or any other of the above verbs are used as main verbs, they form their perfect tense regularly with the past participle:

> *Ich habe das nicht **gekonnt**.*
> *Wir haben das Beste **gewollt**.*
> *Er hat die Suppe nicht **gemocht**.*
> *Hast du das wirklich **gemußt**?*
> *Ich habe mein Buch zu Hause **gelassen**.*
> *Haben Sie das **gehört**?*
> *Er hat das nicht **gebraucht**.*

Past Perfect

B 470 The PAST PERFECT or pluperfect is formed with the PAST TENSE of the helping verbs **haben** or **sein** [→ B 410] and the PAST PARTICIPLE of the main verb [→ B 180, 270]. For the use of *haben* or *sein*, the same rules apply as for the present perfect [→ B 455 ff.]:

> *Ich **hatte** ihm einen Brief **geschrieben**.*
> *Du **hattest** ihm einen Brief **geschrieben**.*
> etc.

> *Ich **war** spät nach Hause **gekommen**.*
> *Du **warst** spät nach Hause **gekommen**.*
> etc.

B 471 Modal verbs and some other verbs use the substitute infinitive instead of the past participle, just as in the present perfect [→ B 468 ff.]:

> *Ich hatte in die Schule **gehen müssen**.*

Future

B 473 German verbs form the FUTURE TENSE with the PRESENT TENSE of the auxiliary verb **werden** [→ B 410] and the INFINITIVE of the main verb.

This infinitive occurs at the end of the main clause:

*Ich **werde** ihm einen Brief **schreiben**.*
*Du **wirst** ihm einen Brief **schreiben**.*
etc.

Future Perfect

The FUTURE PERFECT is formed with the PRESENT TENSE of the auxiliary B 475
verb **werden** [→ B 410] and the PAST INFINITIVE (perfect infinitive)
[→ B 451] of the main verb:

*Ich **werde** ihm einen Brief **geschrieben haben**.*
*Du **wirst** spät nach Hause **gekommen sein**.*
etc.

Past Subjunctive

The PAST SUBJUNCTIVE is formed with the SUBJUNCTIVE I and II of the B 477
auxiliary verbs **haben** or **sein** [→ B 410] and the PAST PARTICIPLE
[→ B 180, 270] of the main verb. For the use of *haben* or *sein*, the same
rules apply as for the present perfect [→ B 455 ff.]:

SUBJUNCTIVE I

*Ich **habe** den Brief **geschrieben**.*
*Du **habest** den Brief **geschrieben**.*
*Er **habe** den Brief **geschrieben**.*
etc.

*Ich **sei** nach Hause **gekommen**.*
*Du **seiest** nach Hause **gekommen**.*
etc.

SUBJUNCTIVE II

*Ich **hätte** den Brief **geschrieben**.*
*Du **hättest** den Brief **geschrieben**.*
*Er **hätte** den Brief **geschrieben**.*
etc.

*Ich **wäre** nach Hause **gekommen**.*
*Du **wärest** nach Hause **gekommen**.*
etc.

Passive

The PASSIVE is formed with the AUXILIARY VERB **werden** [→ B 410] and B 480
the PAST PARTICIPLE [→ B 180, B 270] of the MAIN VERB. The auxiliary
verb may occur in all persons and all tenses of either the indicative or
the subjunctive. The passive infinitive is composed of the past participle
of the main verb and the infinitive of the auxiliary verb. The past

85

participle of *werden*, when used as an auxiliary for the passive, is *worden* [→ B 410]. For meaning and usage of the passive → B 590 ff.

B 481

Forms of the Passive	
INFINITIVE	gebaut werden
PRESENT INDICATIVE	Das Haus wird gebaut.
PAST INDICATIVE	Das Haus wurde gebaut.
PRESENT PERFECT	Das Haus ist gebaut worden.
PAST PERFECT	Das Haus war gebaut worden.
FUTURE	Das Haus wird gebaut werden.
FUTURE PERFECT	Das Haus wird gebaut worden sein.
SUBJUNCTIVE I	Das Haus werde gebaut.
SUBJUNCTIVE II	Das Haus würde gebaut.
PAST SUBJUNCTIVE I	Das Haus sei gebaut worden.
PAST SUBJUNCTIVE II	Das Haus wäre gebaut worden.

B 482 A PASSIVE IMPERATIVE can <u>not</u> be formed with the auxiliary *werden*. In rare cases, mostly in poetic usage, the passive imperative is formed with the imperative of the auxiliary **sein** and the past participle of the main verb:

> *Sei gegrüßt!*   *Seid gegrüßt!*   *Seien Sie gegrüßt!*
> *Sei bedankt!*   *Seid bedankt!*   *Seien Sie bedankt!*

B 483 A passive sentence in various persons is formed by changing the direct object of an action (accusative object) into the grammatical subject:

Active:	*Passive:*
Er sieht **mich**.	**Ich** werde gesehen.
Er sieht **dich**.	**Du** wirst gesehen.
Er sieht **ihn (den Mann, den Berg)**.	**Er (der Mann, der Berg)** wird gesehen.
etc.	

B 484 Intransitive verbs can form a passive only without a subject [→ B 603 ff.], with the auxiliary taking the conjugational form of the 3rd

86

person singular. [For the use of the indefinite pronoun **es** ⤳ B 608, H 053]:

Active:	*Passive:*	
Ich helfe **ihm**.	**Ihm** wurde geholfen.	**Es** wurde **ihm** geholfen.
Sie sprachen **davon**.	**Davon** wurde gesprochen.	**Es** wurde **davon** gesprochen.

MODAL AUXILIARIES do NOT form a passive. Instead, in a passive sentence the modal verb is used in all persons and tenses [⤳ B 421] followed by the passive infinitive of the main verb, i.e. the infinitive of the auxiliary *werden* and the past participle of the main verb [⤳ B 451]:

	Active:	*Passive:*
INFINITIVE	bauen müssen	gebaut werden müssen
PRESENT INDICATIVE	Er muß das Haus bauen.	Das Haus muß gebaut werden.
PAST INDICATIVE	Er mußte das Haus bauen.	Das Haus mußte gebaut werden.
PRESENT PERFECT	Er hat das Haus bauen müssen.	Das Haus hat gebaut werden müssen.
PAST PERFECT	Er hatte das Haus bauen müssen.	Das Haut hatte gebaut werden müssen.
FUTURE	Er wird das Haus bauen müssen.	Das Haus wird gebaut werden müssen.
FUTURE PERFECT	Er wird das Haus gebaut haben müssen.[1]	*No form.*
SUBJUNCTIVE I	Er müsse das Haus bauen.	Das Haus müsse gebaut werden.
SUBJUNCTIVE II	Er mußte das Haus bauen.	Das Haus müßte gebaut werden.
PAST SUBJUNCTIVE I	Er habe das Haus bauen müssen.	Das Haus habe gebaut werden müssen.
PAST SUBJUNCTIVE II	Er hätte das Haus bauen müssen.	Das Haus hätte gebaut werden müssen.

[1] Such forms are extremely rare and should be avoided. They would imply past probability and should be replaced by constructions like: *Er muß das Haus gebaut haben.*

B 486 When modal verbs are used as main verbs, they can not form any passive at all [→ B 598]:[1]

> *Ich konnte heute meine Aufgabe nicht.*
> *Er mag die Suppe nicht.*

Besides the modal verbs, the following verbs can NOT form a passive voice [→ B 598]:

B 487 The verbs **haben**, **sein**, and **werden**, because they describe a process or a state of being:

> *Du hast einen Bleistift.*
> *Das Wetter ist schön.*
> *Der Kranke wird hoffentlich bald wieder gesund.*

B 488 Impersonal verbs, because they describe a process [but → B 495]:

> *Es regnet.*
> *Es gefällt mir sehr gut.*
> *Es geht ihm schlecht.*

B 489 Other verbs which describe a process, like **kommen**, **gehen**, **klingen**, **glänzen**, **schmerzen**, **schimmern**, **freuen**, **lodern**, etc.:

> *Er kommt von Berlin.*
> *Wir gingen nach Hause.*
> *Die neuen Kirchenglocken klingen durch das Tal.*
> *Der Schnee glänzte in der Sonne.*
> *Der Verlust schmerzte ihn sehr.*
> *Die Flamme loderte in die Höhe.*

B 490 Reflexive verbs and verbs with reflexive pronouns [→ D 120, 125]:

> *Er beeilt sich mit seiner Arbeit.*
> *Ich freue mich auf die Ferien.*
> *Das Kind wäscht sich die Hände.*
> *Erinnerst du dich an ihn?*

---

[1] Constructions like *Die Aufgabe wurde von mir nicht gekonnt* or *Die Suppe wird von ihm nicht gemocht* are purely artificial, and should be avoided.

The verbs **hören, sehen, helfen,** and **heißen** ("to bid"), if the object is   B 491
simultaneously the subject of an infinitive phrase [→ H 330 ff.]:

Active	Passive
Ich höre ihn.	Er wird gehört.
Ich höre ihn singen.	*No form.*
Er hilft mir.	Mir wird von ihm geholfen.
Er hilft mir arbeiten.	*No form.*[1]

The verb **lassen** used with the infinitive of another verb, *except* when   B 492
that infinitive describes a state of being:

Active	Passive
Er läßt ihn hereinkommen.	*No form.*
Er ließ das Buch liegen.	Das Buch wurde von ihm liegen gelassen.[2]

Note the difference between the active and the passive sentence in the   B 493
perfect tense:

Active: *Er hat das Buch auf dem Tisch liegen lassen.*
Passive: *Das Buch ist von ihm auf dem Tisch liegen gelassen worden.*

Some verbs which describe a process may also describe an action in   B 495
modern German, and may then form a passive voice, such as:

blitzen: *Es blitzt* (i.e. during a thunderstorm) — no passive.
  Ich blitze (i.e. using a flashbulb) — *Es wird geblitzt.*
brausen: *Der Sturm braust* (i.e. is blowing) — no passive.
  Ich brause (i.e. am taking a shower) — *Es wird gebraust.*

Note that for strong verbs which begin with an inseparable prefix and   B 496
thus do not use **ge-** in the past participle, the infinitive and the past

---

[1] It is of course possible to paraphrase this sentence in the passive: *Mir wird bei meiner Arbeit geholfen.*
[2] This is <u>not</u> a double infinitive [→ B 468].

participle may be identical [→ B 272, 332]. For these verbs, the active future tense and the passive present tense coincide:

Ich werde empfangen. {I will receive.
I am being received.

Er wird behalten. {He will keep.
He is kept.

Du wirst vergessen. {You will forget.
You are being forgotten.

II. USE OF VERB FORMS

⤙ *Introduction*

B 500 Every statement expresses a situation in regard to TIME: the PRESENT, the PAST, or the FUTURE. This time situation must be considered in relation to the speaker or writer of the statement: the time at which the speaker or writer makes the statement is to be considered as present. A verb uses its TENSE forms to express this time relationship.[1]

B 501 German verbs possess both SIMPLE and COMPOUND TENSE forms [→ B 013]. The simple tense forms are PRESENT and PAST. Compound tense forms are the PERFECT, PAST PERFECT, FUTURE, and FUTURE PERFECT. They are formed with an auxiliary verb (**haben**, **sein**, **werden** [→ B 410]) and the past participle or the infinitive of the main verb.

B 502 A verb also expresses an event or a state of being [→ H 005–6]. Events may be classified as actions or processes. Any event or state of being can be expressed by the ACTIVE VOICE:

Action:	*Ich lese die Zeitung. Er geht nach Hause.*
Process:	*Der Motor läuft regelmäßig. Es schneit.*
State of Being:	*Das Wetter ist kalt. Wir schlafen.*

If we want to express an action as a process, we use the PASSIVE VOICE [→ B 590 ff.]:

Action:	*Ich schreibe den Brief.*
Process:	*Der Brief wird geschrieben.*

[1] Note that the grammatical category of tense does not always agree with the actual time situation. [→ B 510 ff.]

When a verb is used to describe reality, it is said to be in the INDICATIVE   B 503
mood. A speaker or writer may express his subjective attitude towards
any statement by using the SUBJUNCTIVE mood [→ B 700 ff.] or by
means of MODAL VERBS [→ B 630 ff.]. The subjunctive may indicate the
potentiality, uncertainty, or nonreality of a statement. There are simple
subjunctive forms, and compound forms which are constructed from
the subjunctive of the auxiliary verb and the infinitive or past participle
of the main verb. The speaker or writer expresses a command, a request,
or a desire by means of the IMPERATIVE of the verb.

There are forms of the verb which do not indicate any relation to   B 504
persons or things, and which by themselves do not express any tense
(INFINITIVE, PARTICIPLE). They are important in the German sentence for
the formation of compound tenses; in addition, they also fulfill a
number of other functions in the sentence [→ B 800 ff.].

TENSE FORMS OF THE VERB

Present Tense

The present tense forms of verbs express a situation [→ H 003] in the   B 510
following relationships to categories of time:[1]

PAST	PRESENT	FUTURE
	B 511–512	
		→
B 514		B 513, B 520
	B 515	
B 516		
B 517		
		B 518

---

[1] In these diagrams, a straight vertical line (|) indicates the beginning or end of a situation,
an arrow (>) indicates an open-ended, continuing situation.

B 511 The situation takes place at the time the statement is made. There need not be any definite indication as to whether the situation began in the past or may continue into the future:[1]

> *Was **machst** du, Karl? Ich **schreibe** einen Brief.*

B 512 Adverbs of time such as **nun**, **jetzt**, **gerade**, **eben** may be used to reinforce the fact that the situation takes place in the present:[2]

> *Ich **schreibe gerade** einen Brief.*
> *Mein Vater **schläft jetzt.***

B 513 For verbs of action, the present tense with the adverb **jetzt** also indicates that the action will begin immediately after the statement:

> *Ich **fahre jetzt** in die Stadt.*
> *Wir **gehen jetzt** essen.*

B 514 Together with a time indication, usually accompanied by **seit** or **schon** (or **schon seit**), the present tense can also express a situation which began in the past and continues in the present. Such situations are expressed in English by the present perfect:[3]

> *Meine Freunde **wohnen** (**schon**) **seit zwei Jahren** in Köln.*
> My friends *have been living* in Cologne for two years.
> *Ich **warte schon eine Stunde.***
> I *have been waiting* for an hour.

B 515 Together with a time indication, the present tense can also indicate a situation which begins in the present and continues into the future:

> *Ich **bleibe zwei Tage** in diesem Hotel.*
> *Wir fahren **auf drei Monate** nach Deutschland.*

B 516 The present tense also expresses the fact that a statement is independent of time and is continuously valid. It is used in proverbs, for general statements, and for actions which are repeated regularly:

> *Es **ist** nicht alles Gold, was **glänzt.***
> *Die Stadt Mainz **liegt** an der Mündung des Mains in den Rhein.*
> *Mein Bruder **geht** jeden Tag ins Büro.*

---

[1] The English progressive present (I am writing) *does not exist* in German. The statement *Ich rauche nicht* may mean either "I do not smoke" or "I am not smoking."

[2] Adverbs of time may of course also be used in other tense forms to reinforce the time situation: *Er war eben angekommen* [→ B 542].

[3] Similarly, (*schon*) *seit* with the German past tense corresponds to the English past perfect: *Er war (schon) seit zwei Wochen in Berlin, als ich ihn besuchte* [→ B 532].

The present tense can also describe a situation which took place entirely   B 517
in the past tense. It is used for lively narrative, after the narrator has
described the events at the beginning of his report in the past tense
[→ B 530], and then reaches the dramatic point of the narrative:

> *Neulich fuhr ich mit meinem Wagen nach Köln. Es war viel Verkehr auf*
> *den Straßen, und ich mußte vorsichtig fahren. Da **kommt** plötzlich an*
> *einer Straßenkreuzung ein Radfahrer von rechts und **fährt** gegen meinen*
> *Wagen. Ich **halte** sofort, **steige** aus und **sehe**, daß er Gott sei Dank*
> *unverletzt **ist**.*

Together with a time indication, the present may also be used to express   B 518
a situation which will begin or take place entirely in the future. Such
statements usually require the future tense in English.

> *Mein Freund **besucht** mich **morgen**.*
> ***In zwei Jahren fahre** ich in meine Heimat zurück.*
> *Ich **bin bald** fertig.*
> *Unser Zug **geht heute** um 4 Uhr nachmittags.*

In the second person singular or plural, the present may be used to   B 520
express a strong or urgent request, as a substitute for the IMPERATIVE
[→ B 790]:

> *Sie **verlassen** sofort mein Haus!*
> *Du **schreibst** jetzt einen Brief an deinen Onkel und **bedankst** dich*
> *bei ihm!*

Past Tense

The PAST TENSE is also called SIMPLE PAST, IMPERFECT, or PRETERITE. This   B 530
verb tense describes an event or a situation which took place entirely in
the past and has no direct relation to the present.

PAST	PRESENT	FUTURE
B 531 >———————| B 532 >———|·····→[1]		

[1] A dotted line indicates a second clause or sentence, showing an extension in time beyond
the range of the situation described in the original statement.

B 531   The past tense is the customary narrative tense, especially in written and formal usage:

> *Im letzten Jahr **war** ich in Hamburg. Mein Aufenthalt **dauerte** leider nur wenige Tage, aber ich **nutzte** die Zeit und **sah** die interessantesten Sehenswürdigkeiten dieser großen Hafenstadt. Jeden Tag **hatte** ich ein bestimmtes Programm: ich **machte** eine Hafenrundfahrt, ich **besuchte** das Opernhaus und **hörte** eine Oper von Mozart, ich **besichtigte** Hagenbecks Tierpark und **ging** in das Vergnügungsviertel von Hamburg, die berühmte Reeperbahn. Jetzt kann ich sagen, daß ich in Hamburg wirklich eine interessante Zeit verbracht habe.*

B 532   The German past tense, usually accompanied by the time indicators **schon** and **seit**, may be used to indicate a continuous situation or action in the past which precedes another, specific past event. Such situations are expressed in English in the past perfect [→ B 514]:

> *Er war (**schon**) **seit** zwei Wochen in Berlin, als ich ihn besuchte.*
> He *had been* in Berlin for two weeks when I visited him.

Present Perfect

B 540   The German verb does not have a simple perfect tense form. The PRESENT PERFECT (often merely called PERFECT) is a compound tense, formed with the present tense of the auxiliary verbs **haben** or **sein** and the past participle of the main verb [→ B 455 ff.]. The present perfect expresses a situation in the following relationships with respect to time:

PAST	PRESENT	FUTURE
B 541		
B 542		
B 543		
		B 545

B 541   The present perfect indicates that a situation ended in the past, but still has a bearing on or a relationship with the present:

94

*Peter **ist** vor einem Jahr nach Berlin **gefahren**. Er studiert dort Medizin.*
*Ich verstehe Französisch. Ich **habe** es in der Schule **gelernt**.*

Together with adverbs of time such as **gerade**, **jetzt**, **eben**, **soeben**, the   B 542
present perfect indicates a situation which ended at or just before the
beginning of the present, immediately prior to the making of the statement:

> *Ich **habe** das Buch gerade **gefunden**.*
> *Er **ist** soeben **angekommen**.*

The present perfect, usually accompanied by the time indicators **schon**   B 543
or **seit**, may also indicate a situation which began in the past and continues in the present:

> *Ich **habe** ihn **seit** zwei Jahren nicht **gesehen**.*
> *Er **hat schon** sechs Monate hier **verbracht**.*

The present perfect is generally preferred as the customary conversa-   B 544
tional form for past events, especially in colloquial usage:

> *Ich **bin** gestern abend ins Kino **gegangen**.*
> ***Hast** du die Zeitung schon **gelesen**?*[1]
> *Was **habt** ihr heute zum Frühstück **gegessen**?*[1]

The present perfect may also be used to indicate that a situation will end   B 545
at a given time in the future. Usually, a definite future time indicator
will accompany the present perfect [→ B 581]:

> *Bis morgen abend **habe** ich meine Arbeit **beendet**.*[2]
> *Richard fährt nach Hause* (or *wird nach Hause fahren*),
>   *wenn er seine Prüfung **gemacht hat**.*

Past Perfect

The PAST PERFECT (or PLUPERFECT) [→ B 470] indicates that a past   B 550
situation precedes another past situation in time.

---

[1] In many statements of this kind, the past tense, while grammatically correct, would be
idiomatically impossible or at the very least extremely stilted: *Lasest du die Zeitung schon?*
Was aßet ihr heute zum Frühstück? With the exception of modals and auxiliaries, the second
person singular or plural rarely occurs in the simple past tense.

[2] In English, many statements of this type have to be expressed in the future perfect:
I'll have finished my work by tomorrow night.

PAST		PRESENT	FUTURE
Past Perfect >‑ ‑ ‑ ‑ ‑ ‑ ‑→	Past Tense ┌· · · · · · · · · · · · ·| ⟨ Present Perfect └· · · · · · · · · · · · ·→		

*Ich ging an die Universität Bonn. Vorher **hatte** ich zwei Semester in Frankfurt studiert.*

*Mein Freund hat mich gestern besucht, nachdem ich ihn schon lange vorher **eingeladen hatte**.*

Future

B 560 German verbs have no simple future tense. The FUTURE is formed with the present tense of **werden** and the infinitive of the main verb [→ B 473]. The future tense expresses a situation in the following relationships with respect to time:

PAST	PRESENT	FUTURE
		B 561 |‑ ‑ ‑ ‑ ‑ ‑ ‑ ‑ ‑ ‑→ B 564.2 |‑ ‑ ‑ ‑ ‑ ‑→
	B 565 |‑ ‑ ‑ ‑ ‑ ‑ ‑ ‑ ‑|	

B 561 The future tense indicates a situation which takes place entirely in the future:

*Mein Freund **wird** mich heute abend **besuchen**.*
*Nächstes Jahr **werde** ich nach Frankreich **fahren**.*

B 562 If it is evident from the context that the situation referred to will take place in the future, the present tense is often used [→ B 517], especially if some time indicator appears in the sentence:

*Mein Freund **besucht** mich **heute abend**.*
*Nächstes Jahr **fahre** ich nach Frankreich.*

B 563 If the auxiliary verb **werden** is stressed in the sentence, the statement is an assertion that the events are definitely expected to happen in the future.

96

*Ich **werde** dir das Geld geben, so schwer es mir auch fällt.*
*Keine Angst, Robert **wird** seine Prüfung bestehen.*

The future often has a modal function. In the first person it indicates   B 564
a future intention, in the second person usually a present request or
encouragement, and in the third person future expectation:

   1. *Ich **werde** morgen um 8 Uhr fahren.*
     *Wir **werden** Ihnen helfen.*

   2. *Du **wirst** jetzt deine Schulaufgaben machen.*
     ***Werdet** ihr wohl sofort herkommen?*
     *Sie **werden** es schon schaffen.*

   3. *Morgen **wird** es nicht regnen.*
     *Meine Schwester **wird** im Juni heiraten.*

The future tense may be used to indicate a present probability or   B 565
likelihood:

*Wo ist Karl? Er **wird** jetzt zu Hause sein.*
*Ich habe einen schönen Hut gesehen, aber er **wird** sicher zu viel Geld kosten.*

Future Perfect

The FUTURE PERFECT expresses a situation in the following relationships   B 580
with respect to time:

	PAST		PRESENT	FUTURE
				B 581–582
				>–––––––|←
	B 583			
>––––––––––––––––––––|–––|			
B 584	Past Tense			
	···········|			
>–––––	Present Perfect			
	···········→			

The future perfect indicates an action which is going to end at or before   B 581
a certain time in the future. (The present perfect is also often used to
indicate a similar time situation. → B 545):

   *Morgen abend **werde** ich meine Arbeit **beendet haben.***
   *Wenn du um 5 Uhr anrufst, **wird** mein Vater schon **zurückgekommen**
   sein.*

B 582   In the same sense, the future perfect can express a likelihood, probability, supposition or assumption. The adverbs **wohl, vielleicht, wahrscheinlich, sicher** are often used in such constructions:

> *Morgen abend* **werde** *ich meine Arbeit sicher* **beendet haben.**
> *Wenn du um 5 Uhr anrufst,* **wird** *mein Vater* **wohl** *schon* **zurückgekommen sein.**

B 583   The future perfect may also express the likelihood or probability that a situation is ending or has ended at the moment the statement is made:

> *Karl ist mit dem 8 Uhr Zug nach München gefahren. Er* **wird** *jetzt schon dort* **angekommen sein.**

B 584   The future perfect may also express a probability or likelihood which took place entirely in the past:

> *Ich klopfte, aber niemand antwortete; er* **wird** *wohl nicht zu Hause* **gewesen sein.**
> *Als wir dich gestern trafen,* **wirst** *du schon lange auf uns* **gewartet haben.**
> *Ich habe meinem Freund letzte Woche einen Brief geschrieben; er* **wird** *ihn sicher schon* **bekommen haben.**

USE OF THE PASSIVE

B 590   We distinguish between the active and the passive voice [→ B 480 ff.].

The ACTIVE VOICE describes an ACTION or a PROCESS. If the subject causes or determines the events, voluntarily or involuntarily, we speak of an action; otherwise the event expresses a process. In addition, the active sentence may also describe a condition, a STATE of BEING.

EVENT		CONDITION (*State of Being*)
ACTION	PROCESS	
Ich schreibe einen Brief.	Ich bekomme einen Brief.	Der Brief ist hier.
Ich setzte mich.	—	Ich saß.
Er wechselt das Geld.	Das Wetter wechselt.	—
Ich schließe die Tür.	Die Tür schließt selbsttätig.	Die Tür schließt nicht gut.

98

The PASSIVE VOICE is a grammatical device for expressing an action as a   B 592
process. A condition or state of being can therefore never be expressed
as a passive.

Almost any action, however, can be regarded as a process and be   B 593
described by means of the passive voice:

ACTIVE	PASSIVE
Ich *schreibe* einen Brief.	Der Brief *wird geschrieben.*
Nach seinem Unfall *halfen* ihm die Passanten.	Nach seinem Unfall *wurde* ihm *geholfen.*
Bei der Feier *gedachte* er des Verstorbenen.	Bei der Feier *wurde* des Verstorbenen *gedacht.*
Wir *haben* zwei Stunden auf meinen Freund *gewartet.*	Auf meinen Freund *ist* zwei Stunden *gewartet worden.*
Auf der Autobahn *fährt* man sehr schnell.	Auf der Autobahn *wird* sehr schnell *gefahren.*

Passive Sentences with Subjects

The person or thing causing an action, i.e. the subject of the active   B 595
sentence, can occur in the passive sentence following the preposition
von [→ H 560].[1] The direct object of the active sentence becomes the
subject of the passive sentence:

ACTIVE	PASSIVE
Ich schreibe den Brief. *Der Wind* treibt die Wolken.	Der Brief wird *von mir* geschrieben. Die Wolken werden *vom Wind* getrieben.

The passive may also be formed from some verbs which already describe   B 596
a process in the active voice. If the subject of the active voice describes

[1] This is called the "agent."

the means through which the event is accomplished rather than the cause of the event, it may occur in the passive sentence after the preposition **durch** [→ H 561]:

ACTIVE	PASSIVE
Die Eltern verwöhnen die Kinder.	Die Kinder werden *von den Eltern* verwöhnt.
Das viele Geld verwöhnt die Kinder.	Die Kinder werden *durch das viele Geld* verwöhnt.
Flieger zerstörten die Festung.	Die Festung wurde *von Fliegern* zerstört.
Bomben zerstörten die Festung.	Die Festung wurde *durch Bomben* zerstört.
Der Junge verursachte großen Schaden.	Großer Schaden wurde *von dem Jungen* verursacht.
Die Explosion verursachte großen Schaden.	Großer Schaden wurde *durch die Explosion* verursacht.

B 597   The preposition **durch** is also used to show some intermediary or medium used to accomplish the process [→ H 561]:

> *Der Brief wurde* **vom** *Minister selbst geschrieben und* **durch** *einen Boten überbracht.*
> *Die Rede wurde* **vom** *Präsidenten gehalten und* **durch** *den Rundfunk übertragen.*

B 598   The following constructions can not form a passive, although they contain an accusative and describe actions:

1. Actions which are expressed by reflexive verbs:

> *Ich wasche* **mich.**
> *Er hilft* **sich** *selbst.*

2. Actions the object of which is a part of the subject's body:

> *Er legte mir* **seine Hand** *auf die Schulter.*
> *Ich habe* **meinen Finger** *verletzt.*

3. Sentences with predicate complements in the accusative, which are closely associated with the verb (often idiomatic phrases):

> *Er erblickte 1938 das Licht der Welt.*
> *Ich spiele oft Klavier.*
> *Er schenkte mir seine ganze Aufmerksamkeit.*

4. Sentences with an accusative object which is simultaneously the subject of an infinitive:

> *Ich sehe meinen Freund kommen.*
> *Wir hören die Kinder singen.*

5. Modal verbs without a dependent infinitive [→ B 485 ff.]:

> *Ich kann meine Aufgabe nicht.*

6. Sentences with an absolute accusative [→ D 926]:

> *Er kam ins Zimmer, den Hut in der Hand.*

7. Sentences with a pleonastic accusative [→ D 925]:

> *Er schlief den Schlaf des Gerechten.*

8. Sentences with an accusative of time or measure [→ predicate modifier D 923] and a personal verb form:[1]

> *Er arbeitete den ganzen Tag.*

9. The verbs **bekommen, erhalten** [→ B 618], and **besitzen**:

> *Ich bekam (erhielt) ein Buch zum Geburtstag.*

To form a passive sentence from an active sentence, the following principles must be applied: B 600

1. The accusative object of the active sentence becomes the subject of the passive sentence.

2. The subject of the active sentence follows the preposition **von** or **durch** in the passive sentence [→ B 595 ff.].

3. The tense of the helping verb **werden** in the passive sentence is identical with the tense of the main verb in the active sentence; in English, the equivalent tense form of the verb "to be" is used.

---

[1] Impersonal passives are possible: *Es wurde den ganzen Tag gearbeitet.*

4. The main verb of the active sentence becomes a past participle in the passive sentence, which appears at the end of the main clause.

5. All other units of the active sentence follow the same sequence in the passive sentence.[1]

ACTIVE	PASSIVE
Der Lehrer fragt den Schüler nach seiner Aufgabe.	Der Schüler wird vom Lehrer nach seiner Aufgabe gefragt.
Gestern bat mich mein Freund dringend um ein Buch.	Gestern wurde ich von meinem Freund dringend um ein Buch gebeten.

Passive Sentences without Subject

B 603   If the active sentence does not have an accusative object, the passive sentence does not have any subject [→ B 484]. In such sentences, **werden** always occurs in the 3rd person singular.

B 604   Sentences with Dative Object:

> *Ich habe viele Briefe geschrieben, aber **mir wurde** nicht **geantwortet**.*
> ***Wurde Ihnen** gestern **geholfen**?*
> *Er hat viel Gutes getan, aber **ihm ist** nicht **gedankt worden**.*
> ***Uns wurde** vom Polizisten **befohlen**, ihm zu folgen.*
> ***Den Eltern wird** immer **vertraut**.*

B 605   Sentences with Genitive Object:

> *Bei der gestrigen Feier **wurde des Verstorbenen gedacht**.*

B 606   Sentences with Prepositional Objects:

> ***Auf den Zug wurde** zwei Stunden **gewartet**.*
> ***Von deinen Problemen wurde** gestern nicht **gesprochen**.*
> ***Vor dem Hund wird gewarnt**.*
> ***Nach dem Dieb ist** eifrig **geforscht worden**.*

---

[1] An expression of time, however, may appear in the passive before the agent introduced by von: *Mein Freund bat mich gestern um ein Buch. — Ich wurde **gestern** von meinem Freund um ein Buch gebeten.*

Sentences without Object:

> *Sonntags* **wird** *nicht* **gearbeitet.**
> *Bei Wanderungen* **wird marschiert** *und* **gesungen.**
> *In dem Café* **wurde** *bis spät in die Nacht* **getanzt.**
> *Bei der Feier* **ist** *viel gegessen und getrunken* **worden.**
> *Hier* **wird** *nicht* **geraucht.**

If no other sentence unit occupies the prefield [→ H 051 ff.] of the declarative sentence in the passive construction, the pronoun **es** takes over the empty prefield position. This pronoun, however, is <u>not</u> the subject of the sentence [→ H 053 ff.]:

> *Es wurde mir nicht geantwortet.*
> *Es ist uns geholfen worden.*
> *Es wurde von deinen Problemen gesprochen.*
> *Es wurde des Verstorbenen gedacht.*
> *Es wird vor dem Hund gewarnt.*
> *Es wird hier nicht geraucht.*
> *Es ist nach dem Dieb geforscht worden.*
> *Es wird sonntags nicht gearbeitet.*

That **es** can not be the subject of the sentence is shown by the fact that it does not appear in sentences without prefield:

> *Wurde dir nicht geantwortet?*
> *Ist nach dem Dieb geforscht worden?*
> *Er erzählte, daß von deinen Problemen gesprochen wurde.*
> *Jeder weiß, daß sonntags nicht gearbeitet wird.*
> *Ich ärgere mich, weil mir nicht geholfen wurde.*

Apparent Passive ("Passive of Being")

The passive voice always expresses a PROCESS. If we want to express the RESULT of an action, i.e. the CONDITION or STATE OF BEING which has been attained, we use the auxiliary verb **sein** with the past participle. This is <u>not</u> a real passive construction; because of its similarity with the passive, however, it is often referred to as an apparent passive or a "passive of being." Nor should this construction be confused with the present or past perfect of the active voice [→ B 460 ff.]; verbs which form their perfect with the auxiliary verb **sein** can not form a passive voice at all. [But → footnote to B 462 for identity of forms.]

The basic difference is simply this: A genuine passive expresses a process, whereas the so-called "apparent passive" describes a condition or a state of being. In the apparent passive, the past participle constitutes a complement of the predicate [→ H 400 ff., 418, 440]. It functions like an adjective and may, in fact, be used as an attributive adjective [→ B 829 ff., J 110]:

> *Die Straße ist breit; sie ist **gepflastert**; die breite,*
> ***gepflasterte** Straße.*
> *Das Buch ist dick; es ist in Leder **gebunden**; das dicke,*
> *in Leder **gebundene** Buch.*

B 611 The following examples will illustrate the difference between a PROCESS (passive) and a STATE of BEING (apparent passive):

PROCESS	STATE OF BEING
Die Arbeit *wird* getan.	Die Arbeit *ist* getan.
Die Türen *wurden* geschlossen.	Die Türen *waren* geschlossen.
Das Auto *ist* gestern verkauft *worden.*	Als wir zum Händler kamen, *war* das Auto schon verkauft.[1]

B 612 The cause or agent of the action (subject of the active sentence) is usually omitted in the apparent passive:

> *Ich schreibe einen Brief. Der Brief wird (von mir) geschrieben.*
> *Jetzt ist der Brief geschrieben.*

Substitute Constructions for the Passive

B 615 Several other grammatical constructions may be used which represent an action as a process. Such constructions are:

B 616 Active sentences with reflexive pronouns [→ D 100 ff., D 165]. In such sentences, the cause or agent of the action can not be identified:

---

[1] As a general rule, the apparent passive occurs only with the present and past tenses of the auxiliary verb *sein.*

PASSIVE	ACTIVE
Der Vorhang *wurde geöffnet.* Das Problem *wird aufgeklärt.*	Der Vorhang *öffnete sich.* Das Problem *klärt sich auf.*

Active sentences containing the verb **lassen** with a reflexive pronoun, and the main verb in the infinitive. Such formations correspond to a passive sentence with the modal verb **können**:   B 617

PASSIVE	ACTIVE

Diese Arbeit *kann* schnell
  beendet werden.
Die Frage *konnte* leicht
  beantwortet werden.
	Diese Arbeit *läßt sich* schnell
	  beenden.
	Die Frage *ließ sich* leicht
	  beantworten.

Active sentences containing verbs like **bekommen** or **erhalten** with the past participle of a verb which expresses the action: B 618

PASSIVE	ACTIVE

Heute *werden* Ihnen die
  Kartoffeln *geliefert.*
Die Ware *wird* Ihnen porto-
  frei ins Haus *geschickt.*
	Heute *bekommen* Sie die
	  Kartoffeln *geliefert.*
	Sie *erhalten* die Ware porto-
	  frei ins Haus *geschickt.*

Active sentences containing verbs like **erfahren,**[1] **finden, gelangen, kommen, gehen,** etc., together with a noun derived from a verb (usually with the suffix **-ung,** a so-called *action noun*). Such constructions are found most frequently in official, business, or journalistic style. The cause or agent of the action can not be designated: B 619

[1] In the sense of "to experience," *not* "to find out, to learn, to discover": *Er hat viel Schlechtes* **erfahren.**

105

PASSIVE	ACTIVE
Sein Wunsch *wurde erfüllt*.	Sein Wunsch *ging in Erfüllung*.
Der Film *wurde aufgeführt*.	Der Film *gelangte (kam) zur Aufführung*.
Das Buch *ist* weit *verbreitet worden*.	Das Buch *hat* große *Verbreitung gefunden*.

B 620 Active sentences containing the verb **sein** with an adjective derived from a verb by means of the suffix **-lich** or **-bar**. These sentences correspond to passive sentences with the modal verb **können**:

PASSIVE	ACTIVE
Diese Frucht *kann* nicht *gegessen werden*.	Diese Frucht *ist* nicht *eßbar*. [→ A 153]
Seine Aussprache *konnte* leicht *verstanden werden*.	Seine Aussprache *war* leicht *verständlich*.

B 621 Similarly, the verb **sein** may be combined with an **infinitive** with **zu**. These sentences also correspond to passive sentences with the modal verb **können**, or the modal verbs **sollen** or **müssen**.

PASSIVE	ACTIVE
Seine Aussprache *konnte* leicht *verstanden werden*.	Seine Aussprache *war* leicht *zu verstehen*.
Dieses Kapitel *muß (soll)* bis morgen *gelesen werden*.	Dieses Kapitel *ist* bis morgen *zu lesen*.

B 623 It is also possible to replace the passive by an active sentence with the impersonal pronoun subject **man**, especially for passive sentences without subject. While technically such sentences describe actions rather than processes, the concept and the effect are the same as with other substitute constructions:

106

PASSIVE	ACTIVE
Sonntags *wird* nicht *gearbeitet.* Es *wurde* nach dem Dieb *geforscht.*	Sonntags *arbeitet man* nicht. *Man forschte* nach dem Dieb.

With some verbs it is possible to form all or almost all of the above   B 625
substitute constructions; at times, however, these may indicate distinct
differences in meaning:

1. *Sein Wunsch wurde erfüllt.*   We are not told who fulfilled the wish, but the action as well as the agent are clearly felt through the process.

2. *Sein Wunsch erfüllte sich.*   The agent is left completely unmentioned and unreferred to; instead, the process is almost treated like an action, as if the wish had a will of its own.

3. *Sein Wunsch läßt sich erfüllen.*   The wish can be fulfilled, but this has not yet been done. Similarly as in 2, but not as strongly, an inherent consent is implied.

4. *Sein Wunsch ging in Erfüllung.*   Completely impersonal statement; existence of agent ignored.

5. *Sein Wunsch ist zu erfüllen.*   Similar to 3, but may also mean that his wish must be or should be (i.e. is to be) fulfilled.

6. *Sein Wunsch ist erfüllbar.*   Similar to 3 and 5, but merely states that the fulfillment of this wish is not impossible.

7. *Ein zu erfüllender Wunsch.*   Like 5. [→ B 815]

8. *Man erfüllte seinen Wunsch.*   Similar to 1. Action clearly expressed, identity of agent deliberately left vague.

USE AND MEANING OF MODAL VERBS

Use of Modal Verbs

Modal verbs are attitude indicators. They usually occur together with   B 630
the infinitive of another verb. Unlike other verbs, they not only indicate
the facts of a situation, but also express an ATTITUDE. When modals are

107

used objectively, they show the attitude of the subject (or an agent unnamed but implied in the sentence) towards the situation (*Ich will Deutsch lernen.* — *Die Kinder müssen um 8 Uhr zu Bett gehen.* — *Die Ware kann ins Haus geliefert werden*). When they are used subjectively, they indicate the attitude of the speaker towards the content of his statement (*Das mag wahr sein.* *Er will fünf Jahre Deutsch gelernt haben*).

B 631   OBJECTIVE STATEMENT

1. The modal verb explains the attitude of the subject towards the situation. This situation is described objectively from the point of view of the speaker.

> *Er kann Deutsch sprechen.*   He has the necessary ability.
> *Er muß jetzt schlafen.*   He is under an obligation.
> *Er mag die Suppe nicht essen.*   He has no desire.

2. When the modal verbs **können, müssen, dürfen,** and **sollen** occur together with a passive infinitive [→ B 485], they do not refer to the subject of the sentence but to the agent who causes the action. This agent may or may not be mentioned in the sentence [→ modifier of person, H 556 ff., 560]:

> *Der Dieb konnte (von der Polizei) verhaftet werden.*
> *Die Arbeit muß (von uns) bis morgen beendet sein.*
> *Der Rasen darf (von Kindern) nicht betreten werden.*
> *Die Tür soll um 8 Uhr geschlossen werden.*

B 632   SUBJECTIVE STATEMENT

The modal verb indicates the subjective attitude of the speaker towards the situation described, i.e. the speaker reports a fact and at the same time indicates his opinion of it:

Er soll aus Berlin kommen.	Other people claim this; the speaker does not know.
Er will aus Berlin kommen.	He claims it; the speaker does not know (in fact, he doubts it).
Er dürfte aus Berlin kommen.	The speaker does not know for sure, but is making a guess.
Er könnte aus Berlin kommen.	The speaker surmises this; it is a possibility.
Er mag aus Berlin kommen.	The speaker draws his conclusion from some evidence.
Er muß aus Berlin kommen.	There is unmistakable evidence.

In the **present tense**, there is NO DISTINCTION in the form of the objective and subjective statements.

Er will viel Geld verdienen therefore may have two different meanings. As an OBJECTIVE statement it indicates that he has the intention (or desire) of becoming rich. As a SUBJECTIVE statement it indicates that he claims to be earning a lot of money, but the speaker doubts the truth of this assertion.

B 633

The **past tense** forms of the two types of statements are different. For OBJECTIVE statements, the modal verbs form the past tense regularly [→ B 421]; the perfect tenses of the modals use the infinitive instead of the past participle [double infinitive → B 468]. In a dependent clause, the conjugated form of the auxiliary verb is placed before the double infinitive:

B 634

> *Er will viel Geld verdienen.*
> *Er wollte viel Geld verdienen.*
> *Er hat viel Geld verdienen wollen.*
> *Ich weiß, daß er viel Geld hat verdienen wollen.*

For SUBJECTIVE statements, the modal verb occurs in the past tense only if the speaker makes his subjective assertion in connection with a report, the events of which lie in the past. The main verb, however, is not in the infinitive, but in the past infinitive [→ B 451]. In a dependent clause, the conjugated form of the modal verb occurs last. Perfect tenses do not exist in subjective statements.

> *Er will viel Geld verdienen, und dabei trägt er so schäbige Kleider.*
> *Er will (wollte) viel Geld verdient haben, hat aber keinen Pfennig sparen können.*
> *Er hatte angeblich früher ein großes Geschäft, wobei er viel Geld verdient haben will (wollte).*

Meaning of Modal Verbs

können

In an OBJECTIVE statement, **können** indicates
1. an ability:[1]

B 635

---

[1] Together with the passive infinitive, it indicates not the ability of the subject, but of the person causing the action [→ B 631.2]: *Endlich konnte der Verbrecher verhaftet werden* (There is no indication as to who was able to do it).

*Ich **kann** Deutsch sprechen.*

*Du **kannst** sehr gut schwimmen.*

*Wir **konnten** ihn nicht verstehen.*

*Er **könnte** der Beste sein* (i.e. he would have the ability), *wenn er fleißiger wäre.*

2. a possibility:

*Mit dem Zug fährt man 12 Stunden bis Hamburg; mit dem Flugzeug **können** wir schon in zwei Stunden dort sein.*

*Wir **könnten** fliegen* (i.e. the possibility is available), *wenn wir es sehr eilig hätten.*

3. a permission:[1]

*Ihr **könnt** heute ins Kino gehen.*

*Ihr **könntet** ins Kino gehen* (i.e. you would get the permission), *wenn ihr wolltet.*

B 636   In a SUBJECTIVE statement, **können** indicates

1. a fairly certain assumption:

*Mein Freund **kann** heute kommen* (i.e. for certain reasons I believe that he will or may come).

*Morgen **kann** das Wetter besser werden* (i.e. from my experience, I am inclined to believe so).

*Er **kann** Deutsch gesprochen haben* (i.e. I assume so, but I did not hear it myself, or did not hear it clearly).

2. a less certain assumption, by using subjunctive II:

*Mein Freund **könnte** heute kommen.*

*Morgen **könnte** das Wetter besser werden.*

*Er **könnte** (vielleicht) Deutsch gesprochen haben.*

3. the conviction of the speaker, that something must be possible (again using subjunctive II):

*Herr Müller **könnte** jetzt wirklich seine Schulden bezahlen.*

*Er **könnte** sein Studium längst abgeschlossen haben.*

dürfen

B 640   In an OBJECTIVE statement, **dürfen** indicates

---

[1] As in English, *können* is sometimes used in the sense of "may": *Kann ich ein Glas Wasser haben?* Correctly, *dürfen* should be used instead. [B 640.1]

1. permission, often with the connotation of a reward:

> *Ihr dürft ins Kino gehen.*
> *Wenn Karls Zeugnis gut ist, darf er eine Reise machen.*
> *Karl hat sich sehr gefreut, weil er eine Reise hat machen dürfen.*

2. in a negative sentence, a specific or general prohibition[1] [→ B 652.2]:

> *Du darfst heute nicht ins Kino gehen.*
> *Autos dürfen hier nicht parken.*
> *Kinder dürfen auf der Straße nicht spielen.*

For use with the passive infinitive, → B 631.2:

> *In der Straßenbahn darf nicht geraucht werden.*
> *Die Vorstellung darf von Jugendlichen nicht besucht werden.*

In a SUBJECTIVE statement, **dürfen** indicates an uncertain assumption, using subjunctive II: B 641

> *Vor einer Stunde ist mein Freund weggegangen; jetzt dürfte er schon zu Hause sein.* (i.e. normally he would not need longer than an hour. I therefore assume that he is already home, but I am not sure.)

wollen

In an OBJECTIVE statement, **wollen** indicates   B 645

1. a wish or desire:

> *Er will zehn Mark von mir haben.*
> *Wolltest du dieses Buch lesen?*
> *Ich freue mich über meine neue Uhr, weil ich schon lange eine solche*
>   *Uhr habe besitzen wollen.*

2. an intention or a plan:

> *Ich will nächsten Sommer nach Italien reisen.*
> *In diesem Jahr will ich unbedingt die Prüfung machen.*

In a SUBJECTIVE statement, **wollen** indicates   B 646

1. an assertion the truth of which the speaker seriously doubts:

> *Er will in Amerika gewesen sein; dabei spricht er kein Wort Englisch!*

---

[1] Note that **nicht dürfen** corresponds to English *must not*.

2. an exclamation of indignation:

*Sie **wollen** ein gebildeter Mensch sein?*

müssen

B 650   The verb **müssen** always indicates that there is only one possibility. In an OBJECTIVE statement, it indicates:

1. compulsion or obligation:

*Kinder **müssen** in die Schule gehen.*
*Man **muß** den Armen helfen.*
*Ich konnte mein Studium nicht vollenden, weil ich arbeiten **mußte**.*
*Ich **müßte** lügen, wenn ich sagte, daß mir das gefällt.*

2. an absolute necessity:

*Alle Menschen **müssen** sterben.*
*Du **mußt** mir helfen.*
*Wir **müssen** uns beeilen, sonst versäumen wir den Zug.*
*Die Arbeit **mußte** gemacht werden.* [→ B 631.2]

3. a paraphrase of the imperative in indirect discourse (usually in the subjunctive) [→ B 761, 765]:

*Er sagte, daß sie sofort kommen **müßten**.*

B 651   In a SUBJECTIVE statement, **müssen** indicates a conviction which the speaker has gained after some reflection or evidence:

*Wer einen so großen Wagen fährt, **muß** sehr reich sein.*
*Er **muß** der Täter gewesen sein, kein anderer kommt in Frage.*
*Der Unfall ließ sich nur so erklären, daß der Fahrer am Steuer eingeschlafen sein **mußte**.*

B 652   The NEGATION of **müssen** can be expressed in several ways:

1. The mere absence of necessity or compulsion is indicated simply by negating the word **müssen** itself:[1]

*Du **mußt** das Buch nicht lesen, wenn du nicht willst* (i.e. nobody is forcing you).
*Um eine Reise zu machen, **muß** man nicht sehr reich sein* (i.e. it is not absolutely necessary).

[1] Note that **nicht müssen** corresponds to English *not to have to*.

112

2. If there is no other choice available, the negation of compulsion becomes a prohibition. This must be expressed by using the verb **dürfen** in the negative:

> *In Deutschland muß man rechts fahren* (i.e. there is no other choice, it is the law). *Man **darf** nicht links fahren.*

3. To indicate that there is no need to do something, the negation of **brauchen**[1] plus an INFINITIVE with **zu** may be used [→ B 468.3]:

> *Ich muß heute abend arbeiten, aber Sie **brauchen** mir nicht zu helfen; ich mache es schon allein fertig.*

sollen

In an OBJECTIVE statement, **sollen** indicates

B 655

1. an order, command, request, or wish of a third person:

> *Gehe zu ihm und sage ihm, daß er zu mir kommen **soll**.*
> *Herr Meier **soll** zum Direktor gehen.*
> *Er dachte nicht mehr daran, daß er einen Brief hatte einwerfen **sollen**.*
> *Der Brief **sollte** sofort eingeworfen werden* [→ B 631.2].
> *Ich **soll** meinem Freund bei der Arbeit helfen* (i.e. somebody — either he himself or someone else — asked me to help him).

2. a moral duty:

> *Zu älteren Leuten **soll** man immer höflich sein.*
> *Ältere Leute **sollen** immer höflich behandelt werden* [→ B 631.2].
> ***Sollte** ich meinem Freund nicht bei der Arbeit helfen?* (i.e. I am asking myself).

3. a commandment (usually religious in nature):

> *Du **sollst** nicht stehlen!*
> *Du **sollst** deine Eltern ehren!*

---

[1] **Brauchen** may be combined with the infinitive only in the following two circumstances:

1. In a **negation**:
> *Sie **brauchen** nicht zu kommen.*

2. When it is restricted by **nur** or **bloß**:
> *Sie **brauchen** **nur** das Geld zu zahlen, und ich lasse Sie in Ruhe.*

In other constructions, *brauchen* is combined with an accusative object:
> *Er **braucht** Geld. Kranke **brauchen** einen Arzt.*

The use of **brauchen** plus an infinitive without **zu** is sometimes found in colloquial speech, but is not considered correct German: *Sie **brauchen** nicht kommen.*

4. In indirect discourse, a paraphrase of the imperative [→ B 761, 765, 795; cf. B 650.3], usually in the subjunctive:

*Meine Freundin hat angerufen und gesagt, ich **solle** sie bald in ihrer neuen Wohnung besuchen.*

B 656   In a SUBJECTIVE statement, **sollen** indicates

1. that the speaker has heard a certain assertion, but assumes no position with regard to its veracity:

*Er **soll** ein sehr reicher Mann sein* (i.e. the speaker does not know it himself, he has only heard it).

*Den Berichten zufolge **soll** der Minister heute in London ankommen* (the speaker has read it).

2. with subjunctive II, a hypothetical possibility in conditional sentences:

*Wenn Sie mein Angebot annehmen **sollten*** (i.e. I am not sure that you will), *so teilen Sie es mir bitte sofort mit.*

3. an astonished question, using subjunctive II:

***Sollten** Sie das wirklich nicht wissen?*
***Sollte** ich ihn so beleidigt haben?*

mögen

B 660   In an OBJECTIVE statement, **mögen** indicates

1. a continuing inclination towards or liking for a thing, a person, or an activity.[1] The modal *mögen* in this sense usually occurs without another verb and forms its perfect tenses with the past participle [→ B 422]:

*Ich **mag** moderne Musik.*
*Ich habe diesen Mann nie **gemocht**.*
***Mögen** Sie Milch in den Kaffee?*
***Magst** du lieber Bier oder Wein?*

2. a momentary inclination or desire for an activity:

*Jetzt **mag** ich keine Musik hören.*
*Weil er gestern seine Aufgabe nicht hat machen **mögen**, muß er heute viel länger arbeiten.*

---

[1] *Mögen* rarely occurs in the affirmative. It is more frequent in the interrogative and especially in negative statements.

114

3. in subjunctive II, a polite form of **wollen**. In this usage, *ich möchte* etc. has present tense meaning; past tenses can be formed only with *wollen*:

> *Ich **möchte** jetzt nach Hause gehen.*
> *Herr Müller **möchte** Sie um 10 Uhr sprechen.*
> ***Möchtest** du mitkommen?*
> but: *Gestern wollte ich in die Stadt fahren.*

4. in indirect discourse, a very polite paraphrase of the imperative [→ B 761, 765, 795; cf. B 650.3, 655.4];[1] present subjunctive I or II may be used (*not* compound tenses):[2]

> *Herr Schmidt hat angerufen und gesagt, man **möge** nicht auf ihn warten.*
> *Ich soll Ihnen Grüße von Frau Meier bestellen und Ihnen sagen, Sie **möchten** sie doch bald besuchen.*

5. a restrictive statement (only present and past tense):

> ***Mag** er auch noch so klug sein, er bekommt die Stellung doch nicht.*
> *Wir **mochten** tun, was wir wollten, wir konnten es ihm nicht recht machen.*

6. a wish which seems capable of fulfillment, particularly in formal or solemn usage (the verb is always in the present subjunctive I or II):[3]

> ***Möge** Gott ihm helfen!*
> *Er **möge** noch lange leben!*
> ***Möchten** sie nur bald kommen!*

7. a permission, whereby the subject is allowed free choice (present tense only):

> *Sie **mag** das Kleid kaufen, wenn es ihr gefällt.*
> *Du **magst** gehen oder bleiben; mache, was du willst.*

---

[1] Also possible in requests addressed to a third person: *Die folgenden Herren **mögen** (**möchten**) bitte zum Direktor kommen.* [→ B 795]

[2] Note the difference between *Er hat gesagt, man möge nicht auf ihn warten* (,,*Bitte, warten Sie nicht auf mich!*“) and *Er hat gesagt, man habe nicht auf ihn warten mögen* (,,*Sie wollten nicht auf mich warten*“).

[3] The term "present subjunctive" is used to indicate that the statement made refers to the present (or future), regardless of the tense form of the verb. For the relationship between tense and time in the subjunctive, → B 716.

115

B 661   In a SUBJECTIVE statement, **mögen** indicates

1. a possibility:

> *Er **mag** jetzt in Berlin sein* (i.e. the speaker considers it possible).
> *Das **mag** wahr sein* (i.e. the speaker is not sure, but concedes the possibility).
> *Er **mag** früher einmal ein großer Schauspieler gewesen sein* (i.e. he doesn't show it now).

2. an approximation or an estimate:

> *Es **mag** zehn Uhr gewesen sein.*
> *Wir **mochten** vielleicht eine Stunde gewartet haben.*

3. a pensive or reflexive question, implying wonderment:

> *Wie **mag** es meinem Freund jetzt gehen?*
> *Wann **mag** das wohl gewesen sein?*

B 670   In colloquial usage, modals often occur in a declarative statement without a dependent infinitive, if a verb of motion (**gehen, fahren,** etc.) is understood or implied [→ H 425 ff.]:

> *Ich **kann** heute ins Kino, denn ich habe Zeit.*
> *Du **darfst** zu deinem Freund; ich erlaube es dir.*
> *Er **will** nach Hause; er ist müde.*
> *Wir **müssen** ins Büro — es ist schon spät.*

B 675   In an answer to a question containing a modal verb, the main verb is usually not repeated. In this case, the modal stands alone in the sentence (usually with the pronoun object **das** or **es**), and forms the perfect tenses with the past participle:

> ***Können** Sie Klavier **spielen**? Nein, das **kann** ich nicht.*
> ***Darfst** du heute ins Kino **gehen**? Ja, ich **darf** es.*
> *Hast du gestern ins Kino **gehen dürfen**? Ja, ich habe es **gedurft**.[1]*

Similarly:

> *Warum kommst du nicht mit uns ins Kino? Weil ich nicht **darf**.*

Summary

B 680   Some modal verbs show different attitudes towards a situation, or various shades or levels of attitudes. Observe the following differences:

---

[1] The form *Ich habe es dürfen* also frequently occurs, especially in colloquial usage.

116

Both **können** or **mögen** may be used to indicate POSSIBILITY: B 681

> *Wir **können** in 2 Stunden in Hamburg sein* [→ B 635.2] indicates the
> OBJECTIVE possibility.
>
> *Das **mag** wahr sein* [→ B 661.1] indicates that the speaker SUB-
> JECTIVELY believes this to be possible.

Können, dürfen, or **mögen** may be used to indicate PERMISSION: B 682

> *Ihr **könnt** ins Kino gehen — ich habe nichts dagegen* [→ B 635.3].
> *Ihr **dürft** ins Kino gehen — ich erlaube es euch zur Belohnung*
> [→ B 640.1].
> *Sie **mag** ins Kino gehen, wenn sie Lust hat* [→ B 660.7].

Both **müssen** and **sollen** indicate NECESSITY or COMMAND, but with a B 683
clear distinction:

> *Du **mußt** die Wahrheit sagen.* (You have no other choice.)
> [→ B 650.1]
> *Du **sollst** die Wahrheit sagen.* (It is your moral duty.) [→ B 655.2]

A SUBJECTIVE statement may show varying degrees of belief: [→ B 632] B 684

> *Sie **muß** 20 Jahre alt sein.* (The speaker is certain.) [→ B 651]
> *Sie **kann** 20 Jahre alt sein.* (The speaker considers it probable.)
> [→ B 636.1]
> *Sie **könnte** (**dürfte**) 20 Jahre alt sein.* (The speaker considers it rather
> likely.) [→ B 636.2, 641]
> *Sie **mag** 20 Jahre alt sein.* (The speaker considers it possible.)
> [→ B 661.1]
> *Sie **soll** 20 Jahre alt sein.* (The speaker has heard it and reports it
> without judgment.) [→ B 656.1]
> *Sie **will** 20 Jahre alt sein.* (She claims it, but the speaker doubts it.)
> [→ B 646.1]

USE OF THE SUBJUNCTIVE

⋟ Introduction

The SUBJUNCTIVE expresses varying degrees of UNCERTAINTY, DOUBT, B 700
and NONREALITY. It may indicate that the speaker is expressing a
hypothesis about a given situation, speculating on what might happen
or might have happened, or that the realization of such a situation
would seem desirable to the speaker, or that the speaker has no

117

first-hand knowledge of the situation, but is merely reporting what he has heard about it.

The German subjunctive exists in one simple tense form only: the present [→ B 716 for relationship between tense and time]. Compound tenses must be constructed with auxiliary verbs.

B 701 Unlike other languages, the use of the subjunctive in German is not required by certain conjunctions or verbs, on which a subjunctive clause might depend. It is exclusively an indication of the relationship or attitude of the speaker towards the situation described. If, in the view of the speaker, a statement is possible, uncertain, or unreal, he may express it in the subjunctive. Accordingly, the indicative or the subjunctive may be used in the same sentence structures to express different attitudes of the speaker to the situation:

> *Hans schrieb, daß er morgen kommt.* (I consider it certain.)
> *Hans schrieb, daß er morgen* **komme** (or **käme**). (I have received the information and am passing it on without judgment.)
>
> *Ich habe gehört, daß er krank ist.* (I do not doubt it.)
> *Ich habe gehört, daß er krank* **sei** (or **wäre**). (I do not know whether this is true.)[1]

B 702 The subjunctive *must* be used in sentences which by their very nature express something unreal: concessive statements, wishes or conditions contrary to fact, hypothetical statements, etc. It is also used in certain requests or commands, and in indirect discourse [→ B 750 ff., 795].

B 703 For the forms of the subjunctive, → B 130 ff., B 240 ff.

Subjunctive I[2]

B 705 In the main clause, SUBJUNCTIVE I is used to indicate a WISH the fulfillment of which is possible. The subjunctive I of the modal verb **mögen** is often used in such sentences [→ B 660.6]:

[1] In colloquial German, such a distinction is not necessarily made. On the other hand, the difference between subjunctive I: *er sei krank* (I am inclined to believe it) and subjunctive II: *er wäre krank* (I doubt it) is largely artificial. They are widely used interchangeably.

[2] The traditional terms subjunctive I and subjunctive II are being used for the sake of convenience. Actually, subjunctive II occurs far more frequently in modern German, especially in colloquial usage. Subjunctive II might thus be called "General Subjunctive," and subjunctive I "Special Subjunctive."

118

*Es **lebe** die Freiheit!*
*Gott **segne** den König!*
*Gott **sei** Dank!*
*Er **möge** noch lange leben!*
***Mögest** du recht viel Erfolg haben!*

Subjunctive I is also used in the main clause to express a request or COMMAND, primarily to the third person singular, very rarely the third person plural. In the first person plural, such commands may be considered either subjunctive or imperative [→ B 129, 238], except for the verb **sein**, where they are clearly subjunctive:

   B 706

*Es **werde** Licht!*
*So **sei** es!*
*Von dieser Medizin **nehme** man dreimal täglich fünf Tropfen.*
***Gehen** wir jetzt!*
***Seien** wir froh, daß alles gut vorüber ist!*

In dependent clauses, subjunctive I is used in RESTRICTIVE or CONCESSIVE clauses [→ B 728]; if the modal verb **mögen** is used, it may appear either in the indicative or in subjunctive I [→ B 660.5]:

   B 710

*Was er auch immer **wünsche**, mir soll es recht sein.*
*Sein Zeugnis **sei** wie es **wolle**, er wird die Stellung doch nicht bekommen.*
*Was immer geschehen **mag** (or **möge**), wir sind vorbereitet.*

Subjunctive I is also used in dependent clauses, if the speaker wants to express the fact that he does NOT NECESSARILY AGREE with someone else's statement:

   B 711

*Paul ist nicht in die Schule gekommen, weil er (wie er sagte) Kopf-schmerzen **habe**.*
*Er will den Zug versäumt haben, weil er kein Taxi **habe** finden können.*

In a dependent clause showing intention or purpose, subjunctive I may also be used after the conjunction **damit** [→ G 130]. The situation on which the clause depends usually lies in the past tense:

   B 712

*Der Vater gab seinem Sohn Geld, **damit** er sich einen Anzug **kaufe**.*
*Ich brachte ihm meinen Regenschirm, **damit** er nicht naß **werde**.*

For use of subjunctive I in indirect discourse, → B 750 ff.

   B 713

119

Subjunctive II

B 715 The subjunctive II form of verbs indicates a situation which one only imagines, but which has not (or not yet) taken place. It expresses a conjecture of what might be (or might have been) possible.

B 716 Although subjunctive II forms are derived from the past tense of verbs, they do not by themselves refer to past events. The following table shows the relationships which exist between the time of the event referred to, and the tense form of the subjunctive: [1]

Situation refers to:	Subjunctive II occurs in:
1. present or future events	main verb or modal auxiliary (or paraphrase with **würde** [2])
2. past events	**haben** or **sein** plus past participle of main verb (or **haben** plus double infinitive for modals [→ B 468, 753]).

1. *Wenn ich Geld **hätte**, **ginge** ich heute ins Theater* (or ***würde** ich heute ins Theater **gehen*** [2]): I have no money (now), therefore I can not go to the theater (now).

   *Wenn du **wolltest**, **könntest** du mir helfen:* If you should want to help me (now or in the future), I am sure that you would be able to do so.

2. *Wenn du mich letzten Sonntag **besucht hättest**, **wären** wir zusammen ins Theater **gegangen**:* You did not visit me, therefore we did not go to the theater together.

   *Wenn er hier **gewesen wäre**, **hätte** ich ihn **sehen müssen**:* He was not here, therefore I could not see him.

B 717 German verbs have no actual conditional form. If the condition is within fact, i.e. if both the condition and the conclusion are capable of fulfillment, we use the indicative:

---

1 Note that there are only two tense forms possible: present or future (identical forms) and past (subjunctive of the auxiliary).

2 The paraphrase with **würde** occurs more frequently in colloquial usage [→ B 719]. The order of the clauses may be reversed: *Ich würde ins Theater gehen, wenn ich Geld hätte.*

120

Wenn ich Zeit habe, komme ich: I may have time; if so, I'll come.

If the condition is contrary to fact, i.e. if fulfillment is not possible, subjunctive II is used:

> *Wenn ich Zeit hätte, käme ich* (or *würde ich kommen): I* have no time; I can not come.
>
> *Wenn ich Zeit gehabt hätte, wäre ich gekommen:* I did not have time; I did not come.

For weak verbs, as well as for some forms of strong verbs which do not take an *Umlaut*, subjunctive II is identical with the indicative past tense [→ B 130 ff., 240 ff.]. In order to recognize the contrary-to-fact nature of a given statement, subjunctive II of *werden* (**würde**) plus the infinitive of the main verb is used in the conclusion, if otherwise the verb would be identical with the indicative: B 718

> *Ich würde mir einen Anzug kaufen, wenn mein Vater Geld schickte.*
> *Wir würden mit unserem Freund ins Theater gehen, wenn er uns besuchte.*
>
> Similarly: *Ich habe nicht geglaubt, daß er die Rechnung je bezahlen würde.*

Whereas the subjunctive is still widely used in written and especially in formal language, the paraphrase with **würde** and the infinitive occurs more and more frequently in the conclusion of a condition, in spoken and colloquial usage, even where the subjunctive forms are clearly distinct from the past indicative. [See examples in B 716 and 717.]   B 719

This is especially true of irregular subjunctive forms of strong verbs [→ B 250]:

> *Wenn er könnte, würde er Ihnen helfen* (not *hülfe er Ihnen*).

Modals and the verbs **haben** and **sein**, however, do not as a rule use this paraphrase, but prefer the subjunctive:

> *Er könnte mir sicher helfen, wenn er wollte.*
> *Wenn er früher angefangen hätte, müßte er sich jetzt nicht so beeilen.*
> *Ich wäre sehr froh, wenn Sie mit uns kämen.*
> *Wenn er fleißiger wäre, hätte er jetzt eine bessere Stellung.*
> [But → B 735]

B 720   As a result, past conditions do not ordinarily use the paraphrase with **würde**:[1]

> *Ich **hätte** ihn gesehen, wenn er hier gewesen wäre.*
> *Wenn ich Zeit gehabt hätte, **wäre** ich gekommen.*

B 721   Substituting the **würde** paraphrase for the subjunctive in the condition (the clause beginning with *if*) is considered poor German by grammatical purists and usually avoided in written and especially formal usage.[2] Nonetheless, it is often found in colloquial language, either with weak verbs, where the subjunctive has no recognizable form, or with irregular (and thus unusual) strong verbs.

> *Wenn ich ihn nur verstehen **würde**, könnte ich ihm helfen.*
> *Ich **würde** mir einen neuen Anzug kaufen, wenn mein Vater mir mehr Geld schicken **würde**.*

B 722   A more acceptable formal substitute for the subjunctive in conditional clauses is a paraphrase with the subjunctive of a modal and the infinitive of the main verb:

> *Der arme Mann! Wenn ihm doch jemand etwas schenken **wollte**.*
> *Wenn ich in der Lotterie gewinnen **sollte**, würde ich mir ein neues Auto kaufen.*
> *Wenn Sie mir helfen **möchten**, wäre ich Ihnen sehr dankbar.*

B 723   Sometimes subjunctive II may appear in independent main clauses, where an ADVERBIAL PHRASE replaces the conditional clause:

> ***Bei schönem Wetter ginge** ich gern spazieren. (Wenn das Wetter schön wäre, . . .)*

[1] Forms like *Ich würde ihn gesehen haben* or *Ich würde gekommen sein* exist, but they are considered awkward and stilted and should be avoided.

[2] The old grammar rule frequently cited in this connection is: *Wenn-Sätze sind würde-los.* This principle, however, is by no means absolute and it is easy to find many literary examples for *wenn — würde* sentences. Only a few are cited here:
Grimmelshausen (*Simplizissimus*): Wenn ich liegen bleiben **würde**, . . .
Lessing (*Laokoön*): Und wenn die alten Artisten bei dem Einwurfe lachen **würden**, . . .
Goethe (*Egmont*): Die sehen nicht aus, als wenn sie so bald Brüderschaft mit uns trinken **würden**!
Raabe (*Akten des Vogelsangs*): Wenn doch der Herr Assessor mal kommen **würde**!
Zuckmayer (*Seelenbräu*): . . ., wenn man sie wieder hinbringen **würde**.
Th. Mann (*Buddenbrooks*): Aber wenn Sie, lieber Herr, uns die Freude machen **würden** . . .
Kafka (*Prozeß*): Wenn er auch natürlich niemals von dieser Rechtfertigung Gebrauch machen **würde**.
Dürrenmatt (*Verdacht*): Es wäre schön, wenn du mir jetzt eine [Zigarre] anbieten **würdest**.
Frisch (*Don Juan*): Wenn du ihn kennen **würdest**!
See Tamsen, "Über ‚Wenn . . . würde' im modernen Deutsch," *Deutschunterricht für Ausländer* IX, 1959, 33 ff.

Mit etwas mehr Mühe könntest du die Arbeit leisten. (Wenn du dich etwas mehr bemühtest, . . .)

An Ihrer Stelle würde ich das nicht tun. (Wenn ich an Ihrer Stelle wäre, . . .)

In many instances, the contrary-to-fact conditional clause is left out, **B 724** when its meaning appears obvious from the context:

*Mein Freund hat sein Studium mit mir begonnen, hat aber nach zwei Semestern nicht weiterstudiert. Jetzt **könnte** er schon Doktor sein.*

*Ich **hätte** den Brief geschrieben, aber ich hatte keine Zeit.*

(Or: *Ich hatte keine Zeit, sonst **hätte** ich den Brief geschrieben.*)

CONTRARY-TO-FACT WISHES also use subjunctive II. These wishes have **B 725** the form of a contrary-to-fact condition with or without **wenn** [→ B 739, G 578, G 582], and usually contain the adverb **doch** or **nur** as an intensifier [→ H 616, 636]:

*Wenn mein Vater nur **käme**! or **Käme** mein Vater doch!*

*Wenn ich diesen Fehler doch nicht gemacht **hätte**! or **Hätte** ich diesen Fehler nur nicht gemacht!*

The conjunctions **als, als ob, als wenn** introduce UNREAL COMPARISONS **B 726** and other statements with the verb in subjunctive II [→ G 049–053]:

*Er gibt so viel Geld aus, **als wäre** er ein Millionär.*

*Tun Sie (so), **als ob** Sie zu Hause **wären**.*

*Es sieht aus, **als wenn** es morgen regnen **würde**.*

If a CONDITIONAL CLAUSE depends on an ADJECTIVE or an ADVERB, it is **B 727** introduced by the conjunction **als daß** and the verb appears in subjunctive II. This indicates the impossibility of a given statement:

*Ich habe zu wenig Geld, **als daß** ich ein Haus kaufen **könnte**.*

*Es ist schon zu spät, **als daß** mein Vater noch im Büro **wäre**.*

In a CONCESSIVE CLAUSE, subjunctive II, often accompanied by *auch*, is **B 728** used to indicate that the speaker does not believe that the situation mentioned in the dependent clause is likely to occur:

*Wenn du mir auch hundert Mark **gäbest**, **täte** ich diese Arbeit nicht (or **würde** ich diese Arbeit nicht tun).*

*Was du mir auch gegeben **hättest**, ich **hätte** diese Arbeit nicht getan.*

123

B 729   Sentences indicating a POSSIBILITY imagined by the speaker contain subjunctive II, usually with the modal auxiliary *können*:

> *Du bist so reich, daß du dir ein neues Auto kaufen **könntest**.*
> *Ich habe jetzt so viel Zeit, daß ich auf Reisen gehen **könnte**.*

B 730   Dependent clauses with the conjunction **ohne daß** [→ G 230] and subjunctive II indicate that a SITUATION which one normally would have expected DID NOT OCCUR:

> *Mein Freund benützte mein Fahrrad, **ohne daß** er mich darum gebeten **hätte**.*
> *Er verließ seine Familie, **ohne daß** er sich weiter um sie gekümmert **hätte**.*

B 731   RELATIVE CLAUSES [→ J 146.1] may contain subjunctive II, if they indicate a wish or a possibility:

> *Ich habe einen Freund, mit dem du nach München fahren **könntest**.*
> *Wenn doch jetzt ein Bekannter **käme**, der mit mir spazieren ginge!*

B 732   Subjunctive II is also used to differentiate between factual and contrary-to-fact statements in the same sentence:

> *Er **müßte** mehr arbeiten, aber er will nicht.*
> *Ich **hätte** ihm geholfen, aber ich konnte nicht.*

B 733   QUESTIONS expressing considerable DOUBT also use subjunctive II:

> *Gäben Sie mir wirklich das Geld?*
> *Hätte das denn etwas geändert?*
> *Sollte er das vergessen haben?*

B 734   Very polite questions and requests are often expressed with subjunctive II, often with **möchte**:

> *Könnten Sie mir bitte Auskunft geben?*
> *Wären Sie so freundlich, mir das Salz zu reichen?*
> *Ich möchte gerne wissen, . . .*

B 735   In this sense, the paraphrase with **würde** and the infinitive of the main verb is often used, even with the verb **sein**:

> *Würden Sie mir bitte das Buch bringen?*
> *Würden Sie so freundlich sein, mir das Salz zu reichen?*

B 736   Subjunctive II of **dürfen** [→ B 643] with the infinitive of the main verb is used to indicate a cautiously phrased supposition:

124

*Mein Freund ist vor einer Stunde weggegangen. Er **dürfte** jetzt schon zu Hause sein.*
*Die junge Dame **dürfte** etwa 25 Jahre alt sein.*

Past forms of subjunctive II with **beinahe** or **fast** are used to indicate   B 737
that an event almost happened, but then did not take place:

*Ich **hätte** die Prüfung beinahe nicht bestanden.*
*Sie **wäre** fast vom Pferd gefallen.*

Subjunctive II is also used to indicate that only a part of the situation   B 738
has been completed:

*Für heute **wären** wir fertig* (i.e. we'll have to continue tomorrow).
*Den größten Teil der Ware **hätte** ich verkauft* (i.e. now I'll have to try to sell the rest, too).
*Das **hätten** wir geschafft!* (Now we'll go on to something else.)

In many conditions, the conjunction **wenn** may be omitted, especially   B 739
in formal usage. [Cf. B 725.] The conditional clause then begins with
the subjunctive form of the verb; the conclusion is usually introduced
by **so** or **dann**:

*Hätte ich Geld, **so** ginge ich ins Theater.*
*Wäre mein Freund gekommen, **dann** hätte er mit uns gehen können.*

Summary of Forms   B 745

	PRESENT CONDITION	PAST CONDITION
Conditional clause (**wenn**)	Subjunctive II	**hätte** or **wäre** + past participle or **hätte** + double infinitive (modals)
Conclusion clause	**würde** + Infinitive or Subjunctive II (primarily **hätte**, **wäre** and modals, as well as a few common verbs like **gehen**, **kommen**, etc.)	

Indirect Discourse

Indirect discourse or indirect quotation is a type of statement in which   B 750
the speaker conveys information given him by a third person. In

125

German, such indirect quotations usually occur in the subjunctive. By using the subjunctive, the speaker stresses his role as a conveyor of secondhand information and declines responsibility for the veracity of the original statement.[1]

B 751 According to strict rules of grammar and style, subjunctive I is preferred for indirect discourse. If, however, subjunctive I forms are identical with the present indicative, subjunctive II *must* be used. From this rule, the following table can be constructed to govern the preferred subjunctive forms of verbs in indirect discourse:[2]

WEAK VERBS	STRONG VERBS	
ich lernte	ich käme	Subj. II
du lernest	du kommest	Subj. I
er lerne	er komme	Subj. I
wir lernten	wir kämen	Subj. II
ihr lernet	ihr kommet	Subj. I
sie lernten	sie kämen	Subj. II

B 752 For most practical purposes, subjunctive I occurs primarily in the third person singular; in the second person singular and plural, its use is considered slightly stilted. As a result, subjunctive II is more and more widely used in all persons for indirect discourse, especially in informal language. The old stylistic principle that subjunctive I is to be preferred unless it is identical with the present indicative has thus in recent years been almost reversed in actual usage, especially in speaking: subjunctive II now occurs frequently, except in those instances where its forms are identical with the past indicative.[3] In any case, it is important to realize that there is no <u>time</u> difference between the two forms [→ B 755 ff.].

B 753 Statements in indirect discourse appear after the introductory statement

---

1 By the same token, of course, the speaker may use the indicative to indicate the unquestionably factual nature of a given statement, or to support a statement. This is especially true if the introductory verb is in the present tense, or is a verb like **wissen**: *Die Zeitung schreibt, daß der Minister in London angekommen ist. Galileo wußte, daß die Erde sich um die Sonne dreht.* In conversational German, the indicative is generally used for indirect statements in the present tense, and frequently in the past tense as well.

2 This does not apply to the verb **sein**, where both subjunctive forms clearly differ from the indicative, and can be used interchangeably. [→ B 140]

3 If both subjunctives are identical with the indicative, subjunctive II *must* be used: *Die Kinder sagten, daß sie in der Schule viel* **lernten.**

in a DEPENDENT CLAUSE introduced by the conjunction **daß**; often, however, this CONJUNCTION is OMITTED and the indirect quotation functions
like a MAIN CLAUSE:

> *Karl schrieb mir,* **daß** *er morgen* **komme** (or **käme**).
> *Karl schrieb mir, er* **komme** (or **käme**) *morgen.*

INTERROGATIVE CLAUSES in indirect discourse follow after the introductory statement as DEPENDENT CLAUSES, with the interrogative acting as
a conjunction. Questions to which the answer is yes or no are introduced in indirect discourse by the conjunction **ob**:

> *Er erklärte mir,* **warum** *er nicht kommen* **könne** (or **könnte**).
> *Sie erzählte uns,* **wo** *sie gewohnt* **habe** (or **hätte**).
> *Ich fragte ihn,* **ob** *er dabei gewesen* **sei** (or **wäre**).

In indirect discourse, there are only THREE TENSE FORMS. If the original
DIRECT QUOTATION is in the PRESENT TENSE [→ B 510 ff.], this indicates
that the action reported within the quotation is SIMULTANEOUS with the
introductory statement:[1] *Er sagte: „Ich arbeite jeden Tag acht Stunden"*
means only that the statement applies to the time when it was made.
We have no indication whether it still holds true now.

Such statements are expressed in indirect discourse by subjunctive
I or II of the main verb or modal verb:

> *Er sagte, daß er jeden Tag acht Stunden* **arbeite.**
> *Er erklärte, daß er darauf nicht antworten* **könne** (or **könnte**) (i.e. he
> could not answer the question at that time).

If the original DIRECT QUOTATION is in the FUTURE TENSE, this indicates
that the action reported in the quotation WILL FOLLOW the time of the
introductory statement [→ B 560 ff.]. In the sentence *Er schrieb: „Ich
werde bald kommen,"* the word *bald* is relative to the time of the introductory statement. We have no indication as to whether the time
referred to has not in fact long since passed.

In indirect discourse, such statements are expressed by the subjunctive I or II of **werden** and the infinitive of the main verb:

> *Er schrieb mir, daß er bald* **kommen werde** (or **würde**).
> *Sie erzählt, daß ihre Eltern sie* **besuchen würden.**

---

[1] It must be remembered that the present tense may be used in German with future implica-
tion [→ B 518]. This also applies to indirect discourse: *Karl erzählte, sein Freund fahre im
Sommer nach Italien.* (Original direct quotation: *„Mein Freund fährt im Sommer nach
Italien."*)

127

B 757   If the original DIRECT QUOTATION occurs in any PAST TENSE form, this indicates that the action reported in the quotation PRECEDED the time of the introductory statement [→ B 530–550]. It does not matter whether the direct quotation was made in the past tense, the present perfect, or the past perfect. In indirect discourse, all such statements are expressed by subjunctive I or II of **haben** or **sein** and the past participle of the main verb, or, in the case of modals, subjunctive I or II of **haben** and the double infinitive [→ B 468]:

> *Ich habe gehört, daß Karl gestern **gekommen sei**.*
> *Er schreibt mir, daß seine Eltern ein Auto **gekauft hätten**.*
> *Die Leute sagten, daß die Polizei den Dieb **habe verhaften können**.*
> (*Die Leute sagten, die Polizei **hätte** den Dieb **verhaften können**.*)

B 758   Note that the tense of the introductory statement has no bearing on the tense of the indirect quotation, nor on the choice of subjunctive I or II:

> *Er **schreibt** mir, er **sei** (or **wäre**) vor einer Woche angekommen.*
> *Er **schrieb** mir, er **sei** (or **wäre**) vor einer Woche angekommen.*

B 759   The following table shows the tense forms of the subjunctive in indirect discourse, and their relationships to the time of the introductory statement:

Original Direct Quotation	Indirect Discourse	Time Relationship
PRESENT TENSE	ich lernte, er lerne ich käme, er komme (käme)	Indirect quotation simultaneous with introductory statement
FUTURE	ich würde lernen (kommen) er werde (würde) lernen (kommen)	Indirect quotation follows after time of introductory statement
ANY PAST TENSE	ich hätte gelernt er habe (hätte) gelernt ich (er) sei (wäre) gekommen	Indirect quotation precedes introductory statement in time

128

In English, similar time relationships apply:

> *Er sagte, er **komme** (or **käme**):* He said he *was* coming.
> *Er sagte, er **werde** (or **würde**) kommen:* He said he *would* come.
> *Er sagte, er **sei** (or **wäre**) gekommen:* He said he *had* come.

The IMPERATIVE is paraphrased in indirect discourse with subjunctive I
or II of the modal verbs **müssen**, **sollen**, or **mögen** and the infinitive of
the main verb [→ B 650.3, 655.4, 660.4]:

> *Ich erklärte ihm, daß er mehr arbeiten **müsse** (**müßte**).*
> *Er schrieb, ich **solle** ihn besuchen kommen.*
> *Karl sagte mir, du **mögest** (**möchtest**) ihn morgen besuchen.*

In any statement reported indirectly, all pronouns and references to
place are changed to correspond to the viewpoint of the narrator:

Direct Discourse	*Indirect Discourse*
Du hast mir gesagt: „*Ich* werde *euch* besuchen.“ Er schreibt: „*Ich* kam mit *meinem* Bruder nach Paris und bleibe drei Wochen *hier*.“	Du hast mir gesagt, *du* würdest *uns* besuchen. Er schreibt, *er* sei (wäre) mit *seinem* Bruder nach Paris gekommen und bleibe (bliebe) drei Wochen *dort*.

If two or more persons are mentioned in the direct quotation, it is better
to use names instead of pronouns in indirect discourse, in order to avoid
misunderstandings:

Direct Discourse	*Indirect Discourse*
Karl schrieb: „Ich bin gestern zu meinem Onkel gefahren. Nachdem ich mit ihm zu Abend gegessen hatte, lud er mich ins Theater ein.“	Karl schrieb, er sei gestern zu seinem Onkel gefahren. Nachdem *er mit seinem Onkel* zu Abend gegessen habe, habe *der Onkel ihn* ins Theater eingeladen. Or: Nachdem *Karl mit ihm* zu Abend gegessen habe, habe *er Karl* ins Theater eingeladen.

Summary

B 765 To convey a statement made by a third person without any judgment on the veracity of its content, the following principles should be observed:

TIME OF ORIGINAL ACTION	*Direct Statement*	*Indirect Discourse*
	TENSE OF MAIN VERB OR MODAL	SUBJUNCTIVE I OR II
1. PRESENT	Present tense	Main verb or modal
2. PAST	Past tense, present perfect, past perfect	**Haben** or **sein** + past participle of main verb or infinitive of modal
3. FUTURE	a. Present [→ B 517]	Main verb or modal
	b. Future tense	**Werden** + infinitive of main verb
4. COMMAND	Imperative [→ B 780]	**Müssen, sollen,** or **mögen** + infinitive of main verb

B 766 Examples:

Direct Discourse	*Indirect Discourse*
Er (schreibt) mir:	Er (schreibt) mir,
1. „*Ich fahre* zu meinen Eltern nach Berlin, denn *ich will* mit meinem Vater sprechen."	*er fahre* zu seinen Eltern nach Berlin, denn *er wolle* mit seinem Vater sprechen.
2. „Gestern *kaufte ich* meine Fahrkarte und heute *bin ich* um 10 Uhr *abgefahren*, nachdem ich meinen Eltern ein Telegramm *geschickt hatte*."	Gestern *habe er* seine Fahrkarte *gekauft* und heute *sei er* um 10 Uhr *abgefahren*, nachdem er seinen Eltern ein Telegramm *geschickt habe*.
„*Ich mußte* mir ein Taxi zum Bahnhof *nehmen*."	*Er habe* sich ein Taxi zum Bahnhof *nehmen müssen*.
3. a. „Nächste Woche *komme ich* wieder zurück."	Nächste Woche *komme er* wieder zurück.
b. „Dann *werde ich* dich *besuchen*."	Dann *werde er* mich *besuchen*.
4. „*Schreibe* mir, wann *du* Zeit *hast*. *Schreibe* aber bitte sofort!"	*Ich solle* ihm *schreiben*, wann *ich* Zeit *hätte*. Ich *müsse* aber sofort *schreiben*.

130

IMPERATIVE

The IMPERATIVE is a form of the verb by means of which a REQUEST or
COMMAND is expressed, which may be directed to one or more persons.
The imperative verb usually stands at the beginning of the sentence,[1]
and the sentence normally ends with an exclamation point:

B 780

> *Hole mir bitte ein Glas Wasser!*
> *Schrei nicht so laut!*
> *Kommt gut nach Hause!*
> *Sprechen Sie etwas deutlicher, bitte!*
> *Seid nett zueinander!*

If the verb needs a reflexive pronoun in the imperative, the pronoun has
the form which corresponds to the person (or persons) addressed:

B 781

> *Wasche **dich** gründlich!*
> *Freut **euch** doch über das schöne Wetter!*
> *Erkundigen Sie **sich** beim Reisebüro!*

If the command is made to a group of persons including the speaker, the
first person plural is used, with the personal pronoun **wir** appearing
immediately after the verb. In the case of the verb **sein**, the form is
clearly subjunctive I; for all other verbs it is identical with the indicative:

B 782

> *Gehen wir jetzt!*
> *Bleiben wir noch!*
> *Seien wir froh, daß alles gut vorüber ist!*

If the request is especially stressed, or in formal usage, the imperative
form of **lassen** and the personal pronoun **uns** may also occur:

B 783

> *Laßt uns jetzt gehen!*
> *Lasset uns beten!*
> *Brüder, **laßt uns** glücklich sein!*

The imperative forms of the second person singular or plural may also
be followed by the personal pronouns **du** and **ihr**; these pronouns are
then stressed and have demonstrative function [→ H 277]:

B 784

> *Mach **du** es doch, wenn du willst!*
> *Helft **ihr** dem armen Mann, ich kann es leider nicht!*

[1] For exceptions → B 785–6.

B 785 A polite request may be followed by the intensifiers [→ H 600 ff.] **bitte**, **doch**, or **doch einmal**. **Bitte** may also occur before the imperative; it is separated from the sentence by a comma only if it is stressed:

> *Komm **doch einmal** her!*
> *Helfen Sie mir **doch**!*
> ***Bitte** geben Sie mir das Buch!*
> *Geben Sie mir **bitte** das Buch!*
> *Geben Sie mir das Buch, **bitte**!*

B 786 In unusual cases, one other sentence element may precede the imperative. This element will always be stressed:

> ***Jetzt** komm einmal sofort her!*
> ***Mich** fragt aber nicht!*

B 787 By using the imperative of **tun** or **machen**, we can give emotional coloring to the request:

> ***Mach**, daß du fortgehst!* (Annoyance)
> ***Tun** Sie mir den Gefallen und bleiben Sie hier!* (Polite request)

B 788 The imperative form of the second person singular, in addition to the general uses of **du** [→ D 020], is also occasionally applied to people in general:

1. In advertisements and slogans:

> ***Kaufe** nur bei Müller und Sohn!*
> ***Trink** Milch und du bleibst gesund!*
> ***Wähle** CDU!*

2. In proverbs, sayings, and idiomatic phrases:

> ***Iß**, was gar ist, **trink**, was klar ist, **sprich**, was wahr ist!*
> ***Üb'** immer Treu und Redlichkeit!*
> *Sein ganzes Vermögen betrug **sage** und **schreibe** nur 100 Mark.*

3. For bibliographical reference (no exclamation point):

> ***Siehe** Seite 9 (s. S. 9). [→ B 233]*
> ***Vergleiche** § 14 (vgl. § 14).*[1]

B 790 A request or command may also be expressed in some ways other than the imperative:

---

[1] The symbol § is the German symbol for paragraph. It corresponds to English "¶."

1. With an infinitive or past participle [→ B 828, 995]:

> *Rechts **gehen**! — Langsam **fahren**! — Nicht **hinauslehnen**!*
> *Rauchen **verboten**! — **Stillgestanden**! — Jetzt **aufgepaßt**!*

2. With certain sentence constructions, in which the conjugated verb is stressed:

Declarative present:	*Ihr **geht** jetzt und **holt** das Buch!*
Interrogative present:	***Kommst** du nun bald?!*
Declarative future:	*Du **wirst** jetzt sofort nach Hause gehen!*
Interrogative future:	***Werdet** ihr endlich anfangen?!*
Interrogative with modal *wollen* in present tense:	***Willst** du jetzt einmal kommen?!* ***Wollen** Sie bezahlen oder nicht?!*
Declarative with modal *sollen* in present tense:	*Das **sollst** du nicht tun!* *Du **sollst** nicht töten!*
Interrogative with subjunctive II of modal *mögen* [→ B 650.4]:	***Möchten** Sie mir bitte das Salz geben?!*

3. With a *daß*-clause standing by itself, sometimes reinforced by *ja*, *nur*, or *nur ja*:

> ***Daß** du pünktlich zu Hause bist!*
> ***Daß** Sie nur nicht zu spät kommen!*
> ***Daß** ihr nur ja keine Dummheiten macht!*

4. With parts of speech other than verbs. Used by themselves, they indicate a very strict command:

> ***Ruhe**! — **Schnell**! — **Los**! — **Fertig**! — **Hierher**! — **Feuer**! — **Zu Hilfe**!*

For paraphrases of the imperative in indirect discourse, → B 761.   **B 791**

A request or a command addressed to a third person is expressed   **B 795**

1. With the present tense of the modal **sollen** or subjunctive I or II of the modal **mögen** [→ B 655.4, 660.4]:

> *Er **soll** heute nachmittag zu mir kommen!*
> *Er **möge** (**möchte**) heute nachmittag zu mir kommen.* (More polite.)

2. With subjunctive I of the main verb and the impersonal pronoun subject **man** [→ B 706] (or a similar impersonal form):

> *Man **merke** sich den Namen gut!*
> *Man **nehme** drei Eier und 100 g Zucker . . .* (no exclamation point)
> *Der Leser **beachte** die folgenden Ausnahmen.* (no exclamation point)

133

PARTICIPLES

B 800   Besides acting as the predicate, the verb can also carry out other functions in the sentence, which are normally expressed by other parts of speech. In these functions the verb appears as a participle. We distinguish two participle forms in German: the PRESENT PARTICIPLE and the PAST PARTICIPLE. [→ B 160 ff., 265 ff.]

Present Participle

B 801   The present participle occurs

1. as an attributive adjective [→ E 050 ff., J 110.7, J 121]:

> das **spielende** Kind, ein **schlafendes** Mädchen, mit **wachsendem** Interesse, die **kommenden** Ereignisse.

2. as a noun derived from the adjective [→ E 500 ff.]:

> ein **Reisender**, die **Genesende**, die **Fliehenden**, etwas **Erschreckendes**

3. as an adverb of manner [→ H 568.3]:

> Die Soldaten marschierten **singend** durch die Stadt.
> **Lächelnd** grüßte mich die Dame.
> **Schwimmend** erreichten wir das Ufer.
> Er kam mir **winkend** entgegen.
> Wir trafen den Patienten **schlafend** an.[1]

B 802   If the present participle is used as an attributive adjective or as a noun, it follows the adjective declension [→ E 050 ff., E 500]:

> Er las das Buch mit **wachsendem** Interesse.
> Auf der Straße sah ich ein **spielendes** Kind.
> **Bellende** Hunde beißen nicht.
> Wecken Sie bitte den **schlafenden** Patienten nicht auf.
> Der **Reisende** nahm ein Zimmer im Hotel.

B 805   Since verbs describe events or states of being, modifiers of the participle

---

[1] Note that *theoretically* this sentence is ambiguous: "sleeping," which is intended to refer to the patient, might be taken to refer to the subject "we." Similarly: *Beiliegend sende ich Ihnen die Rechnung.* [→ B 810]

134

have the character of clauses. Extended participial attributes replace a relative clause:[1]

> *Wir beobachteten die* **stark im Wind schwankenden** *Bäume (die Bäume, die stark im Wind schwankten).*
>
> *Der Direktor lobt seine Mitarbeiter bei jeder* **sich ihm bietenden** *Gelegenheit (bei jeder Gelegenheit, die sich ihm bietet).*
>
> *Die* **vor den feindlichen Soldaten Fliehenden** *wurden in Sicherheit gebracht (die Menschen, die vor den Soldaten flohen).*

In a few verbs, the present participle has taken on its own, limited meaning, which it possesses only in this form and which may differ from the infinitive:

B 807

> *Der Mann ist* **wütend** (**zuvorkommend**)*.*
>
> *Sie ist* **reizend** (**entzückend, bezaubernd**)*.*
>
> *Diese Geschichte ist* **rührend** (**spannend**)*.*

Participles of this kind are the only ones which may not only occur as attributive adjectives (*ein* **wütender** *Mann, ein* **reizendes** *Mädchen, eine* **spannende** *Geschichte*), but also as complements of the predicate, as shown above. These forms have completely lost their verbal character and are looked upon as adjectives; they may even appear in the comparative and superlative:

B 808

> *Sie wird immer* **reizender***.*
>
> *Das ist die* **spannendste** *Geschichte, die ich kenne.*

The progressive form used in English (I am going, he was sleeping) has no counterpart in German at all.

B 809

Used adverbially, the present participle does not in itself designate a certain tense, but describes an event or a state of being which accompanies the event or state of being described in the predicate. It usually shares tense and subject with the predicate:

B 810

> *Die Kinder springen* **lachend** *ins Wasser.*
>
> *Der Polizist hob* **drohend** *den Finger.*
>
> *Die Soldaten sind* **singend** *durch die Stadt marschiert.*
>
> *Wir werden das Ufer* **schwimmend** *erreichen.*

But: *Wir trafen den Patienten* **schlafend** *an.* [→ Footnote B 805]

---

[1] Such constructions occur frequently in journalistic and expository (especially scientific) prose [→ J 163 ff.].

135

B 811   Used attributively, the present participle may contain a tense indication relative to the noun which it modifies. This noun is considered the subject of the action described by the participle (i.e. a barking dog is a dog which barks). If no other expression of time is used, the participle indicates simultaneity with the tense of the predicate. (Note that this need not be present tense):

> *Wir trösten das **weinende** Kind:* We console the child which is presently crying.
>
> *Wir trösteten das **weinende** Kind:* We consoled the child which was crying at the time.

B 812   If the sentence is in the future tense, however, the participle may either indicate a present or a future condition:

> *Wir werden das **weinende** Kind trösten:* At some time in the future, we will console the child which is presently crying.
>
> *Auf dem Spielplatz werden wir viele **spielende** Kinder sehen:* When we get to the playground, we will see many children who will be playing at that time.

B 813   If some other time expression is used, the present participle may indicate past or future conditions:

> *Die **einst blühende** Stadt ist jetzt verlassen:* The city which flourished in the past is abandoned now.
>
> ***Später eintreffende** Personen können nicht aufgenommen werden:* We can not accept anyone who will arrive sometime in the future.

B 815   When the participle is preceded by the preposition **zu**, it indicates something which can be (or could be) done. (This construction is similar to a form of **sein** + **zu** + infinitive [→ B 620, 625.7].)

> *Unsere Reise war ein nicht **zu vergessendes** Erlebnis =*
> *ein Erlebnis, das nicht **zu vergessen** ist.*
>
> *Er sprach ein kaum **zu verstehendes** Deutsch =*
> *ein Deutsch, das kaum **zu verstehen** war.*

Past Participle

B 820   The past participle indicates an action, process, or state of being which is completed or ended. It is used primarily for the formation of compound tense forms with the auxiliary verbs **haben** and **sein**. The present perfect [B 455 ff., 540 ff.], past perfect [B 470–1, 550], and future perfect [B 475, 580 ff.] are formed in this manner.

The past participle is also used with the auxiliary verb **werden** to describe a process in the passive voice [→ B 480 ff., 590 ff.], and with the auxiliary verb **sein** to describe a condition or state of being [→ B 610 ff.].   B 821

In a multiple predicate, the past participle belongs to the second part of the predicate which forms the end of the sentence field [→ H 113.1, 120–1]. The participle usually precedes the infinitive: B 822

> *Er hat uns gestern **besucht**.*
> *Ich bin zu Hause **geblieben**.*
> *Das Haus wurde vor zwei Jahren **gebaut**.*
> *Das Buch ist in Leder **gebunden**.*
> *Er wird wohl schon **angekommen sein**.*

In a dependent clause, where all parts of the predicate come together at the end, the past participle usually precedes the conjugated verb form [→ H 126]:   B 823

> *. . ., daß er uns gestern **besucht** hat.*
> *. . ., weil ich zu Hause **geblieben** bin.*
> *. . ., ob das Haus vor zwei Jahren **gebaut** wurde.*
> *. . ., obwohl das Buch in Leder **gebunden** ist.*
> *. . ., daß er schon **angekommen** sein wird.*

The past participle sometimes occurs together with the verb **kommen** to indicate the manner of motion; it answers the question "how?":[1]   B 825

> *Dort **kommt** mein Freund **gelaufen**.*
> *Ein Vogel **kam geflogen**.*

In this construction, the past participle may be combined with the prefixes **an-**, **heran-**, or **herbei-**, without changing the meaning: B 826

> *Dort kommt mein Freund **herangelaufen**.*
> *Der Vogel kam **herbeigeflogen**.*

---

[1] Note that constructions of this type use the *present* participle in English: He came running.

137

B 827   The word **verlorengehen** is based on a similar construction. Here the past participle *verloren* acts as a modifier of the verb *gehen*:

> *Mein Paß* **ging** *während der Reise* **verloren.**
> *Er ist* **verlorengegangen.**

B 828   Without an auxiliary verb, the past participle may be used to indicate a stern command, which must be carried out at once. [→ Substitute constructions for imperative, B 790.1.] Such a command may be intensified by **jetzt, jetzt aber**, or **nun aber**:

> *Stillgestanden!*
> *Aufgepaßt! Dort kommt ein Auto!*
> *Jetzt schnell eingestiegen!*
> *Nun aber stillgehalten!*

B 829   Like the present participle, the past participle can be used as an attribute to describe a condition attained. In such functions, it follows the adjective declension [→ E 050 ff., E 500 ff.]. It may also be used adverbially:

> *der* **gepflügte** *Acker, frisch* **gebrannter** *Kaffee, ein* **verlorenes** *Buch.*
> *Ich möchte ein Frühstück mit* **geröstetem** *Brot und einem* **weichgekochten** *Ei.*
> *Sie ging* **gekränkt** *aus dem Haus.*

B 830   Nouns formed from past participles also follow adjectival declension:[1]

> *der Verwundete, ein Verwundeter, die Verwundete, die Verwundeten; etwas Geschriebenes*

B 831   Some of these past participles used as nouns or adjectives have almost completely lost their verbal character, so that they can be used only as pure adjectives or nouns. They still follow adjective declension:

> *Er ist mit mir* **verwandt.**
> *Ist Ihnen das nicht* **bekannt**?
> *der* **Bekannte**, *ein* **Verwandter**, *die* **Beamten**[2]

B 832   Similarly to the present participle, past participles used attributively can

---

[1] A few nouns formed from past participles actually have the meaning of present participles *der Bediente* (instead of *der Bedienende*); *der Unterzeichnete* (instead of *der Unterzeichnende*)

[2] The noun *der Beamte* has even formed a feminine equivalent by analogy: *die Beamtin.*

be extended by other modifiers, which have the character of clauses and replace a relative clause [→ B 805, J 163 ff.]:

> *Der **während der Nacht gefallene Schnee** lag auf den Dächern (der Schnee, der während der Nacht gefallen war).*
>
> *Wir befassen uns heute mit der **bereits anfangs erwähnten** Philosophie Nietzsches (mit der Philosophie, die bereits anfangs erwähnt wurde).*
>
> *Das **vor vielen Jahren in der Schule auswendig Gelernte** bleibt mir heute noch im Gedächtnis (die Dinge, die ich vor vielen Jahren auswendig gelernt hatte).*

The past participle of the following verbs can not be used attributively: B 835

1. The past participle of intransitive verbs which form their perfect tenses with **haben**. These verbs describe the duration of an action, a process, or a state of being [→ B 456.3]:

> *Der Mann hat tief **geschlafen*** (No attributive use; only present participle possible: *der **schlafende** Mann*).
>
> *Die Blume hat **geblüht*** (No attributive use; either present participle: *die **blühende** Blume* or a compound: *die **verblühte** Blume*).
>
> *Wir haben dem armen Mann **geholfen*** (No attributive use possible).

Similarly, the past participles of impersonal verbs can not be used attributively: *Es hat **geregnet**.*

2. The past participle of intransitive verbs indicating a change of position (**gekommen, gelaufen, gegangen,** etc.).

However, such participles may sometimes be used attributively if they are extended by a modifier of place:[1]

> *Das **auf die Fahrbahn gelaufene** Kind wurde von einem Auto überfahren.*
>
> *Der **zum Unfallort geeilte** Arzt konnte das Leben des Kindes noch retten.*

3. The past participle of modal auxiliaries.

The past participles **gekonnt** and **gewollt**, however, may be used attributively in a special meaning: *gekonnt* — done with skill and artistry; *gewollt* — intentional, deliberate.

> *Hier sehen Sie ein wirklich **gekonntes** Bild.*
>
> *Diese **gewollte** Beleidigung lasse ich mir nicht gefallen.*

---

[1] English here uses the present participle *having* and the past participle of the main verb: The child having run . . ., the doctor having hurried. . . .

4. The past participle of reflexive verbs (**sich schämen**, **sich freuen**, etc).

A few participles, however, may be used attributively without a reflexive pronoun:

>*sich verirren — das **verirrte** Kind*
>*sich verlieben — der **verliebte** Bräutigam*
>*sich betrinken — der **betrunkene** Gast*
>*sich eignen — bei **geeigneter** Gelegenheit*

B 836   Normally, past participles can not form comparatives. In a few instances, however, where the past participle has lost its verbal character and is considered purely as an adjective, comparative and superlative forms are possible. Such participles are **erfahren, bekannt, angesehen, beliebt, geeignet, vertraut,** etc.

>*Er ist der **erfahrenste** Mensch, den ich kenne.*
>*Wissen Sie, was der **bekannteste** Roman dieses Schriftstellers ist?*
>*Ihre Firma ist eine der **angesehensten** unserer Stadt.*
>*Karl war der **beliebteste** Schüler unserer Klasse.*
>*Er ist **vertrauter** mit diesen Dingen, als ich dachte.*
>*Dieses Mittel ist **geeigneter** als alle anderen.*

Participial Clauses

B 840   In some instances, participles can be modified by other sentence units so that they form a clause of their own, which functions like a dependent clause.[1] These constructions are similar in form to extended participles used attributively [→ B 805, 832].

B 841   Within the sentence, the extended participle may function as an indicator of time [→ H 575 ff.], manner [→ H 580 ff.], or cause [→ H 590 ff.]. The participial phrase or clause always refers to the subject of the sentence in which it occurs.

1. Clauses of Manner:[2]

[1] In English, these would be considered participial phrases. German treats them as clauses.

[2] Note from the three examples that the position of the participial clause within the sentence is flexible, like any dependent clause. Again as in a dependent clause, the verb form appears at the end.

140

Laut um Hilfe schreiend, *lief die Frau durch die nächtlichen Straßen.*

Die Expedition versuchte, **sich mühsam einen Weg durch den Urwald bahnend**, *das geplante Tagesziel zu erreichen.*

Er starrte mich an, **die Augen weit aufgerissen.**

2. Clauses of Cause:

Von einem Pfeil zu Tode getroffen, *stürzte der Vogel zur Erde nieder.*

3. Clauses of Time:

In München angekommen, *begab ich mich sofort zur Universität.*[1]

As an attribute, the extended participle functions in construction and position like a relative clause, without relative pronoun and without inflected verb form. These relative clauses are considered to refer to the noun which is their logical subject:

B 845

Das Wild, **von dem nächtlichen Schuß aufgeschreckt**, *lief eilends in den Wald hinein.*

Die Feuerwehr, **aus den umliegenden Ortschaften herbeigeeilt**, *löschte den Brand schnell.*

It is sometimes difficult to determine whether a given participial clause is to be considered an attributive or relative clause, or whether it is a dependent clause of manner or cause. The position of the clause gives some indication as to its meaning:

Das Wild, **von dem nächtlichen Schuß aufgeschreckt**, *lief eilends in den Wald hinein.* (The deer, which had been frightened by the shot, ran into the woods.)

Das Wild lief eilends in den Wald hinein, **von dem nächtlichen Schuß aufgeschreckt.** (The deer ran into the woods because it had been frightened by the shot.)

In certain constructions which indicate a possible reason or a condition, the past participle, either alone or as a participial phrase, stands at the beginning of the sentence [→ G 577]:

B 846

Angenommen, *dein Vater schickt dir kein Geld; was machst du dann?*

Gesetzt den Fall, *ich habe morgen keine Zeit, zu dir zu kommen, dann gebe ich dir telefonisch Nachricht.*

---

[1] In English, such statements would have to be expressed with the present participle of "to have" and the past participle of the main verb: Having arrived in Munich, . . . Such constructions do not exist in German.

THE INFINITIVE

⩨ *Introduction*

B 900 Besides the participles, the infinitive is also a form of the verb which can occur in functions other than those of the predicate. [For forms of the infinitive, → B 451. Functions of the infinitive within the predicate will be discussed in B 915 ff., other functions in B 926 ff.]

B 901 We distinguish two types of infinitives: the SIMPLE INFINITIVE and the PREPOSITIONAL INFINITIVE (i.e. the infinitive with the preposition **zu**).

lernen	**zu** lernen
fahren	**zu** fahren
können	**zu** können
haben	**zu** haben
sein	**zu** sein
bekommen	**zu** bekommen
vorkommen	vor**zu**kommen

Only the simple infinitive appears in vocabulary and dictionary listings. Which of the two infinitives is used in a sentence depends on the verb which governs the infinitive:

> *Er will uns **besuchen**.*
> *Er wünscht uns **zu besuchen**.*

The prepositional infinitive is always used to modify nouns or adjectives:

> *Meine Hoffnung, reich **zu werden**, wird sich nicht so schnell erfüllen.*
> *Es ist schön **zu reisen**.*

B 902 The simple infinitive is considered part of the predicate and therefore follows the positional rules for multiple predicates [→ H 113]. It belongs to the second part of the predicate which forms the end of the sentence field [→ H 120].

> *Wir **wollen** im Sommer eine Reise nach Italien **machen**.*
> *Ich **werde** heute abend ins Kino **gehen**.*

For so-called double infinitives [→ B 468], the modal infinitive comes at the end of the clause; the dependent infinitive immediately precedes it:

*Er hat in die Schule **gehen müssen.***
*Vom Fenster aus kannst du die Kinder im Garten **spielen sehen.***[1]

In dependent clauses, the conjugated verb occurs after a simple infinitive, but immediately preceding a double infinitive:

*Weißt du, daß ich morgen im Büro **arbeiten muß**?*
*Weißt du, daß ich gestern im Büro **habe arbeiten müssen**?*

The prepositional infinitive is not directly a part of the predicate, since   B 903
it is separated by the preposition **zu**. When it is modified by any other
sentence units, it functions like a dependent clause. Such extended
prepositional infinitives are called INFINITIVE CLAUSES.[2] They can contain any kind of sentence unit other than a subject.

There are two formal differences between an infinitive clause and other   B 904
dependent clauses:

1. The infinitive clause does not have a subject of its own and therefore
no conjugated verb form. (This also applies to participial clauses.
[→ B 840 ff.])
2. It has only two forms to show the time relationship of the events
described:

	Dependent Clause	Infinitive Clause
PRESENT	da er ... kauft	} ... zu kaufen
FUTURE	da er ... kaufen wird	
PAST	da er ... kaufte da er ... gekauft hat da er ... gekauft hatte	} ... gekauft zu haben
	da er ... kam da er ... gekommen ist da er ... gekommen war	} ... gekommen zu sein

---

[1] English uses a present participle here: You can see the children *playing*.

[2] In English, these would be called infinitive phrases.

B 905   The subject of the event which the infinitive describes is either the subject or the object of the sentence of which the infinitive is a part [→ H 330 ff.]:

> *Er will Deutsch **lernen**.* (Subject of sentence and infinitive: he)
>
> *Wie lange mußt du in der Schule **bleiben**?* (Subject of sentence and infinitive: you)
>
> *Hörst du die Kinder draußen **singen**?* (Subject of sentence: you; subject of infinitive: the children)[1]
>
> *Ich sehe Peter im Garten **arbeiten**.* (Subject of sentence: I; subject of infinitive: Peter)[1]

B 908   The TENSE FORM of the infinitive [→ B 451] depends on the tense form of the predicate, i.e. the tense relationship between the event described in the infinitive and that described in the predicate. The infinitive event may be simultaneous with, precede, or follow the predicate event:

> *Ich **höre*** (present) *das Kind **schreien*** (simultaneous).
> *Wir **wollen*** (present) *morgen ins Kino **gehen*** (following).
> *Er **kann*** (present) *diesen Brief nicht **geschrieben haben*** (preceding).
>
> *Wir **wollten*** (past) *damals ein neues Haus **kaufen*** (following).
> *Er **meinte*** (past), *ein Künstler **zu sein*** (simultaneous).
> *Ich **glaubte*** (past) *die Lösung **gefunden zu haben*** (preceding).
>
> *Ich **werde** morgen **versuchen*** (future), *Sie **zu sprechen*** (simultaneous).
> *Ich **werde** ihn **bitten*** (future), *mich nächste Woche **zu besuchen*** (following).
> *Es **wird** Ihnen kaum **gelingen*** (future), *die Arbeit bis dahin **beendet zu haben*** (preceding).

B 910   The infinitive clause (prepositional infinitive plus other sentence units) usually occupies the postfield position [→ H 075].[2] It contains a sentence field [→ H 020] of its own. The sentence field of an infinitive clause, however, contains only one predicate position, the infinitive at the end. The beginning of the sentence field is missing, unless the infinitive clause is introduced by the preposition **um**, **ohne**, or **statt** (**anstatt**):

> *Wir wünschen,   zu Hause in Ruhe   **zu arbeiten**.*
> *Er kam nach Köln, **um** dort an der Universität **zu studieren**.*

---

[1] English would use present participles here. See footnote B 902.

[2] It may also occur in the prefield: ***Ohne mich zu sehen**, trat er ins Zimmer.*

144

Prepositional infinitives or infinitive clauses used attributively [→ J 135] B 911
follow immediately after the noun to which they refer:

> *Er hat keine **Lust zu arbeiten**.*
> *Seine **Hoffnung, eine bessere Stellung zu finden**, erfüllte sich nicht.*

The Infinitive as Part of the Predicate

The simple infinitive, together with the present tense of the auxiliary B 915
verb **werden**, forms the FUTURE [→ B 560 ff.] and the FUTURE PERFECT
[→ B 580] of verbs:

> *Wir **werden** morgen nachmittag einen Spaziergang **machen**.*
> ***Wirst** du das Buch bis Samstag **ausgelesen haben**?*[1]

In the same way, present or past probability may be expressed B 916
[→ B 565, 582], again using the present tense of **werden** and the infinitive (or past infinitive) of the main verb:

> *Peter **wird** jetzt in Berlin **sein**.*
> *Inzwischen **wird** er wohl zu Hause angekommen **sein**.*

The simple infinitive is also used with modal verbs in subjective[2] usage B 917
[→ B 632]. The time of the event itself is indicated by the form of the
infinitive, whereas the time of the supposition, expressed by the modal,
always refers to the present. The modals are used either in the present
or in the past tense indicative, or in the subjunctive. The present indicates an assumption which refers to a present situation, the past
indicates a present assumption about a past situation. Subjunctive
forms may refer to either present or past events:

> *Können Sie mir sagen, wo Herr Müller ist? — Ja, er **muß** (**müßte**) jetzt
> im Büro sein.* (Present)
> *Wie alt war Ihr Freund, als Sie ihn kennenlernten? — Er **konnte**
> (**könnte**) damals etwa 25 Jahre alt gewesen sein.* (Past)

The prepositional infinitive occurs as part of the predicate with the B 918
verbs **haben** and **sein**. Together with **haben**, it expresses the need for an
action. Together with **sein**, it indicates something that can be, must be,

---

[1] This form of the infinitive of **haben** or **sein** plus a past participle is called a PAST INFINITIVE.
[2] For infinitives with modals in objective usage, → B 930.

should be, or is to be done and is one of the substitute constructions for the passive [→ B 621]:[1]

> *Kinder* **haben zu schweigen,** *wenn Erwachsene sprechen.*
> **Haben** *Sie heute viel* **zu arbeiten?** *Nein, ich* **habe** *nichts* **zu tun.**

> *Seine Aussprache* **war** *leicht* **zu verstehen.** (could be)
> *Dieses Kapitel* **ist** *für morgen* **zu lesen.** (must be)
> *Das Material* **ist** *genau* **zu prüfen,** *bevor es für den Bau eines Motors verwendet werden kann.* (should be)
> *Der Vorschlag* **ist zu begrüßen.** (is to be)

B 920 The prepositional infinitive forms part of the predicate with the verbs **brauchen,**[2] **drohen, pflegen, scheinen, vermögen,** and **versprechen,** when they are used like modals. With **brauchen** this construction occurs only if the verb is either negated or limited by adverbs like **nur** and **bloß** [→ B 652.3]:

> *Ich* **brauche** *heute* **nicht zu arbeiten.**
> *Wir* **brauchen keine** *Übungen* **zu schreiben.**
> *Du* **brauchst nur zu kommen,** *wenn du Geld verdienen willst.*
> *Das alte Haus* **drohte einzustürzen.**
> *Er* **pflegt** *bis in die Nacht* **zu arbeiten.**
> *Du* **scheinst** *dich mit diesem Problem viel beschäftigt* **zu haben.**
> *Er* **vermochte** *mir nicht* **zu helfen.**
> *Die Ernte* **verspricht** *gut* **zu werden.**

Compare the use of the verbs **brauchen, pflegen,** and **scheinen** in non-modal functions:

> *Ich* **brauche** *dringend Erholung.*
> *Die Krankenschwester* **pflegte** *den Patienten viele Wochen.*
> *Heute* **scheint** *der Mond.*

B 921 The verbs **drohen** and **versprechen** may also be used with the prepositional infinitive in non-modal functions, if the subject is a person:

> *Der Vater* **drohte,** *seinen Sohn aus der Schule* **zu nehmen.**
> *Der Vater* **drohte** *seinem Sohn, ihn aus der Schule* **zu nehmen.**

---

[1] **Sein** can be used with a prepositional infinitive only if the subject in this construction can also act as the object of the infinitive: *Man konnte seine Aussprache leicht verstehen; wir müssen das Kapitel lesen; er sollte das Material prüfen;* etc.

[2] The use of **brauchen** with the simple infinitive is not considered good German, although it does occur in colloquial speech: *Sie brauchen morgen nicht kommen.*

146

Mein Freund **versprach**, *mir sein Fahrrad* **zu leihen**.
Mein Freund **versprach** *mir, meinem Bruder sein Fahrrad* **zu leihen**.

In some idiomatic phrases, the prepositional infinitive is also used with   B 922
the verbs **geben, stehen, wissen,** and **verstehen**:

> *Das Benehmen dieses jungen Mannes* **gibt zu denken**.
> *Er* **gab** *uns* **zu verstehen**, *daß wir ihn allein lassen sollten*.
> *Du* **weißt** (**verstehst**) **zu reden**.
> *Es* **steht** *kaum* **zu hoffen** (**zu erwarten**), *daß er seine Rechnung bezahlen*
>   *wird*.

THE INFINITIVE AS A SENTENCE UNIT

Subject

The SIMPLE INFINITIVE can act as a SUBJECT. It is then considered a neuter   B 925
noun and is capitalized. Only rarely does it have an article.

> **Irren** *ist menschlich*.
> **Geben** *ist seliger denn* **Nehmen**.
> *Das lange* **Warten** *machte ihn müde*.

If, however, the verb in the infinitive needs to be accompanied by a noun   B 926
to complete the predicate concept [→ H 480 ff.], the infinitive loses its
character as a noun:

> **Unrecht leiden** *ist besser als* **Unrecht tun**.

The PREPOSITIONAL INFINITIVE is used in those instances where the in-   B 927
finitive has been modified by other sentence units and thus has developed
into an infinitive clause [→ B 903 ff.]. The subject of the infinitive
clause, by implication, is understood to be some unnamed person or the
pronoun **man**. If the infinitive clause occurs in the postfield [→ H 070],
the word **es** appears either in the prefield or within the sentence field.

> *Viel* **Kaffee zu trinken** *ist der Gesundheit nicht zuträglich*.
> *Es ist der Gesundheit nicht zuträglich, viel* **Kaffee zu trinken**.
> *Der Gesundheit ist es nicht zuträglich, viel* **Kaffee zu trinken**.
> *Es gehört sich nicht,* **einen alten Mann zu ärgern**. (**Man**
>   *ärgert einen alten Mann nicht*.)

147

B 928 The implied subject of the infinitive phrase can also be determined by the context of the passage:

> *Ich überlegte: Ist es besser **zu fahren** oder **zu bleiben**?*

Object

B 930 The SIMPLE INFINITIVE, when it appears with modal verbs in objective usage [→ B 631], has the function of an object for the modal verb.[1] (The accusative noun or pronoun, if any, in turn acts as the object of the infinitive):[2]

> *Herr Müller **wollte** mit unserem Direktor **sprechen**.*
> *Ihr **sollt** hier Deutsch **lernen**.*
> ***Mußtest** du gestern zu Hause **bleiben**?*
> *Der Vater **will seinen Sohn** nach Berlin **schicken**.*
> *Ich **kann dich** nicht **verstehen**.*

B 931 The simple infinitive also occurs as the object of the verbs **lernen** and sometimes **spielen**:

> *Die Kinder **lernen** in der Schule **schreiben** und **lesen**.*
> *Die Kinder **spielen fangen**.*

B 932 The PREPOSITIONAL INFINITIVE occurs as the object of many transitive verbs (the accusative noun or pronoun again is the object of the infinitive):

> *Langsam begann er, **mich zu verstehen**.*
> *Er schwor, **die Tat** nicht **begangen zu haben**.*
> *Sie fürchtet, zu spät nach Hause **zu kommen**.*

B 933 After many transitive verbs, the prepositional infinitive indicates an event which is to take place later. The most important of these verbs are:

anfangen	erwarten	(nicht) vergessen	versuchen
beabsichtigen	geloben	verheißen	wissen
befehlen	hoffen	verlangen	wünschen
belieben	suchen	vermögen	
beschließen	(nicht) verfehlen	versprechen	

---

[1] For subjective uses of modal verbs, → B 917.

[2] This does not apply to verbs like **lehren, sehen, hören, helfen, lassen**, where the noun or pronoun is the object of the verb and the subject of the infinitive: *Ich hörte ihn kommen.* (I heard him. He came.) [→ B 970]

148

*Ich **hoffe**, in nächster Zeit nach Berlin **zu kommen**.*
*Wir **versuchen**, unsere Arbeit bis morgen **zu beenden**.*
*Er **versprach** mir, meinen Vorschlag **zu unterstützen**.*
*Man **suchte**, ihn noch im Büro zu erreichen.*
*Vergessen Sie nicht, den Brief **aufzugeben**!*

After many other verbs, the prepositional infinitive indicates an event   B 934
which has already begun or is already completed. If the event lies completely in the past, the past infinitive is used. The most important verbs
of this group are:

angeben	erklären	meinen
behaupten	gestehen	versichern
bekennen	glauben	vorgeben
beteuern	leugnen	zugestehen

*Er **glaubt**, im Irrtum **zu sein**.*
*Wir **meinen**, recht **zu haben**.*
*Der Angeklagte **leugnete**, die Tat **begangen zu haben**.*
*Sie **versicherte** uns, nicht dabei **gewesen zu sein**.*

With the following verbs, the indefinite pronoun **es** acts as a substitute   B 935
object and thus anticipates the infinitive clause in the postfield, which
constitutes the genuine object:

ablehnen	ertragen	verdienen
aufgeben	(nicht) erwarten können	vermeiden
aufschieben	finden [1]	versäumen
aushalten	unterlassen	verschieben
beklagen	unternehmen	verschmähen

*Wir **lehnen es ab**, ihm nochmals Geld **zu leihen**.*
*Ich **finde es** nicht **klug** von ihm, sein Haus jetzt **zu verkaufen**.*
*Er kann es kaum **erwarten**, seine Braut **wiederzusehen**.*

With the verbs **lieben, verstehen,** and **wagen** the anticipatory **es** may be   B 936
omitted in the sentence field:

*Ich **wage** (**es**) nicht, meinen Vater **zu fragen**.*
*Verstehst du (**es**), mit kleinen Kindern **umzugehen**?*
*Meine Eltern **lieben** (**es**), am Wochenende an einen See **zu fahren**.*

---

[1] Together with such adjectives as *dumm, klug, töricht, ratsam*, etc.

B 937   By analogy with the transitive verbs, some intransitive verbs may also appear with a prepositional infinitive as an apparent object:

aufhören	(nicht) ermangeln
drohen	gedenken
eilen	zaudern, zögern

*Er **drohte**, dem Lehrer alles **zu sagen**.*
*Warum **zögerst** du, ins Auto **einzusteigen**?*
*Um 8 Uhr **hörte** er **auf zu arbeiten**.*

B 940   After verbs which require a prepositional object, the prepositional infinitive always occurs in the postfield. The preposition which the verb demands is combined with the demonstrative adverb **da(r)-** [→ D 040], and acts as an anticipator to point to the prepositional infinitive following in the postfield. The most important verbs of this type are:

sich abgeben mit	denken an	sich tragen mit
abhängen von	dienen zu	träumen von
absehen auf	sich freuen auf	umgehen mit
abzielen auf	sich freuen über	sich unterhalten mit
ankommen auf	sich gewöhnen an	sich vergnügen mit
es anlegen auf	sich hergeben zu	verhelfen zu
bauen auf	sich machen über	sich verlassen auf
beitragen zu	sich etwas (nichts)	sich verstehen auf (zu)
sich beschäftigen mit	daraus machen	vertrauen auf
bestehen auf	sinnen auf	zwingen zu

*Wir können uns nicht **daran gewöhnen**, jeden Morgen früh **aufzustehen**.*
*Er **beschäftigt** sich **damit**, seinen Garten wieder in Ordnung **zu bringen**.*
*Er will sich nicht **dazu hergeben**, solch eine schmutzige Arbeit **zu tun**.*
*Ich **denke** nicht **daran nachzugeben**.*

B 941   With some verbs, the anticipatory **da-** construction may be omitted:

ablassen von	sich freuen über	prahlen mit
beginnen mit	sich herbeilassen zu	rechnen auf
sich begnügen mit	sich hergeben zu	streben nach
sich bemühen um	sich hüten vor	warnen vor
(sich) erinnern an	klagen über	sich wundern über

*Warum **bemühst** du dich nicht (**darum**), eine Arbeit **zu finden**?*
***Hüten** Sie sich (**davor**), diesem Mann Geld **zu leihen**.*
*Ich **warne** Sie (**davor**), diese Reise **zu machen**.*

150

The prepositional infinitive also occurs as the object of many predicate B 942
adjective constructions, such as

begierig	erfreut	sicher
bekümmert	erstaunt	stolz
bereit	fähig	traurig
betrübt	froh	vergnügt
bewußt (*with dative*)	geeignet	wert
weit entfernt	gerührt	würdig
entzückt	gewiß	zufrieden
	gewohnt[1]	

*Wir sind **bereit**, nach Hause **zu gehen**.*
*Er ist nicht **fähig**, eine fremde Sprache **zu lernen**.*
*Wir sind **traurig**, so viel Geld **verloren zu haben**.*
*Ich bin **erfreut**, Ihre Bekanntschaft **gemacht zu haben**.*
*Bist du dir **bewußt**, uns **beleidigt zu haben**?*
*Wir sind **erstaunt**, so viele Menschen hier **zu finden**.*

Many of these constructions also contain an anticipatory **es** [→ B 935] B 943
or, if they are used with a preposition, an anticipatory **da-** construction
[→ B 940]:

*Wir sind (**es**) nicht **gewohnt**, so schwer **zu arbeiten**.*
*Er ist (**es**) nicht **wert**, sich seinetwegen so viel Mühe **zu machen**.*
*Er war (**damit**) **zufrieden**, gewonnen **zu haben**.*
*Ich bin weit (**davon**) **entfernt**, ihm **zu glauben**.*

Complement of Place

The simple infinitive may occur after verbs of motion like **kommen,** B 950
gehen, fahren, reiten to act as an adverbial complement of place
[→ H 420]. It answers the implied question **wohin**? (where to?):

*Er **geht** jetzt **schlafen** (i.e. he goes to bed).*
*Wir sollen nächsten Sonntag **baden gehen** (i.e. to a lake,*
river, pool, beach, etc.).
*Er **fährt** jeden Tag **spazieren**.*
***Kommst** du mit mir Tennis **spielen**?*
*Meine Mutter **geht** jeden Vormittag **einkaufen**.*
*Wir wollen jetzt **essen gehen**.*

---

[1] Strictly speaking, **gewohnt** should be used as an adjective (*ich bin es **gewohnt***), **gewöhnt** as
a past participle (*ich habe mich daran **gewöhnt***). This distinction is not always strictly
maintained, with **gewöhnt** occasionally appearing as a predicate adjective, but never as an
attributive adjective (*zur **gewohnten** Stunde*).

B 951   After some verbs and expressions, the prepositional infinitive occurs as a complement of place in a figurative sense. A clear-cut distinction between the functions "complement of place" and "prepositional object" [B 940] is not always possible. It depends on the contextual circumstances which of the two functions is used.[1] Since prepositions occur in all these idiomatic expressions, the connection between the verb and the infinitive is made by means of an anticipatory **da-** construction [→ B 940]. Some of these verbs are:

arbeiten an	sich fügen in	dabei sein
ausgehen auf	darangehen	daran sein
beharren auf	kommen an	darauf aus sein
dabei bleiben	sich daranmachen	darüber sein
sich ergeben in	sich darübermachen	drauf und dran sein
sich finden in	pochen auf	darein willigen

*Wir waren gestern **drauf und dran abzureisen**.*
*Ich mache mich jetzt **daran**, den Garten in Ordnung **zu bringen**.*
*Er war **darauf** aus, eine gute Stellung **zu bekommen**.*
*Er kann sich nicht **darein** finden, so früh aufstehen **zu müssen**.*

Complement of Manner

B 955   The simple infinitive of verbs which designate a position or location may be used as a complement of manner [→ H 440] for the verb **bleiben**. Infinitives used in this fashion are: **stehen, liegen, sitzen, hängen, stecken, kleben, haften, wohnen, leben, bestehen**:

*Du **bleibst** immer zu lange im Bett **liegen**.*
*Bitte **bleibt** ruhig **sitzen**!*
*Ich **bleibe** für nächste Woche hier **wohnen**.*
*Er **blieb** vor der Tür **stehen**.*

Predicate Nominative or Accusative

B 960   The simple infinitive may fulfill the function of a predicate nominative [→ H 460] or a predicate accusative [→ H 470]. If the infinitive is

---

[1] *Er arbeitet an der Maschine*, for instance, can mean that he is repairing it (prepositional object), or it may indicate the place where he works (adverbial modifier).

152

modified by other sentence units [→ B 927], the prepositional infinitive is used for the predicate nominative:

> *Ist das **arbeiten**?*
> *Rasten heißt **rosten**.*
> *Das nenne ich Eulen nach Athen **tragen**.*
> *Seine Hoffnung ist, bald in die Heimat **zurückzukehren**.*

Adverbial Modifiers

After the verbs **kommen** and **gehen**, the simple infinitive is sometimes used as an adverbial modifier of purpose [→ H 594]: B 965

> *Hans **kommt** morgen zu uns Fußball **spielen**.*
> *Ich **gehe** zur Post **telefonieren**.*
> ***Komm** mit uns Kaffee **trinken**!*

The prepositional infinitive, appearing in the postfield of a sentence and introduced by the conjunction **um** [→ G 520] also serves to indicate the purpose of an action: B 966

> *Er ist in die Stadt gegangen, **um** Zigaretten **zu kaufen**.*

The subject of the infinitive may be the subject or the object of the sentence:

> ***Ich** kam nach Berlin, **um** Medizin **zu studieren**.*
> *Das Essen genügt **mir**, **um** davon satt **zu werden**.*

An indefinite unnamed subject is also possible:

> *Der Platz ist groß genug, **um** darauf Fußball **zu spielen**.*

Idiomatic phrases, based on a similar construction, also contain an undefined subject of the infinitive:

> ***Um** es kurz **zu sagen**, ich fahre nicht mit.*
> *Ich bin **sozusagen** sein Stellvertreter.*

An infinitive clause introduced by **um** may also show the consequence or effect of an action or situation, if the main clause contains an intensification with **zu** [→ G 521]: B 967

> *Es ist **zu** viel, **um** alles essen **zu können**.*
> *Das ist **zu** wenig, **um** davon **zu leben**.*
> *Es ist **zu** heiß, **um** in der Sonne **zu liegen**.*

B 968   Prepositional infinitives are also used after the conjunctions **(an)statt** (adversative, [→ G 070]) and **ohne** (instrumental, [→ G 435]). The subject of the sentence is also subject of the infinitive:

> *Der Zug fuhr bis Köln, **ohne** einmal **zu halten**.*
> ***Anstatt** (**statt**) **zu arbeiten**, geht Karl jeden Tag auf den Fußballplatz.*

Sometimes the subject may be indefinite:

> *Es ist einfacher zu telefonieren, **statt** einen Brief **zu schreiben**.*

Predicate Infinitive

B 970   The simple infinitive functions as the predicate for the objects of the following verbs: **lassen, spüren, sehen, hören, fühlen, lehren, finden, wissen, haben, legen, schicken, heißen.**[1] In these constructions, the OBJECT of the sentence is the SUBJECT of the infinitive [→ H 330 ff.]:

> *Ich **lasse** den Gast **eintreten**.*
> I give permission — the guest enters.
> ***Siehst** du den Vogel dort **fliegen**?*
> You see the bird — the bird flies.
> *Wir **hörten** das Mädchen ein fröhliches Lied **singen**.*
> We heard the girl — the girl sang the song.
> *Die alte Frau **fühlte** ihren Tod **nahen**.*
> The woman felt death — death was approaching.
> *Sie **hat** viele Kleider im Schrank **hängen**.*
> She has dresses — the dresses are in the closet.
> *Ich **schickte** ihn **einkaufen**.*
> I sent him — he went shopping.
> *Sie **legte** das Kind **schlafen**.*
> She put the child to bed — the child went to sleep.
> *Er **hieß** mich **hereinkommen**.*
> He asked me — I came in.
> *Er **lehrt** uns Deutsch **sprechen**.*
> He teaches us — we speak German.

B 971   For some of these verbs, the infinitive can act as a predicate infinitive without an object actually being mentioned. In such sentences, the object of the action (and thus the subject of the infinitive) can easily be supplied from context:

[1] In the sense of "to bid."

154

Ich höre (jemanden) *klopfen.*
Ich sehe gern (Menschen) *tanzen.*

The prepositional infinitive may be used after some verbs as predicate of   B 973
a dative object. It indicates what the dative object can or should do.
These verbs are:

anheimstellen	empfehlen	raten
aufgeben	erlauben	verbieten
auftragen	freistellen	vorschlagen
befehlen	gebieten	vorschreiben
belieben	gestatten	zumuten

Ich empfehle **dir**, *den neuen Film* **anzusehen**.
Der Offizier befahl **den Soldaten**, *in der Kaserne* **zu bleiben**.
Der Arzt hat **dem Kranken** *verboten, so viele Zigaretten* **zu rauchen**.
Ich möchte **Ihnen** *raten, sich das noch einmal* **zu überlegen**.

The verbs **vergeben** and **verzeihen** are followed by a prepositional past   B 975
infinitive to indicate that the event described by the infinitive lies in the
past:

Wir verzeihen ihm, uns **betrogen zu haben**.

After the verb **helfen**, the prepositional infinitive is used as the predicate   B 976
infinitive for dative objects, if the subject itself does not directly participate in the activity:

Ich helfe **meinem Freund**, *ein Zimmer* **zu finden**.
My friend finds the room.

Helfen Sir **mir**, *mein Auto günstig* **zu verkaufen**.
I am selling my car.

Der Lehrer hilft **den Schülern**, *eine neue Sprache* **zu erlernen**.
The pupils are learning the language.

If, however, the subject of the sentence directly participates in the action   B 977
jointly with the object, the simple infinitive is used at the end of the
sentence field:

Ich helfe **meinem Freund** *die Pakete zur Post* **tragen**.
My friend and I are both carrying packages.

Die Tochter *hilft* **der Mutter** *das Essen* **kochen**.
Mother and daughter are cooking together.

Die Mädchen *haben* **den Bauern** *Kirschen pflücken* **geholfen**.
The farmers and the girls are working jointly.

155

B 978   When the verbs **einbilden** and **vornehmen** are used with a dative re-flexive pronoun, the prepositional infinitive also acts as a predicate infinitive, although this is no longer recognizable because of the identity between the subject and the dative object:

> *Ich nahm **mir** vor, nicht mehr mit ihm **zu sprechen**.*
> *Er bildet **sich** ein, ein reicher Mann **zu sein**.*

B 979   For some verbs, especially **ausreden, erlauben (gestatten), gönnen (mißgönnen), überlassen, verwehren,** the place of the object is often taken by the impersonal pronoun **es,** which acts to anticipate the prepositional infinitive in the postfield [→ B 935]:

> *Ich **erlaube** (**gestatte**) es Ihnen, meine Schreibmaschine **zu benützen**.*
> *Ich **überlasse** es dir, morgen **zu kommen** oder nicht.*
> *Er **gönnt** es mir nicht, im Sommer nach Italien **zu fahren**.*

B 980   The following verbs use the prepositional infinitive as a predicate infinitive. The infinitive here takes the place of a prepositional object or a genitive object [→ H 335]:

abhalten	bezichtigen	treiben
anfeuern	bitten	überführen
anklagen	drängen	überreden
anreizen	ermuntern	veranlassen
anstiften	ermutigen	verbinden
antreiben	ersuchen	verführen
auffordern	gelüsten	verhindern
aufhetzen	gewöhnen	verklagen
aufstacheln	hindern	es verlangt (*impersonal*)
beschuldigen	mahnen (ermahnen)	verleiten
beschwören	nötigen	verpflichten
bewegen	reizen	zwingen

*Ich **bitte** Sie, morgen zu mir **zu kommen** (Ich bitte Sie **um** etwas).*
*Es **verlangt** ihn, ins kühle Wasser **zu springen**. (Es verlangt ihn **danach**.)*
*Man **beschuldigt** den Mann, das Geld gestohlen **zu haben**. (Man beschuldigt ihn **des Diebstahls**.)*

B 981   With these verbs it is possible to form a passive, without making any changes in the prepositional infinitive. The subject of the passive sen-tence is then also the subject of the infinitive:

> *Sie werden gebeten, morgen zu mir **zu kommen**.*
> *Der Mann wurde beschuldigt, das Geld gestohlen **zu haben**.*

156

With many reflexive verbs (reflexive pronoun in the accusative), the B 982
prepositional infinitive is also a predicate infinitive, although this is no
longer recognizable because of the identity between the subject and the
accusative object:

sich in acht nehmen	sich eignen	sich schämen
sich anstrengen	sich entschließen	sich sehnen
sich ärgern	sich erinnern	sich sträuben
sich bedenken	sich freuen	sich unterstehen
sich beeilen	sich fürchten	sich vorsehen
sich bemühen	sich hüten	sich weigern
sich bestreben	sich rühmen	sich wundern

*Das Kind fürchtet **sich**, mit dem fremden Mann **zu sprechen**.*
*Wir freuen **uns**, Sie **wiederzusehen**.*
*Ich erinnere **mich** nicht, dieses Buch je gelesen **zu haben**.*
*Er entschloß **sich**, Medizin **zu studieren**.*
*Warum weigern Sie **sich**, das Geld **anzunehmen**?*

The Infinitive as Attribute

The prepositional infinitive may also appear as part of a sentence unit B 985
[→ J 001 ff.]. It acts as an attribute for nouns which were formed from
infinitives (e.g. **Vergnügen, Streben, Verlangen, Bemühen**), for action
nouns (nouns derived from verbs, e.g. **Wunsch, Hoffnung**), or nouns
derived from adjectives. It follows immediately after the noun to which
it refers. If the noun stands at the end of the sentence field, the prepositional infinitive (infinitive clause) follows in the postfield:

*Ich habe nicht das **Verlangen**, ihn **zu sehen**.*
*Wir gaben endgültig die **Hoffnung** auf, im Sommer nach Italien **zu fahren**.*
*Er hat die **Absicht**, uns morgen **zu besuchen**.*
*Würden Sie bitte die **Freundlichkeit** haben, mir **zu helfen**?*

The expressions **im Begriff, im Falle, in der Lage, auf dem Sprung**, which B 986
act as predicate complements, usually have a prepositional infinitive as
an attribute:

*Wir waren eben **im Begriff abzureisen**, als ein Telegramm kam.*
*Er ist nicht **in der Lage** gewesen, die Rechnung **zu bezahlen**.*
*Ich bin gerade **auf dem Sprung fortzugehen**.*

B 987   The prepositional infinitive can also act as an attribute for some indefinite pronouns and some adverbs:

> *Hier ist **viel** (**wenig, genug, etwas, nichts**) **zu tun**.*
> *Dazu bleibt **viel** (etc.) **zu sagen**.*
> *Ich habe **etwas** (etc.) **einzuwenden**.*
> *Das hat **nichts** (etc.) **zu bedeuten**.*
> *Wo finden wir hier **etwas zu essen** (**zu trinken**)?*

The Infinitive as Noun

B 990   The simple infinitive may take over the function of a noun in a sentence. It is then used exactly like a neuter noun, is capitalized, and may be used with an article and attributes [→ B 925]:

> ***Reden** ist Silber, aber **Schweigen** ist Gold.*
> *Wir lieben das laute **Reden** nicht.*
> *Der Arzt hat mir gesagt, ich solle das viele **Rauchen** aufgeben.*

B 991   If, however, the infinitive is clearly verbal in character and is used together with a predicate complement, it loses its form as a noun [→ B 926].

B 992   A prepositional infinitive may not be used as a noun.

B 993   Some infinitives have completely taken on the character of nouns. They have lost their verbal functions and are understood as nouns. They are given neuter gender, can take on attributes, and even (in many cases) have plural forms. Some such nouns formerly derived from infinitives are:

Andenken	Grauen [1]	Verhalten [1]
Ansehen [1]	Gutachten	Vermögen
Anwesen	Guthaben	Versehen
Behagen [1]	Leben	Versprechen
Benehmen [1]	Leiden	Vertrauen [1]
Betragen [1]	Schreiben	Vorhaben
Einkommen	Unternehmen	Wesen
Entzücken [1]	Verbrechen	Wohlwollen [1]
Erbarmen [1]	Verfahren	
Essen	Vergnügen	

[1] No plural.

158

The Infinitive as Command

If a command is not addressed to a definite person or group of persons, but is a general request, the simple infinitive may be used as a substitute for the imperative [→ B 790.1]:

> *Bitte einsteigen! — Türen schließen! — Rechts fahren!*

Infinitive for Past Participle
(Substitute Infinitive, Double Infinitive)

The simple infinitive replaces the past participle for the modal verbs **dürfen, können, mögen, müssen, sollen,** and **wollen,** when they are used objectively with another infinitive and form a perfect or past perfect. This also applies to a few other verbs [→ B 468]. Such forms are called "double infinitive." In colloquial language, the past participle may be used for verbs other than the modals:

> *Er hat gestern abend **arbeiten müssen**.*
> *Hast du vor drei Jahren schon Deutsch **sprechen können**?*
> *Wir haben die Vögel im Wald **singen hören** (**gehört**).*
> *Paul hat der Dame die Koffer **tragen helfen** (**geholfen**).*

The Infinitive in the Prefield

If a verb in a simple tense form [→ B 013], which normally constitutes the anterior (front) limit of the sentence field [→ H 022], is to be placed in the prefield [→ H 705 ff.], it forms the simple infinitive. The conjugated form of **tun** takes over the position and formal function of the front limit of the sentence field [→ H 125]. The meaning is not changed:

> ***Arbeiten tue** ich nicht gern, lieber faulenzen.*
> ***Lieben tut** er sie nicht, aber er hat sie gern.*

C

❧ The Noun

❧ Introduction

C 001   Nouns are used to designate LIVING BEINGS (**Mann, Freund, Frau, Kind, Hund, Pferd, Fliege**), THINGS or PLACES (**Haus, Tisch, Stadt**), or CONCEPTS (**Glaube, Jahr, Freundschaft**). Nouns are always capitalized.

C 002   All nouns have GENDER [→ C 010 ff.]. German has three genders which are indicated by the article which the noun receives:

der Mann, das Haus, die Freundschaft

C 005   By means of morphological changes, nouns can indicate whether the being, thing, or concept designated refers to only one item (**singular**) or to several items (**plural**). These categories are called NUMBER [→ C 100 ff.]:

Mann — Männer; Pferd — Pferde; Freundschaft — Freundschaften

C 006   The plural does not differentiate gender.

C 008   A noun may fulfill a number of different functions in a sentence. These functions are indicated by the CASE of the noun [→ C 200 ff.]. German

160

has four cases: **nominative, accusative, dative,** and **genitive.**[1] German nouns no longer possess declensional endings for all these cases [→ C 202], and therefore can not unequivocally indicate their function as a sentence unit or attribute in all instances. These functions are therefore indicated most frequently by means of declensional endings of the article [→ D 300 ff.], a pronominal (limiting) adjective [→ D 400 ff.], or a descriptive adjective [→ E 110 ff.]:

Der Mann (nominative) *liest.*
Ich sehe diesen Mann (accusative).
Ich suche ein Zimmer (accusative) *mit fließendem Wasser* (dative).
Die Farbe (nominative) *deiner neuen Schuhe* (genitive) *ist sehr elegant.*

THE GENDER OF NOUNS

In German, nouns are divided into three gender categories which are indicated by the article in the singular. These categories have traditionally been designated as "masculine," "feminine," and "neuter." For the sake of convenience, these designations are being maintained here, even though they can be very misleading. It must be remembered that these are grammatical categories, which do not necessarily coincide with the biological sexual categories of male and female, as far as living beings are concerned. In the case of things and concepts, of course, natural categories of sex do not apply at all; nonetheless, nouns of these types also occur in all three grammatical genders:

C 010

masculine:	*der Mann*	*der Stuhl*	*der Gedanke*
neuter:	*das Kind*	*das Haus*	*das Licht*
feminine:	*die Frau*	*die Stadt*	*die Geduld*

There are no absolute rules for the grammatical gender of nouns. Nouns must therefore be learned with their articles. The following observations, however, may serve as general guidelines:

---

[1] In accordance with modern linguistic practices, all paradigms will be listed in this sequence rather than the traditional nominative, genitive, dative, accusative. Similarly, genders will be listed in the sequence masculine, neuter, feminine. For use of cases, → D 900 ff.

C 015   For living beings, grammatical gender sometimes, but by no means always coincides with the natural gender:

der Mann	das Kind	die Frau
der Löwe	das Lamm	die Kuh

but: *das Weib*, *das Fräulein*; *der Teenager*, *der Backfisch*; *die Schildwache*; *das Roß*

C 018   In certain instances, the grammatical gender can be determined by the meaning of the noun, by its ending, or by the suffix with which it was formed.

Masculine Nouns

C 020   The following groups of nouns are MASCULINE:

※ 1. Male human beings and animals:

der Mann, der König, der Sohn, der Löwe, der Hahn

Exceptions: *die Drohne*, *die Schildwache*, as well as male human beings or animals with the diminutive suffixes **-chen** and **-lein** [→ A 154]: *das Söhnchen, das Häschen, das Männlein, das Bärlein*

※ 2. Names of days of the week, months, seasons, and points of the compass:

der Sonntag, der Mittwoch, der Monat, der März, der Sommer, der Osten

But note: *die Woche*, *das Jahr* (therefore also *das Frühjahr* — but *der Frühling*)

3. Names of stones and minerals:

der Stein, der Diamant, der Basalt, der Granit

Exception: *die Kreide*

4. Names for types of precipitation, winds, and other weather phenomena:

der Regen, der Hagel, der Schnee, der Tau; der Föhn, der Monsun, der Orkan, der Sturm, der Wind; der Blitz, der Donner

Exception: *die Bora*

5. Five nouns ending in -ee:

der Kaffee, der Klee, der See, der Tee; der Schnee (see above)

162

6. Most nouns designating currencies:

> *der Dollar, der Schilling, der Gulden, der Rubel, der Pfennig*

Exceptions: *das Pfund, die Mark, die Krone, die Lira*

7. Names of most mountains:

> *der Olymp, der Vesuv, der Brocken, der Jura, der Himalaja*

Exceptions: *die Eifel, die Sierra Nevada*, and plurals (*die Alpen*, etc.)

⁎ 8. Most nouns derived without suffix, nouns formed with the derivative suffixes **-er, -el, -ling,** and **-s** [→ A 161, A 158, A 175, A 178],[1] and most nouns with the suffix **-en**:[2]

> *der Wurf, der Kauf, der Riß, der Kampf, der Lauf, der Ruf;*
> *der Lehrer, der Kocher, der Wecker*
> *der Schlüssel, der Flügel, der Hebel*
> *der Fremdling, der Säugling, der Feigling*
> *der Schlips, der Knicks, der Schnaps;*
> *der Bogen, der Regen, der Wagen, der Friede(n), der Same(n)*

⤲ 9. Nouns formed with the foreign suffixes **-and, -ant, -ar, -är, -ast, -ent, -eur, -ier** (pronounced *ihr* or *jeh*), **-iker** (sometimes **-ikus**), **-ismus, -ist, -or,** and **-us** [→ A 191]:

> *der Konfirmand, der Spekulant, der Kommissar, der Volontär,*
> *der Gymnasiast, der Palast, der Dirigent, der Spediteur,*
> *der Offizier, der Rentier, der Musiker (Musikus), der Kommunismus,*
> *der Pianist, der Professor, der Motor, der Sozius.*

Neuter Nouns

The following groups of nouns are NEUTER:

C 030

1. Young persons and animals (except those which because of their suffix must have a different gender, e.g. *der Säugling*):

> *das Kind, das Kalb, das Küken, das Lamm, das Fohlen*

[1] This does not apply to nouns ending in **-er** or **-el** where this syllable is part of the stem, rather than a derivational suffix. These nouns often have other genders, e.g. *die Schüssel, die Trommel, die Butter, die Tochter; das Siegel, das Zimmer*. If the suffix **-el** is a diminutive, the noun is neuter: *das Mädel* [→ A 154]. If the ending is part of the suffix **-sel**, the noun is also neuter: *das Rätsel* [→ A 179].

[2] This does not include verb infinitives (*das Singen*) or nouns with the diminutive suffix **-chen** [→ A 154] (*das Männchen*), which are always neuter.

2. Names for animals designating both male and female collectively:

> *das Pferd*, *das Rind*, *das Kamel*, *das Schwein*

✳ 3. Names of cities and towns, continents, and most countries:

> *das alte Berlin*, *das heutige Asien*, *das schöne Italien*, *das südliche Frankreich*

Exceptions: names of countries and regions ending in -**ei** are feminine: *die Türkei*, *die Tschechoslowakei*, *die Mongolei*, *die Lombardei*.

A few other exceptions are: *die Pfalz*, *die Schweiz*, *die Bretagne*, *die Normandie;* *der Irak*, *der Iran*, *der Sudan*, *der Libanon*, *der Balkan;* and some plurals: *die Niederlande*, *die Vereinigten Staaten* [→ D 327].

✗ 4. Names of metals and of chemical elements:

> *das Gold*, *das Silber*, *das Eisen*, *das Nickel*, *das Brom*, *das Uran*

Exceptions: *der Stahl*, *der Schwefel; die Bronze;* and compound nouns such as *der Wasserstoff*, *der Sauerstoff*, *der Stickstoff*

5. Other parts of speech used as nouns, unless they designate persons:

letters are neutral

> *das Essen*, *das Leben*, *das Ich*, *das All*, *das Wenn und Aber*, *das Blau*, *das Neue*, *das ABC*
> but: *der Blinde*, *die Kranke*, etc.

✳ 6. Most collective nouns, except those formed with the suffixes -*schaft* and -*ei* [→ A 157, A 181, C 040.4]:

> *das Volk*, *das Gebirge*, *das Besteck*, *das Dutzend*, *das Gros*, *das Schock*

✳ 7. Nouns derived with the diminutive suffixes -**chen** and -**lein** [→ A 154]:

> *das Fräulein*, *das Männchen*, *das Büchlein*

8. Nouns with the suffixes -**icht, -tel,** and -**tum**:

> *das Dickicht*, *das Röhricht;*
> *das Drittel*, *das Viertel*, etc.
> *das Eigentum*, *das Heldentum*, *das Christentum*

Exceptions: *der Kehricht; der Irrtum*, *der Reichtum*

9. Nouns with the foreign suffixes -**ett, -il, -in,**[1] -**ium, -ma, -ment,** and -**um**:

[1] Do not confuse the foreign neuter suffix -*in* (stressed) with the Germanic feminine suffix -*in* (unstressed) [C 040.1].

das Sonett, das Fossil, das Benzin, das Aquarium,
das Plasma, das Parlament, das Abonnement, das Datum

Exceptions: Nouns ending in **-ett** designating male human beings (e.g.
der Kadett); *der Zement*

Feminine Nouns

The following groups of nouns are FEMININE:

1. Female human beings and animals, often formed with the suffix **-in**[1]   C 040
[→ A 169]:

die Frau, die Tochter, die Kuh, die Ziege; die Lehrerin, die Löwin

Exceptions: Diminutives in *-chen* and *-lein* (e.g. *das Fräulein, das
Mädchen*); *das Weib, das Mannequin; der Backfisch, der Teenager*

2. Numerals used as nouns:

die Eins, die Tausend, die Million, die Null

3. Names of ships and airplanes:

die Bismarck, die Europa, die Caravelle, die Boeing

Exceptions: Animal names usually maintain their proper gender: *der
Kormoran, der Storch, der Condor, das Krokodil.* Some foreign names may
be felt to have a specific gender: *der Starfighter.*

4. Most names of trees and many flowers:

die Eiche, die Tanne, die Linde, die Kiefer, die Palme;
die Rose, die Nelke, die Tulpe, die Narzisse

Exceptions: *der Ahorn*, as well as compounds with *-baum* (*der Tannenbaum,
der Lindenbaum*); *der Flieder, der Krokus, das Vergißmeinnicht*, as well as
diminutives (*das Veilchen*) and compounds (*der Himmelsschlüssel*)

5. Nouns with the derivative suffixes **-ei, -heit, -keit, -schaft, -t(-d), -ung**
[→ A 157, 165, 181, 183, 187]:

die Bäckerei, die Krankheit, die Freundlichkeit,
die Gesellschaft, die Fahrt, die Jagd, die Wohnung

---

[1] See note on p. 164 [C 030.9].

6. Nouns with the foreign derivative suffixes **-a, -ade, -age, -aille, -aise,
-ance, -äne, -anz, -elle, -enz, -esse, -ette, -euse, -ie, -(i)ere, -ik, -ille,
-ine, -ion, -isse, -(i)tät, -itis, -ive, -ose, -sis** (or **-se**), **-ur,** and **-üre** (only
a few examples listed below):

> *die Garage, die Lizenz, die Delikatesse, die Souffleuse,
> die Melodie, die Familie, die Politik, die Nation,
> die Arthritis, die Universität, die Natur*

Special Problems of Noun Gender

⚡ C 050 Some nouns are masculine, but may be used to designate either male or
female persons:

> *der Gast; **der** Lehrling, **der** Liebling, **der** Mensch, **der** Star*

⚡ C 051 Some masculine nouns may be used for female human beings, even
when feminine forms with the suffix **-in** exist. These usually designate
professions:

> *Sie ist **Doktor** (Doktorin) der Philosophie.*
> *Frau Dr. Müller ist **Professor** (Professorin) an der Universität.*
> *Sie ist ein **Landsmann** (eine Landsmännin) von mir.*

⚡ C 055 Compound nouns follow the gender of the stem noun [→ A 201]:

> *das Eisen, die Bahn*   *die Eisenbahn*
> *der Motor, das Boot*   *das Motorboot*
> *das Haus, die Tür, der Schlüssel*   *der Haustürschlüssel*

C 056 There are some exceptions to this principle: *der Mittwoch*, by analogy
to other days of the week [→ C 020.2], and place names ending in **-furt,
-berg, -au, -gau,** and **-stadt,** which are neuter like all place names
[→ C 030.3]:

> *die Furt*   *das bekannte Frankfurt*
> *der Berg*   *das alte Heidelberg*
> *die Au*   *das schöne Reichenau*
> *der Gau*   *das berühmte Oberammergau*
> *die Stadt*   *das reizend gelegene Eisenstadt*

166

Abbreviations usually follow the gender of the unabbreviated noun: C 060

die AG (Aktiengesellschaft), *der VW (Volkswagen)*, *das Auto (Automobil)*

Exceptions: *das Foto (die Photographie)*,[1] *das Kino (der Kinematograph)*, *das Taxi* or *die Taxe (der Taxameter)*

Nouns with Different Genders

Some nouns may be used with two different genders and acquire two C 070 different meanings. These nouns may be derived from the same root, or they may be homonyms of totally different etymological origin.

Some noun pairs with different genders derived from the same root are: C 071

der Band (volume)[2]	*das Band* (ribbon)
der Bund (federation)	*das Bund* (bundle, bunch)
der Erbe (heir)	*das Erbe* (inheritance)
der Gefallen (favor)	*das Gefallen* (pleasure)
der Gehalt (content)	*das Gehalt* (salary)[3]
der Hut (hat)	*die Hut* (protection)
der Junge (boy)	*das Junge* (animal offspring)
der Kristall (mineral)	*das Kristall* (glass)
das Maß (the measure)	*die Maß* (tankard of beer — Bavarian)
der Moment (instant)	*das Moment* (motive, factor)
der Nickel (coin)	*das Nickel* (metal)
der Schild (shield)	*das Schild* (sign)
der See (lake)	*die See* (sea)
das Steuer (rudder, steering wheel)	*die Steuer* (tax)
der Verdienst (earning)	*das Verdienst* (merit)
das Wehr (dam)	*die Wehr* (defense)

In a few instances, normally masculine nouns are given neuter gender C 072 to give the word a pejorative or condescending meaning:

das Ekel, das Mensch, das Pack, das Wurm

Some nouns of different gender which are merely homonyms derived C 073 from different etymological roots are:

---

[1] Both spellings occur.

[2] Modern German slang also allows *die (Jazz)band*, an English loan word.

[3] The masculine form *der Gehalt* is also used for salary, especially in Austria.

der *Alp* (nightmare)	die *Alp* (mountain pasture)
der *Flur* (hallway)	die *Flur* (meadow)
der *Harz* (mountain)	das *Harz* (resin)
der *Heide* (heathen)	die *Heide* (heath)
der *Kiefer* (jaw)	die *Kiefer* (Scots pine)
der *Kunde* (customer)	die *Kunde* (news)
der *Lama* (lama — priest)	das *Lama* (llama — animal)
der *Leiter* (leader)	die *Leiter* (ladder)
der *Mangel* (lack)	die *Mangel* (mangle)
das *Mark* (marrow)	die *Mark* (monetary unit)[1]
der *Marsch* (march)	die *Marsch* (marsh)
der *Mast* (mast)	die *Mast* (force-feeding, fattening)
der *Messer* (surveyor)[2]	das *Messer* (knife)
der *Ohm* (uncle — archaic)	das *Ohm* (ohm — electricity)
der *Otter* (otter)	die *Otter* (adder)
der *Reis* (rice)	das *Reis* (twig)
der *Stift* (pin)	das *Stift* (convent)
der *Tau* (dew)	das *Tau* (rope)
der *Taube* (deaf man)	die *Taube* (dove)
der *Tor* (fool)	das *Tor* (gate)
der *Weise* (wise man)	die *Weise* (manner, melody)

C 074   *Das Gift* (poison) occurs as a feminine noun (with the meaning "gift") only in compounds: *die Mitgift*. *Der Gift* (fury, anger) appears only in South German slang.

C 075   The nouns *Meter* and *Teil* occur both as masculines and as neuters. *Meter*, originally neuter, is frequently used as a masculine in analogy with other nouns ending in *-er*. Compound nouns with *-meter* are always masculine when they indicate a unit of length: **der Millimeter**, **der Kilometer**. When they indicate a measuring device, they are neuter: **das Thermometer**, **das Barometer**.

Teil is usually masculine if it is felt as a component part: **der obere Teil**, **der erste Teil**. It is usually neuter if it designates a share or something separated: *Ich habe mein Teil erhalten*. (Therefore also **das**

[1] Also border country: *die Mark Brandenburg, die Ostmark*; but: *das schöne Dänemark. Der Mark* (horse radish) occurs as East German slang.

[2] Also used in compounds in the sense of "meter": *der Geschwindigkeitsmesser* (the speedometer).

168

Viertel, etc., derived from *das Teil*.) Compounds vary, but are mostly masculine, especially if the modifier is a noun:

> *der Körperteil, der Vorteil, der Bruchteil; das Abteil, das Urteil*

For a few nouns, two (or rarely even all three) genders are possible without any difference in meaning. This is especially the case with foreign words. Some of these words are: C 076

der (*das*) *Barock*	*der* (*das*) *Kompromiß*
der (*das*) *Bonbon*	*der* (*das*) *Lampion*
der (*das, die*) *Dschungel*	*der* (*das*) *Lasso*
der (*das*) *Filter*	*der* (*das*) *Radar*
der (*das*) *Katheder*	*der* (*das*) *Radio*
der (*das*) *Keks*	*das Taxi, die Taxe*

A few Germanic words also occur with two different genders. Some of these are: C 077

der (*die*) *Abscheu*	*der* (*das*) *Mündel*
der (*das*) *Dotter*	*der* (*das*) *Sims*
der (*das*) *Erbteil*	*der* (*die*) *Wulst*
der (*das*) *Knäuel*	*der* (*das*) *Zubehör*

Some nouns may be used with or without the endings **-e** or **-en**; without any ending they are masculine or neuter; with the **-e** ending they are feminine; with the **-en** ending they are masculine. The meanings are related, and often almost identical. Some of these nouns are: C 078

das Eck	*die Ecke*
der Quell	*die Quelle*
das Rohr	*die Röhre*
der Ruin	*die Ruine*
der Schurz	*die Schürze*
der Spalt	*die Spalte*
der Sproß	*die Sprosse*
der Trupp	*die Truppe*
die Backe	*der Backen*
die Karre	*der Karren*
die Posse	*der Possen*
die Streife	*der Streifen*

C 079   Some nouns may be used with or without the endings **-e** or **-(e)n**, without changing their gender or (in most cases) their meaning. Some of these are:

der Gesell, der Geselle; der Same, der Samen; der Friede, der Frieden; der Haufe, der Haufen; der Fels, der Felsen; der Fleck, der Flecken; der Schreck, der Schrecken [→ C 224].

But: *der Bub* (little boy) — *der Bube* (scoundrel)

NUMBER OF NOUNS

C 100   The grammatical category of NUMBER indicates whether a noun refers to one or more living beings, things, or concepts. German has only two number forms: SINGULAR and PLURAL. Not all nouns have a distinct plural form. If they do not, the plural meaning is indicated by the article or the attributes, by verb agreement, or by context. No absolutely valid rules can be stated for the formation of noun plurals; the plural of a noun must be learned together with its singular.

C 101   The plural article for all three genders is **die**.

C 102   Except for some foreign words and loan words [→ C 160], the following categories of plural endings exist:

SINGULAR	PLURAL	DESCRIPTION	DESIGNATION
1 a) der Onkel das Fenster	die Onkel die Fenster	}No plural form [C 105 ff.]	-
b) der Apfel das Kloster die Mutter	die Äpfel die Klöster die Mütter	No ending, *Umlaut*	¨
2 a) der Tag das Jahr die Kenntnis	die Tage die Jahre die Kenntnisse	Ending -e, no *Umlaut* [C 110 ff.]	-e
b) der Sohn das Floß die Hand	die Söhne die Flöße die Hände	Ending -e, *Umlaut*	¨e

(continued)

SINGULAR	PLURAL	DESCRIPTION	DESIGNATION
3 a) der Leib das Kind	die Leiber die Kinder	} Ending **-er**, no *Umlaut* [C 120 ff.]	-er
b) der Mann das Haus	die Männer die Häuser	} Ending **-er**, *Umlaut*	̈er
4 der Hase das Bett die Schule	die Hasen die Betten die Schulen	} Ending **-(e)n**, no *Umlaut* [C 130 ff.]	-(e)n
5 der Streik das Auto die Kamera	die Streiks die Autos die Kameras	} Ending **-s**, no *Umlaut* [C 140 ff.]	-s

Nouns without Plural Ending

MASCULINE and NEUTER nouns ending in unstressed **-el, -en,** and **-er**:[1]   C 105

> *der Hebel — die Hebel; der Wagen — die Wagen;*
> *der Schüler — die Schüler*

> *das Mittel — die Mittel; das Kissen — die Kissen;*
> *das Zimmer — die Zimmer*

Exceptions: *der Muskel, der Pantoffel, der Stachel; der Bauer, der Bayer, der Hummer, der Vetter.* All these form their plural in **-n.**

Some masculine nouns have *Umlaut*:

> *der Apfel — die Äpfel; der Garten — die Gärten;*
> *der Bruder — die Brüder*

Only compounds of *Wasser* and one other neuter noun have *Umlaut*:

> *das Abwasser — die Abwässer; das Kloster — die Klöster*

Two FEMININE nouns ending in **-er**:   C 106

> *die Mutter — die Mütter; die Tochter — die Töchter*

[1] See C 224 for masculine nouns which omit the **-n** in the nominative singular (e.g. *der Buchstabe*).

C 107 NEUTER nouns with the derivative suffixes **-chen, -lein,** and **-sel**:

das Mädchen — die Mädchen; das Tischlein — die Tischlein;
das Rätsel — die Rätsel

C 108 NEUTER nouns with the prefix **Ge-** and the suffix **-e**:

das Gebirge — die Gebirge

C 109 One other masculine noun:

der Käse — die Käse

Nouns with Plural Ending -e

C 110 Most ONE-SYLLABLE MASCULINE nouns, often with *Umlaut* in the plural:

der Stoff — die Stoffe; der Hund — die Hunde; der Arm — die Arme
der Platz — die Plätze; der Fuß — die Füße; der Ton — die Töne
der Brief — die Briefe; der Weg — die Wege

C 111 Many ONE-SYLLABLE NEUTER nouns, usually without *Umlaut* in the plural:

das Heft — die Hefte; das Spiel — die Spiele;
das Jahr — die Jahre; das Boot — die Boote;

However: *das Floß — die Flöße*

C 112 Most ONE-SYLLABLE FEMININE nouns; *Umlaut* wherever possible:

die Stadt — die Städte; die Frucht — die Früchte

C 113 Some POLYSYLLABIC MASCULINE nouns; no *Umlaut* in the plural:

der Besuch — die Besuche; der König — die Könige;
der Monat — die Monate; der Versuch — die Versuche

C 114 MASCULINE nouns derived from COMPOUND NOUNS; *Umlaut* in the plural:

-lassen: der Anlaß — die Anlässe
-stehen: der Bestand — die Bestände; der Vorstand — die Vorstände
-tragen: der Vertrag — die Verträge; der Antrag — die Anträge
-wenden: der Einwand — die Einwände
-drücken: der Ausdruck — die Ausdrücke [1]

[1] Nouns derived from the verb **drucken** (to print), however, do not have *Umlaut* in the plural: *der Abdruck — die Abdrucke.*

172

Nouns with the SUFFIXES **-ling, -nis, -kunft, -s, -sal** (with doubling of the   C 115
final consonant in the case of *-nis*):

> *der Jüngling — die Jünglinge*
> *das Hindernis — die Hindernisse; die Kenntnis — die Kenntnisse*
> *das Schicksal — die Schicksale*
> *die Auskunft — die Auskünfte*
> *der Schlips — die Schlipse*

Nouns with the FOREIGN SUFFIXES — **-an, -ar, -är, -at, -eur, -ier** (if the   C 117
suffix is pronounced *ihr*) [→ C 140], **-il, -iv,** and **-us** [but → C 135, 160]
(final consonant doubled for *-us*), **-ment,** and **-on** [but → C 123, 162]:

> *der Dekan — die Dekane; der Bibliothekar — die Bibliothekare;*
> *der Volontär — die Volontäre; das Sulfat — die Sulfate;*
> *der Friseur — die Friseure; der Offizier — die Offiziere*
> (but *der Bankier — die Bankiers); das Ventil — die Ventile;*
> *das Motiv — die Motive; der Autobus — die Autobusse;*
> *das Temperament — die Temperamente; der Balkon — die Balkone*

Nouns with Plural Ending -er

Most ONE-SYLLABLE NEUTER nouns; *Umlaut* whenever possible: C 120

> *das Amt — die Ämter; das Dorf — die Dörfer;*
> *das Tuch — die Tücher; das Ei — die Eier;*
> *das Kind — die Kinder*

Some ONE-SYLLABLE MASCULINE nouns; *Umlaut* whenever possible:[1]   C 121

> *der Mann — die Männer; der Gott — die Götter;*
> *der Leib — die Leiber; der Ski (Schi) — die Skier (Schier)*

MASCULINE and NEUTER nouns with the SUFFIX **-tum**:   C 122

> *der Irrtum — die Irrtümer; das Fürstentum — die Fürstentümer*

A few foreign words: C 123

> *das Hospital — die Hospitäler; das Regiment — die Regimenter*
> [but → C 117, 162]

---

[1] The following sentence contains the eight most important masculine nouns in this
category: *Der Geist Gottes ist nicht nur im Leib des Mannes, sondern auch im Wurm im
Strauch am Rand des Waldes.*

Nouns with Plural Ending -(e)n (No *Umlaut*)

C 130 All FEMININE nouns ending in **-e** in the singular:

> *die Straße — die Straßen; die Blume — die Blumen*

C 131 Many other polysyllabic and a few monosyllabic feminine nouns:

> *die Schwester — die Schwestern;*
> *die Frau — die Frauen; die Tür — die Türen; die Zeit — die Zeiten*

C 132 MASCULINE nouns ending in **-e**, designating male living beings:

> *der Junge — die Jungen; der Löwe — die Löwen;*
> also: *der Herr — die Herren; der Mensch — die Menschen*

C 133 FEMININE nouns formed with the SUFFIXES **-ei, -heit, -keit, -schaft, -ung,** and **-in** (with doubling of the final consonant):

> *die Bäckerei — die Bäckereien; die Schönheit — die Schönheiten;*
> *die Neuigkeit — die Neuigkeiten; die Freundschaft — die*
> *Freundschaften; die Wohnung — die Wohnungen; die Freundin —*
> *die Freundinnen*

C 134 Nouns formed with the FOREIGN SUFFIXES **-age, -ant, -enz, -ion, -ist, -or,**[1] **-tät,** and **-ur**:

> *die Etage — die Etagen; der Lieferant — die Lieferanten;*
> *die Existenz — die Existenzen; die Nation — die Nationen;*
> *der Kommunist — die Kommunisten; der Doktor — die Doktoren;*
> *die Universität — die Universitäten; die Natur — die Naturen*

C 135 Many MASCULINE nouns ending in **-us**, which change that ending to **-en** in the plural [but → C 117]:

> *der Virus — die Viren; der Typus — die Typen; der Organismus —*
> *die Organismen; der Káktus — die Kaktéen* (note shift in stress)

C 136 A few common NEUTER nouns:

> *das Auge — die Augen; das Bett — die Betten; das Ende — die*
> *Enden; das Herz — die Herzen; das Insekt — die Insekten;*
> *das Juwel — die Juwelen; das Ohr — die Ohren*

---

[1] For most nouns of this type, the suffix *-or* is unstressed in the singular, stressed in the plural: *der Dóktor — die Doktóren; der Proféssor — die Professóren;* but: *der Majóre — die Majóre; der Tenór — die Tenóre* [→ C 223].

Many MASCULINE nouns of the so-called MIXED DECLENSION [→ C 223]:   C 137

> *der Dorn — die Dornen; der Mast — die Masten;*
> *der Schmerz — die Schmerzen; der Staat — die Staaten;*
> *der Untertan — die Untertanen; der Vetter — die Vettern*

Nouns with Plural Ending -s

Many FOREIGN nouns, especially those ending in a vowel: C 140

> *das Auto — die Autos; die Kamera — die Kameras;*
> *das Kino — die Kinos; das Baby — die Babys;*
> *das Hotel — die Hotels; der Park — die Parks;*
> *der Bankier — die Bankiers* [→ C 117]

Some Germanic nouns ENDING in a VOWEL, especially ABBREVIATIONS: C 141

> *die Mutti — die Muttis; der Schupo — die Schupos;*
> *der VW — die VWs; der Uhu — die Uhus*
> but: *der See — die Seen; die Allee — die Alleen;*
> *das Knie — die Knie* [kni–ə]

Words of LOW GERMAN origin, especially NAUTICAL terms: C 142

> *das Deck — die Decks; das Wrack — die Wracks;*
> *das Haff — die Haffs*

FAMILY NAMES: C 143

> *Herr und Frau Müller — die Müllers*

Compound words, if the stem word has no declensional forms: C 144

> *das Stelldichein — die Stelldicheins;*
> *der Dreikäsehoch — die Dreikäsehochs*

In colloquial language, some nouns designating human beings: C 145

> *der Junge — die Jungens* (or *Jungs*)*; der Kerl — die Kerls;*
> *das Fräulein — die Fräuleins; das Mädel — die Mädels*

Special Plural Formations

Irregular plural formations are rare: C 150

175

der Bau — die Bauten; der Sporn — die Sporen

As indicated before [→ C 115, 117, 133], all nouns ending in **-nis** and **-in** and many nouns ending in **-us** double their final consonant:

Hindernisse, Lehrerinnen, Autobusse

C 151 Some nouns have two plural forms of different meanings. This may be a differentiation in the plural only, or it may be the result of two homonyms with different meanings having separate plural forms:[1]

der Balg	*die Bälge* (bellows)	*die Bälger* (brats; coll.)
das Band	*die Bande* (fetters)	*die Bänder* (ribbons)
die Bank	*die Bänke* (benches)	*die Banken* (banks)
der Block	*die Blöcke* (boulders)	*die Blocks* (notepads)[2]
das Ding	*die Dinge* (things)	*die Dinger* (creatures; coll.)
das Gesicht	*die Gesichter* (faces)	*die Gesichte* (visions; obs.)
der Laden	*die Läden* (stores)	*die Laden* (shutters; rare)
das Mal	*die Male* (times)	*die Mäler* (monuments)
der Mann	*die Männer* (men)	*die Mannen* (vassals; arch.)
die Mutter	*die Mütter* (mothers)	*die Muttern* (nuts — for screws)
der Strauß	*die Sträuße* (bouquets)	*die Strauße* (ostriches)
das Wort	*die Worte* (connected)	*die Wörter* (disconnected)

C 152 Nouns with plurals ending in **-e** may coincide with feminine nouns having an **-e** ending in the singular:

die Arme (the arms) — *die Arme* (the poor woman)
die Bande (fetters) — *die Bande* (gang)

C 153 Compound nouns formed with the stem *-mann* change the stem to *-leute* in the plural if they indicate a profession or group:

der Kaufmann — die Kaufleute; der Schutzmann — die Schutzleute;
der Fachmann — die Fachleute; der Landmann — die Landleute

C 154 If individual people are indicated, the plural is formed with the stem *-männer*:

[1] For nouns with different genders *and* different plurals, → C 071–073.

[2] A differentiation is also made between *zwei Bögen* (two bows) and *zwei Bogen Papier* (two sheets of paper) [→ C 190].

176

der Staatsmann — die Staatsmänner; der Schneemann — die Schneemänner; der Weihnachtsmann — die Weihnachtsmänner; der Landsmann — die Landsmänner

Sometimes both plural formations are possible: C 155

der Feuerwehrmann — die Feuerwehrmänner, die Feuerwehrleute
der Ehemann — die Ehemänner (married men),
  die Eheleute (married couple, husband and wife)

Some foreign words have special plural forms [→ also C 135]: C 160

SINGULAR	PLURAL
das Thema	die Themen[1]
das Mineral	die Mineralien
der Atlas	die Atlanten
das Ministerium	die Ministerien
das Konzil	die Konzilien
das Museum	die Museen

The noun *der Saldo* has three plural forms: C 161

die Saldi, die Salden, die Saldos

Some nouns of French origin ending in **-on** or **-ment** can form their C 162 plural either with the ending **-e** or **-s**. Usually, the **-e** ending is used if the word has been sufficiently adopted into German to lose the French pronunciation; if the nasalized vowel is maintained, the **-s** ending is used [→ C 117, 123]:

der Balkon — die Balkone, die Balkons
der Ballon — die Ballone, die Ballons
der Salon — die Salone, die Salons;

das Temperament — die Temperamente
das Medikament — die Medikamente

but: *das Regiment — die Regimenter*
   das Abonnement — die Abonnements

[1] Some foreign nouns in **-a** form their plural in **-ta**: *das Schema — die Schemata.*

177

Nouns without Plurals

C 170　Some categories of nouns can not form any plurals at all. These include names of materials, if they designate the substance itself, not specific types:

> *das Eisen, der Zucker, der Sand, der Beton, der Schnee, der Regen, das Holz, der Wein, die Milch, das Fleisch, das Leder*

C 171　If we wish to distinguish different types of one material or substance, plural forms may be used:

> *Die edelsten Hölzer wurden bei diesem Bau benützt.*
> *Kennen Sie die Weine des Rheintals?*

C 172　In other cases, we have to use compounds with words like **-arten, -sorten** and others [→ C 175, 179] to indicate plurals:

> *der Zucker — die Zuckersorten; der Regen — die Regenfälle;*
> *der Schnee — die Schneemassen*

C 173　General and abstract nouns are usually in the singular:

> *der Hunger, das Glück, die Wärme, die Gesundheit*

C 174　If, however, they are used in a concrete sense, they may have plural forms:

> *das Leiden* — the suffering, no plural;[1]
> > *das Leiden — die Leiden* (various diseases);
> *die Freiheit* — liberty (in a political sense), no plural;
> > *Er nimmt sich viele Freiheiten* (He takes a lot of liberties).

C 175　Sometimes, plurals can be formed by means of compounds [→ C 172] with various stems. Occasionally, new singular forms are then derived from these plurals, which, however, always have a concrete meaning:

SINGULAR	PLURAL	NEW SINGULAR
der Rat	*die Ratschläge*	*der Ratschlag*
das Glück	*die Glücksfälle*	*der Glücksfall*
der Schutz	*die Schutzmaßnahmen*	*die Schutzmaßnahme*

C 176　Verb infinitives used as nouns, and adjectives used as nouns (if they do not indicate persons) as a rule do not form any plural:

---

[1] Except in a poetic sense: *Die Leiden des jungen Werthers.*

178

das Lesen und das Schreiben, das Singen; das Gute, das Blau

Plural forms are possible, however, if the original adjectival character of these nouns is no longer felt: C 177

das Gut, die Güter

Collective nouns also as a rule have no plural:[1] C 178

das Getreide, die Polizei, das Publikum, das Obst, das Vieh

Here again, however, plural forms are possible if we are concerned with different types; sometimes direct plurals are formed, sometimes compounding is necessary [→ C 172, 175]: C 179

die Mannschaft — die Mannschaften;
das Getreide — die Getreidesorten

Proper names in general can not form plurals, unless we wish to designate all members of the same name within a ruling dynasty, such as *die Ottonen*, or members of a family, e.g. *die Meyers* [→ C 143], or unless they are used as common nouns: C 180

Wir sind schließlich keine Krösusse.

Nouns Used Only in the Plural

Certain nouns exist or are used exclusively in the plural, such as C 185

Geschwister, Kosten, Möbel, Eltern, Ferien, Leute,
and compounds with *-waren: Rauchwaren, Schreibwaren*

With other nouns, while a singular theoretically exists, it is never or hardly ever used: C 186

die Ahnen	*die Masern*
die Blattern	*die Scherben*
die Flitterwochen	*die Spesen*
die Gewissensbisse	*die Trümmer*[2]
die Gliedmaßen	*die Vorfahren*
die Hosenträger	*die Zinsen*[3]
die Lebensmittel	*die Zwillinge*

[1] Note that such collective nouns require a singular verb: *Die Polizei **hat** ihn verhaftet* (The police *have* arrested him). *Das Volk **ist** arm* (The people *are* poor).

[2] *Das Trumm* is a South German dialect word.

[3] *Der Zins* may be used in the sense of "rent."

C 187 Nouns designating island groups or mountain ranges are usually in the plural:

> *die Azoren, die Bermudas, die Hebriden, die Kurilen;*
> *die Alpen, die Anden, die Rockies, die Vogesen, die Pyrenäen*

C 188 The plural forms **Weihnachten, Ostern,** and **Pfingsten** are no longer felt as plurals today, but are used as singulars:

> *Weihnachten **ist** das schönste Fest des Jahres.*
> *Ostern **fällt** in diesem Jahr auf den 17. April.*
> *Pfingsten, das liebliche Fest, **war** gekommen.*

C 189 Some other nouns which were originally plurals are now felt as singular: **die Bibel** (from Latin *biblia*: books); **Bayern, Franken, Sachsen** (originally dative plurals: among the Bavarians, etc.). In some instances, it even becomes possible to form new plurals: **der Keks** (from English "cakes") — **die Keks; die Brille** (from MHG *die berille*, plural of the mineral beryll) — **die Brillen.**

C 190 Masculine and feminine nouns designating units of measure, although they possess a plural, are used in the singular when they precede another noun (and often even when used by themselves):

SINGULAR	PLURAL	MEASURING DESIGNATION
der Grad	*die Grade*	*zehn Grad Kälte*
		zehn Grad unter Null
der Mann	*die Männer*	*hundert Mann Polizei*
		alle Mann an Deck!
der Bogen	*(die Bögen)*	*zwei Bogen Papier*
das Glas	*die Gläser*	*zwei Glas Wein*
das Pfund	*(die Pfunde)*	*fünf Pfund*

C 191 Feminine nouns ending in **-e** form plurals even when they are used as measuring units:

SINGULAR	PLURAL	MEASURING DESIGNATION
die Tasse	*die Tassen*	*zwei Tassen Kaffee*
die Flasche	*die Flaschen*	*drei Flaschen Milch*
die Kanne	*die Kannen*	*zwei Kannen Bier*

180

Nouns designating monetary values have no plural form if they indicate   C 192
a price:

> *drei Mark achtzig Pfennig*
> *zwei Dollar*

If they indicate individual coins or bills, a simple plural or, in some
instances, a compound plural is used:

> *vier Pfennige* (individual pieces)
> *drei Markstücke, zwei Dollarscheine*

THE DECLENSION OF NOUNS

The declensional form of a noun depends on the function which the   C 200
noun fulfills in the sentence or clause. It is determined by some other
part of speech (verb, preposition, or another noun) by which the noun
is governed.

By itself, the noun does not have enough declensional forms to show the   C 201
case in which it must stand, and thus to indicate its function in the
sentence unequivocally [→ C 008]. This task is mainly taken up by the
declensional endings of articles [→ D 300 ff.], other limiting adjectives
[→ D 400 ff.], and descriptive adjectives [→ E 110 ff.].

There are four cases in German: NOMINATIVE, ACCUSATIVE, DATIVE, and   C 202
GENITIVE [→ D 900 ff.].[1] To characterize these four cases in all three
genders and in the plural, the German noun possesses only three distinct
declensional case endings: **-(e)s** in the genitive singular masculine and
neuter [→ C 215], **-(e)n** in the accusative, dative, and genitive singular
of some masculine nouns [→ C 220], and **-n** in the dative plural
[→ C 230, 235].

One-syllable masculine and neuter nouns also have an optional **-e** ending   C 203
in the dative singular. This ending, which was formerly required, is no
longer mandatory today and, except in certain idiomatic phrases, is
used mainly in poetic language:

> *zu Hause, auf dem Lande, am Tage, im Jahre des Herrn*

[1] This sequence will be used throughout this book.

Table of Declensional Forms

C 205

		MASCULINE I	MASCULINE II	NEUTER	FEMININE
Sing.	NOM.	der Freund	der Mensch	das Kind	die Mutter
	ACC.	den Freund	den Menschen	das Kind	die Mutter
	DAT.	dem Freund[1]	dem Menschen	dem Kind[1]	der Mutter
	GEN.	des Freundes	des Menschen	des Kindes	der Mutter
Pl.	NOM.	die Freunde	die Menschen	die Kinder	die Mütter
	ACC.	die Freunde	die Menschen	die Kinder	die Mütter
	DAT.	den Freunden	den Menschen	den Kindern	den Müttern
	GEN.	der Freunde	der Menschen	der Kinder	der Mütter

Declensional Endings in the Singular

C 210   MASCULINE NOUNS fall into two categories: some add **-(e)s** in the genitive singular [→ C 215 ff.], others **-(e)n** in the accusative, dative, and genitive singular [→ C 220 ff.]. All NEUTER NOUNS have an **-(e)s** ending in the genitive singular. FEMININE NOUNS have no declensional endings in the singular.

C 215   **-(e)s in the Genitive of Masculine and Neuter Nouns:**
This ending is used for all neuter nouns, as well as all masculine nouns which do *not* form their plural in **-(e)n** [but → C 223]. The **-es** ending is used

1. for nouns ending in **-s, -ß, -tsch, -tz, -x, -z,** and **-zt:**

> *das Gras — des Grases; der Fuß — des Fußes; der Putsch —*
> *des Putsches; der Witz — des Witzes; der Reflex — des Reflexes;*
> *der Scherz — des Scherzes; der Arzt — des Arztes*

2. for most one-syllable nouns, except those which end in a vowel or a silent **h**:

> *der Mann — des Mannes; das Kleid — des Kleides; das Buch —*
> *des Buches;*

but: *der Schnee — des Schnees; der Bau — des Baus; das Vieh — des*
> *Viehs; der Schuh — des Schuhs*

---

[1] For optional **-e** ending (*dem Freunde, dem Kinde*) → C 203 above.

182

Some one-syllable nouns and all polysyllabic nouns (other than those C 216 in C 215.1 above) add an **-s** in the genitive:

> *der Vater — des Vaters; das Geschäft — des Geschäfts;*
> *der Lärm — des Lärms; der Schirm — des Schirms*

If a one-syllable noun becomes the stem word of a compound, it only C 217 adds an **-s** in the genitive:

> *der Stift — des Stiftes; der Bleistift — des Bleistifts*
> *das Buch — des Buches; das Wörterbuch — des Wörterbuchs*

Nouns ending in **-nis** or **-us** double the final consonant (as in the plural, C 218 → C 115, 117) and add **-es**:

> *das Hindernis — des Hindernisses;*
> *der Autobus — des Autobusses*

In some foreign words ending in **-us** and **-os**, however, the genitive C 219 singular has no ending at all:

> *der Rhythmus — des Rhythmus; das Epos — des Epos*

-(e)n in the Accusative, Dative, and Genitive of Masculine Nouns:

This ending is used for all masculine nouns which take the ending **-(e)n** C 220 in the plural:

> *der Mensch, den Menschen, dem Menschen, des Menschen*
> (Plural: *die Menschen*)
> *der Student, den Studenten, dem Studenten, des Studenten*
> (Plural: *die Studenten*)

The **-n** ending is used for nouns ending in **-e** and for a few nouns ending C 221 in **-er** or **-ar** in an unstressed syllable:

> *der Bote, den Boten, dem Boten, des Boten*
> (Plural: *die Boten*)
> *der Junge, den Jungen, dem Jungen, des Jungen*
> (Plural: *die Jungen*)
> *der Bauer, den Bauern, dem Bauern, des Bauern*
> (Plural: *die Bauern*)[1]
> *der Nachbar, den Nachbarn, dem Nachbarn, des Nachbarn*
> (Plural: *die Nachbarn*)

but: *der Husár, den Husaren, dem Husaren, des Husaren*
> (Plural: *die Husaren*)

---

[1] The genitive *des Bauers* is also sometimes used.

C 222 The noun **Herr** has only the ending **-n** in the singular, although it has an **-en** ending in the plural:

> *der Herr, den Herrn, dem Herrn, des Herrn* (Plural: *die Herren*)

Exceptions from the Rule

C 223 Some few masculine nouns have the ending **-en** in the plural, but follow declension I of masculine nouns in the singular:[1]

> der Dorn, des Dorns, die Dornen
> der Fleck, des Flecks, die Flecken
> der Lorbeer, des Lorbeers, die Lorbeeren
> der Mast, des Mastes, die Masten
> der Muskel, des Muskels, die Muskeln
> der Nerv, des Nervs, die Nerven
> der Pantoffel, des Pantoffels, die Pantoffeln
> der Pfau, des Pfaus, die Pfauen
> der Schmerz, des Schmerzes, die Schmerzen
> der Schreck, des Schrecks, die Schrecken
> der See, des Sees, die Seen
> der Staat, des Staates, die Staaten
> der Stachel, des Stachels, die Stacheln
> der Strahl, des Strahls, die Strahlen
> der Typ, des Typs, die Typen
> der Untertan, des Untertans, die Untertanen
> der Vetter, des Vetters, die Vettern
> der Zins, des Zinses, die Zinsen

This also includes two nouns with irregular plurals [→ C 150]:

> *der Bau, des Baus, die Bauten*
> *der Sporn, des Sporns, die Sporen*

and all nouns with the unstressed suffix **-or**[2] [→ C 134]:

> *der Professor, des Professors, die Professoren*
> *der Traktor, des Traktors, die Traktoren*

C 224 Some nouns ending in **-e** have not only the ending **-n** but in addition also the ending **-s** in the genitive. A few of these nouns also occur with

[1] This is called "mixed declension." A similar pattern is followed by a few neuter nouns: *das Auge, das Bett, das Ende, das Insekt, das Juwel, das Ohr.* [For *das Herz* → C 225.]

[2] If the suffix is stressed, the plural is regular: *der Majór, des Majors, die Majore; der Tenór, des Tenors, die Tenöre.*

184

the ending **-en** in the nominative singular [→ C 079]; the plural then coincides with the singular, and the **-s** in the genitive is regular:[1]

der Buchstabe, des Buchstabens	*der Glaube, des Glaubens*
der Drache(n), des Drachen(s)	*der Haufe(n), des Haufens*
der Friede(n), des Friedens	*der Name, des Namens*
der Funke, des Funkens	*der Same(n), des Samens*
der Gedanke, des Gedankens	*der Wille, des Willens*

Only one neuter noun has the plural ending **-en**, the dative and genitive singular ending **-en**, and an additional **-s** ending in the genitive singular: C 225

das Herz, dem Herzen, des Herzens; plural: *die Herzen*

Declensional Endings in the Plural

The plural ending [→ C 100 ff.] is preserved without exception in all   C 230
four cases of the plural. In addition to the plural ending (if any), all nouns, masculine, feminine, or neuter (with the exceptions noted below) must have the ending **-n** in the dative plural. The noun declension does not characterize other cases in the plural in any way:

der Schüler — die Schüler, den Schülern
das Ereignis — die Ereignisse, den Ereignissen
die Hand — die Hände, den Händen
das Haus — die Häuser, den Häusern

The **-n** ending for the dative plural is *not* added   C 235

1. if the nominative plural already ends in **-n**:

der Bauer — die Bauern, den Bauern
das Ohr — die Ohren, den Ohren
die Frau — die Frauen, den Frauen

2. if the nominative plural ends in **-s**:

das Auto — die Autos, den Autos
der Park — die Parks, den Parks
der Uhu — die Uhus, den Uhus
die Müllers — Wir gehen zu Müllers. Bei Müllers ißt
  man gut.[2]

---

[1] Similarly *der Fleck, des Fleckens; der Schreck, des Schreckens.*

[2] By what may be considered reverse analogy, the *-n* is sometimes added in slang expressions in the singular: *Wir gehen zu Muttern. Bei Muttern ißt man gut.*

C 240 Most vocabularies and dictionaries identify declensional forms of nouns by listing the nominative singular, and indicating genitive singular and plural endings: [1]

Listing	Complete Forms
der Vater, -s/⸚	der Vater, des Vaters, die Väter
der Freund, -es/-e	der Freund, des Freundes, die Freunde
der Mann, -es/⸚er	der Mann, des Mannes, die Männer
der Mensch, -en/-en	der Mensch, des Menschen, die Menschen
das Kind, -es/-er	das Kind, des Kindes, die Kinder
die Mutter, -/⸚	die Mutter, der Mutter, die Mütter
das Auto, -s/-s	das Auto, des Autos, die Autos

Replacing the Genitive by the Preposition von

C 245 Since the genitive feminine and plural can not be recognized by any inflectional ending on the noun itself, it is replaced by the preposition **von** with the dative, if it can be indicated neither by an article nor by an attributive adjective [→ D 973, F 694]: [2]

das Heft eines Schülers — die Hefte **von Schülern**
das Heft eines guten Schülers — die Hefte guter Schüler
(or die Hefte **von** guten Schülern)
ein Zeichen der Hoffnung — ein Zeichen **von** Achtung

"Anglo-Saxon Genitive"

C 247 In a noun sequence, the genitive noun is usually second:

die Freunde dieses Mannes

The reverse order is called an "Anglo-Saxon genitive"; it is very rarely used in modern German, except for proper names [→ C 250 ff.], and occurs primarily in poetic language or in proverbs:

dieses Mannes Freunde
Viele Hunde sind des Hasen Tod.

[1] Since feminine nouns never have a genitive ending, this form is often omitted: die Frau, -en.

[2] In spoken and colloquial usage, the paraphrase with von is often used instead of the genitive: Frau Meyers Sohn — der Sohn von Frau Meyer [→ D 950].

186

Genitive of Proper Names

Proper names have no article and no ending in the accusative and dative   C 250
in modern German. The genitive ending -s, however, is added to both
masculine and feminine proper names.[1] The genitive usually precedes
the noun which it modifies ("Anglo-Saxon genitive"); this noun is used
without article:[2]

> *Peters Vater — Evas Mutter — Müllers Garten*
> *Ich kenne Pauls Schwester sehr gut.*
> *Haben Sie Goethes Werke gelesen?*
> *Erikas Arbeit war die beste der ganzen Klasse.*

It is possible, however, to have the proper name come second; it then   C 251
appears in the genitive if there is no article, but without genitive ending
if it follows an article:

> *der Vater Peters — die Werke Goethes*
> *die Rolle des Lohengrin*
> *die Taten des grausamen Nero*[3]

If a person is designated by several names, only the last name has the   C 252
genitive ending:

> *Friedrich Schillers Werke; Wolfgang Amadeus Mozarts Oper*

Proper names ending in -s, -ß, -tz, -x, -z, and sometimes those ending in   C 253
-e, take the extended ending -ens in the genitive. This ending is used only
in formal written language; in colloquial usage they are either replaced
by **von** [→ C 245], by a paraphrase, or by an apostrophe:

> *Hansens Bruder — Maxens Vater — Schulzens Haus*
> *der Bruder von Hans — der Vater von Max — das Haus der Familie*
> *Schulz — die Werke von Aristoteles — Aristoteles' Werke*

Words designating close family relationships (*Vater, Mutter, Onkel,*   C 254

---

[1] Full declension of proper names occurs primarily in religious language, where foreign
declensional endings are preserved:
   die Geburt Jesu Christi; Jesum Christum; Mariä Himmelfahrt; das Evangelium Johanni.

[2] Note that German does not use any apostrophe.

[3] A genitive ending on the proper name is obsolete in such constructions: *Die Leiden des
jungen Werthers.*

Tante, etc. — but not *Bruder* and *Schwester*) and the words *Gott* and *Himmel* are used in the genitive following the rules of proper names:

> *Ich gehe jetzt in Vaters Zimmer.*
> *Das ist Mutters Platz!*
> *Um Gottes (Himmels) willen!*

C 255 If a title (*Frau, Fräulein, General, Direktor, Kaiser*, etc.) is used with a proper name, the title is inflected and the name uninflected, when the title is preceded by an article or adjective [→ J 143]:

> *das Büro des Direktors Müller*
> *die Siege des Generals Blücher*
> *die Krönung des (mächtigen) Kaisers Karl*

C 256 If, however, there is no article or adjective, the title is uninflected and the name has the genitive ending:

> *Frau Maiers Sohn*
> *Direktor Müllers Büro (das Büro Direktor Müllers)*
> *die Siege General Blüchers*
> *die Krönung Kaiser Karls*

C 257 The title **Herr** has a declensional ending in all positions, with or without the article:

> *Herrn Schmidts Sohn — der Sohn des Herrn Schmidt*

C 258 The title **Doktor**, on the other hand, is never inflected:

> *der Vortrag des Herrn Doktor Meyer — Doktor Meyers Vortrag*

C 260 Place names follow the same rules as other proper names. They have no ending other than the genitive **-s**. The genitive may be placed before or after the noun; if it stands before the noun, it is used without article:

> *Deutschlands Hauptstadt — die Hauptstadt Deutschlands*
> *Münchens Straßenbahnen — die Straßenbahnen Münchens*

C 261 The construction with **von** and the dative is often used with place names instead of the genitive. It is always used with names ending in **-s, -x,** or **-z** [→ C 253, D 973]:

> *Die Hauptstadt von Deutschland*
> *die Straßenbahnen von München*
> *die Einwohner von Mainz*
> *die Metro von Paris*

188

Names of countries which must have an article [→ D 327] have full   C 265
declensional forms:

> *Er wohnt in **der** Schweiz.*
> *Die Hauptstadt **des** Kongos ist Leopoldville.*
> *Er wohnt in **den** Niederlanden.*

The genitive **-s** is often omitted with proper names, if the case is indicated   C 270
by an article or attributive adjective:

> *die Geschichte Deutschlands — die Geschichte **des** modernen Deutschland*
> *die Bilder Holbeins — die Bilder **des** jüngeren Holbein*

The names of months often occur in the genitive without ending,   C 275
especially after the word *Monat*:

> *Erinnern Sie sich des schönen Mai?*
> *Während des Monats September ...*

⧽ Pronouns and Pronominal Adjectives

⧽ Introduction

D 001 All pronouns REPLACE NOUNS. In NUMBER and GENDER, they must at all times agree with their ANTECEDENT (the noun to which they refer). The CASE of the pronoun depends on its USE in the sentence:

> *Hier ist ein **Mann**.* ***Er** ist mein Freund.* (Nominative)
> *Sehen Sie **ihn**?* (Accusative)
> *Ich spreche mit **ihm**.* (Dative)
> *Erinnern Sie sich **seiner**?* (Genitive)

D 002 The noun itself lacks the full declensional endings to identify all cases clearly [→ C 200 ff.]; the personal pronoun, however, has a full range of declensional forms [→ D 015] to indicate its function within the sentence.

D 003 Adjectives, on the other hand, do not replace nouns but modify them. The term PRONOMINAL ADJECTIVES thus looks at first like an internal contradiction. We use this term in this chapter and elsewhere to denote

190

certain parts of speech like the article, the possessive, the demonstrative, etc., which precede and modify the noun but which share the pronominal case ending pattern and which can also function as pronouns, when used by themselves. Such adjectives are also called LIMITING ADJECTIVES [→ D 280 ff.].

PERSONAL PRONOUNS

Personal pronouns refer to living beings, things, or concepts. They exist in three PERSONS, two NUMBERS (singular and plural) and, in the third person singular, in three GENDERS (masculine, neuter, feminine).[1] The FIRST PERSON (**ich, wir**) indicates the person or persons SPEAKING, or a group to which the speaker belongs. The SECOND PERSON (**du, ihr, Sie**) indicates the person or persons ADDRESSED or SPOKEN TO. The THIRD PERSON (**er, es, sie;** plural **sie**) indicates the person or persons SPOKEN OF (REFERRED TO). Third person pronouns may also indicate things or concepts, and may refer either to nouns or to entire previously mentioned sentence units.

D 010

Declension of Personal Pronouns

D 015

		SINGULAR		PLURAL	
1st Person	*Nominative*	ich		wir	
	Accusative	mich		uns	
	Dative	mir		uns	
	Genitive[2]	meiner		unser	
2nd Person		*familiar*	*polite*	*familiar*	*polite*
	Nominative	du	Sie	ihr	Sie
	Accusative	dich	Sie	euch	Sie
	Dative	dir	Ihnen	euch	Ihnen
	Genitive[2]	deiner	Ihrer	euer	Ihrer

(continued)

[1] Unlike some other languages, German makes no gender distinction in the plural.

[2] The genitive of personal pronouns is rare in modern German. It occurs primarily in elevated prose or poetic usage: *Wir gedenken **seiner**. Erinnerst du dich **meiner**?* [→ D 060 ff.]

191

	SINGULAR			PLURAL
	masc.	*ntr.*	*fem.*	*masc./ntr./fem.*
3rd Person *Nominative*	er	es	sie	sie
Accusative	ihn	es	sie	sie
Dative	ihm	ihm	ihr	ihnen
Genitive[1]	seiner	seiner	ihrer	ihrer
		(dessen)[2]		(deren)[3]

Dort kommt mein Freund Peter. **Er** *will* **mich** *besuchen.*
Ich *habe einen Bleistift gefunden. Gehört* **er dir**?
Habt **ihr** *das Buch gelesen? Ist* **es** *nicht interessant?*
Kennst **du** *meine Schwester?* **Sie** *kommt heute zu* **mir**.
Das Kind hat die Tasche verloren, die **Sie ihm** *geschenkt*
  haben. **Es** *hat* **sie** *wiedergefunden.*

Second Person of Personal Pronouns

D 020 The personal pronouns **du** and **ihr** are intimate or FAMILIAR forms of
address. They are used

> within the family
> with close friends
> for conversations with or among children (and by small children when
>   addressing adults)
> among equals in certain trades or occupations, especially among
>   laborers, soldiers, athletes, and criminals
> when addressing animals
> in prayer

D 021 The use of **du** and **ihr** normally coincides with addressing people by
their first names:[4]

[1] → footnote 2 on p. 191.
[2] → D 063
[3] → D 060

[4] Schoolchildren, however, are frequently addressed with **du** and the last name: *Hofmüller,
gib mir deine Aufgabe!* This sometimes extends to the military and other adult groups as
well; it often carries a condescending connotation.
  In general, it must be remembered that first-name intimacy (and hence the use of *du*)
is less frequent among Germans than among Americans. See also footnote to D 026.

192

*Was machst **du** heute abend, **Paul**?*
***Hans** und **Marie**, habt **ihr euch** die Hände gewaschen?*

In older literary forms, and in literary works which recreate historical
periods, **du** is used as the general form of address in the second person
singular, especially when addressing equals or people of inferior rank.
It is still used poetically and in proverbs, when addressing things or
concepts (*O sähst **du**, voller Mondenschein, zum letzten Mal auf meine
Pein! — Spare in der Zeit, so hast **du** in der Not*), in some advertising
slogans and other collective uses (*Kauf **deine** Kleider immer bei Brau-
meister!*), in funeral orations, when addressing the dead, and in fables
or fairy tales.   D 022

Similarly, **ihr** (capitalized) occurs in the singular as a polite form of
address to show respect to people of higher rank in older texts and in
works depicting older periods:[1]   D 023

*Glaubt **Ihr Euch** wohl in **Eurem** Rechte?*

In letters, all declensional forms of **du** and **ihr** and their respective possessive forms are always capitalized: D 024

*Lieber Hans! Ich danke **Dir** für **Deinen** Brief, in dem **Du**
schreibst, daß **Du** mich mit **Deiner** Schwester besuchen willst. Ich
erwarte **Euch** Montag abend. Schreibt bitte, wann **Ihr** ankommen
werdet.*

For all other persons, the pronoun **Sie** must be used for both singular
and plural. The verb used with the subject **Sie** is always in the plural.   D 025

The pronoun **Sie** is always capitalized in all its declensional forms,
as well as in its possessive forms [but → D 112 for reflexive pronoun].

The use of **Sie** normally coincides with addressing people by their last
names or title:[2]   D 026

*Was machen **Sie** heute abend, Herr Müller?*
*Wie geht es **Ihnen**, Herr Doktor?*

---

[1] **Ihr** (not capitalized) is also sometimes used in addressing a group of acquaintances, some
of whom would individually be addressed as *Sie*: *Habt **ihr** schon die neuesten Nachrichten
gehört?*

[2] Occasionally, first names (sometimes accompanied by titles like *Herr, Fräulein*) may be
used among younger people together with the pronoun **Sie**: *Fräulein Anna, haben **Sie** heute
abend etwas vor?* Servants are also addressed by first name and **Sie**.

Third Person of Personal Pronouns

D 030 Personal pronouns in the third person singular and plural (**er, es, sie; sie**) may refer to things and concepts as well as to persons. In the singular, the gender of the pronoun must always coincide with the gender of the noun to which it refers:

> *Hier liegt **der** Bleistift. **Er** gehört mir. Ich gebe **ihn** dir.*
> ***Das** Fenster ist offen. Ich schließe **es** jetzt.*
> *Findest du **die** deutsche Grammatik schwer? Ich finde **sie** leicht.*
> *Es gibt **viele** Schwierigkeiten, aber wir werden **ihnen** trotzen.*

D 031 When a neuter noun designates a person (e.g. **das Kind**, or any diminutive ending in **-chen** or **-lein**, such as **das Mädchen**), the pronoun **es** is used.[1] As soon as the name is mentioned, however, the personal pronoun agrees with the biological sex, rather than the grammatical gender. This rule also applies to possessives:

> *Sehen Sie **das** Kind dort? **Es** ist ein sechsjähriges Mädchen. Ich kenne **seine** Mutter. **Es** heißt Elli. **Sie** macht **ihre** Aufgaben immer ohne Fehler.*

D 032 An exception from this principle is the word **Fräulein**, which is always replaced by the personal pronoun **sie**:

> *Dieses **Fräulein** geht ins Büro. **Sie** arbeitet schon 5 Jahre dort. **Ihr** Chef ist Doktor Braun.*

D 035 In texts of the 17th and 18th centuries (and historical works referring to these periods) the personal pronouns **er** and **sie** (always capitalized)[2] are used as forms of address to socially inferior persons:

> *Such' **Er** den redlichen Gewinn!*
> *Was hat **Sie** hier zu schaffen?*

Da- Plus Preposition

D 040 When personal pronouns in the 3rd person refer to things or concepts, they usually do not occur as the object of a preposition. Instead of using the personal pronoun, we combine the demonstrative adverb **da** with

---

[1] Colloquially, however, *das Mädchen* is often replaced by the pronoun *sie*.

[2] When referring to God, however, *er* is usually *not* capitalized.

the preposition [→ E 900 ff.]. If the preposition begins with a vowel, a linking -r- is inserted between the adverb and the preposition.

The most frequent **da(r)-** compounds occur with the following prepositions:

ACCUSATIVE: *dadurch, dafür, dagegen, darum*

DATIVE: *daraus, dabei, damit, danach, davon, dazu*

ACCUSATIVE or *daran, darauf, dahinter, darin, daneben,*
DATIVE: *darüber, darunter, davor, dazwischen*

*Schreibst du mit dem Bleistift? Ja, ich schreibe **damit.***
*Denkst du an deine Arbeit? Ja, ich denke **daran.***
*Freuen Sie sich auf die Ferien? Ja, ich freue mich **darauf.***

In colloquial usage, there often occurs an elision of the -a- in com- **D 041** pounds with prepositions which begin with a vowel:

drum, draus, dran, drauf, drüber, drunter

Some prepositions can not be compounded with **da(r)-**, and the personal **D 043** pronoun must be used. Among these prepositions are all those governing the genitive as well as **ohne, gegenüber, seit,** and a few others:

*Haben Sie Ihren Schirm? Man kann bei diesem Wetter nicht **ohne ihn** ausgehen.*

*Die Post ist in der Sonnenstraße. **Ihr gegenüber** ist das große Kaufhaus.*

*Der Regen wurde immer stärker, aber trotz **dessen** gingen wir aus.[1]*

No absolute rules can be established for the use of the **da(r)-** com- **D 045** pounds. They are used above all with prepositions that do not denote relationships of place (**mit, für,** etc.), and for prepositions denoting spatial relationships when they are used idiomatically or figuratively:

*Ich bin **damit** einverstanden.*
*Er sehnt sich **danach.***
*Wir hoffen **darauf.***
*Denkst du manchmal **daran**?*

If a preposition expresses a spatial relationship, the demonstrative **D 046** adverb compound is used primarily if we are dealing with a relationship in space between specific objects (or an object and a person). If, however,

---

[1] *Trotz dessen* is usually replaced by *trotzdem* in modern usage. [→ F 020, F 023, F 041-2, F 550.]

general space or area locations are to be indicated, the adverb **dort** is generally used:

Das Bild hängt am Nagel.	*Woran hängt es?*	*Es hängt **daran**.*
Das Bild hängt an der Wand.	*Wo hängt es?*	*Es hängt **dort**.*
Er steht auf dem Stuhl.	*Worauf steht er?*	*Er steht **darauf**.*
Er steht auf der Straße.	*Wo steht er?*	*Er steht **dort**.*

D 047 If the preposition **in** is used to indicate location, it can be compounded with **dar-** only to show the place in which a person or a thing is located:

> *Das Geld ist in der Kasse.*   *Es ist **darin** (**drin**).*
> *Mein Vater ist im Zimmer.*   *Er ist **darin** (**drin**).*[1]

D 048 If **in** and **aus** are used to indicate a change of location, the adverbial compounds **hinein, hinaus, herein,** and **heraus** are used instead of the **da-** compounds:[2]

> *Kommst du mit ins Haus?*   *Ja, ich komme **hinein**.*
> *Ich nehme die Tassen aus dem Schrank.*   *Ich nehme sie **heraus**.*

D 049 Since a compound with **da(r)-** may be used to refer to an entire clause or concept [→ E 905], the personal pronoun is used with the preposition if we want to make it clear that the reference is only to an individual word or phrase from the preceding sentence:

> *Der Tag der Prüfung näherte sich. Alle Schüler fürchteten sich **vor ihm*** (i.e. the day). *Alle Schüler fürchteten sich **davor*** (i.e. the examination).
>
> *Mein Vater schenkte mir zum Geburtstag eine goldene Uhr. Ich freute mich sehr **über sie*** (i.e. the watch). *Ich freute mich sehr **darüber*** (i.e. the fact that he gave me a present).

D 050 The prepositions **unter, neben,** and **zwischen** can also be compounded with **da(r)-** when referring to persons, if we are speaking of a certain group:

> *In unserer Klasse waren vierzehn Schüler. **Darunter** waren neun Jungen und fünf Mädchen.*
>
> *Peter sitzt neben Fritz auf der Bank. Ich setze mich **dazwischen**. Ich setze mich **daneben**.*

---

[1] Note the following difference: I stand in front of the office door and ask: "*Ist Herr Meyer drin?*" I call up and want to know whether Mr. Meyer is in the office: "*Ist Herr Meyer dort?*"

[2] This can also be done with **auf**: *Er steigt auf den Baum. Er steigt **hinauf**.*

196

Genitive of Personal Pronouns

As indicated in the footnote to D 015, the genitive of personal pronouns is rarely used. It occurs in the 3rd person plural in certain partitive constructions in elevated language; the form **deren** is substituted for **ihrer** to indicate places or things:

> *Gibt es viele Ausländer an den deutschen Universitäten?*
> *Ja, es gibt **ihrer** viele* (or: *es gibt viele*).
> *In Europa gibt es viele Campingplätze. Ich habe **deren** manche gesehen* (or: *Ich habe manche **von ihnen** gesehen*).

The personal pronoun in the genitive may also appear before the pronouns **all-** and **beid-** [→ D 789, E 656]; these pronouns then take the **-er** ending of the genitive plural for the primary (pronominal) adjective declension [→ E 110]:

> *Peter ist **unser aller** Freund* (*der Freund von uns allen*).
> *Sie ist **euer beider** Tochter* (*die Tochter von euch beiden*).

The personal pronoun in the genitive is used before a cardinal number to indicate a group with a limited size:

> *Es waren **ihrer** drei.*
> *Wir waren **unser** sieben.*

After a verb requiring a genitive object, the genitive **dessen** is used if the personal pronoun **es** refers to an object:

> *Ich erinnere mich **dessen** genau.*

The old forms **mein, dein,** and **sein** occasionally still occur in idiomatic phrases for the genitive personal pronoun forms **meiner, deiner,** and **seiner**:

> ***Sein** werde ich immer gedenken. Ich harre **dein**. Vergißmeinnicht.*

Together with the prepositions **halber, wegen,** and **(um) . . . willen,** the genitive forms of the pronouns end in **-et**:

> *meinethalber, deinethalber, um seinetwillen,*
> *ihretwillen, unseretwegen, euretwegen*

Identical Forms of Personal Pronouns

D 070   There are several personal pronouns which may stand for different persons or which are identical with possessives. The meaning of these words must be distinguished by their context; they include the pronouns **ihr, sie,** and all genitive pronouns.

D 071   The word **ihr** may be

1. 3rd person singular feminine dative:

    *Hier ist eine Studentin. Ich gebe **ihr** ein Buch.*

2. 2nd person plural nominative:

    ***Ihr** seid alle herzlich eingeladen.*

3. a possessive adjective [→ D 602] for the 3rd person singular feminine, 3rd person plural, and (capitalized) formal address:

    *Die Studentin hat **ihr** Buch vergessen.*
    *Herr und Frau Müller und **ihr** Sohn sind bei uns eingeladen.*
    *Herr Meyer, ist **Ihr** Bruder zu Hause?*

D 072   The pronoun **sie** may be

1. 3rd person singular feminine nominative/accusative:

    *Hier kommt meine Tochter mit ihrer Freundin. **Sie** hat **sie** unterwegs getroffen.*

2. 3rd person plural nominative/accusative:

    *Im Sommer haben die Bäume viele Blätter. **Sie** verlieren **sie** im Herbst.*

3. (Capitalized) 2nd person singular and plural of formal address, nominative/accusative:

    *Bitte kommen **Sie** bald, Herr Müller; ich warte auf **Sie**.*
    *Ich habe für **Sie** alle um 8 Uhr einen Tisch im Gasthaus „Zum Goldenen Löwen" bestellt. Ich hoffe, **Sie** werden sich gut unterhalten.*

D 073   The forms **meiner, deiner, seiner,**[1] **unser, euer** may be

1. the genitive of personal pronouns:

[1] The old forms **mein, dein,** and **sein,** of course, are also identical with the possessive adjectives for the respective persons: *Vergißmeinnicht — Hier ist **mein** Freund,* etc.

198

*Erinnert Euch **meiner**. — Wir nehmen uns gern **deiner** an. — Sie schämten sich **seiner**. — Herr, erbarme dich **unser**! — Wir gedenken **euer**.*

2. the possessive adjective [→ D 602] for the respective persons in various cases:

*Ich fahre mit **meiner** Schwester nach München. Das Haus **meiner** Eltern ist dort; der Vater **meiner** Mutter hat es gebaut.*

*Unser Bürgermeister ist sehr stolz auf **unser** neues städtisches Krankenhaus.*

The word **ihrer** may be   D 074

1. 3rd person singular feminine genitive:

*Meine Großmutter ist vor einem Jahr gestorben. Heute gedenken wir **ihrer**.*

2. 3rd person plural genitive:

*Denkt an die Armen und nehmt euch **ihrer** an!*

3. 2nd person genitive singular and plural in formal address (capitalized):

*Sehr geehrter Herr! (Sehr geehrte Herren!) Wir freuen uns auf Ihren Besuch und werden uns **Ihrer** gern annehmen.*

4. Possessive adjective for the 3rd person feminine singular, 3rd person plural, and (when capitalized), for the formal address (singular or plural), if the following noun is genitive or dative feminine or genitive plural:

*Die Frau nimmt das Geld zur Bezahlung **ihrer** Rechnung aus **ihrer** Brieftasche.*

*Die meisten Menschen sind mit **ihrer** Lage nicht zufrieden, da ihr Einkommen zur Erfüllung **ihrer** Wünsche nicht ausreicht.*

*Ich soll Ihnen von **Ihrer** Schwester, von dem Bruder **Ihrer** Frau und von Freunden **Ihrer** Eltern viele Grüße bestellen.*

Use of the Impersonal Pronoun es

The pronoun **es** may be used as subject of verbs which designate natural   D 080
phenomena:

Es regnete den ganzen Tag. Es blitzte und donnerte.

D 081   It is also used for events or feelings the originator of which is unknown:

> *Es klopft an der Tür. — Es rauscht in den Bäumen. —*
> *Es treibt ihn ins Gasthaus.*

D 082   **Es** is also used in certain idiomatic phrases:

> *Wie geht es Ihnen?*
> *Es kommt ganz auf dich an.*
> *In dieser Stadt gefällt es mir.*
> *Es ist uns gelungen, Karten für heute abend zu bekommen.*
> *Was gibt es Neues?*

D 083   **Es** may also be the subject of sentences in which a reflexive construction replaces an impersonal sentence with the modal verb **können**, if these sentences do not contain an accusative object [→ D 166–7]:

> *In diesem Sessel sitzt es sich bequem*
> (i.e. *kann man bequem sitzen*).

D 084   **Es** is used as a filler in the prefield of sentences without subject [→ H 053 ff.]. If some other sentence unit occupies the prefield, the word **es** is omitted.

1. Verbs which express a feeling, as well as predicate adjective constructions indicating feelings:[1]

> *Es friert mich. — Es graut mir vor jenem Mann. —*
> *Es ist mir kalt. — Es wird ihr schlecht. —*
> *Es war mir merkwürdig zumute.*

> But: *Mich friert. — Mir graut vor jenem Mann. —*
> *Gestern wurde ihr schlecht.*

2. Passive sentences containing verbs with objects in the dative or genitive, or with prepositional objects [→ B 608, H 054]:

> *Es wird dem Mann geholfen. — Es wurde auch seines Freundes*
> *gedacht. — Es ist von deinem Vater gesprochen worden.*

> But: *Dem Mann wird geholfen. — Auch wurde seines Freundes*
> *gedacht. — Von deinem Vater ist nie gesprochen worden.*

3. Certain other passive sentences without subject [→ B 608 ff.]:

> *Es wurde bei dem Fest viel gegessen und getrunken.*
> *Es wurde bis in die Nacht gesungen und getanzt.*

---

[1] See also D 086.

But: *Bei dem Fest wurde viel gegessen und getrunken.*
Bis in die Nacht wurde gesungen und getanzt.

In certain idioms, **es** is used as an impersonal object with transitive   D 085
verbs which have no accusative object:

Wir haben es uns bequem gemacht. — Er hat es weit gebracht. —
Sie hat es auf dich abgesehen. — Dieses schöne Haus hat es mir angetan.

For reflexive verbs indicating a feeling, the personal subject may be   D 086
replaced by the impersonal subject **es**; the original subject then becomes
the object, instead of the reflexive pronoun:[1]

Ich ärgere mich, daß das Wetter heute schlecht ist.
Es ärgert mich, daß das Wetter heute schlecht ist.
Er freut sich, daß sein Freund ihn besuchen will.
Es freut ihn, daß sein Freund ihn besuchen will.
Der Vater wundert sich, daß sein Sohn schon wieder Geld braucht.
Es wundert den Vater, daß sein Sohn schon wieder Geld braucht.

The word **es** occupies an empty prefield, if there is no other sentence   D 087
unit there [→ H 053]. The personal form of the verb agrees with the
actual subject, which follows the verb:

Es wartet jemand auf dich. Jemand wartet auf dich.
Es kommen sonntags viele Leute in die Stadt. Sonntags kommen
viele Leute in die Stadt.
Es wird hier ein neues Haus gebaut. Hier wird ein neues Haus gebaut.

The pronoun **es** in the prefield anticipates a following infinitive clause   D 088
or a dependent clause introduced by the conjunction **daß**. This clause is
the actual subject of the main clause:

Es ist möglich, daß mein Freund heute kommt. — Es ist nicht leicht,
eine fremde Sprache zu lernen.

If the dependent clause or infinitive clause occupies the prefield, the
word **es** is omitted:

Daß mein Freund heute kommt, ist möglich. — Eine fremde
Sprache zu lernen, ist nicht leicht.

Similarly, the pronoun **es**, when it occupies the object position in the   D 089
sentence field, may be used to anticipate a dependent clause introduced

---

[1] Similarly D 084.1: *Mich friert. — Es friert mich.*

by **daß** or an infinitive clause, which is the actual object of the main clause:

> *Ich weiß es sicher, daß er morgen kommt. — Ein Ausländer hat es in Deutschland leichter, Deutsch zu lernen.*

If the main clause consists only of subject and predicate, the pronoun **es** is usually omitted:

> *Ich weiß, daß er morgen kommt.*

D 090   The pronoun **es** may also be used in the predicate nominative to anticipate a relative clause:

> *Ich bin es, der geklopft hat.*

REFLEXIVE PRONOUNS

D 100   If the subject and the object of a sentence indicate the same person or thing, a REFLEXIVE PRONOUN is used for the object. No distinct reflexive pronouns exist in the 1st and 2nd person singular and plural in German; the personal pronouns are used instead. The reflexive pronoun for the 3rd person (and for the polite form of address **Sie**) is **sich**.

D 110   **Declension of Reflexive Pronouns:**

	SINGULAR			PLURAL		
	1st person	2nd person	3rd person	1st person	2nd person	3rd person
ACC.	mich	dich	*sich*	uns	euch	*sich*
DAT.	mir	dir	*sich*	uns	euch	*sich*
GEN.	meiner	deiner	*seiner selbst ihrer selbst*	unser	euer	*ihrer selbst*

D 111   The reflexive pronoun **sich** is used for singular and plural; accusative and dative; masculine, neuter, and feminine.

D 112   The reflexive pronoun **sich** is also used for the formal address **Sie** (singular and plural). It is *not* capitalized.

202

The reflexive **seiner selbst** is used in the genitive singular masculine and   D 113
neuter, **ihrer selbst** in the genitive singular feminine and plural; **Ihrer
selbst** is the genitive form for the formal address **Sie**.[1]

Some verbs always have a reflexive pronoun as their object; they are   D 120
called REFLEXIVE VERBS. Some of these verbs are: **sich benehmen, sich
erkälten, sich schämen, sich sehnen, sich ereignen,** etc.:

ich	sehne mich	wir	sehnen uns
du	sehnst dich	ihr	sehnt euch
er, sie, es sehnt *sich*		sie, Sie sehnen *sich*	

> *Ich habe* **mich** *gestern erkältet. — Er schämt* **sich** *seiner Fehler.*

Other verbs may be used reflexively or not reflexively, for example   D 125
(sich) waschen, (sich) erinnern, (sich) vorstellen, etc.:

> *Die Mutter wäscht das Kind. — Ich wasche* **mich.**
> *Er erinnert mich an meinen Vater. — Erinnerst du* **dich** *an ihn?*
> *Ich stelle dir meinen Bruder vor. — Er stellt* **sich** *der Dame vor.*

In many instances, the meaning of the verb changes when it is used   D 126
reflexively, such as **(sich) verlaufen, (sich) stellen, (sich) versprechen,**
(sich) geben, etc.:

> *Der Weg verläuft in gerader Richtung. — Er hat* **sich** *im Wald verlaufen.*
> *Ich stelle den Stuhl an den Tisch. — Stell* **dich** *nicht so dumm!*
> *Er versprach, morgen zu kommen. — Ich habe* **mich** *versprochen.*
> *Er gab mir ein Buch. — Das wird* **sich** *geben.*

Sometimes the construction must be changed, when a verb is to be used   D 127
reflexively; e.g. **(sich) eilen:**

> *Ich bin zu ihm geeilt. — Ich habe* **mich** *geeilt, um zu ihm zu kommen.*

Reflexive verbs are always conjugated with the auxiliary **haben** in the   D 128
perfect tenses:

> *Die Sache* **ist** *gut verlaufen.*
> *Er* **hat sich** *verlaufen.*

---

[1] The word **selbst** is not actually a reflexive, but rather an intensifier. For its use in the sense
of *all alone, no one else, without any help* → D 480; for its use in the sense of *even* → G 440,
J 185.

Special Problems in Usage

D 130 There are some instances in which the reflexive pronoun does *not* refer to the subject:

D 131 In the INFINITIVE CLAUSE, the reflexive pronoun refers to the implied (but unexpressed) subject of the infinitive:

> *Wir forderten ihn auf,* **sich** *zu melden (***er** *solle* **sich** *melden).*
> *Es ist seine Pflicht,* **sich** *pünktlich zur Arbeit einzufinden (daß* **er** *sich . . . einfindet).*
> *Wir hielten es für die Aufgabe dieses Beamten,* **sich** *der Sache mit besonderem Eifer anzunehmen.*

D 132 In a PARTICIPIAL CONSTRUCTION, the reflexive pronoun refers to the following noun:

> *Wir sahen die* **sich** *nähernden Gewitterwolken.*
> *Ich glaube dem* **sich** *selbst lobenden Mann kein Wort mehr.*
> *Sie benützt jede* **sich** *bietende Gelegenheit, um nach Hause zu fahren.*

D 133 If in one of the above constructions (and in connection with attributive adjectives) the pronoun refers to the actual subject of the sentence, the personal pronoun must be used:

> *Wir forderten ihn auf,* **uns** *zu grüßen.*
> *Ich glaube dem* **mich** *lobenden Mann kein Wort.*
> *Sie nützt jede sich* **ihr** *bietende Gelegenheit aus.*
> *Er sah das* **ihm** *vertraute Gesicht vor sich.*

D 135 In the idioms **an sich** and **für sich** (or **an und für sich**), the reflexive has no actual antecedent:

> *Ich wollte* **an** *(***und für***)* **sich** *morgen abreisen, aber ich kann auch später fahren.*
> *Davon sprechen wir nicht. Das ist eine Sache* **für sich***.*

Use of Cases for Reflexive Pronouns

D 140 The reflexive pronoun is in the ACCUSATIVE, if the subject is at the same time the direct object of the action:

204

sich waschen	Ich wasche **mich** im Badezimmer.
sich rasieren	Er rasiert **sich** zweimal täglich.
sich erkälten	Wo hast du **dich** so erkältet?
sich vorstellen	Wir stellen **uns** den Damen vor.
sich nähern	Der Zug nähert **sich** der Grenze.

In many instances, the direct object is only a grammatical idiom and not a factual object: D 141

sich freuen	Ich freue **mich** auf meinen Geburtstag.
sich wundern	Er wundert **sich** über seinen Erfolg.
sich fürchten	Fürchtest du **dich** vor dem Gewitter?

Some verbs with a reflexive pronoun in the accusative describe a situation the conclusion of which is stated in a predicate complement: D 142

*Er hat **sich müde** gearbeitet. — Essen Sie **sich satt**! — Der Kranke muß **sich gesund** schlafen. — Über seine Witze lacht man **sich halb tot**. — Er wird **sich** noch **zu Tode** trinken.*

The reflexive pronoun is in the DATIVE, if the verb can only have a dative object, or if some other direct object exists: D 150

sich widersprechen	Du widersprichst **dir**.
sich helfen	Ich konnte **mir** nicht helfen.
sich etwas einbilden	Das bildet er **sich** nur ein.
sich etwas vorstellen	Kannst du **dir** das vorstellen?
sich etwas ansehen	Haben Sie **sich** diesen Film angesehen?

Similarly: D 151

*Ich kaufe **mir** Zigaretten. — Ich putze **mir** die Schuhe.*

The reflexive pronoun in the dative often shows that the accusative object belongs to the subject of the sentence. This is done especially for parts of the body, where the dative replaces a possessive adjective [→ D 941]: D 152

*Er wäscht **sich** die Hände. (Cf. English: his hands)*
*Sie kämmt **sich** das Haar. (Cf. English: her hair)*
*Ich habe **mir** die Füße erfroren. (Cf. English: my feet)*

205

D 153   The verb **sich getrauen** may have an accusative reflexive pronoun, or a dative reflexive pronoun with an accusative object **es**:

> *Ich getraue **mich** nicht, zum Direktor zu gehen.*
> *Ich getraue es **mir** nicht, zum Direktor zu gehen.*

D 154   Note the difference:

> *Ich wasche **mich**. — Ich wasche **mir** die Hände.*
> *Ich stelle **mich** der Dame vor. — Ich stelle **mir***
> *diese Situation vor.*

D 160   The reflexive pronoun is in the GENITIVE, if the verbal construction requires a genitive complement. The reflexive pronouns in the genitive are identical with the personal pronouns. In the third person, they are accompanied by the intensifier **selbst**, in order to differentiate their reflexive function from the personal pronoun:[1]

> *ich bin **meiner** sicher*   *wir sind **unser** sicher*
> *du bist **deiner** sicher*   *ihr seid **euer** sicher*
>
> *er ist **seiner selbst** sicher*   *sie sind **ihrer selbst** sicher*
> *sie ist **ihrer selbst** sicher*   *Sie sind **Ihrer selbst** sicher*

Other Uses of Reflexives

D 165   The reflexive pronoun is used for processes which are described by an action verb and which occur without a recognizable agent or without an identifiable cause [→ Substitute for Passive B 616]:

> *Das Gewitter entlädt **sich**.*
> *Der Vorhang öffnet **sich**.*
> *Die Tür schloß **sich**.*

D 166   In similar constructions, the reflexive often implies that the action takes place as if by its own volition:

> *Das Buch verkauft **sich** gut.*
> *Diese Schuhe tragen **sich** schlecht.*
> *Die Maschine bedient **sich** leicht.*
> *Sein Wunsch erfüllte **sich** bald.*

D 167   The reflexive is also used as a substitute for impersonal sentences with

---

[1] **Selbst** may also be used after the genitive pronoun in the 1st and 2nd person: *ich bin meiner **selbst** sicher*. For other uses of *selbst* as an intensifier, → D 170 ff. and 480 ff.

man as the subject and the modal **können**. Such sentences indicate a possible situation in which anyone may partake. The personal pronoun **es** is used as the subject [→ D 087]:

> *Hier fährt es sich gut.* (*Hier kann man gut fahren.*)
> *In diesem Sessel sitzt es sich bequem.*
> *Auf dem Lande lebt es sich angenehm.*

The verbs **sich machen** and **sich tun** are used in idiomatic expressions   D 168
which are found only in colloquial language, such as:

> *Die Sache macht sich.* (It's turning out all right.)
> *Er hat sich herausgemacht.* (He turned out better than expected.)
> *Hier tut sich etwas.* (Something is going on.)

Intensification of Reflexives

In order to emphasize the reflexive meaning, the intensifiers **selbst** or   D 170
selber [→ D 480] may be used after the reflexive pronoun in all
persons, genders, and cases:

> *Ich rasiere mich selbst* (or *selber*); i.e. I do not go to the barber.
> *Wir helfen uns selbst* (or *selber*); we do not need anyone else.

As a rule, **selbst** or **selber** are not used if the reflexive pronoun follows a   D 171
preposition which is preceded by **jeder**:[1]

> *Wir lernen jeder für sich.*
> *Heute zahlt jeder für sich.*

Reciprocal Use of Reflexives

In many verbs, the reflexive pronouns have a clearly reciprocal meaning,   D 180
e.g. *sich begrüßen, sich schlagen, sich streiten, sich treffen, sich wieder-*
sehen, etc. The subject is normally in the plural:

> *Die Gäste begrüßen sich.*
> *Die Kinder schlagen sich auf der Straße.*
> *Müßt ihr euch immer streiten?*
> *Wir trafen uns vor dem Rathaus.*
> *Wann sehen wir uns wieder?*

---

[1] In colloquial usage, **selbst** or **selber** may occur in such sentences as well: *Wir lernen jeder für sich selbst. Heute zahlt jeder für sich selber.* This is considered inelegant, however.

207

D 181 Sometimes, the meaning is distributive:

*Die Leute **teilen sich** in die Arbeit.*

D 182 The reflexive pronoun may also be used reciprocally when it is not the object of a verb:

*Die Freunde saßen **sich gegenüber**.*

D 183 When the subject is in the singular, the reflexive pronoun may also sometimes have reciprocal meaning. The person or thing which is in a reciprocal relationship with the subject is made the object of the preposition **mit**:

*Ich habe **mich mit** meinem Freund **gestritten**.*
*Wann willst du **dich mit** Peter **treffen**?*
*Er **duzt sich mit** ihr.*

D 184 In the plural, the meaning of the reflexive is often not quite clear. The context may be reflexive or reciprocal:

Wir rasieren uns.
Reflexive: *Wir rasieren uns **selbst**.* (Each of us shaves himself.)
Reciprocal: *Wir rasieren uns **gegenseitig**.* (Each shaves the other.)

Sie lieben sich.
Reflexive: *Sie lieben sich **selber**.* (Each of them only loves himself.)
Reciprocal: *Sie lieben **einander**.* (Each of them loves the other.)

Other Reciprocal Pronouns

D 190 In order to emphasize the reciprocal meaning, the reciprocal pronoun **einander** may be used instead of the reflexive pronoun [see above]. This is not possible for truly reflexive verbs [→ D 120].

*Wir lieben **uns**. — Wir lieben **einander**.*
*Liebt ihr **euch**? — Liebt ihr **einander**?*
*Sie lieben **sich**. — Sie lieben **einander**.*

D 191 If **einander** follows after a preposition, it is combined with the preposition into one word; it does not, however, have any declensional endings.

208

In such cases, **einander** is usually used together with the reflexive pronoun (especially with all reflexive verbs):

> *Sie verliebten **sich ineinander.***
> *Sie freuen **sich übereinander.***
> *Sie schämen **sich voreinander.***
> *Sie unterhalten **sich miteinander.***
> *Die Zwillinge lassen **sich** nicht **voneinander**
>   unterscheiden.*

Sometimes, the reflexive pronoun is omitted: D 192

> *Die Kinder streiten **miteinander.***

To express the reciprocal action still more clearly, we may use **einer**   D 193
(**jeder**) **den anderen** without the reflexive pronoun, or **gegenseitig** with
the reflexive pronoun:

> *Wir loben **jeder den anderen.** — Wir loben **uns gegenseitig.***
> *Sie widersprachen **einer dem anderen.** — Sie widersprachen **sich gegenseitig.***

INTERROGATIVES

Interrogatives are used in a sentence to inquire after a living being, a   D 200
thing, place, or concept, or an action or process. They may be used by
themselves (INTERROGATIVE PRONOUNS) or attributively (INTERROGATIVE
ADJECTIVES). In a main clause, interrogative pronouns always occupy
the prefield [→ H 051]; in dependent clauses, they act as subordinating
conjunctions [→ G 020]. If the interrogative is the object of a preposition, it follow that preposition:

> *Von **wem** spricht er?*
> *Wissen Sie, von **wem** er spricht?*

The Interrogative Pronoun wer?

The interrogative **wer?** inquires after PERSONS. It is used independently,   D 210
as a pronoun.[1] The verb is usually in the singular, even if the reference
is to more than one person. The answer may be a noun or a pronoun,

[1] But → D 217.

singular or plural, masculine, neuter, or feminine, first, second, or third person:

Wer kommt?	*Ich komme.*	*Wir kommen.*
	Du kommst.	*Ihr kommt.*
	Der Mann (er) kommt.	*Die Männer (sie) kommen.*
	Das Kind (es) kommt.	*Die Kinder (sie) kommen.*
	Die Frau (sie) kommt.	*Die Frauen (sie) kommen.*

D 211   If, however, the interrogative **wer?** acts as a predicate complement of the verb **sein** [→ H 460], the personal form of the verb does <u>not</u> depend on the interrogative pronoun, but on the subject:

*Wer **bin** ich?*	*Wer **sind** wir?*
*Wer **bist** du?*	*Wer **seid** ihr?*
*Wer **ist** dieser Mann?*	*Wer **sind** diese Leute?*

D 215   **Declensional Forms of wer?**

NOMINATIVE	wer?
ACCUSATIVE	wen?
DATIVE	wem?
GENITIVE	wessen?

Wer wohnt in diesem Haus?
Wen hast du heute getroffen? — Für wen arbeitet er?
Wem gab der Lehrer das Buch? — Mit wem hast du gesprochen?
Wessen Buch ist das? — In wessen Auto fährt er?

D 216   After prepositions, **wen?** or **wem?** are used, if the question refers to people; in the answer, the noun or pronoun will occur in the same case:

*Für **wen** arbeitet er? Er arbeitet für **mich**.*
*Mit **wem** hast du gesprochen? Mit **meinem Vater**.*

D 217   In the genitive, **wessen?** does not usually act like a true pronoun, since it modifies a noun. This noun always occurs without any article and normally without any other limiting adjective [→ *dessen* D 520 ff.], and may refer either to a person or a thing. The question itself, to be sure, inquires after a person [but → D 223 for **wessen?** as the genitive of **was?**]:[1]

---

[1] The semi-adjectival character of **wessen** may also be seen in the fact that the answer may be a possessive adjective: *Wessen Buch ist das? Es ist **mein** Buch.*

*Wessen Buch ist das? Das Buch **meines Vaters**.*
*In **wessen** Auto fährt er? In dem Auto **seines Freundes**.*
***Wessen** Verwandter ist er? Er ist ein Verwandter **der Braut**.*

Wessen? may also occur by itself, as a genuine pronoun; such construc-   D 218
tions, however, are fairly rare:

*Wessen erinnerst du dich? Ich erinnere mich **meines Onkels**.*

The Interrogative Pronoun was?

The interrogative **was?** is always a pronoun; it inquires after THINGS,   D 220
CONCEPTS, or ACTIONS. In the nominative, the verb is usually in the
singular [but → D 224]. The answer may be a masculine, neuter, or
feminine noun in the singular or in the plural:

*Was **ist** dort?*	*Dort ist **ein Stuhl**.*	*Dort sind **Stühle**.*
	*Dort ist **das Buch**.*	*Dort sind **Bücher**.*
	*Dort ist **die Tafel**.*	*Dort sind **die Tafeln**.*

The interrogative pronoun **was?** is also used in the accusative. The form   D 221
of the verb depends on the subject. [For use in prepositional constructions, → D 230 ff.]:

*Was **suchst du?** Meinen Bleistift.*

Was? has no dative at all. [But again → D 230 ff. for prepositional   D 222
constructions.]

For a question after a genitive object designating a thing or a concept,   D 223
the form **wessen?** is used. Such constructions are fairly rare [→ D 955
ff. for genitive uses].

*Er ist sich **seines Fehlers** bewußt. **Wessen** ist er sich bewußt?*
*Er wurde **des Diebstahls** beschuldigt. **Wessen** wurde er beschuldigt?*

If the pronoun **was?** is used with the verb **sein** to inquire after a person's   D 224
profession or activity, the verb does <u>not</u> agree with the interrogative
pronoun, but with the subject [→ D 2̅11̅]:

Was ist dein Bruder?[1] Mein Bruder ist Lehrer.
Was sind diese Leute? Sie sind Studenten.

[1] The phrase *von Beruf* is often added: *Was ist er von Beruf?*

D 225   Note the difference:

> *Wer ist dieser Mann? Er ist **Herr Meier**.*
> *Was ist dieser Mann? Er ist **Arzt**.*

D 226   When used with the verb **machen** or **tun**, the interrogative **was?** inquires after an action. The answer to such questions is given by a verb:

> *Was **machen** Sie heute abend? Wir **gehen** ins Theater.*
> *Was **tust** du? Ich **schreibe** einen Brief.*

D 227   If an interrogative sentence with the pronoun **was?** contains a neuter adjective used as a noun, the interrogative pronoun has partitive meaning:

> *Was hast du heute **Gutes** gegessen?*
> *Was kann er **Interessantes** erzählen?*

D 228   The interrogative pronoun **was?** also has partitive meaning when the sentence contains the indefinite pronoun **alles** [→ D 780 ff.]:

> *Was hat er dir **alles** geschenkt?*
> *Was willst du jetzt **alles** tun?*

D 229   A negative sentence beginning with the pronoun **was** and containing the indefinite pronoun **alles** does not actually have an interrogative function; it expresses astonishment and admiration:

> *Was gibt es **nicht alles** in dieser Stadt!*
> *Was haben wir **nicht alles** auf unserer Reise gesehen!*

D 230   As a general rule, the interrogative pronoun **was?** is not used as the object of a preposition [but → D 233, 236]. Instead, the preposition is combined with the interrogative adverb **wo-?** If the preposition begins with a vowel, a linking -**r**- is inserted between the interrogative adverb **wo-?** and the preposition [cf. D 040 ff.].

D 231   The most frequent combinations with **wo(r)-?** occur with the following prepositions:

ACCUSATIVE: *wodurch? wofür? wogegen? worum?*
DATIVE: *woraus? wobei? womit? wonach? wovon? wozu?*
ACC./DATIVE: *woran? worauf? wohinter? worin? worüber? worunter? wovor?*

212

The combinations of **wo(r)-?** and a preposition are used when inquiring   D 232
after a prepositional expression (prepositional object or adverbial
phrase):

> **Woran** *denken Sie? Ich denke* **an** *meine Ferien.*
> **Wofür** *arbeitet der Student? Er arbeitet* **für** *seine Prüfung.*
> **Worüber** *freust du dich? Ich freue mich* **über** *das schöne Wetter.*
> **Wovon** *sprechen die Leute? Sie sprechen* **von** *ihrer Arbeit.*
> **Womit** *schreibt der Lehrer? Er schreibt* **mit** *Kreide.*

Prepositions governing the genitive, and some other prepositions, espe-   D 233
cially **ohne**, can not be compounded with **wo(r)-? Ohne** must therefore
always be used with the interrogative pronoun **was?**; such questions,
however, are rare and usually ask for repetition of a word:[1]

> *Ich bin ohne Hut gekommen.* **Ohne was** *bist du gekommen?*

If the prepositional expression after which we inquire is an adverbial   D 234
phrase of place, we use the interrogatives **wo?**, **wohin?**, or **woher? (von
wo?)** rather than the combinations with a preposition; if it is an adverbial phrase of time, we use **wann?** or **seit wann? (wie lange?)**; if the
adverbial phrase has causal meaning, we use **warum?**:

> *Das Bild hängt* **an der Wand.** *Wo hängt das Bild?*
> *Ich gehe* **in die Schule.** **Wohin** *gehst du?*
> *Er kommt* **aus der Stadt.** **Woher** *kommt er?*
> *Er kommt* **von München.** **Von wo** *kommt er?*
> *Ich mache das* **nach den Ferien.** **Wann** *machst du das?*
> *Sie arbeitet seit drei Stunden.* **Seit wann** (**wie lange**)
>   *arbeitet sie?*
> *Das Kind lachte* **vor Freude.** **Warum** *lachte das Kind?*

The inquiry after a prepositional expression with the preposition **wegen**   D 235
is made with **weswegen? (weshalb? warum?)** [→ E 874]:

> **Wegen** *des Regens konnte ich nicht kommen.* **Weswegen**
> (**weshalb, warum**) *konntest du nicht kommen?*

In colloquial language, the interrogative pronoun **was?** is often used   D 236

---

[1] Questions involving genitive prepositions are extremely rare, except for **wegen** [→ D 235].
They may occasionally occur in cases involving failure to comprehend: *Er trug einen alten
Rock anstatt der Litewka. Anstatt was?* Similar constructions may also be used with other
prepositions which do not combine with **wo?**: *Das Harz sammelte sich zwischen den Lachten
an. Zwischen was?*

with prepositions, especially in the accusative, contrary to the general principle [→ D 230]:[1]

> *An was denkst du? An meine Reise.*
> *Über was habt ihr gesprochen? Über das Wetter.*
> *Um was haben sie gespielt? Um Geld.*
> *Aus was ist dieser Ring gemacht? Aus Gold.*

D 238 The interrogative pronouns **wer?** or **was?** may be combined by means of prepositions with nouns or personal pronouns in the plural or with nouns in the singular which designate a number of persons or things [→ attribute J 150 ff.]. The interrogative pronouns then have partitive meaning:

> *Wer in dieser Klasse kommt aus Köln?*
> *Wem unter euch soll ich helfen?*
> *Was von diesen Sachen willst du deinem Freund schenken?*
> *Was in dieser Tasche gehört dir?*

The Interrogative welch-?

D 240 The interrogative **welch-?** may be used as a PRONOUN or as an attributive LIMITING ADJECTIVE [→ D 280]. It inquires after a definite person or thing within a known group. The interrogative, whether used pronominally or adjectivally, has the declensional endings of the definite article [→ D 305].

D 241 Declensional Forms of **welch-?**:

	SINGULAR			PLURAL
	masculine	neuter	feminine	masc./ntr./fem.
NOM.	welcher?	welches?	welche?	welche?
ACC.	welchen?	welches?	welche?	welche?
DAT.	welchem?	welchem?	welcher?	welchen?
GEN.	welches? welchen?	welchen?	welcher?	welcher?

---

[1] Such constructions are still frowned upon by grammatical purists and are not recommended in formal written language.

214

In the genitive masculine, two adjectival forms are used: **welches** for masculine nouns which do not have any declensional ending in the genitive singular [→ C 220], **welchen** for all other nouns [→ D 242]. The genitive is not used pronominally.

Case Forms of **welch-?** as an Attribute:

D 242

Dort stehen viele Schüler.	*Welcher Schüler kommt aus Berlin?* *Welche Schüler kommen aus Berlin?* *Welchen Schüler haben Sie gestern gesehen?* *Mit welchem Schüler willst du sprechen?*
Ich habe hier zwei Bücher.	*Welches Buch gefällt dir am besten?* *Welches Buch möchtest du haben?* *Von welchem Buch hast du schon gehört?*
Das ist das Buch eines Schülers.	*Das Buch welchen Schülers?*
Das ist das Buch eines Studenten.	*Das Buch welches Studenten?*

Case Forms of **welch-?** as a Pronoun:

D 243

Dort stehen viele Schüler.	*Welcher von ihnen kommt aus Berlin?* *Welche kommen aus Berlin?* *Welchen haben Sie gestern gesehen?* *Mit welchem willst du sprechen?*
Ich habe hier zwei Bücher.	*Welches gefällt dir am besten?* *Welches möchtest du haben?* *Von welchem hast du schon gehört?*

The neuter form of the interrogative pronoun **welch-?** occasionally occurs by itself in the singular as a predicate complement of the verb **sein**. In such cases, the personal form of the verb does <u>not</u> agree with the interrogative pronoun, but with the subject:

D 244

> *Welches sind die wichtigsten Flüsse Deutschlands?*

Descriptive adjectives following **welch-?** usually have secondary (weak) endings [→ E 120]:[1]

D 245

> *Welches neue Buch haben Sie gelesen?*
> *Von welchem neuen Buch haben Sie schon gehört?*
> *Welche neuen Bücher möchten Sie haben?*

[1] In the plural, parallel (strong) endings occasionally occur (*welche neue Bücher*), but are not considered good German.

The Interrogative was für ein-?

D 250   The expressions **was für ein-?** (singular) and **was für?** (plural) are used mostly attributively, with **ein** functioning as a limiting adjective [→ D 280]. The interrogative inquires after an indefinite person or thing within a known group, or after a more detailed description of a person or thing. In the singular, only the indefinite article is declined according to its use in the sentence, not in accordance with the preposition **für** [→ D 256]. The plural has no declensional forms. The answer contains a noun with an indefinite article or an indefinite plural, with or without an attributive adjective:

> *Ich möchte einen Hut kaufen. — **Was für ein** Hut soll das sein? — Ich möchte einen blauen Hut. Ich möchte einen Sommerhut.*
>
> *Sehen Sie die Leute dort? **Was für** Leute sind das? — Das sind Arbeiter.*
>
> ***Was für** Kleider tragen Sie gern? — Moderne Kleider.*

D 251   Notice the difference between **welch-?** and **was für ein-?**:

> ***Welchen** Hut wünschen Sie? — Den blauen Hut* (i.e. a definite hat).
>
> ***Was für einen** Hut wünschen Sie? — Einen blauen Hut* (i.e. any hat of a blue color).

D 252   Before names of materials, the indefinite article is usually omitted:[1]

> ***Was für** Wein trinken Sie? — Ich trinke Rotwein.*
>
> ***Was für** Holz ist das? — Das ist Ahorn.*

D 255   When the expression **was für ein-?** is used pronominally, the indefinite article has the declensional endings of the definite article in all cases [→ D 305]. The plural uses **welche?** instead of the article [→ *was für welche?* D 800]. There is no genitive plural:

	SINGULAR			PLURAL
	masculine	neuter	feminine	masc./ntr./fem.
NOM.	was für einer?	was für eins?	was für eine?	was für welche?
ACC.	was für einen?	was für eins?	was für eine?	was für welche?
DAT.	was für einem?	was für einem?	was für einer?	was für welchen?
GEN.	was für eines?	was für eines?	was für einer?	(No Form)

[1] Colloquial language permits the use of the article here: *Was für einen Wein trinken Sie? Was für ein Holz ist das?*

216

*Ein Herr möchte dich sprechen. — **Was für einer?** —Ein junger Herr.*
*Ich kaufe ein neues Auto. — **Was für eins?** — Einen Sportwagen.*
*Ich lese gern Bücher. — **Was für welche?** — Kriminalromane.*

In the expression **was für?**, the preposition **für** has no influence on any   D 256
article, adjective, or noun following. The case of the entire expression
depends on its use in the sentence. If therefore the entire expression is
preceded by a preposition, this first preposition will govern the declensional form of article, adjective, and noun:

Was für ein Schüler ist er?
Für was für einen Schüler hältst du ihn?
Mit was für einer Person haben Sie gesprochen?
In was für einem Haus wohnen Sie?
In was für ein Haus ist er hineingegangen?
Mit was für dummen Dingen befaßt du dich?

Notice the difference in questions concerning an attributive genitive. If   D 257
we are dealing with a PERSON, we use **wessen?** [→ D 217]; if we are
dealing with a DEFINITE OBJECT,. we use **welch-?** [→ D 241]; if we are
dealing with an INDEFINITE OBJECT, we use **was für ein-?**:

*Das ist das Haus **meines Vaters**. — **Wessen** Haus ist das?*
*Das ist der Turm **der Marienkirche**. — **Welcher** Turm ist das?*
*Das ist der Turm **einer Kirche**. — **Was für ein** Turm ist das?*

Similarly, **was für ein-?** is ordinarily used to inquire after the modifying   D 258
element of a compound noun:

*Das ist ein **Kirchturm**. — **Was für ein** Turm ist das?*
*Das ist ein **Bauernhof**. — **Was für ein** Hof ist das?*

Welch (undeclined) and **was für ein** may also occur in exclamatory   D 265
sentences. If the noun is modified by a descriptive adjective, the indefinite article after **welch** may be omitted:[1]

Welch ein Held! Was für ein Held!
Welch ein schönes Auto! Welch schönes Auto! Was für ein
schönes Auto!

---

[1] The descriptive adjective carries strong (primary) endings [→ E 110].

LIMITING ADJECTIVES

D 280   It is useful to distinguish between descriptive and limiting adjectives. Limiting adjectives do not describe the noun which they modify, but limit or restrict an indefinite category to a definite and precise group or "set" within the category. Thus, phrases like **das Buch, ein Buch, drei Bücher, diese Bücher, meine Bücher,** etc., while not describing the books involved, define the subgroup within the overall category of books.

D 281   Limiting adjectives include NUMERICAL ADJECTIVES [→ E 600], DEFINITE and INDEFINITE ARTICLES [→ D 300 ff.], DEMONSTRATIVES [→ D 400 ff.], POSSESSIVES [→ D 600 ff.], the INTERROGATIVE **welch-?** [→ D 240 ff.], and some others, such as **jed-** [→ D 840] and **all-** [→ D 780], which limit by total inclusion (universal set), and **kein-** [→ D 311, D 857], which limits by total exclusion (zero set).

D 282   Limiting adjectives either have no declensional endings at all (e.g. numerical adjectives and some forms of the indefinite article, **kein**, and the possessives), or the pronominal (primary) endings of the definite article and **dies-** [→ D 305, D 410].

D 283   For declensional endings of descriptive adjectives occurring without limiting adjectives, after an uninflected limiting adjective, or after an inflected limiting adjective, → E 100 ff.

THE ARTICLE

D 300   In the singular, the article indicates the grammatical GENDER (masculine, neuter, feminine) of a noun. The declensional form of the article indicates the NUMBER (singular, plural) and CASE (nominative, accusative, dative, genitive) of the noun. Since nouns themselves no longer possess a full declensional ending pattern [→ C 201 ff.], the article often serves to clarify the function of the noun in the sentence.

FORMS OF THE ARTICLE

D 301   We distinguish between DEFINITE and INDEFINITE articles. The declensional form of attributive adjectives modifying a noun is determined by the declensional pattern of the article [→ E 100 ff.].

218

Declensional Forms of the Definite Article[1]

	SINGULAR			PLURAL
	masculine	neuter	feminine	masc./ntr./fem.
NOMINATIVE:	der	das	die	die
ACCUSATIVE:	den	das	die	die
DATIVE:	dem	dem	der	den
GENITIVE:	des	des	der	der

The definite article has six different declensional forms:

der: nominative singular masculine, dative and genitive singular feminine, genitive plural

das: nominative/accusative neuter

die: nominative/accusative feminine, nominative/accusative plural

den: accusative singular masculine, dative plural

dem: dative singular masculine and neuter

des: genitive singular masculine and neuter

If the singular forms of the definite article are governed by prepositions,   these prepositions may be combined into contractions with the last letter of the following article [→ D 335, F 050]. The most frequent contractions are:

ACCUSATIVE: **das** (ntr.):   *ans, aufs, durchs, fürs, gegens,*[2] *hinters,*[2] *ins, nebens,*[2] *übers,*[2] *ums, unters,*[2] *vors,*[2] *zwischens*[2]

DATIVE: **dem** (masc. & ntr.):   *am, beim, hinterm,*[2] *im, überm,*[2] *unterm,*[2] *vom, vorm,*[2] *zum*

der (fem.):   *zur*

---

[1] The sequences nominative — accusative — dative — genitive and masculine — neuter — feminine — plural in all paradigms make similarities in form immediately apparent. Identical forms are shown in broken-line boxes. Note that distinct accusative forms exist only in the masculine singular.

[2] Mostly colloquial. Contractions with **den** (masc. acc.) are extremely rare: *fürn, übern.* There are no genitive contractions.

D 310 **Declensional Forms of the Indefinite Article**

	SINGULAR			PLURAL
	masculine	neuter	feminine	masc./ntr./fem.
NOMINATIVE:	ein	ein	eine	-
ACCUSATIVE:	einen	ein	eine	-
DATIVE:	einem	einem	einer	-
GENITIVE:	eines	eines	einer	-

D 311 **Negative Forms of the Indefinite Article**

	SINGULAR			PLURAL
	masculine	neuter	feminine	masc./ntr./fem.
NOMINATIVE:	kein	kein	keine	keine
ACCUSATIVE:	keinen	kein	keine	keine
DATIVE:	keinem	keinem	keiner	keinen
GENITIVE:	keines	keines	keiner	keiner

D 312 The indefinite article and its negative form **kein-** [→ D 380 f.] have <u>no</u> ending in the nominative singular masculine and in the nominative/ accusative singular neuter. In all other cases, the endings of the singular correspond to those of the definite article [→ D 305]. Only the negative form of the indefinite article exists in the plural, where the endings are again identical with those of the definite article.

D 313 If the indefinite article or **kein-** are used as pronouns [→ D 800, D 855], the endings of the definite article are used in <u>all</u> cases, including

220

the nominative masculine and the nominative/accusative neuter singular.

Before the indefinite pronominal attributes **ein bißchen (ein wenig)** and **ein paar**, the indefinite article usually appears without any declensional endings [→ D 810, D 870]:

D 314

> *Mit **ein bißchen (ein wenig)** Geduld läßt sich die Sache machen.*
> ***Wegen ein paar** Minuten Verspätung hat er sich so aufgeregt.*

USE OF THE ARTICLE

The article stands before the noun. Adjectives modifying the noun (including participles used as attributes), together with all adverbs or adverbial phrases which in turn modify these adjectives, are placed between the article and the noun [→ J 163 ff. for extended attributes]:

D 315

> | *Der alte Mann* | *wohnt in* | ***einem** sehr entfernt gelegenen Haus* |.

> | *Der schwerverletzte Pilot* | *wurde* | *ins nächste Krankenhaus* | *gebracht.*

> | *Der soeben auf Bahnsteig sechs einfahrende Zug* | *kommt aus Berlin.*

> *Das ist* | ***eine** schwer zu lösende Aufgabe* |.

Use of the Definite Article

The definite article is used to indicate people, things, or concepts which are known or which are defined precisely:

D 320

> *Dort steht ein Mann. **Der** Mann wartet auf seinen Freund.*
> *Auf dem Tisch liegt ein Buch. **Das** Buch gehört mir.*

The definite article may also indicate an abstraction or a general concept [→ D 324]:[1]

D 321

> ***Der** Mensch ist sterblich. — **Das** Leben ist nicht leicht. —*
> *Ich liebe **die** Natur. — **Der** Tod kam schnell. — Er kämpfte für*
> ***die** Freiheit und für **das** Christentum.*

---

[1] English does not use any article in such constructions.

221

D 322   The definite article indicates the particularity or uniqueness of a noun [→ superlative E 342, demonstrative D 410]:

> *Heute ist **der** schönste Tag meines Lebens.*
> *Der Sieg des Skifahrers war **das** Ereignis dieses Winters.*

Specifically, the definite article is used:

D 323   For persons or things in the singular, which represent their type:[1]

> **Das** *Pferd ist ein Reittier.*
> **Der** *Italiener liebt die Musik.*
> **Das** *Auto ist ein Transportmittel.*

D 324   For collective, religious, and ethical concepts or terms which refer to human life [→ D 321]:

> *die Regierung, **die** Menschheit, **das** Christentum, **die** Nation;*
> *die Hölle, **der** Himmel, **die** Sünde;*
> *die Treue, **die** Liebe, **die** Hoffnung, **der** Glaube;*
> *die Geburt, **die** Jugend, **die** Ehe, **der** Tod, **das** Leben*

If, however, two of these concepts are connected in an idiom by the conjunction **und**, the article is usually omitted [→ D 365]:

> *Kirche und Staat — Himmel und Hölle — Liebe und Treue —*
> *Leben und Tod — Geburt und Grab*

D 325   For names of months, seasons, parts of the day, and meals:

> **Das** *Frühstück ist von 7 Uhr 30 bis 9 Uhr.*
> **Der** *Mai ist der schönste Monat des Jahres.*
> **Der** *Winter war ungewöhnlich kalt.*
> **Die** *Nacht kommt jetzt früh.*

If, however, the noun is preceded by an adjective of time, the article may be omitted:

> *Wir sehen uns nächsten Freitag.*
> *Letzten Herbst waren wir in Italien.*

D 326   For names of streets, mountains and mountain ranges, lakes, oceans, and rivers:

---

[1] In the plural, the article is usually omitted: *Pferde sind Reittiere. — Italiener lieben die Musik. — Autos sind Transportmittel.*

die Beethovenstraße — der Kaukasus, die Alpen — die Zugspitze,
der Brocken — der Bodensee — das Mittelmeer, die Nordsee,
der Atlantik — der Rhein, die Donau

For a few names of countries and regions, namely   D 327
1. Feminines and plurals:

die Schweiz, die Türkei, die Tschechoslowakei, die Mongolei,
die Pfalz, die Bretagne, die Normandie;
die Niederlande, die Vereinigten Staaten

2. Some masculines, usually derived from names of mountains, and very few neuters:

der Irak, der Libanon, der Sudan, der Balkan, der Kongo;
das Elsaß, das Baltikum

For proper names modified by an attributive adjective:[1]   D 328

der fleißige Hans, das schöne Italien, die fromme Helene;
Karl der Große

For proper names which designate works of literature or roles in a play,   D 329
or which are used to indicate a type:

Haben Sie den Laokoon gelesen?
Wer spielt heute das Gretchen?
Er ist der Napoleon des zwanzigsten Jahrhunderts.

After the preposition **zu**:   D 330
1. if the verb expresses a development (except if the noun designates a material):

Herr Schulz wurde zum Vorsitzenden gewählt.
Das Gespräch entwickelte sich zur Diskussion.
(Also: zu einer Diskussion)
Man erklärte ihn zum Sieger des Wettkampfes.
Die Szene wird zum Tribunal.
But: *Meine Pläne wurden zu Wasser.*
Was er anfaßt, wird zu Gold.
Der Wein wurde zu Essig.

---

[1] In colloquial language, proper names are often used with the article even if there is no modifying adjective: *Der Meyer ist ein alter Freund von mir. Kennen Sie die Irma?* For last names of women, the article is often used to identify the sex: *die Droste, die Neuber* (or *die Neuberin*).

2. if the expressions indicate the purpose of an action:[1]

> *zum Essen kommen, es zum Spaß machen, etwas zum Beispiel anführen, etwas zum Vergnügen tun*

D 331   After many other prepositions, if they are used concretely:

> *in der Schule, nach der Stunde, von der Heimat, vor der Kirche, während der Arbeit*

But → D 361 for uses without the article.

D 332   In a distributive use of units of measurement:

> *Diese Äpfel kosten 80 Pfennig das Pfund.*
> *Wir fuhren 110 km die Stunde (in der Stunde).*
> *Das Schiff fährt nur zweimal die woche.*

D 333   To replace a possessive adjective [→ D 600 ff.] (especially for parts of the human body), if ownership is clearly evident from the context:[2]

> *Er hat die Hände in den Taschen.*
> *Nimm doch die Pfeife aus dem Mund!*

D 334   To indicate grammatical functions of nouns which otherwise would be used without article:

> *Ich ziehe Kaffee dem Tee vor* (Indicates that tea is the indirect object).
> *Den Hans hat Peter nie gekannt* (Indicates that Hans is the direct object).
> *Er hat sich der Medizin verschrieben* (He is enthusiastic about medicine — to differentiate from *Er hat sich Medizin verschrieben*: He prescribed medicine for himself).

Contraction of Preposition and Article

These contractions [→ D 307] are generally optional, but must be used in the following constructions:

D 335   For many predicate complements [→ H 400 ff.], especially in idiomatic phrases:

> *jemandem ans Leben gehen — jemanden aufs Korn nehmen — etwas ins Auge fassen — beim Wort nehmen — ins Theater, zur Post, zum Bahnhof gehen — zum Geburtstag gratulieren — im klaren sein*

---

[1] The use of **zum** instead of **zu** with an infinitive is considered incorrect German, but occurs colloquially: *Geben Sie mir etwas zum Trinken!*

[2] The indefinite article may be used in a similar manner.

For days of the week, months, seasons, dates, and times of day:

> **am** *Mittwoch,* **im** *August,* **im** *Winter,* **am** *5. März,*
> *Ihr Brief* **vom** *11. April,* **am** *Abend, dreimal* **im** *Monat*

For infinitives used as nouns:

> **beim** *Essen,* **zum** *Essen,* **aufs** *Essen warten —*
> *die Freude* **am** *Tanzen*

For adverbs and predicate adjectives in the superlative:

> **am** *besten,* **aufs** *beste*

If the preposition combines two nouns into a single concept:

> *Frankfurt* **am** *Main — Hotel* **zur** *Post — Gasthaus* **zum** *Bären*

If the definite article, however, functions like a demonstrative [→ D 410]
or if the noun is modified by an attributive clause, the contraction can
not be used:

> *Mein Freund wollte mich Montag besuchen. Gerade* **an dem**
> *Tag war ich aber nicht zu Hause.*
>
> *Ich habe schon viel* **von dem** *Buch gehört, das du mir zum*
> *Geburtstag geschenkt hast.*

Use of the Indefinite Article

The indefinite article is used to indicate an unspecified person or object
in the singular, particularly when it is used for the first time:

> *Haben Sie* **eine** *Zigarette?*
> *Dort steht* **ein** *Mann. Der Mann liest* **ein** *Buch.*

The indefinite article may also generalize the meaning of a noun,
especially in assertive statements:

> **Ein** *Haus kostet viel Geld.*
> **Ein** *Kind sollte immer gut erzogen sein.*

The indefinite article is used especially to indicate unusual characteristics
of a person or thing, or in comparisons:

Er ist **ein** *Held. — Du bist* **ein** *Dummkopf. — Sein Benehmen ist* **eine** *Schande.*

Er arbeitet wie **ein** *Pferd. — Du siehst wie* **ein** *Vagabund aus. — Für* **einen**
Ausländer spricht er sehr gut Deutsch. [→ F 276]

D 348   The indefinite article occurs with proper names when the name is used generically:

*ein Rembrandt, **ein** Opel*

D 349   For **ein-** as an indefinite pronoun, → D 760 ff.

Omission of the Article

D 350   Nouns which have general meaning, and which do not refer to a specific person or thing, are used without an article, especially in proverbs:

Arbeit *macht das Leben süß.*
Glück *und* **Glas***, wie leicht bricht das.*

D 351   The article is always omitted before nouns in the plural, if there is an indefinite article in the singular:

*Dort liegt ein Buch. Dort liegen **Bücher.***

D 352   The article is not used if the noun is preceded by some other limiting adjective [→ D 280 ff.] or an indefinite pronoun:[1]

mein *Bruder und* **seine** *Frau —* **welches** *Kleid? —*
jeder *Mensch —* **diese** *Tür —* **alle** *Leute —* **nichts**
Schönes — **wenig** *Gutes —* **etwas** *Neues*

D 353   However, the indefinite article may be used after uninflected **solch** and **welch** (but not after **manch**):

Solch *ein Ereignis! —* **Welch ein** *schöner Tag!*
Meine Mutter hat **manch** *gülden Gewand. —* **Manch** *liebes Kind.*

The definite article sometimes occurs between **alle** and the noun; it then functions like a demonstrative [→ D 410, D 786]:

Alle die *Leute, die ich sah, schienen froh und zufrieden.*

D 354   The article is also omitted when the noun is preceded by another noun or pronoun in the genitive:

Karls *Vater —* **des Lehrers** *Haus —* **wessen** *Wagen? —*
der Herr, **dessen** *Sohn ich getroffen habe*

---

[1] There are some exceptions from this principle, such as *alle die Leute* or *ein jeder Mensch* [→ D 353, 786, 844].

Specifically, the article is omitted:

For proper names without any attribute [→ D 328]:   D 355

> *Peter wohnt in Berlin. — Deutschland liegt in Europa.*

To designate one's own relatives like **Vater, Mutter, Tante, Onkel,** etc.   D 356
(but not **Bruder** and **Schwester**), and with the word **Gott**, when it is used
monotheistically and without attributive adjective:

> *Vater fährt heute nach Berlin.*
> *Hast du dich schon von Mutter verabschiedet?*
> *Hier wohnt Tante Marie.*
> *Gott verzeiht den Sündern.*
> But: *Der liebe Gott sieht alles. Bin ich ein Gott?*

As a form of address, even if there is an attributive attribute before the   D 357
noun:

> *Lieber Peter! Liebe Inge! Liebe Freunde!*
> *Sehr geehrter Herr Müller!*
> *Verehrte Anwesende!*

For materials, even if preceded by an attributive adjective: D 358

> *Der Ring ist aus (reinem) Gold.*
> *Wir trinken nachmittags immer (schwarzen) Kaffee.*
> *Ich suche ein Zimmer mit fließendem Wasser.*

For titles of books and articles, headlines, and announcements: D 359

> *Kleines Aufsatzbuch*
> *Schwerer Verkehrsunfall in Frankfurt*
> *Eintritt verboten!*
> *Abfahrt 7 Uhr 15.*

In many cases where a noun acts as a predicate complement [→ H 415]:   D 360

> *vor Anker liegen — Atem holen — Haltung annehmen — Hunger*
> *(Durst, Angst) haben — Klavier (Geige, Karten, Fußball) spielen —*
> *Ski laufen — Zeitung lesen*

Some of these expressions have become compound verbs:

> *kopfstehen, maschineschreiben, radfahren*

227

D 361 In many prepositional expressions when they are used attributively, as predicate complements, as adverbial modifiers, or in idioms:

> *ein Mädchen **von** schöner Gestalt — ein Wagen **von** alter Konstruktion — ein Haus **mit** schöner Aussicht — in freundlicher Weise — **aus** großer Sorge — **vor** Freude (Kummer, Schmerz) — in herzlicher Dankbarkeit — **mit** freundlichen Grüßen — **mit** vieler Mühe*

The preposition **ohne** [→ F 490] is frequently used without an article, as are the prepositions **ab, an, aus, außer, bei, nach,** and **vor** [→ F 110 ff., 124 ff., 162 ff., 170 ff., 185, 187, 448, 710], especially when they are used figuratively:

> *Er ist **ohne** Geld (**ohne** Arbeit). — Ich kam **ohne** Hut (**ohne** Mantel).*

> *ab ersten Juli — an Krebs leiden — ein Kind aus erster Ehe — **außer** Gefahr sein — **bei** Gott schwören — Der Wein schmeckt **nach** Faß. — Er zitterte **vor** Angst.*

D 362 In many prepositional expressions with verbs of motion:

> *zu Fuß gehen — zu Bett gehen[1] — zu Lande (zu Wasser) reisen — nach Hause fahren*

By analogy, the same construction is also used in similar prepositional expressions with other verbs:

> *zu Hause sein — zu Bett liegen — in Ruhe lassen*

D 363 For nouns formed from verbs, if they are part of a prepositional expression:

> *Er handelte **auf Befehl.***
> *Er sagte das **mit Angabe** von Gründen.*
> ***Unter Bezugnahme** auf Ihr Schreiben vom . . .*
> ***Bei Berücksichtigung** Ihrer Gründe . . .*

D 364 In general expressions after the verbs **sein** and **werden:**

> *Heute **ist** Tanz. — Ende Januar **ist** großer Ausverkauf. — Im Juni **wird** es Sommer.* (But: *Im Juni beginnt der Sommer.*)

D 365 After the verbs **sein, werden,** and **bleiben** to indicate profession or membership in a certain group [→ predicate nominative H 460], if there is no attributive adjective:[2]

---

[1] Note the difference between *zu Bett gehen* (to go to sleep) and *zum Bett gehen* (to walk toward the bed).

[2] English *does* use the indefinite article in such constructions.

228

*Mein Bruder **ist** Lehrer. — Ich **werde** Ingenieur. — Herr Müller
bleibt Direktor dieser Fabrik. — Er **ist** Spanier. — Ich **bin** Jude.*

But: *Er ist **ein guter** Lehrer.*

In many idiomatic expressions [→ D 324, F 573, F 592]: D 366

*Ebbe und Flut — Mann und Maus — Haus und Hof — Kind und
Kegel — Himmel und Hölle — über Stock und Stein — durch Wald
und Flur — Schlag auf Schlag*

After the conjunction **als** with the meaning "in the capacity of": D 367

*Ich sage dir das **als** (guter) Freund.
Ich bin **als** Student in Paris gewesen.*

With nouns in apposition in the nominative: D 368

*Herr Berg, **Ingenieur** in einer bekannten Fabrik, ...
Herr Müller, **Vorsitzender** unseres Vereins, ...*

The article, however, is possible in the nominative and customary in
other cases:

*Herr Müller, **der** Vorsitzende unseres Vereins, ...
Ich sprach mit Herrn Müller, **dem** Vorsitzenden unseres Vereins.*

With adverbial genitives [→ D 965.3]: D 369

*Er verließ **erhobenen Hauptes** das Zimmer.
Ich kam **frohen Mutes**.*

For the names of certain religious holidays: D 370

Weihnachten, Ostern, Pfingsten

Use of kein-

As the negation of the indefinite article, **kein-** is a limiting adjective D 380
[→ D 280 ff.] which indicates the absence or nonexistence of a person,
thing, or concept. It has the endings of the indefinite article in the
singular and those of the definite article in the plural [→ D 311], and
exists in all cases. It is the equivalent of English *no* (used as a noun
attribute), *not a, none,* or *not any*:

*Er hat **keinen** Sohn, **kein** Kind, **keine** Tochter, **keine** Kinder. —
Ich gehe in **keinen** Zirkus. — Er ist **kein** Freund von mir. — Wir
sprechen mit **keinem** Lügner. — Er war sich **keines** Fehlers
bewußt. — Das tue ich unter **keinen** Umständen.*

D 381   The negation **nicht ein**, which should generally be avoided, is used only when **ein** is emphasized in the sense of "one":

> *Ich habe nicht **eine** Minute Zeit.*
> *Er hat nicht **einen** einzigen Freund.*

D 382   For **kein-** as a pronoun, → D 855.

DEMONSTRATIVES

D 400   Demonstratives point to a person or thing which is already known or one which is to be more fully explained. Demonstratives may either be used independently as pronouns, or attributively as limiting adjectives [→ D 280].

D 401   If the DEMONSTRATIVES are used as PRONOUNS, they replace nouns and their attributes as sentence units; like all pronouns, they must agree with the number and gender of their antecedent, whereas their case depends on their function within the sentence:

> *Dort steht der Wagen unseres Direktors. Ist er nicht elegant? **Den** möchte ich gerne haben!*
> *Hier sind meine Freunde. Mit **denen** mache ich morgen einen Ausflug.*
> *Ich habe mit meiner Schwester gesprochen. Auf **die** kann ich mich verlassen.*
> *Die Polizei sucht **denjenigen**, der das Verbrechen begangen hat.*
> *Es war einmal ein König, **der** hatte eine schöne Tochter.[1]*

D 402   AS DEMONSTRATIVE ADJECTIVES, they function within a sentence unit to modify a noun, and serve to indicate a specific person or thing among a number of similar persons or things; like all adjectives, they agree in number, gender, and case with the noun which they modify:

> *Mein Freund wohnt in einem wunderschönen Haus; er hat sich **dieses Haus** vor einem Jahr gekauft.*
> ***Dieser** Hut gefällt mir nicht.*
> *Hast du mit **jenem** Mann gesprochen, von dem du mir gestern erzählt hast?*

[1] As can be seen from the word order of the second clause, this is not a relative pronoun.

230

The following demonstratives may be used either as pronouns or as demonstrative attributes:

> *der, das, die;* plural *die*
> *dieser, dieses, diese;* plural *diese*
> *jener, jenes, jene;* plural *jene*
> *derselbe, dasselbe, dieselbe;* plural *dieselben*
> *derjenige, dasjenige, diejenige;* plural *diejenigen*
> *solcher, solches, solche;* plural *solche*

The Demonstratives der, das, die

The demonstratives **der, das, die** are the most frequently used demonstrative pronouns. They also occur as limiting adjectives with demonstrative character, although less often. In spoken utterances they differ from the article (in those cases where the forms are identical) by receiving a strong stress. In general, they follow the declensional pattern of the definite article [→ D 305], except that these forms are extended by the syllable **-en** in all genitives and in the dative plural. The declensional endings are thus identical with those of the relative pronouns [→ D 515].[1]

Declension of **der, das, die** as Demonstratives:

	SINGULAR			PLURAL
	masculine	neuter	feminine	masc./ntr./fem.
NOM.:	der	das	die	die
ACC.:	den	das	die	die
DAT.:	dem	dem	der	denen
GEN.:	dessen[2]	dessen[2]	deren	deren
		(des)[2]		derer [→ D 436]

[1] Historically, both the article and the relative pronoun have developed from the demonstrative pronouns.

[2] In the genitive form **dessen**, the s is doubled to obtain a short pronunciation of the vowel e [→ A 032]. The form **des** is archaic: *Des kannst du gewiß sein.*

231

D 421 In the nominative, accusative, and dative, these demonstrative pronouns are used instead of the personal pronouns, if the demonstrative character or effect is to be emphasized. They are usually placed in the prefield of a sentence [→ H 051 ff.], and carry primary stress:

> *Kennst du diese Leute? Ja, **die** kenne ich gut.* (Instead of: *Ich kenne sie gut.*)
> *Arbeiten Sie mit Herrn Müller zusammen? Nein, mit **dem** will ich nichts zu tun haben.* (Instead of: *Ich will mit ihm nichts zu tun haben.*)

D 422 The demonstrative pronoun may be modified by the adverbs **hier, da,** and **dort**, or by a prepositional phrase of location, in order to specify the position of a person or thing:

> *Siehst du die schönen Kleider im Schaufenster? **Das da** gefällt mir am besten.*
> *Welcher ist Ihr Mantel? **Der auf dem Stuhl** gehört mir.*

D 423 The demonstrative adjective may similarly be modified by the adverbs **hier, da,** and **dort**, which will follow immediately after the noun [→ J 115.2]:

> *Hat dein Freund **den** Brief **hier** gelesen?*
> *Geben Sie mir bitte **das** Buch **da**!*
> *Schauen Sie sich einmal **den** Vogel **dort** an!*

D 430 The demonstrative pronoun **das** may also refer to masculine and feminine nouns and to nouns in the plural, if these nouns occur in the predicate nominative [→ H 460 ff.]:

> ***Das** ist Herr Müller.*
> ***Das** ist ein ausgezeichneter Wagen.*
> *Eine schwierige Aufgabe ist **das**!*
> ***Das** waren wirklich schöne Ferien!*

D 431 Similarly, **das** may refer to a general indefinite concept, or to a following dependent clause or infinitive clause [→ J 070 ff.], like the anticipating **es** [→ D 088]:

> ***Das** tut mir leid.*
> *Verstehen Sie **das**?*
> ***Das** freut mich, **daß du mir helfen willst.***
> *Nennen Sie das Höflichkeit, **eine Dame so einen schweren Koffer tragen zu lassen**?*

232

Sometimes **das** occurs together with the indefinite pronoun **all** or **alles**.   D 432
In writing, the demonstrative may be combined with **all** as one word,
often inserting an **-e-** in the dative between **all** and the demonstrative:

> *Ich habe meinem Freund das alles schon gesagt.*
> *Wir haben all das in der Stadt gekauft.*
> *Mit alledem kannst du mir keine Freude machen.*

The genitive forms **dessen** and **deren** are used primarily as demonstrative   D 435
adjectives[1] and serve above all for the clarification of possessive
relationships [→ D 645]; the demonstrative is intended to refer to the
last-mentioned noun:

> *Seine Schwester geht mit ihrer Lehrerin und deren Freundin spazieren*
> (i.e. the teacher's friend).
> *Karl besuchte Herrn Schmidt und dessen Sohn* (i.e. Mr. Schmidt's son).
> *Sie erzählten uns von ihren Eltern und deren Erlebnissen* (i.e. the ex-
> periences of their parents).

The pronoun form **derer** in the genitive plural is used only as the stressed   D 436
antecedent of a following relative clause. By means of this construction,
an attributive clause is included in the genitive relationship. The relative
pronoun associated with the demonstrative pronoun **derer** can only
refer to human beings [→ D 545]:

> *Die Namen derer, die hier begraben sind, werden wir nie vergessen.*
> *Ich bedaure das Schicksal derer, denen man ihren Besitz geraubt hat.*
> *Die Freude derer, deren Kinder nach der Katastrophe wiedergefunden*
> *wurden, war grenzenlos.*

The Demonstrative dies-

The demonstrative **dies-** points to something known or previously   D 440
mentioned. Its demonstrative function is more definite than that of **der,**
das, and **die.** It is therefore used as the most frequent demonstrative
adjective, although it may also occur as a demonstrative pronoun,
especially to make a differentiation with **jener** [→ D 450 ff.]. Whether

---

[1] Demonstrative pronouns in the genitive occur only rarely: *Hier ist die Wohnung dessen,*
von dem ich Ihnen erzählt habe.

used pronominally or attributively, it follows the declensional pattern
of the definite article [→ D 305]:

	SINGULAR			PLURAL
	masculine	neuter	feminine	masc./ntr./fem.
NOM.: ACC.:	dieser diesen	dieses dieses	diese diese	diese diese
DAT.:	diesem	diesem	dieser	diesen
GEN.:	dieses	dieses	dieser	dieser

> *Wer ist **dieser** Herr?*
> *Haben Sie **dieses** Buch gelesen?*
> *Ich wohne in **dieser** Straße.*
> *Mit **diesen** Leuten kann man nicht sprechen.*
> *Wir wollen mit dem 7 Uhr Zug fahren. Mit **diesem** haben wir*
> *eine bessere Verbindung.*

D 441 The neuter form of the demonstrative may be shortened to **dies**:[1]

> ***Dies** ist ein interessantes Buch.*
> ***Dies** Buch ist sehr interessant.*
> *Zieh doch nicht **dies** dunkle Kleid an!*

D 442 The adverbs **hier, da,** and **dort** may be used to indicate the location of a
person or thing more precisely [→ D 422–3]. They may occur either
after the demonstrative pronoun or, in the case of demonstrative
adjectives, after the noun:

> *Welcher Hut gefällt Ihnen am besten? Ich nehme **diesen hier**.*
> *Sehen Sie **dies** neue Auto **dort**?*
> ***Dieses** Kind **da** ist die Tochter unseres Lehrers.*

D 443 The demonstrative pronoun may also be intensified in its function by

---

[1] In most instances, the shortened form **dies** is replaced by **das** in colloquial usage: *Das ist
ein interessantes Buch. Zieh doch nicht **das** dunkle Kleid an!*

234

the word **eben**, which may be spelled together with **dies** as one word if it precedes **dies** and if **dies** is uninflected. **Eben** itself is never inflected.[1]

> *Dieses Kleid ist wirklich elegant. — Ja, **ebendies** (**dies eben**) wollte ich auch sagen.*
>
> *Kann ich Ihnen helfen? Der Herr Direktor hat jetzt leider keine Zeit. — Aber mit **eben diesem** muß ich sprechen!*

When **eben** intensifies a demonstrative adjective, the adjective is always inflected and usually preceded by **eben** (but not spelled as one word). It is possible, however, for **eben** to follow the noun:[1] **D 444**

> *Wir wollen mit **eben diesem** Zug (mit **diesem** Zug **eben**) fahren.*
> *Über **eben diese** Worte (über **diese** Worte **eben**) habe ich mich besonders geärgert.*

The neuter form **dies** or **dieses** may also refer to masculine and feminine singular and to plural nouns in the predicate nominative [→ H 460 ff.]. Such forms are often replaced by **das** [→ D 430]. **D 445**

> *Dies (**das**) ist Herr Müller.*
> *Ist **dies** (**das**) die neue Radiostation?*
> *Dieses (**dies, das**) sind die Töchter meines Kollegen.*

Similarly **dies** or **dieses** may also refer to the entire previous statement; again, **das** is often used in such expressions. **D 446**

> *Ich glaube nicht, daß das Wetter morgen sehr gut sein wird. — Ja, **dies** (**dieses, das**) wollte ich gerade auch sagen.*
> *Er wird die Prüfung sicher gut bestehen. — Natürlich, **dies** (**das**) steht außer Frage.*

Sometimes the demonstrative adjective **dies-** indicates something generally known, usually with a pejorative connotation: **D 447**

> *Hüten Sie sich vor **diesen** Leuten; man kann ihnen nicht trauen.*
> *Was soll ich schon mit **diesem** alten Wagen anfangen?*
> *Was kann man schließlich von **diesem** Herrn Mayer erwarten?*
> *Ich halte nicht viel von **dieser** dummen Politik.*

Generally speaking, the demonstrative ADJECTIVE **dies-** is preferred in **D 448**

---

[1] The word **gerade** may be used in a similar fashion to intensify the demonstrative pronoun or adjective, normally occurring before the demonstrative: *gerade dies — gerade dieses Kleid.*

German, especially in colloquial language, even where English uses *that*. As an indefinite demonstrative PRONOUN, on the other hand, German will often use **das** where English prefers *this*.

The Demonstrative jen-

D 450   The demonstrative **jen-er** (**-es, -e**; plural **-e**) also points to something known or previously mentioned. It occurs either as a demonstrative pronoun or a demonstrative adjective, and has the same declensional pattern as **dies-** [→ D 440]. It does not, however, occur uninflected.

D 451   Generally speaking, **jen-** is used far less frequently than **dies-**, especially in colloquial language, except to differentiate between two items [→ D 455 ff.]. By itself, it is primarily a literary form and refers to people or things more distant in either time or space, or in general more foreign to the speaker:

> *In jenen alten Zeiten herrschten ganz andere Sitten.*
> *Jenes ferne Land blieb lange von der westlichen Kultur unberührt.*
> *An jene Dinge erinnere ich mich nicht gerne.*

D 452   A form of **jen-** may also be used to anticipate a following relative clause:

> *Wir sprechen nicht von **jenen, die immer nur kritisieren wollen.***

D 453   Sometimes **jen-** may also be used to indicate something generally known. The explanation to which the demonstrative pronoun or adjective refers appears in the same sentence unit as an attribute or an attributive clause. In contrast to a similar use of **dies-** [→ D 447], however, **jen-** does not connote any negative attitude on the part of the speaker:

> *Sie besitzt **jene** Zurückhaltung **der Norddeutschen**.*
> *Es herrschte **jene** eigenartige Stimmung, **die man oft vor Gewittern** empfindet.*
> *Er zeigte uns gegenüber **jenes** Benehmen, **das schüchternen Menschen** eigen ist.*

D 454   Like **dies-** [→ D 443], **jen-** may also be intensified by **eben**:[1]

> *Eben jenen Anzug will ich kaufen.*
> *Müssen Sie mit **eben jenem** Herrn (mit **jenem** Herrn **eben**) sprechen?*
> *Eben über jene Worte habe ich mich geärgert.*

---

[1] Again, **gerade** may be used in a similar fashion.

Forms of **jen-** are used coupled with **dies-** to differentiate between two D 455
things, places, or people. This is mainly a literary usage. **Dies-** then
refers to the one closer at hand, **jen-** to the one farther away:

> *Wem gehören die beiden Häuser hier? —* **Dieses** *gehört uns und* **jenes**
> (colloquial: *das andere*) *gehört unseren Freunden.*
> *Ich kaufe* **diese** *Äpfel,* **jene** (colloquial: *die anderen*) *sind mir zu teuer.*

The differences may be made even clearer by using the adverbs **hier, da,** D 456
and **dort**:

> *Wem gehören beiden Häuser? —* **Dieses hier** *gehört uns und* **jenes dort**
> (colloquial: *das dort*) *gehört unseren Freunden.*
> *Ich kaufe* **diese** *Äpfel* **da,** **jene dort** (colloquial: *die dort*) *sind mir zu teuer.*

Similarly, **jen-** refers to the first-mentioned item in a pair (i.e. the one D 457
further removed in time, the former), and **dies-** to the last-mentioned
(i.e. the one closest in time, the latter):

> *Dort kommen Herr Meyer und Herr Müller.* **Dieser** (i.e. Mr. Müller)
> *ist ein Freund von mir,* **jenen** (i.e. Mr. Meyer) *kann ich nicht aus-*
> *stehen.*

To distinguish between two people or things, however, the expressions D 460
der eine and **der andere** are usually preferred [→ E 649]. **Der eine** is used
in the sense of **dieser**, referring to the one closer at hand (the latter),
der andere in the sense of **jener**, to indicate the one further away (the
former):[1]

> *Robert und Paul sind zwei Freunde von mir.* **Der eine** (i.e. *dieser, Paul*)
> *geht noch in die Schule,* **der andere** (i.e. *jener, Robert*) *studiert schon*
> *Medizin.*

In official bureaucratic language, **der erstere** and **der letztere** are often D 461
used to differentiate between two previously mentioned items. The
reference is to the sequence in which the items occurred [→ E 390,
E 715]:

> *Der Bundestag verhandelte gestern über mehrere Gesetzvorschläge*
> *zum Verkehrsrecht und zur Rentenversicherung. Über* **erstere**
> *konnte man sich schnell einigen, über* **die letzteren** *kam es zu*
> *einer langen und lebhaften Debatte.*

---

[1] Note that the sequence is the reverse of the order in which the items originally occurred.

D 465   Pairs of demonstrative pronouns like **der und jener, dieser und jener, dies und das** are used to designate something indefinite or unimportant:

> *Was hat er dir erzählt? — Ach, **dies und das**, aber nichts Wichtiges.*
> *Ich habe **diesen und jenen** (**den und jenen**) im Theater getroffen, aber niemanden, der dich interessieren könnte.*

The Demonstrative derselbe

D 470   The demonstratives **derselbe, dasselbe, dieselbe** (plural **dieselben**) are composites of the article and **selb-**. Together, they may be used as demonstrative pronouns or as adjectives to indicate the identity of several persons or things. The first part follows the declension of the definite article [→ D 305], the second follows weak (secondary) adjective declension [→ E 120]:[1]

	SINGULAR			PLURAL
	masculine	neuter	feminine	masc./ntr./fem.
NOM.: ACC.:	derselbe denselben	dasselbe dasselbe	dieselbe dieselbe	dieselben dieselben
DAT.:	demselben	demselben	derselben	denselben
GEN.:	desselben	desselben	derselben	derselben

> *Wir wohnten in **demselben** Hotel wie im letzten Jahr.*
> *Mein Freund kam zu **derselben** Zeit zurück wie ich.*

D 471   In those cases where the definite article is capable of entering into a contracted form with the preposition [→ D 307, D 335 ff., F 050], **selb-** is separated from the article:

> *Wir wohnten **im selben** Hotel im letzten Jahr.*
> *Mein Freund kam **zur selben** Zeit zurück wie ich.*

---

[1] Note that because of the adjective endings, feminine and plural forms are *not* identical in the nom./acc.

238

Instead of **selb-**, forms of **selbig-** or **nämlich-** are occasionally used; how- ever, these words have an old-fashioned flavor and occur less and less frequently. They are not combined with the article: D 475

> *Kaufe dir diesen Hut! Ich habe mir den **nämlichen** gekauft.*

Note that **derselbe**, etc. indicates identity: D 477

> *Wir sind beide aus **derselben** Stadt* (i.e. from one city).
> *Wir haben nur ein Glas; wir müssen beide aus **demselben** Glas trinken.*
> *Sie besitzt nur ein Kleid; sie hat also jeden Tag **dasselbe** Kleid an.*

The adjective **gleich** is used to express similarity: D 478

> *Meine Freundin trägt das **gleiche** Kleid wie ich, nur hat ihres einen weißen Kragen.*
> *Er hat sich den **gleichen** Wagen gekauft, den mein Vater schon seit langem fährt.*

With concepts, identity and similarity may coincide. In this case either **selb-** or **gleich** may be used: D 479

> *Wir sind beide **derselben** (**der gleichen**) Meinung.*
> *Die beiden Züge kamen zur **selben** (**gleichen**) Zeit an.*

The Demonstrative selbst (selber)

The undeclined demonstrative **selbst** or **selber** follows a noun or pro- noun and acts as an intensifier, excluding all other persons or things: D 480

> *Ich habe ihn **selbst** gefragt.*
> *Mein Freund **selbst** wird morgen mit Ihnen sprechen.* (*Mein Freund wird morgen **selbst** mit Ihnen sprechen*).
> *Ich **selber** muß diese Arbeit machen.* (*Ich muß diese Arbeit **selber** machen.*)

For the use of *selbst* or *selber* as distinguished from reflexives (or as an intensifier of reflexives) → D 170–1.   D 481

In compounds with other words, only **selbst** may be used: D 482

selbstverständlich, selbstredend, selbstgemacht, selbstgefällig, Selbstgespräch

If **selbst** precedes a sentence unit, it acts as an attribute of rank   D 483

239

[→ J 180, 185] similar to **sogar**, and emphasizes this particular sentence unit in a special or unusual way. It corresponds to English "even":[1]

Selbst mein bester Freund konnte mir hier nicht helfen.

Selbst in dieser kleinen Stadt finden regelmäßig Konzerte statt.

Er wird selbst mit dir nicht über seine Sorgen sprechen. (Note that **selbst** refers to **dir** — not even with you.)

The Demonstrative derjenige

D 485   The demonstratives **derjenige, dasjenige, diejenige** (plural **diejenigen**) are used, especially in formal language, if some confusion may arise due to the identity of the article and the demonstratives **der, das, die. Derjenige** etc. is declined in the same manner as **derselbe** [→ D 470], i.e. the first part follows the declension of the definite article [→ D 305], whereas **-jenig-** follows the secondary (weak) adjective declension [→ E 120]. **Derjenige** may occur either as a pronoun or as an adjective, and refers to the following relative clause:

*Die Polizei sucht **denjenigen**, der das Verbrechen begangen hat.*

*Ich helfe **demjenigen** Schüler, der seine Arbeit immer regelmäßig macht.*

D 486   If the demonstrative pronoun and the relative pronoun are in the same case, the forms of **derjenige** plus the relative pronoun may be replaced by **wer, wen,** and **wem** for persons and **was** for objects [→ J 077, 156]:

derjenige, der	} **wer**	*denjenigen, den*	} **wen**	
diejenige, die		*diejenige, die*		
diejenigen, die		*diejenigen, die*		
demjenigen, dem	} **wem**	*dasjenige, das* (Nom. & Acc.)	} **was**	
derjenigen, der				
denjenigen, denen		*diejenige, die* (Nom. & Acc. Pl.)		

Wer diese Frage beanworten kann, soll die Hand heben.

Wen wir heute getroffen haben, kannst du nicht erraten.

Was mich an ihm ärgert, ist sein schlechtes Benehmen.

The Demonstrative solch-

D 490   The demonstrative **solch-** indicates a quality, intensity, or degree in a general way, without designating it specifically. It may be used either as

---

[1] See also G 440.

a pronoun or, more frequently, as an attributive adjective. As a pronoun, it follows the declensional pattern of **dieser** [→ D 440]:

> *Hast du schon einmal **solchen** Wein getrunken? —*
> *Nein, **solchen** habe ich noch nicht getrunken.*

As an adjective, it follows adjectival declensions [→ E 100 ff.], with   D 491
primary (strong) endings if there is no article, after an uninflected
indefinite article, or after definite and indefinite numerical adjectives,
but with secondary (weak) endings after **jeder, alle**, and after inflected indefinite articles:

Primary
> *Ein Kind **solcher** Eltern sollte sich besser benehmen.*
> *Ein **solches** Haus ist heute nicht mehr modern.*
> *Ich habe drei **solche** zu Hause.*
> *Das Lesen **vieler solcher** Texte ist sehr anstrengend.*

Secondary
> *__Jeder solche__ Sonnentag ist für Bauern ein Segen.*
> *In **einem solchen** Zimmer wohne ich gern.*
> *Ich habe noch **keine solchen** Blumen gesehen.*

Solch may occur uninflected before a descriptive adjective:[1]   D 492

> *Ich habe noch nie **solch** interessante Bücher gelesen.*
> *Bei **solch** großem Fleiß sollte er am Ende des Schuljahres seine Prüfung*
> *gut bestehen können.*

It is always uninflected if it stands before the indefinite article:

> *Ich wohne gern in **solch** einem modernen Hotel (in einem **solchen***
> *modernen Hotel).*
> *__Solch__ einen Mantel, wie du ihn hast, möchte ich mir auch kaufen.*

In colloquial usage, **solch-** is often replaced by **so**, occurring either   D 493
before or after the indefinite article, and either with or without a descriptive adjective:

> *ein **so** altes Haus, **so** ein altes Haus, solch ein altes Haus*
> *Ich möchte auch **so** einen Mantel haben.[2]*
> *Hast du schon einmal in **so** einem Hotel gewohnt?*
> *__So__ ein gutes Geschäft wie heute habe ich noch nie gemacht.*

---

[1] The descriptive adjective itself has primary (strong) endings when **solch** is uninflected:
Bei solch großem Fleiß . . . After an inflected form of **solch-**, usage fluctuates. The adjective
may have either primary (strong) or secondary (weak) endings: *Wo haben Sie solche schöne*
(schönen) Blumen gefunden? For a more detailed discussion of adjective endings, → E 150 ff.

[2] If there is no descriptive adjective, **so** always precedes the indefinite article.

D 494 The phrase **so etwas** (colloquially **so was**) is used to replace **ein solches** to refer to a general concept:

> *So etwas habe ich noch nie gehört.*
> *Können Sie sich so was vorstellen?*

Demonstrative Adverbs

D 495 Compounds of **da(r)-** with a preposition are used as demonstrative adverbs, if the first part of the compound is stressed: **dáfür, dámit, dázu,** etc. For the formation and use of these demonstrative adverbs, the same rules apply as for the personal pronouns [→ D 040 ff.]. There are no contractions, however [→ D 041]. These compounds obtain their demonstrative character only through the stress. The adverbs point to a given situation:

> *Weißt du, daß dein Vater heute kommt? Nein, dámit habe ich nicht gerechnet.*
> *Kaufst du dir einen Fotoapparat? Nein, dáfür habe ich kein Geld.*

D 496 Note the difference:

> *Mein Vater gab mir zehn Mark und ich kaufte mir ein Buch dafür.*
> (I bought a book with it.)
> *Mein Vater gab mir nur eine Mark. Dáfür konnte ich mir kein Buch kaufen.* (I couldn't buy a book with that!)

D 497 Compounds of **hier-** with a preposition are also considered as demonstrative adverbs, for example **hierbei, hierunter, hiermit, hiervon, hierzu,** etc.[1] These, however, do not refer to persons or things, but only to concepts, processes, or general logical connections:

> *Ich kann Ihnen die Grammatik nicht erklären, denn hiervon verstehe ich nichts.*
> *Mein Vater hat mir diesen Monat kein Geld geschickt. Hierdurch bin ich in große Schwierigkeiten geraten.*
> *Hiermit übersende ich Ihnen die monatliche Abrechnung.*
> *Hat der Direktor etwas über die neue Fabrik gesagt? Nein, hierüber hat er nicht gesprochen.*

---

[1] The use of **hie-** is archaic and rarely occurs in modern German.

RELATIVE PRONOUNS

A relative pronoun introduces an attributive clause [→ J 145] which modifies a noun or a pronoun.   D 500

Since the relative pronoun replaces the noun or pronoun for which it stands, it must have the SAME NUMBER and the same grammatical GENDER as the noun or pronoun to which it refers. We call this noun or pronoun the ANTECEDENT of the relative pronoun.   D 501

The declensional form (i.e. the CASE) of the relative pronoun, on the other hand, depends on the FUNCTION which it performs within the attributive (relative) clause [→ D 515].   D 502

The most frequently used relative pronouns are **der, das, die** and their inflectional forms; **wer** and **was** are also used as relative pronouns in special functions [→ D 550 ff.]. The forms of the relative pronoun **welch-** [→ D 570 ff.] are used rather infrequently in modern German.   D 503

The Relative Pronouns der, das, die

The relative pronouns **der, das, die** (plural **die**) are used in almost all instances. Their declensional forms correspond to those of the demonstrative pronoun **der, das, die** [→ D 420] in all cases except for the genitive plural, for which only the form **deren** exists.   D 510

Declensional Forms of Relative Pronouns   D 515

	SINGULAR			PLURAL
	masculine	neuter	feminine	masc./ntr./fem.
NOM.:	. . ., der	. . ., das	. . ., die	. . ., die
ACC.:	. . ., den	. . ., das	. . ., die	. . ., die
DAT.:	. . ., dem	. . ., dem	. . ., der	. . ., denen
GEN.:	. . ., dessen	. . ., dessen	. . ., deren	. . ., deren

243

*Kennen Sie den Mann, **der** mich gestern besucht hat?*
*(**Der** Mann hat mich gestern besucht.)*
*Der Mann, **den** du gesehen hast, wohnt nicht mehr hier.*
*(Du hast **den** Mann gesehen.)*
*Hier ist die Adresse des Herrn, **dem** dein Vater schreiben will.*
*(Dein Vater will **dem** Herrn schreiben.)*
*Dort sind meine Freunde, mit **denen** ich zur Schule ging.*
(Ich ging mit meinen Freunden zur Schule.)
*Die Mitarbeiter, **deren** wir heute gedenken, waren zehn Jahre hier tätig.*
*(Wir gedenken **der** Mitarbeiter.)*

D 520   If the relative pronoun replaces an attributive genitive, it does not actually function as a genuine pronoun, but rather as a possessive attribute before the noun to which the genitive attribute belongs. The noun then appears without article [→ D 217, D 352]:

*Dort steht das Haus, **dessen Bild** ich dir gezeigt habe.*
*(Ich habe dir **das Bild des Hauses** gezeigt.)*
*Der Schüler, **dessen Vater** der Lehrer schrieb, ist krank.*
*(Der Lehrer schrieb **dem Vater des Schülers**.)*

D 521   If the noun, which follows the relative pronoun in the genitive, is preceded by a descriptive adjective, the adjective has primary (strong) declensional endings [→ E 110 ff.]:

*Mein Freund, **dessen** ältester Sohn in Berlin wohnt, besuchte mich heute.*
(Der älteste Sohn meines Freundes wohnt in Berlin.)
*Die Schüler, **deren** gute Arbeiten gelobt wurden, waren sehr stolz.*
(Die guten Arbeiten der Schüler wurden gelobt.)

D 522   The relative pronoun in the genitive often replaces a possessive adjective:

*Ich habe den Schriftsteller, **dessen** Bücher ich gut kenne, in Paris getroffen.*
*(Ich kenne **seine** Bücher gut.)*

D 525   If the word, which the relative pronoun replaces, functions as a prepositional object in the dependent clause, the preposition stands before the relative pronoun at the beginning of the relative clause:

*Der Mann, **mit dem** ich gesprochen habe, ist mein Freund.*
*(Ich habe **mit dem Mann** gesprochen.)*
*Die Familie, **bei der** er wohnt, ist sehr freundlich.*
*(Er wohnt **bei der Familie**.)*

Instead of a preposition with a relative pronoun in the dative, a com-   D 526
bination of **wo(r)-** plus the preposition may sometimes be used, if the
reference is to things or places [→ **da(r)-** plus preposition, D 040 ff.]:

> *Hier ist das Hotel, **in dem** ich gewohnt habe.*
> *Hier ist das Hotel, **worin** ich gewohnt habe.*
>
> *Das ist die Feder, **mit der** ich schreibe.*
> *Das ist die Feder, **womit** ich schreibe.*

To indicate location, the adverb **wo** [→ E 860 ff.] may be used by itself   D 527
to replace the preposition **in** followed by a relative pronoun in the
dative:

> *Hier ist das Hotel, **in dem** ich gewohnt habe.*
> *Hier ist das Hotel, **wo** ich gewohnt habe.*
>
> *Er will mir die Schule zeigen, **in der** er Deutsch lernt.*
> *Er will mir die Schule zeigen, **wo** er Deutsch lernt.*

The adverb **wo** is always used when we refer to names of places or   D 528
countries:

> *Er fährt morgen nach Paris, **wo** er drei Jahre studiert hat.*
> *Wir sind gestern aus Italien zurückgekommen, **wo** wir den Sommer
> verbracht haben.*

If the relative pronoun combines relative clauses with the personal   D 530
pronouns **ich, du, wir,** or **ihr,** and if these personal pronouns are the
subject of the relative clause, the pronouns are repeated in order to
obtain agreement with the verb [→ H 275 ff., J 151.9]:

> **Ich**, *der **ich** schon zehn Jahre hier wohne, verlasse diese Stadt nicht.*
> *Er fragt **dich**, der **du** seine Sorgen kennst, um Rat.*
> *Er hat **uns**, die **wir** ihm geholfen haben, gedankt.*[1]
> *Der Lehrer ist mit **euch**, die **ihr** so fleißig seid, zufrieden.*

If the personal pronouns in the singular (**ich, du**) are not repeated, the   D 531
verb in the relative clause has the inflectional ending of the 3rd person
singular:

> **Ich**, *der schon zehn Jahre hier wohnt, verlasse diese Stadt nicht.*
> *Er fragt **dich**, der seine Sorgen kennt, um Rat.*

---

[1] For the 1st person plural, the pronoun may be omitted without changing the sentence:
Er hat uns, die ihm geholfen haben, gedankt.

D 532 The same happens in sentences, where the subject is the personal pronoun **ich** or **du**, if the impersonal pronoun **es** occurs as a predicate
nominative [→ D 090]:

> *Ich bin **es**, **der** geklopft hat.*
> *Warst **du es**, **der** mich um das Buch gebeten hatte?*

D 533 The personal pronoun **Sie** must appear in the relative clause. By the
choice of the relative pronoun, we distinguish between singular and
plural, as well as between masculine and feminine:

> SINGULAR: *Ich danke Ihnen, **der** (**die**) Sie mir geholfen haben.*
> PLURAL: *Ich danke Ihnen, **die** Sie mir geholfen haben.*

D 540 If a relative clause refers to a noun or personal pronoun in the plural,
similarities between the people or things referred to may be emphasized
by the pronoun **alle** [→ D 780], which occurs after the relative pronoun
and has the same declensional form:

> *Er hatte drei Söhne, **die alle** im gleichen Jahr gestorben sind.*
> *Die Leute, **denen allen** der Film gefallen hatte (**denen** der Film **allen***
>   *gefallen hatte), gingen zufrieden nach Hause.*
> *Wir, **die** (**wir**) **alle** in diesem Haus wohnen, kennen uns gut.*

D 545 A relative clause may refer to the demonstrative pronouns **der, das, die;**
die [→ D 410]. In the genitive plural, the demonstrative pronoun then
has the form **derer** [→ D 436]:

> *Bist du **die**, **der** ich das Buch gegeben habe?*
> *Kennen Sie **den**, **dessen** Arbeit den ersten Preis gewonnen hat?*
> *Das Leben **derer**, **die** blind sind, ist sehr schwer.*

D 546 If a relative clause has a demonstrative pronoun as its antecedent, the
demonstrative often has the extended form with **-jenig-** [→ D 485]:

> *Bist du **diejenige**, **der** ich das Buch gegeben habe?*
> *Kennen Sie **denjenigen**, **dessen** Arbeit den ersten Preis gewonnen hat?*
> *Das Leben **derjenigen**, **die** blind sind, ist sehr schwer.*

The Relative Pronouns wer and was

D 550 The relative pronoun **wer** (**wen, wem, wessen**) designates persons who
are not precisely defined. It corresponds to English "he who, whoever,

246

anyone who." The relative clause usually appears before the main clause, which often begins with the demonstrative pronoun **der** (**den, dem, dessen**) [→ D 486, J 157]:

> *Wer den ganzen Tag arbeitet,* **der** *ist abends sehr müde.*
> *Wen wir lieben,* **den** *möchten wir nicht verlieren.*
> *Wer mir hilft,* **dem** *bin ich dankbar.*

If the relative pronoun is in the same case as the noun or pronoun in the following clause,[1] to which it refers, the main clause may begin without the demonstrative pronoun: **D 551**

> *Wer den ganzen Tag arbeitet, ist abends sehr müde.*
> *Wen wir lieben, möchten wir nicht gern verlieren.*

The demonstrative pronoun is not used if the relative clause follows the main clause: **D 552**

> *Glücklich ist,* **wer** *vergißt, was nicht mehr zu ändern ist!*

The adverbs **auch, immer,** and **auch immer** may be used after the relative pronoun **wer** to intensify its general character: **D 555**

> *Wer mir* **auch immer** *hilft, dem gebe ich eine Belohnung.*

The relative pronoun **was** is used if the antecedents of the relative clause are indefinite pronouns or numerals, or adjectives used as neuter nouns: **D 560**

> *Ist das* **das Beste,** **was** *Sie für mich tun können?*
> *Du hast* **etwas** *gemacht,* **was** *verboten ist.*
> *Er schenkt ihr* **alles,** **was** *sie sich wünscht.*
> *Wir wissen* **nichts,** **was** *dich interessieren könnte.*
> *Es war* **wenig,** **was** *Richard von seiner Reise erzählte.*
>   (**Was** *Richard von seiner Reise erzählte, war sehr wenig.*)

As the last sentence above indicates, **was** may also be used in the sense of "that which" or "whatever"; in this sense, it may be reinforced by **auch, immer,** or **immer auch**:[2]   **D 561**

> *Was Sie erzählten, war sehr interessant.*
> *Was* **immer** *er* **auch** *sagt, glaube ich ihm nicht.*

---

1 Such relative clauses are either subject clauses or object clauses [→ H 270–2, H 320].

2 The same intensification may be used after interrogative adverbs: *wo auch, wann immer, wie auch immer,* etc.

D 562   If the relative clause refers to the entire concept contained in the main clause, the relative pronoun **was** is also used:

> *Er war sehr krank,* **was** *uns allen leid tat.*
> *Mein Freund zeigte mir die Sehenswürdigkeiten der Stadt,* **was** *mich sehr freute.*

D 563   Compare the following:

> *Er hatte* **ein Buch** *geschrieben,*   *(Viele Leute haben* **das Buch** *gelesen,*
> **das** *viele Leute gelesen haben.*   **das** *er geschrieben hat.)*

> **Er hatte ein Buch geschrieben,**   *(Viele Leute haben gelesen,* **daß er**
> **was** *viele Leute gelesen haben.*   **ein Buch geschrieben hat.)**

D 565   If a relative clause refers to the entire situation referred to in the main clause, and the relative pronoun must appear together with a preposition, the adverb **wo(r)-** plus the preposition is used instead of the relative pronoun [→ D 040 ff., D 526]:

> *Ich ging mit meinem Freund durch die Stadt,* **wobei** *er mir alle Sehens-würdigkeiten erklärte.*
> *Er half uns bei der Arbeit,* **worum** *wir ihn gebeten hatten.*

D 566   The word **wie** may be used in a relative function, if the relative clause modifies an indefinite predicate complement or an adverbial phrase:

> *In der Form,* **wie** *er sich entschuldigte, lag fast etwas Beleidigendes.*
> *Es regnete in einem Ausmaß,* **wie** *es für diese Jahreszeit ganz unge-wöhnlich war.*

The Relative Pronoun welcher

D 570   The relative pronoun **welch-** follows the declensional pattern of **dieser** [→ D 440], but has no genitive forms. These relative pronouns are rather rarely used in modern German.

D 571   Forms of **welch-** are used as relative pronouns primarily to avoid mis-understandings which might arise if several nouns or pronouns in one sentence are modified by relative clauses:

> *Anna spielt nicht mehr mit Peter,* **der** *den Ball,* **welcher** *ihr gehörte, verloren hatte.*

248

Such constructions are considered inelegant, however, and should be avoided.

Another use for **welch-** as a relative pronoun in written language[1] is to avoid repetitions of identical forms: D 572

> *Sie ist die, **welche** die Kinder erzogen hat.* (Instead of *Sie ist die, **die** die Kinder erzogen hat.*)
>
> *Sind Sie nicht der, **welcher** der Frau das Geld gab?* (Instead of *Sind Sie nicht der, **der** der Frau das Geld gab?*)
>
> *Er plante ein großes Unternehmen, **welches** das Gesicht des ganzen Stadtteils ändern sollte.*

Forms of **welch-** may be used attributively with a noun which sum-   D 573
marizes the content of the situation described in the preceding clause:

> *Ich schrieb ihm, er müsse das Geld zu dem festgesetzten Termin zurück-zahlen, von **welcher** Forderung ich nicht abgehen würde.*

POSSESSIVES

Possessives indicate a relationship of ownership or belonging between   D 600
one person or thing and another person or thing. Possessives may be
used as independent pronouns or attributively as limiting adjectives
[→ D 280 ff.]:

Das Haus gehört mir.	*Es ist **mein** Haus.*
Sie ist Französin.	*Frankreich ist **ihr** Vaterland.*
Der Baum hat viele Blüten.	***Seine** Blüten sind weiß.*
*Hier ist **unser** Sohn.*	*Wo ist **deiner**?*

Possessive adjectives precede the noun; they take the place of the article   D 601
and follow the declensional pattern of the indefinite article [→ D 310].

The following table shows the declensional pattern of the possessive   D 602
adjectives and their relationships to personal pronouns:

---

[1] In spoken language, the repetition is less objectionable, since stress and intonation serve to distinguish between the different functions of identical words.

249

PERSONAL PRONOUN		SINGULAR			PLURAL
		masc.	neuter	fem.	masc./ntr./fem.
ich	NOM.	mein	mein	meine	meine
	ACC.	meinen	mein	meine	meine
	DAT.	meinem	meinem	meiner	meinen
	GEN.	meines	meines	meiner	meiner
du	NOM.	dein	dein	deine	deine
	ACC.	deinen	dein	deine	deine
	DAT.	deinem	deinem	deiner	deinen
	GEN.	deines	deines	deiner	deiner
er, es, man	NOM.	sein	sein	seine	seine
	ACC.	seinen	sein	seine	seine
	DAT.	seinem	seinem	seiner	seinen
	GEN.	seines	seines	seiner	seiner
sie	NOM.	ihr	ihr	ihre	ihre
	ACC.	ihren	ihr	ihre	ihre
	DAT.	ihrem	ihrem	ihrer	ihren
	GEN.	ihres	ihres	ihrer	ihrer
wir	NOM.	unser	unser	unsre[1]	unsre
	ACC.	unsren[1]	unser	unsre	unsre
	DAT.	unsrem	unsrem	unsrer	unsren
	GEN.	unsres	unsres	unsrer	unsrer
ihr	NOM.	euer	euer	eure[1]	eure
	ACC.	euren[1]	euer	eure	eure
	DAT.	eurem	eurem	eurer	euren
	GEN.	eures	eures	eurer	eurer
sie	NOM.	ihr	ihr	ihre	ihre
	ACC.	ihren	ihr	ihre	ihre
	DAT.	ihrem	ihrem	ihrer	ihren
	GEN.	ihres	ihres	ihrer	ihrer
Sie	NOM.	Ihr	Ihr	Ihre	Ihre
	ACC.	Ihren	Ihr	Ihre	Ihre
	DAT.	Ihrem	Ihrem	Ihrer	Ihren
	GEN.	Ihres	Ihres	Ihrer	Ihrer

(Rows grouped: **ich**, **du**, **er, es, man**, **sie** under SINGULAR; **wir**, **ihr**, **sie**, **Sie** under PLURAL.)

[1] **Unser** and **euer** lose the **-e-** of the stem, if the ending begins with an **-e**. The full forms, however, are also possible: **unseren, eueren,** etc. (but not **euerer**). It is also possible for the endings **-en** and **-em** to lose the **-e-**: **unsern, unserm, euern, euerm.**

250

As the bold-faced endings indicate, the declension of the possessive adjective follows the pattern of the indefinite article **ein**. It is identical with that of the demonstrative **dieser** [→ D 440], except in the NOMINATIVE MASCULINE and the NOMINATIVE/ACCUSATIVE SINGULAR, where there is NO ENDING AT ALL [cf. indefinite article, D 312].[1]

D 603

When used as pronouns, the possessives have full declensional endings in all genders and cases [→ D 620 ff.].

D 604

Notice the difference between the personal pronoun **ihr** (fem. sgl. dat., 2nd ps. pl. nom.) and the possessive adjective **ihr**:

D 606

> *ich zeige **ihr** ein Buch; **ihr** arbeitet, **ihr** kamt;*
> ***ihr** Vater, **ihr** Kind*

Similarly, we must distinguish between the genitive of the personal pronouns **meiner, deiner, seiner, ihrer, unser, euer, Ihrer,** and the corresponding forms of the possessives [→ D 073–4]:

D 607

> *drei **ihrer** Kinder* (possessive adjective: three of **her** children)
> *Es waren **ihrer** drei* (personal pronoun: three of **them**).
> *Sie gedachten **unser**.*
> *Das ist **unser** Haus.*

We must also differentiate between the possessive adjectives **ihr** (singular), **ihr** (plural), and **Ihr** (polite) [→ D 071]:

D 608

> *Die Mutter liebt **ihr** Kind* (**her**, i.e. the mother's child).
> *Die Eltern lieben **ihr** Kind* (**their**, i.e. the parents' child).
> *Herr Müller, **Ihr** Sohn möchte Sie sprechen*
> (**your**, i.e. Mr. Müller's son).

The CHOICE of the POSSESSIVE ADJECTIVE in the THIRD PERSON (**sein, ihr**) depends on its ANTECEDENT, i.e. the preceding noun to which it refers. **Sein** is used, if the antecedent is masculine and neuter (his, its), **ihr** if the antecedent is feminine or plural (her, their). The ENDINGS, however, depend on the GENDER, NUMBER, and CASE of the NOUN which FOLLOWS and which the possessive adjective modifies:

D 610

---

[1] Because of the similarity of inflectional endings, the indefinite article, **kein**, and the possessive adjectives are often referred to as *ein-words*.

his: *Der Vater liebt **seinen** Sohn, **sein** Kind, **seine** Tochter, **seine** Kinder.*

its: *Das Kind liebt **seinen** Vater, **sein** Brüderchen, **seine** Mutter, **seine** Eltern.*

her: *Die Mutter liebt **ihren** Sohn, **ihr** Kind, **ihre** Tochter, **ihre** Kinder.*

their: *Die Eltern lieben **ihren** Sohn, **ihr** Kind, **ihre** Tochter, **ihre** Kinder.*

D 611 The same principle also applies if the antecedent is an inanimate object. The choice of **sein** or **ihr** is again determined by the gender of the antecedent, even though in English both masculine and feminine forms correspond to "its"; for a plural antecedent, **ihr** must be used.

*Der Tisch und **seine** Farbe:* the table and *its* color

*Das Buch und **seine** Farbe:* the book and *its* color

*Die Lampe und **ihre** Farbe:* the lamp and *its* color

*Die Häuser und **ihre** Farbe:* the houses and *their* color

D 615 If we want to emphasize a relationship of ownership, the adjective **eigen** may be used after the possessive adjective:

*Ich wohne in **meinem eigenen** Haus.*
*Er hat es mit **seinen eigenen** Augen gesehen.*
*Sie hat **ihr eigenes** Kind verlassen.*

D 620 If the possessive is used as an independent pronoun, it may be preceded by the definite article. It then follows the adjective declension with secondary (weak) endings [→ E 120]:

*Hier ist mein Heft. Wo hast du **das deine**?*
*Ich habe meinen Bleistift vergessen. Kannst du mir **den deinen** geben?*
*Grüße deine Frau von **der meinen**!*
*Wir besuchten meine Freunde und **die seinen*** (i.e. my friends and his).

D 621 If the possessive refers to one's family, it is capitalized:

*Grüße bitte die **Deinen** von mir!*
*Ich schreibe heute an die **Meinen**.*
*Wir besuchten meine Freunde und die **Seinen*** (i.e. my friends and his family).

Capitalization also occurs in certain idiomatic usages: D 622

> *Jedem das **Seine**!*

The possessive pronoun with the definite article also has an extended D 625
form with the infix **-ig-**. It is capitalized and usually refers to family.
Other usages are possible, but sound stilted and should be avoided:

> *Ich schreibe heute an die **Meinigen**.*
> *Hier ist mein Heft. Wo ist das **Deinige**?*

If the possessive pronoun is used without an article, it follows the de- D 630
clensional ending of **dieser** [→ D 440] in all cases. [But → D 640]:

> *Hier liegt ein Bleistift. Ist es **deiner**? Ich habe **meinen** in der Tasche.*
> *Hier ist mein Heft. Wo ist **deines**?*

In colloquial language, the abbreviated forms **meins, deins,** etc., may D 631
also be used, if the possessive adjective refers to a neuter noun:

> *Hier ist mein Heft. Wo hast du **deins**?*

The possessive pronoun has NO ENDINGS when it is used as a predicate D 640
nominative [→ D 911] with the verbs **sein, werden,** and **bleiben**, or as a
predicate accusative with verbs like **nennen, heißen,** etc. [→ H 470]:

> *Du bist **mein** und bleibst **mein**.*
> *Das Haus wird morgen **dein**.*
> *Endlich kann ich diesen Ring **mein** nennen!*

If we want to distinguish the possessive relationship of two different D 645
nouns in the third person singular, we use the possessive adjective to
refer to the subject of the sentence, and **dessen** (masc./ntr.) or **deren**
(fem./pl.) to refer to something other than the subject [→ D 435]:

> *Peter spricht mit seinem Freund und **seiner** Schwester*
> (i.e. Peter's sister).
> *Peter spricht mit seinem Freund und **dessen** Schwester*
> (i.e. the friend's sister).
>
> *Anna spricht mit ihrer Freundin und **ihrer** Schwester*
> (i.e. Anna's sister).
> *Anna spricht mit ihrer Freundin und **deren** Schwester*
> (i.e. the girl friend's sister).

253

D 650   In letters, all possessive adjectives referring to the person or persons addressed are capitalized [→ D 024]:

> *Ich habe heute **Deinen** Brief bekommen.*
> *Wie geht es **Euren** Eltern?*

D 655   The adverbial idiom **seinerzeit** (previously, at that time, a long time ago) is always unchanged:

> *Ich habe mir **seinerzeit** vorgenommen, mir einmal die Welt anzusehen.*

D 660   The possessive adjective may be replaced by the so-called dative of possession [→ D 941]:

> ***Mir** klopfte das Herz.*
> *Willst du **dir** die Hände waschen?*

D 665   The possessive adjective may also be replaced by the definite article, if ownership is clearly established [→ D 333]:

> *Er hat **die** Hände in **den** Taschen.*
> *Nimm doch **die** Pfeife aus **dem** Mund!*

INDEFINITE PRONOUNS AND ATTRIBUTES

⤜ *Introduction*

D 700   Indefinite pronouns or attributes are used to indicate persons, things, or concepts which we can not or do not want to define precisely.

D 710   Some of these pronouns ALWAYS indicate PERSONS: **man, jemand, niemand, jedermann, irgendwer**; others ALWAYS indicate THINGS or CONCEPTS: **nichts, etwas**. None of these can be used attributively. [For an exception → D 772.]

D 720   Another group of indefinite pronouns may indicate PERSONS, THINGS, or CONCEPTS; they may also be used attributively as indefinite adjectives.[1]

[1] Most of them function as limiting adjectives [→ D 280 ff.]; some, however, like **einig-, ander-, viel-, wenig-, mehrer-,** are treated like descriptive adjectives. See D 747, D 749, and individual entries.

254

Pronouns or attributes of this type are used to indicate   D 721

> a totality: *all-*, *ganz-*, *sämtlich*
> a large indefinite quantity: *viel-*, *lauter*, *eitel*
> an indefinite quantity: *ander-*
> a small indefinite quantity: *einig-*, *etlich-*, *einzeln-*, *etwas*, *ein bißchen*, *ein paar*, *wenig-*, *manch-*, *mehrer-*
> a partitive number: *jed-*, *jeglich-*
> a single indefinite item: *ein-*
> a nonexisting item: *kein-*

A few words are so similar in usage to indefinite pronouns that they   D 725
should be included here, although they can only be used as attributes:

> *ganz*, *sämtlich-*, *lauter*, *eitel* (archaic)

Beide, which is sometimes treated in this context, is not really an   D 727
indefinite pronoun or attribute. [→ Numerals, E 656–7]

Some indefinite pronouns and attributes have no or incomplete de-   D 730
clensional forms; most of the ones which may be used attributively lack
genitives.

The following indefinite pronouns and attributes have NO DECLENSIONAL   D 731
FORMS:

> *man*, *etwas*, *was*, *nichts*, *ein bißchen*, *ein paar*, *mehr*, *lauter*, *eitel*

The pronoun **jedermann** has only one inflectional form: an **-s** ending in   D 732
the genitive. **Jemand** and **niemand** may occur with or without declensional endings in the accusative and dative.

The other indefinite pronouns or attributes follow the declensional   D 733
pattern of **dieser** [→ D 440].[1] The following, however, may occur with
or without declensional endings:

> *all*, *ganz*, *manch*, *viel*, *wenig*

Some indefinite pronouns or attributes may be used after a definite or   D 734
indefinite article or some other limiting adjective; they then follow the
appropriate adjective declension:

> *ander-*, *ein-*, *einzel-*, *ganz-*, *jeglich-*, *sämtlich-*, *viel-*, *wenig-*

The declension of **irgendwer** follows the pattern of the interrogative   D 735

---

[1] **Ein-** and **kein-**, of course, follow the indefinite article declension [D 310 f.] when used
attributively.

pronoun **wer?** [→ D 215]; **kein-** used attributively follows the declension of **ein** [→ D 311].

D 737   Pronouns which indicate persons have the reflexive pronoun **sich** and the possessive **sein.**

D 740   When an indefinite pronoun is followed by an adjective,[1] this adjective is considered as a noun and is capitalized after **jemand, niemand, irgendwer, alles, etwas, was, einiges, etliches, einzelnes, manches, viel,** and **wenig.** The adjective **ander-,** however, is never capitalized.

D 741   Such adjectives carry PRIMARY (strong) adjective endings [→ E 110] after **irgendwer, nichts, etwas, was,** and after undeclined forms of **jemand, niemand, manch, viel,** and **wenig.**

D 742   These adjectives carry SECONDARY (weak) adjective endings [→ E 120] after **alles, einiges, einzelnes, etliches, jegliches, manches, vieles, weniges,** and inflected forms of **jemand** and **niemand.**

D 745   If an indefinite adjective modifying a noun is followed by another (descriptive) attributive adjective,[1] this second adjective carries PRIMARY endings after **etwas, ein bißchen, ein paar, lauter, manch, viel,** and **wenig,** and after uninflected **ein** or **kein.**

D 746   The descriptive adjective carries SECONDARY endings after **all-, jed-, jeglich-,** and inflected forms of **ein-** or **kein-.**

D 747   In general, descriptive adjectives following **ander-, einig-, einzeln-, etlich-, viel-,** and **wenig-** have the same ending as the indefinite adjective itself [→ E 150 ff.]. After **manch-,** usage varies, with secondary forms predominating in the singular [→ E 153–4].

D 749   **Indefinite Pronouns** (See Table on pp. 258–9)

D 750   **man**

N.	man
A.	einen
D.	einem
G.	—

The indefinite pronoun **man** always refers to persons. It exists only in the nominative. For the dative and the accusative, the corresponding forms of **ein-** [→ D 800] are used. There are no plural forms; after **man** the verb is in the 3rd person singular. In a second occurrence in

---

[1] See chapter E for details on adjective endings.

the same sentence, the word **man** is repeated and not, as in English, replaced by *he*.

There is no genitive; instead the possessive adjective **sein** is used.

> *Sonntags arbeitet **man** nicht.*
> *Wenn **man** fleißig ist, kann **man** viel lernen.*
> *Peter ist unhöflich. Er grüßt **einen** nicht und gibt **einem** nicht die Hand.*
> *Da kann **man seine** Geduld verlieren.*

jedermann

N.	jedermann
A.	jedermann
D.	jedermann
G.	jedermanns

The indefinite pronoun **jedermann** always refers   D 755
to persons. It exists only in the singular and has
no declensional forms except for the genitive. The
verb appears in the 3rd person singular. The
genitive always precedes the noun to which it
refers; this noun then loses the article [→ D 352].

> *In unserem Dorf geht sonntags **jedermann** in die Kirche.*
> *Er grüßt **jedermann** auf der Straße.*
> *Er erzählt **jedermann** seine Sorgen.*
> *Moderne Musik ist nicht **jedermanns** Geschmack.*

jemand, niemand

N.	jemand
A.	jemand(en)
D.	jemand(em)
G.	jemand(e)s

The indefinite pronouns **jemand** and its negative   D 760
counterpart **niemand** always refer to persons, and
occur only in the singular. The inflectional endings
correspond to the masculine indefinite article, but
may be omitted in the dative and accusative.[1] The
genitive, which is rarely used, precedes the noun which it modifies.

> *Ist **jemand** dort? Nein, **niemand** ist dort.*
> *Wir haben im Garten **niemand**(en) gesehen.*
> *Er spricht mit **jemand**(em).*
> *Dieses Land ist **niemands** Besitz.*

Instead of the genitive, the preposition **von** is often used. In this con-   D 761
struction, the declensional ending of the pronoun may not be omitted:

> *Hier liegt ein Buch **von jemandem**! Wem gehört es?*

---

[1] The uninflected forms occur more frequently in the accusative than in the dative, and more frequently for **jemand** than for **niemand.**

Table of Indefinite Pronouns and Attributes

	INDEFINITE PRONOUNS			
	For People	For Things	Declension	Declension of Nominal Adjective
man	*man*	—	—	—
jedermann	*jedermann*	—	gen. only	—
jemand	*jemand*	—	acc./dat. opt.	primary
niemand	*niemand*	—	acc./dat. opt.	primary
irgendwer	*irgendwer*	—	like *wer*	primary
	irgend- welche	*irgendwelche*	like *welche*	—
etwas (was)	—	*etwas* (*was*)	—	primary
nichts	—	*nichts*	—	primary
all-	*alle* (*alles*)	*alle, -s*	def. art.	secondary
ander-	*andere*	*andere, -s*	def. art.	—
ein-	*eine, -r*	*ein(e)s*	def. art.	—
	welche	*welche*	(after art. like adj.)	—
ein bißchen	—	*ein bißchen*	—	—
einig-	*einige*	*einige, -s*	def. art.	secondary
einzeln-	*einzelne*	*einzelne, -s*	def. art.	secondary
etlich-	*etliche*	*etliche, -s*	def. art.	secondary
jed-	*jede, -r*	*jedes*	def. art.	secondary
jeglich-	*jegliche, -r*	*jegliches*	adjective	secondary
kein-	*keine, -r*	*keine, -s*	def. art.	—
manch-	*manche, -r*	*manche, -s*	def. art.	secondary
		manch	—	primary
mehrer-	*mehrere*	*mehrere, -s*	def. art.	—
ein paar	*ein paar*	*ein paar*	—	primary
viel-	*viele*	*viel, -e, -es*	def. art.	prim. or sec.
wenig-	*wenige*	*wenig, -e, -es*	def. art.	prim. or sec.
mehr	*mehr*	*mehr*	—	primary
ganz	—	—	—	—
sämtlich-	—	—	—	—
eitel, lauter	—	—	—	—

Declension (by itself)	With Def. Art.	With Indef. Art.	Declension of Descr. Adject.	Paragraph
—	—	—	—	D 750
—	—	—	—	D 755
—	—	—	—	D 760
—	—	—	—	D 760
—	—	—	—	D 765
def. art.	—	—	secondary	D 765
—	—	—	primary	D 770
—	—	—	—	D 775
def. art.	(after *all*-)	—	secondary	D 780
def. art.	secondary	prim. or sec.	like *ander*-	D 795
indef. art.	secondary	—	prim. or sec.	D 800
—	—	—	—	D 800
—	—	—	primary	D 810
def. art.	—	—	fluctuates	D 820
def. art.	secondary	prim. or sec.	like *einzeln*-	D 830
def. art.	—	—	primary	D 835
def. art.	—	prim. or sec.	secondary	D 840
def. art.	—	prim. or sec.	secondary	D 850
indef. art.	—	—	prim. or sec.	D 855
def. art.	—	—	fluctuates	D 860
manch	—	—	primary	D 862
def. art.	—	—	like *mehrer*-	D 865
—	—	—	primary	D 870
like adj.	secondary	—	like *viel*-	D 875
like adj.	secondary	—	like *wenig*-	D 875
—	—	—	primary	D 885
like adj.	secondary	prim. or sec.	like *ganz*-	D 890
like adj.	secondary	—	secondary	D 895
—	—	—	primary	D 896

D 762 If **jemand** or **niemand** is followed by an adjective, the pronoun as a rule appears without inflection. The adjective is then capitalized and carries strong (primary) masculine endings [→ E 110]. Before the adjective **ander-** (never capitalized), **jemand** and **niemand** are almost always uninflected.

> *Das Kind spricht mit **jemand Fremdem*** (or: ***jemandem Fremdem***).[1]
> *Ich habe **niemand Interessanten** gesehen.*
> *Ich möchte mit **jemand anderem** sprechen.*
> *Kannst du **niemand anderen** fragen?*

D 763 In such constructions, the adjectives in the nominative and accusative are sometimes used with neuter declensional endings, even though they refer to persons. In colloquial usage, **anders** may occur in the dative as well:

> *Hast du **jemand Bekanntes** gesehen?*
> ***Niemand anders** kommt dafür in Frage.*
> *Ich habe dich gestern mit **jemand anders** gesehen.*

D 764 The indefinite nature of the pronoun **jemand** may be intensified by the use of **irgend**, written either jointly or separately:

> *Wir werden schon **irgend jemand**(*en*) (***irgendjemanden***) treffen.[2]*

D 765 **irgendwer, irgendwelche**

N.	irgendwer
A.	irgendwen
D.	irgendwem
G.	—
N.	irgendwelche
A.	irgendwelche
D.	irgendwelchen
G.	—

The pronoun **irgendwer** is declined like the interrogative **wer?** in the singular; forms of **irgendwelche** (declined like **welche**) are used in the plural. The genitive is not used. The singular refers to persons only; the plural may be used to refer to things [→ D 803]. Nominal adjectives are rarely used after **irgendwer**; if they occur, they are capitalized and have neuter primary endings [→ E 110]. After **irgendwelche**, they have plural primary endings.

> ***Irgendwer** wollte dich sprechen.*
> *Frage **irgendwen**, aber nicht mich!*

---

[1] The form *mit jemandem Fremden* also exists.
[2] The spelling **irgendjemand** is rejected by some grammarians.

*Sie geht mit **irgendwem** zum Tanzen.*
*Dort kommen **irgendwelche**.*
***Irgendwer Bekanntes** sprach heute im Radio.*
*Gestern sind **irgendwelche Fremde** angekommen.*

Forms without **irgend** occur in colloquial usage in the sense of "some- D 766
one." They are mostly unaccompanied by adjectives except for **ander-**,
which carries masculine primary endings:

*Ich hätte geantwortet, wenn mich **wer** gefragt hätte.*
*Wenn du **wen** sprechen willst, mußt du dich beeilen.*
*Könnte dir vielleicht **wer anderer** helfen?*

etwas

The indefinite pronoun **etwas** (negative **nichts** [→ D 775]) is used for D 770
things or concepts. It is always singular and has no declensional forms.
The short form **was** occurs frequently, especially in colloquial usage.
The following adjective is capitalized (except for **ander-**), and carries
neuter primary endings [→ E 110]:

*Ich habe **etwas** für Sie.*
*Hat er Interesse an **etwas**?*
*Er will dir **was** sagen.*
*Meine Mutter will heute **etwas Gutes** kochen.*
*Haben Sie nicht **was Billigeres**?*
*Er sprach von **etwas anderem**.*

In colloquial language, **etwas Kleines** may be used to refer to a newborn D 771
child:

*Müllers haben letzte Woche **etwas Kleines** (**was Kleines**) bekommen.*

Etwas may be used as an indefinite attribute before singular nouns D 772
designating things or concepts. It has partitive character and corresponds to English "some." The abbreviated form **was** may not be used.
Descriptive adjectives carry primary endings [→ E 110]:

*Geben Sie mir bitte **etwas Brot**!*
*Mit **etwas Geduld** kann man mehr erreichen.*
*Haben Sie **etwas kaltes Wasser**?*

D 773 A PREPOSITIONAL or NOMINAL INFINITIVE may be used after **etwas** [→ B 987]:

> *Haben Sie etwas zu essen?*[1]
> *Hier hast du etwas zum Spielen.*[1]
> *Bring mir was zu lesen!*

D 774 The indefinite character of **etwas** or **was** may be stressed by using **irgend**. **Irgendwas** is spelled as one word, **irgend etwas** must be spelled separately:

> *Kann ich Ihnen mit **irgend etwas** eine Freude machen?*
> *Bring mir **irgendwas** zu lesen!*

nichts

D 775 The indefinite pronoun **nichts** is the negative of **etwas** [→ D 770]. It refers to things or concepts and has no declensional forms. It is used only in the singular. Adjectives following **nichts** are capitalized and carry neuter primary endings [→ E 110].

> *Ich schenke ihm **nichts** zum Geburtstag.*
> *Mit **nichts** kann man **nichts** kaufen.*
> *Du bist zu **nichts** zu gebrauchen.*
> *In der Zeitung steht **nichts** Neues.*
> *Man kann dir mit **nichts** Schönem eine Freude machen.*

D 776 A prepositional infinitive may depend on **nichts**; such constructions may be expanded by the use of **mehr**:

> *Ich habe **nichts zu lesen.***
> *Jetzt haben wir **nichts mehr zu tun.***

D 777 In colloquial language, such infinitives are also used as nouns:

> *Die Kinder haben **nichts zum Spielen.***
> *Haben Sie **nichts mehr zum Trinken?***

Indefinite Pronouns and Attributes

all-

D 780 The indefinite pronoun **all-** is used to refer to a totality of things or objects in the plural which are already known or which were previously mentioned. **All-** follows the declension of the definite article in the plural.

---

[1] Notice the difference: *etwas zu essen* — something to eat, something which can be eaten; *etwas zum Spielen* — something to play with, something for the purpose of playing.

*Hier liegen die Bücher. Sind das **alle**?*
*Ich habe keine Äpfel mehr; ich habe **alle** gegessen.*
*Die Kinder gehen bald. Hast du mit **allen** gesprochen?*
Der Lehrer hat die Aufgaben der Schüler korrigiert. Die Arbeiten
*   **aller** waren gut.*

If **alle** (plural) refers to a noun or pronoun which has not been speci- D 781
fically mentioned before, it always designates persons:

*   **Alle** sind schon nach Hause gegangen.*
*   Ich habe **alle** gesehen.*
*   Hast du mit **allen** gesprochen?*
*   Er arbeitet zum Wohle **aller**.*

Alles (singular, neuter only) refers primarily to things or concepts: D 782

*   **Alles** ist in Ordnung.*
*   Hast du **alles** verstanden?*
*   Er ist mit **allem** zufrieden.*

In the nominative, however, **alles** may also be used for persons, if the D 783
totality of a group is to be stressed. If the verb is conjugated, it is in the
singular:

*   **Alles** einsteigen!*
*   **Alles** hört auf mein Kommando.*
*   Mein Freund machte einen Scherz, und **alles** lachte.*

Adjectives following **alles** (always referring to things or concepts) are D 784
capitalized and carry weak (secondary) adjective endings [→ E 120]:

*   **Alles Moderne** gefällt mir.*
*   Ich wünsche dir **alles Gute**!*
*   Er hat mir von **allem Wichtigen** erzählt.*

All- may also be used as an indefinite attribute, declined like the definite D 785
article in all genders, singular and plural:

*   **Aller** Anfang ist schwer.*
*   Sie hat **alles** Geld verloren.*
*   Er ist mit **aller** Vorsicht gefahren.*
*   Er hat mir **alle** Bücher geschenkt.*
*   Ich habe mit **allen** Kollegen gesprochen.*
*   Die Arbeiten **aller** Schüler waren gut.*

263

D 786   If the noun is modified by an article, demonstrative or possessive, **all-** precedes the other limiting adjectives and has the same inflectional ending:

> *Ich habe **alle die** Bücher schon gelesen.*
> ***Alle diese** Leute sind Studenten.*
> *Peter hat mich mit **allen seinen** Freunden besucht.*

D 787   In such constructions, **all** may also appear without inflection:

> *Wo hast du **all die** schönen Sachen gekauft?*
> *Er hat mich mit **all seinen** Freunden besucht.*
> ***All diese** Leute sind Studenten.*
> *Er hat mir **all das** Geld geschenkt.*

D 788   Descriptive adjectives following **all-** (or the article, possessive, or demonstrative) take weak (secondary) endings [→ E 120]:

> ***Alle meine alten** Freunde besuchten mich.*
> *Bei **allem guten** Willen konnte er die Arbeit doch nicht beenden.*
> *Er schenkte mir **alle diese schönen** Bücher.*

D 789   In the plural, **all-** often occurs following a plural personal pronoun. The genitive of **all-** after personal pronouns precedes the noun to which the genitive refers [→ D 061]:

> *Mein Freund hat **uns alle** eingeladen.*
> *Ich wünsche **Ihnen allen** viel Glück.*
> *Es ist **unser aller** Wunsch, daß du bald wieder gesund wirst.*

D 790   If **all-** refers to a noun or pronoun subject which precedes the verb, **all-** may precede or may follow the verb. It may also follow after an accusative object, if the totality of the group is to be stressed:

> ***Wir** sind **alle** ins Kino gegangen. — **Wir alle** sind ins Kino gegangen.*
> ***Sie alle** müssen **mich** morgen besuchen. — **Sie** müssen **mich alle** morgen besuchen.*
> *Ich habe **alle die** Bücher schon gelesen. — Ich habe **die Bücher alle** schon gelesen.*

D 793   If **alle** occurs as a predicate complement after the verbs **sein** or **werden**, it has the idiomatic meaning of "gone," "used up," or "finished."

*Mein Geld ist **alle**.*

*Das Essen ist **alle**.*

*Die Dummen werden nicht **alle**.*

ander-

The indefinite pronoun or attribute **ander-** indicates a difference between two persons or things. It follows the declension of a descriptive adjective [→ E 100 ff.]:   D 795

*Es war ein **anderer** (Junge).*

*Das ist etwas **anderes**.*

*Ich will mit keinem **anderen** (Mann) sprechen.*

After the personal pronouns **wir** and **ihr**, it usually follows the weak (secondary) declension [→ E 120]:   D 796

*Wir (ihr) **anderen** . . .*

Before an **-n**, the **-e-** of the ending is often omitted; before other endings, the **-e-** of the stem may be dropped: D 797

*Ich habe keinen **anderen** gesehen.*

*Hast du ein **andres** Buch?*

*Das waren **andre** Zeiten.*

The form **anders** is used as the neuter adverb or predicate adjective; it may also occur as a pronoun after **jemand** or **niemand** instead of the masculine form: D 798

*Er war wo **anders**.*

*Das Wetter ist heute **anders**.*

*Er sprach mit **jemand**(em) **anders** (mit **jemand anderem**, mit **jemandem anderen**).*

*Niemand **anders** (niemand **anderer**) war hier.*

Descriptive adjectives following **ander-** usually have the same declensional ending as **ander-** itself [→ E 150]:   D 799

*Hast du ein **anderes interessantes** Buch?*

*Hast du **andere interessante** Bücher?*

*Ich habe keine **anderen interessanten** Bücher.*

*Er besitzt eine große Anzahl **anderer interessanter** Bücher.*

265

ein-

D 800

	m.	n.	f.
N.	einer	ein(e)s	eine
A.	einen	ein(e)s	eine
D.	einem	einem	einer
G.	—	—	—
N./A.	welche		

As an indefinite pronoun, **ein-** only has singular forms and no genitive. Masculine and feminine usually refer to persons, neuter to things or concepts. Note that the pronoun carries the full endings of the definite article, including the nom. masc. and the nom./acc. ntr. For the plural, **welche** is used in nominative and accusative only.

*Auf der Straße steht **einer** und wartet.*
*Soeben hat man wieder **einen** ins Krankenhaus gebracht.*
*Das Auto gehört **einem** unserer Freunde.*
***Eine** von diesen Studentinnen ist meine Kusine.*
*Sag mir nur **ein(e)s**, was hast du gestern gemacht?*

*An der Haltestelle stehen **welche** und warten auf den Bus.*
*Ich möchte eine Schachtel Zigaretten. — Was für **welche**, bitte?*

D 801

The pronoun **ein-** may also follow the definite article; it then carries weak (secondary) adjective endings [→ E 120], including plural forms:

*Sag mir nur **das eine**, was hast du gestern gemacht?*
***Der eine** kam und der andere ging.*
***Die einen** kamen und die anderen gingen.*

D 802

If **ein-** refers to a previously mentioned noun, it may replace either persons or things, and agrees with the gender of the noun antecedent. In this usage, the neuter nominative/accusative form is **eins**:

*Siehst du einen Schüler? Ja, ich sehe **einen**.*
*Hast du einen Bleistift? Ja, ich habe **einen**.*
*Hast du ein Heft? Ja, ich habe **eins**.*
*Haben Sie Bücher? Ja, ich habe **welche**.*
*Sind Kinder im Garten? Ja, dort sind **welche**.*

D 803

The indefinite nature of **ein-** or **welche** may be stressed by the use of **irgend**:

***Irgendeiner** muß es doch getan haben!*
*Haben Sie keine Bücher? Ich nehme **irgendwelche**!*

As an attribute, **ein-** functions as the indefinite article [→ D 345 ff.].   D 805
Welche exists as an attribute only in its interrogative function
[→ D 240].

Descriptive adjectives after **irgendein** follow the rules of the indefinite   D 806
article [→ E 130 ff.]:

>*Hast du irgendein neues Buch?*
>*Er nahm Geld aus irgendeiner inneren Tasche.*

Descriptive adjectives after **irgendwelche** usually have strong (parallel)   D 807
endings [→ E 110]:[1]

>*Er hat mir irgendwelche dumme Geschichten erzählt.*

ein bißchen [2]

The indefinite pronoun **ein bißchen** is used for things or concepts which   D 810
have been previously mentioned. By itself, it has no declensional forms
[but → D 816–7].

>*Möchten Sie Zucker in den Kaffee? Ja, ein bißchen.*
>*Hast du Angst? Ja, ein bißchen.*
>*Haben Sie nicht zuviel Salz in den Salat getan? Nein, ich habe nur*
>*ein bißchen genommen.*

Ein bißchen may also be used as an indefinite attribute. Adjectives fol-   D 815
lowing **ein bißchen** carry strong (primary) endings [→ E 110].

>*Geben Sie mir bitte ein bißchen Suppe!*
>*Haben Sie noch ein bißchen Geduld!*
>*Mit ein bißchen Mut kann man viel erreichen.*
>*Sie würzt die Speisen immer mit ein bißchen schwarzem Pfeffer.*
>*Ich habe gern ein bißchen Grünes am Fenster.*

The adjective **klein**, inserted between **ein** and **bißchen**, may be used to   D 816
indicate a very small quantity. **Klein** may be undeclined, or carry
primary endings [→ E 110]; in the dative, however, **ein** is declined and
klein carries secondary endings [→ E 120]:

>*Geben Sie mir bitte ein klein bißchen (ein kleines bißchen) Suppe!*
>*Haben Sie noch ein klein bißchen (ein kleines bißchen) Geduld!*
>*Mit einem kleinen bißchen Mut kann man viel erreichen.*

---

[1] Weak (secondary) endings are also possible: *irgendwelche dummen Geschichten* [→ E 150].
[2] *Ein wenig* may be used instead of *ein bißchen* [→ D 883].

D 817   If **ein** is replaced by the definite article, a possessive, or a demonstrative, these attributes must be declined. **Ein** is also declined if it is preceded by **so**:

> *Mit **meinem bißchen** Geld kann ich keine weite Reise machen.*
> *Mit **dem bißchen** Wasser kann man kein Geschirr spülen.*
> *Mit **diesem bißchen** Arbeit werden Sie bald fertig werden.*
> *Mit **so einem bißchen** Butter kannst du kein Brot streichen.*

einig-

D 820   The indefinite pronoun **einig-** is used in the plural for previously mentioned or previously known persons or things; it carries the endings of the definite article:

> *Sind alle deine Freunde schon da? Nein, **einige** sind nicht gekommen.*
> *In unserer Bibliothek stehen viele interessante Bücher. In **einigen** habe ich schon gelesen.*

D 821   In the singular, **einiges** refers only to things or concepts. A following nominal adjective carries weak (secondary) endings [→ E 120]:

> *Ich war gestern in der Stadt und habe **einiges** gekauft.*
> *Er hat in seinem Leben schon **einiges Schwere** mitgemacht.*
> *Es gefällt mir hier sehr gut, mit **einigem** jedoch bin ich nicht zufrieden.*

D 825   As an indefinite attribute, **einige** occurs primarily in the plural. A descriptive adjective following carries primary endings, identical with those of **einige** itself [→ E 150]:

> *Ich habe **einige gute** Bücher gelesen.*
> *Durch Briefe **einiger guter Bekannter** habe ich von Ihrem Erfolg erfahren.*
> *Er sprach mit **einigen alten** Freunden.*

D 826   With abstract nouns, **einig-** also occurs in the singular. Descriptive adjectives following carry weak (secondary) endings:

> *Er wohnt seit **einiger** Zeit in Berlin.*
> *Mit **einigem guten** Willen könnten Sie das schon machen!*

D 828   Before cardinal numbers, **einige** is used as an adverb in the sense of "approximately" or "some":

> *Im Bus saßen **einige** zwanzig Reisende.*
> *Sie ist schon **einige** dreißig Jahre alt.*

268

einzeln-

Einzeln-, which very rarely occurs in the singular, follows the same rules D 830
as **einig-**:

> *Sind alle Schüler fleißig? — Die meisten ja, aber **einzelne** sind nicht*
> *sehr fleißig* [→ D 820].
> *Die Geschichte hat mich sehr interessiert. **Einzelnes** war mir neu*
> *[→ D 821].*
> *Ich habe gestern **einzelne alte Bekannte** getroffen* [→ D 825].

After an article, possessive, or demonstrative, **einzeln-** is declined like D 832
an adjective:

> *In den **einzelnen** Städten, die wir besucht haben, haben wir viele*
> *Sehenswürdigkeiten gesehen.*

Other descriptive adjectives following **einzeln-** carry the same endings D 833
as **einzeln-** itself [→ E 150].

etlich-

Etlich- follows the same rules as **einzeln-**, but is not normally used after D 835
articles, possessives, or demonstratives. [See examples in D 830, for
which **etlich** may be substituted.]

Etlich- is occasionally used in the neuter singular, followed by a D 836
nominal adjective with secondary declension:

> *Wir haben auf unserer Reise **etliches** (Neue) gesehen.*[1]

jed-

The indefinite pronoun **jed-** occurs only in the singular. Masculine and D 840
feminine forms refer only to persons. **Jed-** follows the ending pattern of
the definite article, but has no genitive:

> *Jeder muß arbeiten.*
> *Er fragte jeden.*
> *Er tanzt mit jeder. — Sie tanzt mit jedem.*

As an indefinite attribute, **jed-** has all singular forms,[2] including the D 841

---

[1] A primary ending on the following adjective is also possible: *etliches Neues.*

[2] Plurals exist only in colloquial expressions as a substitute for **alle**: *Er kommt jede paar*
Minuten mit etwas anderem.

269

genitive, and occurs in all three genders. A following adjective carries secondary endings:

Jeder Mensch muß arbeiten.
Ich arbeite jeden Tag.
Wir sprechen nicht mit jedem fremden Menschen.
Die Taten jedes guten Menschen werden belohnt.
Jedes normale Kind muß in die Schule gehen.
Die Schüler haben jede Woche einen Tag frei.

D 842   Forms of **jed-** (either pronouns or attributes) may be preceded by the indefinite article **ein-** to strengthen the partitive meaning. In such constructions, a genitive is possible for the pronoun as well. **Jed-** follows the regular adjective declension:

Ein jeder (Mann) muß arbeiten.
Der Lehrer fragt einen jeden (Schüler) in der Klasse.
Wir sprechen nicht mit einem jeden (Menschen).
Es ist die Pflicht eines jeden (guten Bürgers), sein Vaterland zu verteidigen.

D 843   Similarly, the indefinite pronoun or attribute **einzeln-** may follow **jed-** as an intensification. **Jed-** then has primary endings [→ E 110], **einzeln-** and other adjectives secondary endings [→ E 120]:

Jeder einzelne (Mensch) war bereit, uns zu helfen.
Der Lehrer fragt jeden einzelnen (Schüler).
Es ist die Pflicht jedes einzelnen (guten Bürgers), sein Vaterland zu verteidigen.

D 844   If the indefinite article **ein-** precedes **jed- einzeln-**, **jed-** has regular adjective endings, primary or secondary [→ D 842]; **einzeln-** and any other following adjectives again carry secondary endings [→ E 120]:

Ein jeder einzelne (gute Bürger) muß seine Pflicht tun.
Ich wollte mit einem jeden einzelnen (neuen Schüler) sprechen.

D 845   The indefinite attribute **jed-** is sometimes also used with abstract nouns:

Er behandelt mich mit jeder Freundlichkeit.
Wir haben die Arbeit ohne jede Schwierigkeit beendet.[1]

D 846   **Jed-** also occurs in the compounds **jedesmal** and **jedenfalls**:

---

[1] A plural form (*ohne jede Schwierigkeiten*) is not considered good German.

270

*Er hat mich **jedesmal** besucht.*
*Es ist **jedenfalls** besser, wenn er kommt.*

When **jed-** is combined with ordinal numbers, it expresses a definite sequence: **D 847**

*Er bekommt **jeden zweiten** Tag einen Brief.*
***Jeder zehnte** unter uns will weiter studieren.*

To designate all individual parts of a group, **jed-** is followed by a genitive plural, if the group is a noun, and by the proposition **von** if it is a pronoun: **D 848**

***Jeder der Gäste** hat ein Einzelzimmer.*
***Jedes der Kinder** gab dem Bettler ein Almosen.*
*Ich schenkte **jedem meiner Freunde** ein Buch zum Geburtstag.*
***Jeder von uns** hofft, daß du bald wieder gesund wirst.*
*Wir gaben **jedem von ihnen** eine Mark Trinkgeld.*

Jed- may also be used in the same meaning in apposition [→ J 137] for nouns and pronouns in the plural. It follows the verb (or, in the case of inversion, the subject), and has the case ending corresponding to the singular of the noun or pronoun to which it refers: **D 849**

*Die Gäste haben **jeder** ein Einzelzimmer.*
*Wir hoffen **jeder**, daß du bald wieder gesund wirst.*
*Meinen Freunden schenkte ich **jedem** ein Buch zum Geburtstag.*

jeglich-

The indefinite pronoun or attribute **jeglich-** occurs as a synonym for **jed-** in elevated style only. It follows the same rules as **jed-**, but is most frequently used with the indefinite article [→ D 842]: **D 850**

*Sie kamen **ein jeglicher** aus seiner Stadt.*
*Wir fragten **einen jeglichen** nach dem Weg.*

kein-

The indefinite pronoun **kein-** refers to previously known or previously mentioned nouns. It follows the same rules as the indefinite pronoun **ein-** [→ D 800 ff.], but does have plural forms. It takes the endings of the definite article in all genders and cases: **D 855**

*Das weiß **keiner**!*
*Hast du ein Buch? Nein, ich habe **kein(e)s**.*
*Wir sahen **keinen** und sprachen mit **keinem**.*
*Haben Sie Kinder? Nein, wir haben **keine**.*

271

D 856   For **kein-** as an attribute, → D 311, 380.

D 857   Adjectives following **kein-** have the same endings as adjectives after **ein-** [→ E 130 ff.]:

> *Er ist **kein guter** Schüler.*
> *Warum gibst du mir **kein interessantes** Buch?*
> *Wir haben **keine schönen** Bilder.*

manch- [1]

D 860   As an indefinite pronoun, **manch-** refers to persons and follows the masculine and feminine forms of the definite article, singular and plural, but without a genitive:

> ***Manche** lernen langsam, und **mancher** lernt es nie.*
> *Ich habe schon **manchen** getroffen, der viele fremde Sprachen sprechen konnte.*
> *Wir haben mit **mancher** gesprochen, die mit diesem Hotel sehr zufrieden war.*

D 861   In the neuter singular, **manch-** refers only to things or concepts. Nominal adjectives following **manches** are capitalized (except for **ander-**), and carry secondary endings: [2]

> *Ich habe schon **manches** (**andere**) gesehen.*
> *Wir haben schon **manches** (**Gute**) von ihm gehört.*

D 862   As an indefinite attribute, **manch-** may either be uninflected [3] (also in compounds, such as **manchmal**), or follow the declensional pattern of the definite article:

> *Ich war **manchmal** nicht ganz sicher.*
> *Er hat **manche** Zeit damit verbracht.*
> *Ich erinnere mich **manches** Menschen aus meiner Jugendzeit.*
> ***Manche** Leute können das nicht verstehen.*

D 863   Descriptive adjectives following uninflected **manch** have primary endings. [3] Secondary endings predominate after inflected forms of **manch-**

---

[1] In the plural, **manch-** has the meaning of "some"; in the singular, it has the meaning of "many a (person or thing)."

[2] Uninflected **manch** followed by a neuter primary ending occurs rarely: *manch Gutes, manch anderes.*

[3] This occurs mainly in poetic usage: *manch armer Mann, manch schönes Kind, manch bunte Blumen,* etc.

in the singular; in the plural, however, primary endings (i.e. parallel endings with **manch-** itself) occur more frequently in modern German, although secondary endings are still used [→ E 150]:

> *Er hat **manches wertvolle** Buch geschrieben.*
> *Ich bin schon mit **manchem berühmten** Mann zusammengetroffen.*
> *In **mancher einsamen** Stunde hilft ein gutes Buch.*
> *Er hat **manche fremde** Länder (or **manche fremden** Länder) gesehen.*
> *Die Galerie enthält Bilder **mancher großer** (or **großen**) Maler.*

Before **ein-**, **manch** is always uninflected. If an adjective follows, its ending depends on the form of **ein-** [→ E 130 ff.]:   D 864

> ***Manch einer** hält sich für klüger, als er ist.*
> *Er hat schon an **manch einem** Sportwettkampf teilgenommen, und hat auch **manch einen** gewonnen.*
> ***Manch ein junger** Mann hat vorschnelle Entschlüsse bereut.*

mehrer-

As a pronoun or an attribute, **mehrer-** follows the same rules as **einig-** [→ D 820 ff.]. It hardly ever occurs in the singular.   D 865

> *Hast du dir Bücher gekauft? — Ja, ich habe **mehrere** gekauft.*
> *Hier sind die Geschenke **mehrerer guter** Freunde.*

Do not confuse **mehrere** (several) with **mehr** (more) [→ D 885].   D 866

ein paar

Ein paar is undeclined. It occurs only in the plural, usually attributively. If an adjective follows, it has primary endings [→ E 110]:   D 870

> *Haben Sie heute Bananen? — Ja, ich habe noch **ein paar**.*
> *Ich kaufte **ein paar billige** Bücher.*
> *Wir kamen vor **ein paar** Tagen in Berlin an.*
> *Sie sprach mit **ein paar alten Bekannten**.*

If the word **paar** is not preceded by **ein**, but by the definite article, demonstrative, or possessive, these are declined, and the following adjective has secondary endings [→ E 120]:   D 871

> *Er hat mir **seine paar neuen** Bilder gezeigt.*
> *In **den paar schönen** Tagen des Sommers sind wir an die See gefahren.*

Do not confuse **ein paar** (a few, a couple of) with **ein Paar** (a pair).   D 872

273

viel-, wenig-

D 875 As indefinite pronouns, **viel-** and **wenig-** in the plural refer to persons. They follow the declension of the definite article:

> *Gestern haben mich **viele** besucht, aber nur **wenige** sind bis Mitternacht geblieben.*
>
> *Er hat mit **vielen** gesprochen, aber er wurde nur von **wenigen** verstanden.*

D 876 **Viel-** and **wenig-** may refer to things in the plural, if they have been previously mentioned:

> *Hat er viele Bücher? — Ja, er hat **viele**, aber er hat nur **wenige** davon gelesen.*

D 877 In the singular, **viel** and **wenig** occur either uninflected or with neuter endings and refer to things or concepts:

> *Er hat in der Schule **viel(es)** gelernt, aber nur **wenig(es)** behalten.*
>
> *Ich bin schon mit **wenig(em)** zufrieden.*

D 878 Adjectives following these indefinite pronouns are capitalized and carry primary neuter endings [→ E 110]. The pronouns themselves are then usually undeclined:

> *Ich habe nur **wenig Neues** gehört.*
>
> *Er hat sich mit **viel Interessantem** beschäftigt.*

D 879 If **viel** is inflected, however, the nominal adjective has secondary endings [→ E 120]:

> *Er ist zu **vielem Bösen** fähig.*
>
> *Er hat **vieles Gute** getan.*

D 880 As indefinite attributes, **viel-** and **wenig-** in the plural are declined like adjectives;[1] any other descriptive adjective following has the same ending as **viel-** or **wenig-** [→ E 150]:

> *Ich habe **viele gute** Freunde in dieser Stadt.*
>
> *Hast du die **vielen** Menschen gesehen?*
>
> *Ich war nur **wenige kurze** Stunden hier, aber sie gehören zu **meinen wenigen schönen** Erlebnissen dieses Jahres.*

D 881 In the singular, **viel** and **wenig** are usually undeclined in attributive use.[1]

---

[1] The uninflected attributive form also occurs occasionally in the plural: *Er darf nur **wenig süße** Sachen essen.* Usually, however, uninflected forms in the plural are adverbs rather than adjectives: *viele ältere Männer* — many older men; *viel ältere Männer* — much older men.

Descriptive adjectives which follow carry primary endings [→ E 120]:

> *Ich nehme nur **wenig** Milch in den Kaffee.*
> *Wir haben **wenig** Geld.*
> *Mit **viel gutem** Willen kann er die Sache machen.*
> *Trink nicht so **viel kaltes** Wasser!*

In the dative singular, **viel-** and **wenig-** often have primary declensional   D 882
endings [→ E 110]. They have secondary endings if they follow articles,
possessives, or demonstratives [→ E 120]. Other descriptive adjectives
have the same endings as **viel-** and **wenig-** [→ E 150]:

> *Er war mit **vieler** Freude bei der Arbeit.*
> *Ich bin mit **wenigem** Geld durch Europa gefahren.*
> *Mit **meinem wenigen** Geld kann ich nicht viel kaufen.*
> *Was willst du mit **der vielen guten** Milch?*
> ***Dieses wenige kalte** Wasser genügt nicht zum Wäschewaschen.*

Wenig- may be preceded by the indefinite article **ein**, which is not   D 883
declined, similar to **ein bißchen** [→ D 810]:

> *Können Sie mir **ein wenig** Geld leihen?*
> *Ich nehme nur **ein wenig** Zucker in den Kaffee.*
> *Mit **ein wenig** gutem Willen erreicht man mehr.*

When **viel-** occurs together with other words, undeclined forms are   D 884
written as one word and declined forms are written separately:

> ***Wieviel** Uhr ist es?*
> *Ich habe **zuviel** Arbeit.*
>
> ***Wie viele** Schüler sind in der Klasse?*
> *Ich bekomme **zu viele** Briefe.*

mehr

Mehr is the comparative of **viel**. It may be used either attributively or as   D 885
a pronoun, but has no declensional forms. Adjectives following **mehr**
have primary endings [→ E 120]:

> *Ich habe etwas Geld, aber ich brauche **mehr**.*
> *Du mußt mit **mehr** Energie arbeiten.*
> *In Deutschland gibt es jetzt **mehr moderne** Fabriken als früher.*
> *Ich trinke **mehr dunkles** Bier als helles.*

275

Indefinite Attributes

ganz-

D 890   As an indefinite attribute, **ganz-** is used like an adjective. It occurs primarily in the singular, but may sometimes be used in the plural. Other adjectives following **ganz-** have parallel inflection [→ E 130 ff.]:

> *Das **ganze große** Haus war in Aufregung.*
> *Ich habe gestern einen **ganzen** Tag frei gehabt.*
> *Das Wetter war die **ganzen langen** Wochen schön.*
> *Sie sucht Arbeit für **ganze** Tage.*

D 891   Before names of cities, countries, or continents, **ganz** is used without declensional endings, if there is no definite article:

> *In **ganz** Köln feiert man Karneval.*
> *Es schneite gestern in **ganz** Österreich.*
> ***Ganz** Europa interessierte sich für die politische Entwicklung der letzten Tage.*

D 892   If there is a definite article, however, **ganz-** must be declined:

> ***Das ganze** Europa interessierte sich für die politische Entwicklung der letzen Tage.*
> *Es schneite gestern in **der ganzen** Schweiz.*

sämtlich-

D 895   The indefinite attribute **sämtlich-** is declined like an adjective. Other adjectives, if any, usually have secondary endings [→ E 120 ff.]:

> *Ich besuchte **sämtliche wichtigen** Museen in Berlin.*
> *Meine **sämtlichen alten** Freunde gratulierten mir zum Examen.*

lauter, eitel

D 896   As indefinite attributes, **lauter** and **eitel** (poetic usage only) are undeclined[1] and occur without an article. **Lauter** may be followed by some other adjective with primary endings [→ E 120; → also indefinite numerical attributes ending in **-erlei**, E 807].

> *Auf dem Ball traf ich **lauter alte** Bekannte.*
> *Über seine Worte empfand ich **eitel** Freude.*

D 897   Do not confuse **lauter** with declined forms of **laut**:

> *Er sang vor **lauter** Freude. — Er sang mit **lauter** Stimme.*

---

[1] In the sense of "pure," **lauter** has inflectional endings: *Er sprach die **lautere** Wahrheit. Der Ring ist aus **lauterem** Gold.* Similarly, **eitel** also exists as an adjective in the sense of "vain."

276

THE USE OF CASES

Cases are used to designate the FUNCTION of a NOUN or PRONOUN in the sentence. German has four cases: nominative, accusative,[1] dative, and genitive. These cases can be recognized by the declensional endings of nouns and their attributes, and the declensional endings of the pronouns. These endings, however, are not always unequivocal; since the four cases do not suffice as unambiguous function indicators, prepositions are often used to make additional differentiations [→ F 001 ff.].   D 900

According to their function within the sentence, we distinguish between SENTENCE UNIT CASES (i.e. subject, object) and ATTRIBUTIVE CASES. The case of a sentence unit is determined by the use of the unit within the sentence, and by the verb in the predicate. The case of an attribute is determined by the noun or adjective which the attribute modifies, as well as by the nature of the attribute.   D 901

Subject Case [→ H 250 ff.]   D 902

NOM.: *Der Lehrer fragt den Schüler. — Den Mann habe ich um Auskunft gebeten.*

Object Cases [→ H 300 ff.]   D 903

ACC.: *Ich besuche dich morgen. — Wir lesen ein Buch.*
DAT.: *Helfen Sie mir! — Ich gebe dem Lehrer mein Heft.*
GEN.: *Wir gedenken seiner. — Man beschuldigt ihn des Diebstahls.*

All cases may be found in PREDICATE COMPLEMENTS [→ H 220] and in PREDICATE MODIFIERS [→ H 230]. Which case is used depends on the type of complement or the type of modifier: D 904

NOM.: *Peter ist mein bester Freund. — Wir sind die letzten.*
ACC.: *Sie nennt ihn ihren Retter. — Wir warteten eine Stunde.*
DAT.: *Ich hebe dir die Zeitung bis morgen auf.*
GEN.: *Eines Tages schrieb er mir einen Brief.*

Cases are determined not only by the function of a sentence unit in the sentence, but also by PREPOSITIONS. We thus speak of **prepositional cases**   D 908

---

[1] The accusative as a separate case form exists only in the 1st and 2nd person singular, and in the 3rd person singular masculine. 1st and 2nd person plural forms are identical with the dative; 3rd person singular neuter and feminine, as well as all 3rd person plurals, are identical in form with the nominative.

(accusative, dative, genitive). These prepositions determine the case of a noun and its attributes or the case of a pronoun, without regard to its function in the sentence.

We can differentiate between two groups of prepositions:

1. Prepositions which determine the case of a noun or pronoun entirely by themselves. They exist in the accusative, the dative, and the genitive [→ D 927, 945, 975]:

ACC.: *Hier ist ein Brief **für dich**. — Darf ich **um das Salz** bitten?*
DAT.: *Ich wohne **bei meinem Onkel**. — Ich gehe **mit ihm** spazieren.*
GEN.: *Wir lernen **während des Unterrichts** viel. — **Meinetwegen** kannst du schwimmen gehen.*

2. Prepositions which determine the case of a noun or pronoun with the help of a verb. These prepositions may be followed by either the dative or the accusative [D 928, 947]:

*Wir **gehen in die** Schule. — Wir **bleiben** zwei Stunden **in der** Schule.*
*Ich **stelle** die Tasse **auf den** Tisch. — Die Tasse **steht auf dem** Tisch.*

Nominative

D 910   The nominative is the case of the SUBJECT. It agrees with the personal form of the verb in the predicate [→ H 250 ff., H 275 ff.]. It answers the question **who?** for persons, **what?** for things or concepts.

> *Der Schüler arbeitet fleißig.*
> *Wir lernen Deutsch.*
> *Der Kranke muß im Bett liegenbleiben.*
> *Dieses Haus kostet viel Geld.*

D 911   The predicate nominative appears as the PREDICATE COMPLEMENT of the verbs **sein, werden, bleiben, scheinen, heißen, (sich) dünken**. It answers the question **what?** [→ H 460 ff.]:

> *Herr Müller ist **ein guter Lehrer**.*
> *Sein Sohn ist nach langem Studium **Arzt** geworden.*
> *Dr. Meier ist im neuen Kabinett **Minister** geblieben.*
> *Ich heiße **Karl**.*

278

> *Er dünkt sich **ein kluger Mensch.***
> *Das scheint mir **eine gute Lösung.**[1]*

The nominative also appears as a COMPLEMENT OF MANNER after the D 912
conjunctions **als** and **wie** to designate a qualification of the subject
[→ H 465]. It answers the question **in what capacity?** (*als*) or **how?**
(*wie*):

> *Ich spreche zu dir **als dein bester Freund.**[2]*
> *Das Adjektiv gebraucht man in diesem Satz **als Nomen.***

> *Ich spreche zu dir **wie dein bester Freund.**[2]*
> *Er kämpfte **wie ein Held.***

In passive constructions of the verbs **nennen, schelten, schimpfen, taufen,** D 913
titulieren, the original object of the active sentence is also in the
nominative [→ D 918 for these verbs in the active voice]. It answers
the question **how?** or **what?**

> *Paul wurde von seinem Freund **ein Dummkopf** genannt.*
> *Er wird von seinem Lehrer **ein Faulpelz** gescholten.*

Accusative

The accusative is the OBJECT CASE[3] [→ H 325 ff.] for transitive verbs, D 915
indicating the immediate recipient of the action. It answers the question
whom? for persons, **what?** for things and concepts:

> *Ich habe **einen Brief** geschrieben.*
> *Der Lehrer fragt **den Schüler.***
> *Sie liebt **mich.***

The verbs **lehren** and **kosten**[4] have two accusative objects, one indicating D 916
a person and the other a thing or concept:

> *Die Mutter lehrte **ihr Kind ein gutes Benehmen.***
> *Das neue Auto hat **mich viel Geld** gekostet.*

---

[1] If this sentence is expanded to *Das scheint mir eine gute Lösung zu sein*, the phrase *eine
gute Lösung* technically becomes the predicate complement of *zu sein* rather than of *scheint*.

[2] Note the difference: *als dein bester Freund* — in my capacity as your friend; *wie dein
Freund* — like your friend (the way your friend would).

[3] The term "direct object" is deliberately avoided here. [→ D 931–2, H 302–6]

[4] The double accusative with **lehren** is considered stilted and is often avoided. In colloquial
usage, **kosten** occurs with a personal object in the dative: *Das neue Auto hat mir viel Geld
gekostet.* This is not considered good German.

D 917 The verbs **fragen, bitten,** and **angehen** may also have two accusative objects, one of which is a neuter or indefinite numerical pronoun:[1]

> *Das Kind fragte **den Vater vieles**.*
> *Sie fragte **mich dieses und jenes**.*
> *Ich bitte **dich nur eines**.*
> *Er bat **mich dies und das**.*
> *Das geht **Sie nichts** an.*

D 918 The verbs **nennen, schelten, schimpfen, taufen, titulieren** may have two personal objects [→ D 913 for passive voice]:

> *Er schimpfte (schalt) **den Mann einen Narren**.*
> *Seine Mutter nannte **ihn ihren Liebling**.*

D 920 The accusative is always used after the idiom **es gibt** (singular or plural):

> *In dieser Stadt gibt es **ein gutes Theater**.*
> *Gibt es in deiner Heimat **viele hohe Berge**?*

D 921 Note the difference in meaning between **es gibt** on the one hand and **es ist** or **es sind** on the other: **Es ist** or **es sind** refers to a specific group or entity in a specified place. (*Es ist ein Fehler in diesem Satz. Es waren dreißig Menschen im Saal*.) **Es gibt** refers to general existence, usually indefinite in number and in an unspecified place. (*Es gibt einen Gott. Es gab viele Schwierigkeiten*.) **Es ist kein Arzt hier** means that no doctor is present in the room. **Es gibt keinen Arzt hier** means that there is no doctor in this area at all — for example after the death of the former village physician. The use of **es gibt** with reference to specific things or places should be avoided.[2]

There are, to be sure, some important differences in form between the two idioms as well:

1. **Es gibt** is always followed by the accusative, **es ist** or **es sind** by the nominative.

2. Since **es** is the genuine impersonal subject of the phrase **es gibt**, the verb is always in the singular, even when referring to a plurality of

---

[1] In other constructions, there is a direct personal object and a prepositional object: *Das Kind fragte den Polizisten **nach dem Weg**. Er bat mich **um baldige Antwort**.*

[2] The one exception to this principle is a phrase such as " *Was gibt es heute zum Frühstück?* "

280

concepts. In the phrase **es ist** or **es sind**, **es** anticipates the genuine subject, with which the verb must agree in number.

3. In the phrase **es gibt**, **es** may occupy the prefield or a position within the sentence field:

> *Es gibt heute viel zu tun. — Heute gibt es viel zu tun.*

In the phrase **es ist** or **es sind**, **es** only occurs in the prefield, but disappears if the sentence begins with some other part of speech:

> *Es sind heute viele Leute hier. — Heute sind viele Leute hier.*

Both idioms may occur in all tenses.

The accusative appears in PREDICATE COMPLEMENTS or MODIFIERS as ⟨ D 923 ⟩

1. Accusative of Place: for intransitive verbs which indicate a change of position. It answers the question **where?**

> *Wir gehen **den Berg** hinauf.*
> *Er kommt **die Treppe** herunter.*
> *Gehen Sie **diese Straße** entlang und dann **die zweite Straße** rechts!*

2. Accusative of Time: to designate a definite point in time (answering the question **when?**) or a duration of time (answering the question **how long?**):

> *Nächsten Sonntag besuche ich meinen Onkel.*
> *Ich besuche ihn **jede Woche**.*
> *Ich habe **den ganzen Nachmittag** gearbeitet.*
> *Wir blieben **drei Wochen** in Berlin.*

Similarly, dates are indicated in letters or news releases:

> *München, **den 5. März** 1960.*

3. Accusative of Measure: to designate units of measurement, weight, value, or age (answering the question **how much?, how many?, how old?** etc.). Besides the verbs, such accusatives may also depend on adjectives such as **alt, breit, dick, entfernt, hoch, lang, schwer, tief, weit**:

> *Die Maschine wiegt **eine Tonne**.*
> *Die Straße ist **einen Kilometer** lang.*
> *Diese Sache ist **keinen Pfennig** wert.*
> *Das Kind ist **zwei Jahre und einen Monat** alt.*

D 925   Some normally INTRANSITIVE verbs are accompanied by an accusative, if together they form a verbal concept (sometimes called pleonastic accusative):

> *Wir tanzten **einen Tango**.*
> *Er schlief **den Schlaf** des Gerechten.*

D 926   The accusative is also used in ELLIPTIC CONSTRUCTIONS as so-called "absolute accusative" or in greetings:

> *Er kam ins Zimmer, **den Hut** in der Hand [haltend].*
> *[Ich wünsche dir einen] **guten Morgen, guten Tag, guten Abend**.*

D 927   As a PREPOSITIONAL CASE, the accusative always follows certain prepositions which are said to "govern" the accusative [→ F 010]; these are **bis, durch, für, gegen, ohne, um, wider**:[1]

> *Wir fahren **durch die Stadt**.*
> *Er geht heute **ohne seinen Freund** spazieren.*
> *Ich bleibe **bis nächsten Montag**.*

D 928   Following the prepositions **an, auf, hinter, in, neben, über, unter, vor,** and **zwischen**, the accusative occurs only if the prepositions are used in a concrete sense and the verb in the predicate indicates a change of position or motion towards a place (answering the question **wohin?**) [→ D 947, F 030]:

> *Er legt das Buch **auf den Tisch**.*
> *Wir gehen **in die Schule**.*

D 929   The accusative is also used when a noun or pronoun precedes one of the following POSTPOSITIONS [→ F 005]: **entlang, hindurch, lang,**[2] **über**:[2]

> *Er ging **die Straße entlang**.*
> *Ich schlief **die ganze Nacht hindurch**.*
> *Er hat **sein Leben lang** gearbeitet.*
> *Was hast du **den Tag über** getan?*

Dative

D 930   The DATIVE is used as an OBJECTIVE CASE if the verb describes an action which is directed to or benefits a person or (less frequently) a thing or

---

[1] For **ab**, → F 110.

[2] **Lang** and **über** may be looked upon as adverbs.

concept. The question **whom? (to whom? for whom?)** is possible only for persons or for concepts regarded as persons [→ D 221].

The dative object is often called the "indirect object"; this term, how- D 931 ever, is misleading, since there are many verbs (the so-called "intransitive" verbs) which can only take a dative object [→ D 933–4]. Such objects, which may be persons, things, or concepts, are no less "direct" than any other object (*Ich gratuliere* **Ihnen**; *er folgt* **meinem Befehl**, etc.). The terms "primary" and "secondary" objects are therefore used: the PRIMARY object indicates the person or thing with which the action or process is immediately concerned; the SECONDARY object indicates the person towards whom the action is directed [→ H 302 for a full explanation of these terms].

Many verbs (so-called "transitive" verbs) may occur with both an D 932 accusative and a dative object. This indicates that the subject (nominative) performs an operation with an object (accusative) which concerns another object (dative). The accusative (primary) object is normally a thing or a concept, answering the question **what?** (occasionally a person, answering the question **whom?**); the dative (secondary) object is normally a person, answering the question **to whom** or **for whom** (occasionally **from whom?**). Most of the verbs which can take both accusative and dative objects are verbs of giving or taking, and verbs conveying or refusing information.[1] Only a few examples are listed here: **berichten, bieten, bringen, empfehlen, erlauben, geben, kaufen, leihen, liefern, melden, mitteilen, nehmen, rauben, retten, sagen, schenken, schreiben, senden, verbieten, verdanken, verheimlichen, verschaffen, versprechen, verweigern, widmen, wünschen, zeigen**, etc.:[2]

> *Ich bringe* **meinem Freund** *ein Buch.*
> *Ich gebe (schenke) es* **ihm**.
> *Der Mann hat* **mir** *Geld genommen (gestohlen).*
> *Der Arzt hat* **dem Kind** *das Leben gerettet.*
> *Das Kind verdankt* **ihm** *sein Leben.*
> *Das kann ich* **Ihnen** *nicht erlauben.*
> *Ich wünsche* **dir** *alles Gute!*

[1] Note that these verbs may occur with an accusative (primary) object only; they can generally not occur with a dative (secondary) object only [but → D 933].

[2] In a German sentence, the dative object usually precedes the accusative object, unless the accusative object is a pronoun [→ H 711 ff.].

D 933 There are a few verbs which often occur with only a dative object; thus, they appear to be intransitive verbs. They are, however, capable of a direct object, although it is sometimes limited to indefinite pronouns like **es** or **das**. Some such verbs are: **antworten** (and its synonyms), **befehlen, danken, sich denken, nützen, raten, vergeben (verzeihen)**, etc. [→ H 351]:

> *Was hat er **dir** geantwortet?*
> *Er hat es **mir** befohlen.*
> *All das danke ich nur **ihm**.*
> *Das glaube ich **Ihnen** nicht.*
> *Kannst du **ihm** seinen Fehler verzeihen?*
> *Das dachte ich **mir** schon.*

D 934 A number of verbs are genuinely INTRANSITIVE and can only take dative objects, but no accusative.[1] Some of these verbs are: **ähneln, begegnen,**[2] **dienen, drohen, fehlen, fluchen, folgen, gleichen, gratulieren, helfen, lauschen, schaden, schmeicheln, (ver)trauen, trotzen, weh tun, winken** [→ H 351]. The objects of these verbs may be persons or things:

> *Ich bin **ihm** auf der Straße begegnet.*[3]
> *Er diente **der Familie** seit vielen Jahren.*
> *Womit willst du **mir** drohen?*
> *Folgen Sie **diesem Wagen**!*
> *Ein Ei gleicht **dem anderen**.*
> *Er gratulierte **mir** zum Geburtstag.*
> *Ich kann **Ihnen** nicht helfen.*
> *Das viele Rauchen wird **deiner Gesundheit** schaden.*
> *Er winkte **ihr** mit dem Taschentuch.*

D 935 The dative object is often found after verbs with the prefixes **aus-, bei-, ent-, entgegen-, ge-, nach-, vor-, wider-, zu-**, and **zuvor-** [→ H 351]. The objects may be persons or things:

---

[1] Many of these verbs may be made transitive (i.e. take an accusative object) with the prefix **be-** or **ver-**: *Der Sohn folgt **dem Rat** seines Vaters. Der Sohn befolgt **den Rat** seines Vaters. — Die Polizei folgte **dem Dieb**. Die Polizei verfolgte **den Dieb**.*

[2] **Begegnen** is an exception from the general rule that verbs with the prefix **be-** are transitive [→ A 301].

[3] Note that since **begegnen** is an intransitive verb of motion, it takes the helping verb **sein** in the perfect tenses [→ B 460].

284

*Er ist **einer Antwort** ausgewichen.*
*Ich stimmte **seiner Meinung** bei.*
*Das entspricht **meinen Erwartungen**.*
*Ich bin **meinem Freund** entgegengefahren.*
*Gehört dieses Buch **Ihnen**?*
*Die Polizei lief **dem Dieb** nach.*
*Ich habe **mir** nichts vorzuwerfen.*
*Widersprich **dem Lehrer** nicht!*
*Wir hörten **der Musik** lange zu.*
*Er ist **allen unseren Wünschen** zuvorgekommen.*

The dative also follows many IMPERSONAL EXPRESSIONS, such as **es fällt** D 936 **ein, es fällt schwer, es fehlt, es gefällt, es geht, es gelingt, es geschieht, es tut leid, es scheint, es schmeckt, es kommt vor,** etc. The objects are always persons:

*Wie geht es **deinem** Vater?*
*Gefällt es **Ihnen** hier?*
*Es gelang **mir**, Theaterkarten zu bekommen.*
*Es kam **ihm** vor (schien **ihm**), als habe er das alles schon einmal gesehen.*
*Was ist **dem Mann** eingefallen?*

Many ADJECTIVES are also used with the dative [→ E 550, H 353, D 938 H 441]. The following (as well as their opposites and many of their synonyms) are among the most frequent: **ähnlich, angenehm, behilflich, bekannt, billig,**[1] **böse, dankbar, feindlich, fremd, freundlich, gehorsam, gleich,**[2] **gleichgültig, gnädig, lästig, leicht, lieb, möglich, nachteilig, nahe, nützlich, peinlich, recht, schädlich, schuldig,**[3] **teuer, treu, überlegen, unbegreiflich, verhaßt, wert, willkommen:**

*Er sieht **seinem Vater ähnlich**.*
*Dieser Mann ist **mir** nicht **bekannt**.*
*Ich bin **Ihnen** sehr **dankbar**.*
*Ist **dir** das nicht **peinlich**?*
*Was **dem einen recht** ist, ist **dem anderen billig**.*
*Das Lernen fremder Sprachen ist **jedem nützlich**.*
***Mir** ist es **unmöglich**, morgen zu kommen.*

---

[1] In the sense of "proper, appropriate."
[2] In the sense of "equal to" or "indifferent."
[3] In the sense of "indebted."

285

D 940 The dative is also used to indicate the interest or concern of a person about an action in which this person is not a direct participant. This construction is called a DATIVE OF INTEREST [→ H 557]: [1]

> *Öffnen Sie **der Dame** die Tür.*
> *Das ist **mir** eine große Freude.*
> *Ich hebe **dir** die Zeitung bis morgen auf.*
> *Mein Lehrer schrieb **mir** einen Brief an die Universität.*

Note the difference between the following two examples:

> *Mein Lehrer schrieb **mir** einen Brief.* (Dative object)
> *Mein Lehrer schrieb **mir** einen Brief an die Universität.* (Dative of interest)

In the first example, the teacher wrote a letter, which he then sent to me, and in which he informed me of something. **Einen Brief** is the direct object, **mir** the indirect object.

In the second example, the teacher wrote a letter for me (in my interest), which he then sent to the university, and in which he informed them about me.[2] **Mir** indicates the person affected by the action.

D 941 The dative frequently indicates an object, especially a part of the body, which belongs to a person [→ H 558]. This is known as a DATIVE OF POSSESSION.

1. Subject:

> ***Mir** klopfte **das Herz**. (Mein Herz klopfte.)*
> ***Die Füße** sind **ihm** geschwollen. (Seine Füße sind geschwollen.)*

2. Accusative Object:[3]

> *Er hat **mir das Leben** schwer gemacht (= mein Leben).*
> *Willst du **dir die Hände** waschen (= deine Hände)?*
> *Ich werde **der Dame die Koffer** tragen (= die Koffer der Dame).*

---

[1] The dative of interest may be replaced by a prepositional phrase: *Das ist eine große Freude für mich. Mein Lehrer schrieb für mich einen Brief an die Universität.*

[2] It is, of course, theoretically possible for the second example to mean that the teacher wrote a letter to me, addressed at the university. This distinction will be made clear by the context.

[3] The possessive adjective is often replaced by the definite article: *Er hat die Hände in den Taschen. — Nimm doch die Pfeife aus dem Mund.* [→ D 333, D 665]

3. A prepositional phrase of location:[1]

> *Sie sprang **ihm an den Hals*** (= *an seinen Hals*).
> *Die Sonne schien **mir ins Gesicht*** (= *in mein Gesicht*).

Normally, the dative of possession is preferred to the corresponding   D 942
possessive adjective or genitive construction. Thus,

> *Ich wasche **mir** die Hände.*   Not: *Ich wasche **meine Hände**.*
> *Sie wäscht **dem** Kind die Haare.*   Not: *Sie wäscht die Haare **des Kindes**.*

The possessive adjective is used, however, in a few idiomatic expressions:

> *Ich wasche **meine Hände** in Unschuld.*

The dative is used in constructions where the statement made in the   D 943
sentence refers to or shows a relationship with a person, usually other
than the subject. This is known as a DATIVE OF REFERENCE [→ H 559].
If the dative of reference is omitted, the meaning of the sentence does
not change.

> *Du arbeitest **mir** zu langsam.*
> *Ich gehe nicht gern mit ihm spazieren; er geht **mir** immer zu schnell.*
> *Der Lehrer hat sich über die Klasse beklagt; sie ist **ihm** zu laut.*
> *Du gehst **mir** heute nicht ins Kino!*
> *Das war **dir** ein Kerl!*
> *Ich nahm **mir** kaum die Zeit, Frühstück zu essen.*

As a PREPOSITIONAL CASE, the dative always follows certain prepositions   D 945
[→ F 020]. The most frequent of these are: **aus, außer, bei, mit, nach**
(in the sense of "after" or "towards"), **seit, von, zu:**

> *Ich komme eben **aus der** Stadt.*
> *Er wohnt **bei seinem** Onkel.*
> *Gehst du **mit mir**?*
> *Wir sind **seit drei Tagen** in Berlin.*

The dative is also used when a noun or pronoun precedes one of the   D 946

---

[1] A few verbs may use a prepositional phrase of location with an accusative rather than a
dative, which then has the same meaning: *Ich nahm sie bei der Hand. — Er stieß mich in den
Rücken*. Sometimes, either dative or accusative are possible: *Der Kopf schmerzt mir (mich).
— Der Hund biß ihm (ihn) ins Bein.*

following POSTPOSITIONS [→ F 005]: **entgegen, gegenüber, gemäß, nach** (in the sense of "according to"), **zufolge, zuwider:**

> *Er handelte **meinen Anweisungen entgegen** (**zuwider**).*
> ***Dem Bahnhof gegenüber** ist ein neues Hotel.*
> ***Deinem Wunsche gemäß** bin ich pünktlich erschienen.*
> ***Meiner Meinung nach** wird es morgen regnen.*
> ***Seinem Brief zufolge** hat er die Prüfung bestanden.*

D 947 Following the prepositions **an, auf, hinter, in, neben, über, unter, vor,** and **zwischen**, the dative is used only if the preposition indicates a concrete location and the verb in the predicate does not indicate a change of position or motion towards a place (answering the question **wo?**) [→ D 928, F 030]:

> *Das Buch liegt **auf dem Tisch**.*
> *Wir lernen **in der Schule**.*

D 948 The dative may also be used with the above prepositions and verbs of motion, provided that the predicate does not indicate motion towards a goal:

> *Wir tanzen **im** Saal.*
> *Ich gehe hinter **meinem** Freund.*
> *Er schwimmt **im** See.*
> *Ich fahre **im** Auto.*

Note the difference:

> *Das Flugzeug fliegt über **die** Stadt* — The airplane passes over the city.
> *Das Flugzeug fliegt über **der** Stadt* — The airplane circles above the city.
>
> *Wir fuhren in **der** Straßenbahn* — We were riding in the streetcar.
> *Wir fuhren in **die** Straßenbahn* — We were inside a car and drove into (i.e. collided with) the streetcar.

The Genitive

D 950 The genitive is primarily a noun case. Genitive pronoun forms are rather rare and survive primarily either in certain fixed expressions, such as **meinethalber, deinetwegen, um seinetwillen**, etc., or in elevated language, such as **Wir gedenken seiner**. In colloquial language, the genitive is often replaced by the dative (**wegen mir, trotz dem Regen**) or by a prepositional construction with **von**. Its most frequent use is to indicate a relationship between two nouns, normally expressed in English by the preposition "of" [→ D 970].

As an OBJECTIVE CASE, the genitive exists only after a few verbs, many of which belong to legal terminology [→ H 380 ff.]; the genitive object always indicates a concept. Among these verbs are the following:

D 955

anklagen	entbehren	entsetzen [2]
bedürfen	entbinden [1]	ermangeln
berauben	entheben	überführen
beschuldigen	entledigen	versichern
bezichtigen	entraten	zeihen

*Er wurde **des Diebstahls angeklagt** (**bezichtigt, beschuldigt, überführt**).*
*Das **entbehrt jeder Grundlage**.*
*Der Minister wurde **seines Amtes enthoben** (**entsetzt**).*
*Ich **versichere** Sie **meiner Hochachtung**.*

A genitive object (indicating a concept) occurs in a few idiomatic verbal expressions:

D 956

sich eines Besseren (anderen) besinnen
seines Amtes walten
der Ruhe pflegen
jeder Beschreibung spotten
jemanden keines Blickes (Grußes, Wortes, keiner Antwort) würdigen
eines Besseren belehren

A genitive object also occurs after some REFLEXIVE VERBS, for a few of which the object may be a person.

D 957

sich annehmen	sich enthalten	sich erwehren
sich bedienen	sich erbarmen	sich rühmen
sich befleißigen	sich erfreuen	sich schämen
sich bemächtigen	sich erinnern	sich vergewissern

*Nehmen Sie sich **des Mannes** an!*
*Wir konnten uns **des Feindes** nicht erwehren.*
*Ich **schäme** mich **meiner bösen Worte**.*

---

[1] Only in the sense of "to release from," not "to give birth to."
[2] Only in the sense of "to suspend" (see example), not "be horrified."

D 958   Two other verbs may also take a person as a genitive object; they are **bedürfen** and **gedenken**:

> *Die Gesunden bedürfen **des Arztes** nicht.*
> *Wir gedenken **seiner**.*

D 960   Genitive objects also occur together with certain ADJECTIVES used as verbal complements [→ E 440, H 386]. (The genitive object precedes the adjective.)[1]

bar	gewärtig	(un)sicher
bedürftig	(un)gewiß	teilhaftig
(un)bewußt	(un)kundig	überdrüssig
eingedenk	mächtig	verdächtig
(un)fähig	müde[3]	verlustig
froh	satt[3]	voll, voller[4]
gewahr[2]	(un)schuldig	(un)wert
		(un)würdig

> *Du bist **keiner schlechten Tat fähig**.*
> *Er ist **seines Erfolges sicher** (**gewiß**).*
> *Ich bin **des Lernens überdrüssig** (**satt**).*
> *Diese schmutzige Arbeit ist **deiner** nicht **würdig**.*

D 965   The genitive also occurs as an ADVERBIAL MODIFIER:

1. In expressions of time which indicate indefinite time or repeated events:

> *Eines Tages besuchte mich mein Freund.*[5]
> *Wir gingen **des Abends** (**abends**) immer in ein Restaurant.*
> *Letzten Endes tut er immer, was er will.*

2. In some expressions of place:

---

[1] In colloquial usage, the genitive is often replaced by prepositional constructions, e.g. **fähig zu, froh über, müde von, schuldig an** (dative), **voll mit**: *Er ist schuldig an dem Mord. Du bist zu keiner schlechten Tat fähig.*

[2] **Gewahr** is used only with the verb **werden**. It also occurs with the accusative: *Er wurde seines Irrtums (seinen Irrtum) gewahr.*

[3] **Müde** and **satt** often occur with the accusative: *Ich habe es satt.*

[4] **Voller** precedes the genitive expression: *Er kam **voller** guter Absichten.*

[5] By analogy, expressions like **nachts, des Nachts, eines Nachts** may also be used: *Im Sommer gingen wir des Nachts (nachts) oft spazieren.* This can not be done if **Nacht** is preceded by an attributive adjective: *in einer schönen Nacht.*

290

> *Gehen Sie diese Straße entlang, dann sehen Sie **linker Hand** das neue Hotel.*
>
> *Laß ihn **seines Weges** gehen!*

3. In some idiomatic expressions of manner:

[handwritten: can't get the same meaning from parts 966]

> *Ich fahre immer **erster Klasse**.*
> ***Meines Wissens** fährt nachts kein Zug nach Salzburg.*
> *Er ging **frohen Mutes** (**guter Laune**) weiter.*
> ***Schweren Herzens** beschloß er abzufahren.*
> ***Meines Erachtens** hätte die Arbeit beendet sein müssen.*

4. As a remnant in some adverbs: **links, rechts, meinerseits, jedenfalls, keineswegs, gewissermaßen, glücklicherweise,** etc.

The genitive is found as a predicate complement of the verb **sein**: D 967

> *Ich bin ganz **deiner Meinung**.*
> *Er ist **voller Freude**.*
> *Wir sind **anderer Ansicht**.*

The genitive occurs most frequently as the case of a NOUN ATTRIBUTE D 970
of another noun. The noun in the genitive usually follows the noun
which it modifies[1] and may have one of the following relationships
with it:

1. The genitive indicates a relation of ownership, part and whole, membership, property, feature, or characteristic, etc. (GENITIVE OF POSSESSION):[2]

> *das Haus **meines Vaters**, das Dach **des Hauses**, der Kopf **des Tieres**, der Glanz **seiner Augen**, ein Mitglied **dieses Vereins***

2. The genitive acts as subject for an action noun (SUBJECT GENITIVE):

> *der Tanz **der Kinder*** — *die Kinder tanzen*
> *die Freundlichkeit **der Frau*** — *die Frau ist freundlich*
> *der Befehl **des Offiziers*** — *der Offizier befiehlt*

---

[1] The so-called "Anglo-Saxon genitive," in which the genitive noun precedes, is fairly rare. It occurs primarily with proper names (*Herrn Müllers Haus, Maries Onkel*), or in elevated style: *Er ist keines Menschen Freund.* [→ C 247, 250]

[2] This is the reason why the genitive is sometimes referred to as the possessive case. This terminology is misleading, however.

3. The genitive acts as the object for an action noun (OBJECT GENITIVE):

die Beantwortung **des Briefes** — man beantwortet den Brief
die Lösung **des Problems** — man löst das Problem
der Besitz **eines Hauses** — man besitzt ein Haus

Notice the difference:

die Entdeckung **des Forschers** — der Forscher entdeckt etwas
die Entdeckung **Amerikas** — man hat Amerika entdeckt

D 971 The genitive may also be the noun attribute of some other part of speech. It then has partitive meaning (PARTITIVE GENITIVE).[1]

The partitive genitive may occur with the following parts of speech:

indefinite pronoun:	jeder **der** Schüler
cardinal numbers:	zwei **meiner** Freunde
ordinal numbers:	das dritte **dieser** Bücher
indefinite numerals:	viele **deiner** Briefe
adjectives in comparative:	der ältere **der** beiden Brüder
adjectives in superlative:	der beste **der** Schüler

D 972 The partitive genitive is **not** used in the following constructions:

1. the names of cities and months, and for dates:

die Stadt Berlin, der Monat Juni, der 24. Dezember

2. <u>units of measurement</u>:[2]

drei Pfund Äpfel, zwei Glas Bier, eine Flasche Wein,
eine Tasse Kaffee, ein Stück Kuchen, ein Blatt Papier

D 973 If in the attributive use of a genitive, the case can not be recognized by an inflectional ending, it must be replaced by a prepositional expression with the preposition **von** [→ C 245, 253, 261].[3] This happens primarily

---

[1] The partitive genitive may be replaced by the preposition **von** [→ F 697] (zwei **von** meinen Freunden, viele **von** deinen Büchern), or by the preposition **unter** [→ F 622] (der beste **unter** den Schülern, das teuerste **unter** diesen Kleidern).

[2] With units of measurement, the genitive of nouns preceded by an attributive adjective is possible but sounds stilted: ein Glas kalten Wassers. Usually, the adjectival phrase is considered to be in apposition to the unit of measurement and is in the same case: Ich trinke ein Glas **kaltes** Wasser (eine Tasse **schwarzen** Kaffee). Er kam mit einem Glas kaltem Wasser (einer Tasse schwarzem Kaffee).

[3] The genitive must be used if the second noun is preceded by an article: die Gärten **des** schönen Paris. It may also be used if the second noun is preceded by an adjective: der Bau neuer Straßen; die Produktion **reinen** Stahls. It is also possible in these constructions to replace the genitive by **von** (der Bau **von** neuen Straßen; die Produktion **von** reinem Stahl).

1. with nouns in the indefinite plural without attributes:

> *der Bau von Straßen, die Arbeiten von Studenten*

2. with names without genitive forms:

> *die Gärten von Paris, die Küste von Tunis*

3. with the names of materials without attributes:

> *die Produktion von Stahl, die Gewinnung von Torf*

As a PREPOSITIONAL CASE, the genitive occurs after a number of preposi-   D 975
tions [→ F 040]; the most frequent ones are **(an)statt, trotz, während,**
and **wegen**:

> *Mein Freund kam **trotz des schlechten Wetters**.*
> ***Während meiner Reise** lernte ich viele Städte kennen.*

The construction **um . . . willen** encloses the genitive object [→ F 046];   D 976
the prepositions **ungeachtet** and **wegen** may also occur as postpositions
[→ F 042]; **halber**[1] always functions as a postposition [→ F 044]:

> ***Um** Gottes **willen**!*
> ***wegen** des schlechten Wetters — des schlechten Wetters **wegen***
> ***ungeachtet** seiner Krankheit — seiner Krankheit **ungeachtet***
> *der Ordnung **halber***

[1] After pronouns, the form **-halben** (sometimes **-halb**) is used: *meinethalben.*

E

ⅹ Adjectives and Adverbs

DESCRIPTIVE ADJECTIVES

ⅹ Introduction

E 001 Adjectives are used to modify nouns and to characterize living beings, places, things, or concepts.

E 005 We distinguish between LIMITING ADJECTIVES [→ D 280 ff.] and DE-SCRIPTIVE ADJECTIVES. Limiting (or pronominal) adjectives include definite and indefinite articles [→ D 300 ff.], demonstratives [→ D 400 ff.], possessives [→ D 600], numerical adjectives [→ E 600], the interrogative **welch-** [→ D 240 ff.], as well as **all-, jed-,** and **kein-.**

All other adjectives are called descriptive adjectives.[1] It is important to keep this distinction in mind.

E 010 The adjective may function as an ATTRIBUTE [→ J 110.6], as a PREDICATE COMPLEMENT [→ H 411], PREDICATE NOMINATIVE [→ H 461.2], or PREDICATE ACCUSATIVE [→ H 471.2].

[1] For **manch-** and **solch-** and indefinite attributes like **andere, einige, mehrere, viele, wenige,** etc., → individual entries in Chapters D and E 150 ff.

294

An adjective may also function adverbially as a PREDICATE MODIFIER   E 011
[→ E 800 ff.]. As such, it modifies verbs, adjectives, or other adverbs
and acts as an indicator of manner [→ H 568.2], answering the question **how?**

Adjectives are declined only if they are used as attributes preceding a   E 012
noun, if they follow an article as a predicate nominative, accusative, or
complement, or if they are used as nouns. Otherwise, they are uninflected [cf. E 220, 230, 240]:

> *Sie hat einen **neuen blauen** Hut.*
> *Die heutige Lage ist eine **kritische**.*
> *Lesen Sie ein deutsches Buch? Nein, ich lese ein **englisches**.*
> *Helfen Sie dem **Blinden**!*

> *Dieses Kleid ist sehr **schön**.*
> *Ich nenne diese Arbeit **ausgezeichnet**.*
> *Er lag **krank** im Bett,*
> *Hänschen **klein**.*

Adjectives used adverbially are always uninflected: E 013

> *Das Auto fährt **schnell**.*
> *Heute ist es **bitter** kalt.*
> ***Tief** unten im Tal fließt ein Bach.*

Adjectives and Adverbs

UNINFLECTED ADJECTIVES and ADVERBS may be IDENTICAL in FORM but   E 050
clearly DIFFER in FUNCTION.[1] It is useful to keep this distinction in mind.
In a sentence such as **Das Mädchen ist schön**, **schön** is an adjectival
attribute which describes a quality of the girl herself. In the sentence
Das Mädchen singt schön, on the other hand, the word **schön** describes
the quality of her singing; in terms of function, **schön** should be classified as an adverb of manner and as such is functionally interchangeable
with other adverbs of manner, for instance **gern**: **Das Mädchen singt
gern**.

The functional and semantic difference between adjective and adverb   E 051
can also be seen by contrasting such phrases as **eine junge verheiratete**

---

[1] Many modern German grammars deny this distinction on purely formal grounds. This
practice, however, is confusing from an English point of view, where the differentiation is
essential and is indicated by the ending *-ly* (beautiful, beautiful*ly*).

Frau (a young married woman) where **jung** (ADJ.) modifies **Frau**, and **eine jung verheiratete Frau** (a recently married woman — not necessarily a young woman at all) where **jung** (ADV.) modifies **verheiratet**.[1]

E 055   Where adjectives and adverbs have common features, such as comparative and superlative forms, they will be treated under the same heading. For a full discussion of adverbs, → E 800 ff.

DECLENSION OF DESCRIPTIVE ADJECTIVES

Basic Principles

E 100   LIMITING adjectives may be completely uninflected, such as the numerical adjectives; they may have inflected and uninflected forms (**all, solch, manch, welch,** etc.); or they may have no endings in certain cases, such as the indefinite article, **kein**, and the possessives (the so-called "**ein**-words" [→ D 600 ff.]). When limiting adjectives have inflectional endings, they follow the pattern of the definite article [→ D 305] and **dies-** [→ D 410].[2]

These endings are called PRIMARY or pronominal (strong) endings.[3] They serve as function indicators and show number, gender, and case of the noun following (or understood).

E 102   If no such function indicator precedes the descriptive adjective, the DESCRIPTIVE adjective itself carries the PRIMARY endings. This happens if there is no limiting adjective at all, or if the limiting adjective is uninflected.[4]

E 105   If, however, the descriptive adjective is preceded by an inflected limiting adjective, the descriptive adjective itself carries so-called SECONDARY (weak) endings, which no longer serve as function indicators.

---

[1] To be sure, there are formal differences here as well: the adjective is inflected (*junge*), and the two adjectives are usually separated by a comma: *eine junge, verheiratete Frau*.

[2] For details of individual patterns, see individual entries in Chapter D.

[3] The traditional terms "strong" and "weak" have been replaced by the more descriptive and meaningful labels "primary" and "secondary."

[4] There are two exceptions from this principle: adjectives in the genitive singular masculine and neuter have secondary endings, since the noun acts as a function indicator [→ E 110]; and descriptive adjectives after uninflected **dies** have secondary endings: *dies alte Buch*.

296

There are only two secondary endings: **-e** in the nominative singular   E 106
(and, of course, the accusative singular feminine and neuter, since these
forms are always identical with the nominative), **-en** for all other cases
of the singular and all plurals.

Primary Adjective Endings

The descriptive adjective has PRIMARY ENDINGS if the noun which it   E 110
modifies is NOT preceded by any article or other limiting adjective.

The primary adjective endings are identical with the endings of
dies- [→ D 410]. In the genitive singular masculine and neuter, however,
the adjective has the ending **-en**, since the noun itself has the function-
indicating **-s** ending of the genitive:

	Singular			Plural
	Masc.	Ntr.	Fem.	Masc./Ntr./Fem.
NOM.	-er	-es	-e	-e
ACC.	-en	-es	-e	-e
DAT.	-em	-em	-er	-en
GEN.	**-en**	**-en**	-er	-er

		Masculine	Neuter	Feminine
Sing.	NOM.	alt-**er** Wein	rot-**es** Licht	kühl-**e** Luft
	ACC.	**-en** Wein	**-es** Licht	**-e** Luft
	DAT.	**-em** Wein	**-em** Licht	**-er** Luft
	GEN.	**-en** Weines	**-en** Lichtes	**-er** Luft
Pl.	NOM.	**-e** Weine	**-e** Lichter	**-e** Lüfte
	ACC.	**-e** Weine	**-e** Lichter	**-e** Lüfte
	DAT.	**-en** Weinen	**-en** Lichtern	**-en** Lüften
	GEN.	**-er** Weine	**-er** Lichter	**-er** Lüfte

Er brachte eine Flasche mit altem Wein.
Das Aroma alten Weines ist sehr stark.
Kühle Luft ist manchmal ungesund.
Im Zimmer brannte rotes Licht.
Im Zimmer brannten rote Lichter.

E 111 The descriptive adjective also has primary endings after numerical adjectives [→ E 670], after uninflected forms of indefinite attributes such as **manch, solch, welch, viel, wenig, etwas, mehr** [→ D 700 ff.] and uninflected **ein**-words [→ E 130], after personal pronouns,[1] and after genitive forms [→ **wessen** and **dessen** D 217, D 521].

*Dort stehen **drei** alte Frauen.*
*Mit **solch** großem Fleiß wird er viel lernen.*
*Bei **etwas** besserem Wetter könnten wir den Ausflug machen.*
*Er ist **ein** alter Mann.*
*Sie haben **mir** armer Frau viel Freude gemacht.*
*Wir fuhren in **Roberts** neuem Wagen an die See.*
*Der Dichter, **dessen** neues Buch ich gelesen habe, ist ein Franzose.*
***Wessen** rotes Tuch hängt dort?*

Secondary Adjective Endings

E 120 The descriptive adjective has SECONDARY endings if it follows after an inflected limiting adjective, such as the definite article. The secondary ending is **-e** after **der** (masc., nom. only), **das** (ntr., nom./acc.), and **die** (fem. sgl., nom./acc.). In all other cases of the singular and plural, the secondary ending is **-en**.

	Singular			Plural
	Masc.	Ntr.	Fem.	Masc./Ntr./Fem.
NOM.	-e	-e	-e	-en
ACC.	-en	-e	-e	-en
DAT.	-en	-en	-en	-en
GEN.	-en	-en	-en	-en

[1] But → E 160.

		Masculine	Neuter	Feminine
Sing.	NOM.	der alt-**e** Mann	das klein-**e** Haus	die jung-**e** Frau
	ACC.	den **-en** Mann	das **-e** Haus	die **-e** Frau
	DAT.	dem **-en** Mann	dem **-en** Haus	der **-en** Frau
	GEN.	des **-en** Mannes	des **-en** Hauses	der **-en** Frau
Pl.	NOM.	die **-en** Männer	die **-en** Häuser	die **-en** Frauen
	ACC.	die **-en** Männer	die **-en** Häuser	die **-en** Frauen
	DAT.	den **-en** Männern	den **-en** Häusern	den **-en** Frauen
	GEN.	der **-en** Männer	der **-en** Häuser	der **-en** Frauen

Der alte Mann ist mein Großvater.
Sehen Sie das kleine Haus dort drüben?
Ich sprach mit der jungen Frau.
Ich bin der Enkel des alten Mannes.
Sehen Sie die kleinen Häuser dort drüben?
Ich sprach mit den jungen Frauen.

The descriptive adjective also has secondary endings after **dies-, jen-,** E 121
solch-,[1] **derjenig-, derselb-** [→ demonstratives D 440, 450, 470], **welch-**[1]
[→ interrogatives D 240], **all-, jed-, manch-**[1] [→ indefinite attributes
D 780, 840, 860], inflected forms of **ein**-words [→ E 130], and after
beide [→ E 656]:

Dieser junge Mann ist mein Freund.
Haben Sie jenes bekannte Buch gelesen?
Mit welcher schönen Frau hast du gesprochen?
Er liest jedes wichtige Buch.
Aller gute Wille nützt nichts.
Er hat keine guten Manieren.
Die Väter beider jungen Menschen sind gute Freunde.

Note that primary and secondary endings coincide in the feminine E 122
singular nominative/accusative (**-e**), the masculine singular accusative
(**-en**), and the dative plural (**-en**):

Kühle Luft ist manchmal ungesund. Ich vertrage die kühle Luft nicht.
Er trinkt roten Wein. Mögen Sie diesen roten Wein?
Wir helfen armen Leuten. Wir helfen den armen Leuten.

[1] For fluctuations in endings after **manch-, solch-,** and **welch-,** → E 153–4.

Mixed Adjective Endings

E 130 The category of "mixed adjective endings" is included here only because it is traditionally used to describe endings of descriptive adjectives after the so-called "**ein** words" (indefinite articles, **kein-**, and the possessives). In actuality, of course, there is no such category. Descriptive adjectives have primary endings if the preceding **ein**-word is uninflected (masculine singular nominative and neuter singular nominative/accusative); they have secondary endings if the preceding **ein**-word is inflected (all other cases).

E 131 In actual practice, this means that after **ein**-words, the descriptive adjective ends in **-er** in the masc. nom. [→ E 110], **-es** in the ntr. nom./ acc. [→ E 110], **-e** in the fem. nom./acc. [→ E 120], and **-en** in all other cases of the singular and all plurals [→ E 120].

	Singular			Plural
	Masc.	Ntr.	Fem.	Masc./Ntr./Pl.
NOM.	**-er**	**-es**	**-e**	**-en**
ACC.	**-en**	**-es**	**-e**	**-en**
DAT.	**-en**	**-en**	**-en**	**-en**
GEN.	**-en**	**-en**	**-en**	**-en**

		Masculine	Neuter	Feminine
Sing.	NOM.	ein alt **-er** Mann	ein klein**-es** Haus	eine jung**-e** Frau
	ACC.	einen **-en** Mann	ein **-es** Haus	eine **-e** Frau
	DAT.	einem **-en** Mann	einem **-en** Haus	einer **-en** Frau
	GEN.	eines **-en** Mannes	eines **-en** Hauses	einer **-en** Frau
Pl.	NOM.	keine **-en** Männer	keine **-en** Häuser	keine **-en** Frauen
	ACC.	keine **-en** Männer	keine **-en** Häuser	keine **-en** Frauen
	DAT.	keinen **-en** Männern	keinen **-en** Häusern	keinen **-en** Frauen
	GEN.	keiner **-en** Männer	keiner **-en** Häuser	keiner **-en** Frauen

300

*Ich lese **ein** deutsches Buch.*
*Sie ist **eine** alte Frau.*
***Sein** alter Vater hat heute Geburtstag.*
*Wir haben **kein** deutsches Geld.*
*Ich habe **keinen** großen Hunger.*
*Er kam mit **einem** jungen Mädchen.*
*Haben Sie **keine** besseren Bücher?*

Note that the **-er** ending on words like **dieser, jener, welcher, keiner,** etc.   E 132
is an inflectional ending and that the following descriptive adjective
therefore has a secondary ending; the syllable **-er** on the words **unser**
and **euer,** however, is part of the stem. These words are uninflected and
the following descriptive adjective therefore has a primary ending:

primary secondary
Dieser alte Mann ist unser Vater.

primary
Unser alter Vater hat heute Geburtstag.

Summary of Rule

> If the PRIMARY ending has NOT occurred PRIOR to the descriptive   E 135
> adjective, it will occur ON the descriptive adjective.[1] If the primary
> ending HAS occurred prior to the descriptive adjective, the de-
> scriptive adjective has SECONDARY endings (**-e** or **-en**).

Adjectives in Sequence

If a noun is preceded by several descriptive adjectives, they all have the   E 140
same declensional ending:

ein armer, alter Mann
das große, neue Haus
meine lieben, guten Freunde

An attributive adjective may sometimes be considered as forming a   E 141
unified concept with a noun. In such cases, other descriptive adjectives
preceding a noun without an article have parallel primary endings in the

[1] For exception in the genitive sing. masc./ntr. → footnote E 102.

301

nominative and accusative, but may have secondary endings in the dative singular masculine and neuter:[1]

> *Hier ist guter roter Wein. — Ein Prosit mit gutem roten Wein!*
> *Das Zimmer hat fließendes warmes und kaltes Wasser. — Er*
> *sucht ein Zimmer mit fließendem warmen und kalten Wasser.*

E 142   Some few descriptive adjectives may take on demonstrative character when they have primary endings. Any following descriptive adjective then has secondary endings in the singular:[2]

> *Beiliegendes kleine Geschenk soll Ihnen Freude machen.*

E 143   Nouns are rarely preceded by more than one limiting adjective. When this happens, however, all the limiting adjectives have primary endings; the distinction is made between limiting adjectives on the one hand (primary endings), and descriptive adjectives on the other (secondary endings):

limiting	descriptive
alle meine	*lieben alten Freunde*
alle diese	*interessanten deutschen Bücher*

E 144   When **jeder (jeglicher), solcher,** and **einzelner** are preceded by un-inflected **ein,** they (as well as following descriptive adjectives) have primary endings. After an inflected form of **ein-,** however, they have secondary endings:

> *Ein jeder guter Bürger soll seinem Vaterland helfen.*
> *Es ist die Pflicht eines jeden guten Bürgers, seinem Vaterland zu helfen.*

Indefinite Adjectives

E 150   In general, indefinite adjectives in the plural, such as **ähnliche, andere, derartige, einige, einzelne, etliche, folgende, gewisse, letztere, mehrere, obige, sämtliche, sogenannte, sonstige, ungezählte (unzählbare, unzählige,**

---

[1] The feminine and all plurals also have parallel endings. In the masculine and neuter genitive, the **-en** ending must be used [→ E 110]: *das Aroma guten roten Weines.* Parallel endings are also possible in the masculine and neuter dative: *mit fließendem warmem und kaltem Wasser; mit gutem rotem Wein.*

[2] The plural has parallel endings: *beiliegende kleine Geschenke,* or better: *die beiliegenden kleinen Geschenke.*

zahllose, zahlreiche), verschiedene, viele, weitere, wenige, etc., are treated like descriptive adjectives, since a limiting adjective, by definition, must define a given category in a precise way [→ D 280 ff.].

The indefinite adjectives themselves therefore have primary endings if unpreceded by an inflected limiting adjective, secondary endings if they follow an inflected limiting adjective. Other descriptive adjectives which follow them have parallel inflection, i.e. the same ending as the indefinite adjective:[1]

primary	secondary
viele gute Freunde	— **meine** *vielen guten Freunde*
andere alte Männer	— **die** *anderen alten Männer*
sonstige neue Bücher	— **alle** *sonstigen neuen Bücher*
folgende interessante Sätze —	**diese** *folgenden interessanten Sätze*

In the singular, where these indefinite adjectives occur less frequently, usage fluctuates. In general, secondary endings on descriptive adjectives predominate after inflected primary forms of **einig-, etlich-, folgend-, manch-, sämtlich-, solch-, viel-, welch-,** and **wenig-.** Parallel primary endings do occur, however: E 151

	but also:
mancher arme Mann	*weniges gutes Essen*
bei einigem guten Willen	*einiges slawisches Blut*
sämtliches vorhandene Material	*vieler schöner Schmuck*
vieles alte Zeug	etc.
folgender interessante Bericht	
etc.	

After uninflected forms, to be sure, the descriptive adjective always has primary endings [→ E 111]: E 152

viel *gutes Essen*
welch *netter Mensch!* (**welch ein** *netter Mensch!*)
manch *bunte Blumen*
mit (ein) **wenig** *gutem Willen*

After **manch-** and **solch-** in the plural, traditional grammatical rules call for secondary endings. However, **manche** and **solche** are no longer felt E 153

---

[1] This is especially true in the nominative and accusative. In the dative, primary and secondary endings coincide: *vielen guten Freunden.* In the genitive, which occurs rarely, usage fluctuates: *die Stimmen anderer alter* (or *alten*) *Männer.*

to be strictly limiting adjectives. Consequently, parallel primary endings occur very frequently on the following descriptive adjective, and today tend to predominate after **manch-**:

> *manche zarte Bande*
> *solche geheimnisvolle Kräfte*

E 154   After **welch-** in the plural, secondary endings predominate. Primary endings occur, but rather rarely, and are not considered good German. Primary endings, however, tend to predominate after **irgendwelch-** in the plural:

> ***Welche*** *neuen Bücher haben Sie gelesen?*
> *Haben Sie **irgendwelche** neue Bücher gelesen?*

E 155   **Beide** [→ E 656] is felt to be a limiting adjective, and the following descriptive adjective therefore usually has secondary inflection. Parallel primary endings occur, but are rare:[1]

> ***beide*** *alten Männer*
> *die Söhne **beider** alten Männer*
> ***beide*** *geschlossene Augen*

E 160   After personal pronouns, where the rule would require primary endings [→ E 111], usage sometimes fluctuates, especially after **wir, mir,** and **dir**; primary forms predominate after **ich, du,** and **Sie** (singular), secondary forms after **ihr**[2] and **Sie** (plural):

> *wir Deutsche(**n**); dir krank**em** (kranken) Mann; mir alt**er** (alten) Frau*
> *ich Arm**er**, du Arm**er**, Sie Arm**er** (masc.), Sie Arm**e** (fem.)!*
> *ihr Arm**en**, Sie Arm**en** (pl.)!*

Special Problems of Adjective Declension

E 200   In adjectives ending in **-el,** the **-e-** of the final stem syllable is omitted before the ending:

---

[1] After some other inflected limiting adjective, both **beide** and the following descriptive adjective have secondary endings: *die beiden alten Männer, die Söhne dieser beiden alten Männer.*

[2] After the possessive **ihr,** to be sure, primary endings must be used: *ihr neues Kleid.*

dunkel — das dunkle Zimmer
im dunklen Zimmer

If the ending is **-en**, it is possible for the stem to remain intact, while the **-e-** of the ending is omitted: E 201

im dunklen Zimmer — im dunkeln Zimmer

Similarly, adjectives ending in **-er** and **-en** may lose the **-e-** of the final stem syllable before an ending: E 202

bitter — ein bitterer Kaffee   *— ein bittrer Kaffee*
einen bitteren Kaffee — einen bittren Kaffee

teuer — ein teueres Auto   *— ein teures Auto*
eines teueren Autos   — eines teuren Autos

offen — eine offene Tür   *— eine offne Tür*
einer offenen Tür   — einer offnen Tür

For adjectives ending in **-er** (but not those ending in **-en**), the ending **-en** may also be shortened to **-n**:   E 203

einen bittren Kaffee   — einen bittern Kaffee
eines teuren Autos   — eines teuern Autos

The adjective **hoch** loses the **-c-** of the stem before an **-e-** in the ending: E 210

*Das Haus ist **hoch** — das **hohe** Haus — ein **hohes** Haus*

Some descriptive adjectives have NO DECLENSIONAL ENDINGS even when they are used attributively. These include   E 220
1. Foreign words ending in **-a**, especially adjectives of color:

*Das Mädchen trug ein **rosa** Kleid.*
*Sie hatte ein **lila** Band im Haar.*
*Auf dem Markt können Sie **prima** Obst kaufen.*

2. Adjectives ending in **-er** derived from the names of cities. These adjectives are always capitalized:

die Frankfurter Straße   — in der Frankfurter Straße
der Kölner Dom   — vor dem Kölner Dom
das Straßburger Münster — das Portal des Straßburger Münsters

305

E 230   Attributive descriptive adjectives may occur WITHOUT ENDINGS in the
following circumstances:[1]

1. In poetic usage:

> *Meine Mutter hat manch* **gülden** *Gewand.*
> *Wir wollen sein ein* **einzig** *Volk von Brüdern.*
> **Schön** *Rosmarin.*

2. In certain idiomatic or proverbial expressions:

> *auf* **gut** *Glück*
> **ruhig** *Blut*
> *ein* **halb** *Dutzend*
> **arabisch** *Eins,* **römisch** *Zwei*

E 240   Descriptive adjectives FOLLOWING THE NOUN which they modify have
no declensional endings:[2]

> *Hänschen* **klein**
> *Röslein* **rot**
> *Ich sah ein Mädchen,* **jung** *und* **schön**.
> *Der Genitiv* **maskulin** *hat die Endung -es.*

E 250   Some adjectives have no declensional endings and can not be used
attributively, but only as verbal complements. Some of these adjectives
are **allein, barfuß, gewärtig, gram, leid, quitt, schade, schuld,** etc.
[→ J 035]. Some of these adjectives exist today only in fixed idiomatic
phrases, i.e. **abspenstig machen, gewahr werden.**

> *Ich bin* **allein.**
> *Die Angelegenheit ist (tut) mir* **leid.**
> *Die Kinder waren (gingen)* **barfuß.**

E 251   It is often possible to form derivatives from these adjectives by adding
the syllable **-ig.** The derivative adjectives can be used attributively and
are inflected:

> *Das ist seine allein**ig**e Schuld.*
> *Es war eine leid**ig**e Angelegenheit.*
> *Die barfüß**ig**en Kinder spielten im Garten.*

---

[1] Adjectives used as adverbs are always uninflected [→ E 013].
[2] Descriptive adjectives in the predicate are also uninflected [→ E 012].

Adjectives denoting NATIONALITY may be used as independent sentence   E 255
units (i.e. other than as noun attributes) only if they designate something
characteristic or typical for this nation. Otherwise they have to be
paraphrased:

> *Das Werk dieses Malers hat typisch **französische** Züge. Das Werk
> dieses Malers ist echt **französisch.***
> *Diese drei Jungen sind **spanische** Studenten. Diese drei Studenten sind
> **Spanier.***
> *Ich lese ein **englisches** Buch. Es ist ein Buch **in englischer Sprache.***

When such adjectives describe a language and are used with verbs   E 256
denoting speaking, writing, understanding, etc., they are capitalized.[1]
[→ E 500 ff. for adjectives used as nouns.]

> *Er lernt (kann, versteht, schreibt) **Deutsch.***
> *Er spricht gut **Deutsch.***

After the preposition **auf**, however, the adjective is usually not capitalized   E 257
and uninflected:

> *Wie sagt man das **auf deutsch**?*

Adjectives formed from adverbs of time by the addition of the ending   E 260
-ig may only be used attributively:

> *heute, gestern:*   *Ist das die heut**ige** Zeitung oder die gest**rige**?*
> *vor:*   *Ich sah ihn vor**ige** Woche.*
> *hier:*   *Wir besuchten die hies**igen** Museen.[2]*

Adverbs of time with the suffix **-s** lose this ending before the adjective   E 261
suffix **-ig**:

> *damals:*   *Bei unseren damal**igen** Besprechungen war er nicht anwesend.*
> *ehemals:*   *Die ehemal**igen** Bewohner dieses Hauses sind weggezogen.*

Similarly, adjectives may be formed by adding the ending **-er** to adverbs   E 265

---

[1] This does not apply to certain idiomatic usages: *Mit dem muß man deutsch reden* — One
has to be (brutally) frank with him. In other instances, lower case is also sometimes used in
modern German.

[2] Note the stem change from **-r** to **-s**.

of place, often with a slight change in the stem of the adverb. Such adjectives can also be used attributively only [1] [→ E 393]:

> vorn: *Bitte benützen Sie den **vorderen** Eingang!*
> außen: *Schon die **äußere** Form dieses Buches gefällt mir.*
> unten: *Wer wohnt hier im **unteren** Stockwerk?*
> innen: *Die Fenster gingen auf den **inneren** Hof.*

E 268   The words **rechts, links,** and **anders** [→ E 391] lose the suffix **-s** when they are used attributively before nouns. This also applies to the adverb **besonders** when it is used as an attributive adjective:

> *Die Glocke ist **rechts**. — Er gab mir die **rechte** Hand.*
> *Gehen Sie die erste Straße **links**. — Das Geschäft ist auf der **linken** Straßenseite.*
> *Heute sind die Verhältnisse **anders**. — Die **anderen** Verhältnisse machen die Arbeit leichter.*
> *Die Sache ist **besonders** wichtig. — Die Sache ist von **besonderer** Wichtigkeit.*

COMPARISON OF ADJECTIVES AND ADVERBS

E 300   In the comparison of adjectives and adverbs there are two levels, both of which are derived from the base form of the adjective, the so-called POSITIVE. These two levels are called COMPARATIVE and SUPERLATIVE.

E 301   The comparative of descriptive adjectives and adverbs is formed with the affix **-er**, the superlative with the affix **-st**. These are added to the stem of the adjective and are followed by the declensional endings. [2]

    The superlative is usually preceded by the definite article or a possessive, never by the indefinite article or an indefinite limiting adjective.

> *Heute ist ein schöner Tag, aber gestern war es **schön-er**. Gestern war ein **schön-er-er** Tag. Der **schön-st-e** Tag dieser Woche war Sonntag.*
> *Mein Vater hatte ein schnelles Motorboot, aber das meines Onkels war **schnell-er**. Mein Vater kaufte auch ein **schnell-er-es** Motorboot. Jetzt hat er das **schnell-st-e** Boot auf dem See.*

---

[1] These forms look like, but do not function as, comparatives.

[2] Technically, the comparative affix **-er** and the superlative affix **-st** thus become infixes.

German adjectives and adverbs use the comparative and superlative   E 302
affixes regardless of their length:

> *Dieses Buch ist viel interessanter als das andere.*
> *Er ist der fleißigste Schüler.*
> *Er sprach noch verworrener als gewöhnlich.*

For special uses of **mehr**, → E 365. **Meist** is not used to form super-   E 303
latives, except in compounds such as **meistgeliebt**. For absolute superlatives, → E 385 ff.

Special Declensional Forms

If the adjective ends in **-d, -t, -tz, -s, -ß,**[1] **-st, -x,** or **-z,** the superlative   E 310
suffix is **-est**. This usually also applies to adjectives ending in **-sch**:

gesund	*(der, das, die) gesündeste*
weit	*(der, das, die) weiteste*
heiß	*(der, das, die) heißeste*
fix	*(der, das, die) fixeste*
kurz	*(der, das, die) kürzeste*
frisch	*(der, das, die) frischeste* or *frischste*

Exceptions from this rule include multisyllabic adjectives ending in   E 311
-isch, present participles, and past participles of verbs with a stem
ending in **-t** [→ B 180]:[2]

> *malerisch:*   *Das ist der malerischste Platz unserer Reise.*
> *brennend:*   *Dies ist im Augenblick meine brennendste Sorge.*
> *gefürchtet:*   *Er ist der gefürchtetste Beamte in dieser Behörde.*

Adjectives ending in **-el** always lose the **-e-** of the last stem syllable in the   E 315
comparative; for adjectives ending in **-en** and **-er**, this omission is
optional:

> *dunkel:*   *Die Straße ist heute **dunkler** als sonst.*
> *trocken:*   *In diesem Sommer ist das Wetter **trockner** (**trockener**) als im*
>   *vorigen Jahr.*
> *teuer:*   *Das Obst ist hier **teurer** (**teuerer**) als in anderen Geschäften.*

---

[1] Exception: *groß, der größte.*

[2] Past participles of other weak verbs *do* insert the linking -e- in the superlative: *geschickt, der geschickteste.*

E 316　For past participles of strong verbs, however, the full **-en** ending is maintained in the comparative:

> *gelungen:　Diese Feier war **gelungener** als alle früheren.*

E 320　Many one-syllable adjectives take UMLAUT in the comparative and superlative:

alt	*älter*	*(der, das, die) älteste*
jung	*jünger*	*(der, das, die) jüngste*
groß	*größer*	*(der, das, die) größte*

E 321　Adjectives with **-au-** in the stem, however, do not take *Umlaut*:

laut	*lauter*	*(der, das, die) lauteste*

E 322　Several adjectives may form their comparative and superlative either without or (less frequently) with *Umlaut*:[1]

bang, blaß, glatt, naß, schmal, fromm, rot, krumm

E 325　Only a few adjectives have irregular comparison:

groß	*größer*	*(der, das, die) größte* [→ E 310 note]
hoch, hoh-	*höher*	*(der, das, die) höchste* [→ E 210]
nah	*näher*	*(der, das, die) nächste*
gut	*besser*	*(der, das, die) beste*
viel	*mehr*	*(der, das, die) meiste*

E 326　The adjective/adverb **wenig**, besides its regular comparison, also has the irregular forms **minder** (used only as an adverb to modify adjectives), **(der, das, die) mindeste**, and the verb modifier **im mindesten**. These forms occur infrequently [→ E 824].

> *Diese Angelegenheit ist **minder** wichtig.*
> *Er gab sich nicht die **mindeste** Mühe.*
> *Die Frage interessiert mich nicht **im mindesten**.*

E 327　The comparative forms **mehr** and **weniger** have NO ADJECTIVE DECLENSION [→ D 885]:

> *Paul hat **mehr** Geld als Peter.*
> *Mein Freund hat **mehr** Bücher als ich.*
> *Ich habe **weniger** Zeit als du.*
> *Unser Haus hat **weniger** Zimmer als sein Haus.*

[1] For **gesund**, on the other hand, comparative forms with *Umlaut* are more frequent.

310

Adjectives used adverbially as PREDICATE MODIFIERS have the compara-   E 330
tive ending **-er**, always UNINFLECTED [→ E 820 ff.]. In the superlative,
they use the preposition **am** and the ending **-sten**. [For absolute superlative, → E 386.]

> *Marie singt schön. Anna singt **schöner**. Ilse singt **am schönsten**.*

For adverbs with irregular comparative forms → E 824.   E 331

Comparison of Adjectives as Predicate Complements

The comparative forms of predicate adjectives correspond to those of   E 340
attributive adjectives [→ E 305 ff.].

Predicate adjectives in the comparative have NO DECLENSIONAL ENDINGS   E 341
[→ E 012]:

> *Das Haus ist groß. — Dein Haus ist **größer** als meines.*

Predicate adjectives in the superlative always have declensional endings.   E 342
If the predicate superlative refers to a specific noun (or if it is followed
by some complement), the definite article is used and the adjective
carries secondary endings.[1] Otherwise, it follows the preposition **am**
and takes the ending **-en** [for **auf . . . -ste**, → E 386, E 821]:

> *Der letzte Monat war sehr schön, aber dieser ist **der schönste**.*
> *Diese Wochen waren **die schönsten** des Jahres.*
> *Gestern war es schön, aber heute ist es **am schönsten**.[2]*

Note the difference between the **-er** ending of the uninflected predicate   E 345
comparative, and the primary **-er** ending of the inflected attributive
positive: [3]

primary
Dieser Junge ist klein. Er ist ein klein⟦er⟧ Junge. (positive)

primary
Dieser Junge ist noch kleiner. Er ist ein kleiner⟦er⟧ Junge. (compar.)

---

[1] If the article is replaced by an undeclined form of a possessive adjective, primary endings must be used: *Ich habe drei Söhne; Peter ist mein jüngster* (or *Jüngster*).

[2] As a general rule of thumb, the use of the definite article in the superlative predicate corresponds to English usage.

[3] Some adjectives, of course, already contain the syllable **-er** in the (uninflected) stem (*heiter, sicher, tapfer*, etc.). They may still have an **-er** suffix for the comparative and another as an inflectional ending: *Dieser Mann ist tapfer. Er ist ein tapferer Mann. Mein Freund ist noch tapferer. Er ist ein tapfererer Mann.* Fortunately, such constructions are rare.

Uses of the Comparative

E 350   When a comparison is made to describe an INEQUALITY (or the absence of an inequality) between two persons or things, we use the conjunction **als** and the comparative [→ G 045]:

> *Er ist **älter als** ich.*
> *Heute ist das Wetter **nicht besser als** gestern.*
> *Ich habe ein **billigeres** Buch gekauft **als** du.*

E 351   The second unit of the comparison may also be a dependent clause [→ G 048]:

> *Der Zug kam **früher an, als ich erwartet hatte.***
> *Der Film war **besser, als man nach der Kritik annehmen konnte.***

E 352   If an adjective is used in the predicate nominative to describe a noun with the conjunction **als**, elevated style uses the conjunction **denn** in the comparison, to avoid excessive repetition of the same conjunction (**als**):

> *Er ist **als** Wissenschaftler bedeutender **denn als** Lehrer.*

E 355   When a comparison is made to describe an EQUALITY (or the absence of an equality), we use the construction **so ... wie** or **ebenso ... wie** and the positive of the adjective [→ G 595 ff.]. The second unit of the comparison may be a dependent clause:

> *Ich bin (**eben**)**so alt wie** er.*
> *Dieses Buch ist **nicht so interessant wie** das andere.*
> *Die Reise dauerte **so lange, wie ich gedacht hatte.***

E 356   The use of **wie** with the comparative is considered incorrect German, although it sometimes occurs in colloquial language, especially in Southern Germany, Switzerland, and Austria:[1]

> *Er ist **älter wie** du.*

E 360   The adverb **weniger** may be used together with the conjunction **als** and the positive of the adjective in a comparison involving an inequality (or the absence of an inequality):

> *Mein Sohn ist **weniger fleißig als** meine Tochter.*
> *Berlin ist **nicht weniger schön als** München.*

---

[1] The use of **als** with the positive occurs very rarely, primarily in Austria. It is considered poor German and should be avoided: *Er ist so alt als ich.*

The construction **mehr . . . als** with the positive may be used to compare two (adjectival) characteristics of the same person or thing: E 365

> *Dieses Bild ist **mehr interessant als schön**.*
> *Er war **mehr tot als lebendig**.*
> *Sie ist **mehr traurig als ärgerlich*** (i.e. she is annoyed, too, but primarily sad).

To stress the absence of the second of two such qualities, the construction **eher . . . als** with the positive may be used:[1] E 366

> *Sie ist **eher traurig als ärgerlich*** (i.e. she is sad rather than annoyed).

A relationship between two comparatives is expressed by **je . . . je**, **je . . . desto**, or **je . . . umso**: E 370

> *Je früher je lieber.*
> *Je mehr ich arbeite, **desto** müder bin ich.*
> *Je besser die Arbeit, **umso** größer der Lohn.*

Another form of comparison may be made by expressions such as **noch einmal so . . . wie, doppelt so . . . wie, zweimal so . . . wie**, etc.: E 371

> *Er ist **noch einmal** (**nochmal, doppelt, zweimal**) so reich **wie** ich.*
> *Berlin ist **zehnmal** so groß **wie** unsere Stadt.*

A repetition of a comparative with the conjunction **und** occurs primarily in narratives for the same of emphasis. Usually, however, it is replaced by **immer** and the comparative:[2] E 375

> *Die Tage wurden **länger und länger**. Die Tage wurden **immer länger**.*
> *Immer größer, immer besser, immer schöner, immer mehr, etc.*
>   (bigger and bigger, better and better, etc.).

Absolute Comparative

The so-called ABSOLUTE COMPARATIVE expresses a general rather than a specific comparison and indicates a certain amount of the quality indicated, usually somewhere between a concept and its opposite. Paradoxically, it indicates something less than the positive: E 380

> *Er ist ein **älterer** Herr* (i.e. not a young man, but not an old man either — an elderly man).

---

[1] The distinction between **mehr . . . als** and **eher . . . als** is not always strictly observed.
[2] Similarly, *immer wieder* (again and again).

*Ich habe eine **längere** Reise gemacht* (i.e. not exactly a short trip, but not a very long trip).
*Er ist ein **höherer** Beamter* (not really a high official).
*die **nähere** Umgebung* (the not too distant surroundings).
*eine **größere** Stadt* (a fairly large city).
*die **höhere** Schule*[1] (higher than elementary school).

Absolute Superlative

E 385 The ABSOLUTE SUPERLATIVE designates a very high degree of a given quality. For adjectives, it usually occurs as an attribute without the article:

> ***Liebster** Vater! **Teuerste** Mutter!*
> *Es war **höchste** Zeit.*
> ***Herzlichsten** Dank für Ihre freundliche Einladung.*
> *Ich komme mit **größtem** Vergnügen.*
> *Er legte **schärfsten** Protest dagegen ein.*

E 386 The absolute superlative of adverbs is uninflected if the adverb stands alone or modifies an adjective; it is used with the ending **-stens** or with the preposition **aufs** and the ending **-ste** if it precedes a verb [→ E 821]:

> *Er kam **eiligst** (**schleunigst**) nach Hause.*
> *Das weiß ich **längst**.*
> *Die Sache ist **äußerst** wichtig.*
> *Sie war **tiefst** betrübt.*
> *Dieses Buch ist **höchst**[2] interessant.*
> *Das Rauchen ist **aufs strengste** (**strengstens**) verboten.*
> *Diesen Stoff kann ich Ihnen **wärmstens** (**aufs wärmste**) empfehlen.*

E 387 The strongest form of the absolute superlative uses the prefix **aller-** before the adjective in the superlative:

> *Gestern war der **allerschönste** Tag meines Lebens.*
> *In der Zeitung stehen die **allerneuesten** Nachrichten.*

---

[1] Note that *höhere Schule* is a secondary school and corresponds to "high school." *Hochschule* designates an institution of "higher education" on the university level. *Hohe Schule* is used only in the training of horses, as well as in a few idioms: *Die Hohe Schule der Liebe, der Diplomatie*, etc.

[2] Forms like *höchstens* (at the most), *wenigstens* (at the least), *meistens* (most of the time), etc. also have absolute superlative functions.

314

Less emphatic forms of intensification are constructed with the adverbs **sehr, besonders, recht**, etc. and the adjective in the positive:

> *Wir haben eine **sehr interessante** Reise gemacht.*
> *Haben Sie **recht herzlichen** Dank!*
> *Er war ein **besonders fleißiger** Schüler.*

E 388

Adjectives may also be intensified by using a noun as a prefix:

E 389

> **tod**krank, **toten**bleich, **kohl**schwarz, **schnee**weiß, **kern**gesund, **kreuz**fidel, **stock**taub, **stroh**dumm, **splitter**nackt, **sternhagel**voll (completely drunk), **blitz**sauber, **spindel**dürr, etc.

Special Comparisons

A comparative of the ordinal number **erst** can be formed to indicate one of two people or things: **der (das, die) erstere**. The other member of the pair is designated by **der (das, die) letztere** [→ D 461, E 715].

E 390

Anders [→ E 268] is used to show inequality (or absence of inequality); it is used like the comparative with the conjunction **als**:

E 391

> *Heute ist das Wetter (**nicht**) **anders als** gestern.*
> *Ich habe **andere Sorgen, als** du glaubst.*

Adverbs of place may form attributive adjectives by using the ending **-er** [→ E 265]. These adjectives are not felt to have comparative meaning, but are used as positives.[1] They may form superlatives (but not comparatives) of their own. Note the changes in the stem:

E 393

PREDICATE ADVERB	ATTRIBUTIVE ADJECTIVE	
	Positive	Superlative
vorn	vorder-	(der, das, die) vorderste
hinten	hinter-	hinterste
mitten in	mittler-	mittelste
oben	ober-	oberste
unten	unter-	unterste
außen	äußer-	äußerste
innen	inner-	innerste

[1] In English, on the other hand, such forms as upper, lower, inner, outer, etc., are felt to be comparatives, and can form superlatives only by adding -most.

> *Unsere Freunde sind **vorn**.*
> *Wir gehen durch die **vordere** Tür.*
> *Er sitzt in der **vordersten** Reihe.*

E 395   There are some adjectives which do not normally lend themselves to comparisons, i.e. color adjectives and other concepts for which only an opposite, but not a comparative, is conceivable. They will have comparative and superlative forms only in unusual circumstances. Such adjectives include **weiß, schwarz, nackt, tot, lebendig, krank, leer, voll, dreieckig, neunfach**, etc.

> *Malen Sie die Zukunft nicht noch **schwärzer** als nötig!*
> *Der Junge ist viel **lebendiger** als seine Schwester.*
> *Ich habe den Saal schon **voller** gesehen, ich habe ihn schon **leerer** gesehen, aber ich habe ihn nie so voller Lehrer gesehen.*

E 396   Normally, intensification of such adjectives is accomplished by compounding them with a noun prefix [→ E 389]:

> *schneeweiß, splitternackt, mausetot*

E 397   In other compound adjectives, only one of the two parts is capable of comparison. If both parts are adjectives and have maintained their original meaning, only the modifier is compared:

> *Das Haus wurde an den **Meist**bietenden verkauft.*
> *Er ist der **best**gehaßte Mann in der Stadt.*

E 398   If the compound of two adjectives has aquired a unified meaning (usually figurative), the base word is compared as if it were a single word:

> *kaltblütig**st**, weitsichtig**st**, hartgesotten**st**, freisinnig**st***

USE OF ADJECTIVES

E 400   The adjective may function in a sentence either as an ATTRIBUTE or as a COMPLEMENT.

E 401   As an ATTRIBUTE [→ J 110.6], the adjective usually stands before the noun or, although very infrequently, after the noun. If the adjective precedes the noun, it must be inflected [→ E 100 ff. for adjective declension]. If the adjective is the only attribute preceding the noun, it

316

must also serve as function indicator, carrying the appropriate primary ending to characterize number, gender, and case of the noun [→ D 900 ff.]:

> *Der* **reiche** *Kaufmann kaufte ein* **neues** *Auto.*
> *Die Erfindungen* **großer** *Wissenschaftler bilden die*
> *Grundlagen der* **heutigen** *Technik.*

An attributive adjective may either be essential for the comprehension of the sentence (*Herr Müller ist ein* **tüchtiger** *Mensch*) or it may serve merely to add detailed information to the statement (*Ein* **alter** *Mann kam die* **breite** *Straße herunter*).   E 402

If the attributive adjective follows the noun [→ E 240, J 115.1], it is uninflected. If several adjectives follow a noun, they are separated from the noun by a comma: E 405

> *Röslein* **rot**. — *Genitiv* **maskulin**.
> *Es war einmal ein König,* **alt und grau**.

An adjective may also be used as an attribute of a previously mentioned noun which is understood, but not repeated: E 410

> *Mein Hut ist schon sehr alt. Ich brauche einen* **neuen**.[1]

As a PREDICATE COMPLEMENT, the adjective normally has no declensional ending. It appears in the predicate nominative or the predicate accusative [→ H 411]:   E 420

> *Der Mann ist* **alt**.
> *Das Wetter wird* **schön**.
> *Viele Menschen bleiben ihr ganzes Leben* **arm**.
>
> *Seine vielen Fragen machen mich* **krank**.

The adjective is declined in the predicate nominative   E 422
1. If it indicates a classification, or designates a contrast:

> *Ihr Hut ist* **ein sehr altmodischer**.[2]
> *Diese Schuhe sind* **nicht die richtigen** *für dieses Wetter.*

---

[1] Note that such adjectives are not capitalized, unless they refer to human beings. Capitalization could result in confusion in a sentence such as: *Ich suche eine neue Wohnung, denn ich bin mit meiner* **alten** *nicht zufrieden. Mit meiner* **Alten** would be a slang reference to my wife.

[2] Or: *Ihr Hut ist sehr* **altmodisch**.

2. In the superlative:

> *Peter ist **der jüngste**.*

3. If the adjective has a demonstrative function:

> *Seine Worte waren **folgende:** . . .*
> *Es ist jeden Tag **das gleiche**.*
> *Er schien plötzlich **ein ganz anderer**.*

4. For ordinal numbers:

> *Wir sind **die ersten**.*
> *Du bist **der dritte**.*
> *Er war **der letzte**.*

E 440   Adjectives may govern certain cases [→ D 923.3, 938, 960] or certain prepositional constructions [→ F 070]:

ACCUSATIVE:	*gewohnt*	*Wir sind **diese Arbeit** gewohnt.*[1]
	tief	*Das Wasser war **einen Meter** tief.*
DATIVE:	*ähnlich*	*Die Tochter ist **dem Vater** ähnlich.*
	recht	*Diese Sache ist **mir** recht.*
GENITIVE:	*verdächtig*	*Er ist **des Diebstahls** verdächtig.*
	sicher	*Ich bin **meiner Sache** sicher.*
PREPOSITION:	*besorgt um*	*Die Mutter ist **um ihren Sohn** besorgt.*
	zufrieden mit	*Der Lehrer war **mit ihm** zufrieden.*

Dictionaries usually indicate which case a given adjective governs.

E 450   Some adjectives may be used either with a simple case object, or with a prepositional phrase:

dankbar + dat. (person)	*Ich bin **ihm** dankbar.*
+ *für* (thing)	*Ich bin **für das Geschenk** dankbar.*
gewohnt + acc.	*Wir sind **diese Arbeit** gewohnt.*[1]
+ *an* (acc.)	*Wir sind **an diese Arbeit** gewohnt.*
gleich + dat.	***Mir** ist es gleich, ob er es tut oder nicht.*
+ *für*	***Für mich** ist es gleich, ob er es tut oder nicht.*

[1] For the form **gewöhnt**, → B 942, footnote.

nützlich	+ dat.	*Seine Arbeit ist **allen** nützlich.*
	+ *für*	*Seine Arbeit ist **für alle** nützlich.*
fähig	+ gen.	*Er ist **einer solchen Gemeinheit** nicht fähig.*
	+ *zu*	*Er ist **zur Leitung** dieses Geschäftes nicht fähig.*

PARTICIPLES USED AS ADJECTIVES

Both present participles [→ B 800 ff.] and past participles [→ B 820 ff.]   E 470
of verbs may be used as noun attributes. They are then treated like other
descriptive adjectives and follow regular inflectional patterns, taking
either primary or secondary endings.

PRESENT PARTICIPLES used as attributes [→ B 801 ff.] indicate the   E 471
transitory or momentary character of the action or characteristic
indicated:

> *das **spielende** Kind*
> *ein **weinendes** Mädchen*
> *mit **wachsendem** Interesse*
> *ein **wütender** Mann*

In some instances, these participles have completely lost their verbal   E 472
character and are felt to be regular adjectives; they are thus capable of
comparative and superlative forms [→ B 807]:

> *Ich kenne eine noch **spannendere** Geschichte.*
> *Er ist der **zuvorkommendste** Mensch, den ich kenne.*

PAST PARTICIPLES used as attributes [→ B 829] indicate the completion   E 475
of the action or state indicated:

> *der **gepflügte** Acker*
> *frisch **gebrannter** Kaffee*
> *mit **ausgestreckten** Armen*

Some past participles have also lost their verbal character and can   E 476
therefore form comparatives and superlatives [→ B 836]:

> *Dieses Mittel ist **geeigneter** als viele andere.*
> *Er war der **beliebteste** Schüler unserer Klasse.*

319

E 480 For further details, → B 802 ff. for present participles, B 829 ff. for past participles, and J 163 ff. for extended (participial) modifiers.

ADJECTIVES FUNCTIONING AS NOUNS

E 500 Many adjectives, as well as participles used as adjectives, may function as nouns. They are then capitalized, but otherwise maintain their adjectival character, and follow the normal declensional pattern for descriptive adjectives. They are capable of forming comparatives and superlatives. Such adjectives are called NOMINAL ADJECTIVES.[1]

E 501 **Declensional Patterns of Nominal Adjectives**

		Masculine	Feminine	Neuter
Sing.	NOM.	der Krank-**e**	die Krank **-e**	das Gut-**e**
	ACC.	den **-en**	die **-e**	das **-e**
	DAT.	dem **-en**	der **-en**	dem **-en**
	GEN.	des **-en**	der **-en**	des **-en**
Pl.	NOM.	die **-en**	die **-en**	
	ACC.	die **-en**	die **-en**	—
	DAT.	den **-en**	den **-en**	
	GEN.	der **-en**	der **-en**	

		Masculine	Feminine	Neuter
Sing.	NOM.	ein Krank-**er**	eine Krank-**e**	ein Gut-**es**
	ACC.	einen **-en**	eine **-e**	ein **-es**
	DAT.	einem **-en**	einer **-en**	einem **-en**
	GEN.	eines **-en**	einer **-en**	eines **-en**
Pl.	NOM.	**-e**	**-e**	
	ACC.	**-e**	**-e**	—
	DAT.	**-en**	**-en**	
	GEN.	**-er**	**-er**	

[1] Occasionally, a nominal adjective may be preceded by another descriptive adjective: *Der mitleidige Reiche hat einer armen Kranken geholfen.* Note the parallel endings.

In the SINGULAR MASCULINE and FEMININE, as well as in the PLURAL,   E 505
nominal adjectives usually designate PEOPLE:[1]

> *Der Reiche hat einer Armen geholfen.*
> *Kranke brauchen die Hilfe des Arztes.*
> *Dem (den) Tüchtigen gehört die Welt.*

A nominal adjective in the NEUTER SINGULAR indicates a THING or a   E 510
CONCEPT. This usage has no plural:

> *Er hat in seinem Leben viel Gutes getan.*
> *Ich habe etwas Interessantes von ihm gehört.*
> *Das Schönste im Leben währt oft nicht lange.*

Many nominal adjectives and participles [→ B 801.2, B 831] are not   E 515
felt as adjectives any more and are used as feminine and masculine
nouns. In such instances, they may sometimes designate things or concepts, and may be modified by other descriptive adjectives:

> *der Abgeordnete, der (die) Angeklagte, der Beamte (die Beamtin), der*
> *(die) Bekannte, der (die) Fremde, der (die) Gefangene, der Gesandte,*
> *der (die) Heilige, der (die) Irre, der (die) Reisende, der (die) Verwandte,*
> *der (die) Vorsitzende*

> *die Elektrische (Straßenbahn); die Linke, die Rechte (Hand, Partei);*
> *die Moderne (Kunst, Literatur); die Gerade, die Senkrechte, die*
> *Horizontale, die Diagonale (Linie), etc.*

> *Der Beamte ist ein guter Bekannter von mir.*
> *Ich sprach mit dem deutschen Gesandten.*
> *Haben Sie viele Verwandte in dieser Stadt?*
> *Er fuhr mit der Elektrischen.*

In contrast to other nationalities, which are designated by regular   E 516
nouns, **der Deutsche** (fem.: **die Deutsche**, pl.: **die Deutschen**) is also a
nominal adjective:

> *Ein Deutscher und ein Franzose trafen sich auf einer Reise.*
> *Der Deutsche saß neben dem Franzosen.*
> *Im Ausland leben viele Deutsche.*
> *Ist es wahr, daß alle Deutschen blonde Haare und blaue Augen haben?*

---

[1] Notice the difference: *der Alte* (the old man). *Ich kaufe mir einen neuen Hut. Der alte*
(the old hat) *ist schon sehr schäbig* [→ E 410].

E 520   When adjectives denoting nationality are used to indicate the language, two neuter nominal adjectives may be formed:

> secondary ending: *das **Deutsche**, das **Italienische**, das **Englische***
> no ending: *das beste **Deutsch**, das klassische **Latein***

E 521   The secondary ending occurs only after the definite article and without an attribute:

> *Wir übersetzen aus **dem Deutschen** ins **Spanische**.*
> *Im Mittelalter war das **Lateinische** die Sprache der Gelehrten.*

E 522   The nominal adjective is uninflected if it occurs without an article or with an attribute:[1]

> *Ich lernte **Latein** in der Schule.*[2]
> *In Paris spricht man **das beste Französisch**.*
> ***Mein Deutsch** ist noch nicht einwandfrei.*
> ***Deutsch** und **Englisch** sind verwandte Sprachen.*

E 525   Similarly, two different neuter nominal adjectives may be formed from color adjectives, with secondary endings and without endings. Unlike adjectives denoting languages, the uninflected form may also occur after the definite article without attribute to denote the color itself:

> *Wir fahren ins **Grüne**. — **Das Grün** der Wälder wechselte mit **dem dunklen Grau** der Felsen.*
> *Der Schütze hat ins **Schwarze** getroffen. — **Das schlichte Schwarz** der Trauergäste bildete einen Gegensatz zu dem farbenprächtigen Sommertag.*
> *Er rollte die Augen, so daß man **das Weiße** sehen konnte. — Der beschneite Berg glänzte in herrlichem **Weiß**.*

E 526   It is also possible to form regular feminine nouns from color adjectives, as from other adjectives [→ A 156]:

> *die **Bläue**, die **Schwärze**, die **Röte***

E 530   After **etwas, nichts, viel, wenig, mehr**, the neuter nominal adjective occurs in the singular with PRIMARY endings [→ D 770, 775, 875, 885]; after **alles**, it has SECONDARY endings [→ D 783]:[3]

---

[1] The adjective is usually not capitalized after the preposition **auf** (*auf deutsch*) and in certain idiomatic usages [→ E 256–7].

[2] The use of **Lateinisch** in sentences such as the above should be avoided.

[3] The adjective **ander-** follows the same rules of inflection, but it is never capitalized: *nichts anderes, alles andere*, etc.

*Meine Mutter hat heute **etwas Gutes** gekocht.*
*Ich habe nicht **viel Neues** gehört.*
*Er hat mir von **nichts Wichtigem** erzählt.*

*Ich wünsche dir **alles Gute**!*
*Er hat mir von **allem Wichtigen** erzählt.*

NUMERICAL ADJECTIVES

We distinguish between two basic types of numerical adjectives: ORDINAL NUMBERS and CARDINAL NUMBERS. All numerical expressions are derived from these two groups.

E 600

CARDINAL NUMBERS

Cardinal numbers denote a precise quantity. They answer the question **wieviel?** when the noun is in the singular, **wie viele?** when the noun is in the plural. In general, numerical adjectives have no declensional endings [but → E 645 ff., 655 ff., 660].

E 601

The German cardinal numbers are:

E 602

0 *null*	10 *zehn*	20 *zwanzig*	30 *dreißig*
1 *eins*	11 *elf*	21 *einundzwanzig*	40 *vierzig*
2 *zwei*	12 *zwölf*	22 *zweiundzwanzig*	50 *fünfzig*
3 *drei*	13 *dreizehn*	23 *dreiundzwanzig*	60 *sechzig*
4 *vier*	14 *vierzehn*	24 *vierundzwanzig*	70 *siebzig*
5 *fünf*	15 *fünfzehn*	25 *fünfundzwanzig*	80 *achtzig*
6 *sechs*	16 *sechzehn*	26 *sechsundzwanzig*	90 *neunzig*
7 *sieben*	17 *siebzehn*	27 *siebenundzwanzig*	100 *hundert (einhundert)*
8 *acht*	18 *achtzehn*	28 *achtundzwanzig*	101 *hunderteins*
9 *neun*	19 *neunzehn*	29 *neunundzwanzig*	139 *hundertneununddreißig,*

etc.

200 *zweihundert*	1000 *tausend (eintausend)*
300 *dreihundert*	1101 *tausendeinhunderteins*
900 *neunhundert*	1999 *tausendneunhundertneunundneunzig*
999 *neunhundertneunundneunzig*	2000 *zweitausend* etc.

999.999 *neunhundertneunundneunzigtausendneunhundertneunundneunzig* [1]

---

[1] A period or a space is used to separate groups of three digits: 24.163 or 24 163. A comma is used to indicate decimals [→ E 641].

E 603   When numbers from 1 to 999 999 are spelled out, they are always written as one word.

E 604   Years are usually read as follows:

1968: *neunzehnhundertachtundsechzig*[1]

Years between 1000 and 1099 are read like normal ordinal numbers:

1030: *(ein)tausenddreißig.*

This also applies to years projected into the future beyond the year 2000:

Das Jahr 2001 (zweitausendeins)
Im Jahre 3500 (dreitausendfünfhundert)

E 605   Note the following variations in pronunciation and spelling:

1 *eins*	but	21 *einundzwanzig*, 41 *einundvierzig*, etc. (no **s**)
3 *drei*		30 *dreißig*, 31 *einunddreißig*, etc. (**ß**, not **z**)
6 *sechs* [**chs = ks**]		16 *sechzehn*, 60 *sechzig*, etc. (**ch**, no **s**)
7 *sieben*		17 *siebzehn*, 70 *siebzig*, etc. (no **en**)[2]

E 610   To distinguish between **zwei** and **drei** in oral communication (e.g. on the telephone), the form **zwo** is sometimes used instead of **zwei**. In writing, however, **zwei** must always be used.

E 611   Numerical units from 1 to 9 are called ones (*der Einer*);[3] 10, 20, 30, 40 etc. are called tens (*der Zehner*); 100, 200, 300, etc., are called hundreds (*der Hunderter*); 1000, 2000, etc. are called thousands (*der Tausender*).

E 612   Both in speaking and when the numbers are written out, the ones precede the tens from 13 on; after 21, they are combined by **und**; **und** is NOT used between hundreds and tens or between hundreds and ones:[4]

---

[1] In formal language, *eintausendneunhundertachtundsechzig* may be used. In informal usage, on the other hand, *neunzehn achtundsechzig* may occur in spoken communication, but not in writing.

[2] Forms like *siebenzig* are obsolete.

[3] Do not confuse *der Einer*, which denotes a digital unit in the decimal system, with *der Einser*, the highest grade in the German school marking system (an "A") [→ E 694.3], or with *die Eins*, the name for the numeral itself [→ E 690 ff.].

[4] Note that this differs from English usage: one hundred *and* twenty nine — *hundertneunundzwanzig*; three hundred *and* five — *dreihundertfünf.*

14 *vierzehn* (4/10)

25 *fünfundzwanzig* (5/+/20)

102 *hundertzwei* (100/2) — less frequently *einhundertzwei* (1/100/2)

387 *dreihundertsiebenundachtzig* (3/100/7/+/80)

537.829 *fünfhundertsiebenunddreißigtausendachthundertneunundzwanzig*
(5/100/7/+/30/1000/ /8/100/9/+/20)

In compounds preceding other digits, the numeral 1 is always pro-   E 613
nounced and written **ein-**:

21 *einundzwanzig*   1028 *eintausendachtundzwanzig*

31 *einunddreißig*

51 *einundfünfzig*

At the end of a group of digits, however, the numeral 1 is pronounced
and written **eins**:

101 *hunderteins* (*einhunderteins*)

2001 *zweitausendeins*

Telephone numbers are not pronounced as a whole number, but either   E 614
singly or in groups of two:

3159 *drei eins fünf neun* (3-1-5-9)

2438 *vierundzwanzig achtunddreißig* (24-38)

29563 *neunundzwanzig fünf dreiundsechzig* (29-5-63)

Except for prices, time of day, measurements, and mathematical usage,   E 617
numbers below ten are always written out, numbers below twenty
usually. In addition, numbers are often written out in financial trans-
actions, to avoid errors and forgeries:

*Der Junge ist **neun** Jahre alt.*

*Wir blieben **vierzehn** Tage in Paris.*

*Zahlen Sie Herrn Meyer DM 386.- (**dreihundertsechsundachtzig** Mark) aus!*

*Sie schulden uns einen Betrag von $126.- (in Worten: **einhundertsechsundzwan-
zig** Dollar).*

Approximations or estimates are also written out: E 618

*Es waren sicher **zweihundert** Leute da* (i.e. I did not count them, I only guessed).

*Von dem über **hundert*** (not: 100) *Meter hohen Turm hat man eine schöne
Aussicht.*

325

E 620   Names of numbers above 999 999, for every three digits, are considered FEMININE NOUNS and have an **-en** ending in the plural:

> 1.000.000   *eine Million*
> 2.000.000   *zwei Millionen*
> 1.000.000.000   *eine Milliarde (tausend Millionen)* [1]
> 1.000.000.000.000   *eine Billion (tausend Milliarden)* [1]

E 621   These numbers are not written as one word with numbers of a lower order:

> 1.500.000   *eine Million fünfhunderttausend*

E 625   When indicating dates, the numeral showing the year is either used by itself or after the prepositional phrase **im Jahre**: [2]

> *Goethe wurde **1749** geboren und starb **1832**.*
> *Goethe wurde **im Jahre 1749** geboren und starb **im Jahre 1832**.*

E 626   Historical dates may use the following abbreviations:

v. Chr.	*— vor Christus*	*n. Chr.* *— nach Christus*
v. Chr. G.	*— vor Christi Geburt*	*n. Chr. G.* *— nach Christi Geburt*
v. Zr.	*— vor der Zeitrechnung*	*n. Zr.* *— nach der Zeitrechnung*

The abbreviation *A.D.* (*Anno Domini*) may also be used.

E 630   When pronouncing or writing out prices, **Mark** is always in the singular. **Pfennig** occurs in the plural (**Pfennige**) only if a number of individual coins is to be indicated [→ C 192]; otherwise it remains a singular:

> DM   1,40   *eine Mark vierzig* [3]
> DM   12,23   *zwölf Mark dreiundzwanzig*
> DM   −,51   *einundfünfzig Pfennig*
> DM   3,01   *drei Mark eins*

---

[1] Note that the German word **Milliarde** corresponds to the American "billion" (10^9), and the German **Billion** to the American trillion (10^{12}). Consequently, the German **Trillion** equals the American quadrillion (10^{15}), etc. Numbers of that magnitude, to be sure, occur very infrequently. The term **Myriade** (originally 10,000) is used today to indicate a large quantity.

[2] The preposition **in** should never be used by itself with the year.

[3] DM stands for **Deutsche Mark**, and is the international symbol for the official currency of the Federal Republic of Germany. In colloquial language, however, only the word **Mark** is used. A 10-**Pfennig** piece is sometimes colloquially called **der Groschen**. Do not confuse this with Austrian currency, where 1 **Schilling** = 100 **Groschen**.

326

To tell time, we distinguish between official usage and colloquial usage. E 632
Both answer the question **Wie spät ist es?** or **Wieviel Uhr ist es?** In
designating time, **Uhr** is always in the singular. Official time is indicated
on a 24-hour basis:

8.15 Uhr: *acht Uhr fünfzehn* (*Minuten*)[1] (8:15 a.m.)
12.32 Uhr: *zwölf Uhr zweiunddreißig* (12:32 p.m.)
20.45 Uhr: *zwanzig Uhr fünfundvierzig* (8:45 p.m.)
24.00 Uhr: *vierundzwanzig Uhr* (midnight)
0.25 Uhr: *null Uhr fünfundzwanzig* (12:25 a.m.)

In colloquial language, the following methods for telling time are used: E 633

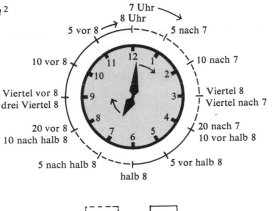

7.00 Uhr: *sieben Uhr*
7.05 Uhr: *fünf* (*Minuten*) *nach sieben*
7.10 Uhr: *zehn* (*Minuten*) *nach sieben*[2]
7.15 Uhr: (*ein*) *Viertel nach sieben*
    or: (*ein*) *Viertel acht*
7.20 Uhr: *zwanzig nach sieben*
    or: *zehn vor halb acht*
7.25 Uhr: *fünf vor halb acht*[3]
7.30 Uhr: *halb acht*
7.35 Uhr: *fünf nach halb acht*
7.40 Uhr: *zehn nach halb acht*
    or: *zwanzig vor acht*
7.45 Uhr: (*ein*) *Viertel vor acht*
    or: *drei Viertel acht*
7.50 Uhr: *zehn vor acht*[3]
7.55 Uhr: *fünf* (*Minuten*) *vor acht*
8.00 Uhr: *acht Uhr*

In case of doubt, adverbs of time may be used together with the clock E 634
time:

    *Ich komme um 7 Uhr **morgens** (**abends**) an.*
    *Er hat bis 12 Uhr **mittags** (**mitternachts**) gearbeitet.*

---

[1] Note that German uses a period, not a colon, between hour and minutes. The use of the
word *Minuten* is optional.
[2] Forms like *fünf Minuten vor Viertel acht* may occur occasionally, but should be avoided.
[3] Or: *in fünf Minuten halb acht, in zehn Minuten acht*, etc.

327

E 635 The word **Uhr** may be used with full hours; it is rarely used when minutes are indicated, or with quarter and half hours:

es ist ein Uhr   or   es ist eins
es ist zwei Uhr   or   es ist zwei
es ist 10 (Minuten) nach 3 (Uhr)
es ist drei Viertel sieben
es ist halb neun

E 636 The expression **Ich habe drei Uhr** may be used to mean that my watch shows three o'clock. It answers the question **Wieviel Uhr haben Sie?** or **Wie spät haben Sie?**

Note the difference between

Ich habe ein Uhr   — My watch shows that it is one o'clock.
Ich habe eine Uhr   — I own a watch.

Ich habe zwei Uhr   — My watch shows that it is two o'clock.
Ich habe zwei Uhren — I own two watches.

E 640 Mathematical expressions are written and spoken as follows:

$5 + 3 = 8$ 5 und (plus) 3 ist (sind) 8
$8 - 3 = 5$ 8 weniger (minus) 3 ist 5
$3 \cdot 5 = 15$ }
$3 \times 5 = 15$ }   3 mal 5 ist 15
$12 : 4 = 3$ 12 (geteilt) durch 4 ist 3
$6^2 = 36$ 6 hoch 2 (6 Quadrat) ist 36
$6^3 = 216$ 6 hoch 3 (6 zur dritten) ist 216
$\sqrt{36} = 6$ (Die) Quadratwurzel aus 36 ist (gleich) 6
$\sqrt[3]{216} = 6$ (Die) Kubikwurzel aus 216 ist (gleich) 6
n_6 n sechs
$\dfrac{n}{6}$ n über sechs
$3(n + m)$ 3 mal Klammer n plus m

E 641 Decimals are indicated in German by a comma, not by a period [→ footnote E 602 for the use of periods to separate groups of three digits]. They are written and spoken as follows:

32,8   zweiunddreißig Komma acht
0,25   Null Komma fünfundzwanzig

328

The words *Hundertstel, Tausendstel,* etc. may also be used [→ E 760 ff.].

The numerical adjective *eins*

Before a noun, the number one is identical with the indefinite article and has full declensional endings for all cases and all genders [→ D 310]. The numerical adjective receives vocal stress to differentiate it from the indefinite article:[1]   E 645

> *Wir haben alle aus **einem** Glas getrunken.*

If the numeral one occurs in last place in compounds with hundreds or thousands and stands before a noun, it is declined, usually written separately, and connected with the other number by means of the conjunction **und**. The noun always appears in the singular: E 646

> *Meine Reise hat genau **hundert und einen** Tag gedauert.*
> *Die Märchen aus **Tausendundeiner** Nacht.*

When **ein** as a numerical adjective follows the definite article, a demonstrative or possessive, or a relative pronoun, it is used like an adjective and has the appropriate primary or secondary endings [→ E 110, 120]:   E 647

> *Der **eine** Mann, der ihm helfen konnte, war nicht zu erreichen.*
> *Schon bei diesem **einen** Unfall hat es viele Verletzte gegeben.*
> *Der alte Mann geriet mit seinem **einen** Bein in ein Loch und stürzte.*
> *Der Wagen, dessen **eines** Rad zerbrochen war, lag auf der Straße.*

If **ein** is used as a pronoun, it has the full declension endings [→ D 800]:   E 648

> ***Einer** der Reisenden fuhr mit mir nach Hamburg.*
> *Ich fragte **eine** der Frauen, die dort standen, nach dem Weg.*
> *Er ging mit **einem** von ihnen ins Theater.*

The expression **der (das, die) eine** is often used in contrast to **der (das, die) andere** [→ D 460]:   E 649

> *Wer sind die Frauen dort? — **Die eine** ist Frau Müller, **die andere** kenne ich nicht.*

In this usage, it is possible to have **die einen** occur in the plural:

> *Wir haben viele Schüler. **Die einen** sind fleißig, **die anderen** sind faul.*

---

[1] In print, spacing is used to indicate this emphasis: *Wir haben alle aus e i n e m Glas getrunken.*

E 650 Uninflected **ein** is used
1. before fractions and the noun **Uhr**:

> *Er kam vor **ein Uhr**.*
> *Wir multiplizieren drei Viertel mit **ein Fünftel**.*

2. in compound idioms with **zwei, ander,** and **derselbe**:

> *Er kommt in **ein oder zwei** Tagen.*
> *Wir sprachen mit **ein und dem anderen**.*
> *Sie wohnen in **ein und derselben** Straße.*

zwei and **drei**

E 655 Like all other numerical adjectives, **zwei** and **drei** are usually undeclined. They may, however, sometimes occur with primary plural endings [→ E 110] in the dative (optional) or genitive:

> *Ich habe mich gestern mit zwei(**en**) aus unserer Klasse unterhalten.*
> *Man kann nicht zwei(**en**) Herren gleichzeitig dienen.*
> *In diesem Hotel wohnen Diplomaten dreier verschiedener Länder.*

E 656 The adjective **beide** is used to designate two previously mentioned persons or things, or to indicate that there are two and no more than two of a certain type. The singular form **beides** may be used only to refer to concepts or processes and to things:

> *Siehst du die zwei Herren dort? Ich kenne sie **beide**.*
> *Ich habe zwei interessante Bücher gesehen und **beide** gekauft.*
> *Seine **beiden** Söhne kamen ihm entgegen.*
> *Ich sollte Brot und Butter holen, aber ich habe **beides** vergessen.*

E 657 Descriptive adjectives following **beide** [→ E 155] usually have secondary (weak) endings, although parallel primary endings also occur occasionally:

> **beide** *alten Männer* (rare: **beide** *geschlossene Augen*)

E 658 If the noun or pronoun which is modified by **beide** is the subject of the sentence and stands in the prefield, **beide** may appear after the verb in the sentence field:

> *Die Geschwister kamen **beide** zur gleichen Zeit.*
> *Wir haben **beide** den Geburtstag unserer Tante vergessen.*

330

The noun **das Paar** (**die Paare**) designates two persons or things which form a unit.[1] E 659

> *ein Paar Schuhe, ein Paar Strümpfe, zwei Paar braune Socken*
> *das Ehepaar, das Liebespaar, ein Brüderpaar*

Inflection of Other Cardinal Numbers

In a few instances, numbers from four upwards (but hardly ever above ten) may have primary adjectival endings in the plural [→ E 110]. They are usually found in idiomatic expressions: E 660

> *Der Hund streckte alle **viere** von sich.*
> *Der Verletzte kroch auf allen **vieren**.*
> *Früher fuhren die Fürsten mit **vieren** oder mit **sechsen*** (i.e. with four or six horses).
> *Er ließ alle **fünfe** gerad sein.*
> *Beim Kegeln kann man nicht immer alle **neune** schieben.*

The preposition **zu** and the ending **-en** may be used to indicate the size of a group:[2] E 661

> *Wir gingen **zu sechsen** spazieren.*
> *Die Soldaten marschierten **zu dreien** in einer Reihe.*

The ending **-er** may be added to cardinal numbers to indicate years: E 665

> *Dieser Wein ist ein **dreiundsechziger*** (*Jahrgang*).
> *In den **zwanziger** Jahren kam es zu einer großen Krise.*

This ending occasionally occurs in other uses as well:

> *eine **fünfundzwanziger** Birne* (a 25-watt bulb)

Adjectives after Cardinal Numbers

Descriptive adjectives following cardinal numbers have primary (strong) inflectional plural endings [→ E 110]: E 670

> ***drei** alte Männer*

---

[1] Do not confuse the noun **ein Paar** with the indefinite pronoun **ein paar** [→ D 870]. For the case of the second noun, → D 972.

[2] The more common form, ending in **-t**, is actually an ordinal number: **zu zweit, zu dritt**, etc. [→ E 730]. Groups may also be indicated by the genitive of a personal pronoun preceding the cardinal [D 062]: *Wir waren **unser** sechs.*

E 671   If, however, the cardinal is preceded by an inflected limiting adjective (article, demonstrative, possessive, **alle**, etc.), the following descriptive adjective has secondary (weak) endings [→ E 120]:

> **die drei** *alten Männer*
> **meine zwei** *besten Freunde*

E 675   For adjectives after **ein-**, → E 130 ff. For adjectives following **beide**, → E 657.

E 680   **je** and **pro**
Before cardinal numbers, **je** indicates an equal distribution of things. For prices and other units, **pro** is used after the numeral and before the unit; the definite article may also be used [→ D 332]:

> *Ich hatte sechs Mark bei mir und gab den drei Kindern* **je** *zwei Mark.*
> *Die Äpfel kosten DM 2.-* **pro** *Kilo (**das** Kilo).*

Cardinal Numbers as Nouns

E 690   All cardinal numbers can be used as nouns. They are usually feminine and have no inflectional endings in the singular; the plural, which ends in **-en**, is extremely rare [→ E 693–5]:

> **Die Sieben** *ist eine Glückszahl.*
> *Der große Uhrzeiger steht auf* **der Fünf***, der kleine zwischen* **der Acht** *und* **der Neun***.*
> *Er brachte ein Zeugnis mit zwei* **Einsen** *nach Hause.* (North German only [→ 694.3])

E 691   These numerical nouns are used primarily
1. For streetcar and bus lines:

> *Die* **Vier** *ist gerade abgefahren. Nehmen Sie die* **Zehn***!*

2. For grades in school, especially in North Germany [→ E 694.3]:[1]

> *Hans hat im Rechnen eine* **Drei** *bekommen. In Deutsch hat er eine* **Eins** *geschrieben.*
> *Ein Zeugnis mit drei* **Einsen** *ist sehr gut.*

---

[1] The numerical system differs in various German states. The following numbers may be used: 1 *sehr gut*, 2 *gut*, 3 *genügend*, 4 *nicht genügend*; 3 *befriedigend*, 4 *mangelhaft*, 5 *nicht genügend*; 3 *befriedigend*, 4 *ausreichend*, 5 *mangelhaft*, 6 *ungenügend*.

3. For teams, especially soccer:

*Die Münchener **Elf** spielt heute gegen Köln.*

4. To indicate age:

*Sie hat die **Zwanzig** lang überschritten.*
*Wenn man die **Siebzig** erreicht hat, sollte man sich zur Ruhe setzen.*

It is also possible to form masculine nouns from cardinal numbers by adding the ending **-er**. These may occur in the plural, without any additional ending.   E 693

They are found primarily in the following uses: E 694
1. To indicate a group characterized by that number:

*Man liest die **Einer** vor den **Zehnern** [→ E 612].*
*Geben Sie mir eine **Zehnerpackung** Zigaretten!*
*Die Turner zogen in **Sechserreihen** durch die Stadt.*

2. For bills, small coins, and stamps, often in idioms:

*Können Sie mir einen **Hunderter** wechseln?*
*Geben Sie mir bitte eine Mark in **Zehnern**!*
*Ich brauche ein paar Briefmarken: drei **Zwanziger** und zwei **Fünfer**.*
*Für einen **Sechser** (5-Pfennig piece) kann man nicht viel kaufen.*
*Das ist keinen **Dreier** wert (old 3-Pfennig piece, i.e. a red farthing).*

3. For grades in school, especially in Southern Germany [→ E 691.2]:

*Er hat einen **Vierer** in Mathematik, aber einen **Einser** in Geschichte.*

4. For approximate age:

*Er ist ein rüstiger **Fünfziger**.*
*Sie ist in den **Vierzigern**.*

The numbers **Hunderte** and **Tausende** are used as plural nouns to indicate large groups, usually people. These forms have primary inflectional endings [→ E 110]:   E 695

*In der Fabrik arbeiten **Hunderte** von Arbeitern.*
*Der Politiker hat zu **Tausenden** gesprochen.*
*Der Straßenbau braucht die Arbeitskraft **Hunderter** von Menschen.*

ORDINAL NUMBERS

E 700   Ordinal numbers are used to assign to a person or thing a definite order or rank within a series. They are formed by adding the affix **-t** or **-st** to the cardinal number, followed by inflectional endings.

E 701   The ordinals from 2 to 19 use the affix **-t**, numbers from 20 to 100 the affix **-st**.[1] Ordinals may have primary or secondary endings, like all other adjectives [→ E 101, 102].

The ordinals **der (das, die) erste**; **der (das, die) dritte**; **der (das, die) achte** are irregular. For **sieben**, there are two forms: **der (das, die) siebte** or **siebente**.

*der, das, die **erste***	*der, das, die elfte*
zweite	*zwölfte*
dritte	*dreizehnte*, etc.
vierte	*zwanzigste*
fünfte	*einundzwanzigste*
sechste	*zweiundzwanzigste*, etc.
sieb(en)te	*hundertste*
achte	*hundert(und)erste*
neunte	*hundertzweite*, etc.
zehnte	*tausendste*, etc.

*Nehmen Sie die **dritte** Straße links. Ich wohne im **sechsten** Haus auf der linken Seite im **ersten** Stock.*
*Er hat sich ein **zweites** Auto gekauft.*
*Beim Wettschwimmen war er an **vierter** Stelle.*

E 702   In compound numbers, only the last number receives the ending **-t** or **-st**:[2]

*der fünfundachtzig**ste***
*der zweihundertdrit**te***
*der fünftausenddreihundertvierundzwanzig**ste***

[1] After 100, 101 is irregular (see above). 102 to 119 again use **-t**, 120 to 200 **-st**, etc.

[2] Actually, the rule governing affixes could thus be formulated as follows: One is irregular, 2 to 12 add **-t**, all other tens and larger units add **-st**.

Ordinal numbers answer the question **der (das, die) wievielte?**: E 703

> *Der **wievielte** ist heute? Heute ist **der fünfzehnte**.*

When written in numbers, the ordinals are indicated by a period after E 704
the cardinal number:

> der 1. *der erste*
> der 3. *der dritte*
> der 25. *der fünfundzwanzigste*

After the names of rulers, roman numerals are used: E 705

> NOM.: Georg V. *Georg der Fünfte*
> ACC.: Georg V. *Georg den Fünften*
> DAT.: Georg V. *Georg dem Fünften*
> GEN.: Georgs V. *Georgs des Fünften*

For **erst** as an intensifier, → H 620. E 710

The expression **der erste** is used in contrast to the expression **der letzte**: E 715

> *Wir wohnen im **letzten** Haus der Straße, nicht im **ersten**.*

Das (das, die) erste and **der (das, die) letzte** also have a comparative E 716
form [→ E 390], if two persons or things are contrasted:

> *Karl und Fritz sind meine Freunde. Der **erstere** wohnt in Berlin und der*
> ***letztere** in Köln.*

Plural forms are used to distinguish groups of people or things: E 717

> *Meine Verwandten und Freunde besuchen mich heute. Die **ersteren** kommen*
> *am Vormittag und die **letzteren** am Abend.*
> *Wir haben einige Flaschen Bier und drei Flaschen Wein gekauft. **Erstere***
> *waren billig, aber die **letzteren** waren sehr teuer.*

Dates always use the masculine form of the ordinals, referring either to E 720
the noun **Tag** or to the name of the month. The day always precedes
the month.

The question **Welcher Tag ist heute?** usually inquires after the day
of the week. **Der wievielte ist heute?** asks for the day of the month. In
dates, the day is always written in numbers. The month is usually

335

written out, sometimes omitted altogether, and written in numbers (occasionally roman numerals) in official or business communications:

14. 11. (14. XI.) der vierzehnte elfte, vierzehnter elfter, der vierzehnte November, vierzehnter November
am 6. 8. (6. VIII.) am sechsten achten, am sechsten August

Ich bestätige mit bestem Dank Ihr Schreiben vom 28. 10.[1]
Herr Müller, geboren am 18. VII. 1925, war vom 1. IV. 1956 bis 31. X. 1959 in unserer Firma als Buchhalter beschäftigt.
Der wievielte ist heute? Heute ist der 10. (der 10. Mai). (Den wievielten haben wir heute? Heute haben wir den 10.)
Wann wurde Goethe geboren? Am 28. August 1749.

E 721 Dates on letter heads are indicated as follows:

München, den 17. 9. 1959 (den 17. IX. 1959).

E 722 If the day of the week is used before the date, the day of the week is in the dative, the date usually in the accusative; if the day of the week follows, they are both in the dative:

am Freitag, den 16. August
am 16. August, einem Freitag

E 725 Ordinals without declensional endings are combined with superlatives to indicate an order of ranking:

Der Watzmann ist der zweithöchste Berg Deutschlands.
Mein Freund ist der drittbeste Schüler in der Klasse.

E 730 The uninflected ordinal is used after the preposition **zu** to indicate a numerically defined group:[2]

Die Kinder spielten zu zweit.
Wir gingen zu sechst spazieren.
Die Soldaten marschierten zu dritt in einer Reihe.

E 735 To indicate a definite series or sequence, the indefinite pronoun **jed-** is used preceding the ordinal number [→ D 847]:

Er kommt jeden zweiten Tag.[3]

---

[1] The form *Ihr Brief vom 28. ds.* (the 28th of this month) is sometimes used commercially.
[2] For use of **zu** plus the ending **-en**, → E 661.
[3] The equivalent of the English expression "every *other* day" is not used in German.

OTHER FORMS OF NUMERALS

Classifying Numerals

Classifying numerals indicate a certain sequence. They are formed by   E 750
adding the ending **-ens** to ordinal numbers. They are adverbs and have
no inflectional forms.

When they are written as numerals, they do not differ from ordinals:
they use a period after the number [→ E 704]:

1. *erstens*	10. *zehntens*	20. *zwanzigstens*
2. *zweitens*	11. *elftens*	30. *dreißigstens*
3. *drittens*	15. *fünfzehntens*	31. *einunddreißigstens*. etc.

Heute gehe ich nicht ins Kino. **Erstens** *kostet es zu viel Geld,* **zweitens**
habe ich keine **Zeit,** *und* **drittens** *kenne ich den Film schon.*

Dieser neue Staubsauger hat drei Vorteile. Er ist 1. sehr preiswert,
2. sehr einfach zu handhaben, 3. sehr sparsam im Stromverbrauch.

Fractions

Fractions designate a part of a whole. They are derived from a con-   E 760
traction of the ordinal numbers and the noun **Teil**, and are themselves
considered nouns (**der dritte Teil** > **das dritte Teil** > **das Drittel**). They
are formed from ordinals from three on by adding the ending **-el**.

Fractions are mostly written as numbers:

$\frac{1}{3}$	*ein Drittel*	$\frac{3}{100}$ *drei Hundertstel*[1]
$\frac{2}{5}$	*zwei Fünftel*	$\frac{1}{250}$ *ein Zweihundertfünfzigstel*
$\frac{5}{16}$	*fünf Sechzehntel*	$\frac{13}{1000}$ *dreizehn Tausendstel*[1]

Fractions are usually neuter nouns, without any plural ending: E 761

das Drittel, das Hundertstel
Ich habe das erste Viertel meines Studiums beendet.
Teilen Sie den Kreis in Sechstel!

[1] Fractions expressed in hundredths, thousandths, etc., may of course also be written as
decimals: $\frac{3}{100} = 0{,}03$; $\frac{13}{1000} = 0{,}013$ [→ E 641].

337

E 762   Sometimes, fractions are considered as uninflected adjectives modifying a noun; in this use, the two numbers are written as one word:

> *Er hat **dreiviertel** Liter Bier getrunken.*
> *Der Käse wiegt **dreiviertel Kilo**.*

E 763   The upper numeral in a fraction is an ordinal number and is called **der Zähler** (the numerator); **1** is pronounced **ein**. The lower numeral is the actual fraction and is called **der Nenner** (the denominator):

> $\frac{1}{5}$ *ein* (numerator) *Fünftel* (denominator)

E 765   The fraction $\frac{1}{2}$ is either an inflected adjective, pronounced **halb**, or a feminine noun, **die Hälfte**:

> *Er war **ein halbes** Jahr (**das halbe** Jahr) in Berlin.*
> *Was ist **die Hälfte** von 24?*

E 766   Similarly, the fraction $\frac{1}{1}$ (or any other fraction in which numerator and denominator are identical) is either the inflected adjective **ganz** or the neuter noun **das Ganze**:

> *Die Reise dauerte **ein ganzes** (**das ganze**) Jahr.*
> *Teilen Sie **das Ganze** durch 5!*

E 770   So-called improper fractions, i.e. whole numbers followed by a fraction, are pronounced without **und**. The noun is in the plural, unless it is a masculine or neuter unit of measurement:

> $1\frac{3}{4}$ *Stunden*   *ein dreiviertel Stunden*
> $2\frac{1}{3}$ *Kilogramm*   *zwei eindrittel Kilogramm*

E 771   When an improper fraction contains **halb** after the whole number, it is written as one word and not inflected.

> *Seine Reise dauerte **eineinhalb** Jahre ($1\frac{1}{2}$ Jahre).[1]*
> *Ich habe **zweieinhalb** Pfund Obst gekauft ($2\frac{1}{2}$ Pfund).*

E 772   It is also possible (although less common) to combine $\frac{1}{2}$ with the preceding whole number by **und**. They are then written as separate words, and the noun is in the singular [→ E 646]:

> *Seine Reise dauerte **ein und ein halbes** Jahr.*

[1] Instead of **eineinhalb**, the form **anderthalb** is also used:
> *Seine Reise dauerte **anderthalb** Jahre.*

Generally, this construction occurs only if the preceding numeral is 1 or 2, and the following noun is in the nominative or accusative.

Generic Numbers

Generic numbers designate a quantity of different kinds or types. They are formed by adding the suffix **-erlei** to the cardinal numbers. They are adverbs and remain uninflected [→ E 806].

E 780

Generic numbers answer the question "how many kinds?" (**wievielerlei?**). This interrogative is infrequently used. If the following noun designates a material or a unit of measurement, it is in the singular:

> *Wievielerlei Mahlzeiten gibt es in Deutschland? Es gibt dreierlei Mahlzeiten: Frühstück, Mittagessen und Abendessen.*
> *Sie hat ein Kleid aus zweierlei Stoff.*
> *Man darf nicht mit zweierlei Maß messen.*
> *Für unseren Ausflug gibt es viererlei Möglichkeiten: wir gehen zu Fuß, wir fahren mit der Bahn, mit dem Bus oder mit dem Auto.*

Generic numbers formed from high cardinal numbers (100, 1000) do not designate a specific number, but only very many different people or things:[1]

E 781

> *Es gibt hunderterlei Möglichkeiten, diese Sache zu machen.*
> *Mein Sohn hat immer tausenderlei Fragen.*

Repetitive Numbers

Repetitive numbers indicate how often something is repeated. They are formed from cardinal numbers by adding the suffix **-mal**. They answer the question **wie oft?** or (less frequently) **wievielmal?** By themselves, they are uninflected adverbs. It is possible, however, to form adjectives from repetitive numbers by adding the ending **-ig**: *einmal, zweimal, dreißigmal, hundertmal — einmalig, zweimalig, dreißigmalig, hundertmalig.*

E 790

> *Wie oft hast du deiner Mutter geschrieben? Ich habe ihr dreimal geschrieben.*
> *Wievielmal bist du in München gewesen? Ich bin schon viermal dort gewesen.*
> *Nach zweimaligem Versuch hatte er Erfolg.*

---

[1] In analogy to the generic numbers, indefinite numerical adverbs may be formed with the suffix **-erlei**: *allerlei, mancherlei, vielerlei.*

Duplicating Numbers

E 795 Duplicating numbers are similar to repetitive numbers and indicate a certain quantity of identical things or actions. They are adjectives formed from cardinal numbers by adding **-fach**, and answer the question **wie oft?** or (infrequently) **wievielfach?**: *einfach, zweifach, zehnfach,* etc.

> *Wie oft (**wievielfach**) muß ich diese Formulare ausfüllen? Füllen Sie sie **dreifach** aus.*
> *Der Motor hat eine **zweifache** Sicherung.*

E 796 **Zweifach** is often replaced by **doppelt**. An older form, very rarely used today, is **zwiefach**.

E 797 In elevated literary style, duplication or repetition may also be indicated with the suffix **-fältig**, especially with high cardinal numbers:

> *Was du den Armen gibst, wird Gott dir **tausendfältig** wiedergeben.*

ADVERBS

E 800 Adverbs belong to the category of words which CAN NOT CHANGE THEIR FORM. (These words are sometimes called particles.) The adverb may be used as a verb complement, as a verb modifier, or as an attribute for nouns, pronouns, adjectives, and other adverbs. As a modifier, it follows the verb. As a verb complement, it constitutes the second part of the predicate. As an attribute, the adverb follows the nouns and pronouns which it modifies [→ J 210, J 220], but precedes adjectives and other adverbs[1] [→ J 230, J 240].

> *In Deutschland fahren die Autos **rechts**.*
> *Der Herr **dort** ist der Vater meines Freundes.*
> *Du **hier** gehst jetzt und holst die Kreide.*
> *Dieses Buch ist **besonders** interessant.*
> *Ich habe diese Arbeit schon **sehr** oft gemacht.*

[1] Adverbs ending in **-erlei** as noun attributes precede the noun. They may be formed from ordinal numbers [→ E 780] or from indefinite numerical adjectives: *Er hat mir **vielerlei** Aufträge gegeben.*

340

Forms of Adverbs

We distinguish between several types of adverbs, according to their derivation:

1. Uninflected Adjectives Used Adverbially E 805

Almost all descriptive adjectives may be used adverbially in their uninflected form to serve as predicate modifiers [→ E 013]:

> *Das Auto fährt **schnell**.*
> *Heute ist es **bitter** kalt.*
> ***Tief** unten im Tale fließt ein Bach.*

2. Simple Adverbs: ja, heute, hier, her, sehr, oft, etc.: [1] E 806

> *Kommst du **heute** zu mir? **Ja**, ich komme.*
> ***Hier** liegen deine Bücher.*
> *Kommen Sie bitte **her**!*
> *Ich habe mich über Ihren Brief **sehr** gefreut.*

3. Derived Adverbs E 807

Adverbs may be derived from other parts of speech by means of the suffixes **-s, -lich, -erlei, -falls,** and, much more rarely, **-lings**. The suffix **-e** occurs infrequently today; it is still found in colloquial language or in poetic usage [→ A 156]: *gerne, balde, stille.*

> *Das neue Hotel liegt hier **rechts**.*
> *Wir haben nur **morgens** Unterricht.*
> *Meine Eltern waren **kürzlich** in Spanien.*
> *Sie haben dort **mancherlei** gesehen.*
> *Er kann **bestenfalls** um 3 Uhr hier sein.*
> *Das Kind fiel vor Schreck **rücklings** zu Boden.*
> *Du hast mich **lange** warten lassen.*

Adverbs may also be derived from descriptive adjectives, numerical E 808
adjectives, pronouns, or prepositions with the suffixes **-weise, -maßen, -mal(s)** [→ E 790], **-wärts, -art,** etc.:

> ***Glücklicherweise** haben wir noch Theaterkarten für heute abend bekommen.*
> *Bei **einigermaßen** schönem Wetter machen wir einen Ausflug.*
> *Ich danke **vielmals**.*
> *Unser Weg ging steil **aufwärts**.*

[1] Sometimes called "pure" adverbs.

E 809 **4. Compound Adverbs**

An adverb may be compounded with a preposition, an adjective, or another adverb acting as modifier [→ A 205, 206]:

> *Wer kommt **zuerst**?*
> *Sie können **überall** Arbeit finden.*
> *Gehen Sie immer **geradeaus**!*
> *Ich lege das Buch **hierher**.*

Use of Adverbial Adjectives

E 810 When descriptive adjectives in their uninflected form are used adverbially, they normally do not modify nouns or pronouns, but only verbs, adjectives, or other adverbs [→ E 805].

E 811 Adjectives used as nouns may be modified by adverbial adjectives, if they refer to a quality and not to the person or thing expressed by the noun [→ J 134]:

> *der **wahrhaft** Reiche*
> *die **links** Gehenden*
> *das **alt** Bewährte*
> *das **gut** Brauchbare*

E 812 Adverbial adjectives may also be used as attributes of present or past participles:

> *ein **gut** gehendes (or **gut**gehendes) Geschäft*
> *ein **blau** gestreiftes (**blau**gestreiftes) Kleid*[1]

E 813 When such participles are used as nouns, they may again be preceded by adjectives used adverbially:

> *die **jung** Verheirateten* (the newlyweds, *not* the young married)

E 815 Adverbial adjectives may also be used as predicate modifiers [→ H 550 ff.]. In this function, they describe the manner or the circumstances under which a certain situation takes place:

---

[1] Note the difference between **ein blaugestreiftes Kleid** (the stripes are blue, but we don't know the color of the dress) and **ein blaues gestreiftes Kleid** (the dress is blue, but we don't know the color of the stripes).

342

*Der Vorhang öffnet sich **langsam**.*
*Ich bin **gut** in München angekommen.*
*Wir sind **geduldig** sitzen geblieben.*

Comparison of Adverbs

Adjectives used as adverbs use the ending **-er** in the comparative; in the superlative they use the preposition **am** and the ending **-sten** [→ E 330]: E 820

*Marie singt **schön**. Anna singt **schöner**. Ilse singt **am schönsten**.*

In the absolute superlative [→ E 386], the adverb may be used with the ending **-st, -stens,** or the preposition **aufs** and the ending **-ste**: E 821

*Das ist **höchst** interessant.*
*Rauchen ist **strengstens** (**aufs strengste**) verboten.*

For irregular comparison forms, → E 325. E 822

Adverbs not derived from adjectives normally have no comparative and superlative forms. For superlative adjectives derived from adverbs of place (**oben — der oberste**, etc.) → E 393. E 823

A comparative and superlative meaning is possible for the following adverbs, where the comparative and superlative uses different forms: E 824

Positive	Comparative	Superlative
bald	{ früher / eher	{ am frühesten / am ehesten / baldigst
gern[1]	lieber	am liebsten
sehr / viel	mehr	am meisten[2]
wohl	besser	{ am besten / bestens
wenig[3]	minder	{ am mindesten / mindestens

[1] **Gern**, being an adverb, can only modify a verb. If the object of the concept "to like" is a person or a thing, the verb **haben** must be used: *Ich habe meinen Onkel sehr gern.*

[2] The form **meistens** means "most of the time."

[3] The regular comparative forms **weniger** and **am wenigsten** (**wenigstens**) are used more frequently than the irregular forms.

> *Ich trinke* **gern** *Kaffee; ich trinke* **lieber** *Bier;* **am liebsten** *trinke ich Wein.*
>
> *Daß du kommst, freut mich* **sehr***; es würde mich noch* **mehr** *freuen, wenn deine Frau auch käme; und* **am meisten** *freut es mich, daß es euch allen gut geht.*

Types of Adverbs

We can distinguish adverbs according to meaning by the following categories:

E 830
1. Adverbs of Place
These adverbs function in the sentence as INDICATORS of LOCATION or DIRECTION [→ H 420, H 571]. They determine the place at which the action occurs, or the place towards which or from which the action progresses. They answer the question **wo?, wohin?,** or **woher?:** [1]

> *Sehen Sie* **dort** *das neue Hotel?*
> *Wir gehen den Berg* **hinauf.**
> *Die Sportler kamen von* **überallher.**

E 831
The adverbs may be attributes of nouns or pronouns [→ E 800] and indicate their position. They may also be used together with other adverbs of place to give a more precise location:

> *Das Haus* **hier** *gehört meinem Vater.*
> *Ihr* **dort** *könnt nach Hause gehen.*
> *Die Familie Müller wohnt* **dort oben.**
> *Seht ihr das kleine Haus* **dahinten?**

E 832
Some adverbs of place may follow or precede a prepositional expression of location or direction. Again, they serve to define or emphasize the position more precisely:

> **Oben unter dem Dach** *unseres Hauses ist ein Vogelnest.*
> **Hinten am Waldrand** *steht eine kleine Hütte.*
> *Wir haben* **auf dem Berg oben** *übernachtet.*
> **Von Osten her** *wehte ein eisiger Wind.*

---

[1] The adverb **da** may function either as an adverb of place (*Da ist mein Hut*) or as an adverb of time (*Da geschah es plötzlich, . . .*) [→ E 899].

2. Adverbs of Time

These adverbs function as TIME INDICATORS [→ H 430, H 575]. They answer such questions as **wann?, bis wann?, seit wann?, wie lange?, wie oft?,** etc.:

> *Wir sind **kürzlich** in Paris gewesen.*
> *Mein Freund wird **einstweilen** bei mir wohnen.*
> *Die Zeitung kommt **täglich.***
> *Der Unterricht findet **vormittags** statt.*

Occasionally, these adverbs may function as noun attributes. They may also be used together with another adverb of time to give a more precise definition of time:

> *Der Mann **gestern** war wirklich unhöflich.*
> *Diese Arbeit **heute** war sehr langweilig.*
> *Wir haben **gestern nachmittag** keinen Unterricht gehabt.*

Adverbs of time may sometimes precede a prepositional expression of time, again to define the time more precisely:

> ***Heute in einem Monat** ist mein Geburtstag.*
> ***Gestern vor acht Tagen** sind wir in Berlin angekommen.*

Adverbs of time coordinate a statement according to tense categories as follows:

PRESENT: **jetzt, nun; gegenwärtig; heutzutage, heutigentags;** (simultaneous with another event) **gleichzeitig; da** [→ E 899]

PAST: **gerade, eben, soeben, vorhin; kürzlich, neulich,**[1] **jüngst; früher, einst, einstmals; damals;** (preceding another event) **vorher, seinerzeit, ehedem**

FUTURE: **demnächst, nächstens,**[1] **zukünftig, dereinst;** (following another event) **nachher, dann, später; zunächst**[1]

3. Adverbs of Manner

These adverbs function in the sentence as INDICATORS OF MANNER [→ H 440, H 580]. They describe the way or mode in which the

---

[1] Note that **neulich** means "recently," *not* "newly." **Nächstens** means "shortly, very soon," **zunächst** means "first of all"; neither corresponds to English "next" (**der Nächste, als nächstes**).

situation or activity occurs. They may also indicate DEGREE, QUALITY, QUANTITY, or INTENSITY, and answer the questions **wie?**, **wie sehr?**, etc.:

> *Ich danke Ihnen **sehr** für Ihren Brief.*
> *Er fiel **kopfüber** ins Wasser.*
> *Wir trinken **gern** Bier.*

E 841 Adverbs of NEGATION [→ H 650, H 760] are also considered as adverbs of manner:

> *Bist du morgen **nicht** zu Hause?*
> *Er war mit der Arbeit **keineswegs** zufrieden.*

E 842 The so-called INTENSIFIERS [→ H 600] are also classified as adverbs of manner. They indicate the subjective attitude of the speaker to the event described, and express such feelings as surprise, emphasis, uncertainty, etc.:

> *Das wissen Sie **ja**.*
> *Er ist **doch** gekommen.*
> *Du hast **wohl** deinen Verstand verloren.*
> *Das kann **vielleicht** (**möglicherweise**) stimmen.*

E 843 As ATTRIBUTES OF RANK, adverbs of manner may be used to evaluate a sentence unit or another attribute either positively or negatively, depending on the subjective attitude of the speaker [→ J 180 ff.]:

> *Ich habe **nur** einen Apfel gegessen.*
> ***Auch** hier wird viel gebaut.*
> ***Erst** mein Freund konnte diese Maschine reparieren.*

E 844 Adverbs of manner may be used as attributes before adjectives or other adverbs:

> *Ich finde das Bild **sehr** schön.*
> *Wir haben das Theater **sehr** oft besucht.*

E 845 **4. Adverbs of Cause**

These adverbs function in the sentence as INDICATORS of CAUSE [→ H 590 ff.] and describe the REASON or the PURPOSE of an action, or the MEANS or the CONDITION on which the situation depends. They

346

answer questions like **warum?, weshalb?** (causal, consecutive); **wodurch?, womit?** (instrumental); **unter welcher Bedingung?** (conditional); **wozu?, wofür?, zu welchem Zweck?** (final):

> *Ich bin **deinetwegen** nach Köln gefahren.*
> *Wir müssen den Jungen **nötigenfalls** bestrafen.*
> *Wir übersenden Ihnen **hiermit** unsere Rechnung für die gelieferte Ware.*
> *Er mußte gestern arbeiten und konnte **daher** nicht kommen.*
> *Wir haben ihn **jedenfalls** eingeladen.*
> ***Schlimmstenfalls** werde ich zum Arzt gehen.*

Adverbs as Conjunctions

Some adverbs may take over the function of conjunctions [→ G 001 ff.]. They differ from genuine conjunctions by the fact that they themselves act as a sentence unit and therefore may occupy a position in the pre-field or within the sentence field:[1]

E 850

> *Ich habe heute noch viel zu tun,[2] **deshalb** kann ich nicht mit euch ins Kino gehen. (Or: ich kann **deshalb** nicht mit euch ins Kino gehen).*
> *Er fährt nach Wien, **außerdem** hat er noch die Absicht, Innsbruck zu besuchen.*
> ***Zwar** hat mir mein Vater Geld geschickt, ich kann euch aber **trotzdem** keines leihen.*

The conjunctional adverbs **doch, jedoch,** and **indessen** [→ G 275, 350, 375] may sometimes assume the function of genuine coordinating conjunctions. They are then in an isolated position in front of the sentence, and do not affect word order:

E 851

> *Ich möchte mit dir gehen, **jedoch** ich habe jetzt keine Zeit.[3]*
> *Jener Mann ist sehr reich, **doch** er ist nicht glücklich.*
> *Wir haben ihm unsere Hilfe angeboten, **indessen** hat er sie abgelehnt.*

---

[1] Genuine conjunctions either stand isolated outside of the sentence (coordinating), or form the front limit of the sentence field (subordinating) [→ H 115].

[2] The so-called "comma splice" is permissible in German.

[3] The alternate forms **jedoch habe ich jetzt keine Zeit** and **ich habe jedoch jetzt keine Zeit** are of course also possible.

Relative Adverbs

E 860   The adverbs of place **wo, wohin,** and **woher** may be used as relative adverbs to relate an expression of place [→ H 420, H 571, J 170.5] to an event which has the same location [→ D 526–8]:

> *Wir kommen jetzt in das Zimmer,* **wo** *der Dichter seine größten Werke geschrieben hat.*
> *Die Leute stehen da,* **wo** *gestern der Verkehrsunfall passiert ist.*
> *Ich zeige dir hier auf der Karte die Gegend,* **wohin** *wir fahren wollen.*
> *Dort,* **wohin** *wir morgen fahren wollen, gibt es viele interessante Dinge zu sehen.*
> *Italien ist das Land,* **woher** *Deutschland das meiste Obst importiert.*

E 861   If the relative adverb is parallel in form with the adverb of place to which it refers, the antecedent adverb of place may be omitted [→ J 171]:

> *Ich schlafe (***dort***),* **wo** *du gestern geschlafen hast.*
> *Er kommt (***daher***),* **woher** *wir auch kommen.*
> *Sie fährt (***dorthin***),* **wohin** *ihr Mann gefahren ist.*

E 862   If the attributive clause (clause of location) occupies the prefield, it comes before the adverb of place to which it refers; the adverb of place may be omitted:

> **Wo** *er wohnt, (***dort***) möchte ich auch wohnen.*
> **Wo** *du* **hin***gehst, (***da***) will ich auch* **hin***gehen.*

Interrogative Adverbs

E 870   Interrogative adverbs are used in INFORMATIONAL QUESTIONS [→ H 007] to inquire after the completion of the predicate or other expressions which are still missing in the sentence. According to the sentence unit for which they elicit information, they can be differentiated into the following categories of meaning:

E 871   PLACE: **wo?** (location), **wohin?** (direction, destination), **woher?** (origin) [→ E 881, 882]:

> **Wo** *liegt der Bleistift? Auf dem Tisch.*
> **Wohin** *fahren Sie am Sonntag? Nach Wien.*
> **Woher** *kommen Sie? Aus Amerika.*

348

TIME: **wann?** (point or space of time), **wie lange?** (duration), **wie oft?** E 872
(repetition):

> *Wann hast du Geburtstag? Am 3. Februar.*
> *Wann war die Zeit der Kreuzzüge? Im Mittelalter.*
> *Wie lange bleiben Sie? Drei Wochen.*
> *Wie oft gehst du ins Kino? Jede Woche einmal.*

MANNER: **wie?:** E 873

> *Wie war gestern das Wetter? Schön.*
> *Wie gefällt dir mein neuer Hut? Sehr gut.*

CAUSE: **warum?,**[1] **weshalb?, weswegen?** (causal: reason); **wozu?** (final: E 874
purpose); **womit?, wodurch?** (instrumental: means):

> *Warum kommst du heute so spät? Weil ich verschlafen habe.*
> *Weshalb fragst du mich? Ich dachte, du weißt es.*
> *Wozu lernst du Fremdsprachen? Damit ich eine bessere Stellung*
> * bekomme.*
> *Womit schreiben Sie? Mit einem Kugelschreiber.*
> *Wodurch hat er im Leben so großen Erfolg gehabt? Durch seinen Fleiß*
> * und seine Ausdauer.*

Directional Adverbs

The directional adverbs **her** and **hin** are used when a predicate indicates E 880
an action or a process which moves in a certain direction. These adverbs
may often function as separable verb prefixes [→ A 250 ff., B 300 ff.].

Usually, these directional adverbs indicate the manner in which a
motion, an action, or a process is viewed from the standpoint of the
speaker. **Her** indicates a direction TOWARDS THE SPEAKER, and **hin** a
direction AWAY FROM THE viewpoint of the SPEAKER:[2]

> *Geht Hans morgen auch ins Theater? Ja, er geht auch **hin**.*
> *Komm bitte **her** und hilf mir!*

---

[1] Note the difference between **warum?** and **worum?**: *Sie spielten zum Vergnügen.* **Warum**
spielten sie? — Sie spielten um Geld. **Worum** *spielten sie?*

[2] Note that **hier, da,** and **dort** are position indicators and can never be used to describe
direction [→ E 895 ff.].

349

E 881 In questions, these directional adverbs are combined with the interrogative adverb **wo?**:

> *Wohin bringt ihr die Bücher?*
> *Woher kommt dieser Mann?*

E 882 If we are less interested in the action or process itself, and more in the goal (**hin**) or origin (**her**), the directional adverbs may be separated from the interrogative adverb and placed at the end of the sentence:

> *Wo bringt ihr die Bücher **hin**?*
> *Wo kommt dieser Mann **her**?*

E 883 The directional adverbs are often combined with prepositions, sometimes preceding and sometimes following them. The entire compound may function as a separable verb prefix. The preposition **in** changes to **ein**:

> **her**ab, **her**auf, **her**aus, **her**bei, **her**über, **her**unter, **her**vor, **her**ein, etc.
> **hin**ab, **hin**auf, **hin**aus, **hin**über, **hin**unter, **hin**ein, etc.
> hinter**her**, nach**her**, neben**her**, seit**her**, vor**her**
> neben**hin**, vor**hin**

> *Die Kinder gehen **hinaus**.*
> *Er gibt das Geld nicht **heraus**.*
> *Sie ging die Treppe **hinauf**.* (The observer is downstairs.)
> *Sie ging die Treppe **herauf**.* (The observer is upstairs.)

E 884 Some of these compounds are used mainly as adverbs of time:

> *Was willst du **nachher** tun?*[1]
> *Meinen Freund habe ich letztes Jahr gesehen. **Seither**[2] habe ich nichts mehr von ihm gehört.*
> *Ich habe endlich eine Wohnung gefunden. **Vorher** habe ich im Hotel gewohnt.*
> ***Vorhin** hat jemand nach dir gefragt.*

E 885 The adverb **her** may also be used by itself as an adverb of time:

> *Es sind jetzt drei Monate **her**, daß ich dich das letzte Mal gesehen habe.*

---

[1] Note the difference between **nach** (preposition), **nachdem** (conjunction), and **nachher** (adverb).

[2] **Seitdem**, originally a conjunction, is now used as a synonym of **seither**.

350

In colloquial usage, the directional adverbs in compounds are often   E 886
abbreviated. **Her-** is then shortened to **r-**, and the same form is also
used for the compound with **hin-**, regardless of the actual direction:
raus, rüber, rein, runter, ran, rauf, etc.

> *Komm doch raus! — Raus!* (i.e. *Hinaus!*)
> *Er geht die Treppe runter. — Er kommt die Treppe runter.*
> *Wir kommen rein. — Er ging ins Geschäft rein.*

In many verbal compounds, the directional adverbs have lost their   E 887
original meaning and are only used figuratively:

> *Der Verlag bringt ein neues Buch heraus.*
> *Sie läßt sich nicht dazu herab, mit ihm zu sprechen.*
> Similarly: *Sein ganzes Vermögen ist hin.*
> *Wo denken Sie hin?*

If a sentence already contains an indication of place, **her** and **hin** are used   E 888
to indicate the position of the observer in relation to the situation
described:

> *Peter kommt vom Bahnhof her.*
> *Das Geräusch kommt von unten her.*
> *Die Prozession bewegt sich zur Kapelle hin.*

Sometimes, the directional adverb **hin** is used to indicate the viewpoint   E 889
of the subject rather than that of the observer:

> *Sie war müde und legte sich ein wenig hin.*
> *Sein rechter Fuß schmerzt ihn. Er ist gestern hingefallen.*
> *Er singt (spricht, murmelt, schimpft) vor sich hin.*

The directional adverb **her** may be used to designate a movement with   E 890
unchanging local relationship between persons or things mentioned in
the sentence:

> *Peter fuhr mit seinem Motorrad neben dem Zug her.*
> *Der Hirt treibt seine Herde vor sich her.*
> *Warum läufst du immer hinter mir her?*
> *Der Hauptmann marschierte vor seiner Kompanie her.*

351

Positional Adverbs

E 895   The adverbs of location **hier, dort,** and **da** [1] designate the place at which an event occurs. They are called POSITIONAL ADVERBS and, in contrast to the directional adverbs **her** and **hin**, are never used to indicate direction.

     Hier designates the place at which the speaker is located, whereas **dort** designates a place at some distance from the speaker. **Da** has no clearly definable local relationship to the speaker; it indicates a position somewhere between **hier** and **dort**, and has primarily a demonstrative character:

> *Mein Vater ist jetzt nicht **hier**.*
> ***Dort** steht Herr Müller.*
> *Ist Frau Meier heute **da** (= hier)?*
> ***Da** (= dort) kommt mein Freund.*

E 896   Positional adverbs may occur together with other adverbs of place. In such usage, **da** is synonymous with **dort** and has demonstrative character:

> **hier** oben, **hier** unten, **hier** vorn, **hier** hinten, etc.
> **dort** oben, **dort** unten, **dort** vorn, **dort** hinten, etc.
> **da** oben, **da** unten, **da** vorn, **da**hinten (one word), etc.

> *Siehst du das Haus **dort unten**?*
> *Mein Arbeitszimmer ist **hier vorn**.*
> ***Dahinten** kommt Karl.*

E 897   **Da** may form contractions with some adverbs of place, and thereby lose its demonstrative character; e.g. **droben, drunten, drinnen, draußen,** etc.: [2]

> *Wir waren auf dem Berg, aber wir haben **droben** niemanden gesehen.*
> ***Drunten** im Tal liegt ein kleines Bauernhaus.*
> *Die Straßenbahnhaltestelle ist nicht auf dieser Straßenseite, sondern **drüben**.*

E 898   In order to reestablish the demonstrative character, **da** may be placed before these contractions:

---

[1] Since English only makes the bipolar distinction between here and not-here, i.e. there, German **da** sometimes corresponds to English "here" and sometimes to English "there," depending on the context.

[2] Note the difference between **draußen** and **außen, drinnen** and **innen**: Draußen and **drinnen** refer to something outside or inside an enclosure, whereas **außen** and **innen** refer to the outside or inside of surfaces which form the enclosure: *Drinnen im Zimmer ist es warm, aber draußen ist es kalt. — Die Schachtel ist **außen** schwarz und **innen** weiß.*

352

> **Da droben** steht ein kleines Haus.
> **Da drüben** kommen zwei Männer.

As an extension of its demonstrative function, **da** may often be used in   E 899
a temporal sense, meaning "then, at that moment, at that point in
time":

> *Ich saß ruhig in meinem Zimmer.* **Da** *klopfte plötzlich jemand an die Tür.*
> **Da** *geschah es, . . .*

Da as a Pronominal Adverb

Because of its demonstrative character, **da** may replace a sentence unit   E 900
(or phrase), if the unit core is a noun which designates a thing or a concept. This, however, is possible only if the function of the sentence unit
is introduced in the sentence by one of the following prepositions
[→ D 495]: **an, auf, aus, bei, durch, für, gegen, hinter, in, mit, nach,
neben, über, um, unter, von, vor, wider, zu, zwischen.**

The adverb **da** is compounded with the preposition which character-   E 901
izes the function. If the preposition begins with a vowel, a linking
-r- is inserted: **dabei, dadurch,** etc., but **daran, darauf, daraus,** etc.
[→ D 040 ff.]:

> *Fährst du morgen* **mit deinem neuen Fahrrad***? Ja, ich fahre* **damit** *an den*
> *See.*
> *Hast du dich nicht* **über seinen Besuch** *gefreut? Doch, ich habe mich sehr*
> **darüber** *gefreut.*

In a question, the interrogative adverb **wo?** is combined in a similar   E 903
manner with the preposition characterizing the function. The linking
-r- is again inserted if the preposition begins with a vowel, e.g. **wofür?,**
womit?, wozu?, but **worüber?, worum?,** etc.[1]

> **Worauf** *warten Sie? Ich warte* **auf den Bus.**
> **Wovon** *hat Herr Berger gesprochen? Er hat* **von seiner Reise** *gesprochen.*
> **Worüber** *freust du dich? Ich freue mich* **über das schöne Wetter.**

---

[1] The use of **was** with the preposition, which frequently occurs in colloquial speech, is
considered inelegant: *Auf was warten Sie?*

E 905   **Da-** is used within the sentence field to anticipate dependent clauses in the postfield [→ H 785]. Together with the preposition which characterizes the function of the dependent clause, **da-** occupies the position in the sentence which corresponds to its function:

> *Der Lehrer hat* **davon** *gesprochen,* **daß wir mit unserer Klasse bald einen Ausflug machen.**
> *Er wartet* **darauf, daß ich ihm helfe.**
> *Hast du noch* **damit** *gerechnet,* **daß dein Vater dir Geld schickt?**

E 906   Similarly, **da-** with a preposition may anticipate infinitive clauses [→ B 940] which occur in the postfield:

> *Ich freue mich schon* **darauf, dich wiederzusehen.**
> *Wir haben uns alle* **danach** *gesehnt,* **auf Urlaub fahren zu können.**
> *Ich denke nicht* **daran, ihm ein Geschenk zu geben.**

E 908   With some verbs which normally demand a prepositional object, **da-** and the preposition may be omitted in the sentence field, if there can be no doubt about the relationship between the predicate and the dependent clause or infinitive clause [→ B 941]:

> *Ich freue mich* (**darauf**), **daß mein Freund mich morgen besucht.**
> *Er hofft* (**darauf**), **daß wir ihm bei seiner Arbeit helfen.**
> *Er beginnt morgen* (**damit**), *eine neue Fremdsprache* **zu lernen.**
> *Ich habe mich* (**darüber**) *gefreut,* **Sie wiedergesehen zu haben.**

E 910   If the dependent clause is to occupy the prefield, the compound of **da-** and the preposition also moves into the prefield in front of the dependent clause, in order to emphasize the relationship between the preposition and the clause [→ G 121, G 133]:

> **Dadurch, daß du ihm unser Geschäftsgeheimnis verraten hast,** *ist uns großer Schaden entstanden.*
> **Dafür, daß er mir bei meinen Schwierigkeiten geholfen hat,** *werde ich ihm immer sehr dankbar sein.*

E 911   In order to emphasize the demonstrative character of **da**, the compound of **da-** and the preposition may be placed into the prefield, while the dependent clause follows in the postfield:

354

*Damit haben wir nicht gerechnet, **daß du noch kommst.***
*Davon hast du mir nichts gesagt, **daß ich dir bei der Arbeit helfen soll.***

The adverb **hier** is similarly, but less frequently, combined with preposi-   E 915
tions to form the following compounds: **hierauf, hieraus, hierbei,
hierdurch, hierfür, hiergegen, hierin, hiermit, hiernach, hierüber, hierunter,
hierzu** [→ D 497]:[1]

Hiermit übersenden wir Ihnen die Rechnung.
Hierin muß ich dir recht geben.
Hierzu ließe sich noch vieles sagen.

[1] Combinations with **hie-** are archaic and rarely occur in modern German.

F

✣ Prepositions

✣ Introduction

F 001 Prepositions, like declensional forms, are FUNCTION INDICATORS. Since German has a limited number of declensional endings for pronouns, nouns, and noun modifiers, the possibilities of indicating a large variety of functions can be extended considerably by the use of prepositions. Specifically, the prepositions serve to indicate the function and meaning of sentence units (words or phrases) within a sentence, or the function and meaning of attributes within a sentence unit. They may occur either together with declensional endings, or as a substitute for them, in such instances where the absence of declensional forms (i.e. for proper names and adverbs) does not permit any indication of function other than by means of prepositions.

F 002 Prepositions themselves are UNDECLINABLE, but they demand certain declensional forms of declinable words with which they are associated. Prepositions are said to "govern" certain cases.[1]

[1] German grammatical terminology uses the word **Rektion** for the concept of "governing" a case.

356

Most prepositions (as the word literally indicates) precede the word to   F 005
which they refer, usually a noun or a pronoun. Some of them, however,
may follow their referent. These are sometimes called POSTPOSITIONS.

CASE AND POSITION OF PREPOSITIONS

The following prepositions and postpositions govern the ACCUSATIVE:[1]   F 010

ab, bis, durch, entlang, für, gegen, ohne, um, wider

> *Er geht **durch den** Park.*
> *Was kann ich **für dich** tun?*
> *Wir sitzen **um den** Tisch.*

ab governs the accusative if it is used in a temporal sense; otherwise it   F 011
requires the dative [→ F 105]:[2]

> *Ab nächsten Montag habe ich eine neue Stellung.*

bis may be used alone or together with another preposition. In that case   F 012
the second preposition determines the declensional form:

> *Bis dreißigsten Dezember.*
> *Bis zum dreißigsten Dezember.*
> *Der Weg geht **bis an den** Rand des Waldes.*
> *Der Weg geht **bis zu dem** Rand des Waldes.*

entlang governs the accusative if it is used as a postposition. If it precedes   F 013
the noun, it requires the genitive:

> *Die Straße entlang stehen viele Bäume.*
> *Entlang der Straße stehen viele Bäume.*

Sometimes, a noun is preceded by the preposition **an** and followed by   F 014
the postposition **entlang**. In that case, the declensional form is determined by **an** [→ F 030]:

> *An der Straße entlang stehen viele Bäume.*

Durch may also occur as a postposition: F 015

> *Er arbeitete den ganzen Tag **durch**.*

---

[1] The prepositions **gen** and **sonder** are archaic.
[2] The dative occasionally occurs in a temporal use as well: *ab erstem Juli* [→ F 020].

357

F 016 **Außer** with the accusative is extremely rare:

*Ich geriet **außer mich**.*

F 020 The following prepositions and postpositions govern the DATIVE:[1]

ab [→ F 011], **aus, außer** [→ F 016, F 025], **bei, binnen, dank, entgegen, fern, gegenüber, gemäß, längs, laut, mit, nach, nächst, nebst, samt (mitsamt), seit, trotz, von, zu, zufolge, zu(un)gunsten, zuwider**

*Er ging eben **aus dem** Haus.*
*Ich schreibe **mit einem** Bleistift.*
*Kommst du morgen **zu mir**?*

F 021 **entgegen, gegenüber, gemäß, zufolge,** and **zuwider** usually follow the noun or pronoun to which they refer:

*Den **Bedingungen gemäß** bezahlte ich meine Rechnung pünktlich.*
*Seinem **Brief zufolge** hat er die Prüfung bestanden.*
*Er saß **mir gegenüber**.*

F 022 If **zufolge** precedes the noun, it governs the genitive:[2]

*Zufolge **des Gesetzes** wurde sein Vermögen einzogen.*

F 023 **binnen, dank, längs, laut,** and **trotz** are often used with the genitive [→ F 041]:[3]

*Wir machten **trotz des** schlechten Wetters einen Ausflug.*
*Dank **seines Fleißes** kam er gut vorwärts.*

F 024 When **nach** is used in the sense of "according to," it often follows the noun [→ F 447]:

*Meiner **Meinung nach** ist das nicht richtig.*

F 025 **Außer** may sometimes occur with the genitive in certain constructions. This usage is considered old-fashioned:[4]

[1] The archaic preposition **ob** usually governs the dative, sometimes the genitive.

[2] Similarly, **zugunsten (zuungunsten)** is used with the dative after the noun, with the genitive preceding the noun.

[3] In modern German, particularly in colloquial usage, the dative has become more frequent, even though **trotz** is traditionally listed among the prepositions governing the genitive [→ F 550–1].

[4] **Außer** with the accusative is also possible [→ F 016].

358

*Er ging **außer** Landes.*

The following prepositions govern either the **DATIVE** OR the **ACCUSATIVE**
[→ D 928, 947–8]:   F 030

an, auf, hinter, in, neben, über, unter, vor, zwischen

They require the ACCUSATIVE when the verb indicates a DIRECTION or a   F 031
change of position (motion towards a place), and when they answer the
question **wohin?**:

> *Die Kinder gehen **in die** Schule. (**Wohin** gehen die Kinder?)*
> *Er hat die Tasse **auf den** Tisch gestellt. (**Wohin** hat er die Tasse gestellt?)*
> *Ich setze mich **auf den** Stuhl. (**Wo** setze ich mich **hin**?)*

With verbs indicating a position or LOCATION, these prepositions require   F 032
the DATIVE. They then answer the question **wo?**:

> *Die Kinder lernen **in der** Schule. (**Wo** lernen die Kinder?)*
> *Die Tasse steht **auf dem** Tisch. (**Wo** steht die Tasse?)*
> *Ich sitze **auf dem** Stuhl. (**Wo** sitze ich?)*

With verbs of motion, these prepositions use the accusative to indicate   F 033
the goal or destination of the movement; they use the dative to indicate
the place where the action occurs:

> *Er geht **in das** Zimmer.*
> *Er geht **im** Zimmer auf und ab.*
> *Wir fahren **aufs** Land.*
> *Wir fahren **auf einem** Schiff.*

The verbs **schreiben** and **klopfen**, although they do not actually indicate   F 034
a change of position, are also generally used with the accusative:

> *Er schreibt etwas **an die** Tafel, **auf ein** Blatt Papier, **in sein** Heft.*[1]
> *Ich klopfe **an die** Tür, **auf den** Tisch.*[1]

If these prepositions are not used to express spatial relationships, **über**   F 035
is followed by the accusative; **hinter, neben, unter, vor,** and **zwischen**

[1] Dative constructions are also possible, although rare: *Es klopft **an der** Tür. Der Specht klopft **am** Baum. Er schreibt **an einem** Roman. Ich schreibe **auf der** Schreibmaschine.*

usually by the dative. The prepositions **an, auf,** and **in** may be followed by the dative or the accusative, if they are used in a figurative sense:

*Wir sprechen **über ihn.***
*Er wohnt schon **über eine** Woche hier.*

***Unter den** Schülern sind einige Ausländer.*
*Er warnte mich **vor der Gefahr.***

*Ich zweifle **an seinem** guten Willen.*
But: *Ich kann mich **an dieses** Klima nicht gewöhnen.*
*Er wartet **auf mich.***
But: *Ich bestehe **auf meinem** Recht.*
*Er verliebte sich **in ein** junges Mädchen.*
But: *Sie antwortete **in einem** freundlichen Ton.*

F 036 When the prepositions **in, an,** and **vor**[1] are used in a temporal sense, they always require the dative:

***Am** Sonntag gehen wir spazieren.*
***In einer** Stunde kommt der Zug.*
***Vor einem** Jahr war ich in Berlin.*[1]

F 037 When the preposition **an** follows verbs like **denken, (sich) erinnern, glauben,** etc., the accusative is used:

*Ich glaube **an seine** Worte.*
*Erinnerst du dich **an ihn?***
*Niemand denkt **an mich.***

F 040 The following prepositions govern the GENITIVE:[2]

abseits, angesichts, anhand, anläßlich, anstatt, anstelle, aufgrund, außerhalb, beiderseits, betreffs, bezüglich, binnen, dank, diesseits, einschließlich, entlang [→ F 013], halber, hinsichtlich, infolge, inmitten, innerhalb, jenseits, kraft, längs, laut, mangels, mittels, oberhalb, seitens, statt, trotz, um ... willen, unfern, ungeachtet, unterhalb, unweit, vermittels, vermöge, während, wegen, zeit, zufolge [→ F 022], zu(un)gunsten [→ F 022 footnote], zwecks

***Jenseits des** Flusses steht ein kleines Haus.*
***Kraft meines** Amtes eröffne ich hiermit die Ausstellung.*

---

[1] Note that the German preposition **vor** in a temporal sense corresponds to the English "ago."

[2] Many genitive prepositions are gradually becoming obsolete. The archaic forms **behufs** and **unerachtet** also govern the genitive. The archaic preposition **ob** is used either with the dative or the genitive. For **außer** with the genitive, → F 025.

The prepositions **binnen, dank, längs, laut,** and **trotz** may be used with the genitive or with the dative [→ F 023]:

F 041

> *binnen einem Monat, binnen eines Monats*
> *trotz des Regens, trotz dem Regen*

The prepositions **statt (anstatt), während,** and **wegen** occasionally occur with the dative, partly in colloquial usage,[1] partly in the plural, where the genitive has no inflectional ending:

F 042

> *Nun muß ich die Arbeit (an)statt ihm machen.*
> *Während zehn Monaten . . .*
> *Wegen dem Wetter . . .*
> *Wegen Geschäften . . .*

The preposition **entlang** governs the accusative when it follows a noun [→ F 013]; **zufolge** and **zu(un)gunsten,** when used as postpositions, govern the dative [→ F 022]:

F 043

> *Dem Wetterbericht zufolge soll die Kälte andauern.*

The prepositions **wegen** and **ungeachtet** may also occur as postpositions governing the genitive:

F 044

> *Des schlechten Wetters wegen sind wir zu Hause geblieben.*
> *Des schlechten Wetters ungeachtet gingen wir spazieren.*

The preposition **halber (-halben, -halb)** always follows the noun or pronoun:

F 045

> *Der Ordnung halber will ich noch meine Arbeit beenden.*

In the constructions **um . . . willen** and **von . . . wegen,** the genitive stands between the two parts:

F 046

> *Um Gottes willen!*
> *Von Rechts wegen sollte so etwas nicht geschehen.*

When the postpositions **halb(en), wegen,** and **willen** are combined with pronouns, they are written together as one word. The pronouns then have special forms:

F 047

---

[1] The dative occurs especially with pronouns, and is particularly frequent in Austria and Switzerland.

ich	meinethalben	meinetwegen	um meinetwillen
du	deinethalben	deinetwegen	um deinetwillen
er, es	seinethalben	seinetwegen	um seinetwillen
sie	ihrethalben	ihretwegen	um ihretwillen
wir	unsrethalben	unsretwegen	um unsretwillen
ihr	eurethalben	euretwegen	um euretwillen
Sie	Ihrethalben	Ihretwegen	um Ihretwillen
was?	weshalb?	weswegen?	um wessentwillen?
das	deshalb	deswegen	um dessentwillen

Contractions

F 050   Some prepositions may be combined with the definite article in contracted forms [→ D 307, D 335 ff.]. The most common contractions are:[1]

Preposition + **dem** (dat.):   *am, beim, hinterm,*[2] *im, überm,*[2] *unterm,*[2] *vom, vorm,*[2] *zum*

Preposition + **das** (acc.):   *ans, aufs, durchs, fürs, gegens,*[2] *hinters,*[2] *ins, nebens,*[2] *übers,*[2] *ums,*[2] *unters,*[2] *vors,*[2] *zwischens*[2]

Preposition + **der** (dat.):   *zur*

IDIOMATIC PREPOSITIONAL PHRASES

F 060   Many verbs, nouns, and adjectives require certain prepositions by means of which the relation to the following noun or pronoun is established. Often different prepositions result in different meaning, such as *Er hat Angst **vor** Dieben; er hat Angst **um** sein Geld. — Ich freue mich **auf** meinen Geburtstag; ich freue mich **über** meine Geschenke.*

F 061   It is important to learn the prepositions which are idiomatically associated with certain verbs, nouns, or adjectives.[3] Some important constructions with verbs and prepositions are:[4]

---

[1] Contractions with **den** (acc.) are very rare: *fürn, übern.* There are no genitive contractions.

[2] Mostly colloquial.

[3] See individual listings of prepositions, F 100 ff.

[4] These listings are merely examples and are not to be considered exhaustive.

362

use of wie *(p. 310)

GERMAN GRAMMAR — APPLIED LINGUISTICS

DATE	TOPIC	PAGES
Monday, December 1	Adjective Endings	296 – 308
Wednesday, December 3	Adjectives used as nouns	320 – 323
	Extended Adjective constructions	618 – 620
Friday, December 5	Comparison of adjectives & adverbs	308 – 316
Monday, December 8	TEST?? (Or: Prepositions)	356 – 407
Wednesday, December 10	Prepositions	356 – 407

Final Examination: NO Principle parts or limited

dǫ → acc.

*= exceptions

arbeiten an (dat.) ✻ *glauben an* (acc.)
denken an (acc.) *sich halten an* (acc.)
sich erinnern an (acc.) *leiden an* (dat.) ✻
erkennen an (acc.) *teilnehmen an* (dat.)✻
sich gewöhnen an (acc.) *zweifeln an* (dat.) ✻

achten auf (acc.) *schwören auf* (acc.)
antworten auf (acc.) *vertrauen (sich verlassen) auf* (acc.)
bestehen auf (dat.) ✻ *verzichten auf* (acc.)
hoffen auf (acc.) *warten auf* (acc.)

bestehen aus *sich etwas (nichts) machen aus*

bleiben bei *schwören bei*

danken für *schwärmen (sich begeistern) für*
halten für *sorgen für*

sich fügen (schicken) in (acc.) *sich verlieben in* (acc.)

sich begnügen mit *sich verloben (verheiraten) mit*
sich beschäftigen mit *wetten mit*
handeln mit *winken mit*

fragen (sich erkundigen) nach *sich sehnen nach*
riechen (schmecken) nach *streben (suchen) nach*

klagen über (acc.) *sprechen über* (acc.)
lachen über (acc.) *streiten über* (acc.)
nachdenken über (acc.) *sich wundern über* (acc.)

bitten um *sich kümmern (sorgen) um*
sich handeln um *wetten um*

halten von *handeln von*

sich fürchten vor (dat.) ✻ *warnen vor* (dat.) ✻
schützen vor (dat.) ✻ *zittern vor* (dat.) ✻

Some important idiomatic combinations of nouns and prepositions are: F 065

Bedarf an (dat.) *Lust an* (dat.)
Bitte an (acc.) *Mangel an* (dat.)
Freude an (dat.) *Schuld an* (dat.)
Interesse an (dat.) *Vergnügen an* (dat.)

Anspruch auf (acc.) *Recht auf* (acc.)
Aussicht auf (acc.) *Wut (Zorn) auf* (acc.)

Interesse für *Vorliebe für*
Verständnis für *Schritt für Schritt, Tag für Tag*, etc.

363

*Mitleid **mit***	*Streit **mit** (jemandem)*
*Verlangen **nach***	*Sehnsucht **nach***
*Freude **über** (acc.)*	*Zorn **über** (acc.)*
*Angst (Sorge) **um***	*Streit **um** (etwas)*
*Achtung (Ehrfurcht) **vor** (dat.)*	*Angst (Furcht) **vor** (dat.)*

F 066   Often, the idiomatic meaning of a noun phrase depends on which of two different prepositions is used. Some such constructions are:

*Der Bauer arbeitet **auf dem Feld**. — Der Soldat steht **im Feld**.*
*Der Page lebt **am Hofe** des Königs. — Der Knecht arbeitet **auf dem Hof** des Bauern.*
*Sein Schicksal liegt mir **am Herzen**. — Ich habe noch etwas **auf dem Herzen**.*
*Viele Menschen waren **auf der Straße**. — **In welcher Straße** wohnst du?*
*Die Sterne stehen **am Himmel**. — Die Engel sind **im Himmel**.*
*Er macht Forschungen **im Gebiet** der Sahara. — Er macht Forschungen **auf dem Gebiet** der Technik.*
*Wir sind seit drei Jahren **im Land**. — Wir wohnen im Sommer **auf dem Land**.*
*Er hielt das Buch **in der Hand**. — Er hielt das Kind **bei der Hand**.*
*Der Preis wurde **auf drei Mark** erhöht. — Der Preis wurde **um drei Mark** erhöht.*

F 070   Adjectives may also be combined with certain prepositions. Since many of them are identical with a similar noun construction (e.g. **Schuld an, schuldig an**), only a few of them are listed here:

*interessiert **an** (dat.)*	*reich **an** (dat.)*
*gespannt **auf** (acc.)*	*vorbereitet **auf** (acc.)*
*stolz **auf** (acc.)*	*zornig **auf** (acc.)*
*bekannt **für***	*dankbar **für***
*gerecht **gegen***	*gleichgültig **gegen***
*besorgt **um***	*schade **um***
*überzeugt **von***	*voll **von***
*bereit **zu***	*fähig **zu***

USE AND MEANING OF PREPOSITIONS

F 100   The use of prepositions is highly idiomatic. Attempts to establish one-to-one lexical relationships between English and German prepositions are rarely successful, except in the most concrete applications. A variety of usages and meanings are listed below for each preposition. Such a list, to be sure, can never be complete; the English equivalents listed for each preposition are merely suggestions.

ab

PLACE: beginning, starting point. English equivalent: "from." DATIVE   F 105
[→ F 683 **von . . . ab**]. The noun usually follows without an article:

> *Der Preis des Wagens beträgt **ab** Fabrik DM 5700.-*
> ***Ab** hier ist die Straße gesperrt.*

TIME: beginning. English equivalent: "from . . . on." ACCUSATIVE   F 106
[→ F 687 **von . . . ab**].

> ***Ab** Dienstag ist wieder Schule.*
> ***Ab** fünften Mai bin ich zu Hause.*
> ***Ab** nächste Woche habe ich eine neue Stellung.*

abseits (GENITIVE)
PLACE: location off to the side. English equivalent: "away from."   F 110

> *Das Dorf liegt **abseits** aller Verkehrswege.*
> *Das Gasthaus steht **abseits** der Straße.*

an

PLACE: Actual or apparent contact along one side (or from below)   F 115
[→ F 145, 460, 620 **auf, neben, unter**]. English equivalent: "at, to, on,[1] from." ACCUSATIVE (**wohin?**) for verbs which indicate a direction, goal, or motion towards the location indicated:

> *Ich setze mich **ans** Fenster.*
> *Er hängt das Bild **an die** Wand.[1]*
> *Wir fahren **an den** See.*
> *Der Lehrer schreibt **an die** Tafel.[1]*
> *Sie klopft **an die** Tür.*

DATIVE (**wo?**) for all other verbs, indicating a position or a spatial   F 116
relationship with the location indicated:

> *Ich sitze **am** Fenster.*
> *Das Bild hängt **an der** Wand.*

---

[1] Even in the few instances when **an** corresponds to English "on," the concept "along the side" is maintained. Do not confuse this function with the concept "on top of" [→ F 145 **auf**].

365

> *Wir wohnen **am** See.*
> *Die Lampe hängt **an der** Decke.*
> *Er steht **an der** Straßenecke.*
> *Sie geht **am** Haus vorbei.*[1]

F 117   Figurative local use [→ F 037]. English equivalent: "of, at, to." Accusative-dative distinction is made by figurative implication:

> *Ich denke **an dich**.*
> *Sie schreibt **an ihren** Vater.*   } Implied direction; acc.
>
> *Wir hängen **an unseren** Eltern.*
> *Ihre Gesundheit liegt uns **am Herzen**.*   } Implied position; dat.

F 118   TIME: Point or space of time. This preposition is used for days of the week, dates, parts of the day, and similar time indications [→ F 335 ff. in]. English equivalent: "on, at, in." DATIVE. **An dem** always contracted to **am**.

> *Er besucht mich **am** Mittwoch.*
> ***An einem** schönen Abend saßen wir in unserem Garten.*
> ***Am** 5. März habe ich Geburtstag.*
> ***An** Sonn- und Feiertagen ist das Büro geschlossen.*
> *Ich komme **am** Ende der Woche.*
> ***Am** Nachmittag gingen wir spazieren.*

F 119   CAUSE (especially for sickness or death). The noun follows without an article, unless there is an attributive adjective in the singular [→ D 361]. English equivalent: "from, of." DATIVE.

> *Er leidet **an** Rheumatismus.*
> *Ich litt **an** heftigen Kopfschmerzen.*
> *Sie starb **an einem** schweren Leiden.*

F 120   POSSESSION (or lack) of a certain quality. The noun follows without an article. English equivalent: "in" (or no preposition). DATIVE.

> *Sie ist reich **an** Ideen.*
> *Ich zweifle **an** seinem Fleiß.*
> *Das Problem nimmt ständig **an** Wichtigkeit zu.*
> *Es fehlt ihm **an** Mut.*

---

[1] In sentences of this type, **an ... vorbei** has the English equivalent "past": She walks past the house.

366

INTEREST or participation. English equivalent: "in." DATIVE. F 121

> *Wir sind **am** Kauf dieses Wagens interessiert.*
> *Ich beteilige mich **am** Ausflug.*

Action or event IN PROGRESS. English equivalent: "at." DATIVE. F 122

> *Wir sind **an der** Arbeit.*
> *Das Wasser ist **am** Kochen.*

SUPERLATIVE of adverbs and predicate adjectives. No English equivalent. F 123
DATIVE. Always contracted to **am**.

> *Er trinkt **am** liebsten Bier.*
> *Im Herbst ist das Wetter **am** schönsten.*

Approximate MEASUREMENT. In this construction, the phrase **an die** has F 124
no influence on the declensional form of the following noun; the
expression stands isolated from the noun. English equivalent: "about."

> *Gestern waren **an die** fünfhundert Personen im Theater.*
> *Wir haben **an die** vierzig Schüler in der Klasse.*
> *Das Auto kostet **an die** viertausend Mark.*
> *Ich muß heute Briefe von **an die** zwanzig Freunden und*
>   *Bekannten beantworten.*

angesichts (GENITIVE)
CONSIDERATION of a certain fact. English equivalent: "in view of." F 125

> ***Angesichts dieser** Tatsache verstummte er.*

anhand (GENITIVE)
MEANS or aid of accomplishing a purpose. English equivalent: "by F 130
means of."

> ***Anhand des** belastenden Materials gelang es dem Staatsanwalt, den*
>   *Angeklagten des Verbrechens zu überführen.*

anläßlich (GENITIVE)
Cause or occasion. English equivalent: "at the occasion of." F 135

> ***Anläßlich des** Geburtstags des Präsidenten waren alle Schulen*
>   *geschlossen.*

anstatt
SUBSTITUTION, replacement [→ F 540 **statt**]. Usually GENITIVE, but F 140

367

dative occurs colloquially, especially with pronouns. English equivalent: "instead of."

*Er erhielt für seine Arbeit **anstatt des** Lohnes nur Dank.*

F 141   **anstelle** is occasionally used in place of **anstatt**.

auf

F 145   PLACE: Actual or apparent contact from above or motion towards the top [→ F 560, F 115 **über, an**]. English equivalent: "on, up." ACCUSATIVE (**wohin?**) for verbs which indicate a direction or goal.[1]

*Ich lege das Buch **auf den** Tisch.*
*Wir gehen **auf die** Straße.*
*Mein Freund steigt **auf den** Berg.*

F 146   The directional quality of the preposition is emphasized by the expression **auf . . . zu**. English equivalent: "towards, up to."

*Der Gast kam **auf** mich **zu**.*
*Die Flugzeuge flogen **auf** die Stadt **zu**.*
*Gehen Sie **auf** dieses Haus **zu**!*

F 147   DATIVE (**wo?**) for verbs indicating location or position. English equivalent: "on, in."

*Die Lampe steht **auf dem** Tisch.*
*Ich bin **auf der** Straße.*
*Die Bauern arbeiten **auf dem** Feld.*
*Die Hütte steht **auf dem** Gipfel des Berges.*

F 148   Figurative local use. Accusative-dative distinction is made by implication. English equivalent: "on, onto, of, towards."

*Das Fenster geht **auf die** Straße.*
*Hier ist ein schöner Blick **auf den** Berg.* ⎱ Implied direction; acc.

*Er ist **auf dem** Heimweg.*
*Er kam **auf der** Durchreise von Hamburg*
nach Wien in München an. ⎱ Implied location; dat.

---

[1] In certain expressions, upward motion is no longer actually expressed, merely direction toward a goal: *Ich gehe **auf die** Bank, **aufs** Postamt.*

TIME: Duration of time, definite point of time. English equivalent: "for, on, at, to." ACCUSATIVE.

> *Wir fahren **auf** zwei Monate nach Deutschland.*
> ***Auf die** Dauer können wir hier nicht wohnen.*
> *Seine Ankunft fällt **auf den** elften Mai.*
> *Man soll seine Arbeit nicht **auf die** letzte Minute verschieben.*
> *In der Nacht von Sonntag **auf** Montag wurde ein Auto gestohlen.*
> *Meine Uhr geht **auf die** Minute genau.*

A relatively long duration of time in the future is indicated by **auf ... hinaus**. English equivalent: "for."

> *Hier haben wir noch **auf** Jahre **hinaus** Arbeit.*

An impending point of time is indicated by **auf ... zu** [→ F 688 **von ... auf**]. English equivalent: "towards."

> *Wir müssen uns beeilen, denn es geht schon **auf** Mitternacht **zu**.*

PURPOSE or DESIRE. English equivalent: "for." ACCUSATIVE.

> *Er bereitet sich **auf die** Prüfung vor.*
> *Ich hatte Appetit (Lust) **auf** Pilze.*

BELIEF, CONFIDENCE, or EXPECTATION. English equivalent: "for, in, of, on, to." ACCUSATIVE.

> *Wir hoffen **auf eine** Nachricht von unseren Eltern.*
> *Er vertraut **auf meine** Ehrlichkeit.*
> *Ich freue mich **auf die** Ferien.*
> *Sie ist stolz **auf ihre** Arbeit.*
> *Wir verlassen uns **auf** dich.*
> *Warten Sie schon lange **auf** mich?*

FRAME OF MIND or attitude directed towards a person. English equivalent: "at, with, of." ACCUSATIVE.

> *Ich bin zornig **auf** ihn.*
> *Er ist nicht gut **auf** mich zu sprechen.*

MANNER. English equivalent: "in." ACCUSATIVE.

> *Er hat mir **auf** englisch **geschrieben**.*
> *Sagen Sie es bitte **auf** deutsch.*
> *Ich werde ihn **auf** jeden Fall besuchen.*

F 156   MEASUREMENT or DISTRIBUTION. English equivalent: "to, for." ACCUSA-
TIVE.

> *Sein monatlicher Verdienst kommt **auf** 1000 Mark.*
> *Nehmen Sie von dieser Medizin fünf Tropfen **auf ein** Glas Wasser.*
> *So viel kommt nicht **auf dich**.*

F 157   INSISTENCE. English equivalent: "on." DATIVE.

> *Er besteht **auf** meinem Besuch.*

F 158   The form **aufs** is followed by the superlative adverb [→ E 386]. No English equivalent.

> *Rauchen ist **aufs** strengste verboten.*

F 159   The phrase **auf Grund** (sometimes spelled as one word **aufgrund**) is usually followed by the GENITIVE, sometimes by **von** and the DATIVE. English equivalent: "on the basis of."

> ***Auf Grund** (**aufgrund**) seines Geständnisses wurde der Angeklagte verurteilt.*
>
> ***Auf Grund** (**aufgrund**) **von** Zeugenaussagen wurde der Angeklagte verurteilt.*

aus (DATIVE)

F 160   PLACE: Origin [→ F 680 **von**]. English equivalent: "from, out of."

> *Der Herr ging **aus dem** Haus.*
> *Richard kommt **aus** Berlin.[1]*
> *Wir trinken Kaffee **aus einer** Tasse.*
> *Wir kamen um 10 Uhr **aus dem** Theater.*

F 161   TIME: Origin. English equivalent: "from."

> *Diese Stadt hat noch Bauwerke **aus dem** Mittelalter.*
> *Sie zeigte uns Bilder **aus ihrer** Kindheit.*

F 162   Figurative ORIGIN or source. The noun follows without article [→ D 361]. English equivalent: "from" (or no preposition).

> ***Aus** welchem Werk von Schiller stammt dieses Zitat?*
> *Der junge Mann stammt **aus** guter Familie.*

---

[1] Note the difference between *Er kommt **aus** Berlin* (i.e. he is a Berliner) and *Er kommt **von** Berlin* (he just arrived here from Berlin).

*Sie ist ein Kind **aus** seiner ersten Ehe.*
*Wir haben das Auto **aus** zweiter Hand gekauft.*

REASON or CAUSE. The noun follows without article. English equivalent: F 163
"from, out of" [→ D 361].

*Er hat mir den Brief nur **aus** Höflichkeit geschrieben.*
*Wie ich **aus** Erfahrung weiß, sind Schüler nicht immer fleißig.*
*Sie schenkt dem Armen **aus** Mitleid ihr letztes Geld.*
***Aus** Liebe zu ihren Eltern verzichtete sie auf ihr Glück.*

MATERIAL. The noun follows without article. English equivalent: F 164
"(made) of."

*Dieser Ring ist **aus** purem Gold.*
*Er hat ein Herz **aus** Stein.*
***Aus** welchem Material besteht dieser Schmuck?*

SEPARATION. English equivalent: "out of." F 165

*Ich bin **aus dem** Verein ausgeschieden.*
*Dieses Kleid ist schon lange **aus der** Mode gekommen.*
*Er hat Klavierspielen gelernt, doch er ist jetzt **aus der** Übung.*
*Er ist vor Wut **aus der** Haut gefahren.*

außer (DATIVE)

PLACE: Position outside an area. The noun follows without article F 170
[→ D 361]. English equivalent: "out of, outside of." The genitive
occurs occasionally but is considered old-fashioned:

*Mein Vater ist seit zwei Stunden **außer** Hause.*
*Das Flugzeug kannst du nicht mehr sehen, es ist **außer** Sichtweite.*
*Er ging **außer** Landes.*

Figurative location: outside a realm or possibility. The noun follows F 171
without article. English equivalent: "out of, beside."

*Der Kranke ist jetzt **außer** Gefahr.*
*Daß ich dir helfen kann, steht **außer** Frage.*
*Er ist so schnell gelaufen, daß er **außer** Atem ist.*
*Diese Maschine ist **außer** Betrieb.*
*Ich war **außer mir** vor Schreck.*[1]

---

[1] The accusative is sometimes possible: *Ich geriet **außer mich**.*

F 172   EXCEPTION: Exclusion of all other possibilities. English equivalent: "except for." [→ H 071]

> *Alle meine Freunde **außer dir** haben mir geholfen.*
> *Wer **außer dem** Lehrer kann so gut Französisch sprechen?*
> *Außer diesem Garten habe ich schon alle Grundstücke hier gekauft.*

F 173   INCLUSION in addition to something else. Often intensified by **auch, auch noch.** English equivalent: "besides."

> *Auf meiner Reise werde ich **außer** München auch (noch) Nürnberg besuchen.*
> *Außer der jungen Dame saßen auch (noch) drei Herren im Abteil.*
> *Ich möchte **außer diesem** Roman auch noch etwas Lyrisches lesen.*

außerhalb (GENITIVE)

F 175   PLACE: Location outside an area. English equivalent: "outside of."

> *Mein Garten liegt **außerhalb der** Stadt.*
> *Dieser Paß gilt nicht für Länder **außerhalb** Europas.*

F 176   TIME: Outside a time span. English equivalent: "outside of."

> *Die Schüler müssen auch **außerhalb der** Unterrichtszeit lernen.*
> *Außerhalb der Bürozeit können Sie mich in meiner Privatwohnung sprechen.*

F 177   EXCLUSION: Outside the realm of the possible. English equivalent: "outside of."

> *Diese Entwicklung liegt **außerhalb** meines Einflusses.*

behufs

F 180   PURPOSE. Archaic and legalistic. English equivalent: "for the purpose of, on behalf of." GENITIVE.

> *Behufs der Kinderfürsorge wurde im Gemeinderat der folgende Beschluß gefaßt.*

bei (DATIVE). (General concept: "in conjunction with.")

F 185   PLACE: Spatial proximity without contact[1] [→ F 115 **an**]. English equivalent: "near."

---

[1] Occasionally, contact may be indicated: *Sie hielt das Kind bei der Hand.* Here, and in such phrases as **beim Fenster, bei** corresponds to English "by."

*Das Hotel liegt **beim** Bahnhof.*
*Wir verbringen den Sommer in Bad Reichenhall **bei** Salzburg.*
*Ich wohne **bei der** Kirche.*
*Sie saß **beim** Fenster.*

Presence at somebody's place or home. English equivalent: "at, with."   F 186

*Er ist Lehrling **bei der** Firma Müller und Co.*
*Wir kaufen unser Fleisch **bei** Herrn Francke.*
*Ich wohne **bei** meinen Eltern.[1]*
*Der Arzt ist jetzt **bei** seinen Patienten.*
*Ich habe das Buch **bei** meinem Freund liegen lassen.*
*Haben Sie Ihren Paß **bei** sich?*
*Ich war gestern **beim** Bäcker.*

Placement in a group. English equivalent: "among, in, with."   F 187

***Bei den** Studenten herrschte große Aufregung.*
***Bei uns** in Deutschland ist das nicht üblich.*
*Er war Offizier **bei der** Luftwaffe.*
*Ich bin Ingenieur **bei einer** Autofirma.*

TIME: Point in time. English equivalent: "at, upon."   F 188

***Bei** meiner Ankunft in Köln holte mich mein Freund vom Bahnhof ab.*
*Er hinterließ **bei** seinem Tod ein großes Vermögen und kleine Kinder.*
***Bei** Beginn der Theatervorstellung geht das Licht im Zuschauerraum aus.*

Simultaneity of action. English equivalent: "during."   F 189

*Ich war **bei der** Prüfung sehr aufgeregt.*
*Dürfen wir **bei der** Arbeit rauchen?*
*Er trank viel Wasser **beim** Essen.*

Duration of time. English equivalent: "at, during."   F 190

*Haben Sie Paris schon **bei** Nacht gesehen?*

MANNER or condition. English equivalent: "in."   F 191

***Bei** diesem Licht kann man nicht lesen.*

---

[1] Note the difference: *Ich wohne **bei** meinem Freund* — I am staying at his apartment. *Ich wohne **mit** meinem Freund* — We share an apartment.

F 192 Physical or mental CONDITION. The noun follows without article. English equivalent: "in."

> *Er ist **bei** bester Gesundheit.*
> *Wir waren gestern **bei** guter Laune.*

F 193 ORIGIN (literary source). English equivalent: "in (the works of)."

> *Ich habe dieses Zitat **bei** Goethe gelesen.*[1]

F 194 AFFIRMATION or oath. English equivalent: "to, upon."

> *Ich schwöre **bei** Gott.*
> ***Bei** meiner Ehre, ich sage die Wahrheit.*

F 195 REASON. English equivalent: "with, because of."

> ***Bei** seinem Fleiß muß er im Leben viel Erfolg haben.*

F 196 EVENTUALITY. English equivalent: "in case of, at."

> ***Bei** schlechtem Wetter findet das Konzert im Saale statt.*
> *Sie können mir das Geld **bei** passender Gelegenheit zurückgeben.*

F 197 CONCESSION. English equivalent: "in spite of." Usually expanded to **bei all**.

> ***Bei all** seiner Mühe hat er doch immer Mißerfolg.*
> ***Bei** seinem Alter ist er noch sehr rüstig.*
> *Man muß ihn **bei all** seinem Reichtum bemitleiden.*

beiderseits

F 200 LOCATION on two sides of an area. Infrequently used. English equivalent: "on both sides." GENITIVE.

> ***Beiderseits** des Flusses wuchsen Trauerweiden.*

betreffs

F 205 REFERENCE. Mainly business and legal term. English equivalent: "concerning." GENITIVE.

> ***Betreffs** dieser Angelegenheit haben wir Ihnen bereits*
> *zweimal geschrieben.*

bezüglich

F 206 REFERENCE. Similar in usage to **betreffs** [→ above]. GENITIVE.

---

[1] This is not to be confused with the English phrase "by Goethe" (*von Goethe*).

binnen

TIME: Space of time. English equivalent: "within." GENITIVE or DATIVE   F 210
(dative used almost exclusively for plurals) [→ F 375 **innerhalb**].

> *Binnen eines Monats (einem Monat) muß ich die Arbeit beenden.*
> *Ich bitte Sie, die Rechnung binnen drei Tagen zu begleichen.*

bis (ACCUSATIVE)

PLACE: Limit or goal of an action or process; extent or dimensions.   F 220
English equivalent: "to."

> *Ich fahre nur bis Stuttgart.*
> *Er war von oben bis unten schmutzig.*

Usually, **bis** is followed by other prepositions which in their turn govern   F 221
the declensional form of the noun or pronoun. These compounds define
movement or extension in space by stating its limits. English equivalent:
"to, up to, down to."

> *Wir stiegen bis zur Spitze des Berges hinauf.*
> *Er füllt die Gläser bis zum Rand.*
> *Herr Müller begleitete seinen Gast bis an die Tür.*
> *Das Wasser ist so klar, daß man bis auf den Grund sehen kann.*

TIME: Limits of time span. English equivalent: "until."   F 222

> *Die Geschäfte sind bis 7 Uhr abends geöffnet.*
> *Bis Ende des Jahres muß ich meine Arbeit beendet haben.*
> *Wir können bis nächsten Sonntag (bis elften Mai) bleiben.*

In this sense, **bis** is often followed by the prepositions **in** or **zu**. which   F 223
then govern the declension of the noun.

> *Sein Großvater war bis ins hohe Alter gesund.*
> *Die jungen Leute haben bis in die Nacht getanzt.*
> *Bis zum Jahre 1918 war Deutschland eine Monarchie.*

LIMITATION: extreme extent. **Bis** is used with other prepositions which   F 224
determine declensional endings. English equivalent: "up to, down to."

> *Ich habe mich bis aufs äußerste angestrengt.*
> *Er ist konservativ bis in die Knochen.*
> *Wir haben in Italien bis zum Überdruß Spaghetti gegessen.*
> *Ich bin bereit, einen Betrag bis zu 1000 Mark zu bezahlen.*

F 225   EXCEPTION: **bis auf** [→ F 172 **außer**]. ACCUSATIVE. English equivalent: "except for."

> *Jetzt sind die Gäste **bis auf einen** gekommen.*
> *Bei der Flugzeugkatastrophe sind alle **bis auf** zwei Passagiere umgekommen.*

dank

F 230   CAUSE. English equivalent: "due to, thanks to, owing to." DATIVE or GENITIVE.

> ***Dank** unermüdlichem Einsatz der Feuerwehr konnte der Brand bald gelöscht werden.*
> ***Dank** seines Fleißes bestand er die Prüfung gut.*

diesseits

F 235   PLACE: Location at the side of the speaker [→ F 380 **jenseits**]. English equivalent: "at this side of." GENITIVE.

> ***Diesseits** des Tales liegt ein schönes Schloß.*

durch (ACCUSATIVE)

F 240   PLACE: Movement in space from one side to another, from one end to another, or the position at which an area may be entered or left. English equivalent: "through."

> *Ich gehe **durch den** Park.*
> *Er schwamm **durch den** Fluß.*
> *Wir reisen **durch** Deutschland.*
> *Der Dieb stieg **durch das** Fenster ins Haus.*
> *Gehen Sie **durch diese** Tür!*

F 241   TIME: An entire span of time. In this usage, **durch** usually acts as a postposition (following the noun). The longer form **hindurch** is often used. English equivalent: "long, through" (postposition).

> *Er mußte sein ganzes Leben **durch** (**hindurch**) schwer arbeiten.*
> *Es regnete letztes Jahr **den** ganzen Sommer **durch** (**hindurch**).*
> *Ich könnte **den** ganzen Tag **hindurch** schlafen.*

F 242   Occasionally, the preposition also precedes the noun. It is then frequently expanded by **hindurch** which follows the noun. English equivalent: "through."

376

*Durch viele Jahre (**hindurch**) müssen die Eltern ihre Kinder ernähren.*

Time (on the clock) which is just passed. Postposition. (This is a col- **F 243** loquial usage.) English equivalent: "past."

> *Es ist drei Uhr **durch**.*

CAUSE: Means, in a passive construction [→ B 596 ff., F 692 **von**]. **F 244** English equivalent: "by (means of)."

> *Er wurde **durch einen** Unfall verletzt.*
> *Die Stadt wurde **durch ein** Erdbeben zerstört.*

INTERMEDIARY or MEANS in active sentences. English equivalent: **F 245** "through, by (means of)."

> *Ich habe das Zimmer **durch einen** Freund gefunden.*
> *Er muß seinen Lebensunterhalt **durch** Handarbeit verdienen.*
> *Wir haben das Geheimnis **durch eine** List erfahren.*

einschließlich

INCLUSION. English equivalent: "including." GENITIVE. **F 250**

> *Das Zimmer kostet **einschließlich** Bedienung 18 Mark.*

entgegen (DATIVE)

OPPOSITE. The preposition often follows the noun. English equivalent: **F 255** "contrary to."

> ***Entgegen der** Bitte seines Freundes sprach er doch mit dem Lehrer.*
> ***Entgegen meinen** Erwartungen (meinen Erwartungen **entgegen**) war das Wetter gestern sehr schön.*

In the sense of "against" or "towards," **entgegen** is a separable verb **F 256** prefix and not a postposition:

> *Er **kam** mir **entgegen**. (Er **kam** mir gestern auf der Straße **entgegen**.)*

entlang

PLACE: Parallel with or accompanying a line. English equivalent: **F 260** "along." GENITIVE when it is used as a preposition:

> ***Entlang des** Zaunes stehen schöne Bäume.*
> *Siehst du die Häuser **entlang der** Straße?*

377

F 261 ACCUSATIVE when it is used as a postposition:

> *Den Zaun **entlang** stehen schöne Bäume.*
> *Die ganze Straße **entlang** sieht man viele moderne Häuser.*

fern (DATIVE)

F 265 DISTANCE. English equivalent: "far away from." Rarely used.

> *Er war **fern der** Heimat.*

für (ACCUSATIVE)

F 270 TIME: Time span, sequence of time, regularity. English equivalent: "for, by, after."

> *Darf ich Sie **für einen** Augenblick sprechen?*
> *Er will **für** immer hier wohnen.*
> *Tag **für** Tag denkt er an seine Eltern.* [→ F 273]

F 271 PURPOSE, aim, or interest. English equivalent: "in, for."

> *Ich bereite mich **für die** Prüfung vor.*[1]
> *Interessieren Sie sich **für** moderne Musik?*

ADVANTAGE or disadvantage; reference. English equivalent: "for."

> *Er arbeitet **für seine** Familie.*
> *Die Arbeit ist zu schwer **für ihn.***
> *Zigaretten sind nicht **für** Kinder.*
> *Milch ist gut **für die** Gesundheit.*

F 273 SEQUENCE: **für** stands between two identical nouns which are not preceded by an article. English equivalent: "by."

> *Ich habe den Brief **Satz für Satz** ins Deutsche übersetzt.*
> *Wir gingen **Schritt für Schritt** vorwärts.*

F 274 QUALIFICATION. English equivalent: "for."

> *Er ist **für diese** Arbeit nicht geeignet.*

F 275 SUBSTITUTION. English equivalent: "for."

> *Ich werde den Brief **für dich** schreiben.*

F 276 COMPARISON. English equivalent: "for."

---

[1] The preposition **auf** may also be used in this sense [→ F 152].

378

Für einen Ausländer sprechen Sie sehr gut Deutsch.
Er versteht für einen Laien sehr viel von Musik.

REMEDY [→ F 284 **gegen**]. English equivalent: "for, against."   F 277

Hier habe ich gute Tabletten für Magenschmerzen.
Für seine Krankheit gibt es kein Mittel.

PRICE, quantity, reward. English equivalent: "for."   F 278

Ich habe das Auto für 5000.- Mark gekauft.
Geben Sie mir für 80 Pfennig Äpfel.
Für seine Hilfe erfuhr er nur Undank.

gegen (ACCUSATIVE)

PLACE: Motion in a direction to the point of contact. English equivalent: F 280
"against."

Die Soldaten marschierten gegen den Feind.
Das Auto fuhr gegen einen Baum.

Direction towards a goal, often intensified by **hin**, following the noun,   F 281
or in opposition to some force [→ F 285]. English equivalent: "towards,
against."

Wir fuhren gegen Süden.
Das Segelboot kam gegen das Ufer hin.
Die Fußballmannschaft mußte gegen den Wind spielen.

TIME: Indefinite point or span of time [→ **um**. F 585–8]. English equiva-   F 282
lent: "about."

Kommen Sie gegen 10 Uhr in mein Büro!
Ich reise gegen Ende des Jahres nach Frankreich.

ATTITUDE or relationship [→ F 292 **gegenüber**]. English equivalent: F 283
"towards."

Du warst nicht sehr freundlich gegen den alten Mann.
Seid immer hilfsbereit gegen die Armen!
Der Vater ist streng gegen seinen Sohn.

REMEDY [→ **für** F 277]. English equivalent: "against."   F 284

Wir haben ein gutes Mittel gegen Rheumatismus.

F 285   OPPOSITION [→ F 281]. English equivalent: "against."

> *Sie kämpften **gegen den** Feind.*
> *Ich bin **gegen diesen** Vertrag.*

F 286   COMPARISON. English equivalent: "compared to." [→ F 293 **gegenüber**]

> *Du hast viel Geld, aber **gegen diesen** Mann bist du arm.*
> ***Gegen** früher stehen jetzt viel mehr Häuser in dieser Straße.*

F 287   EXCHANGE. English equivalent: "against (to, for)."

> *Ich möchte diese Briefmarke **gegen diese** zwei anderen tauschen.*
> *Ich wette eins **gegen** zehn, daß ich recht habe.*
> *Zahlen Sie **gegen diesen** Scheck 1000 Mark aus.*

F 288   Approximate number [→ F 124 **an die**]. English equivalent: "about."

> *Gestern waren **gegen** hundert Personen im Saal.*
> *Sie ist **gegen** dreißig Jahre alt.*

F 289   The shortened form **gen** is archaic and occurs only in poetic usage in the sense of direction, approximate time, or opposition:

> ***gen** Norden, **gen** Abend*
> *Wir ziehen **gen** Engelland.*

gegenüber (DATIVE)

F 290   PLACE: Location on the opposite side. English equivalent: "opposite."

> ***Gegenüber dem** Bahnhof steht ein modernes Hotel.[1]

F 291   **Gegenüber** usually acts as a postposition. It always follows personal pronouns:

> ***Dem** Bahnhof **gegenüber** steht ein modernes Hotel.*
> *Er saß **mir gegenüber**.*

F 292   ATTITUDE [→ F 283 **gegen**]. It usually acts as a postposition for nouns, always for personal pronouns. English equivalent: "towards."

> *Er ist **alten Leuten gegenüber** immer freundlich.*
> *Der Vater ist **seinem Sohn gegenüber** sehr streng.*

---

[1] In colloquial usage, **gegenüber** is often followed by **von**: *Gegenüber vom Bahnhof steht ein modernes Hotel.*

> *Mir gegenüber ist er immer hilfsbereit.*
> *Ich bin seinem Plan gegenüber skeptisch.*

COMPARISON [→ F 286 **gegen**]. In this usage, **gegenüber** always acts as a   F 293
postposition. English equivalent: "compared to."

> *Ein Autofahrer ist einem Motorradfahrer gegenüber im Vorteil.*
> *Ein Mann hat einer Frau gegenüber bessere Berufsaussichten.*

gemäß (DATIVE)

AGREEMENT. Occurs primarily in official language, either as a preposi-   F 300
tion or as a postposition. It is rarely used with a pronoun, where it
would have to be postpositive. English equivalent: "according to."

> *Gemäß den Bestimmungen dürfen hier keine Lastwagen fahren.*
> *Den Bestimmungen gemäß dürfen hier keine Lastwagen fahren.*
> *Wir werden demgemäß handeln.*

gen → F 289 **gegen**   F 305

halber (GENITIVE)

REASON or cause. Acts as a postposition. English equivalent: "because   F 310
of, due to, on account of, for the sake of."

> *Dieses Haus ist besonderer Umstände halber zu verkaufen.*
> *Er fährt seiner Gesundheit halber an die See.*

After personal pronouns, the preposition changes to **halben**. [For special   F 311
forms → F 047.] English equivalent sometimes: "for all (I) care."

> *Meinethalben brauchen Sie nicht zu kommen.*

hindurch → F 242 **durch**   F 315

hinsichtlich (GENITIVE)

REFERENCE. Rarely used. English equivalent: "with regard to, con-   F 320
cerning."

> *Hinsichtlich der Lieferung des Materials verweisen wir Sie auf
> unseren Brief vom 21. März.*

hinter

PLACE: Location at or motion towards the rear of an area, a person, or   F 325

381

an object. English equivalent: "behind." Accusative (**wohin?**) for verbs which indicate a direction or a goal:

> *Ich gehe **hinter das** Haus.*
> *Sieh **hinter dich**!*
> *Er stellte sich **hinter seinen** Freund.*

F 326   Dative (**wo?**) for verbs indicating position or unchanging motion parallel with a point of reference:

> *Der Garten liegt **hinter dem** Haus.*
> *Er steht hinter **seinem** Freund.*
> *Ein Mann kam (ging) **hinter mir** her.*

F 327   Time: Backwardness. The noun or pronoun is usually followed by **zurück**. English equivalent: "behind." Dative.

> *Die Stadt ist **hinter der** Zeit **zurück**.*
> *Er ist mit seinen Ansichten weit **hinter uns zurück**.*

F 328   Support, help. English equivalent: "behind." Dative.

> *Der Politiker hat seine Partei **hinter sich**.*
> *Ich habe mit meinen Wünschen meine Freunde **hinter mir**.*

F 329   Inferiority. English equivalent: "behind." Dative.

> *Wir wollen an Mut nicht **hinter ihm** zurückstehen.*

in

F 330   Place: Position or motion inside an area, or entering that area from outside. English equivalent: "in, into, to." Accusative (**wohin?**) for verbs indicating a direction or a goal, also before names of countries with article [→ F 440 **nach**].

> *Ich werfe den Ball **in die** Luft.*
> *Wir gingen oft **ins** Theater. [→ F 755 **zu**]*
> *Die Wespe stach ihn **in den** Arm.*
> *Sie schreibt die Regeln **in ihr** Heft.*
> *Wir fahren **in die** Türkei (**in die** Vereinigten Staaten).*

F 331   Dative (**wo?**) for verbs indicating a position or location.

382

*Der Tisch steht **im** Zimmer.*
*Er hat eine Narbe **im** Gesicht.*
*Wir schwimmen **im** See.*

TIME: Point of time. English equivalent: "in, at." DATIVE. F 335

*Mitten **in der** Nacht begannen die Glocken zu läuten.*
*Wir haben die Nachricht **im** letzten Moment erhalten.*

Future space of time. English equivalent: "in." DATIVE. F 336

*Kommen Sie **in einer** Woche wieder!*

Past duration of time. English equivalent: "in, during." DATIVE. F 337

*Er war **in seiner** Kindheit oft krank.*

Indication of age. English equivalent: "at." DATIVE. F 338

*Er ist **in hohem** Alter gestorben.*
*Ich kam **im** Alter von zehn Jahren nach Chicago.*

Indication of year, season, or month. English equivalent: "in" F 339
[→ F 118 **an**]. DATIVE. **In dem** is always contracted to **im**.

*Im **Jahre** 1918 wurde Deutschland eine Republik.[1]*
*Im **Frühling** blühen die ersten Blumen.*
*Unsere Ferien beginnen **im** Juli.*

FIELD of action or subject matter. English equivalent: "in." DATIVE. F 340

*Ich habe **in dieser** Arbeit wenig Erfahrung.*
*Der Schüler ist **in** Mathematik besonders gut.*

CHANGE or beginning of a condition or activity. English equivalent: F 341
"into." ACCUSATIVE.

*Ich habe den Brief **ins** Deutsche übersetzt.*
*Peter hat sich **in ein** junges Mädchen verliebt.[2]*
*Morgen tritt das Gesetz **in** Kraft.*
*Mein Freund ist **in** Schulden geraten.*

[1] The German preposition **in** can *not* be used immediately before a numeral indicating the year. **In 1918** is an anglicism.
[2] English here corresponds to "*in* love *with*."

383

F 342   MANNER. English equivalent: "in." DATIVE.

> *Du mußt mir alles im einzelnen erklären.*
> *Er antwortete mir in einem freundlichen Ton.*

infolge (GENITIVE)

F 350   CONSEQUENCE. English equivalent: "as a result of."

> *Infolge seines Fleißes hatte er in der Prüfung gute Noten bekommen.*

inmitten (GENITIVE)

F 360   PLACE: Location in the midst of an area or a group of people. English equivalent: "in the middle (midst) of, among."

> *Inmitten des Sees liegt eine kleine Insel.*
> *Der Lehrer steht inmitten seiner Schüler.*

innerhalb (GENITIVE)

F 370   PLACE: Location inside an area. English equivalent: "inside of."

> *Innerhalb dieser Stadt gibt es viele Parkanlagen.*

F 375   TIME: Space of time [→ F 210 **binnen**]. English equivalent: "within."

> *Innerhalb eines Monats werde ich meine Arbeit beenden.*[1]

jenseits (GENITIVE)

F 380   PLACE: At the other side, beyond (literal and figurative) [→ F 235 **diesseits**]. English equivalent: "across, beyond."

> *Jenseits des Flusses steht ein großer Bauernhof.*
> *Das ist jenseits meiner Möglichkeiten.*

kraft (GENITIVE)

F 390   MEANS. Used mainly in legal terminology. English equivalent: "by virtue of."

> *Kraft seines Amtes hat er viele Vollmachten.*
> *Er wurde kraft des Gesetzes zu drei Jahren Gefängnis verurteilt.*

längs (DATIVE or GENITIVE)

F 400   PLACE: Parallel with or accompanying a line [→ F 260 **entlang**]. English equivalent: "along."

[1] The dative is used for plural nouns: *innerhalb drei Monaten.*

> *Wir fuhren **längs der** Küste.*
> ***Längs der** Straße stehen viele schöne Bäume.*
> *Die Straße verläuft **längs dem** Flußufer (**längs des** Flußufers).*

laut (GENITIVE or DATIVE)

AGREEMENT. Used mainly in official and commercial documents. The F 410
noun often appears without article and without inflectional ending.
English equivalent: "according to."

> ***Laut des** Gesetzes (**laut Gesetz**) vom 12. Mai 1927 sind Sie ver-*
> *pflichtet, dem Finanzministerium folgende Abgaben zu entrichten.*
> *Ich übersende Ihnen **laut** Rechnung vom 5.3.67 den Betrag von DM 255.-*
> ***Laut** ärztlichem Befund muß er ein Sanatorium besuchen.*

mangels (GENITIVE)

LACK. Infrequently used. English equivalent: "for the want of." F 415

> ***Mangels** näherer Informationen ist dieser Bericht noch unvollständig.*

mit (DATIVE)

PLACE: In the same direction. English equivalent: "with." F 420

> *Unser Boot fuhr **mit dem** Strom.*
> *Wir flogen **mit dem** Wind.*

TIME: Point or span of time, simultaneity. English equivalent: "with, F 421
in, at the age of."

> *Er machte sein Doktorexamen **mit** 25 Jahren.*
> ***Mit der** Zeit lernt man viele Probleme verstehen.*
> *Die Natur ändert sich **mit der** Jahreszeit.*
> ***Mit der** Morgendämmerung beginnt der Tag.*

RELATIONSHIPS between persons, things, or concepts: togetherness, F 422
commonness, reciprocity, possession, property. English equivalent:
"with, to."

> *Ich bin **mit ihm** befreundet.*
> *Wir unterhielten uns **mit dem** alten Mann.*
> *Ich streite mich nicht **mit dir**.*
> *Peter ist **mit der** Tochter des Kaufmanns verlobt.[1]*

[1] Note that German usage differs from English: *verliebt in* [→ F 341], *verlobt mit*,
verheiratet mit.

Warum vergleichst du mich immer **mit meinem** *Bruder?*
Er beschäftigt sich **mit** *Mathematik.*
Ich habe **mit ihm** *Platz getauscht.*
Du hast dir **mit dieser** *Arbeit sicher viel Mühe gegeben.*
Wir suchen ein Zimmer **mit** *fließendem Wasser.*
Ich esse Eier **mit** *Schinken gern.*
Er wohnt **mit** *seinem Freund.*[1]
Ich sah ein Mädchen **mit** *blonden Haaren.*

F 423   MEANS or instrument. English equivalent: "with, by."

Er fährt **mit dem** *Auto nach München.*
Ich schreibe **mit der** *Schreibmaschine.*
Du mußt das Fleisch **mit dem** *Messer schneiden.*

F 424   MANNER. English equivalent: "with."

Mit *Freundlichkeit erreicht man mehr.*
Er hat mich **mit der** *Absicht besucht, über sein Geschäft zu sprechen.*
Kannst du das Haus **mit dem** *bloßen Auge erkennen?*
Unterschreiben Sie den Scheck **mit** *Vor- und Familiennamen!*
Das Auto fuhr **mit** *hoher Geschwindigkeit durch die Straßen.*
Er hat sein Ziel **mit** *großem Erfolg erreicht.*
Ich verbleibe **mit** *herzlichen Grüßen Dein Freund Karl.*

F 425   **mitsamt** (DATIVE) → F 500 **samt**

mittels (GENITIVE)

F 430   MEANS or instrument. English equivalent: "by means of."

Die Waren können **mittels eines** *Aufzugs nach oben befördert werden.*

F 431   **vermittels** is sometimes used instead of **mittels** [→ F 660].

nach (DATIVE)

F 440   TIME: Sequence in time. English equivalent: "after."

Nach *Regen folgt Sonnenschein.*
Nach mir *die Sintflut!*
Es ist jetzt zehn Minuten **nach** *fünf Uhr.*
Ich habe meinen Freund **nach 20 Jahren** *wiedergesehen.*

---

[1] For the difference between *Er wohnt* **mit** *seinem Freund* and *Er wohnt* **bei** *seinem Freund*
→ F 181 footnote.

386

PLACE: Direction towards a goal. Used for names of geographic loca- F 441
tions, i.e. cities, countries, continents [→ F 330 **in** for names of countries with article], points of the compass, and adverbs of location
[→ F 750 **zu**]. English equivalent: "to, towards."

> *Er fährt* **nach** *England (***nach** *London,* **nach** *Europa).*
> *Im Winter fliegen viele Vögel* **nach dem** *Süden.*
> *Der Ballon steigt* **nach** *oben.*
> *Er ging* **nach** *hinten.*
> *Wir schauten* **nach** *allen Seiten: erst* **nach** *rechts, dann* **nach** *links.*

Destination in the idiom **nach Hause** [→ F 752 **zu Hause**]. F 442

> *Ich gehe um 5 Uhr* **nach Hause**.[1]

AIM or PURPOSE of an action or an inquiry. English equivalent: "for, F 443
after, about."

> *Er hat sich* **nach der** *Abfahrt des Zuges erkundigt.*
> *Hat jemand* **nach mir** *gefragt?*
> *Die Mutter ging in die Küche und sah* **nach dem** *Essen.*
> *Ich habe den Wunsch* **nach** *Ruhe.*
> *Der Vater telefonierte* **nach einem** *Arzt.*
> *Ich suche* **nach einem** *Buch, aus dem ich Französisch lernen kann.*

SEQUENCE [→ F 462 **neben**]. English equivalent: "next to." F 444

> **Nach dem** *Direktor ist er der wichtigste Mann in der Fabrik.*
> **Nach** *Berlin ist Hamburg die größte Stadt Deutschlands.*

MODEL. English equivalent: "after, by, from." F 445

> *Er zeichnet* **nach der** *Natur.*
> *Der Sohn ist* **nach dem** *Vater geraten.*
> *Ich spiele* **nach** *Noten.*

SENSE PERCEPTION. The noun usually follows without article. English F 446
equivalent: "of, like."

> *Hier riecht es* **nach** *Fisch.*
> *Das Essen schmeckt* **nach** *Zwiebeln.*
> *Sieht es heute* **nach** *gutem Wetter aus?*
> *Es hört sich nicht* **danach** *an.*

---

[1] Note that this idiom is not transferable to other expressions. **Nach der Schule**, for
example, means "after school" [→ F 440].

F 447 LOGICAL SEQUENCE or origin [→ F 300, F 410, F 770 **gemäß, laut, zufolge**]. **Nach** may act as a preposition or as a postposition. English equivalent: "judging by, according to."

Seinem Brief nach (***nach seinem Brief***) *wird er morgen ankommen.*
Deutschem Recht nach (***nach deutschem Recht***) *ist ein solches Benehmen strafbar.*

F 448 In many instances, **nach** acts as a postposition in the sense of "according to."

Meinem Gefühl nach ist es schon zu spät.
Seinem Benehmen nach hat er keine gute Erziehung gehabt.
Dem Wetterbericht nach soll es morgen regnen.
Wie wird die Sache deiner Ansicht nach (***deiner Meinung nach***) *weitergehen?*
Meiner Erfahrung nach muß das Experiment gelingen.
Er ist nur dem Namen nach Lehrer.
Bitte treten Sie der Reihe nach ein!

nächst (DATIVE)

F 450 PLACE: Immediate vicinity. English equivalent: "next to."

Nächst dem Bahnhof steht ein modernes Haus.

neben

F 460 PLACE: Lateral vicinity without contact [→ F 115 **an**, F 180 **bei**]. English equivalent: "beside."

ACCUSATIVE (**wohin?**) for verbs which indicate a direction or goal.

Stellen Sie den Stuhl neben das Fenster!
Er setzte sich neben mich.

F 461 DATIVE (**wo?**) for verbs indicating location or position, or unchanging motion parallel to a point of reference:

Neben dem Hotel ist eine Bäckerei.
Mein Vater sitzt neben meiner Mutter.
Wir gingen durch die Stadt, und mein Freund ging neben mir.

F 462 RANK or SEQUENCE [→ F 444 **nach**]. English equivalent: "next to." DATIVE.

Neben dem Direktor ist er der wichtigste Mann in dieser Fabrik.
Neben Kaffee trinke ich Tee am liebsten.

nebst (DATIVE)

ADDITION: Something accessory or supplementary to some other object. F 470
English equivalent: "together with." The noun usually follows without
article.

> *Der Fotoapparat **nebst** Tasche kostet nur DM 250.-*

ob (DATIVE or GENITIVE)

REASON. Archaic, used only in poetic language. English equivalent: F 475
"for, because of."

> *Er tadelte sie **ob** ihrer Faulheit.*
> *Er schämte sich **ob** dieses Ausspruchs.*

PLACE: Location on the banks of a river. Very rare. DATIVE. English F 476
equivalent: "on."

> *Rothenburg **ob der** Tauber.*

oberhalb (GENITIVE)

PLACE: On the upper side of or above a certain location. English F 480
equivalent: "above."

> ***Oberhalb des** Tales liegt ein einsamer Bauernhof.*

ohne (ACCUSATIVE)[1]

LACK, ABSENCE. The noun usually follows without article. English F 490
equivalent: "without."

> *Er ist seit zwei Jahren **ohne** Arbeit.*
> ***Ohne** Geld kann man nicht leben.*
> *Er hat sie **ohne** Grund beleidigt.*
> ***Ohne** meinen Bruder fühle ich mich sehr einsam.*
> *Wir mußten **ohne dich** anfangen.*

EXCLUSION, EXCEPTION: Things not included. English equivalent "not F 491
including."

> *Das Essen kostet 4.55 Mark **ohne** Getränke.*
> *Er bezahlte für sein Zimmer **ohne** Heizung DM 80.-*

---

[1] The use of **ohne** with the dative is obsolete and survives only in the expression **ohnedem**
and in humorous poetry: *Bescheidenheit ist eine Zier, doch weiter kommt man ohne ihr.* It
is considered incorrect German today.

F 495   UNREAL CONDITION: If it had not been for . . . The verb is in subjunctive II [→ B 131, B 240]. English equivalent: "without."

> *Ohne meinen Freund hätte ich keine Arbeit gefunden.*
> *Er könnte ohne seine Frau nicht leben.*
> *Ohne die Hilfe dieses Rechtsanwalts säße er jetzt im Gefängnis.*

samt, mitsamt (DATIVE)

F 500   Collectivity: things belonging together, accessories, members of a group. The noun often follows without article. English equivalent: "along with."

> *Der Dampfer ist bei dem Sturm samt Passagieren und Mannschaft gesunken.*

F 501   **mitsamt**, used less frequently, often has slightly derogatory connotations. English equivalent: "together with."

> *Er ist mitsamt all seinem Kram gekommen.*

seit (DATIVE)

F 510   TIME: Duration or time span. The beginning of the action lies in the past; if the statement is in the present tense, it corresponds to the English present perfect; if it is in the past tense, it corresponds to the English past perfect. The adverb **schon** is often used as an intensifier. English equivalent: "for."

> *Ich lerne schon seit drei Jahren Deutsch.*
> *Peter liegt seit vier Tagen im Krankenhaus.*
> *Er war schon seit zwei Wochen in Berlin, als ich ihn besuchte.*

F 511   Point of time in the past, seen as the beginning of an action. Present tense in German corresponds to present perfect in English. English equivalent: "since."

> *Es regnet schon seit Montag.*
> *Ich wohne seit dem 1. Mai in meiner neuen Wohnung.*
> *Seit wann sind Sie in Deutschland? Seit letztem Sommer.*

seitens (GENITIVE)

F 520   ORIGINATOR (mainly in official documents). English equivalent: "from, by."

> *Seitens des Gerichts ist in dieser Sache nichts unternommen worden.*
> *Seitens meines Bruders sind keine Schwierigkeiten zu erwarten.*

390

sonder (ACCUSATIVE)

EXCLUSION, LACK. Archaic synonym for **ohne** [→ F 490–91]. English F 530
equivalent: "without."

> *Er war ein Held sonder Fehl.*

statt

SUBSTITUTION, REPLACEMENT. Shortened form of **anstatt** [→ F 140]. F 540
Usually GENITIVE, but DATIVE is occasionally used, especially in colloquial language, before pronouns, and before plural nouns. English
equivalent: "instead of."

> *Er schickte mir statt des Briefes nur eine Postkarte.*
> *Statt seines Vaters (statt seinem Vater) kam sein Onkel.*
> *Statt Worten will ich Taten sehen.*
> *Willst du nicht statt mir gehen?*

trotz

WITHOUT CONSIDERATION. DATIVE or GENITIVE (dative in such expres- F 550
sions as **trotzdem, trotz allem,** before pronouns, before plural nouns,
and generally in colloquial usage; genitive in elevated style.) English
equivalent: "despite, in spite of."

> *Trotz dem schlechten Wetter (trotz des schlechten Wetters) gingen
> heute viele Leute zum Stadion.*
> *Ich werde es trotz Ihnen tun.* (Colloquial)
> *Trotz Einwänden seiner Freunde setzte er seine Arbeit fort.*

CONCESSION. GENITIVE. English equivalent: "in spite of." F 551

> *Trotz seines Fleißes hat er keinen Erfolg erzielt.*

über

PLACE: Location or movement over or above a point, surface, or space, F 560
without contact [→ F 145 **auf**]. English equivalent: "over, above."
ACCUSATIVE (**wohin?**) with verbs which indicate a direction or goal.

> *Ich hänge das Bild über das Sofa.*
> *Ein Gewitter zog über das Land.*

DATIVE (**wo?**) for all other verbs. F 561

> *Die Lampe hängt über dem Sofa.*
> *Herr Meyer wohnt im dritten Stock, gerade über mir.*

F 562   Crossing an area. ACCUSATIVE. English equivalent: "over, across."

> *Das Boot fährt **über den** See.*
> *Nur bei grünem Licht darf man **über die** Straße gehen.*

F 563   Position at (DATIVE) or motion towards (ACCUSATIVE) the other side of an obstacle. English equivalent: "across."

> *Das Gasthaus liegt **über dem** Fluß.*
> *Der Dieb entkam mit dem Geld **über** alle Berge.*

F 564   Intermediate station on a road or journey. ACCUSATIVE. English equivalent: "via, by way of, over."

> *Wir reisen von Deutschland **über** Österreich und Jugoslawien nach Griechenland.*
> *Er fährt **über den** Sankt Bernhard Paß in die Schweiz.*

F 565   TIME: Surpassing a time limit. English equivalent: "over, beyond, more than, past." ACCUSATIVE.

> *Die Konferenz dauert schon **über** zwei Stunden.*
> *Er studierte **über** sechs Jahre Medizin.*
> *Er ist schon drei Tage **über die** festgesetzte Zeit fort.*
> *Dieser Herr muß **über** 60 Jahre alt sein.*

F 566   End of a time span. English equivalent: "in, from." ACCUSATIVE.

> *Ich besuche dich morgen **über eine** Woche.*
> ***Übers** Jahr werden sie heiraten.*

F 567   Duration of time. In this sense, **über** follows the noun [→ F 241 ff., **durch, hindurch**]. English equivalent: "long, through" (postposition), "throughout." ACCUSATIVE.

> *Wir hatten **den ganzen Winter über** viel Schnee.*
> *Er hat **die Nacht über** gearbeitet.*
> *Mein Bruder lebte **das ganze Jahr über** auf dem Land.*

F 568   Clock time past the hour. Colloquial [→ F 442 **nach**]. English equivalent: "after, past." ACCUSATIVE.

> *Es ist schon zehn Minuten **über** 5 Uhr.*
> *Es ist ein Viertel **über** acht.*

F 569   EXCESS. Surpassing a certain amount [→ F 565]. English equivalent: "over, above, beyond, more than." ACCUSATIVE.

392

*Er hat **über** 5000 Mark gewonnen.*
*Sie liebt ihre Heimat **über alles**.*
*Der alte Mann arbeitete **über seine** Kräfte.*

EXEMPTION. Outside of a concept. English equivalent: "beyond, above." F 570
ACCUSATIVE.

*Er ist **über allen** Tadel erhaben.*

TOPIC, subject matter. English equivalent: "about." ACCUSATIVE. F 571

*Wir haben uns **über die** Mode unterhalten.*
*Sagen Sie mir Ihre Meinung **darüber**!*
*So sollte man nicht **über die** Leute sprechen.*
*Ich las ein Buch **über das** Leben dieses Komponisten.*
*Er hält einen Vortrag **über** Philosophie.*

CAUSE of a mood or feeling. English equivalent: "about." ACCUSATIVE. F 572

*Sie lachte **über den** Witz.*
*Wir freuen uns **über das** schöne Wetter.*
*Er ist zornig **über seinen** Mißerfolg.*
*Sie sind glücklich **über ihre** Heirat.*

REPETITION. In this sense, **über** stands between two identical nouns F 573
without article. English equivalent: "after." ACCUSATIVE. [→ F 273
für, F 592 **um**]

*Das Kind stellt Fragen **über** Fragen.*
*Er machte Schulden **über** Schulden.*

AMOUNT. Exact sum of money. English equivalent: "in the amount of, F 574
for." ACCUSATIVE.

*Er gab mir eine Rechnung **über** DM 50.-*
*Hier ist eine Quittung **über** zehn Mark.*

um (ACCUSATIVE)

PLACE: Position or circular motion around a point or an area. English F 580
equivalent: "around, about."

*Wir sitzen **um den** Tisch.*
*Die Straße geht **um die** Stadt.*
*Das Rad dreht sich **um seine** Achse.*
*Sieh **um dich**!*

F 581   In this sense, the preposition **um** may be intensified by the adverbs **herum** following the noun or pronoun:

> *Wir sitzen **um** den Tisch **herum**.*
> *Die Straße geht **um** die Stadt **herum**.*
> *Sieh **um** dich **herum**!*

F 582   Position or motion to one side, especially street corners. English equivalent: "around."

> *Er geht **um die** Ecke.*
> *Das Hotel steht rechts **um die** nächste Straßenecke.*
> *Das Auto fuhr **um die** Kurve.*

F 585   TIME: Approximate time. English equivalent: "around, about."

> *Um Ostern bekamen wir Besuch.*
> *Der Kaiser lebte **um** Christi Geburt (**um das** Jahr eintausend).*
> *Ich bin morgen **um diese** Zeit wieder zu Hause.*

F 586   In order to stress the indefinite nature of the time statement, **herum** may be used following the noun:

> *Um Ostern **herum** bekamen wir Besuch.*
> *Ich bin morgen **um diese** Zeit **herum** wieder zu Hause.*

F 587   Exact clock time. English equivalent: "at."

> *Der Zug fährt **um** 15 Uhr 35 ab.*
> *Der Unterricht beginnt **um** 9 Uhr.*
> *Hans kam **um** halb acht.*

F 588   Indefinite or approximate clock time may be indicated by using **um ... herum** [→ F 282 **gegen**]. English equivalent: "about, around."

> *Der Unfall ereignete sich gestern **um** 8 Uhr **herum**.*
> *Ich komme **um** 9 Uhr **herum** wieder nach Hause.*

F 590   AIM, goal, or purpose of an action. English equivalent: "for, about" (or no preposition):

> *Er bat mich **um das** Buch.*
> *Wir spielten gestern **um** Geld.*
> *Die Mutter kümmerte sich nicht **um ihre** Kinder.*
> *Ich beneide dich **um dein** neues Auto.*

394

*Der Kampf **ums** Dasein ist schwer.*
*Er lief **um sein** Leben.*

GAIN or LOSS. No exact English equivalent: sometimes no preposition, sometimes paraphrased. F 591

*Sein Freund ist bei einem Unfall **ums** Leben gekommen.*
*Er hat mich **um mein** Geld gebracht.*
*Der Arzt machte sich **um das** Wohl der Menschheit verdient.*
*Wir wetteten **um** zehn Mark.*

SEQUENCE or series [→ F 273 **für**, F 573 **über**]. English equivalent: "after." F 592

*Jahr **um** Jahr verging.*
*Er besucht mich einen Tag **um den** anderen.*
*Bei dem letzten Spiel gewann er Zug **um** Zug.*

VALUE or price. English equivalent: "for." F 593

*Dieses Klavier ist **um** 400 Mark zu verkaufen.*
*Ich habe **um** 6 Mark Obst gekauft.*

DIFFERENCE. English equivalent: "by" or no preposition. F 594

*Das Thermometer ist seit gestern **um** 10 Grad gefallen.*
*Sein Auto ist **um** tausend Mark teurer als meines.*
*Die Tochter ist nur **um** 19 Jahre jünger als die Mutter.*
*Wir kamen **um eine** Stunde zu spät.*

APPROXIMATE NUMBER. The noun is usually accompanied by the definite article [→ F 129 **an die**]. English equivalent: "about." F 595

*Es waren gestern nur **um die** hundert Personen hier.*

um . . . willen (GENITIVE)

REASON, advantage for a person or thing. English equivalent: "for the sake of, for (someone's) sake." [For the form of personal pronouns, → F 047.] F 600

*Um Gottes **willen**! Um Himmelswillen!*
*Um seines Erfolges **willen** vernachlässigte er seine Gesundheit.*
*Die Frau opferte **um** ihrer Kinder **willen** ihr ganzes Vermögen.*
*Ich habe das nicht **um deinetwillen** getan.*

unbeschadet (GENITIVE)

F 605   WITHOUT REGARD, concern, or prejudice. English equivalent: "in spite of."

> *Unbeschadet dessen will ich dir doch meine Meinung sagen.*

unfern (GENITIVE)

F 610   → F 650 **unweit**

ungeachtet (GENITIVE)

F 615   WITHOUT CONSIDERATION. English equivalent "regardless of."

> *Ungeachtet der Schwierigkeiten lernte er die deutsche Sprache sehr gut.*

F 616   **unerachtet** is an archaic and rare alternate form for **ungeachtet**.

unter

F 620   PLACE: Position or motion below a point, a surface, or an area. English equivalent: "under, below, beneath, underneath." ACCUSATIVE (**wohin?**) for verbs which indicate a direction or a goal.

> *Sie stellte die große Vase **unter das** Fenster.*
> *Er legte den Teppich **unter den** Tisch.*

F 621   DATIVE (**wo?**) for all other verbs, when location is indicated.

> *Wir saßen zusammen **unter einem** Baum.*
> *Sie trägt die Tasche **unter dem** Arm.*
> *Ich bin zehn Meter **unter** Wasser geschwommen.*[1]

F 622   Figurative location amidst a number of similar persons or things. English equivalent: "among." DATIVE.

> ***Unter den** Schülern waren viele Ausländer.*
> *Wir blieben den ganzen Tag **unter uns**.*
> ***Unter den** Büchern meines Freundes sind viele interessante Romane.*
> *Es herrschte große Freude **unter den** Kindern.*

F 623   Destination: movement towards or inclusion into a group of persons or things. English equivalent: "among." ACCUSATIVE.

---

[1] Even though the dative is not distinguishable in this example, the concept is one of location and answers the question **wo?**

396

*Ich komme selten **unter die** Leute.*
*Reihen Sie dieses Buch **unter die** Kriminalromane ein.*
*Hölderlin gehört **unter die** Klassiker.*

Figurative location under some influence or authority. English equiva-   F 624
lent: "under." DATIVE.

*Wir arbeiteten **unter einem** fähigen Ingenieur.*
*Der Fahrer war **unter dem** Einfluß von Alkohol.*

Figurative movement towards inclusion under some influence or   F 625
authority. English equivalent: "under." ACCUSATIVE.

*Er kam **unter die** Aufsicht der Polizei.*
*Diese Tat fällt **unter die** Amnestie.*

TIME: Location at or within a span of time. English equivalent: "under   F 630
(the date of), during." DATIVE.

*Ich habe Ihren Brief **unter dem** 12. dieses Monats erhalten.*
    (Commercial style; **vom** preferred [→ F 685]).
*Er lebte **unter** Kaiser Friedrich (**unter der** Zeit Kaiser Friedrichs).*
*Ich besuche meinen Freund oft **unter der** Woche.*

SIMULTANEITY of two actions. English equivalent: "under, among."   F 631
DATIVE.

*Die Soldaten marschierten **unter dem** Jubel der Bevölkerung in die*
    Stadt ein.
*Er hat die Arbeit **unter großen** Schwierigkeiten beenden können.*

MANNER [similar to F 631 above]. English equivalent: "under."   F 632
DATIVE.

*Wir müssen die Arbeit **unter allen** Umständen beenden.*
***Unter** welchen Bedingungen wollen Sie das Haus verkaufen?*

REASON. English equivalent: "because of, under." DATIVE.   F 633

*Er wurde **unter dem** Verdacht des Diebstahls verhaftet.*

LOWER VALUE, amount, or position. English equivalent: "under, below,   F 635
beneath, less than." DATIVE, except for numbers.

*Ich suche ein Zimmer (für) **unter** 90 Mark Miete.*
*Es waren nur **unter** hundert Zuschauer im Theater.*
*Das ist **unter** meiner Würde.*

unterhalb (GENITIVE)

F 640 PLACE: Position below a point of reference. English equivalent: "below, underneath."

> *Unterhalb des Daches befindet sich der Speicher.*

unweit (GENITIVE)

F 650 PLACE: Proximity. English equivalent: "not far from."

> *Unweit der Stadt liegt ein schöner, großer See.*

F 651 **unfern** is a less frequent alternate form for **unweit**.

vermittels (GENITIVE)

F 660 Means or intermediary [→ F 430 **mittels**]. Very rarely used. English equivalent: "by means of."

> *Der Ertrunkene wurde vermittels einer Stange aus dem Wasser gefischt.*

vermöge (GENITIVE)

F 670 CAUSE or reason. Rarely used. English equivalent: "due to, by virtue of, by dint of."

> *Vermöge seiner Sprachkenntnisse bekam er eine sehr gute Stellung.*

von (DATIVE)

F 680 PLACE: Motion from a point of origin. English equivalent: "from, off."

> *Mein Freund kommt von Berlin.[1]*
> *Das Glas fiel vom Tisch.*
> *Ich hole mein Geld von der Bank.*

F 681 Point of origin [→ F 160 **aus**]. English equivalent: "from."

> *Dieser Brief ist von meinem Vater.*
> *Sein Vermögen stammt von seiner Familie.*

F 682 Distance. English equivalent: "from."

---

[1] For the difference between **Er kommt von Berlin** and **Er kommt aus Berlin** → F 160 footnote.

*Wie weit liegt Altona **von** Hamburg entfernt?*
Meine Wohnung ist nur eine kurze Strecke (nur 10 Minuten)[1]
  ***von** der Universität.*
*Das ist nicht weit **von** hier.*

Starting point of a line: **von ... ab** [→ F 105]. English equivalent: F 683
"from ... on."

> *Von hier **ab** ist die Straße gesperrt.*

TIME: Indication of date. English equivalent: "of."   F 685

> *Ihren Brief **vom** 11. Mai habe ich dankend erhalten.*
> *In Ihrem Schreiben **vom** 5. 3. teilten Sie mir mit, daß ...*

Indication of age. English equivalent: "of."   F 686

> *Er ist ein junger Mann **von** 25 Jahren.*
> *Im Alter **von** 18 Jahren verließ ich die Schule.*

Beginning of a time span: **von ... ab (an)** [→ F 106]. English equiva-   F 687
lent: "from ... on."

> *Von morgen **ab** (**von** morgen **an**) arbeite ich bei einer anderen Firma.*
> *Vom 1. Juli **ab** (**an**) haben wir eine neue Adresse.*

Beginning and end of a time span: **von ... auf**; **von ... bis**. English   F 688
equivalent: "from ... to, from ... till."

> *In der Nacht **von** Montag **auf** Dienstag hatten wir ein Gewitter.*
> *Wir haben **von** 9 Uhr **bis** 12 Uhr Unterricht.*

SEPARATION. English equivalent "from, against."   F 690

> *Das Land wurde **von seinen** Unterdrückern befreit.*[2]
> *Er hat sich **von den** Strapazen seiner Reise erholt.*
> *Sie rät mir **von dieser** Tätigkeit ab.*

MATERIAL [→ F 163 **aus**]. The noun follows without article. English   F 691
equivalent: "(made) of."

> *Dieser Ring ist **von purem** Gold.*
> *Er hat ein Herz **von** Stein.*

---

[1] Time is used here as a measure of distance.

[2] Only context can distinguish such sentences from passives [→ F 692]. The land was
obviously freed *from* its oppressors, not *by* them.

F 692   AGENT, originator, or cause of an action, especially in passive sentences [cf. **durch** F 244, B 596 ff.]. English equivalent: "by."

> *Der Student wurde **von dem** Professor geprüft.*
> *Das Haus ist **von einem** berühmten Architekten gebaut worden.*
> *Du bist **von der** Sonne schön gebräunt.*

F 693   ORIGINATOR in active sentences, to take the place of an attributive genitive [→ D 973] (often felt as a passive). English equivalent: "by."

> *Wir haben gestern ein Drama **von** Schiller gelesen.*
> *In dem Museum hängen viele Bilder **von** Rembrandt.*
> *Das ist eine Sonate **von** Mozart.*

F 694   SUBSTITUTE FOR GENITIVE for nouns without article [→ D 973]. English equivalent: "of."

> *Die Kleider **von Kindern** muß man oft waschen.*
> *Es ist ein Zeichen **von Achtung**.*

F 695   PARTITIVE.[1] English equivalent "of."

> *München ist eine Stadt **von einer** Million Einwohnern.*
> *Ich gab ihm **von meinem** Geld.*
> *Er ist der reichste **von allen** Kaufleuten dieser Stadt.*
> *Trinken Sie von diesem Wein!*

F 696   DESCRIPTION [→ J 115.3]. The noun usually follows without article [→ D 361]. English equivalent "of."

> *Sie war ein Mädchen **von** schöner Gestalt.*
> *Ich habe für Sie eine Nachricht **von** großer Wichtigkeit.*
> *Er ist ein Mann **von** mittlerer Größe.*

F 697   COMPLETION of ADJECTIVE constructions. English equivalent: "of, from."

> *Er ist müde **von der** Arbeit.[2]*
> *Sie ist voll **von** Ideen.*
> *Ich bin überzeugt **davon**.*

F 698   **von . . . wegen** (GENITIVE) → **wegen** F 735.

[1] In general, partitives are rare in German. The partitive "of" is usually omitted: **ein Stück Kuchen, eine Tasse Kaffee, die Stadt Berlin**, etc.
[2] Not tired *of* work (**der Arbeit müde**), but tired *from* working.

400

vor

PLACE: Frontal position or movement. English equivalent: "in front   F 700
of, before." ACCUSATIVE (**wohin?**) for verbs which indicate a direction or
goal:

> *Ich stelle meine Schuhe **vor die** Tür.*
> *Wir fahren **vor das** Hotel.*
> *Sie pflanzte die Blumen **vor das** Haus.*

DATIVE (**wo?**) for all other verbs.   F 701

> *Die Schuhe stehen **vor der** Tür.*
> *Der Wagen hält **vor dem** Hotel.*
> *Viele schöne Blumen wachsen **vor dem** Haus.*

Immediate proximity or presence. English equivalent "outside of,   F 702
before, at." DATIVE.

> *Unser Haus steht **vor der** Stadt.*
> *Die Pianistin spielte **vor vielen** Zuhörern.*
> *Die Zeugen mußten **vor** Gericht Aussagen machen.*
> *Das Schiff liegt **vor** Anker.*

Distance from a goal. English equivalent: "before, from." DATIVE.   F 703

> *Ich hatte mit meinem Wagen zehn Kilometer **vor** München*
> *einen Unfall.*

TIME: Point of time in the past lying a specified distance from the   F 705
present. English equivalent: "ago" (postposition). DATIVE.

> *Ich bin **vor drei Jahren** in England gewesen.*
> *Er hatte heute **vor vierzehn Tagen** Geburtstag.*

Time span prior to the stated time. English equivalent "before."   F 706
DATIVE.

> ***Vor meinem** zwanzigsten Lebensjahr wohnte ich in New York.*
> *Mein Freund kann mich nicht **vor** Montag besuchen.*

Exact clock time prior to the full hour. English equivalent: "before."   F 707
DATIVE.

> *Jetzt ist es genau 17 Minuten **vor** 9 Uhr.*
> *Er kam ein Viertel **vor** zehn.*

401

F 710   CAUSE of a FEELING. The noun usually stands without an article if it designates a concept. English equivalent: "because of, from, with." DATIVE.

> *Er wurde rot vor Wut.*
> *Sie ließ vor Schrecken die Tasse fallen.*
> *Die Kinder schrien vor Begeisterung.*
> *Wir konnten vor Dunkelheit die andere Straßenseite nicht sehen.*
> *Ich konnte vor Müdigkeit nicht mehr arbeiten.*

F 711   ATTITUDE or feeling towards something or someone. English equivalent: "of, for." DATIVE.

> *Wir haben große Achtung vor dir.*
> *Sie hatte Angst vor dem Tod.*
> *Fürchtest du dich vor dem Hund?*

F 715   PROTECTION, warning, defense. English equivalent "of, from, before." DATIVE.

> *Er warnte mich vor ihm.*
> *Die Stadtbewohner flohen vor dem Feind.*
> *Er schützte sich vor Ansteckung.*
> *Hüten Sie sich vor diesem Menschen!*
> *Wir suchten vor dem Gewitter Schutz.*

während (GENITIVE)[1]

F 720   TIME: Simultaneity. English equivalent: "during."

> *Während meines Studiums in Berlin traf ich viele interessante Menschen.*
> *Während des Unterrichts ist das Rauchen verboten.*
> *Ich war während des Sommers am Meer.*

wegen

F 730   REASON. English equivalent: "because of." Usually GENITIVE, but DATIVE occurs colloquially.

> *Wegen des Regens (wegen dem Regen) blieben wir zu Hause.*
> *Das Geschäft ist wegen der Krankheit des Besitzers geschlossen.*
> *Der Vater will wegen seines Sohnes mit dem Lehrer sprechen.*
> *Der Angeklagte wurde wegen Diebstahls verurteilt.*

---

[1] The dative occurs in the expression **währenddem** and with noun plurals: *während zehn Jahren.*

402

The DATIVE is always used before indefinite pronouns and neuter F 731
nominal adjectives. It also occurs frequently before personal pronouns.

> *Ich wollte Sie **wegen** etwas anderem sprechen.*
> *Ich bin in großer Sorge **wegen dem** Gefährlichen dieses Unternehmens.*
> *Ich tue das nur **wegen dir**.*

If **wegen** functions as a postposition, it always governs the GENITIVE. F 732

> *Der Vater will **seines Sohnes wegen** mit dem Lehrer sprechen.*
> *Er arbeitet nur **des Geldes wegen**.*

When **wegen** occurs as a postposition with personal pronouns, it is F 733
written together with the pronoun which takes a special form [→ F 047]:

> *Er kam eigens **meinetwegen** in die Stadt.*

Colloquially, such compounds with personal pronouns often have the F 734
meaning "for all (I) care."

> ***Meinetwegen** kannst du tun, was du willst.*

In the combination **von . . . wegen**, the noun is governed by **wegen** and F 735
takes the genitive case. English equivalent: "according to, by."

> ***Von** Rechts **wegen** dürfte so etwas nicht erlaubt werden.*

wider (ACCUSATIVE)[1]

CONTRAST, opposite [→ F 280 ff., **gegen**]. Rarely used; occurs primarily F 740
in certain idiomatic phrases or in elevated language. English equivalent:
"against."

> *Er handelte **wider das** Gesetz.*
> *Ich habe den Fehler **wider** mein besseres Wissen begangen.*
> *Das ist eine Sünde **wider den** Geist.*
> ***Wider** (ihren) Willen gehorchte sie.*

willen (GENITIVE)

Postposition. → **um . . . willen** F 600. F 745

zeit (GENITIVE)

TIME: The entire time span. English equivalent: "during." Occurs only F 750
in fixed idioms.

> *Er war **zeit** seines Lebens ein armer Mann.*

---

[1] Do not confuse **wider** (against) with **wieder** (again).

zu (DATIVE)

F 755   PLACE: Motion or direction towards a goal. Not used for names of cities and countries [→ F 330 **in**, F 440 **nach**]. English equivalent: "to."[1]

> *Er fährt zu seinen Eltern.*
> *Ich spreche zu dir.*
> *Wir beten zu Gott.*
> *Gehen Sie zum Bahnhof?*
> *Sie sieht zum Fenster herein.* (English "through the window.")
> *Er kam mit dem Autobus zur Schule.*

F 756   LOCATION. Old-fashioned and rare usage, except in the idiom **zu Hause**. English equivalent: "at, on, in" [→ F 440–1 **nach**].

> *Die Stadt liegt zu beiden Seiten des Flusses.*
> *Er wurde zu Berlin geboren.*
> *Gestern war ich nicht zu Hause.*

F 757   TYPE of MOTION. The noun follows without article, except for feminine singular nouns. English equivalent: "on, by, at."

> *Wir gehen immer zu Fuß in die Schule.*
> *Die Feinde kamen zu Land und zu Wasser.*
> *Mein Vater fährt zur See.*

F 760   TIME: Point or space of time. English equivalent: "for, at, in."

> *Die deutschen Schulkinder erhalten ihre Zeugnisse zu Ostern.*
> *Dieses Buch habe ich zum Geburtstag bekommen.*
> *Er kam gerade zur rechten Zeit.*
> *Zu unserer Zeit gab es solche Dinge noch nicht.*

F 761   AIM, PURPOSE, BELONGING. English equivalent: "to, for."

> *Dieser Mann eignet sich nicht zum Kaufmann.*
> *Ich möchte mich zum Studium anmelden.*
> *Mein Freund ist mir zu Hilfe gekommen.*
> *Der Garten gehört zum Haus.*[2]

---

[1] German clearly distinguishes between zu (up to) and in (into): *Ich gehe zum Theater* (in the direction of the theater) — *Ich gehe ins Theater* (into the building) [→ F 330].

[2] Note the difference: *Der Garten gehört zum Haus* — The garden belongs to (is part of) the house. *Der Garten gehört mir* — The garden belongs to (is owned by) me.

Der Dieb wurde zu drei Jahren Gefängnis verurteilt.
Ich habe eine Einladung zu seinem Geburtstag.
Die Musik spielt zur Unterhaltung.

PURPOSE (before abstract nouns). English equivalent: "as, in." F 762

Er schenkte ihr Blumen zum Beweis für seine Liebe.
Zum Dank für deine Hilfe lade ich dich ein.
Die Kapelle spielte zu Ehren des Gastes.

CHANGE, development, appointment, election. English equivalent: "to, F 763
into" (or none).

Er entwickelte sich zu einem Künstler.
Er wurde zum Offizier befördert (zum Präsidenten gewählt,
*   zum Vorsitzenden ernannt, zum Kaiser ausgerufen, etc.)*
Wien wurde ihm zur zweiten Heimat.

PRICE or PART. English equivalent: "for, at." F 764

Zu welchem Preis wollen Sie das Haus verkaufen?
Dort stehen ein Paar Schuhe zu 50 Mark.
Ich habe das Buch schon zum größten Teil (zur Hälfte) gelesen.

COMPARISON. English equivalent: "to." F 765

Das Fußballspiel endete 3:2 (drei zu zwei).
Ich wette 10 zu 1, daß er heute kommt.

DISTRIBUTIVE, MEASUREMENT, dimension. English equivalent: "at, by." F 766

Geben Sie mir fünf Briefmarken zu 10 Pfennig.
Die Feinde kamen zu Tausenden ins Land.
Wir gingen zu dritt.
Er zeichnete ein Rechteck von 10 cm zu 5 cm.

FOOD or DRINK for meals. English equivalent: "for, with." F 767

Zum Frühstück esse ich immer ein Ei.
Zum Braten trinkt man Rotwein.

zufolge

CONSEQUENCE or effect. (Preposition.) English equivalent: "as a result F 770
of." GENITIVE.

Zufolge des internationalen Abkommens ist der Zoll zwischen den
*   beteiligten Ländern aufgehoben.*

F 771 AGREEMENT. (Postposition.) English equivalent: "according to." DATIVE.

> *Der Zeitungsmeldung **zufolge** ist der Minister wieder abgereist.*
> *Dem Gerücht **zufolge** soll der König abgedankt haben.*

zu(un)gunsten

F 775 BENEFIT (or DETRIMENT). English equivalent: "to the (dis)advantage of." Rarely used. GENITIVE as a preposition, DATIVE as a postposition.

> *Was wir auf Erden Gutes tun, kommt **dem** Reiche Gottes **zugunsten**.*
> *Die Schlacht fiel **zuungunsten der** Römer aus.*

zwecks (GENITIVE)

F 780 PURPOSE. Fairly rare. English equivalent: "for the purpose of."

> *Er fuhr **zwecks** Erholung für drei Wochen an die See.*

zwischen

F 790 PLACE: Location or motion between two or more people, objects, or places. English equivalent: "between, among." ACCUSATIVE (**wohin?**) for verbs which indicate a direction or goal.

> *Setzen Sie sich **zwischen** meinen Bruder und meine Schwester!*
> *Ich stelle den Stuhl **zwischen die** Tür und **das** Sofa.*
> *Er steckte die Zeitung **zwischen die** Bücher.*

F 791 DATIVE (**wo?**) for all other verbs.

> *Meine Schwester sitzt **zwischen mir** und meinem Vater.*
> *Mein Haus steht **zwischen** vielen schönen Bäumen.*

F 795 TIME: Interval in time. English equivalent: "between." Usually DATIVE.

> *Die Geschäfte sind **zwischen** 12 Uhr und 14 Uhr geschlossen.*
> ***Zwischen dem** 8. März und **dem** 11. März ist der Arzt verreist.*

F 796 ACCUSATIVE may be used, however, if the basic meaning of the verb implies a direction or motion towards a goal:

> *Wir legen die Konferenz **zwischen den** 5. und 20. Juli.*

F 797 RELATIONSHIP. English equivalent: "between." DATIVE.

> *Morgen findet eine Unterredung **zwischen dem** Präsidenten und **dem** Botschafter statt.*
> ***Zwischen** uns beiden ist es aus.*

406

Approximate number; upper and lower limits of an estimate. English   F 798
equivalent: "between."

> *Es waren gestern zwischen 25 und 30 Gäste bei uns.*
> *Die Temperatur schwankte zwischen 30 und 35 Grad.*

FOREIGN PREPOSITIONS

German uses a number of foreign prepositions, such as **inklusive (inkl.),**   F 900
exklusive (exkl.), per, pro, via, vis-à-vis, etc. Nouns following without
article are uninflected:

> *per Flugzeug, exklusive Verpackung, inklusive Bedienung, pro Stück,*
> *via München*

When the noun is preceded by a modifier, the inflection follows a Ger-   F 901
man model:

> *inklusive (einschließlich) aller Portokosten*
> *per (zum, für den) fünfzehnten Februar*
> *vis-à-vis (gegenüber) dem Hotel*

G

✵ Conjunctions

✵ Introduction

G 001 Conjunctions are uninflected. They connect words, phrases, clauses or sentences with one another and thus establish logical and grammatical relationships between these units:

> *Mein Freund kommt morgen. Seine Schwester kommt morgen.* →
> *Mein Freund **und** seine Schwester kommen morgen.*

> *Peter ist faul. Hans ist fleißig.* →
> *Peter ist faul, **aber** Hans ist fleißig.*

> *Wir bleiben zu Hause. Das Wetter ist schlecht.* →
> *Wir bleiben zu Hause, **weil** das Wetter schlecht ist.*

G 002 Conjunctions determine the syntax of the clause to which they belong and identify the logical relationship of this clause to the other clause with which the conjunction connects it:

> clause I | clause II
> *Wir bleiben zu Hause,* | ***denn** das Wetter ist schlecht.*
> clause I | clause II
> *Wir bleiben zu Hause,* | ***weil** das Wetter schlecht ist.*
> clause I | clause II
> *Wir bleiben zu Hause,* | ***obwohl** das Wetter schön ist.*

408

clause I | clause II
Das Wetter ist schön, | *deshalb bleiben wir nicht zu Hause.*[1]

clause I | clause II
Das Wetter ist schön, | *trotzdem bleiben wir zu Hause.*[1]

TYPES OF CONJUNCTIONS

We distinguish between **coordinating** and **subordinating** conjunctions. G 003

COORDINATING CONJUNCTIONS connect a clause with another (parallel) clause of equal type, i.e. they combine a main clause with a main clause or a dependent clause with another dependent clause:[2]

main clause I | main clause II
Ich gehe heute nicht spazieren, | *denn ich habe keine Zeit.*

main clause I | main clause II
Paul macht einen Ausflug, | *aber Hans bleibt zu Hause.*

main clause | dependent clause I |
Wir bleiben heute zu Hause, | *weil das Wetter schlecht ist* | *und*

dependent clause II
(weil) wir auch keine Zeit haben.

main clause | dependent clause I |
Ich gehe mit dir spazieren, | *wenn du auf mich wartest* | *oder*

dependent clause II
(wenn du) mir jetzt bei meiner Arbeit hilfst.

SUBORDINATING CONJUNCTIONS combine dependent clauses with main G 004
clauses. The dependent clauses are subordinate[3] to the main clauses, and replace a sentence unit (word or phrase) of the main clause. They may function as subject, as object, as a predicate complement, or as an adverbial modifier [→ H 040, H 780 ff.]:

| *Die gestrige Ankunft des Ministers in Berlin* | *wurde gemeldet.* → |

Es wurde gemeldet, | *daß der Minister gestern in Berlin angekommen ist.*

---

[1] In English, each of the last two examples would be considered as containing two complete sentences, requiring a period or a semicolon between them. In German, however, this so-called "comma splice" is permissible. In general, the term conjunction is broader in German than it is in English and covers concepts which English would consider adverbial in nature [→ E 850].

[2] Coordinating conjunctions, to be sure, also operate below the clausal level, connecting words or phrases. See individual entries, G 030 ff.

[3] The terms "dependent clause" and "subordinate clause" are being used interchangeably.

409

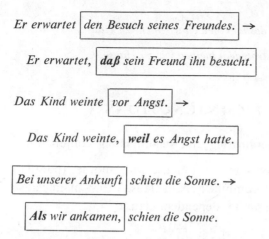

G 005 Subordinating conjunctions may also connect dependent clauses with other dependent clauses. They then subordinate the dependent clause which they introduce to the preceding subordinate clause. Again, the second dependent clause as a whole replaces a sentence unit of the first dependent clause. In this way, several dependent clauses may be linked together, each subordinated to the preceding one:

main clause	dependent clause I	dependent clause II
Ich war traurig,	*als er mir sagte,*	*daß er nicht kommen konnte.*

main clause	dependent clause I	
Die Zeitung berichtete,	*daß der Minister freudig begrüßt wurde,*	

dependent clause II
als er auf dem Bahnhof ankam.

main clause	dependent clause I	
Es ist möglich,	*daß wir zusammen spazieren gehen,*	*wenn du mir*

dependent clause II		dependent clause III
bei meiner Arbeit hilfst,	*indem du mit mir das Zimmer aufräumst,*	

dependent clause IV
bevor meine Mutter kommt.

G 006 **Sequence of clauses**

A dependent clause may often occupy either the prefield or the postfield of the main clause [→ H 050 ff., H 075]. If the dependent clause is in the prefield, the subject of the main clause must necessarily follow its own inflected verb form. (An easy way to remember this principle is by the simple rule: If the main clause comes second, its subject comes second):

410

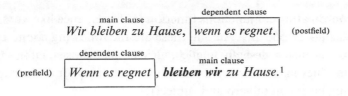

POSITION OF THE CONJUNCTIONS

In combining two clauses, conjunctions may function in various syntactical ways.

Coordinating Conjunctions

Some of these conjunctions (**allein, denn, oder, sondern, und**) are INDE-PENDENT and always stand ISOLATED OUTSIDE the sentence as a unit. They therefore have no effect whatsoever on word order:

G 008

Wir gehen jetzt nach Hause, | **denn** *unsere Eltern warten auf uns.*[2]

There are other coordinating conjunctions which can either stand ISOLATED BEFORE the sentence or WITHIN the sentence (e.g. **aber**). Even when they are within a sentence, however, they do not constitute a sentence unit and have no effect on word order:

G 009

Karl geht in die Schule, | **aber** *Hans bleibt zu Hause.*

Karl geht in die Schule, | *Hans* **aber** *bleibt zu Hause.*

Karl geht in die Schule, | *Hans bleibt* **aber** *zu Hause.*

There are other coordinating conjunctions (e.g. **also, doch**) which either stand ISOLATED BEFORE the sentence, or occupy the PREFIELD [→ H 705] as a sentence unit. In isolation, they do not affect word order; if they are considered as constituting the prefield, they require inversion of verb and subject:

G 010

Ich habe ihm Geld angeboten, | **doch** *er wollte es nicht.*

Ich habe ihm Geld angeboten, | **doch** *wollte* **er** *es nicht.*

---

[1] Note the characteristic word order: FINITE VERB — COMMA — FINITE VERB at the juncture of the two clauses.

[2] Conjunctions not affecting word order are shown in a shaded box.

G 011 Most coordinating conjunctions function in the sentence like ADVERBIAL MODIFIERS [→ H 550 ff.]. Among these are the following conjunctions: **allerdings, demnach, deshalb, folglich, gleichwohl, indessen, infolgedessen, trotzdem**. They may occur WITHIN the SENTENCE FIELD, or in the PREFIELD (requiring inversion of verb and subject):[1]

> *Das Wetter ist schlecht,* | ***deshalb** bleibe **ich** zu Hause.*
> *Das Wetter ist schlecht,* | *ich bleibe **deshalb** zu Hause.*

G 012 TWO-PART CONJUNCTIONS usually function in their respective clauses as ADVERBIAL MODIFIERS, occurring either in the PREFIELD or within the SENTENCE FIELD.[2] Some of these two-part conjunctions are: **entweder . . . oder, weder . . . noch, nicht nur . . . sondern auch, zwar . . . aber, bald . . . bald, teils . . . teils, einerseits . . . and(e)rerseits**, etc.

> ***Einerseits** möchte ich Ihnen helfen,* | ***and(e)rerseits** habe **ich** wenig Zeit.*

> *Unser Direktor arbeitet **nicht nur** sehr viel,* | **sondern** *er spielt **auch** jeden Tag Tennis.*

Subordinating Conjunctions

G 015 Subordinating conjunctions introduce dependent clauses. They form the FRONT LIMIT of the SENTENCE FIELD within the dependent clause [→ H 115 ff.]. The verb moves to the end of the dependent clause (transposed word order):

> main clause
> dependent clause
> *Wir gehen spazieren,* | ***weil** das Wetter schön **ist**.*

G 016 The only exception to this rule is the conjunction **als** in implied conditions. The conjunction then occupies the prefield, requiring inversion of subject and verb [→ G 049 ff.]:

> main clause
> dependent clause
> *Er spricht Deutsch,* | ***als wäre er** in Deutschland geboren.*

G 017 For many subordinating conjunctions, the dependent clause may come first in the sentence, occupying the prefield of the entire sentence (i.e.

[1] From the point of view of English grammar, these are not coordinating conjunctions, since English would consider the resulting combination two separate sentences. They *are* conjunctions in German, however [→ G 002].

[2] The conjunctions **aber, oder,** and **sondern** continue to act as isolated words outside or inside their sentence unit; **entweder** may also be isolated before its clause [→ G 313].

the prefield of the main clause). This requires inversion of subject and verb in the main clause [→ G 006, H 075]:

dependent clause	main clause
***Wenn** wir nach Wien fahren,*	*besuchen **wir** die Oper.*

Often a sentence unit or a part of a sentence unit in the main clause anticipates the following dependent clause. Such words or phrases which point to the following clause are sometimes called **correlates**. G 018

*Ich gehe **deshalb** nicht ins Kino,* | ***weil** ich kein Geld habe.*

*Er spricht **so** schnell,* | ***daß** man ihn nur schwer verstehen kann.*

The prepositions **ohne, (an)statt,** and **um** are used as a special type of subordinating conjunction. They are always followed by an INFINITIVE CLAUSE,[1] the subject of which is only mentioned in the main clause. Infinitive clauses always use the infinitive with **zu**. G 019

Er hat mein Fahrrad genommen, | ***ohne** mich vorher darum **zu bitten.***
(Er hatte mich vorher nicht darum gebeten).

Er geht nur seinem Vergnügen nach, | ***(an)statt** zu Hause **zu arbeiten.***
(Er sollte stattdessen zu Hause arbeiten).

Er ist nach Deutschland gekommen, | ***um** hier Medizin **zu studieren.***
(Er will hier Medizin studieren).

In many respects, relative pronouns, interrogative pronouns, and interrogative adverbs function like subordinating conjunctions [G 700 ff.]. G 020

RELATIVE PRONOUNS [→ D 500 ff.] introduce attributive clauses [→ J 146.1]:

Kennen Sie den Mann, | ***der** dort an der Straßenecke steht?*

INTERROGATIVE PRONOUNS [→ D 200 ff.] and INTERROGATIVE ADVERBS

---

[1] These are called "infinitive phrases" in English. In German, however, they function as clauses.

413

[→ E 870 ff.] are used to form subordinate clauses or attributive clauses [→ J 146.2]:

Sagen Sie mir bitte, |*wer dieser Herr ist!*|

Wissen Sie, |*wohin dieser Weg führt?*|

Er hat die Frage, |*wohin sein Bruder gefahren ist,*| *nicht beantworten können.*

FUNCTION OF THE CONJUNCTIONS

G 021   Conjunctions establish relationships between two situations. Coordinating conjunctions relate two situations of equal significance to each other, and clarify the logical connections between the two situations.

Subordinating conjunctions are function indicators for clauses the contents of which have the role of sentence units. The situation specified in the dependent clause, together with the other sentence units of the main clause, serve to describe a total situation and the circumstances accompanying it. The dependent clause thus plays a subordinate role to the main clause.

Coordinating Conjunctions

G 022   SEQUENCE, AMPLIFICATION, EXPANSION (copulative):
Additive: **und; sowohl . . . als auch (wie auch); nicht nur . . . sondern auch** (stressed additive); **weder . . . noch** (negative additive), etc.
Explicative: **und auch (außerdem, dazu, überdies, zudem), sowie; ja, ja sogar** (stressed explicative); **geschweige denn** (negative explicative), etc.
Proportional: **um so, desto.**

G 023   CONTRAST (disjunctive):
Alternative: **oder, oder auch; entweder . . . oder** (emphatic), etc.
Adversative: **aber, dagegen, hingegen, indessen,** etc.
Comparative: **als (denn)** (unequal); **wie** (equal).
Corrective: **(zwar) aber, doch, jedoch; allein, nur** (stressing a limitation);

414

allerdings, freilich (polite limitation); **wenigstens, zumindest** (weakening of an assertion); **sondern, sondern vielmehr** (corrective after negative statement); **aber vielmehr** (corrective after positive statement).
Assertive: **aber, dennoch, dessenungeachtet, (und) doch, gleichwohl, immerhin, indessen, nichtsdestoweniger, trotzdem,** etc.
Restrictive: **(in)sofern, (in)soweit**

REASON, CONSEQUENCE (consecutive): G 024
Reason: **denn, nämlich; ja, eben** (acquiescent); **doch** (emphatic).
Cause: **also, folglich, mithin, (und) somit, so ... denn, demnach, nun, daher, darum, deshalb, deswegen, infolgedessen,** etc.
Conditional: **andernfalls, sonst.**

Subordinating Conjunctions

PLACE, DIRECTION (local): G 025
wo (location), **woher** (origin), **wohin** (destination); **soweit** (extension).[1]

TIME (temporal): G 026
als, wie (point in time); **solange, während, indes, indem**[2] (duration); **sooft, wenn** (repetition); **als, nachdem, seitdem, sobald, wie, wenn** (referring to previous events); **bis, bevor, ehe** (referring to impending events).

CAUSE, REASON: G 027
Concessive (insufficient reason): **obgleich, obschon, obwohl, obzwar, wenn auch, wenngleich, wennschon, wiewohl; ohne daß** (negative).
Conditional (possible reason): **falls, wenn, sofern, wo(fern), angenommen (daß), im Falle daß, vorausgesetzt daß.**
Causal (actual reason): **da, weil, deswegen weil; umsomehr als, zumal** (decisive reason).

PURPOSE, CONSEQUENCE: G 028
Final (purpose, goal): **damit, daß; auf daß** (elevated style); **um** (with infinitive clause).
Consecutive (consequence, effect): **daß, so daß, weshalb; ohne** (with

---

[1] **Soweit** may also be used in a figurative sense: *soweit ich weiß* (as far as I know).
[2] **Indem** is a combination of simultaneity and instrumentality [→ G 340].

infinitive clause), **ohne daß** (non-occurring consequence); **als daß** (impossible consequence).

G 029   MANNER:

Comparative: **wie** (equality); **als** (inequality); **soviel, soweit** (degree); **wie wenn** (comparison within fact); **als ob, als wenn** (comparison contrary to fact).

Adversative (contrast): **während, indes, indessen, wohingegen; (an)statt** (with infinitive clause), **statt daß** (substitute).

Instrumental (means, accompanying circumstance): **indem,**[1] **dadurch daß; ohne daß** (negative).

Proportion: **je ... desto, je ... je, je ... umso, umso ... je, je nachdem.**

USE AND MEANING OF CONJUNCTIONS[2]

aber

G 030   The conjunction **aber** has CONTRASTING (ADVERSATIVE) meaning and is used to combine sentence units (words or phrases) and clauses.

G 031   SENTENCE UNITS:

> *Dieser alte Mann ist arm,* **aber** *glücklich.*
> *Das Haus ist alt,* **aber** *schön.*

G 032   In negative sentences, the conjunction **aber** is not used, if two mutually exclusive items are contrasted [→ **sondern** G 470].[3] It is used, however, if the contrast is not based on mutual exclusion:

> *Dieser alte Mann ist* **nicht** *reich,* **sondern** *arm.*
> *Dieser alte Mann ist* **nicht** *reich,* **aber** *glücklich.*
>
> *Das Haus ist* **nicht** *neu,* **sondern** *alt.*
> *Das Haus ist* **nicht** *neu,* **aber** *schön.*

G 033   In negative sentences, the adversative meaning of **aber** may be intensified by **wohl** (preceding) or **doch** (following):

[1] **Indem** is a combination of simultaneity and instrumentality [→ G 340].

[2] Neither the list of conjunctions nor the various meanings and usages are intended to be exhaustive. Only the most common forms are listed.

[3] If the second clause is negative, **aber** must be used: *Das Haus ist neu,* **aber nicht** *schön. Das Haus ist nicht neu,* **aber auch nicht** *alt.*

416

*Dieser alte Mann ist **nicht** reich, **wohl aber** glücklich.*
*Das Haus ist **nicht** neu, **aber doch** schön.*

CLAUSES: The conjunction **aber** stands ISOLATED outside the second G 034
clause, which limits or expands the preceding clause in a contrastive
manner:

> *Mein Freund hat mich nicht besucht, **aber** er hat mir einen*
> *Brief geschrieben.*
> *Peter wollte die Prüfung machen, **aber** er hat sie nicht bestanden.*
> *Richard war fleißig, **aber** Hans war faul.*
> *Diese Bilder sind teuer, **aber** schön sind sie nicht.*

In the same meaning, **aber** may follow the subject, the conjugated part G 035
of the predicate, or (less frequently) some other sentence unit. Even
then, however, it remains isolated and is not considered a sentence unit.

> *Karl geht in die Schule, Hans **aber** bleibt zu Hause.*
> *Karl geht in die Schule, Hans bleibt **aber** zu Hause.*

> *Peter hat Deutsch gelernt, er kann **aber** nicht gut Deutsch*
> *sprechen.*
> *Peter hat Deutsch gelernt, Französisch kann er **aber** nicht.*
> *Peter hat Deutsch gelernt, gut sprechen kann er es **aber** nicht.*

The adverbial modifier **zwar** in the preceding clause may be used to G 036
qualify or weaken the adversative meaning:

> *Peter hat **zwar** Deutsch gelernt, **aber** er kann es nicht gut*
> *sprechen.*

If the preceding clause is negative, **wohl** (preceding) or **doch** (following) G 037
may be used to intensify the adversative meaning of **aber** [→ G 033].
Doch may also be used if the first clause is positive and the second
negative; **zwar** is then frequently used in the first clause.

> *Mein Freund hat mich **nicht** besucht, **wohl aber** hat er mir einen*
> *Brief geschrieben.*
> *Er hat **nicht** viel gearbeitet, die Prüfung hat er **aber doch***
> *bestanden.*
> *Er hatte es mir **zwar** versprochen, **aber** er hatte es **doch nicht***
> *getan.*

For **aber** as an intensifier → H 610. G 038

allein

G 040 The conjunction **allein** has a meaning similar to **aber** [→ G 030 ff.], indicating some special LIMITATION, but may only be used to connect MAIN CLAUSES. Like **aber**, **allein** is isolated outside the clause. It is used primarily in poetic language. The sentence stress does not fall on **allein**, but either on the word immediately following or on the verb.

> *Ich hatte es dir schon immer sagen wollen,* **allein** *nie hatte ich Gelegenheit dazu.*
> *Er hat vielen Menschen Unglück gebracht,* **allein** *das Schlechte wollte er nicht.*
> *Er wollte das schon immer tun,* **allein** *er konnte es nicht.*[1]

als

G 045 The conjunction **als** connects sentence units or sentences. It may be used in a comparison to establish INEQUALITY [→ E 350 ff.].[2]

G 046 SENTENCE UNITS (English "than"):

> *Peter ist größer* **als** *Karl.*
> *Er hat ein teureres Haus gekauft* **als** *wir.*
> *Sein Bild ist weniger schön* **als** *mein Bild.*
> *Wir fühlten uns nirgends glücklicher* **als** *zu Hause.*

G 047 The conjunction **als** may also follow words which express dissimilarity through negation, difference, or contrast, e.g. **nichts, niemand, ander-, sonst, entgegengesetzt, umgekehrt,** etc. (English "but"):

> *Er wollte* **nichts** *tun* **als** *arbeiten.*
> *Sie ist alles* **andere als** *schön.*
> *Wir sahen* **niemanden als** *deinen Freund.*

G 048 CLAUSES: The conjunction **als** introduces a DEPENDENT CLAUSE, the content of which is in opposition to the situation described in the main clause. The main clause always contains a comparative or the adverb **anders** (English "than"):

---

[1] Do not confuse the above sentence, in which **allein** corresponds to English "however," with *Er* **allein** *konnte es nicht*, where **allein** (stressed) means "alone." See also J 190.

[2] The use of **wie** in comparisons establishing inequality is not considered standard German, although it occurs colloquially, especially in Bavaria and Austria [→ G 595 ff. **wie**].

*Das Wetter war **schöner**, **als** wir gehofft hatten.*
*Ich verstehe Deutsch **besser**, **als** ich es sprechen kann.*
*Er machte die Sache **anders**, **als** wir sie gemacht hatten.*

Als occurs in the prefield of a clause which expresses a contrary-to-fact   G 049
comparison. In such unreal comparisons, the verb usually appears in
subjunctive II[1] [→ B 726] (English "as if"):

*Er spricht Deutsch, **als wäre** er ein Deutscher.*
*Sie sieht aus, **als hätte** sie geweint.*
*Er ißt, **als könnte** er nicht genug bekommen.*

In the main clause, the correlate **so** may be used to anticipate the fol-   G 050
lowing comparison:

*Der Mann aß **so** schnell, **als** könnte er nicht genug bekommen.*
*Tun Sie **so**, **als** wären Sie zu Hause.*

The same meaning of comparison contrary-to-fact is also obtained by   G 051
beginning the dependent clause with the double conjunction **als ob**. The
verb again appears in the subjunctive; however, it moves to the end of
the dependent clause.

*Er spricht Deutsch, **als ob** er ein Deutscher **wäre**.*
*Sie sieht aus, **als ob** sie geweint **hätte**.*

The unreal comparison may be intensified by placing **gleichsam** before   G 052
the conjunction **als**:

*Er behandelt mich, **gleichsam als** wäre er mein Vater.*
*Er behandelt mich, **gleichsam als ob** er mein Vater wäre.*

The expressions **als wenn** or **wie wenn** are sometimes used instead of   G 053
als ob.

The conjunction **als** introduces a subordinate clause of TIME, the situa-   G 055
tion of which occurred simultaneously with the situation of the main
clause in the past (English "when"). Unlike **wenn** [→ G 571], **als** refers

---

[1] Subjunctive I is also occasionally used: *Er spricht Deutsch, **als sei** er ein Deutscher. Sie
sieht aus, als **habe** sie geweint. Er ißt, als **könne** er nicht genug bekommen.* Note that these
clauses do NOT have dependent word order [→ G 016].

to SINGLE PAST EVENTS. The verb in the dependent clause is usually in the simple past tense, sometimes in the perfect.

> *Wir trafen unseren Lehrer, **als** wir am Sonntag im Theater waren.*
> *Die Sonne schien, **als** ich in München ankam.*

G 056   If the dependent clause occupies the prefield,[1] it serves as a contact unit [→ H 705 ff.] with adverbial function:

> ***Als** wir Sonntag im Theater waren, trafen wir unseren Lehrer.*
> ***Als** ich in München ankam, schien die Sonne.*

G 057   The statement of the subordinate clause in the prefield of the whole sentence may be summarized by the adverb **da** as the first element of the main clause. In this usage, **da** is considered as forming the prefield of the main clause:

> ***Als** Robert in Köln ankam, **da** wartete sein Freund schon auf dem Bahnhof.*
> ***Als** wir am Sonntag im Theater waren, **da** trafen wir unseren Lehrer.[2]*

G 058   In lively narrative, the verb may appear in the present tense. This, however, does not change the construction in any way, since the situation is still understood to be in the past [→ B 516].

G 059   The conjunction **als** may also introduce a dependent clause of time, in which the situation precedes that of the main clause. In such cases, the verb in the main clause is in the past tense or the present perfect, the verb in the subordinate clause is in the past perfect [→ G 392 **nachdem**]:

> ***Als** Robert seine Prüfung **beendet hatte, fuhr** er nach Hause.*
> ***Als** wir in München **angekommen waren, haben** wir ein Hotelzimmer **gesucht**.*

G 060   The following time relations apply:

Simultaneity: Verb in Main Clause: past tense (present perfect)
                Verb in Subordinate Clause: past tense (present perfect)

Time Sequence: Verb in Main Clause: past tense or present perfect
                Verb in Subordinate Clause: past perfect

---

[1] → G 006, H 075.

[2] Note that **da** is used in a temporal sense. In the sentence: *Als wir Sonntag im Theater waren, trafen wir **da** unseren Lehrer*, it would have local meaning.

420

The expression of manner **insofern** or **insoweit** in the main clause imparts   G 062
limiting (RESTRICTIVE) meaning to the subordinate clause in the postfield. The subordinate clause is introduced by the conjunction **als**
(English "as"):

> *Insofern war ich mit dem Hotel zufrieden, als das Essen immer gut
> war.*
>
> *Ich war mit dem Hotel insoweit zufrieden, als das Essen immer gut
> war.*

The phrase **als da sind** is an old-fashioned expression which follows the   G 063
noun and has the same meaning as **unter anderem** or **zum Beispiel**
[→ G 085]:

> *Deutschland produziert viele Maschinen, **als da sind**: Lokomotiven,
> Flugzeugmotoren, Traktoren, usw.*

also

The conjunction **also** acts as a circumstantial modifier in the prefield or   G 065
the sentence field of a main clause. It has CONSECUTIVE meaning, explain-
ing the results or consequences arising from the situation in the preceding main clause:

> *Mein Freund kann nicht mit mir in die Ferien fahren, **also muß** ich
> allein fahren.*
>
> *Wir haben kein Geld, wir können dir **also** nicht helfen.*[1]

If **also** appears in the sentence field, the introductory particle **so** may   G 066
occupy the prefield:

> *Wir haben kein Geld, **so** können wir dir **also** nicht helfen.*

The consecutive meaning of **also** within the sentence field may be re-   G 067
inforced by the adverb **auch**:

> *Wir haben kein Geld, wir können dir **also auch** nicht helfen.*

For **also** as an intensifier, → H 611.   G 068

anstatt (statt)

The conjunction **anstatt** introduces an ADVERSATIVE INFINITIVE CLAUSE.   G 070
The infinitive clause explains the situation which had been expected in

---

[1] Again, it should be pointed out that these would be considered "run-on sentences" in
English, rather than a relationship between main and subordinate clause. Such use of
parataxis is very common in modern German.

421

contrast to what is actually happening, as stated in the main clause. The subject of the main clause is also the implied subject of the infinitive clause [→ B 904]. The shortened form **statt** is often used for **anstatt**. These conjunctions must not be confused with the prepositions **anstatt** [→ F 140] and **statt** [→ F 540].

> *Peter geht ins Kino,* **anstatt** *für die Schule zu arbeiten.*
> *Wir sind zu Hause geblieben,* **statt** *nach Italien zu reisen.*

G 071   **anstatt daß** → G 175.

ausgenommen

G 075   → G 586 **außer wenn**.

bald . . . bald

G 080   The double conjunction **bald . . . bald** has PARTITIVE meaning (English "now . . . now"), and connects sentence units or clauses.

G 081   SENTENCE UNITS:

The conjunction immediately precedes the parallel sentence units. If the conjunction refers to the subject, however, it occupies the prefield:

> *Er fährt* **bald** *nach Frankfurt,* **bald** *nach Berlin.*[1]
> *Sie schreibt mir* **bald** *Briefe,* **bald** *Postkarten.*
> **Bald** *kommt er,* **bald** *sein Bruder.*

G 082   CLAUSES:

If the double conjunction serves to connect clauses, each part occupies the prefield of its own clause:

> **Bald** *schreibt sie mir einen Brief,* **bald** *telefoniert sie mit mir.*
> **Bald** *fährt er mit dem Auto,* **bald** *fliegt er mit dem Flugzeug.*

zum Beispiel

G 085   The phrase **zum Beispiel** is an explanatory expression and combines words and clauses.

G 086   WORDS:

Zum Beispiel usually occurs in the postfield preceding the explanatory words. In this usage it is usually abbreviated **z.B.**:

---

[1] A position in the prefield is also possible: *Bald fährt er nach Frankfurt,* **bald** *nach Berlin.*

422

*Wir haben auf unserer Reise viele Städte gesehen, **z.B.** Köln, Frankfurt, Hamburg, Berlin, usw.*

CLAUSES: G 087

When **zum Beispiel** combines clauses, it stands in the prefield or within the sentence field of the second clause. In this function, the abbreviation **z.B.** is not used:

> *Der Mann war sehr unfreundlich, **zum Beispiel** wollte er mir keine Auskunft über den richtigen Weg geben.*
> *Der Mann war sehr unfreundlich, er wollte mir **zum Beispiel** keine Auskunft über den richtigen Weg geben.*

bevor

The conjunction **bevor** introduces DEPENDENT CLAUSES of TIME, the G 090 situation of which follows the situation of the main clause in time (succession). The subordinate clause may appear in the prefield or in the postfield [→ G 006, H 075]:

> ***Bevor** ein Ausländer in Deutschland studieren kann, muß er Deutsch lernen.*
> *Ein Ausländer muß Deutsch lernen, **bevor** er in Deutschland studieren kann.*

The CONJUNCTION **bevor** must not be confused with the PREPOSITION **vor** G 091 [→ F 706] or the ADVERB **vorher** [→ E 838]:

> ***Vor** seinem Studium in Deutschland muß man Deutsch lernen.*
> *Er will in Deutschland studieren, aber **vorher** muß er Deutsch lernen.*

The conjunction **ehe** may introduce the same subordinate clauses as G 092 **bevor** [→ G 301]. It is, however, a literary form and rarely used.

beziehungsweise

The conjunction **beziehungsweise** is an EXPLANATORY expression and has G 095 the meaning of "or, or else, to be more precise."[1] It indicates an alternative and connects words or phrases. It is usually abbreviated in writing to **bzw.**:

> *Sprechen Sie mit dem Direktor, **bzw.** mit seiner Sekretärin.*

---

[1] Only rarely does **beziehungsweise** have the meaning of "respectively": *Meine Schwestern Anna und Marie haben drei, **bzw.** vier Kinder.*

bis

G 100   The conjunction **bis** introduces DEPENDENT CLAUSES of TIME. The situation of the main clause ends when the situation in the subordinate clause begins.

    The subordinate clause may be placed in the prefield or in the postfield [→ G 006, H 075]. If it occupies the postfield, the expanded conjunction **bis daß** may be used in elevated language:

> *Wir warten vor dem Kino,* **bis** *ihr kommt.*
> **Bis** *du mich wieder besuchst, habe ich das Buch ausgelesen.*
> *Bei der Trauung verspricht das Brautpaar, einander treu zu bleiben,* **bis daß** *der Tod die beiden scheide.*

G 101   For the preposition **bis**, → F 220.

bloß

G 105   → G 410 ff. **nur** (restrictive, limiting).

da

G 110   The conjunction **da** introduces a DEPENDENT CLAUSE of CAUSE, which indicates a generally known reason for the situation of the main clause [→ G 565 **weil**].[1] The conjunction occurs almost exclusively in written language.

    In general, the subordinate clause introduced by **da** occupies the prefield [→ H 075]:

> **Da** *Paris seit Jahrhunderten Frankreichs Hauptstadt ist, ist die Stadt auch das Kulturzentrum des Landes.*
> **Da** *ich gestern — wie Sie wissen — keine Zeit hatte, konnte ich Sie leider nicht besuchen.*

G 115   For **da** in a temporal sense together with **als**, → G 057.

G 116   Note that both **da** and **seit** [→ G 440 ff.] correspond to English "since." **Da**, however, refers to CAUSE and **seit** to TIME:

> **Da** *er Deutsch lernt, kann er viel verstehen.*
> (His study of German is the cause of his ability to comprehend.)
> **Seit** *er Deutsch lernt, kann er viel verstehen.*
> (His ability to comprehend dates from the time of his German studies.)

---

[1] The distinction between **da** and **weil** is not strictly maintained.

424

da(r) plus preposition [1]

The compound **da(r) + preposition** [→ D 040–050] occupies the pre- G 117
field of a main clause and connects it with the preceding clause. It
expresses a relationship which is common to the two situations:

> *Auf dem Tisch liegt meine Tasche,* **darin** *findest du dein Buch.*
> *Dort ist das Hotel,* **daneben** *ist gleich meine Wohnung (gleich* **daneben**
> *ist meine Wohnung).*

dadurch [1]

The conjunction **dadurch** occupies the prefield of an INSTRUMENTAL G 120
MAIN CLAUSE which explains the consequences arising from the situation
of the preceding main clause:

> *Der Schüler war klug und lernte immer fleißig,* **dadurch** *wurde er der*
> *Beste in der Klasse.*
> *Ich habe im letzten Jahr viel Geld verdient,* **dadurch** *konnte ich mir*
> *jetzt endlich ein Auto kaufen.*

The combination **dadurch daß** [1] introduces an INSTRUMENTAL DEPENDENT G 121
CLAUSE which occupies the prefield [→ G 006, H 075]; the situation
described by the subordinate clause indicates the reason or cause for
the situation of the following main clause [G 370 ff. **indem**]. No comma
is used to separate **dadurch** and **daß**:

> **Dadurch daß** *jeder seine Pflicht tat, wurde das gute Ergebnis erreicht.*
> **Dadurch daß** *der Arzt den Kranken sofort operierte, rettete er ihm*
> *das Leben.*

The same meaning is obtained by having **dadurch** as a correlate in the G 122
sentence field of the main clause, anticipating the instrumental subordinate clause which then follows in the postfield and is introduced by
daß:

> *Das gute Ergebnis wurde* **dadurch** *erreicht,* **daß** *jeder seine Pflicht tat.*
> *Der Arzt rettete dem Kranken* **dadurch** *das Leben,* **daß** *er ihn sofort*
> *operierte.*

daher

→ G 265 **deshalb** and G 140 **darum** G 125

---

[1] In English, such **da**-compounds are not considered conjunctions. **Dadurch daß**, however,
is a genuine conjunction; it is often equivalent to the English construction "by ... ing"
(By operating immediately, the doctor saved his life).

damit

G 130 The conjunction **damit** introduces DEPENDENT CLAUSES of PURPOSE (final clauses). The subordinate clause explains the purpose of the situation in the main clause [→ G 520 **um**]: [1]

> *Mein Vater hat mir Geld geschickt, **damit** ich mir einen neuen Anzug kaufen kann.*
> *Die Eltern schicken die Kinder zur Schule, **damit** sie fremde Sprachen lernen.*

G 131 **Damit** may also occupy the prefield of an INSTRUMENTAL MAIN CLAUSE. [2] The main clause with the conjunction **damit** indicates the result of a situation described by the preceding main clause. The two clauses are usually separated by a semicolon:

> *Ich habe gestern mein Examen gemacht; **damit** habe ich mein Studium an der Universität beendet.*

G 132 If a dependent clause with the conjunction **daß** occupies the postfield, **damit** stands as a correlate within the main clause, anticipating the subordinate clause [→ **dadurch daß** G 122]. The main clause explains the result of the situation described in the subordinate clause:

> *Ich habe mein Studium an der Universität **damit** beendet, **daß** ich gestern mein Examen gemacht habe.*

G 133 The expression **damit, daß** may also be used to introduce a DEPENDENT CLAUSE, describing a situation the result of which is contained in the following main clause [→ G 121 **dadurch daß**]:

> ***Damit, daß** ich gestern mein Examen gemacht habe, habe ich mein Studium an der Universität beendet.*

dann

G 135 The conjunction **dann** stands in the prefield or within the sentence field

---

[1] In this use, **da<u>mit</u>** is always stressed on the second syllable; it corresponds to English "so that."

[2] In this use, **da<u>mit</u>** is usually (but not always) stressed on the first syllable; it corresponds to English "with that" or "thereby," and would not be considered a conjunction in English. (Note word order compared with G 130.)

of a MAIN CLAUSE, the situation of which follows that of a preceding main clause in TIME:[1]

> *Wir machen jetzt unsere Aufgaben, **dann** gehen wir spazieren.*
> *Wir machen jetzt unsere Aufgaben; wir gehen **dann** spazieren.*

In the prefield of a main clause, the conjunction **dann** may impart CONDITIONAL meaning to the preceding main clause: G 136

> *Du mußt fleißig arbeiten, **dann** hast du im Leben Erfolg.*
> *Der Kranke soll die Medizin regelmäßig nehmen, **dann** wird er bald wieder gesund.*

Similarly, **dann** often appears in the prefield of a main clause following a conditional subordinate clause introduced by **wenn**:   G 137

> ***Wenn** Sie es nicht wünschen, **dann** machen wir es auch nicht.*
> ***Wenn** mein Freund gestern gekommen wäre, **dann** hätten wir ins Theater gehen können.*

In conditional statements in which the conjunction **wenn** is omitted, the following main clause is usually introduced by **so** or **dann**:   G 138

> ***Wäre** mein Freund gestern gekommen, **dann** (or **so**) hätten wir ins Theater gehen können.*

darum

The conjunction **darum** occupies the prefield of a MAIN CLAUSE and explains the PURPOSE of or reason for that action in order to attain the results stated in the preceding main clause.   G 140

    The conjunctions **daher, dazu, deshalb** [→ G 265], and **deswegen** may be used with the same meaning.

> *Richard will in Deutschland studieren, **darum** lernt er jetzt Deutsch.*
> *Morgen fahre ich in die Ferien, **darum** brauche ich Geld.*

das heißt

The expression **das heißt** is an EXPLANATORY phrase which connects sentence units or clauses. It is usually abbreviated **d.h.**   G 145

---

[1] In this usage, the English equivalent "then" would not be considered a conjunction, but an adverb of time.

427

G 146   SENTENCE UNITS:

>   *Wir, **d.h.** meine Freunde und ich, werden heute ins Kino gehen.*

G 147   CLAUSES:

When **das heißt** connects clauses, it stands isolated outside its clause and does not affect word order.

>   *Wir werden morgen einen Ausflug machen, **d.h.** wir fahren zuerst mit dem Bus und wandern dann durch den Wald.*

daß

G 150   The conjunction **daß**, alone or together with prepositions, other conjunctions, and other parts of speech, introduces DEPENDENT CLAUSES of various meanings.

G 151   **Daß** may introduce dependent clauses which in their entirety constitute the subject of the main clause. These are called SUBJECT CLAUSES. If the subject clause introduced by the conjunction **daß** appears in the postfield, the impersonal pronoun **es** occupies the prefield of the sentence [→ H 053 ff.]:[1]

>   ***Daß** der Sohn in der Schule gut lernt, macht den Eltern Freude.*
>   ***Es** macht den Eltern Freude, **daß** der Sohn in der Schule gut lernt.*
>
>   ***Daß** der Minister morgen in unsere Stadt kommt, ist unwahrscheinlich.*
>   ***Es** ist unwahrscheinlich, **daß** der Minister morgen in unsere Stadt kommt.*

G 152   **Daß** may also introduce dependent clauses which in their entirety constitute the direct (accusative) object of the main clause. Such clauses are called OBJECT CLAUSES. If the object clause occupies the postfield, the impersonal pronoun **es** may appear in the place of the object within the sentence field of the main clause:

>   ***Daß** das Auto zu schnell gefahren ist, habe ich sofort gesehen.*
>   *Ich habe (**es**) sofort gesehen, **daß** das Auto zu schnell gefahren ist.*

G 153   This usage of **daß** is especially frequent after verbs of saying, thinking, knowing, etc.:

---

[1] If some other element occupies the prefield, the anticipatory **es** follows the verb: *Den Eltern macht **es** Freude, **daß** ihr Sohn gut lernt.*

*Er sagte, **daß** er nicht kommen könnte.*
*Meinen Sie, **daß** es morgen regnen wird?*
*Ich weiß, **daß** du recht hast.*

If the verb in the main clause requires a PREPOSITIONAL OBJECT, a com-   G 154
pound of **da(r)-** with the appropriate preposition [→ D 040 ff.]
occupies the position of the object in the sentence field: [1]

*Er hat **davon** gesprochen, **daß** er nach Italien fahren will.*
*Ich bestehe **darauf**, **daß** Sie mir helfen.*
*Ich habe mich **darüber** gefreut, **daß** du mich besuchen konntest.*

If the verb which requires a prepositional object indicates a feeling or   G 155
emotion, the **da(r)-** construction may be omitted in the sentence field of
the main clause, before a subordinate clause introduced by **daß**:

*Ich habe mich gefreut, **daß** du mich besuchen konntest.*

A subordinate clause introduced by **daß** may also replace an ADVERBIAL   G 156
EXPRESSION. In this usage, the compound of **da(r)-** with a preposition
explains and anticipates the nature of the adverbial expression. The
da(r)- construction may not be omitted:

*Er hat mich dauernd **damit** aufgehalten, **daß** er mich immer wieder*
um meine Hilfe bat.
*Eine große Schwierigkeit auf unserer Reise sehe ich **darin**, **daß** wir*
so viel Gepäck mitnehmen müssen.

The conjunction **daß** also introduces dependent clauses which explain   G 157
the PURPOSE of the situation contained in the main clause [→ **damit**
G 130]. In the main clause, **deshalb** [→ G 265] may be used as a correlate to anticipate the dependent clause:

*Euer Vater hat euch das Geld nicht **deshalb** gegeben, **daß** ihr es für*
nutzlose Dinge ausgebt.

Darum, dazu, dafür, or the expressions **in der Absicht, zu dem Zweck,**   G 158
etc., may be used instead of **deshalb**:

*Ich habe dir das Buch **in der Absicht** gegeben, **daß** du etwas davon*
lernst.

---

[1] English may replace such a construction by the phrase "the fact that," by a gerund, or it
may omit it altogether: He spoke of *the fact that* he was going to Italy. I insist on your
helping me. I was glad that you were able to visit me.

G 159   **Daß** may also introduce ATTRIBUTIVE clauses which explain a certain situation, usually after nouns:

> *Der Glaube, **daß** wir in Gottes Hand sind, macht uns stark.*

If the noun is part of an idiomatic construction containing a preposition [→ F 065], the compound of **da(r)-** plus the preposition is used before the subordinate clause:

> *Aus Freude **darüber**, **daß** sein Sohn endlich die Prüfung bestanden hatte, schenkte er ihm ein Motorrad.*

abgesehen davon, daß

G 160   → G 185 **außer daß**

als daß

G 165   The conjunction **als daß** introduces a CONSECUTIVE SUBORDINATE CLAUSE containing a verb in subjunctive II. The dependent clause explains that the situation described in the main clause does not permit the result which would normally be anticipated, usually because of some excessive circumstance. In the main clause, **zu** (or intensified as **allzu**) points to the negative consequences to be expected:

> *Er sprach **zu** schnell, **als daß** ich ihn verstehen könnte.*
> *Die Wohnung ist **zu** klein, **als daß** er dort mit seiner Familie leben könnte.*
> *Er ist noch **zu** krank, **als daß** er schon alles essen dürfte.*
> *Das Wetter war **allzu** schön, **als daß** wir zu Hause geblieben wären.*

angenommen, daß

G 170   → G 577 **wenn** (conditional).

anstatt daß

G 175   The conjunction **anstatt daß** (or its shortened form **statt daß**) introduces an ADVERSATIVE SUBORDINATE CLAUSE, which indicates what situation had been expected in contrast to the actual situation depicted in the main clause [→ G 070 **anstatt**]. The dependent clause may appear either in the prefield or in the postfield [→ G 006, H 075]:

> *__Anstatt daß__ der Vater mit dem Lehrer spricht, geht die Mutter zu ihm.*
> *Peter geht zu oft ins Kino, **anstatt daß** er mehr für die Schule arbeitet.*

430

ausgenommen, daß

→ G 186 **außer daß**; G 585 **außer wenn** (conditional).

außer daß

The conjunction **außer daß** introduces RESTRICTIVE SUBORDINATE CLAUSES which limit the statement made by the main clause. The dependent clause may appear in the prefield or in the postfield:

G 185

> *Der Schüler ist immer zum Unterricht gekommen,* **außer daß** *er einmal wegen Krankheit gefehlt hat.*

Subordinate clauses with the same meaning may be introduced by the conjunction **nur daß** and by the expressions **abgesehen davon, daß; ausgenommen, daß; mit der Einschränkung, daß**:

G 186

> *Der Schüler ist immer zum Unterricht gekommen,* ***ausgenommen, daß** er einmal wegen Krankheit gefehlt hat.*
> ***Abgesehen davon, daß** er einmal wegen Krankheit gefehlt hat, ist der Schüler immer zum Unterricht gekommen.*

unter der Bedingung, daß

→ G 577 **wenn** (conditional).

G 190

bis daß

→ G 100 **bis**.

G 195

dadurch daß

→ G 121, 122 **dadurch**.

G 200

damit, daß

→ G 132, 133 **damit**.

G 205

es sei denn, daß

The expression **es sei denn, daß** introduces RESTRICTIVE SUBORDINATE CLAUSES. The dependent clause has conditional meaning and limits the statement of the main clause [→ G 585 **außer wenn**]:

G 210

> *Ich kann meine Schulden nicht bezahlen,* ***es sei denn, daß** mir mein Vater Geld schickt.*

im Falle, daß

→ G 579 **wenn** (conditional).

G 215

kaum daß

G 220 → G 383 **kaum**; G 458 **sobald**.

nur daß

G 225 → G 186 **außer daß**.

ohne daß

G 230 The conjunction **ohne daß** introduces a SUBORDINATE CLAUSE which expresses the fact that the situation of the main clause did not, as should be expected, result from the situation of the dependent clause[1] [→ G 735 **ohne**]:

> *Der Schüler bestand die Prüfung, **ohne daß** er sich darauf vorbereitet hatte.*
> *Er fährt nach Spanien, **ohne daß** er vorher Spanisch lernt.*

so daß

G 235 The conjunction **so daß** introduces CONSECUTIVE SUBORDINATE CLAUSES. The dependent clause expresses the consequences resulting from the preceding main clause:

> *Als er am späten Abend in Köln ankam, waren die Hotels schon alle besetzt, **so daß** er kein Zimmer mehr bekommen konnte.*

G 236 If the consecutive subordinate clause does not refer to the entire situation of the main clause, but only to one specific part, this concept in the main clause is preceded by **so, dermaßen,**[2] or **solch**; the dependent clause begins with the conjunction **daß**. **So** and **dermaßen** are used before adjectives and adverbs, **solch** before nouns [→ D 490 ff.]:

> *Der Schüler hatte **so** gut gelernt, **daß** er die Prüfung glänzend bestand.*
> *Wir haben gestern einen **so** schönen Film gesehen, **daß** wir ganz begeistert waren.*
> *Wir haben gestern **solch** einen schönen Film gesehen, **daß** wir ganz begeistert waren.*
> *Das Mittagessen war **dermaßen** reichlich, **daß** wir jetzt nichts mehr essen können.*

G 237 **So** may also appear by itself at the end of the sentence field of the main

---

[1] Subjunctive II may be used [→ B 730].
[2] Used infrequently.

432

clause, with the dependent clause (beginning with **daß**) expressing a consequence:

>*Er benahm sich **so**, **daß** alle Leute auf ihn aufmerksam wurden.*

statt daß

→ G 175 **anstatt daß**.   G 240

vorausgesetzt, daß; unter der Voraussetzung, daß

→ G 577 **wenn** (conditional).   G 245

dazu

→ G 140 **darum** (final).   G 250

denn   G 255

The COORDINATING conjunction **denn** stands ISOLATED outside a CAUSAL MAIN CLAUSE, without affecting the word order. This clause expresses the reason for the preceding main clause [→ G 110 **da**; G 565 **weil**[1]]:

>*Robert muß Deutsch lernen, **denn** er will in Deutschland studieren.*
>*Ich bleibe heute zu Hause, **denn** mein Freund wird mich besuchen.*

The use of **denn** as a synonym for **als** in comparing inequal concepts [→ G 075 ff.] is extremely rare and is restricted almost exclusively to poetic or Biblical language: G 256

>*Geben ist seliger **denn** nehmen.*

For **so ... denn**, → G 451.   G 257

For **denn** as an intensifier, → H 615.   G 258

dennoch

→ G 515 **trotzdem**.   G 260

deshalb

The conjunction **deshalb** occupies the prefield of a CONSECUTIVE MAIN CLAUSE which explains the consequences arising from the preceding main clause [→ G 156]:   G 265

>*Der Schüler hat seine Arbeit ohne Fehler geschrieben, **deshalb** lobt*
>   *ihn der Lehrer.*
>*Heute ist das Wetter schlecht, **deshalb** gehe ich nicht spazieren.*

---

[1] Note, however, that **da** and **weil** are *subordinating* conjunctions.

G 266   The conjunctions **daher, darum, deswegen,** and **folglich** may be used with the same meaning.

deswegen

G 270   → G 140 **darum** (final); G 266 **deshalb** (consecutive).

doch

G 275   The conjunction **doch** may appear either ISOLATED before an ADVERSATIVE MAIN CLAUSE, or in the PREFIELD of such a clause.[1] In either case, it expresses a CONTRAST with the statement made in the preceding main clause:

> *Richard ist fleißig,* **doch** *Peter ist faul.*
> *Diese Bilder sind teuer,* **doch** *sie sind nicht alle schön. — Diese Bilder sind teuer,* **doch** *sind sie nicht alle schön.*

G 276   The expanded form **jedoch** may be used in the same meaning as **doch**; most of the time, **jedoch** stands isolated before or within the clause:

> *Er hat ein feierliches Versprechen gegeben,* **jedoch** *er hat sein Wort nicht gehalten (. . ., er hat sein Wort* **jedoch** *nicht gehalten).*

G 277   For **doch** as an intensification of **aber,** → G 033, 037.

G 278   For **doch** as a general intensifier, → H 616.

dort, dorther, dorthin

G 280   These adverbs may be used as conjunctions to indicate the COMMON LOCATION, origin or direction of two clauses:

> *Robert geht zum Bahnhof,* **dort** *erwartet er seine Eltern. — Robert geht zum Bahnhof, er erwartet* **dort** *seine Eltern.*[2]
> *Wo du hingehst,* **dorthin** *will ich auch gehen. — Wo du hingehst,* **dort** *will ich auch* **hingehen.**

ebenso

G 285   The conjunction **ebenso** appears in the prefield of a COMPARATIVE MAIN CLAUSE which is preceded by another main clause. The conjunction expresses the fact that the situation of the second clause is identical, similar, or comparable to that of the first clause:

---

[1] Only if both clauses have the same subject.
[2] Considered two independent sentences in English.

434

*Er spricht mehrere europäische Sprachen, **ebenso** kennt er einige afrikanische Sprachen.*

ebensosehr, ebensowenig

The conjunction **ebensosehr** stands in the prefield of a COMPARATIVE G 290
MAIN CLAUSE which is preceded by another main clause. The conjunction expresses an identity or similarity of degree between the situation indicated in the two clauses:

> *Mein Freund begeistert sich für die Kunst, **ebensosehr** liebt er auch die Musik.*

If the first main clause is negative, the conjunction **ebensowenig** is used G 291
in the prefield of the second clause, giving this second main clause a negative meaning as well:

> *Ich kann seine Bücher nicht verstehen, **ebensowenig** kann ich seinen Vorlesungen folgen.*

ebenso wie (auch)

→ G 490 **sowie (auch)**. G 295

ehe

The conjunction **ehe** introduces a SUBORDINATE CLAUSE. It expresses the G 300
idea that the action of the main clause is being preferred to the action of the dependent clause (English "before" or "rather than"):

> ***Ehe** ich ihn um Geld bitte, verzichte ich lieber auf das Vergnügen.*

For **ehe** in a temporal sense (used primarily in elevated style) → G 090 G 301
bevor.

einerseits . . . and(e)rerseits (. . . aber auch)

This two-part conjunction stands in the prefield of PARTITIVE MAIN G 305
CLAUSES, and contrasts two different, often opposing situations with each other:

> ***Einerseits** freue ich mich auf die Reise, **and(e)rerseits** möchte ich **(aber auch)** hierbleiben.*

entweder . . . oder

The two-part conjunction **entweder . . . oder** has ALTERNATIVE meaning. G 310
It excludes one of two possibilities, without specifying which of these

435

possibilities applies. **Entweder ... oder** occurs before sentence units, or before main clauses.

G 311   SENTENCE UNITS:

Oder always precedes the word or phrase which it refers to. **Entweder** may occur either before its referent, or in the prefield of its clause:

> *Er ist **entweder** im Büro **oder** im Lager. — **Entweder** ist er im Büro **oder** im Lager.*
>
> *Ich fahre **entweder** mit dem Zug **oder** mit dem Auto. — **Entweder** fahre ich mit dem Zug **oder** mit dem Auto.*

G 312   **Entweder** may also occur isolated before the sentence, without affecting word order:

> ***Entweder** er ist im Büro **oder** im Lager.*
>
> ***Entweder** ich fahre mit dem Zug **oder** mit dem Auto.*

G 313   CLAUSES:

Entweder occurs either in the prefield or within the sentence field of its clause; **oder** always stands isolated before the second clause. If the subject is repeated or if the second clause has a different subject, a comma is used before **oder**:[1]

> ***Entweder** gehst du nach Hause **oder** bleibst hier.*
>
> *Du gehst **entweder** nach Hause **oder** bleibst hier.*
>
> *Du gehst **entweder** nach Hause, **oder** du bleibst hier.*
>
> ***Entweder** zahlst du die Rechnung, **oder** ich muß sie bezahlen.*

G 314   If **entweder** is in the isolated position before the sentence, the two clauses are always separated by a comma and the subject (if it is the same) must be repeated:

> ***Entweder** du gehst nach Hause, **oder** du bleibst hier.*
>
> ***Entweder** du zahlst die Rechnung, **oder** ich muß sie bezahlen.*

etwa

G 315   **Etwa** is an EXPLANATORY conjunction which expands and specifies words or phrases more precisely, especially nouns (English "such as"):

> *Für den Erfolg im Beruf braucht man heutzutage Fremdsprachen, **etwa** Französisch, Spanisch, usw.*

[1] If the two clauses have different subjects, the subject usually carries primary stress.

falls

→ G 577 **wenn** (conditional).   G 320

folglich

→ G 265 **deshalb** (consecutive).   G 325

geschweige (denn)

The conjunction **geschweige** and the expanded expression **geschweige**   G 330
denn are used to combine sentence units. They refer to a negative concept, and INTENSIFY the NEGATION with the word or phrase following
(English "let alone"):

> *Die alten Leute gehen kaum mehr aus dem Haus, **geschweige** (**denn**)
> aus ihrem Dorf.*

gesetzt den Fall

→ G 577 **wenn** (conditional).   G 335

indem

The conjunction **indem** introduces DEPENDENT CLAUSES of MANNER. The   G 340
subordinate clause explains the process or the method by means of
which the situation of the main clause is accomplished. **Indem** combines
the concept of simultaneity and means, and is usually expressed in
English with the verbal phrase "by (do)ing (something)" [→ G 121
dadurch daß], if the two clauses have the same subject. The dependent
clause may occupy the prefield or the postfield [→ G 006, H 075]:

> *Der Lehrer erklärte die Aufgabe, **indem** er sie an die Tafel schrieb.*
> *Man kann im Leben nur Erfolg haben, **indem** man viel arbeitet.*
> ***Indem** er mich unterstützte, zeigte er sich als wahrer Freund.*

Sometimes, simultaneity is combined with cause rather than with   G 341
means (English "as" or "while"). The two clauses may have different
subjects:

> ***Indem** er sich bückte, verlor er (entfiel ihm) seine Brieftasche.*

Occasionally, **indem** is used merely to indicate simultaneity of action.   G 342
Such usage, however, is not recommended as good style and **während**
[→ G 550] is preferred:

> *Er zündete sich eine Zigarette an, **indem** er sich niedersetzte.*

437

indes

G 345 The conjunction **indes** stands isolated before ADVERSATIVE MAIN CLAUSES. The main clause introduced by **indes** indicates a situation different from that expected from the content of the preceding main clause (English "however") [→ G 030 **aber**; G 275 **doch**]:

> *Ich habe ihm geraten, mehr zu arbeiten, **indes** er tat es nicht.*

indessen

G 350 The conjunction **indessen** may introduce ADVERSATIVE MAIN CLAUSES [→ G 345 above]. **Indessen** may either appear in the prefield (requiring inverted word order) or — less frequently — in isolation (without affecting word order):

> *Ich habe ihm geraten, mehr zu arbeiten, **indessen** tat er es nicht.*
> *Ich habe ihm geraten, mehr zu arbeiten, **indessen** er tat es nicht.*

G 351 **Indessen** may also combine two MAIN CLAUSES in a temporal sense; it indicates the SIMULTANEITY of the two actions, whereby the action of the second clause is of somewhat shorter duration than that of the first clause. **Indessen** may appear in the prefield or within the sentence field of the second clause:[1]

> *Der Vater holt das Auto aus der Garage, die Mutter packt **indessen** das Essen ein.*
> *Die Familie hörte eine interessante Rundfunksendung, **indessen** stahlen Einbrecher im Schlafzimmer den Schmuck.*

G 352 The conjunctions **unterdessen** [→ G 545], **inzwischen, währenddem,** and **währenddessen** have the same meaning. They may also occur in the prefield or within the sentence field.

G 353 In the sense of simultaneity, **indessen** may also be used as a SUBORDINATING CONJUNCTION; this usage, however, is not considered good style:

> *Der Vater holt das Auto aus der Garage, **indessen** die Mutter das Essen einpackt.*

insofern, insoweit

G 355 The conjunctions **insofern** and **insoweit** occur in the prefield of a

---

[1] In this sense, the English equivalent "meanwhile" would be considered an adverb of time, and not a conjunction.

438

RESTRICTIVE main clause which limits the statement of the preceding main clause:

> *Das Essen war immer gut, **insofern** war ich mit dem Hotel zufrieden.*
> *Er hat mir das Geld jetzt zurückgegeben, **insoweit** ist alles in Ordnung.*

Insofern and **insoweit** may occur in the prefield or in the sentence field of a main clause followed by a dependent clause introduced by **als** [→ G 060]:

G 356

> ***Insofern** war ich mit dem Hotel zufrieden, **als** das Essen gut war.*
> *Ich war **insoweit** mit dem Hotel zufrieden, **als** das Essen gut war.*
> *Ich war mit dem Hotel **insofern** zufrieden, **als** das Essen gut war.*

For **insofern** and **insoweit** as subordinating conjunctions in a restrictive conditional sense, → G 460 **sofern** (**soweit**).

G 357

inzwischen

→ G 351–2 **indessen**, G 545 **unterdessen**.

G 360

je + comparative **. . . desto** (**je, umso**) + comparative [1]

The two-part conjunction **je . . . desto** (**je, umso**) combines a COM-PARATIVE dependent clause with a comparative main clause. **Je** acts as a SUBORDINATING CONJUNCTION, whereas **desto** (**je, umso**) stands in the prefield of the main clause. The entire construction indicates that the situation in the main clause increases or decreases in the same degree as the situation in the dependent clause (English "the + comp. . . . the + comp."):

G 365

> ***Je** länger er in Deutschland lebt, **desto** besser spricht er Deutsch.*
> ***Je** besser ich sie kenne, **je** lieber habe ich sie.*
> ***Je** mehr ein Schüler arbeitet, **umso** mehr lernt er.*

If the main clause comes at the beginning, with **immer** + comparative in the prefield, and the dependent clause in the postfield is introduced by the conjunction **je**, it expresses a constantly progressing increase or decrease:

G 366

> ***Immer** müder wurde ich, **je** länger ich warten mußte.*

[1] The form **desto . . . desto** is not considered good style.

439

G 367   The same meaning is also occasionally expressed by two identical comparatives combined with **und** in the prefield of the main clause (literary style):

> *Müder und müder wurde ich, je länger ich warten mußte.*

je nachdem

G 370   The conjunction **je nachdem** introduces DEPENDENT CLAUSES which express various possibilities arising out of a situation, corresponding to similar possibilities in the main clause. The dependent clause occupies the prefield:

> *Je nachdem er mich heute oder morgen besucht, kann ich mit ihm spazierengehen oder nicht.*

G 371   If the different possibilities in the subordinate clause are not specifically designated, **je nachdem** is used with an interrogative adverb. In this construction, the dependent clause may occur in the postfield:

> *Je nachdem wie teuer die Reise ist, fahre ich mit der Bahn oder mit dem Bus.*
> *Er besucht mich heute oder morgen, je nachdem wann er Zeit hat.*

G 372   The form **je nachdem ob** is also occasionally used:

> *Er besucht mich heute oder morgen, je nachdem ob er Zeit hat.*

jedoch

G 375   → G 276 **doch**.

kaum

G 380   The conjunction **kaum** occurs in the prefield or within the sentence field of a MAIN CLAUSE of TIME, which is followed by a second main clause usually containing **so** or **da** in the prefield. The construction **kaum . . . so (da)** expresses the fact that the situation in the second main clause begins immediately after the situation in the first main clause ends. The verb in the first clause (containing **kaum**) is usually in the past perfect, the verb in the second clause in the simple past or present perfect [→ B 530, 540, 550].

> *Kaum hatte er im Kino Platz genommen, so ging das Licht aus.*
> *Er hatte kaum im Kino Platz genommen, da ging das Licht aus.*

440

The immediate time sequence of the two clauses may be intensified by G 381 the expression **auch schon** in the second main clause. The tense forms of the verbs follow the same rules as for the conjunction **sobald** [→ G 455]. When **auch schon** is used, **da** or **so** may be omitted.

> *Kaum* hatte er im Kino Platz genommen, **(da)** ging **(auch schon)** das Licht aus.

The second main clause may be replaced by a dependent clause with the G 382 conjunction **als**. The time sequence and the meaning remain the same:

> *Er hatte **kaum** im Kino Platz genommen, **als (auch schon)** das Licht ausging.*

When **kaum** together with the conjunction **daß** introduces a dependent G 383 clause, this clause must occupy the prefield. The adverb **so** or **da** is not used in this construction:

> *Kaum daß er im Kino Platz genommen hatte, ging (**auch schon**) das Licht aus.*

The conjunction **sobald** [→ G 455] may be used to replace **kaum daß**; G 384 the verb in the dependent clause introduced by **kaum daß**, however, must always be in some past tense form.

mal . . . mal

→ G 080 **bald . . . bald**, for which **mal . . . mal** is a colloquial substitute: G 385

> *Mal ist er freundlich, mal hat er schlechte Laune.*

nachdem

The conjunction **nachdem** introduces DEPENDENT CLAUSES of TIME. The G 390 situation described in the subordinate clause precedes that of the main clause. The subordinate clause may occupy either the prefield or the postfield [→ G 006, H 075].

The tense forms of the verbs in the main and dependent clauses stand in G 391 the following relationship:

DEPENDENT CLAUSE	MAIN CLAUSE
Past Perfect	Simple Past or Present Perfect
Present Perfect	Present Tense
Present Perfect	Future

> *Nachdem* er Deutsch **gelernt hatte**, **verbrachte** er einen Sommer in Europa (**hat** er einen Sommer in Europa **verbracht**).
> *Nachdem* er Deutsch **gelernt hat**, **verbringt** er einen Sommer in Europa.
> Er **wird** einen Sommer in Europa **verbringen**, *nachdem* er Deutsch **gelernt hat**.

G 392   It is important not to confuse the conjunction **nachdem** with the preposition **nach** [→ F 442] or the adverb **nachher** [→ E 838]:

> *Nachdem* er Deutsch gelernt hatte, verbrachte er einen Sommer in Europa.
> *Nach* seinem Deutschstudium verbrachte er einen Sommer in Europa.
> Erst lernte er Deutsch und *nachher* verbrachte er einen Sommer in Europa.

G 393   The conjunction **als** [→ G 059] may be used in the same meaning as **nachdem**, if the dependent clause is in the past perfect:

> *Als* er Deutsch gelernt hatte, verbrachte er einen Sommer in Europa.

G 394   For **je nachdem** → G 371-2.

namentlich (aber) [1]

G 395   The conjunction **namentlich**, frequently intensified by **aber**, is used to combine words and phrases. It explains and SPECIFIES:

> Alle Leute, **namentlich** (**aber**) die Kinder, hatten unter der Kälte zu leiden.
> Er hat im letzten Jahr, **namentlich** (**aber**) in den Ferien, viel an seinem neuen Roman gearbeitet.

nämlich [1]

G 400   **Nämlich** is an EXPLANATORY conjunction, introducing a list of words as examples:

> Die Kinder müssen in der Schule viele Dinge lernen, **nämlich** Rechnen, Schreiben, Lesen, usw.

G 401   **Nämlich** may also occur within the sentence field of causal main clauses

[1] Although dictionaries sometimes translate both **namentlich** and **nämlich** as *namely*, they are by no means identical and should be clearly distinguished: **namentlich** is English *especially* or *particularly*, whereas **nämlich** corresponds to *that is to say*, or *for instance*.

442

which explain the reason for the statement made in the preceding main clause:[1]

> *Robert muß Deutsch lernen, er will **nämlich** in Deutschland studieren.*
>
> *Ich bleibe heute zu Hause, meine Eltern wollen mich **nämlich** besuchen.*
>
> *Mein Freund fährt nach Hamburg, er hat dort **nämlich** eine neue Stellung gefunden.*

noch

Noch is an ALTERNATIVE conjunction, occurring only after negative statements, and in itself has negative meaning [→ G 560 **weder ... noch**]. It may be used to combine sentence units or clauses.   G 405

SENTENCE UNITS: G 406

> *Ich kenne dieses Buch nicht, **noch** die anderen Werke dieses Dichters.*

CLAUSES: G 407
Noch occurs in the prefield of the second clause, requiring inversion:

> *Er arbeitet nicht, **noch** tut er sonst etwas Nützliches.*
> *Er gibt mir kein Geld, **noch** hilft er mir auf andere Art.*

nur

The conjunctive adverb **nur** combines sentence units and clauses and has RESTRICTIVE meaning.   G 410

SENTENCE UNITS: G 411

> *Ich bin nicht krank, **nur** müde.*
> *Sie liebt auch moderne Musik, **nur** weniger als klassische.*

Nur may also be used as an intensifier for individual words or phrases [→ H 636]:   G 412

> *Mein Freund hat mir immer geholfen, **nur** Geld gab er mir nie.*

CLAUSES: G 413
Nur may occur in the prefield or within the sentence field of RESTRICTIVE

---

[1] In this usage, **nämlich** would not be considered a conjunction in English, but an adverb occurring within the second (independent) clause.

MAIN CLAUSES which limit the statement made in the preceding main clause:

> *Ich kaufe dieses Buch,* **nur** *muß ich zuerst mein Geld holen.*
> *Ich kaufe dieses Buch, ich muß* **nur** *zuerst mein Geld holen.*
> *Mein Freund hat mir immer geholfen,* **nur** *gab er mir nie Geld.*
> *Robert lernt in der Schule gut,* **nur** *macht ihm die Grammatik Schwierigkeiten.*

G 414   **Bloß** may be used as a synonym for **nur** in elevated style.

ob[1]

G 415   The conjunction **ob** introduces DEPENDENT CLAUSES which act as the accusative object of the main clause (OBJECT CLAUSES). The main clause is either negative or interrogative in nature, and the dependent clause introduced with the conjunction **ob** is an indirect question derived from a direct question without interrogative pronoun. These are called ALTERNATIVE questions, to which only an affirmative or negative answer is possible. The subordinate clause may occupy either the prefield or the postfield of the sentence [→ G 006, H 075]:

> *Weißt du,* **ob** *dein Freund morgen kommt?*
> *Ich fragte ihn,* **ob** *seine Eltern aus Berlin kommen.*
> **Ob** *er die Prüfung bestanden hatte, sagte er nicht.*

G 416   If the object clause appears in the postfield, the impersonal pronoun **es** may occupy the position of the object in the main clause as a correlate, anticipating the dependent clause:

> *Ich weiß* **es** *noch nicht,* **ob** *ich dich nächste Woche besuchen kann.*

G 417   For **als ob** → G 051 ff.

ob . . . oder

G 420   The dual conjunction **ob . . . oder** combines sentence units or clauses and has CONCESSIVE meaning.

G 421   SENTENCE UNITS:

> *Ich trinke alles,* **ob** *Bier* **oder** *Wein.*

---

[1] Although frequently translated as "if," **ob** actually corresponds to English "whether," except in the phrase **als ob**.

CLAUSES: G 422

The conjunction **ob** introduces CONCESSIVE DEPENDENT CLAUSES, in which two similar sentence units are connected by **oder**. The dependent clause itself stands isolated before a declarative statement and does not affect the word order of the main clause:

> **Ob** *Sie mich **oder** meinen Bruder fragen, Sie erhalten keine Auskunft.*

The concessive clause is thus not in itself a sentence unit of the follow- G 423
ing main clause, but must be considered as a subordinate clause in the postfield of an implicit preceding main clause:

> *(Es ist gleichgültig),* **ob** *Sie mich **oder** meinen Bruder fragen. Sie erhalten keine Auskunft.*

The conjunction **oder** with its sentence unit may also follow after the G 424
verb, occupying the postfield of its own clause:

> **Ob** *Sie mich fragen **oder** meinen Bruder, Sie erhalten keine Auskunft.*

obwohl

The conjunction **obwohl** introduces a CONCESSIVE SUBORDINATE CLAUSE. G 425
The statement made in the dependent clause reinforces the statement made in the main clause, which took place in spite of it.

> *Er wollte sich nicht entschuldigen, **obwohl** er im Unrecht war.*
> *Der Sohn macht die Reise, **obwohl** sein Vater es verboten hat.*

The subordinate clause may occupy the prefield of the sentence G 426
[→ G 006, H 075]. In this case, the statement made in the dependent clause may be summarized with the adverb **so** in the prefield of the main clause, followed by the adverb **doch** within the sentence field of the main clause:

> **Obwohl** *Peter kein fleißiger Schüler war,* **(so)** *hat er die Prüfung* **(doch)** *bestanden.*

The conjunctions **obgleich, obschon,** and (less frequently) **obzwar** may G 427
be used in place of **obwohl** [→ G 580 **wenn auch**; G 516 **trotzdem**; G 034 **zwar . . . aber**].

445

oder

G 430   The conjunction **oder** combines sentence units or clauses. It has ALTER-
NATIVE meaning, i.e. it offers a choice between two or more possibilities.

G 431   SENTENCE UNITS [→ H 291]:

> *Er kommt heute **oder** morgen.*
> *Wurde die Arbeit von dir **oder** von deinem Freund gemacht?*

G 432   CLAUSES:

Oder connects MAIN CLAUSES. If the subject in the two clauses is the
same, they are not separated by comma. If the second clause does
contain a subject, **oder** stands isolated before the clause and does not
affect word order:

> *Ich schreibe ihm einen Brief **oder** besuche ihn in den nächsten Tagen.*
> *Du mußt mir helfen, **oder** die Arbeit wird nicht rechtzeitig fertig.*

ohne

G 435   The conjunction **ohne** introduces INSTRUMENTAL INFINITIVE CLAUSES.[1]
The infinitive clause explains that the situation in the main clause takes
place regardless of the situation in the infinitive clause, which would
normally be expected to have taken place. The subject of the main clause
is also by implication subject of the infinitive clause [→ B 904 ff.]:

> *Der Schüler bestand die Prüfung, **ohne** vorher viel gelernt zu haben.*

G 436   For the preposition **ohne**, → F 490 ff.

G 437   For **ohne daß** → G 230.

seit, seitdem[2]

G 440   The conjunctions **seit** or **seitdem** introduce DEPENDENT CLAUSES of
TIME. The conjunction expresses the fact that the situation of the main
clause begins at the same time with the situation of the subordinate
clause. The verbs in both clauses have the same tense form:

> ***Seit (seitdem)** Robert in Deutschland lebt, lernt er besser Deutsch.*
> ***Seitdem (seit)** Robert in Deutschland lebte, lernte er besser Deutsch.*

---

[1] Considered an infinitive phrase in English.
[2] For the difference between **da** and **seit**, → G 116.

446

If, however, the situation of the dependent clause has already ended, the   G 441
following relationship applies for the verbs in the two clauses:

DEPENDENT CLAUSE	MAIN CLAUSE
Present Perfect Past Perfect	Present Simple Past

Seitdem wir ein Auto gekauft haben, machen wir viele Reisen.
Seitdem wir ein Auto gekauft hatten, machten wir viele Reisen.

Seit Peter die Schule verlassen hat, arbeitet er in einer Fabrik.

The distinction between preposition, conjunction, and adverb, which is   G 442
very clear for **vor, bevor, vorher** [→ G 091], for **nach, nachdem, nachher**
[→ G 392], and for **trotz** and **trotzdem** [conjunction *and* adverb,
→ G 510 ff.], is not as well defined in this instance. Only **seit**, to be
sure, may be used as a preposition [→ F 510]. Both **seit** and **seitdem**,
however, function interchangeably as conjunctions; **seitdem** may also
be used adverbially, as a synonym for **seither** [→ E 883]:

> *Er war letzte Woche bei mir zu Besuch, aber* **seither** (**seitdem**) *habe ich ihn nicht mehr gesehen.*

selbst

Selbst is used only before individual words or phrases; it INTENSIFIES the   G 445
statement with reference to the expression which it precedes (English
"even") [→ J 185]:

> *Diese Arbeit war zu schwer für uns,* **selbst** *für Peter, der der Stärkste von uns ist.*

In a negative statement, **selbst** is often replaced by **auch nicht** (**auch ...**   G 446
nicht); this corresponds to English "not even":

> *Die Arbeit war nicht leicht für uns,* **auch nicht** *für Peter* (**auch** *für* Peter **nicht**), *der der Stärkste von uns ist.*

Sogar may be used as a synonym for **selbst**.   G 447

so

The conjunction **so** stands in the prefield of a CONSECUTIVE MAIN CLAUSE,   G 450 which explains the consequences of the preceding main clause [→ G 065 **also**, G 265 **deshalb**, etc.]:

> *Mein Freund kam gestern nicht zu mir, so ging ich allein spazieren.*

G 451 The consecutive meaning may be intensified by adding **also** or **denn** in the sentence field. **Denn** is used mainly in elevated style:

> *Du hast deine Schulaufgaben gemacht, so kannst du also auch mit deinen Freunden spielen gehen.*
> *Heute ist das Wetter schlecht, so gehe ich denn nicht spazieren.*

G 452 If the conjunction **so** appears in the prefield, it imparts conditional meaning to a preceding imperative clause or a main clause with **sollen** ... **nur** or **brauchen** ... **nur**. **Dann** [→ G 136] may be used in a similar manner.

> *Hilf dir. selbst, so wird dir Gott helfen.*
> *Peter braucht seinen Vater nur um Geld zu bitten, so schickt er es ihm sicher.*
> *Er soll nur fleißig lernen, so wird er schon Erfolg haben.*

G 453 **So** is also frequently used in the prefield of a main clause following a subordinate conditional clause introduced by **wenn** or **wenn auch** [→ G 581 f.]. In conditional statements where the conjunction **wenn** is omitted, the following main clause is almost always introduced by **so** or **dann** [→ G 137]:

> *Wäre mein Freund gestern gekommen, so (dann) hätte er mit uns ins Theater gehen können.*

G 454 If **so** with an adjective or adverb introduces a subordinate clause and the main clause contains **auch** or **auch immer**, so has CONCESSIVE meaning ("no matter how"). If the dependent clause comes at the beginning of the sentence, it stands isolated before the main clause and does not affect its word order [cf. G 422–3 **ob**]:

> *Er fährt morgen nach München, so schlecht das Wetter auch (immer) sein möge.*
> *So schwer die Arbeit auch ist, ich werde sie beenden.*

sobald

G 455 The conjunction **sobald** introduces DEPENDENT CLAUSES of TIME. The situation of the main clause begins immediately after the end of the

448

situation in the subordinate clause. The dependent clause may occupy either the prefield or the postfield [$\rightarrow$ G 006, H 075].

The verbs in the two clauses have the following tense relationships: G 456

TIME REFERENCE	DEPENDENT CLAUSE	MAIN CLAUSE
Past	Past Perfect	Simple Past
Future	Present Perfect	Present
Future	Present Perfect	Future

Sobald Paul die Schule beendet hatte, begann er seine Arbeit in einer Fabrik.

Sobald Paul die Schule beendet hat, beginnt er seine Arbeit in der Fabrik.

Sobald Paul die Schule beendet hat, wird er seine Arbeit in der Fabrik beginnen.

If the situation in the main clause and in the subordinate clause occur at G 457 approximately the same time, the tense forms in both clauses are identical (except for the third example below):

TIME REFERENCE	DEPENDENT CLAUSE	MAIN CLAUSE
Past	Simple Past	Simple Past
Present or Timeless Statement	Present	Present
Future	Present	Future

Sobald der Lehrer in die Klasse kam, begann der Unterricht.
Sobald der Lehrer in die Klasse kommt, beginnt der Unterricht.
Sobald der Lehrer in die Klasse kommt, wird der Unterricht beginnen.

The conjunctions **sowie** and **kaum daß** indicate the same time relation- G 458 ship as **sobald**.

In contrast to English, all conjunction compounds with **so-** (**sobald,** G 459 **sofern, solange, sooft, soviel, sowie, soweit,** etc.) are written as one word and are normally not followed by **als** or **wie**.

449

sofern (soweit)

G 460 The conjunctions **sofern** or **soweit** introduce RESTRICTIVE DEPENDENT CLAUSES with CONDITIONAL meaning. The subordinate clause limits the statement of the main clause:

> *Er kann seine Schulden bezahlen, **sofern** sein Vater ihm Geld schickt.*
> *Soweit es Paul möglich ist, hilft er seinem Freund.*

G 461 The alternate forms **insofern** and **insoweit** are sometimes used.

solange

G 465 The conjunction **solange** (sometimes **solang**) introduces DEPENDENT CLAUSES of TIME. The situation in the subordinate clause runs simultaneously with the action of the main clause, and ends at the same time. The dependent clause usually (but not always) occupies the prefield [→ H 075].

> ***Solang** ich in Deutschland war, habe ich kein Wort Englisch gesprochen.*
> *Wir müssen zu Hause bleiben, **solange** es regnet.*

G 466 The conjunction **solange** may also give a secondary conditional meaning to the dependent clause:

> ***Solange** er mir das Geld nicht zurückgibt, kann er von mir keine Hilfe erwarten.*

sondern

G 470 The conjunction **sondern** has ADVERSATIVE meaning and expresses a contrast, opposite, or contradiction. It combines sentence units or clauses, and occurs after a negative statement [→ G 032 **aber**] to express two ideas which are mutually exclusive.[1] If the contrast is not based on mutual exclusion, **aber** is used.

SENTENCE UNITS:

> *Das Kleid ist nicht schwarz, **sondern** dunkelblau.*
> *Das Kleid ist nicht schwarz, **aber** elegant genug.*[2]
> *Er ist nicht zu Hause, **sondern** im Café.*

[1] The idea expressed by **sondern** corresponds to English "but instead, but rather, but on the contrary."

[2] If the second phrase or clause is negative, **aber** *must* be used: *Das Kleid ist schwarz, **aber** nicht elegant.* Such constructions never refer to mutually exclusive concepts.

In the expression **nicht nur ... sondern auch, sondern** does not indicate   G 471
mutual exclusion. Instead, it has ADDITIVE function, similar to **sowohl**
... als auch [→ G 495]:

> *Er ist **nicht nur** dumm, **sondern auch** arrogant.*

CLAUSES: G 472

If **sondern** combines two MAIN CLAUSES with the same subject, the subject
need not be repeated. If the two subjects are not the same, **sondern**
stands isolated before the second main clause and does not affect its
word order:

> *Er arbeitet heute nicht im Büro, **sondern** besucht seine Eltern.*
> *Ich besuche ihn heute nicht, **sondern** er besucht mich.*

Sondern may also express a LIMITATION; in this case the adverb **nur**   G 473
occurs either immediately after **sondern** or within the sentence field of
the second clause:

> *Sie hat kein Geld, **sondern nur** Grundbesitz.*
> *Wir wollen das Haus nicht kaufen, **sondern** besichtigen es **nur**.*

Occasionally, **sondern** occurs not only after negative clauses, but also   G 474
after expressions which have negative meaning:

> *Ich vermied es, etwas zu sagen, **sondern** schwieg.*

sonst

The conjunction **sonst** occurs in the prefield of a MAIN CLAUSE and im-   G 475
parts a NEGATIVE CONDITIONAL meaning to the preceding main clause
[→ G 579 **wenn ... nicht**]:

> *Du mußt fleißig arbeiten, **sonst** hast du im Leben keinen Erfolg!*
> *Das kranke Kind soll die Medizin regelmäßig nehmen, **sonst** wird es*
>   *nicht gesund.*
> *Mach jetzt deine Schulaufgaben, **sonst** darfst du nicht zum Schwimmen*
>   *gehen!*

The conjunction **ander(e)nfalls** may be used as a synonym for **sonst** in   G 476
this meaning.

Sonst may also occur in the prefield of RESTRICTIVE MAIN CLAUSES which   G 477

451

limit the statement of the preceding main clause. Usually, **aber** occurs within the sentence field of the clause introduced by **sonst**:

> *Mein Freund gab mir nie Geld,* **sonst** *hat er mir* **aber** *in jeder Beziehung geholfen.*
>
> *Robert kann die Grammatik nicht verstehen,* **sonst** *ist er* **aber** *ein guter Schüler.*

G 478 The restrictive meaning of **sonst** may be reinforced either by placing **zwar** in the first main clause, or by placing the conjunction **aber** immediately before **sonst**:

> *Mein Freund gab mir* **zwar** *Geld,* **aber sonst** *hat er mir in keiner Beziehung geholfen.*
>
> *Robert kann* **zwar** *die Grammatik verstehen,* **aber sonst** *ist er kein guter Schüler.*

G 479 **Sonst** may also be used in a TEMPORAL sense in the meaning of "usually, in the past." It occurs either in the prefield or within the sentence field of the second clause:[1]

> *Mein Freund besucht mich nicht mehr,* **sonst** *kam er immer nachmittags zu mir.*
>
> *Heute bist du aber sehr schlechter Laune, du bist doch* **sonst** *sehr vergnügt.*

sooft

G 480 The conjunction **sooft** introduces DEPENDENT CLAUSES of TIME, the situation of which is repeated again and again simultaneously with the main clause. The subordinate clause may occupy either the prefield or the postfield [→ G 006, H 075]:

> *Herr Müller bittet mich um Geld,* **sooft** *ich ihn auf der Straße treffe.*
>
> **Sooft** *Peter vom Schwimmen kommt, ist er erkältet.*

soviel

G 485 The subordinating conjunction **soviel** introduces RESTRICTIVE CLAUSES which limit the applicability of the main clause to the condition stated in the dependent clause:

> **Soviel** *ich weiß, ist er ein sehr braver Junge.*
>
> *Die Sache ging,* **soviel** *ich sehen konnte, recht gut.*

---

[1] In English, these would be looked upon as separate sentences, rather than clauses joined by conjunction. In German, they may be either sentences or clauses.

The limitation may, but need not be, of a quantitative nature: G 486

> *Er nahm, **soviel** er konnte.*

sowie (auch)

The conjunction **sowie** or **sowie auch** combines SENTENCE UNITS and has G 490
SUPPLEMENTARY function. It is often used in order to avoid repetitive
occurrences of **und**:

> *Wir besuchten meine Eltern und meine Geschwister **sowie auch**
> meinen Bruder.*
> *Kinder und Studenten **sowie** Militär zahlen ermäßigte Eintrittspreise.*
> *Mein Freund **sowie auch** mein Bruder studieren in München.*

For **sowie** as a subordinating conjunction in the sense of **sobald**, G 491
→ G 455.

sowohl . . . als auch

The conjunction **sowohl . . . als auch** connects SENTENCE UNITS. It com- G 495
bines TWO POSSIBILITIES into the statement made in the sentence, which
do not automatically or necessarily occur jointly.[1] Often this conjunction is contained in an answer to a question with the conjunction **oder**:

> *Er ist **sowohl** dumm **als auch** arrogant.*
> *Fährt dein Vater nach Köln oder nach Mainz? Mein Vater fährt
> **sowohl** nach Köln **als auch** nach Mainz.*

statt (daß)

→ G 070, G 175 **anstatt, anstatt daß** G 500

stattdessen

The conjunction **stattdessen** appears in the prefield of an ADVERSATIVE G 501
MAIN CLAUSE, the content of which stands in contrast with the content
of the preceding main clause:

> *Er hat versprochen, mir einen Brief zu schreiben, **stattdessen** schickt
> er nur eine Postkarte.*
> *Meine Freundin und ich wollten miteinander arbeiten, **stattdessen**
> haben wir geplaudert.*

---

[1] The English equivalent "as well as" occurs before the second element. "Both . . . and"
may also be used in English.

G 502 **Stattdessen** may also occur either in the prefield or within the sentence field of adversative main clauses which contrast a situation that did not take place with the actual situation in the preceding main clause. The verb in the adversative clause appears in subjunctive II:

> *Peter geht oft ins Kino,* **stattdessen** *sollte er mehr für die Schule arbeiten (. . . , er sollte* **stattdessen** *mehr für die Schule arbeiten).*

G 503 The form **stattdem** occurs occasionally in colloquial usage, but is not considered acceptable.

teils . . . teils

G 505 The conjunction **teils . . . teils** has partitive meaning and connects both sentence units and clauses.

G 506 SENTENCE UNITS:

The second part of the conjunction with the word or phrase it introduces usually occupies the postfield:

> *Teils hat der Schüler die Arbeit selber gemacht,* **teils** *auch sein Vater.*

G 507 CLAUSES:

Each part of the conjunction appears in the prefield of a MAIN CLAUSE:

> *Teils will er sein Haus verkaufen,* **teils** *will er es aber auch behalten.*
> [→ G 305 **einerseits . . . and(e)rerseits**].

trotzdem

G 510 The conjunction **trotzdem** appears in CONCESSIVE MAIN CLAUSES, usually in the prefield, sometimes within the sentence field. The concessive main clause indicates a consequence different from that which one would normally expect from the content of the preceding main clause:

> *Karl war kein guter Schüler,* **trotzdem** *hat er die Prüfung gut bestanden.*

G 511 The concessive function may be intensified by placing **aber** or **und** before **trotzdem**:

> *Der Zug hatte Verspätung,* **aber trotzdem** *kam ich rechtzeitig ins Theater (. . . , ich kam* **aber trotzdem** *rechtzeitig ins Theater)* *(. . . ,* **und trotzdem** *kam ich rechtzeitig ins Theater).*

G 512 It is possible for **aber** (**und**) and **trotzdem** to be separated within the sentence:

454

*Er war kein guter Schüler, **aber** er hat **trotzdem** die Prüfung bestanden (. . . , **und** er hat **trotzdem** die Prüfung bestanden).*

If the subject in the two clauses is the same and **aber trotzdem** does not occupy the prefield, the subject need not be repeated: G 513

*Er war kein guter Schüler, hat **aber trotzdem** die Prüfung bestanden.*

Often the adverbs **zwar, wohl, freilich** within the sentence field of the preceding clause serve to anticipate the concessive clause with the conjunction **trotzdem** which follows: G 514

*Er war **zwar** kein guter Schüler, hat aber **trotzdem** die Prüfung bestanden.*

The conjunctions **doch** [→ G 275], **dennoch**, or **gleichwohl** may be used as synonyms for **trotzdem**. G 515

Trotzdem may also be used as a SUBORDINATING conjunction introducing a concessive dependent clause indicating that an event took place in spite of the situation in the subordinate clause [→ G 425 **obwohl**]:[1] G 516

__Trotzdem__ er kein guter Schüler war, hat er die Prüfung bestanden.

um

The conjunction **um** introduces FINAL INFINITIVE CLAUSES.[2] The infinitive clause explains the purpose of the situation described in the main clause. The subject of the main clause is also understood to be the subject of the infinitive clause [→ G 130 **damit**; B 904]: G 520

*Er ist nach Deutschland gefahren, **um** dort Deutsch zu lernen.*
*Herr Müller hat die Uhr gekauft, **um** sie seiner Frau zu schenken.*

The infinitive clause following the conjunction **um** has consecutive function, if in the main clause **zu** or **allzu** before an adjective or adverb is used to anticipate the infinitive clause. The infinitive clause then explains certain impossible consequences which a factor in the main clause does not permit [→ G 165 **als daß**]: G 521

*Er ist noch **zu** krank, **um** schon alles essen zu dürfen.*

[1] This usage is widespread, although traditional grammars still frown upon it and require the use of **trotzdem daß** as a subordinating conjunction. **Trotzdem daß**, however, is very rarely used and **trotzdem** has won out, in analogy with **seitdem, indem,** and **nachdem,** which developed in the same manner.

[2] Considered an infinitive phrase in English.

G 522   For the preposition **um** → F 580 ff.

um so mehr, als

G 525   The expression **um so mehr, als** introduces a strongly stressed CAUSAL SUBORDINATE CLAUSE. The dependent clause explains the reason for the situation in the preceding main clause:

> *Der Dieb muß streng bestraft werden,* **um so mehr,** *als er schon einmal wegen Diebstahls im Gefängnis war.*
>
> *Hans sollte seinem Freund helfen,* **um so mehr,** *als sein Freund ihm auch oft geholfen hat.*

G 526   The phrase **um so mehr** may also appear within the sentence field of the preceding main clause. If there is an adjective in the comparative, **mehr** is omitted and the adjective is preceded by **um so (umso)**:

> *Hans sollte seinem Freund* **um so mehr** *helfen,* **als** *sein Freund ihm auch oft geholfen hat.*
>
> *Der Dieb muß* **umso strenger** *bestraft werden,* **als** *er schon einmal wegen Diebstahls im Gefängnis war.*

um so weniger, als

G 530   The expression **um so weniger, als** introduces a strongly stressed CAUSAL SUBORDINATE CLAUSE [→ G 525 **um so mehr, als**]. The preceding main clause is always negative:

> *Das Kind darf heute* **nicht** *spielen gehen,* **um so weniger,** *als es noch erkältet ist.*
>
> *Ich kann dir* **kein** *Geld leihen,* **um so weniger,** *als du mir noch von letzter Woche 5 Mark schuldest.*

G 531   The phrase **um so weniger** may also appear within the sentence field of the preceding main clause. In this case, the main clause does not contain a negation, since the expression **um so weniger** in itself already has a negative meaning:

> *Das Kind darf heute* **um so weniger** *spielen,* **als** *es noch erkältet ist.*

und

G 535   The conjunction **und** combines PARALLEL sentence units or clauses. It has COPULATIVE function.

456

> *Peter **und** seine Kameraden fuhren nach Salzburg **und** nach Wien.*
> *Mein Freund **und** ich gingen zuerst ins Kino **und** dann in ein Café.*
> *Er starb arm, einsam **und** unglücklich.*[1]

The conjunction **und** may also be used to combine several sentence units   G 537
in groups of two each:

> *Viele Menschen hoffen auf Glück **und** Reichtum, Erfolg **und** Ruhm.*

CLAUSES: G 538

The conjunction **und** always combines equal units, i.e. it connects main
clauses with main clauses and subordinate clauses with subordinate
clauses. It always stands isolated outside the clause and does not affect
word order:

> *Mein Freund brachte mir die Zeitung, **und** ich las die neuesten*
> *Nachrichten.*
> *Als wir den Saal betraten **und** bevor wir noch unsere Plätze finden*
> *konnten, ging schon das Licht aus **und** das Konzert begann.*
> *Ich fahre im Sommer nach Deutschland, wo ich meine Familie*
> *besuchen **und** viele alte Freunde wiedersehen werde.*[2]

If the subject is the same for both clauses, and if the second clause does   G 539
not have some other expression in the prefield, the subject is not repeated in the second clause, and the two clauses are not separated by
a comma:[3]

> *Der Lehrer kam ins Klassenzimmer **und** begann den Unterricht.*
> *Ich gehe zur Universität **und** höre dort eine Vorlesung.*
> *Wir werden in unsere Heimatstadt fahren **und** alle unsere alten*
> *Freunde besuchen.*[4]

---

[1] Note that in contrast to English usage, **und** is NOT preceded by comma when it introduces
the last element in a series.

[2] Note that the subject of the second subordinate clause is omitted if it is identical with the
first and if the conjunction applies to both clauses [→ G 539], and that the auxiliary verb
at the end of the second subordinate clause refers to both dependent clauses [cf. footnote 4].

[3] If the first clause has some other expression in the prefield, the subject may nevertheless
be omitted in the second clause: ***Dann kam der Lehrer ins Klassenzimmer und begann den***
Unterricht. [But → G 540.]

[4] Note that auxiliary verbs which apply to both clauses are also omitted in the second
clause: *Ich habe den Brief geschrieben **und** gleich zur Post gebracht.* But: *Ich **bin** zur Univer-*
*sität gegangen und **habe** dort eine Vorlesung gehört.*

G 540   If, however, the prefield of the second clause is occupied by some other expression, the subject of the second clause must be repeated (or replaced by a pronoun), and the two clauses separated by a comma:

> *Der Lehrer kam ins Klassenzimmer,* **und dann** *begann er den Unterricht.*
>
> *Heute fahren wir nach Wien,* **und morgen** *gehen wir dort ins Theater.*

G 541   If the two main clauses do not have the same subject, a comma is used before **und**:

> *Karl geht in die Schule,* **und** *Hans bleibt zu Hause.*
>
> *Er fragte,* **und** *sie antwortete.*

G 542   If the conjunction **und** connects a declarative statement with a preceding imperative clause, the imperative clause attains conditional meaning:

> *Hilf dir selbst,* **und** *Gott wird dir helfen.*
>
> *Gebt uns ein Schiff,* **und** *wir fahren über das Meer.*

G 543   Sometimes a declarative statement or an imperative clause after **und** replaces a subordinate clause with **daß** [→ G 150 ff.] or an infinitive clause:

> *Er ist dazu imstande* **und** *läßt uns eine Stunde warten.* (*Er ist dazu imstande, uns eine Stunde warten zu lassen.*)
>
> *Es fehlte nicht viel,* **und** *ich hätte mir ein neues Auto gekauft.* (*Es fehlte nicht viel, daß ich mir ein neues Auto gekauft hätte.*)
>
> *Seien Sie bitte so freundlich* **und** *helfen Sie mir!* (*Seien Sie bitte so freundlich, mir zu helfen!*)

unterdessen

G 545   The conjunction **unterdessen** occurs in the prefield or within the sentence field of a MAIN CLAUSE of TIME. It expresses the fact that simultaneously with the action expressed in the preceding main clause, another shorter action is taking place:

> *Der Lehrer spricht mit dem Schuldirektor,* **unterdessen** *schreiben die Schüler ihre Arbeiten (. . . , die Schüler schreiben* **unterdessen** *ihre Arbeiten).*[1]

G 546   The conjunctions **indessen** [→ G 351], **inzwischen, währenddem,** and **währenddessen** may be used in the same meaning.

---

[1] These would be considered two separate sentences in English.

während

The conjunction **während** introduces SUBORDINATE CLAUSES of TIME   G 550
(English "while"). It expresses the fact that the situation of the main
clause and that of the dependent clause occur simultaneously and last
for the same time. The dependent clause may occupy either the prefield
or the postfield [→ G 006, H 075]:

> *Ich lernte viel Italienisch, **während** ich in Italien war.*
> ***Während** der Lehrer die Regel erklärte, hörten die Schüler aufmerksam
> zu.*

Während may also introduce ADVERSATIVE SUBORDINATE CLAUSES, which   G 551
indicate a contrast to the situation of the main clause (English "whereas"). The second clause always contains the concept which is to be
stressed:

> *Im Herbst ist das Wetter in den Bergen meist schön, **während** es im
> Sommer recht unbeständig ist.*
> ***Während** das Wetter in den Bergen im Herbst meist schön ist, ist es im
> Sommer recht unbeständig.*

> *Richard ist sehr nervös, **während** sein Bruder ein sehr ruhiger Mensch
> ist.*
> ***Während** Richard sehr nervös ist, ist sein Bruder ein sehr ruhiger
> Mensch.*

währenddem, währenddessen

→ G 545 **unterdessen**.   G 555

weder . . . noch

The conjunction **weder . . . noch** combines sentence units and parallel   G 560
main clauses. It has ALTERNATIVE function, and both parts carry
NEGATIVE meaning [→ G 405 **noch**]. It is the negative form of **entweder
. . . oder** [→ G 310 ff.], or of **sowohl . . . als auch** [→ G 495].

SENTENCE UNITS: G 561
If **weder . . . noch** combines two parts of the subject, the conjugated
verb is in the plural.

> *Ich spreche **weder** Italienisch **noch** Französisch.*
> ***Weder** ich **noch** mein Bruder haben Französisch gelernt.*
> *Er arbeitet **weder** in einer Fabrik **noch** in einem Büro.*

459

G 562 CLAUSES:

Weder usually appears within the sentence field of the first clause; **noch** always occupies the prefield of the second clause:

> *Er arbeitet **weder** in einer Fabrik, **noch** geht er in ein Büro.*

G 563 If the negative meaning is to be emphasized, **weder** may also occur in the prefield of the first clause:

> ***Weder** arbeitet er in einer Fabrik, **noch** geht er in ein Büro.*

weil

G 565 The conjunction **weil** introduces CAUSAL SUBORDINATE CLAUSES stating a reason for the situation of the main clause, which was not assumed to have been known previously [→ G 110 **da**].[1]

> *Robert lernt Deutsch, **weil** er in Deutschland studieren will.*
>
> *Wir gehen heute ins Kino, **weil** man dort einen interessanten Film spielt.*

G 566 If the causal subordinate clause is to be stressed, **darum, deshalb,** or **deswegen** may appear within the sentence field of the preceding main clause to anticipate the dependent clause:

> *Ich bleibe heute **deshalb** zu Hause, **weil** mich meine Freundin besuchen will.*
>
> *Er ist **deswegen** nach Berlin gefahren, **weil** dort die Filmfestspiele stattfinden.*

G 567 The dependent clause may occupy either the prefield or the postfield [→ G 006, H 075].

wenn

G 570 The conjunction **wenn** introduces DEPENDENT CLAUSES of TIME. The situation in the main clause and that in the subordinate clause occur simultaneously.

G 571 **Wenn** is used for PRESENT events, FUTURE events, and REPEATED PAST EVENTS. The conjunction **als** [→ G 054] is used for single past events.[2]

> ***Wenn** Paul in die Schule geht, trifft er unterwegs viele Kameraden.*

[1] The distinction between **da** and **weil** is *not* strictly maintained.
[2] But → G 058.

460

Wenn mein Freund morgen ankommt, werde ich ihn vom Bahnhof abholen.

Meine Mutter freute sich immer sehr, wenn ich sie besuchte.

If the dependent clause occupies the prefield of the entire sentence [→ G 006, H 075], the statement contained in it may be summarized by **dann** in the prefield of the main clause [→ G 137]:   G 572

Wenn mein Freund morgen ankommt, dann hole ich ihn vom Bahnhof ab.

Wenn ich meine Mutter besuchte, dann freute sie sich immer sehr.

In order to emphasize the repetitive nature of the situation, **wenn** may be preceded by **immer** or **jedesmal**. **Immer** may also occur within the sentence field of the main clause: G 573

Immer wenn wir einen Ausflug machen wollten, regnete es.

Jedesmal wenn wir ihn einladen, hat er keine Zeit.

Wenn ich nach Berlin komme, besuche ich immer meine alten Freunde.

The conjunction **wenn** also introduces CONDITIONAL SUBORDINATE CLAUSES, which state the circumstances on which the action of the main clause depends. The dependent clause often occupies the prefield: G 574

Man lernt eine Fremdsprache schnell, wenn man fleißig ist.

Wenn ich morgen Zeit habe, besuche ich dich.[1]

If the condition is assumed, unreal, or contrary-to-fact, SUBJUNCTIVE II is used in both clauses [→ B 715 ff.]:   G 575

Wenn mein Freund jetzt käme, gingen wir zusammen ins Theater.

Wenn mein Freund gestern gekommen wäre, hätten wir zusammen ins Theater gehen können.

If the dependent clause occupies the prefield of the entire sentence, **so** [→ G 453] or **dann** [→ G 137, 572] may be used to summarize the statement made in the conditional clause: G 576

Wenn mein Freund jetzt käme, so gingen wir zusammen ins Theater.

Wenn Sie jetzt einverstanden wären, dann könnte der Vertrag unterschrieben werden.

In order to differentiate between the temporal and the conditional use   G 577

---

[1] Theoretically, an ambiguity exists between the conditional and the temporal use of **wenn** [→ G 571]. If the context does not make the meaning clear, a synonym for **wenn** may be used [→ G 577].

461

of **wenn**, the conjunction **falls** or the expressions **unter der Bedingung, daß; im Falle, daß; vorausgesetzt, daß** may be used as synonyms for conditional dependent clauses.

The expressions **angenommen** or **gesetzt den Fall** may also be used in the same meaning; the conditional clause, however, then has the word order of a main clause and must come first in the sequence. The second (actual) main clause then has **so** or **dann** in its prefield:

> **Falls** *ich morgen Zeit habe, besuche ich dich.*
> **Vorausgesetzt,** *daß der Schüler fleißig ist, lernt er die neue Fremdsprache schnell.*

> **Angenommen,** *mein Freund käme jetzt,* **so** *gingen wir zusammen ins Theater.*

> **Gesetzt den Fall,** *mein Freund* **wäre** *gestern gekommen,* **dann** *hätten wir zusammen ins Theater gehen können.*

G 578   The conjunction **wenn** may also introduce WISHES (usually contrary-to-fact or incapable of fulfillment), which have the form of subordinate clauses, even though they are neither followed nor preceded by a main clause. The verb is in subjunctive II, and the sentence ends with an exclamation point. **Wenn** is intensified by **nur** following either immediately or within the sentence field, or by **doch** within the sentence field:

> **Wenn nur** *mein Freund gestern hier gewesen wäre!*
> **Wenn** *ich* **nur** *wieder jung sein könnte!*
> **Wenn** *es* **doch** *morgen* **nur** *nicht regnen würde!*

G 579   **Wenn** is also used to introduce a RESTRICTIVE subordinate clause with conditional meaning, if the dependent clause contains a negation. In this case it limits the negative statement of the preceding main clause:

> *Ich kann meine Miete nicht bezahlen,* **wenn** *du mir kein Geld leihst.*
> **Wenn** *du deine Schularbeiten nicht machst, darfst du nicht Ball spielen gehen.*

G 580   **Wenn . . . auch** (sometimes **auch wenn**)[1] is used to introduce CONCESSIVE

---

[1] Note that **wenn . . . auch** corresponds to either "even though" or "even if" in English. The distinction in German is not made by means of vocabulary, but by means of MOOD: in the sense of "even though," the indicative is used, in the sense of "even if" subjunctive II: *Wenn deine Worte auch wahr* **waren,** *so* **konntest** *du mich damit nicht verletzen.* (Your words, even though true, could not hurt me). — *Wenn deine Worte auch wahr* **wären, könntest** *du mich damit nicht verletzen.* (Your words, even if true, could not hurt me).

462

SUBORDINATE CLAUSES which emphasize the statement made in the main clause:

> *Peter hat die Prüfung gut bestanden, **wenn** er **auch** kein guter Schüler war.*

If the dependent clause with **wenn . . . auch** occupies the prefield of the entire sentence, **so** is used in the prefield of the main clause to summarize the statement of the subordinate clause [→ G 576]. The adverb **doch** often appears within the sentence field of the main clause: G 581

> ***Wenn** die Reise **auch** sehr teuer war, **so** bereuen wir es **doch** nicht, sie gemacht zu haben.*

In all usages listed from G 574 on (but NOT in the temporal sense of **wenn**), the conjunction **wenn** may be omitted and its position occupied by the conjugated form of the verb [→ H 025.2, 025.3]. The dependent clause, which begins with the verb, always appears in the prefield of the entire sentence; **so** (or sometimes **dann**) usually occurs in the prefield of the main clause [→ G 453, 138]:   G 582

> ***Hilfst** du dir, **so** hilft dir Gott. [→ G 574]*
>
> ***Wäre** mein Freund gestern gekommen, **dann** hätten wir zusammen ins Theater gehen können. [→ G 575]*
>
> ***Könnte** ich nur wieder jung sein! [→ G 578]*
>
> ***War** die Reise auch sehr teuer, **so** bereuen wir es **doch** nicht, sie gemacht zu haben [→ G 581].*

The verb **sollen** in subjunctive II may also replace the conjunction **wenn**, if the main clause follows and the situation expressed in the conditional dependent clause indicates a future possibility. **So** often occurs in the prefield of the main clause: G 583

> ***Sollte** ich morgen nicht zu Hause sein, **so** kannst du mich im Büro anrufen.*
>
> ***Sollten** meine Eltern am Sonntag kommen, **so** werde ich den Ausflug nicht mitmachen können.*

außer wenn

The conjunction **außer wenn** introduces a RESTRICTIVE DEPENDENT CLAUSE with CONDITIONAL meaning. The dependent clause limits the negative statement of the main clause: G 585

> *Morgen wollen wir einen Ausflug machen, **außer wenn** es regnet.*

G 586   The expressions **ausgenommen, wenn; es sei denn, daß** [→ G 210], and **wenn ... nicht** [→ G 579] impart a similar meaning to the dependent clause.

bloß wenn, nur wenn

G 590   The double conjunctions **bloß wenn** and **nur wenn** introduce CON-DITIONAL DEPENDENT CLAUSES with LIMITING meaning. The subordinate clause occurs in the prefield,[1] and states precisely limited conditions:

> *Nur **wenn** du mir hilfst, kann ich die Arbeit rechtzeitig beenden.*
> ***Bloß wenn** das Wetter morgen schön ist, machen wir einen Ausflug.*

The same meaning is obtained by having **nur** or **bloß** (possibly intensified by **dann**) within the sentence field of the main clause, and the dependent clause introduced by **wenn** in the postfield:

> *Ich kann die Arbeit **nur (dann)** rechtzeitig beenden, **wenn** du mir hilfst.*
> *Wir machen **bloß dann** einen Ausflug, **wenn** das Wetter schön ist.*

wie

G 595   The conjunction **wie** is used in COMPARISONS to express EQUALITY or similarity [→ **als** G 045 ff.].[2] It is used to combine sentence units and clauses. Adjectives or adverbs are preceded by **so** or **ebenso** [→ E 355].

G 596   SENTENCE UNITS:

> *Er ist **so** alt **wie** mein Bruder.*
> *Ich fahre **ebenso** gern mit dem Flugzeug **wie** mit dem Schiff.*

G 597   CLAUSES:

The dependent clause occupies the postfield:

> *Die Prüfung war nicht so schwer, **wie** ich gedacht hatte.*
> *Mein Freund brachte mir das Buch, **wie** er es mir versprochen hatte.*

G 598   **wie** (+ adjective or adverb) **... auch (immer)** introduces CONCESSIVE SUBORDINATE CLAUSES. The dependent clause usually occupies the postfield:

---

[1] If **bloß** or **nur** appear within the sentence field of the subordinate clause, the meaning is changed to an intensified condition or an implied wish: *Wenn du mir **nur** hilfst. ... Wenn **bloß** das Wetter morgen schön ist, ...*

[2] The use of **wie** in comparisons expressing inequality is considered incorrect German, although it sometimes occurs colloquially in Southern Germany and Austria.

> *Er fährt morgen nach Frankfurt, **wie** schlecht das Wetter **auch** (**immer**) sein möge.*

If the main clause follows, the dependent clause stands isolated before it and does not affect word order. [For a similar construction, cf. **ob . . . oder**, G 420, 423]:   G 599

> *Wie schwer **auch** die Arbeit sein mag, ich muß sie beenden.*

Wie may also have EXPLANATORY function, introducing a series of words or examples in the meaning of "such as":   G 600

> *Bauern haben viele Haustiere, **wie** Pferde, Kühe, Schweine, Schafe, Hühner, usw.*

wie auch is used to combine sentence units; it has SUPPLEMENTARY function [→ G 490 **sowie auch**; G 495 **sowohl . . . als auch**]:   G 601

> *Mein Freund **wie auch** ich studierten in München.*
> *Mein Vater fährt nach Köln **wie auch** nach Mainz.*

wie wenn

→ G 053 **als ob**.   G 605

wo

The conjunction **wo** may be used to introduce concessive subordinate clauses which express an unfulfilled expectation. The dependent clause is often intensified by **doch**:   G 610

> *Warum hast du mir nicht geschrieben, **wo** ich dich so darum gebeten habe?*
> *Peter ist über das schlechte Ergebnis seiner Prüfung sehr enttäuscht, **wo** er **doch** immer so fleißig gelernt hatte.*

wo, woher, wohin

These conjunctions introduce DEPENDENT CLAUSES of PLACE,[1] which serve to define the local relationship to the statement made in the main clause: G 615

> *Ich wohne, **wo** mein Vater vor zehn Jahren gewohnt hat.*
> *Wir folgen dir, **wohin** du auch immer gehst.*
> *Dies ist das Dorf, **woher** er kommt.*

[1] **Wo** as a conjunction of time is a colloquialism: *In dem Augenblick, **wo** . . .* ; *jedesmal, **wo** . . .*

465

G 616　Often an adverb of location appears in the main clause to anticipate the subordinate clause:

> *Ich wohne **dort**, **wo** mein Vater vor zehn Jahren gewohnt hat.*

G 617　The adverb of location must appear in the main clause, if the actions in the two clauses do not occur in the same direction:

> *Wir fahren **dorthin**, **wo** wir zusammen studiert haben.*
> *Er kam **daher**, **wohin** ich heute fahren will.*

zumal

G 620　The conjunction **zumal**, which is rarely used today, introduces a strongly stressed CAUSAL SUBORDINATE CLAUSE, which explains the reason for the situation in the main clause [→ G 525 **um so mehr, als**]:

> *Der Dieb muß streng bestraft werden, **zumal** er schon einmal wegen Diebstahls im Gefängnis war.*

und zwar

G 625　The conjunction **und zwar** has explanatory and supplementary function (English "namely, that is"). It connects sentence units:

> *Ein Juwelier verkauft viele wertvolle Dinge, **und zwar** Uhren, Ringe, Schmuck, usw.*
> *Das Konzert findet morgen statt, **und zwar** um 8 Uhr abends im Stadttheater.*
> *Er hatte einen Autounfall, **und zwar** einen so schweren, daß er seit Wochen im Krankenhaus liegt.*

zwar ... aber

G 630　→ G 034 **aber**

Interrogatives as Conjunctions

G 700　Interrogative pronouns (**wer, was, welcher, was für ein,** etc.) and interrogative adverbs (**wann, warum, wie, wo, woher, wohin**) may also act as subordinating conjunctions. They introduce so-called indirect questions, which function in every respect like dependent clauses:

> *Ich wußte nicht, **was** ich tun sollte.*
> *Er fragte mich, **wer** eben gekommen sei.*

*Ich möchte wissen, **warum** er nicht geschrieben hat.*
*Können Sie mir sagen, **wann** der nächste Zug ankommt?*
*Er überlegte sich, **wohin** er gehen sollte.*[1]

The interrogative pronoun or adverb may be preceded by a preposition, without changing its conjunctive function: G 701

*Ich wußte nicht, **mit wem** ich gesprochen hatte.*
*Er fragte mich, **seit wann** ich in Berlin sei.*

Relative Pronouns

Although relative pronouns are not, properly speaking, conjunctions, they do perform a very similar function. Like the subordinating conjunctions, they introduce dependent clauses, which in the case of the relative pronouns have attributive meaning. For a full discussion of the forms and uses of relative pronouns, → D 500 ff. For relative clauses, → J 145 ff.   G 750

For dependent clauses in indirect discourse without introductory conjunction, → H 061.   G 770

INTERJECTIONS

⅓ *Introduction*

Interjections are not parts of speech in the strict meaning of the term. They are exclamations, utterances which convey a certain feeling or sensation, or which attempt to imitate various non-linguistic sounds (onomatopoeia). They are uninflected and have no etymology or derivation, although it is possible for other parts of speech to be derived from them (e.g. **ächzen** from **ach!**, **miauen** from **miau**).   G 800

By their very nature, interjections and exclamations are basically part of the spoken language. When they occur as written forms, their spelling fluctuates.

Unlike other words, interjections and exclamations do not constitute part of a sentence, but are actually complete utterances in themselves.   G 801

---

[1] **Her** or **hin** may also occur as verb prefixes: *Er überlegte sich, wo er hingehen sollte.*

They do occur in front of or — less frequently — within a sentence, but they remain isolated from the structure of the sentence and do not affect word order in any way.

G 802 The following lists do not in any way claim to be exhaustive, neither in the number of interjections listed nor in the range of their possible meanings. They are merely intended as illustrations of the most frequent occurrences.[1]

G 810 SENSATIONS, FEELINGS, etc.

ach	pleasure, pain, regret, longing, astonishment, annoyance
ah	pleasure, surprise, satisfaction
aha	surprise, agreement, satisfaction, triumph
ätsch	mockery
au, autsch, auweh	pain
bah, bäh	disgust, contempt
ei*	pleasure, surprise
eia (poppeia)*	tenderness
ha	annoyance, anger
haha, hehe, hihi, hoho, höhö	laughter, snickering, derision
he	exclamation, appellation (!); question (?)
hei, heisa*	pleasure
herrje(mine)*	sorrow, regret
hm	doubt, reflection
hoppla	surprise
hu	coldness, fear
juchhe, juchhei (rasa)*	pleasure
na	reluctant consent; doubt (?)
nanu	surprise
o, oh, oweh	pain, regret, longing
oho	astonishment, anger
oje (mine)*	regret, surprise
paperlapapp*	rejection, derision

[1] Forms which are no longer in current usage, but may still be found in literature, folk songs, etc., are indicated by an *.

Under no circumstances should these examples be construed as an attempt to be prescriptive. A non-native speaker should exercise extreme caution in the use of interjections.

pfui	disgust
topp*	agreement
uff	surprise, relief
uh	fear

REQUESTS G 820

he, heda, holla*	request for attention or identification
hopp, hops, hopsasa	request to jump
ho ruck	rhythmic pulling movement
hüh	(to draft animals) request to start moving
kusch	(mainly to dogs) lie down, be quiet
prrr	(to draft animals) request to stop
pst, sch	request for silence

IMITATION of HUMAN SOUNDS G 830

äh	hesitation in speech
hatschi	sneezing
hem	clearing of throat
hick	hiccoughs or drunkenness
trallala	humming
uff	heavy breathing

IMITATION of ANIMAL SOUNDS G 840

iah	donkey
kikeriki	rooster
mäh	sheep
miau	cat
muh	cow
wauwau	dog

IMITATION of OTHER SOUNDS G 850

bim bam bum	church bells, chimes
bum	drum
bums	loud noise
holterdipolter*	falling, stumbling
hui, husch	wind (or wind-like speed)
klingeling	bell ringing
knacks	breaking
patsch, platsch	splashing
piff paff puff	shooting

plumps	dropping into water
rips raps	tearing
ritsch ratsch	tearing
ritze ratze	sawing
schnipp schnapp	cutting
schwups	spilling
tapp tapp	steps
tick tack	clock
trara	trumpet
wupps	dropping or spilling

H

❧ The Sentence

❧ Introduction

Language serves the purposes of expression and communication. Different functions of language can be recognized by the various types of
linguistic utterances. We distinguish between four main categories:

H 001

1. Statement (declarative)
2. Question (interrogative)
3. Command (imperative)
4. Exclamation (exclamatory)

The **statement** is the most important type of linguistic expression, and
provides information of a factual or assumed nature. Each statement
describes a SITUATION or a number of situations, which in their totality
and in their relationship to one another make up the content of the
declarative statement.

H 002

The linguistic form in which a statement is made is an UTTERANCE.
An utterance (or discourse) is made up of one or more SENTENCES,
which are the essential grammatical units of speech. Sentences in turn
consist of one or more CLAUSES, each of which contains SENTENCE UNITS

(words or phrases) which can be recognized as constituent members of the sentence. These sentence units are placed into a grammatical and logical relationship to one another by means of a predicate (verbal concept).

H 003   Each SITUATION described in a sentence or clause can be divided into

1. an event or a state of being, which is designated as the SENTENCE CORE (predicate), and
2. AGENTS, i.e. persons, things, or concepts which participate in the event or state of being described (subject or object).

A given situation can usually be described in various grammatical ways, according to the manner in which it is being observed or in which it is to be considered (Predicate in **bold print**):

> *Der Kopf* **schmerzt** *ihm. — Er* **hat** *Kopfschmerzen.*
> *Sie* **ängstigt sich** *dauernd. — Sie* **lebt** *in* **ständiger Angst.**
> *Ich* **freue mich** *über das Geschenk. — Das Geschenk* **macht** *mir* **Freude.**
> *Die Pferde* **ziehen** *den Wagen. — Der Wagen* **wird** *von den Pferden* **gezogen.**

H 004   In addition to the essential components of any situation (predicate and subject[1]), a statement may be expanded by including a description of the CIRCUMSTANCES under which the situation takes place. These circumstances describe place, time, reason, condition, manner, etc.

H 005   The sentence core describes either an EVENT or a STATE OF BEING. An *event* describes an *action* or a *process*, involving movement or change. *States of being* describe an *unchanging condition* or situation. Both are expressed in the sentence either through the PREDICATE itself [→ H 110 ff.], or through the predicate together with a PREDICATE COMPLEMENT [→ H 400 ff.].

Events:

> *Er* **schließt** *die Tür.*
> *Ich* **setze** *mich.*
> *Sie* **dankte** *mir.*
> *Die Wohnung* **wird** *neu* **gemalt.**

---

[1] There are German sentences without an explicit subject, such as dative passive constructions: *Dem Mann kann geholfen werden*, or statements like: *Mich friert.*

472

States of Being:

> *Die Tür schließt schlecht.*
> *Ich sitze auf meinem Stuhl.*
> *Sie war mir dankbar.*
> *Die Wohnung steht leer.*

Events may be divided into ACTIONS and PROCESSES. An event is called   H 006
an action when the agent of the event, appearing as the subject of the
sentence [→ H 250], intentionally or unintentionally causes the event to
happen. All other events are called processes.

Actions:

> *Die Pferde ziehen den Wagen.*
> *Ich gehe in die Schule.*
> *Er steigt auf den Berg.*
> *Meine Mutter kocht das Essen.*
> *Man baut dort ein schönes Haus.*

Processes:

> *Die Wolken ziehen nach Westen.*
> *Meine Uhr geht genau.*
> *Die Temperatur steigt auf 60 Grad.*
> *Das Wasser kocht.*
> *Dort wird ein schönes Haus gebaut.*

Many events may be described *either* as actions *or* as processes. It is up
to the speaker to decide how he sees the event described, or how he
wants to have it considered:

> *Der Hund erschreckt das Kind. — Das Kind erschrickt vor dem Hund.*
> *Die Arbeiter asphaltieren die Straße. — Die Straße wird neu
> asphaltiert.*
> *Er öffnet die Tür. — Die Tür öffnet sich.*

A statement is caused by a desire on the part of the speaker to express a   H 007
concept or to provide some other person with some information. This
information or expression may also be elicited by the other participant
in the linguistic situation. Such a request for a statement is called a
question. All questions are indicated by question marks. If a question
inquires after the *veracity* of an *entire situation* and all its accompanying

473

circumstances, it is called an ALTERNATIVE QUESTION. Alternative questions do not use any interrogative pronouns or adverbs, and may be answered by **ja** (affirmative), **nein** (negative), or **doch** (emphatic affirmative after a negative question):

> *Hat dir Peter einen Brief geschrieben? **Ja**, er hat mir gestern geschrieben.*
> *Gehen Sie jetzt ins Büro? **Nein**, ich gehe erst um 10 Uhr.*
> *Bei diesem schlechten Wetter macht ihr wohl keinen Ausflug? **Doch**, wir gehen trotzdem.*[1]

If a question inquires only after a given *unit* within the *situational context* (i.e. predicate, subject, object, or any circumstances accompanying the situation), it is called an INFORMATIONAL QUESTION. Such questions are introduced by *interrogative pronouns* (eliciting as their answer predicate, subject, or object) or *interrogative adverbs* (inquiring after a circumstance):[2]

> ***Wer** hat dir den Brief geschrieben?*
> ***Wen** wollen Sie sprechen?*
> ***Wem** gehört dieses Buch?*
> ***Was** hast du gestern gemacht?*

> ***Warum** sind Sie nicht gekommen?*
> ***Wann** geht der nächste Zug?*
> ***Wo** bist du gestern gewesen?*

H 008 A **command** is a form of linguistic utterance which requests a certain behavior or action from another person. Its purpose is to bring about a desired situation.[3] Commands are indicated by exclamation marks. The command may be addressed to one or more persons present:

> ***Hilf** mir bei meiner Arbeit!*
> ***Seid** ruhig!*
> ***Schließen** Sie bitte die Tür!*
> *Ihr **geht** sofort ins Bett, Kinder!*

[1] **Doch** in this sense has no exact English equivalent. It can be rendered by "yes indeed" or by placing vocal stress on the auxiliary verb: "Oh yes, we *are* going — we *do* go —we *will* go anyway."

[2] An interrogative may be preceded by a preposition: *Seit wann lernen sie Deutsch?*

[3] The form of the verb may either be in the imperative or in subjunctive I. (Occasionally, the indicative may be used.) [→ B 782 ff.]

Such commands may also include the speaker himself:

> **Gehen wir** *jetzt ein wenig in den Garten!*
> **Laßt uns** *beten!*

A command may also be a general wish or request, or may be addressed to a third person:

> *So **sei** es!*
> *Es **werde** Licht!*
> *Lang **lebe** der König!*
> *Er **möge** hereinkommen!*
> *Der Leser **beachte** vor allem die folgenden Regeln:*

The command or request may also emanate from a third person:

> *Sie sollen zum Direktor kommen!*
> *Du mögest morgen bei Hans vorbeikommen!*

An **exclamation** is a spontaneous utterance intended to express a feeling   H 009
or describe a situation. Like all linguistic utterances, it presupposes a
listener (at least by implication) from whom, however, no response is
expected.[1] Exclamations are also indicated by exclamation marks.

> *(Zu) Hilfe!*
> *Welch ein heißer Tag!*
> *Wie nett von Ihnen!*
> *Wie schön es hier ist!*
> *Da sind doch diese Leute schon wieder!*

TYPES OF SENTENCES

According to the four basic types of linguistic utterances, we distinguish   H 010
four corresponding types of sentences:

1. **Declarative Sentences**, which may be constituent parts of connected utterances [→ H 051 ff. and H 705 ff.].
2. **Interrogative sentences** [→ H 025.4].
3. **Imperative sentences** [→ H 025.1].
4. **Exclamatory sentences** [→ H 009].

[1] As the first three examples indicate, an exclamation need not be a complete sentence.

H 011   These four types of sentences are characterized not only by their grammatical form, but also by punctuation marks, by vocal stress, and by
sentence intonation [→ K 001 ff.].

FORMS OF SENTENCES

H 015   Sentences may consist of one or more clauses. A sentence of two or
more clauses is called a COMPOUND sentence if it consists of two main
(or independent) clauses; it is called a COMPLEX sentence if it consists of
a main clause and one or more dependent (subordinate) clauses:

Compound sentence:[1]

main clause I   conj.   main clause II

*Ich war letzten Sommer in Berlin | und | dort besuchte ich meine
Freunde.*

Complex sentence:[1]

main clause   conj.   subordinate clause

Ich besuchte meine Freunde, | als ich letzten Sommer in Berlin war.

H 016   As their names indicate, INDEPENDENT or MAIN clauses are able to form
a complete sentence when standing by themselves:

> *Ich war letzten Sommer in Berlin.*
> *Dort besuchte ich meine Freunde.*

H 017   DEPENDENT or SUBORDINATE clauses, however, can not stand by themselves; in order to form a complete sentence, they require a main clause,
for which they provide some kind of supplementary information
[→ subject clauses H 270, object clauses H 320, adverbial clauses
H 568.8].

H 018   One of the most important grammatical features of the German language is the differentiation between main and subordinate clause in
terms of the POSITION of the PREDICATE, which always appears at the
end of subordinate clause [→ H 040].

H 019   In fact, the form of a German sentence in general is determined by the
position of the predicate [→ H 120 ff.]. The different parts of the

---

[1] See G 001 ff. for coordinating and subordinating conjunctions.

476

predicate constitute the skeleton of the sentence and thus the focal points around which the position of all sentence units [→ H 700 ff.] is organized.

THE SENTENCE FIELD

The characteristic feature of the German sentence is the phenomenon of the SPLIT PREDICATE in main clauses. The term split predicate indicates that any compound predicate (i.e. a verbal concept which consists of two or more units) will be divided and will occupy two separate positions in the main clause.

H 020

The part of the predicate which conveys the major or precise meaning is found at the end of the clause. In the beginning of the main clause, we find the inflected (conjugated, finite) verb. In the case of a compound predicate this may be an auxiliary verb having only a formal role as a function indicator, which acts to modify the second (major) part of the predicate, the meaning indicator. In the case of verbs with separable prefixes, the first part of the predicate indicates the general (stem) meaning, which is then made more specific — or in many cases completely altered — by the second part.

H 021

The two parts of the predicate constitute the front and rear (ANTERIOR and POSTERIOR) limits of the SENTENCE FIELD, within which other sentence units are arranged:

H 022

anterior limit	sentence field	posterior limit
V_1[1]	. . . .	V_2[1]

V_1	Sentence Field	V_2
Hast	*du das Buch gestern abend*	*gelesen?*
Wird	*Hans morgen mit dir ins Kino*	*gehen?*
Steigen	*Sie bitte schnell in den Zug*	*ein!*
Fängt	*der Unterricht pünktlich um 10 Uhr*	*an?*

If the predicate consists of a SIMPLE VERB (or a verb with an inseparable prefix) in the present or past tense, the position of the second part of the predicate (the POSTERIOR LIMIT of the sentence field) remains

H 023

[1] The letter V is used as an abbreviation for "verbal unit" in order to avoid confusion with adverbial modifiers of place (P). See H 709 for complete list of symbols.

UNOCCUPIED. It nonetheless exists latently by implication, and will be occupied by the second part of the verb which carries the major meaning, as soon as the predicate is given a different form:

V_1	Sentence Field	(V_2)
Geht	*Hans morgen mit dir ins Kino*	(...)?
Verstehen	*Sie mich nicht*	(...)?
Wird	*Hans morgen mit dir ins Kino*	*gehen?*
Können	*Sie mich nicht*	*verstehen?*

H 024   If the clause is contained entirely within the sentence field (i.e. if the clause begins with V_1), the subject (S) usually follows immediately after the first part of the predicate (V_1):[1]

V_1	S	Sentence Field	V_2
Hast	*du*	*das Buch gestern abend*	*gelesen?*
Wird	*Hans*	*morgen mit dir ins Kino*	*gehen?*

H 025   The following sentences or clauses contain all sentence units within the sentence field:

1. IMPERATIVE SENTENCES:[1]

	Sentence Field	
Vergiß	*deine alten Freunde nicht!*	
Gehen	*Sie durch diese Tür!*	
Steigen	*Sie bitte schnell in den Zug*	*ein!*
Fangen	*wir unsere Arbeit*	*an!*
Bringt	*mir bitte auch mein Buch*	*mit!*

2. WISHES without the conjunction **wenn**:

	Sentence Field	
Käme	*doch morgen mein Freund!*	
Brächte	*er mir nur das Geld*	*mit!*
Hätte	*ich doch nur meine Aufgabe besser*	*vorbereitet!*

[1] Imperative sentences in the familiar second person singular and plural do not explicitly contain a subject. The word **du** or **ihr** is implied.

478

3. CONDITIONAL clauses without the conjunction **wenn**:

.... Sentence Field ....

Kommt　　*morgen kein Besuch zu mir,*　　　　...
Will　　　*Hans nicht mit uns ins Kino*　　**gehen,** ...
Hätte　　*ich meine Aufgabe besser*　　**vorbereitet,** ...

4. INTERROGATIVE sentences containing ALTERNATIVE questions:

.... Sentence Field ....

Geht　　　*Hans morgen mit uns ins Kino?*
Kommt　　*der Zug um 5 Uhr in München*　　**an?**
Hat　　　*Peter seine Arbeit schon*　　　**beendet?**
Können　*Sie mich nicht*　　　　　　　**verstehen?**

5. DECLARATIVE sentences containing EMPHATIC statements:

.... Sentence Field ....

Waren　　*es doch schon viele Jahre,*
Hatte　　*ich mir doch lange schon ein neues Auto* **gewünscht** ...

The ANTERIOR LIMIT of the sentence field (V_1) is occupied by the form of the verb which carries the PERSONAL ending. This is known as the inflected, conjugated, or finite part of the verb [→ examples in H 022 ff. above]. H 030

The POSTERIOR LIMIT of the sentence field (V_2) is occupied by the predicate complement. This may be a PAST PARTICIPLE: H 031

Hast　*du das Buch gestern abend*　**gelesen?**
Ist　　*Hans mit euch ins Kino*　　**gegangen?**

It may also be occupied by a SIMPLE or a PREPOSITIONAL INFINITIVE: H 032

Können　*Sie mich nicht*　　　**verstehen?**
Wirst　　*du morgen ins Kino*　　**gehen?**
Lassen　*Sie sich die Haare*　　**schneiden!**

Wünschen　*Sie, morgen länger*　　**zu schlafen?**
Versuche,　*ihn telephonisch*　　**zu erreichen!**

479

H 033   SEPARABLE PREFIXES of compound verbs also occupy the posterior end of the sentence field:

Steigen	*Sie bitte schnell in den Zug*	*ein!*
Fängt	*die Klassenstunde pünktlich um 10 Uhr*	*an?*
Stell	*dir nur meine Überraschung*	*vor!*

H 034   Adjectives and nouns in the PREDICATE NOMINATIVE, i.e. the completion of the copulative verbs **sein, werden,** and **bleiben,** are also found in the V_2 position:

Bist	*du mit deiner Arbeit noch nicht*	*fertig?*
Wird	*es im Sommer wirklich erst um 9 Uhr*	*dunkel?*
Bleiben	*Sie bitte trotz aller Schwierigkeiten*	*mein Freund!*
Sei	*doch nicht dein ganzes Leben lang*	*ein Narr!*

H 035   In many verbal idioms, such as **Klavier spielen, Deutsch sprechen, Pech haben, Auto fahren, einen Spaziergang machen, Rücksicht nehmen,** etc., what appears to be a direct object is actually felt to be a PREDICATE complement which expresses the major meaning of the verbal concept. It therefore moves to the end of the sentence field to occupy the V_2 position [→ predicate complements H 725 ff.].[1]

Spielt	*Fritz jeden Nachmittag zwei Stunden*	*Klavier?*
Nimm	*doch bitte auf mich*	*keine Rücksicht!*
Hat	*der Zug in Köln wirklich nur 3 Minuten*	*Aufenthalt?*
Schenkt	*dem Lehrer in der Schule immer*	*Aufmerksamkeit!*

H 036   The second part of the predicate may contain a combination of various elements. For examples, → H 120 ff.

H 040   For **dependent** (subordinate) clauses, the position otherwise filled by the first part of the predicate (V_1) at the anterior limit of the sentence field is occupied by a CONNECTING LINK (**C**), which indicates the function of the dependent clause and its relation to the main clause. Such connecting links are subordinating conjunctions [→ G 025 ff.], relative pronouns [→ D 500 ff.], relative adverbs [→ E 860 ff.], interrogative

---

[1] The distinction between a direct object and a verbal complement is not always easy to make and depends on a feeling for what constitutes a conceptual unit: *Er spricht seine Rolle sehr gut* (direct object). — *Er spricht sehr gut Deutsch* (verbal complement) [→ H 233].

480

pronouns [→ D 200 ff.], interrogative adverbs [→ E 870 ff.], and prepositions followed by interrogatives. The entire predicate is placed at the end of the sentence field, with the inflected part (V_1) following the uninflected part (V_2):

C . . . . Sentence Field		V (V_2 – V_1)
. . . , **weil**	*Hans heute abend ins Kino*	**geht.**
. . . , **da**	*er auch seine Schwester*	**mitbringt.**
. . . , **wenn**	*sie von mir Geld*	**haben will.**
. . . , **dessen**	*Vater in der Fabrik*	**gearbeitet hatte.**
. . . , **was**	*dir der Lehrer gestern in der Schule*	**gesagt hat.**
. . . , **wo**	*das Hotel zum Goldenen Löwen*	**zu finden ist.**
. . . , **von wem**	*du dieses Buch*	**bekommen hast.**
Wenn	*ich mit meiner Arbeit fertig*	**bin, . . .**
Da	*wir heute Besuch*	**bekommen werden, . . .**

Sentence Units Before and After the Sentence Field

It is possible for sentence units to occur outside the sentence field, either in the PREFIELD (before the sentence field, i.e. the first part of the predicate) or in the POSTFIELD (after the sentence field, i.e. the second part of the predicate). Each position may be occupied by only one sentence unit [→ H 065]. This sentence unit, in addition to the function which it normally fulfills within the sentence, plays an additional role: it either serves to establish interest, or it operates as a CONTACT UNIT with a preceding or following statement [→ H 705]. H 050

The Prefield

DECLARATIVE STATEMENTS normally have one sentence unit preceding the first part of the predicate.[1] This unit in the prefield of the sentence fulfills the function of a contact member with the preceding sentence of a connected utterance or discourse, or serves to arouse interest by referring to a particular concept. It neither loses its grammatical and H 051

---

[1] For declarative statements without a prefield, in which the finite part of the verb occupies a position of strong emphasis, → H 025.5.

logical function within the sentence, nor its claim to its normal position within the sentence field [→ H 710 ff.], to which it reverts if the sentence assumes a different form. The basic diagram of the regular declarative sentence or main clause is as follows:[1]

Prefield		Sentence Field
. . . .	V_1	. . . . (V_2)

In the illustrative examples below, the item in parentheses indicates the position which this particular sentence unit would assume if it were not located in the prefield.

Prefield	. . . .	Sentence Field . . . .
Hans	geht	(Hans) heute abend ins Kino.
Heute abend	geht	Hans (heute abend) ins Kino.
Ins Kino	geht	Hans heute abend (ins Kino).
Der Zug	kommt	(der Zug) um 5 Uhr in München **an.**
Um 5 Uhr	kommt	der Zug (um 5 Uhr) in München **an.**
In München	kommt	der Zug um 5 Uhr (in München) **an.**
Peter	hat	(Peter) seine Arbeit noch nicht **beendet.**
Seine Arbeit	hat	Peter (seine Arbeit) noch nicht **beendet.**
Noch	hat	Peter seine Arbeit (noch) nicht **beendet.**
Beendet	hat	Peter seine Arbeit noch nicht **(beendet).**
Er	will	(er) morgen mit mir nach Köln **fahren.**
Morgen	will	er (morgen) mit mir nach Köln **fahren.**
Mit mir	will	er morgen (mit mir) nach Köln **fahren.**
Nach Köln	will	er morgen mit mir (nach Köln) **fahren.**

H 052   As can be seen from the examples above, any sentence unit (other than the negation **nicht**)[2] may occupy the prefield. It is important to emphasize, however, that ONLY ONE SENTENCE UNIT may appear in that position, which is always followed by the first part of the predicate. Under no circumstances can two different sentence units occupy the prefield:

---

[1] It is important to realize that the so-called "inverted" word order (i.e. subject following the first part of the predicate) is really the **normal** German sequence. What traditional grammars have called "regular" word order occurs only if the subject occupies the prefield (see illustrative sentences). Most German sentences in fact do *not* begin with the subject.

[2] **Nicht** may appear in the prefield as part of a sentence unit but not as a complete sentence unit by itself: *Nicht oft hat man solch eine Gelegenheit.*

	Prefield	
English: He never works.	German: *Er*	*arbeitet nie.*
	Nie	*arbeitet er.*
English: Yesterday he came.	German: *Er*	*kam gestern.*
	Gestern	*kam er.*

If a declarative statement uses no contact unit, and puts no special emphasis on any part of the sentence, a non-stressed **es** occupies the prefield position, in order to give the sentence the form of the normal declarative statement. In such sentences, **es** merely serves as a filler or anticipatory unit, and fulfills no grammatical function. The verb therefore does not agree with **es**, but with the genuine subject of the sentence. **Es** immediately disappears if some other sentence unit assumes contact function or receives special emphasis, or if the sentence assumes a form other than that of a declarative statement: **H 053**

Prefield	. . . . Sentence Field		
Es	*kommen*	*dort viele Leute.*	
Dort	*kommen*	*viele Leute.*	
Es	*sind*	*gestern viele Besucher im Theater*	*gewesen.*
Gestern	*sind*	*viele Besucher im Theater*	*gewesen.*
Es	*ist*	*heute nicht viel*	*zu tun.*
—	*Ist*	*heute nicht viel*	*zu tun?*

The anticipatory **es** may not appear in the prefield, if the subject of the sentence is a personal pronoun:[1] **H 054**

> *Sie kommen dort.*
> *Wir sind gestern im Theater gewesen.*

In passive sentences without a subject [→ B 607], the anticipatory **es** must not be confused with a subject. The formal agreement with the personal form of the verb [→ H 275 ff.] is only apparent. **Es** again disappears as soon as some other sentence unit occupies the prefield: **H 055**

Prefield	. . . . Sentence Field		
Es	*wurde*	*im Café die ganze Nacht*	*getanzt.*
Die ganze Nacht	*wurde*	*im Café*	*getanzt.*
Es	*wird*	*hier nicht*	*geraucht.*
Hier	*wird*	*nicht*	*geraucht.*

[1] Note that English "It is I" corresponds to German *Ich bin es.*

483

H 056   If a subject clause [→ H 270 f.] occupies the postfield [→ H 070 ff.], the anticipatory **es** usually appears in the prefield:

Prefield	.... Sentence Field	Postfield
Es	*gefällt* *mir nicht,*	*daß ich am Sonnstag arbeiten muß.*
Es	*ist* *noch nicht bekannt,*	*wann der Minister ankommt.*
Es	*ist* *nicht gut für dich,*	*wenn du so viel rauchst.*
Es	*ist* *unmöglich gewesen,*	*die Arbeit zu beenden.*

H 057   The anticipatory **es** again disappears if the subject clause is moved from the sentence field (or the postfield) into the prefield:

Prefield	..... Sentence Field .....
Daß ich am Sonntag arbeiten muß,	*gefällt* *mir nicht.*
Wann der Minister ankommt,	*ist* *noch nicht bekannt.*

H 058   The personal form of the verb in the 3rd person singular in H 055 and H 056 is not actually in agreement [→ H 275 f.] with the anticipatory **es**, since **es** is not the subject of the sentence. The 3rd person singular is used even in sentences without a subject, because it is the only personal form which can also express indefinite concepts [→ *man sagt, man liest* D 750 ff.].

H 060   A COMMAND [→ H 008] may also have the form of a declarative statement:

Prefield	.... Sentence Field	
Jetzt	*gehst* *du zu deinem Vater!*	
Sie	*sollen* *morgen zum Direktor*	*kommen!*
Ihr	*bringt* *bitte eure Freunde*	*mit!*
Du	*wirst* *jetzt deine Schulaufgaben*	*machen!*

H 061   Clauses reporting a verbal statement indirectly (INDIRECT DISCOURSE) may also have the form of declarative statements, although grammatically and semantically they depend on the introductory main clause. (The conjunction **daß** is here omitted):

	Prefield	... Sentence Field ...	
Er erzählte mir,	*seine Schwester*	*sei* *jetzt Studentin*	*geworden.*
Ich glaube,	*er*	*hat* *die Wahrheit*	*gesagt.*

For INFORMATIONAL QUESTIONS [→ H 007], the interrogative pronoun, interrogative adverb, or interrogative phrase occupies the prefield of the sentence. The answer, however, is not normally placed in the prefield, but as close to the end of the sentence field as possible: H 062

Questions:

Prefield		.... Sentence Field......	
1. *Wen*	**willst**	*du morgen*	**besuchen?**
2. *Was*	**habt**	*ihr in Köln*	**getan?**
3. *Wann*	**kommt**	*der Zug hier*	**an?**
4. *In welcher Stadt*	**wohnt**	*Ihr Freund?*	

Answers:
1. (*Ich will morgen*) **meinen Freund** (*besuchen*).
2. (*Wir haben in Köln*) **das Münster besichtigt**.
3. (*Er kommt*) **um 7 Uhr 30** (*an*).
4. (*Er wohnt*) **in Berlin**.

Coordinating conjunctions (**und, aber, oder,** etc.), appellations (**Mutter, Herr Meyer,** etc.), exclamations (**ach, oje,** etc.), or words like **ja, nein, doch, bitte, danke,** etc., are NOT considered as part of the prefield and do not affect word order in any way. H 065

The Postfield

A further position for a sentence unit outside of the sentence field is in the POSTFIELD. All types of sentences may have one sentence unit appear in the postfield. H 070

Main Clause:

Prefield V₁ ...... Sentence Field ...... V₂   Postfield

Dependent Clause: [→ H 040]
C ..... Sentence Field ...... V₂ ... V₁   Postfield

Sentence units introduced by the conjunctions **als** or **wie** and the preposition **außer** often occupy the postfield: H 071

Prefield		.... Sentence Field		Postfield
In Italien	**blühen**	*die Blumen im Januar*		*wie bei uns im Mai.*
Ich	**habe**	*mit keinem anderem*	**gesprochen**	*als mit ihm.*
Niemandem	**will**	*ich aus dem Urlaub*	**schreiben**	*außer dir.*

485

H 072   A corrected or amended statement following either **nicht** or **sondern** also frequently appears in the postfield:

Prefield	.... Sentence Field			Postfield
Nicht heute	**wollen**	*wir ans Meer*	**fahren,**	*sondern morgen.*
Morgen	**wollen**	*wir ans Meer*	**fahren,**	*nicht heute.*
Nicht Peter	**hat**	*diesen Brief*	**geschrieben,**	*sondern ich.*
Ich	**habe**	*diesen Brief*	**geschrieben,**	*nicht Peter.*

H 073   Supplementary and additional statements, or sentence units which are intended to create a particular impression, are also occasionally found in the postfield:

Prefield	.... Sentence Field			Postfield
Ich	**habe**	*gestern noch im Büro*	**gearbeitet**	*bis spät in die Nacht.*
Nach München	**kommen**	*jedes Jahr viele Touristen,*		*besonders zum Oktoberfest.*

H 075   Dependent clauses [→ J 070 ff.] are also often found in the prefield or in the postfield. They may be complete clauses with their own subject, or infinitive clauses [→ B 910] without subject:[1]

Prefield	...... Sentence Field		
Als mein Freund auf dem Bahnhof ankam,[2]	**erwartete**	*ich ihn bereits.*	
Wenn du mir Geld gibst,[2]	**bringe**	*ich dir Zigaretten*	**mit.**
Daß es morgen regnen soll,[2]	**kann**	*ich nicht*	**glauben.**
Um die Prüfung zu bestehen,[2]	**muß**	*man viel*	**lernen.**

Prefield	...... Sentence Field			Postfield
Ich	**erwartete**	*meinen Freund,*		*als er auf dem Bahnhof ankam.*
Ich	**bringe**	*dir Zigaretten*	**mit,**	*wenn du mir Geld gibst.*
Ich	**kann**	*es nicht*	**glauben,**	*daß es morgen regnen soll.*
Man	**muß**	*viel*	**lernen,**	*um die Prüfung zu bestehen.*

H 076   Attributive (relative) clauses [→ J 145 ff.] occupy the postfield, if they modify the last sentence unit within the sentence field:

---

[1] Considered infinitive phrases in English.

[2] Note the sequence *verb — comma — verb* at the juncture of the two clauses. This is the characteristic feature of sentences with a dependent clause in the prefield.

Prefield ..... Sentence Field			Postfield

Er **sieht** *sich den Film* **an,**   *den wir ihm empfohlen haben.*

Ist *der Herr*   **gekommen,** *der gestern geschrieben hat?*

Note that subordinate clauses may have a postfield of their own: H 078

      Dependent Clause

.... Sentence Field ....   Postfield

Als Richard nach Deutschland kam, um Medizin zu studieren, |
     main clause
sprach er noch kein Wort Deutsch.

      Dependent Clause

.... Sentence Field .....   Postfield

Wenn du mir morgen hilfst, wie du mir versprochen hast, |
     main clause
werde ich dir immer dankbar sein.

LIMITS OF SENTENCE FIELD

The two parts of the predicate (V_1 and V_2), or the connecting link **C** and   H 100
the predicate **V**, form the ANTERIOR (front) and POSTERIOR (rear) LIMITS
of the sentence field [→ H 021 ff.]. They represent the stable positions
in the German sentence, and therefore determine the position and
sequence of all other sentence units.

The Predicate

The PREDICATE is the most essential functional unit of a sentence, and   H 110
includes all verbal forms of the sentence as well as many verbal complements. It fulfills three functions: 1) It describes the event or state of
being which the sentence expresses, and thus forms the SENTENCE CORE
[→ H 005 f.]. 2) It locates the situation with respect to time. 3) It
imparts to the sentence its grammatical form. The function of the
predicate is performed by verbs and other parts of speech acting as verb
complements [→ H 400 ff.].

Form of the Predicate

The predicate consists of at least one verb in the present or past (the so-   H 112
called "simple tenses"), in an INFLECTED form. Since verb inflections
(also called conjugations) are used to indicate tense and person,

487

inflected verb forms are also known as personal verb forms or finite verb forms — as opposed to nonfinite or nonpersonal forms, such as participles or infinitives.[1]

> *Ich habe (hatte) kein Geld.*
> *Er ist (war) bei mir.*
> *Willst (wolltest) du das Buch?*
> *Wir gehen (gingen) ins Kino.*
> *Es wird (wurde) kalt.*

H 113   Often the predicate is composed of two or more verb forms: a FINITE VERB (present or past) and a NONFINITE FORM. The finite verb constitutes the anterior limit, the nonfinite form the posterior limit of the sentence field in main clauses [→ **split predicate** H 020 ff., H 120 ff.]:

1. Auxiliary[2] + Past Participle: *Ich habe einen Brief geschrieben.*
   Er ist in die Schule gekommen.
   Das Essen wird um 12 Uhr serviert.
   Ich bin von Herrn Müller geschickt worden.[3]

2. Auxiliary + Infinitive: *Wir werden im Sommer nach Europa fahren.*
   Bis Montag werde ich das Buch gelesen haben.[4]
   Sie wird im Kino gewesen sein.[4]
   Er hat gestern leider nicht kommen können.[5]

3. Modal Verb[6] + Infinitive: *Wir wollen ins Theater gehen.*
   Sie kann damals 25 Jahre alt gewesen sein.
   Er muß meinen Brief schon bekommen haben.

---

[1] Do not confuse the term NONPERSONAL (i.e. uninflected) verb form with the concept of IMPERSONAL verbs (e.g. **regnen**); similarly, NONFINITE refers to several nonconjugated forms, of which the INFINITIVE is only one.

[2] The verbs **haben, sein,** and **werden** are called auxiliaries.

[3] A passive sentence in a perfect tense contains two past participles, of which the second one is **worden.**

[4] Forms like **gelesen haben** or **gewesen sein** are called "perfect infinitives."

[5] Modals and the verb **lassen** use so-called "double infinitives" in the perfect tenses.

[6] The verbs **dürfen, können, mögen, müssen, sollen,** and **wollen** are called modal auxiliaries or simply modals.

488

4. Other Verbs + Infinitive:[1] *Ich sehe die Kinder im Garten spielen.*
   Er geht heute Abend tanzen.
   Ihr lernt in der Schule schreiben.

5. Other Verbs + Prepositional *Du brauchst morgen nicht zu kommen.*
   Infinitive: *Ich wünsche nicht gestört zu werden.*[2]

6. Auxiliary + Prepositional *Er hatte den ganzen Tag nichts zu tun.*
   Infinitive: *Sie haben nur den Befehl zu befolgen!*
   Da ist nichts mehr zu machen.
   Diese Sätze sind nicht schwer zu verstehen.

7. Verb + Separable Prefix:[3] *Der Zug fährt pünktlich um 5 Uhr ab.*
   Ich trete meine neue Stellung am Montag an.
   Ich lernte gestern eine reizende junge Dame kennen.

In dependent clauses (subordinate clauses, attributive clauses, relative H 115
clauses) [→ J 070 ff., J 145 ff.], the connecting link C (conjunction,
relative pronoun, relative adverb, etc.) constitutes the anterior limit,
the predicate with all its verb forms the posterior limit of the sentence
field. Except for double infinitives [→ H 126–7], the finite (inflected)
form follows the nonfinite (unconjugated) verb form:

C		V
. . . . Sentence Field		
Weißt du, daß	*dein Freund gestern im Theater*	*gewesen ist?*
" , *wer*	*mich heute morgen zu Hause*	*besucht hat?*
" , *wohin*	*wir nächstes Jahr in den Ferien*	*fahren werden?*
Du weißt, daß	*ich nicht*	*gestört zu werden wünsche!*

[1] In English, such constructions may take simple infinitives, prepositional infinitives (with "to"), or present participles.

[2] Forms like **gestört zu werden** are called "passive infinitives."

[3] Other verb complements [→ H 035, H 400 ff., H 725 ff.] function like separable prefixes; in some instances (e.g. **maschineschreiben**) they have actually become part of the verb.

Position of the Various Predicate Parts

H 120 In independent clauses, the so-called MAIN CLAUSES, the personal form of the verb constitutes the first part of the predicate (V_1) and thus designates the anterior limit of the sentence field. For simple verb forms, the meaning of the predicate is thereby defined. In compound verb forms, this first part of the predicate is mainly a function indicator, carrying the conjugational endings and forms to indicate tense and person. The full meaning of the verb is indicated or specified by the second part of the predicate (V_2) which contains a nonfinite form (infinitive or past participle) or a verbal complement (separable prefix, etc.). This second part of the predicate constitutes the posterior limit of the sentence field:

Prefield	V_1	Sentence Field	V_2	
	(finite)		(nonfinite)	
Er	**kommt**	*morgen.*	—	
Er	**ist**	*gestern*	**gekommen.**	(Past Participle)
Er	**will**	*morgen*	**kommen.**	(Infinitive)
Er	**kommt**	*um 5 Uhr*	**an.**	(Complement)

H 121 If the second part of the predicate (V_2) consists of several verb forms, they are normally arranged in the following sequence:[1] VERB COMPLEMENT — PAST PARTICIPLE[2] — INFINITIVE[3] [but → H 130 ff.].

Prefield	V_1 ...	Sentence Field	V_2	
	(finite)		(nonfinite)	
Er	**hat**	*seinen Hut*	**ab·genommen.**[4]	(Complement — Past Participle)
Er	**wird**	*seinen Hut*	**ab·nehmen.**	(Complement — Infinitive)

[1] As the examples illustrate, the sequence is exactly the reverse of that followed in English. In order to rearrange the sequential pattern of nonfinite verb forms from German to English, it is necessary to begin at the end and work forward.

[2] In passive constructions, where there are two past participles, the participle of the main verb comes first, followed by **worden** (NOT *geworden*) as the past participial form of **werden**.

[3] This may be either a simple or a prepositional infinitive.

[4] The raised dot between the prefix and the verb stem (**ab·nehmen**) is merely a typographical device to separate the two functions. In writing, they constitute a single word.

490

Er	**kann**	*den Hut*	**genommen haben.**	(Past Participle — Infinitive)
Er	**muß**	*den Hut*	**ab·genommen haben.**	(Complement — Past Participle — Infinitive)
Der Hut	**ist**	*von ihm*	**genommen worden.**	(Past Participle — Past Participle)
Der Hut	**wird**	*von ihm*	**ab·genommen worden sein.**[1]	(Complement — Past Participle — Past Participle — Infinitive)

In the case of the perfect tenses of modals, the infinitive of the modal is used as a substitute for the past participle [→ B 996]. In these so-called double infinitive constructions, the modal infinitive occurs after the infinitive of the main verb:[2]   H 122

> Ich habe gestern nicht arbeiten können.

In unusual cases, the second part of the predicate may occupy the pre-field as a contact member [→ H 051], or for the sake of special emphasis or contrast: H 123

> **Gegeben** *habe ich ihm das Buch nicht; er hat es sich selbst genommen.*
> **Arbeiten** *sollen Sie hier, nicht herumspielen!*
> **Auf** *steigt der Strahl.*

In such constructions, predicate complements [→ H 400 ff.], which are part of the event or state of being which the sentence expresses, may occupy the prefield together with the second part of the predicate: H 124

> **Bankrott gemacht** *hat er nicht, aber in finanziellen Schwierigkeiten ist er doch.*
> **Ratschläge geben** *will er immer, aber selbst befolgt er keine.*

With simple predicates [→ H 023], the main verb which forms the first (and only) part of the predicate may also move into the prefield for reason of special emphasis. In such constructions, the verb must assume infinitive form, and the verb **tun** takes over the functional   H 125

---

[1] Unusual construction. For other dependent infinitives, → H 130 ff.

[2] Even though the substitute or participial infinitive here comes *after* the regular infinitive, German word order is still the exact reverse of that used in English.

491

purpose (i.e. personal inflection, tense) of the first part of the predicate:[1]

> *Lieben **tut** er sie nicht, aber er hat sie gern.*
> *Arbeiten **tue** ich nicht gerne, sondern lieber faulenzen.*
> *Ansehen **täte** ich mir den Film schon, wenn ich nur genug Geld hätte.*

H 126   In DEPENDENT CLAUSES [→ J 070 ff. and J 145 ff.], where the entire predicate forms the posterior limit of the sentence field, the parts of the verb are arranged in the following sequence: Verb Complement — Past Participle — Infinitive — Finite Verb:[2]

Connector	Sentence Field	Predicate
..., *daß*	*er den Hut*	*nimmt*
..., *daß*	*er den Hut*	*ab·nimmt*
..., *daß*	*er den Hut*	*genommen hat*
..., *daß*	*er den Hut*	*nehmen will*
..., *daß*	*er den Hut*	*ab·genommen hat*
..., *daß*	*er den Hut*	*ab·nehmen wird*
..., *daß*	*er den Hut*	*genommen haben muß*
..., *daß*	*er den Hut*	*ab·genommen haben kann*
..., *daß*	*der Hut von ihm*	*ab·genommen worden ist*[3]

H 127   If the predicate of the dependent clause contains a double infinitive, i.e. the infinitive of a main verb and the infinitive of a modal acting as a substitute for the past participle [→ B 996, H 122], the finite form stands at the beginning of the multiple predicate:[3]

> ..., *daß er den Hut **hat nehmen wollen***
> ..., *daß er den Hut **hat ab·nehmen müssen***

H 128   Predicate complements [→ H 400 ff.] in dependent clauses are enclosed between the finite verb and the double infinitive:[3]

> ..., *ob er sich **wird zur Verfügung stellen wollen**.*
> ..., *daß er dem Kranken **hätte Hilfe leisten sollen**.*
> ..., *weil er sich nicht **habe gut benehmen können**.*
> ..., *daß er damals **habe Wort halten müssen**.*
> ..., *daß sie sofort **haben die Flucht ergreifen wollen**.*

---

[1] Similarly, in substandard colloquial usage and in certain poetic expressions, **tun** may constitute the first part of the predicate (V₁) with the main verb in the infinitive at the posterior limit of the sentence field (V₂): *Vor allen Gefahren **tut** er uns **bewahren**. Ich **tät'** lieber fleißiger **arbeiten**, wenn ich an Ihrer Stell' wär'!*

[2] All footnotes to H 121 apply to dependent clauses as well.

[3] These constructions are somewhat clumsy, and are generally avoided, especially in colloquial usage.

Predicate with Dependent Infinitives

Verbs in the infinitive may occur in a sentence in a function other than that of the predicate itself [→ B 950, 955, 970]. These are called DEPENDENT INFINITIVES. If the predicate consists only of a finite verb and such a dependent infinitive, the infinitive occupies the posterior limit of the sentence field (V_2):   H 130

> *Meine Mutter* **geht** *jeden Vormittag* **einkaufen.**
> *Er* **blieb** *vor der Tür* **stehen.**
> **Komm** *mit uns Kaffee* **trinken!**
> **Siehst** *du den Vogel dort* **fliegen?**
> *Wir* **hörten** *das Mädchen ein fröhliches Lied* **singen.**

If the second part of the predicate contains some other verb form, the dependent infinitive stands at the end of the sentence field before the second part of the predicate. The following examples will illustrate various possibilities.[1]   H 131

Verb in the predicate in the **present** or **past** tense (MAIN and DEPENDENT CLAUSES):   H 132

Er **geht**	*heute*	**tanzen.**
. . . , ***daß***	*er heute*	**tanzen** *geht.*
Er **sieht**	*Karl*	**kommen.**
. . . , ***daß***	*er Karl*	**kommen** *sieht.*
Er **ließ**	*das Buch*	**liegen.**
. . . , ***daß***	*er das Buch*	**liegen** *ließ.*
Er **brauchte**	*heute nicht*	***zu*** **kommen.**
. . . , ***daß***	*er heute nicht*	***zu*** **kommen** *brauchte.*

Verb in the predicate in the **present perfect** or **past perfect** (MAIN CLAUSES):   H 133

Er **ist**	*heute*	**tanzen** *gegangen.*
Er **hat**	*Karl*	**kommen** *sehen.*[2]
Er **hatte** *das Buch*		**liegen** *lassen.*[2]
Er **hätte** *heute nicht*		***zu*** **kommen** *brauchen.*[2]

---

[1] Except for double infinitives in dependent clauses, the principle that the German verb sequence is the exact reverse of English word order still applies.

[2] The verbs **sehen, hören, lassen, helfen, lehren, lernen heißen** (in the sense of "to bid") and **brauchen** form double infinitives in the perfect tenses (**brauchen** usually with a prepositional infinitive) [→ B 468, 996]. With **sehen** and **lassen** the past participle occurs colloquially (*. . . kommen gesehen, . . . liegen gelassen*), but is considered inelegant. With **hören**, either the infinitive or the past participle may be used: *Ich habe ihn singen* **hören** (*singen* **gehört**). With **helfen, lehren,** and **lernen,** the past participle is preferred by most speakers. *Ich habe ihm die Koffer tragen geholfen.* **Heißen** occurs very infrequently.

H 134   Verb in the predicate in the **future** (MAIN CLAUSES):[1]

Er wird heute	**tanzen** *gehen.*
Er wird Karl	**kommen** *sehen.*
Er wird das Buch	**liegen** *lassen.*
Er wird heute nicht	*zu* **kommen** *brauchen.*

H 135   In a DEPENDENT CLAUSE in the **present perfect, past perfect,** or **future,**[2] the dependent infinitive precedes all other elements in the second part of the predicate, with the finite verb coming last.

With verbs using double infinitives, however [→ H 133], the finite verb form precedes the other predicate elements in the perfect tenses.

. . . , daß er heute	**tanzen** *gegangen ist.*	
. . . , daß er Karl	***hat*** **kommen** *sehen.*	(Double infinitive)
. . . , daß er Karl	**kommen** *gesehen* ***hat.***	
. . . , daß er das Buch	***hatte*** **liegen** *lassen.*	(Double infinitive)
. . . , daß er das Buch	**liegen** *gelassen* ***hatte.***	
. . . , daß er heute nicht	***hätte*** *zu* **kommen** *brauchen.*	(Double infinitive)
. . . , daß er heute	**tanzen** *gehen wird.*	
. . . , daß er Karl	**kommen** *sehen wird.*	
. . . , daß er das Buch	**liegen** *lassen wird.*	
. . . , daß er heute nicht	*zu* **kommen** *brauchen wird.*	

H 136   For PASSIVE CONSTRUCTIONS in the **present tense, past tense, present perfect,** and **past perfect,** the basic principles of H 131 ff. apply for both MAIN CLAUSES and DEPENDENT CLAUSES:

Das Buch **wird** *(***wurde***) von ihm*	**liegen** *gelassen.*
. . . , daß das Buch von ihm	**liegen** *gelassen* **wird** *(***wurde***).*
Das Buch **ist** *(***war***) von ihm*	**liegen** *gelassen worden.*
. . . , daß das Buch von ihm	**liegen** *gelassen worden* **ist** *(***war***).*

H 137   For PASSIVE CONSTRUCTIONS in the **future tense,**[3] the basic principles of

---

[1] Future perfect constructions are rare: *Er wird gestern tanzen gegangen sein* [→ H 150].

[2] Again, the future perfect occurs rarely: *. . . , daß er tanzen gegangen sein wird.* It usually expresses a supposition and has subjective meaning [→ H 150].

[3] Future perfect passive sentences are almost exclusively theoretic constructions: *Das Buch* **wird** *von ihm* **liegen** *gelassen worden sein. Er sagt, daß das Buch von ihm* **liegen** *gelassen worden sein wird* [→ H 151].

H 131 ff. apply for main clauses. In dependent clauses, the finite form of the verb may occur either at the beginning or at the end of the multiple predicate:

Das Buch **wird** *von ihm*	**liegen** *gelassen werden.*
... , *daß das Buch von ihm*	**liegen** *gelassen werden wird.*
... , *daß das Buch von ihm* **wird**	**liegen** *gelassen werden.*

If MODAL VERBS in OBJECTIVE STATEMENTS [→ B 631] in the **present** or **past** tense are used with a dependent infinitive, this dependent infinitive is the first element in the second part of the predicate, and is followed by the infinitive to which the modal refers. In a dependent clause, the modal verb appears at the very end: [1]

H 140

Er **will** (**wollte**) *heute*	**tanzen** *gehen.*
Er **kann** (**konnte**) *Karl*	**kommen** *sehen.*
Er **muß** (**mußte**) *das Buch*	**liegen** *lassen.*
... , *daß er heute*	**tanzen** *gehen will* (*wollte*).
... , *daß er Karl*	**kommen** *sehen kann* (*konnte*).
... , *daß er das Buch*	**liegen** *lassen muß* (*mußte*).

If MODAL VERBS in OBJECTIVE STATEMENTS [→ B 631] in the **present perfect** or **past perfect** are used with dependent infinitives, the modal infinitive (as a substitute for the past participle) always occurs at the very end. In dependent clauses, the finite verb form precedes all other parts of the multiple predicate [→ H 127]:

H 141

Er **hat** *heute*	**tanzen** *gehen wollen.*
Er **hat** *Karl*	**kommen** *sehen können.*
Er **hat** *das Buch*	**liegen** *lassen müssen.*
... , *daß er heute*	**hat** **tanzen** *gehen wollen.*
... , *daß er Karl*	**hat** **kommen** *sehen können.*
... , *daß er das Buch* **hat**	**liegen** *lassen müssen.*

If MODAL VERBS in OBJECTIVE STATEMENTS [→ B 631] in the **future tense** [2] are used with dependent infinitives, the modal infinitive also occurs at

H 142

---

[1] Again, the verbal sequence is the exact reverse of English word order.

[2] Once again, the future perfect is listed only for the sake of theoretic completeness: *Er* **wird** *heute* **tanzen** *gehen wollen haben.* Such a construction, however, would never occur in actual usage.

the very end. In dependent clauses, the finite verb again precedes all other parts of the multiple predicate:

*Er **wird** heute*	**tanzen** *gehen wollen.*
*Er **wird** Karl*	**kommen** *sehen können.*
*Er **wird** das Buch*	**liegen** *lassen müssen.*

*. . . , **daß** er heute*	***wird** tanzen gehen wollen.*
*. . . , **daß** er Karl*	***wird** kommen sehen können.*
*. . . , **daß** er das Buch **wird** liegen lassen müssen.*	

H 143 If MODAL VERBS in an OBJECTIVE STATEMENT are used in a PASSIVE CON-STRUCTION in the **present** or **past** tense with a dependent infinitive, the so-called passive infinitive [→ B 451 f.] of the verb to which the modal refers occurs at the end of the main clause. In the dependent clause, the finite form of the modal verb comes last:

> *Das Buch **muß** (**mußte**) (von ihm) **liegen** gelassen werden.*
> *, . . . **daß** das Buch (von ihm)   **liegen** gelassen werden **muß** (**mußte**).*

H 144 If MODAL VERBS in an OBJECTIVE STATEMENT are used in a PASSIVE con-struction in the **present perfect** or **past perfect** with a dependent infinitive, the modal infinitive always occurs at the very end. In a dependent clause, the finite form of the helping verb precedes all other parts of the multiple predicate:[1]

> *Das Buch **hat** (von ihm)   **liegen** gelassen werden müssen.*
> *. . . , **daß** das Buch (von ihm) **hat** liegen gelassen werden müssen.*

H 145 The same principle also applies to MODAL verbs in OBJECTIVE statements in **future** PASSIVE constructions with a dependent infinitive:[2]

> *Das Buch **wird** (von ihm)   **liegen** gelassen werden müssen.*
> *. . . , **daß** das Buch (von ihm) **wird** liegen gelassen werden müssen.*

H 148 If MODAL VERBS in SUBJECTIVE STATEMENTS [→ B 632] are used in the **present** or **past** tense with dependent infinitives to refer to past events, the *past infinitive* [→ B 451 f.] of the verb to which the modal refers

---

[1] Such constructions are clumsy and are usually avoided, as are those in H 145.

[2] A modal in the future perfect passive with a dependent infinitive is an utterly fantastic construction: *Das Buch **wird** (von ihm) **liegen** gelassen worden sein müssen.* [→ H 149, 150 for subjective statement.]

496

comes at the end of the sentence field of main clauses. In dependent clauses, the finite form of the modal comes last:

*Er **mag** heute*	**tanzen**	*gegangen sein.*
*Er **will** Karl*	**kommen** *gesehen haben.*	
*Er **muß** das Buch*	**liegen**	*gelassen haben.*
*. . . , **daß** er heute*	**tanzen**	*gegangen sein mag.*
*. . . , **daß** er Karl*	**kommen** *gesehen haben will.*	
*. . . , **daß** er das Buch* **liegen**	*gelassen haben muß.*	

If MODAL verbs are used in SUBJECTIVE statements in the **present** or **past** tense to express a PASSIVE construction referring to past events, involving dependent infinitives, the *past perfect infinitive* [→ B 451 f.] constitutes the posterior limit of the sentence field in main clauses, following the dependent infinitive. In dependent clauses, the finite form of the modal comes at the end: **H 149**

> *Das Buch **muß** von ihm*   **liegen** *gelassen worden sein.*[1]
> *, . . . , **daß** das Buch von ihm* **liegen** *gelassen worden sein muß.*

If the auxiliary **werden** in the present tense is used in a SUBJECTIVE statement [→ presumption B 565] together with a dependent infinitive to refer to a past event, the *past infinitive* appears at the end of main clauses, followed by the finite form of **werden** in dependent clauses: **H 150**

*Er **wird** heute*	**tanzen**	*gegangen sein.*
*Er **wird** Karl*	**kommen** *gesehen haben.*	
*Er **wird** das Buch*	**liegen**	*gelassen haben.*
*. . . , **daß** er heute*	**tanzen**	*gegangen sein wird.*
*. . . , **daß** er Karl*	**kommen** *gesehen haben wird.*	
*. . . , **daß** er das Buch* **liegen**	*gelassen haben wird.*	

If the auxiliary **werden** in the present tense is used in a SUBJECTIVE statement to refer to a past event in the passive voice, together with a dependent infinitive, the *past passive infinitive* appears at the end of main clauses, followed by the finite form of **werden** in the dependent clause:[1]   **H 152**

> *Das Buch **wird** von ihm*   **liegen** *gelassen worden sein.*
> *. . . , **daß** das Buch von ihm* **liegen** *gelassen worden sein wird.*

---

[1] Note the difference in meaning: Objective — The book had to be left there (i.e. he had no choice); Subjective — The book must have been left there by him (i.e. I am making an assumption).

TABLE OF PREDICATE SEQUENCES

H 155 **List of Abbreviations:**

C	Connector (conjunction, relative pronoun, etc.)
F_v	Finite form of main verb
F_a	Finite form of auxiliary (**haben** or **sein**)
F_h	Finite form of **haben**
F_s	Finite form of **sein**
F_w	Finite form of **werden**
F_m	Finite form of modal
Pr	Separable prefix (or other verb complement)
P.P.	Past participle
I	Infinitive of main verb
I_a	Infinitive of auxiliary (**haben** or **sein**)
I_h	Infinitive of **haben**
I_s	Infinitive of **sein**
I_w	Infinitive of **werden**
I_m	Infinitive of modal
Dp.I.	Dependent infinitive
S.I.	Substitute infinitive (**lassen, sehen,** etc., used instead of past participle)
wd	**worden**
Pres	present
Pft	perfect (present and past perfect have identical sequence)
Fut	future
Obj	objective statement
Sub	subjective statement

Single Verb

H 160   1. ACTIVE VOICE

	Main Clause [H 120–1]	Dependent Clause [H 126]
Pres⎱ Past⎰	F_v .... Pr	C .... Pr — F_v
Pft	F_a .... Pr — P.P.	C .... Pr — P.P. — F_a
Fut	F_w .... Pr — I	C .... Pr — I — F_w
Fut Pft	F_w .... Pr — P.P. — I_a	C .... Pr — P.P. — I_a — F_w

498

2. PASSIVE VOICE

	Main Clause [H 120–1]	Dependent Clause [H 126]
Pres ⎞ Past ⎠	F_w . . . . Pr — P.P.	C . . . . Pr — P.P. — F_w
Pft	F_s . . . . Pr — P.P. — wd	C . . . . Pr — P.P. — wd — F_s
Fut	F_w . . . . Pr — P.P. — I_w	C . . . . Pr — P.P. — I_w — F_w
Fut Pft	F_w . . . . Pr — P.P. — wd — I_s	C . . . . Pr — P.P. — wd — I_s — F_w

Single Verb and Modal

1. ACTIVE VOICE

	Main Clause [H 122]	Dependent Clause [H 126–7]
Pres ⎞ Past ⎠	F_m . . . . Pr — I	C . . . . Pr — I — F_m
Pft Obj [1]	F_h . . . . Pr — I — I_m	C . . . . F_h — Pr — I — I_m
Pft Sub [1]	F_m . . . . Pr — P.P. — I_a	C . . . . Pr — P.P. — I_a — F_m
Fut	F_w . . . . Pr — I — I_m	C . . . . F_w — Pr — I — I_m
Fut Pft [2]	F_w . . . . Pr — P.P. — I_h — I_m	C . . . . F_w — Pr — P.P. — I_h — I_m

2. PASSIVE VOICE

	Main Clause [H 122]	Dependent Clause [H 126–7]
Pres ⎞ Past ⎠	F_m . . . . Pr — P.P. — I_w	C . . . . Pr — P.P. — I_w — F_m
Pft Obj [1]	F_h . . . . Pr — P.P. — I_w — I_m	C . . . . F_h — Pr — P.P. — I_w — I_m
Pft Sub [1]	F_m . . . . . . Pr — P.P. — wd — I_s	C . . . . Pr — P.P. — wd — I_s — F_m
Fut	F_w . . . . . . Pr — P.P. — I_w — I_m	C . . . . F_w — Pr — P.P. — I_w — I_m
Fut Pft [2]	F_w . . Pr — P.P. — wd — I_s — I_m	C . F_w — Pr — P.P. — wd — I_s — I_m

[1] Note the difference between the objective perfect (e.g. *Er hat den Brief schreiben müssen —* he had to write the letter) and the subjective perfect (e.g. *Er muß den Brief geschrieben haben* — he must have written the letter). → B 630–2.

[2] The future perfect is extremely rare and usually has subjective meaning (e.g. *Er wird den Brief geschrieben haben müssen*).

Verbs with Dependent Infinitives[1]

H 170   1. ACTIVE VOICE [→ H 132–5]

	Main Clause	Dependent Clause
Pres⎫ Past⎭ Pft[2] Fut[3]	F_v .... Dp.I. ⎧F_a .... Dp.I. — P.P. ⎩F_h .... Dp.I. — S.I. F_w .... Dp.I. — I	C .... Dp.I. — F_v ⎧C .... Dp.I. — P.P. — F_a ⎩C .... F_h — Dp.I. — S.I. C .... Dp.I. — I — F_w

H 171   Modal Constructions in Objective Statements [H 140–2]

	Main Clause	Dependent Clause
Pres⎫ Past⎭ Pft Fut	F_m .... Dp.I. — I F_h .... Dp.I. — I — I_m F_w .... Dp.I. — I — I_m	C .... Dp.I. — I — F_m C .... F_h — Dp.I. — I — I_m C .... F_w — Dp.I. — I — I_m

H 172   Modal Construction in Subjective Statement (Action in Past) [H 148]

	Main Clause	Dependent Clause
Pres⎫ Past⎭	F_m .... Dp.I. — P.P. — I_a	C ..... Dp.I. — P.P. — I_a — F_m

H 173   **Werden** in Subjective Statement (Action in Past) [H 150]

	Main Clause	Dependent Clause
Pres	F_w .... Dp.I. — P.P. — I_a	C ..... Dp.I. — P.P. — I_a — F_w

[1] For the sake of simplification, prefixes are no longer included in these tables. Their position corresponds to that in H 160–166.

[2] S.I. used instead of participle for **lassen, sehen,** etc. ⌊→ H 133]

[3] Future perfect forms are not listed; → H 173 for subjective use of **werden** (supposition) in active voice, H 178 in passive voice.

500

2. PASSIVE VOICE [H 136–7]

	Main Clause	Dependent Clause
Pres⎱ Past⎰	F_w .... Dp.I. — P.P.	C ....Dp.I. — P.P. — F_w
Pft	F_s .... Dp.I. — P.P. — wd	C ..... Dp.I. — P.P. — wd — F_s
Fut[1]	F_w .... Dp.I. — P.P. — I_w	⎰C...... Dp.I. — P.P. — I_w — F_w ⎱C...... F_w — Dp.I. — P.P. — I_w

Modal Constructions in Objective Statements [H 143–5]

	Main Clause	Dependent Clause
Pres⎱ Past⎰	F_m .... Dp.I. — P.P. — I_w	C ..... Dp.I. — P.P. — I_w — F_m
Pft	F_h ..... Dp.I. — P.P. — I_w — I_m	C .. F_h — Dp.I. — P.P. — I_w — I_m
Fut	F_w ..... Dp.I. — P.P. — I_w — I_m	C ... F_w — Dp.I. — P.P. — I_w — I_m

Modal Constructions in Subjective Statements (Action in Past) [H 149]

	Main Clause	Dependent Clause
Pres⎱ Past⎰	F_m .... Dp.I. — P.P. — wd — I_s	C ... Dp.I. — P.P. — wd — I_s — F_m

Werden in Subjective Statements (Action in Past) [H 152]

Pres	F_w .... Dp.I. — P.P. — wd — I_s	C .. Dp.I. — P.P. — wd — I_a — F_w

Note that in dependent clauses the finite (personal) form stands before H 180
all other parts of the predicate with substitute infinitives in the present
or past perfect, and with modal infinitives in objective statements in the
present or past perfect and in the future. (See tables.)

[1] → H 137 for two alternate forms in dependent clause.

TYPES OF SENTENCE UNITS

⸙ Introduction

H 200   Each sentence describes a situation, the core of which is an event (action or process) or a state of being (condition). Within the grammatical structure of the sentence, this core has the function of the predicate.

H 201   In German, the part of speech used to express the predicate is the verb and its complements. Form and meaning of the verb must therefore indicate the nature of the situation within the context of the sentence.

H 202   In order to complete the description of a situation, it is necessary to identify the living beings, things, or concepts which take part in the event or state of being and without which the situation is not possible. These persons, things, or concepts are the AGENTS within the situation, and appear in the sentence as functional sentence units which are called SUBJECT or OBJECT.

H 203   For an event, up to three agents are possible (one subject and two objects), the exact number depending upon the type of event described. For a state of being, however, only one agent is possible: the subject.[1]

1. Subject – Object

H 210   Among agents, we distinguish between SUBJECT and OBJECTS. This differentiation has both a formal and a functional basis.

H 212   The **subject** is the sentence unit which originates the action or condition indicated by the verb. In form, it must agree with the finite (personal, inflected, conjugated) part of the verb in the predicate [→ H 275]. It differs from the object through its NOMINATIVE form.[2] We inquire after the subject with the interrogative **wer?** for persons or **was?** for things or concepts [→ H 250]:

[1] Except for sentences with no explicit subject: *Mir ist kalt. Mich friert.*

[2] The nominative may also occur as a predicate complement, the so-called predicate nominative [→ H 406]: *Dieses Haus ist **ein Hotel**.*

502

Events: *Mein Vater arbeitet in seinem Büro.* (Action)
       Die Sonne geht in dieser Jahreszeit um 5 Uhr auf. (Process)

States of Being: *Die Kinder schlafen in ihren Betten.*
       Die Läden sind am Sonntag geschlossen.

An event may have one or two agents other than the subject. These are   H 213
called **objects**; their number is determined by the nature of the event.
The object indicates the living being, thing, or concept to which the
predicate refers. The form of the object depends on the verb which
performs the predicate function. Objects may be characterized by the
accusative, the dative, the genitive, or a preposition.

We therefore distinguish four types of objects: H 215

      Accusative Object [→ H 325]:

          *Ich sehe **einen Mann**.*   Question: *wen?*
          *Er bringt **einen Brief**.*   Question: *was?*

      Dative Object [→ H 350]:

          *Er dankt **seinem Vater**.*   Question: *wem?*

      Genitive Object [→ H 380]:

          *Wir gedachten **des Dichters**.*   Question: *wessen?*

      Prepositional Object [→ H 390]:

          *Ich denke **an meinen Vater**.*   Question: *an wen?*
          *Ich denke **an meine Arbeit**.*   Question: *woran?*

2. Predicate Complements

Because of the large variety of events and states of being, as well as the   H 220
need of describing these as exactly or vividly as possible, the number of
verbs available to a language does not suffice by itself to fulfill the
predicate function [→ H 110] in its complete extent. Therefore, the
task of describing the events or states of being in detail is often taken
over by other sentence units acting as PREDICATE COMPLEMENTS, since
these sentence units with their greater possibilities of variety are better
suited to the description of different aspects of a situation than the
formally rather rigid predicate. Such predicate complements are part
of the sentence core [→ H 003].

H 221   In a sentence with a predicate complement, the task of defining the sentence field [→ H 020 ff.] remains within the predicate, with the predicate complement acting as the first unit within the posterior limit of the sentence field [→ H 031 ff.].[1]

H 222   Predicate complements may be distinguished according to their CONTENT:

Complement of place [→ H 420]:

*Mein Freund wohnt **in einem Hotel**.*   Question: *wo?*

Complement of time [→ H 430]:

*Das Fest dauerte **bis zum Morgen**.*   Question: *wie lange?*

Complement of manner [→ H 440]:

*Die Kinder benahmen sich **schlecht**.*   Question: *wie?*

Complement of cause [→ H 455]:

*Das Feuer entstand **durch Leichtsinn**.*   Question: *warum?*
wodurch?

according to their CASE FORM:

Predicate nominative [→ H 460]:

*Dieses Haus ist **ein Hotel**.*   Question: *wer? was?*

Predicate accusative [→ H 470]:

*Sie nennt ihn **ihren Freund**.*   Question: *wie? was?*

or according to their GRAMMATICAL FUNCTION in the sentence:

Predicate subject [→ H 475]:

*Heute findet hier **ein Konzert** statt.*   Question: *was?*

Predicate object [→ H 480]:

*Der Zug hat hier **keinen Aufenthalt**.*   Question: *was?*

H 223   Predicate complements may be nouns, pronouns, adjectives, adverbs, prepositional phrases, or subordinate clauses [→ H 410 ff.].

---

[1] Nonconjugated verb parts follow the predicate complement [→ H 222]; *Mein Freund wird **in einem Hotel** wohnen. Das Fest dauerte **bis zum Morgen** an. Die Kinder haben sich **schlecht** benommen.*

3. Predicate Modifiers

A sentence may also contain one or several sentence units beyond those   H 230
functional units which are essential for the description of the situation.
These additional sentence units contain information about the CIRCUM-
STANCES under which the situation takes place, or about persons who
are affected by the situation or have an influence upon it.

Since these units are not absolutely essential for the description of   H 231
the situation, but add supplementary information which modifies the
situation in various ways, they are called PREDICATE MODIFIERS. They
can be distinguished according to their CONTENT:

Modifier of place [→ H 571]:

> *Ich will **in Berlin** meinen Freund
> besuchen.*   Question: ***wo?***

Modifier of time [→ H 575]:

> *Wir haben **heute** einen Brief
> geschrieben.*   Question: ***wann?***

Modifier of manner [→ H 580]:

> *Der Zug fährt **langsam** in den
> Bahnhof ein.*   Question: ***wie?***

Modifier of cause [→ H 590]:

> *Wir blieben **wegen des schlechten
> Wetters** zu Hause.*   Question: ***warum?***

Modifier of person [→ H 556 ff.]:

> *Ich hebe **dir** die Zeitung bis morgen
> auf.*   Question: ***wem?***
> *Komme **mir** nicht zu spät nach   ***für wen?***
> Hause!*
>
> *Hans schreibt **seinem Freund** einen
> Brief an die Universität.*
>
> *Ich gehe **für dich** zur Post.*

Modifiers of place, time, manner, and cause may be adverbs or preposi-   H 232
tional phrases. Modifiers of person may be nouns, pronouns, or
prepositional phrases.

505

H 233   The distinction between modifiers and predicate complements is not always easy to make. The basic principle is that a predicate complement adds an essential component to the statement, without which the sentence would be grammatically incomplete, while a modifier merely provides grammatically unessential additional information: *Mein Freund wohnt in Berlin* — predicate complement. (*Mein Freund wohnt* is not a complete sentence.) *Ich besuche meinen Freund in Berlin* — modifier. (*Ich besuche meinen Freund* is a complete sentence.) Modifiers are located within the sentence field [→ H 020 ff.] or in the prefield.

H 235   A special type of modifiers are the so-called INTENSIFIERS or PARTICLES, which do not describe the situation or the accompanying circumstances, but characterize the SUBJECTIVE ATTITUDE of the speaker [→ H 600 ff.]:

> *Ich gehe ja. — Was machst du denn?*

SUBJECT AND OBJECT

The Subject

H 250   The SUBJECT [→ H 212] performs the following operations within the situational context of a sentence:

H 251   For ACTIONS [→ H 006] the subject designates the AGENT (i.e. living being) which causes the action to happen:

> *Der Gärtner verbrennt die alten Sträuche.*
> *Ein Dieb hat das Geld gestohlen.*
> *Der Hund bellt.*
> *Herr Müller fährt den Wagen in die Garage.*

H 252   For PROCESSES [→ H 006], the subject designates the CAUSE of the event, i.e. the thing or concept which brings about the process:

> *Das Feuer vernichtet den Wald.*
> *Die Sonne geht morgens um 5 Uhr auf.*
> *Der Pfeil hat das Ziel getroffen.*
> *Die Maschine stellt in der Stunde Tausende von Zigaretten her.*

H 253   The subject may also indicate the person, thing, or concept which is included in the process or with which the process is concerned:

506

Das Feuer brennt.
Das Wasser kocht.
Die alten Sträucher brennen.
Die Sträucher werden verbrannt.
Der Dieb wurde verhaftet.
Hans hat heute einen Brief bekommen.
Ich habe gestern meinen Freund getroffen.

For STATES of BEING, the subject designates a person, thing, or concept   H 254
to which a certain characteristic or attribute is ascribed or which is found
to be in a certain condition or state:

Peter ist mein Freund.
Herr Müller ist Arzt.
Die Blumen blühen.
Die Tür schließt schlecht.
Das Holz ist verbrannt.
Das Kind war krank.
Wir sind zu Hause.

Form of the Subject

The subject may be a noun (proper name or common noun) or pronoun,   H 255
or words belonging to other parts of speech which are treated as nouns.[1]

PROPER NAMES: H 256

Hans hat heute einen Brief bekommen.
Herr Müller ist Arzt.
Tante Marie kam uns gestern besuchen.
Amerika wurde 1492 von Kolumbus entdeckt.

COMMON NOUNS: H 257

Der Schüler schreibt einen Brief.
Die Kinder spielen im Garten.
Der Direktor und *der Ingenieur* gehen durch die Fabrik.
Die Großeltern, die Eltern und *die Kinder* sitzen im Zimmer.
Das Feuer brennt.
Pünktlichkeit ist eine Tugend.

---

[1] These nouns or pronouns may of course be extended by attributes [→ J 100 ff.].

PRONOUNS

Ich fahre nächste Woche nach Wien.
Ihr arbeitet im Büro.
Fahren Sie mit dem Auto?
Karl braucht Geld, denn er will eine Reise machen.
Wer hat heute telefoniert?
Was steht dort auf dem Tisch?
Einer von euch könnte mir helfen.
Das gefällt mir nicht.
Man wandert im Sommer viel.
Keiner blieb zu Hause.
Beide Hüte sind schön, aber dieser gefällt mir am besten.

H 259   Other parts of speech used as nouns:

1. ADJECTIVES:

Der Alte ist schon seit Wochen krank.
Das Blau des südlichen Himmels fasziniert die Touristen.

2. NUMERALS:

Die Drei ist eine Glückszahl.
Alle fünf waren gestern im Kino.

3. POSSESSIVES:

Die Seinen (i.e. his family) *wollten ihn besuchen.*

4. VERBS *in the* INFINITIVE:[1]

Das Rauchen ist ungesund.
Reden ist Silber, Schweigen ist Gold.

5. ADVERBS:

Mich interessiert nur das Heute und nicht das Morgen.

6. PREPOSITIONS:

Das Auf und Ab der Preise ist kein gutes Zeichen für die Wirtschaft.

---

[1] If the infinitive is modified by some other element, it becomes an infinitive clause [→ B 903] which in its entirety acts as the subject [→ subject clause H 270]: *Starken Kaffee zu trinken*, (*Das Trinken starken Kaffees*) *ist der Gesundheit schädlich.*

7. CONJUNCTIONS:

> *Das ständige **Wenn** und **Aber** dieses Mannes gefällt mir nicht.*

8. LETTERS *of the* ALPHABET:

> ***Das A** und **O** des Lernens ist die Wiederholung.*
> ***Das Z** ist der letzte Buchstabe des Alphabets.*

9. PHRASES:

> ***Das Vergißmeinnicht** ist eine schöne Blume.*
> ***Ein Taugenichts** (**ein Tunichtgut**) wird im Leben keinen Erfolg haben.*

All parts of the sentence which define the subject more closely or which depend on the subject are considered part of the subject. They are either ATTRIBUTES [→ J 100 ff.] or phrases in APPOSITION [→ J 137]. Attributes may either follow or precede the subject; phrases in apposition always follow: H 260

> ***Dieser junge Mann** hat gestern einen Unfall gehabt.*
> ***Der Vater dieses kleinen Mädchens** ist ein reicher Kaufmann.*
> ***Der soeben einfahrende Schnellzug** kommt aus Berlin.*
> ***Die Studenten aus dem Ausland** wollten die Museen der Stadt besichtigen.*
> ***Das kleine Haus in der Gartenstraße** gehört uns.*
> ***Karl der Große** lebte im achten und neunten Jahrhundert.*
> ***Herr Müller, der Chefingenieur dieser Textilfabrik,** hat eine interessante Erfindung gemacht.*

ATTRIBUTIVE CLAUSES may also be used to define the subject more precisely. Such clauses are introduced by relative pronouns, relative adverbs, or conjunctions. They may also be infinitive clauses [→ J 145 ff.]:   H 265

> ***Der Schnellzug,*** | ***der soeben in den Bahnhof einfährt,*** | *kommt aus Berlin.*

> ***Die Studenten,*** | ***die aus dem Ausland kommen,*** | *wollen die Museen dieser Stadt besichtigen.*

> ***Das kleine Haus,*** | ***das in der Gartenstraße steht,*** | *gehört uns.*

509

Herr Müller, | *der der Chefingenieur dieser Textilfabrik ist,* | *hat eine interessante Erfindung gemacht.*

Der Junge, | *dessen Mutter krank geworden ist,* | *kommt heute nicht in die Schule.*

Der Herr, | *mit dem Sie eben gesprochen haben,* | *ist ein alter Bekannter von mir.*

Der Garten, | *den du dort siehst,* | *gehört meinen Eltern.*

Derjenige, | *der das Verbot übertritt,* | *wird bestraft.*

Wer nicht fleißig lernt, | *(der) hat im Leben wenig Erfolg.* [→ H 270]

Das Land, | *wo es die meisten Hochhäuser gibt,* | *ist Amerika.*

Die Frage, | *ob mein Freund heute kommt,* | *ist schwer zu beantworten.*

Die Sorge, | *ihr Kind zu verlieren,* | *machte die Mutter fast wahnsinnig.*

H 266   Pronoun subjects replace the entire sentence units with all modifiers:

Das kleine Haus in der Gartenstraße | *gehört uns. Gefällt* es *Ihnen?*

Herr Müller, der Chefingenieur dieser Textilfabrik, | *hat eine interessante Erfindung gemacht.* Er *hat schon viele Jahre daran gearbeitet.*

Der Junge, dessen Mutter krank geworden ist, | *kommt heute nicht in die Schule, denn* er *muß zu Hause helfen.*

H 268   There are some processes, especially those referring to weather phenomena, as well as some other idiomatic expressions, in which no

510

agent [→ H 003, 200 ff.] is either present or mentioned. The impersonal pronoun **es** then appears as the formal subject:

> *Es blitzt und donnert.*
> *Es regnet.*
> *Es friert.*
> *Es dämmert.*
> *Es wurde dunkel.*
> *Es klopft an die Tür.*
> *Es geht mir gut.*
> *Es gefällt ihm bei uns.*
> *Es ist mir kalt.*[1]

Subject Clause

If a complete clause becomes the subject of a statement, it is expressed   H 270
by a subordinate clause, which then functions as the subject of the main
clause. Such dependent clauses are called SUBJECT CLAUSES. Subject
clauses are introduced by conjunctions, interrogative pronouns, or
interrogative adverbs:

> **Daß nächsten Samstag Unterricht ist,** *gefällt den Schülern nicht.*
> **Daß der Minister morgen in unsere Stadt kommen soll,** *stand in allen Zeitungen.*
> **Wann der Minister hier eintrifft,** *ist noch nicht bekannt.*
> **Ob mein Freund morgen kommt,** *ist noch ungewiß.*
> **Wer nicht mit uns mitkommen will,** *soll es jetzt sagen.*
> **Was Sie erzählten,** *war sehr interessant.*
> **Weshalb er an der Tagung nicht teilgenommen hat,** *ist mir nicht bekannt.*

INFINITIVE CLAUSES which act as the subject of the entire sentence are   H 271
also included among the subject clauses [→ H 259.4 footnote]:[2]

> **Starken Kaffee zu trinken,** *ist der Gesundheit schädlich.*
> **Nach München zu fahren,** *war mir leider nicht möglich.*

Subject clauses usually occupy the postfield. If no other sentence unit   H 272

---

[1] This sentence may appear colloquially without a subject: *Mir ist kalt.*

[2] In English, these would be considered infinitive phrases. German classifies them as clauses.

fulfills the function of a contact link in the prefield [→ H 051], an anticipatory **es** is used in the prefield to fill this position [→ H 053 ff.]: [1]

> *Es gefällt den Studenten nicht,* **daß nächsten Samstag Unterricht ist.**
> *Es ist noch nicht bekannt,* **wann der Minister hier ankommt.**
> *Es ist noch ungewiß,* **ob mein Freund morgen kommt.**
> *Es ist der Gesundheit schädlich,* **starken Kaffee zu trinken.**
> *Es war mir leider nicht möglich,* **nach München zu fahren.**

Agreement of Subject and Predicate

H 275   There must be an AGREEMENT IN FORM between the subject and the conjugated part of the predicate, which must correspond with the subject in NUMBER (singular or plural) and PERSON (1st, 2nd, or 3rd person) [→ B 011 ff.]: [2]

PRESENT TENSE

	Singular		Plural	
1st person	ich	lerne	wir	lernen
2nd person	du	lernst	ihr	lernt
3rd person	der Mann⎫ er ⎪ das Kind ⎬ lernt es ⎪ die Frau ⎪ sie ⎭		die Männer⎫ die Kinder ⎪ die Frauen ⎬ lernen sie ⎪ Sie [3] ⎭	

H 276   Since the conjugational forms of the verb by themselves do not always suffice to identify person and number unequivocally, the subject (noun

---

[1] Note the difference between the anticipatory **es** and **es** as the formal subject in impersonal constructions [→ H 268]: The impersonal subject **es** may appear in the prefield or within the sentence field (*Heute regnet es*). The anticipatory **es** disappears as soon as some other sentence unit occupies the prefield [→ H 055 fff.].

[2] The German grammatical term for the agreement between subject and predicate is **Kongruenz.**

[3] From the point of view of formal analysis, **Sie** is 3rd person plural, even though it is used to designate 2nd person singular and plural.

or pronoun) must always be mentioned.[1] Note the identity of verb forms for different persons:

> *er lernt — ihr lernt*
> *wir lernen — sie lernen*
> *ich lernte — er lernte*
> *ich kam — er kam*
> *wir kamen — sie kamen*

In imperative forms in the 2nd person singular and plural, however, the personal pronoun subject is omitted, since the endings are sufficient to identify the subject: **H 277**

> ***Geh****(e) jetzt nach Hause!* ***Nimm*** *deinen kleinen Bruder mit!*
> ***Geht*** *in die Schule!* ***Bringt*** *mir mein Buch wieder zurück!*

In the imperative, the subject is mentioned only if it is to receive special stress or emphasis. The pronoun then has demonstrative character [→ B 784]: **H 278**

> *Bring* ***du*** *mir das Buch! (Nicht ein anderer.)*
> *Helft* ***ihr*** *dem alten Mann, ich kann es leider nicht tun.*

Multiple Subjects

If the subject is represented by two or more nouns, the verb form is in the plural:[2] **H 280**

> | ***Karl, Peter und Richard*** | *gehen in die Schule.* |

> | ***Der Vater und der Sohn*** | *besuchten die Mutter im Krankenhaus.* |

Exceptions from this rule are phrases which contain closely related

---

[1] In colloquial usage and in certain poetic forms, the subject pronouns are sometimes omitted: *Hast du schon so eine Frechheit gesehen? Geht einfach hin und* ***nimmt*** *sich ein Stück Kuchen! — Bin allein auf dieser Welt,* ***habe*** *weder Gut noch Geld.*

[2] Note the difference: | *Der Jäger* | *mit seinem Hund geht auf die Jagd.* —

| *Der Jäger und sein Hund* | *gehen auf die Jagd.*

concepts or which are part of an idiom. Such concepts or idioms are considered a unit and therefore use the singular verb form:

> **Sein Hab und Gut** *ging verloren.*

> **Lust und Liebe** *zum Abenteuer* **trieb** *den Forscher auf diese gefährliche Expedition.*

H 281 When the personal pronoun **es** occupies the prefield to anticipate the grammatical subject, it has no influence on the personal form of the verb [→ H 053]:

> *Es* **kommen** *sonntags immer viele Leute in die Stadt.*

H 282 Multiple infinitives, infinitive clauses, or verbal nouns as subjects take a singular verb:

> **Das Lärmen und Singen** *dauerte die ganze Nacht.*

> **Im Regen zu stehen und auf die Straßenbahn zu warten** *ist kein Vergnügen.*

> **Das Betreten des Fabrikgeländes und der Aufenthalt vor der Einfahrt** *ist Unbefugten verboten.*

H 283 When subjects in the singular are connected by the conjunctions **oder** and **entweder . . . oder**, the personal form of the verb is in the singular:

> **Robert oder Peter** *besucht mich heute.*

> **Entweder Karl oder seine Schwester** *muß heute zu Hause bleiben.*

H 284 With the conjunction **weder . . . noch**, the verb is usually in the plural, although the singular sometimes occurs:

> **Weder mein Vater noch meine Mutter** *haben* (**hat**) *mir geantwortet.*

> **Weder Mondlicht noch Sternenschein** *waren* (**war**) *am Himmel zu sehen.*

514

If the subject contains a unit of measurement or quantity in the singular   H 285
(e.g. **Anzahl, Gruppe, Herde, Kompanie, Menge, Pfund,** etc.), the personal
form of the verb may be either in the singular or in the plural. In the
singular, the verb refers to the unit of measurement itself, in the plural
it refers to the noun which is being measured:

> *Dort **liegt eine Menge** Bücher auf dem Tisch.*
> *Dort **liegen** eine Menge **Bücher** auf dem Tisch.*

> ***Eine Gruppe** junger Leute **spielte** auf dem Platz Fußball.*
> *Eine Gruppe **junger Leute spielten** auf dem Platz Fußball.*

> ***Ein Pfund Äpfel kostet** jetzt sechzig Pfennig.*
> ***Ein Pfund Äpfel kosten** jetzt sechzig Pfennig.*

The same rule applies when the unit of measurement is in the plural and   H 286
the noun to be measured in the singular:

> ***Zehn Liter** Wein **kosten** 35 Mark.*
> *Zehn Liter **Wein kostet** 35 Mark.*

Similarly, a singular may be used, even though the unit of measurement   H 287
is in the plural, if the amount measured is a unit:

> | ***Zwanzig Mark*** | ***wird** kaum reichen.* |

> | ***Zehn Prozent** des Materials* | ***ging** verloren.* |

> | ***Zwei Drittel** der Mannschaft* | ***wurde** gerettet.* |

Collective nouns as subjects demand singular verbs in German, even   H 288
where corresponding English nouns demand a plural:

> | ***Die Polizei*** | ***hat** den Dieb gefangen.* |

> | ***Das Volk*** | ***war** von der Rede des Präsidenten begeistert.* |

When pronouns (or a pronoun and a noun) referring to different gram-   H 290
matical persons are used as subjects and are combined by an additive
conjunction (**und, sowohl . . . als auch,** etc.), the personal form of the
verb is in the first person plural if one of the two subjects is in the first

515

person, otherwise in the second person plural. Often, the two subjects are combined and repeated by a single common pronoun:

$$
\left.\begin{array}{l}
ich + du \\
ich + er\ (sie,\ es) \\
ich + ihr \\
ich + sie\ (Sie) \\
wir + sie\ (Sie)
\end{array}\right\} = wir
\qquad
\left.\begin{array}{l}
du + er\ (sie,\ es) \\
du + sie\ (Sie) \\
ihr + sie\ (Sie)
\end{array}\right\} = ihr
$$

Du und ich *gehen* heute ins Kino. (*Du und ich,* **wir** *gehen* . . .)

Du und meine Schwester *seid* Freundinnen. (*Du und sie,* **ihr** *seid* . . .)

Ihr und eure Freunde **könnt** *tun, was* **ihr** *wollt.*

H 291   When different grammatical persons are used as subjects and are connected by alternative conjunctions (e.g. **oder, entweder . . . oder**), the personal form of the verb agrees with the pronoun closest to the verb:

Sollst **du oder ich** *die Arbeit machen? —* **Soll** **ich oder du** *die Arbeit machen?*

Entweder kommst **du** *zu mir* **oder er.** *—* **Entweder kommt** **er** *zu mir* **oder du.**

H 292   The same rule may also be applied to **weder . . . noch**; generally, however, the verb will be in the plural [→ H 284, G 561]:

Weder ich noch mein Bruder **hat** (**haben**) *studiert.*

Weder er noch du *gehst* (*gehen*) *heute ins Kino.*

H 293   If the subject appears within the sentence field, the personal form of the verb may remain in the singular, even though an additional subject may follow:

Heute **besuchte** *mich* **mein Freund und seine Frau.**

Ihm **gehört** **das Haus und der Garten.**

516

The personal form of the verb may appear in the plural in forms of H 294
address which are intended to express extreme politeness, even though
only one person is being addressed:

> *Was befehlen **Herr Major**?*
> *Was wünschen **der Herr**?*
> ***Euer Exzellenz** haben mich gerufen.*
> ***Gnädige Frau** wollten um 7 Uhr geweckt werden.*

In RELATIVE CLAUSES which refer to the 1st or 2nd person, the subject is H 295
often repeated [→ D 530]. The personal form of the verb agrees with
the personal pronoun:

> ***Ich, der ich** den ganzen Tag gearbeitet **habe,** wünsche abends meine*
> *Ruhe.*
> *Warum fragst du **mich, der ich** keine Ahnung **habe**?*
> ***Dir, der du** mir immer geholfen **hast,** bin ich sehr dankbar.*

If the pronoun subject is not repeated, the verb has the ending of the H 296
third person singular [→ D 531]. Such constructions, however, are rare:

> ***Dir, der** mir immer geholfen **hat,** bin ich sehr dankbar.*
> ***Ich, der** den ganzen Tag gearbeitet **hat,** wünsche abends meine Ruhe.*

If an anticipatory **es** appears before the relative clause, the personal H 297
pronoun is not repeated and the verb agrees with the relative pronoun:

> ***Ich** war **es, der** dich gefragt **hat.***
> *Warst **du es, die** mich gestern besuchen **wollte**?*
> *Wart **ihr es, die** mich gestern besuchen **wollten**?*

Objects

All agents in a situation described by the sentence [→ H 003], which do H 300
not have any effect on the personal form of the predicate and thus do
not function as the subject [→ H 275 ff.], are classified as sentence units
with the function of OBJECTS.

Objects are necessary parts of certain situations without which the H 301
sentence would not be complete. Actions and processes may have one or
two objects, their number depending upon the type of predicate. If a
sentence contains two objects, we must distinguish between a "primary"
and a "secondary" object.

H 302   The traditional terms "direct" and "indirect" object are misleading, since the so-called direct object is usually equated with the accusative and the so-called indirect object with the dative. This, however, is not consistent with the German grammatical point of view, nor does it correspond to English equivalents. In many verbs, dative and genitive objects follow immediately after the verb (*Er dankt* **mir**; *wir gedenken* **des verstorbenen Dichters**) and are thus in a sense "direct" objects in German as well as in English. The terms "primary" and "secondary" object are better suited to describe the actual phenomena of the language. A PRIMARY object, regardless of case, indicates the person or thing with which the action or process is directly concerned and which fulfills the verbal concept. (For some verbs, this may even be a prepositional object: *Er bittet* **um Brot**.) A SECONDARY object, regardless of case, indicates the person towards whom the action is directed.

A verb may have a primary object without a secondary object:

> *Ich lese* **die Zeitung**.
> *Der Schüler antwortet* **dem Lehrer**.
> *Er bedarf* **des Trostes**.

It may not, however, have a secondary object without a primary object:

> *Mein Freund gab* **mir** ...
> *Ich kaufte* **meiner Frau** ...
> *Der Bettler bat* **die Leute** ...

The above sentences are fragmentary and need a primary object (or a predicate object [→ H 480 ff.]) to complete the thought:

> *Mein Freund gab mir* **ein Geschenk**.
> *Ich kaufte meiner Frau* **Blumen**.
> *Der Bettler bat die Leute* **um eine Gabe**.

H 303   In the following examples, the primary object is indicated by the number (1), the secondary object by (2):

Fritz kauft	→ **einen Anzug**. (1)
Der Lehrer fragt	→ **einen Schüler**. (1)
Inge bringt	→ **das Buch**. (1)
Der Vater schreibt	→ **einen Brief**. (1)
Mein Freund hilft	→ **mir**. (1)
Wir gedenken	→ **des verstorbenen Dichters**. (1)
Er wartet	→ **auf seinen Vater**. (1)

518

Der Lehrer gibt ——	*dem Jungen* (2) ← *das Buch.* (1)	
Der Dieb stahl ——	*dem Mann* (2) *das Geld.* (1)	
Ich kaufte ————	*meinem Freund* (2) ← *ein Geschenk.* (1)	
Der Bettler bat ——	*die Leute* (2) ← *um eine Gabe.* (1)	

We distinguish the following types of objects, according to their declension: H 305

> Accusative object [→ H 325]
> Dative object [→ H 350]
> Genitive object [→ H 380]
> Prepositional object [→ H 390]

The verb in the predicate determines the form which the object of the sentence must take. The verb **fragen,** for instance, requires an ACCUSATIVE object, **antworten** a DATIVE object, **gedenken** a GENITIVE object, and **warten** requires a PREPOSITIONAL object, i.e. the verb connects the object with a preposition, which determines the case of the object: H 306

Accusative object:	*Der Mann fragt*	**den Jungen.**
		das Kind.
		die Frau.
		die Schüler.
Dative object:	*Der Mann antwortet*	**dem Jungen.**
		dem Kind.
		der Frau.
		den Schülern.
Genitive object:	*Der Mann gedenkt*	**des Jungen.**
		des Kindes.
		der Frau.
		der Schüler.
Prepositional object:	*Der Mann wartet*	**auf den Jungen.**
		auf das Kind.
		auf die Frau.
		auf die Schüler.
	Der Mann spricht	**von dem Jungen.**
		von dem Kind.
		von der Frau.
		von den Schülern.

519

Form of Objects

H 310   Objects may be either nouns or pronouns, as well as other parts of speech used as nouns:

Accusative object:	*Ich besuchte **Karl** gestern.*
	*Sehen Sie **den Mann?***
	*Ich kenne hier **niemanden.***
	*Wo ist der Brief, **den** ich heute bekommen habe?*
	*Wir lieben **kein Wenn und Aber.***
Dative object:	*Ich gab **Anna** ein Geschenk.*
	*Der Schüler antwortet **dem Lehrer.***
	*Das Haus gefällt **mir.***
	*Er hilft **niemandem.***
	*Dort steht das Kind, **dem** ich Schokolade geschenkt habe.*
Genitive object:[1]	*Wir gedenken **des verstorbenen Dichters.***
	*Er rühmt sich **seines Erfolges.***
Prepositional object:	*Ich habe mich **über Franz** sehr geärgert.*
	*Wir fürchten uns **vor nichts.***
	*Glaubst du **an deinen Erfolg?** Ja, ich glaube **daran.***

H 311   After **modal** verbs and the verbs **helfen, lehren,** and **lernen,** INFINITIVES may take the place of an accusative object [→ B 931, 976]:

> *Wir wollen heute ins Kino **gehen.***
> *Peter lernt **schwimmen.***
> *Herr Müller lehrt **maschineschreiben.***
> *Wir helfen **aufbauen.***

H 312   In some situations a PREPOSITIONAL INFINITIVE may constitute the object. If this infinitive is expanded to include modifiers of its own, it is separated by a comma and becomes an INFINITIVE CLAUSE. An infinitive clause always occupies the postfield.

PREPOSITIONAL INFINITIVE

> *Wir haben uns entschlossen **zu gehen.***
> *Er versuchte **zu antworten.***

---

[1] Proper names and pronouns occur very rarely in genitive objects: *Erinnern sie sich Herrn Müllers? Er harret **meiner.***

INFINITIVE CLAUSE[1]

Accusative object:

*Der Arzt empfiehlt, **den Kranken sofort zu operieren.** (Der Arzt empfiehlt **die sofortige Operation des Kranken.**)*

*Ich hoffe, **dich bald wiederzusehen.***

*Er hat mir versprochen, **mir für die Reise sein Auto zu leihen.***

Genitive object (rare):

*Er hat sich enthalten, **viel Alkohol zu trinken.** (Er hat sich **des Genusses von Alkohol** enthalten.)*

Prepositional object:[2]

*Ich freue mich **darauf, nach Italien zu reisen.** (Ich freue mich **auf die Reise nach Italien.**)*

Object Clause

When a complete clause is used as the object within a situational con-   H 320
text, a dependent clause (OBJECT CLAUSE)[2] is formed, which occupies the
postfield:

*Der Arzt empfiehlt, **daß der Kranke sofort operiert wird.***
*Ich weiß nicht, **ob wir morgen einen Ausflug machen können.***
*Wissen Sie, **wann der Zug von hier abfährt?***

*Ich antworte, **wem ich will.***

*Wir freuen uns (**darauf**), **daß ihr uns morgen besucht.***
*Ihr habt euch nicht **darum** gekümmert, **ob es uns gut geht.***

The Accusative Object

The most frequent case for objects is the ACCUSATIVE. Verbs which take   H 325
accusative objects are called "transitive." A large number of verbs
demand accusative objects, above all inseparable verbs with the prefixes
be-, durch-, er-, hinter-, über-, um-,[3] all causative verbs, such as **stellen,
setzen, legen, hängen, stecken, tränken, fällen,** etc., and many others.
For verbs with two accusative objects → D 916 ff., H 347.

---

[1] Infinitive clauses can not function as dative objects.

[2] Prepositional object clauses are often anticipated in the main clause by **da** + preposition
[→ B 940].

[3] This need not apply to separable verbs with the same prefixes: *Wir **übergehen** die nächste
Frage.* But: *Wir **gehen** zur nächsten Frage **über.***

H 326　Since the nominative and the accusative of nouns and third person pronouns differ only in the singular masculine, subject and object often can not be differentiated by their form. Therefore, the following rule applies:

If nominative and accusative have the same form, the accusative (object) must always follow the nominative (subject). In such instances, the accusative may not occupy the prefield of a declarative statement [→ H 711 f.]:

> [s]*Das* *Kind fragt* [o]***die Mutter.*** *Fragt das* [s]*Kind* [o]***die Mutter?*** *Ja, es* [s]*fragt*
> [o]*sie. Fragt es* [s]*sie?* [o]*Ich höre, daß das Kind* [o]***die Mutter*** *fragt. Ich höre,*
> *daß es* [s]*sie* [o]*fragt.*

H 327　This rule does not apply in the following three cases:

1. The agreement between verb and subject [→ H 275] clearly identifies the subject:

> [o]*Die* ***Mutter*** *fragen die* [s]*Kinder nie.*

2. The nature of the verb allows no doubt about the relationship between subject and object:

> [o]*Das* ***Buch*** *hat* [s]*sie schon längst gelesen.*

3. Context makes the situation absolutely clear:

> [o]*Das* ***Zimmer*** *reinigte das* [s]*Mädchen.*
> [o]*Die* ***Maus*** *hat die* [s]*Katze gefressen.*

H 328　Most reflexive verbs use the reflexive pronoun as an accusative object:[1]

> *Ich freue **mich** über dein Geschenk.*
> *Er ärgert **sich** über seinen Fehler.*
> *Ich begnüge **mich** nicht mit diesem Geld.*
> *Erkundigst du **dich** nach meinem Befinden?*

H 329　The idiom **es gibt** is also followed by an accusative object [→ D 920–1]:

> *Es gibt **keinen guten Grund** dafür.*

---

[1] There are some reflexive verbs with only a dative object, e.g. **sich helfen**, others with a dative and an accusative object, e.g. **sich (etwas) überlegen, sich (etwas) denken**. Note the difference between *Ich stelle **mich** vor* and *Ich stelle **mir** etwas vor*, or between *Hast du **dich** gewaschen?* and *Hast du **dir** die Hände gewaschen?*

Predicate Infinitive

Verbs of perception (e.g. **sehen, hören, fühlen**) and of causation (e.g.   H 330
lassen, heißen [to bid], **lehren, schicken**) may have an accusative object
followed by an infinitive. In these constructions, the ACCUSATIVE OBJECT
is the SUBJECT of the INFINITIVE action; the infinitive is the predicate for
the object of the finite verb. The infinitive is therefore called a PREDICATE
INFINITIVE: [1]

*Ich sehe **meinen Freund kommen**.*	*Ich sehe meinen Freund. Mein Freund kommt.*
*Wir hören **die Schüler singen**.*	*Wir hören die Schüler. Die Schüler singen.*
*Sie fühlte **den Tod nahen**.*	*Sie fühlte den Tod. Der Tod nahte.*
*Ich schicke **das Mädchen einkaufen**.*	*Ich schicke das Mädchen. Das Mädchen geht einkaufen.*
*Ich lege **mich schlafen**.*	*Ich lege mich nieder. Ich schlafe ein.*

If the predicate infinitive has modifiers of its own, they are placed   H 331
between the accusative object and the predicate infinitive:

*Er hat **drei Anzüge im Schrank hängen**.*	*Er hat drei Anzüge. Die Anzüge hängen im Schrank.*
*Ich lasse **den Schüler den Brief schreiben**.*	*Der Schüler schreibt den Brief auf meine Veranlassung.*

With the verb **lassen** (sometimes used with a dative or accusative re-   H 332
flexive), the predicate infinitive describes a process in the PASSIVE. The
infinitive is a substitute for the past participle [→ B 468 for substitute
infinitive in the perfect tenses of modals and **lassen**]:

*Ich lasse **den Brief schreiben**. (Der Brief wird geschrieben.)*

*Ich lasse **den Brief von einem Schüler schreiben**. (Der Brief wird von einem Schüler geschrieben.)*

*Ich ließ **mir einen Anzug machen**. (Der Anzug wurde für mich gemacht.)*

*Ich habe **mich rasieren** lassen. (Ich bin rasiert worden.)*

*Der Vater läßt **seinem Sohn die Haare** schneiden. (Dem Sohn werden die Haare geschnitten.)*

---

[1] See also B 970–82.

H 333   Note the following constructions:

> *Der Vater läßt **einen Brief schreiben.***
> (*Der Brief wird geschrieben.*)
> *Der Vater läßt **seinen Sohn einen Brief schreiben.**[1]*
> (*Der Sohn schreibt den Brief.*)
> *Der Vater läßt **seinem Sohn einen Brief schreiben.***
> (*Der Brief wird an den Sohn geschrieben.*)
> *Der Vater läßt **die Mutter dem Sohn einen Brief schreiben.**[1]*
> (*Die Mutter schreibt einen Brief an den Sohn.*)

H 335   With many verbs, the predicate infinitive is formed by a PREPOSITIONAL INFINITIVE or by an INFINITIVE CLAUSE [→ B 980]. Infinitive clauses always occupy the postfield:

> *Ich bitte **dich zu kommen.***   (*Du sollst kommen.*)
> *Ich habe **dich** gebeten **zu kommen.***
> *Ich bitte **dich, morgen nachmittag zu mir zu kommen.***
> *Ich habe **dich** gebeten, **morgen nachmittag zu mir zu kommen.***
>
> *Er zwingt **mich zu arbeiten.***   (*Ich muß arbeiten.*)
> *Er hat **mich** gezwungen **zu arbeiten.***
> *Er zwingt **mich, sonntags in seinem Garten zu arbeiten.***
> *Er hat **mich** gezwungen, **sonntags in seinem Garten zu arbeiten.***

Modifiers of Manner with an Accusative Object

H 340   Verbs of perception, judgment, report, etc. (such as **sehen, finden, wissen, glauben, melden**) may have an accusative object followed by a modifier of manner [→ H 580]. The modifier (usually an adjective) indicates the condition in which the accusative object finds itself. It answers the question **wie?**

> *Ich sehe **ihn fröhlich.***   (*Ich sehe ihn. Er ist fröhlich.*)
> *Wir fanden **ihn schlafend.**[2]*   (*Wir fanden ihn. Er schlief.*)
> *Er traf **mich krank** an.*   (*Er traf mich an. Ich war krank.*)

---

[1] In order to avoid accumulations of pure case forms, it is possible to use prepositional constructions: *Der Vater läßt einen Brief von seinem Sohn schreiben. Der Vater läßt die Mutter einen Brief an den Sohn schreiben.*

[2] *Ich fand ihn fröhlich* may have two meanings: *Ich fand ihn, und er war fröhlich* or *Ich dachte, daß er fröhlich war.*

524

Note: These are considered modifiers of manner, since they provide additional information about the basic situation: *Ich sehe ihn. Ich sehe ihn fröhlich.* In the explanatory sentence in parentheses, however, *fröhlich* (as well as any other similar sentence unit) is a predicate complement.

Similar constructions are also found with some other verbs in which the modifier of manner describes the NATURE of the object: **H 341**

> *Wir pflücken **die Tomaten reif*** (i.e. *die reifen Tomaten*).
> *Ich trinke **den Kaffee bitter*** (i.e. *den bitteren Kaffee*).
> *Er ißt **das Obst roh*** (i.e. *das rohe Obst*).

The modifier may also describe the STATE into which the object is BROUGHT. In some verbs, such a modifier is so intimately connected with the verb that it is written together with the infinitive of the verb and is considered a verb prefix (e.g. **sattessen, totschlagen**): **H 342**

> *Sie färbt **ihr Kleid grün**.* (*Das Kleid wird grün.*)
> *Ich lasse **meinen Freund allein**.* (*Mein Freund bleibt allein.*)
> *Wir stellen **den Pfahl aufrecht**.* (*Der Pfahl wird aufrecht gestellt.*)
> *Ihr eßt **euch satt**.* (*Ihr werdet satt.*)

Some verbs connect the modifier of manner to the object by means of the prepositions **als** or **für**: **H 343**

> *Wir kennen **diesen Mann als ehrlich**.*
> *Ich halte **diesen Studenten für sehr intelligent**.*

Modifiers of Place with an Accusative Object

For verbs of perception and similar verbs (e.g. **sehen, hören, fühlen, finden**, etc.), a modifier of place [→ H 571] may be added to the accusative object. It designates the location at which the accusative object is found: **H 345**

*Ich fand **das Buch im Schrank**.*	(*Ich fand das Buch. Das Buch war im Schrank.*)
*Er fühlte **einen Schmerz im Magen**.*	(*Er fühlte einen Schmerz. Der Schmerz war im Magen.*)
*Wir hören **den Lehrer im Zimmer**.*	(*Wir hören den Lehrer. Der Lehrer ist im Zimmer.*)
*Ich habe **dich auf der Straße** gesehen.*	(*Ich habe dich gesehen. Du warst auf der Straße.*)

525

Double Accusative Object

H 347   Some verbs may take two accusative objects [→ D 916–18]. The first accusative object designates a person, the second a thing. These verbs include **kosten** [but → H 362], **lehren,** and (less frequently) **bitten** and **fragen**:[1]

> *Diese Reise kostete **ihn keinen Pfennig.***
> *Er lehrt **mich die deutsche Sprache.***
> *Ich bitte **dich nur eines.***
> *Er fragte **den Lehrer die dümmsten Dinge.***

H 348   The verbs **nennen, schimpfen** (or **schelten**), **taufen,** and **titulieren** (archaic) may take two accusative objects designating persons [→ predicate accusative H 470]:

> *Die Mutter nennt **ihn ihren Liebling.***
> *Er schimpfte (schalt) **mich einen Narren.***

The Dative Object

H 350   Many verbs require a dative object [→ D 931 ff.]. These are primarily verbs which indicate an action that implies an actual or figurative direction either toward the dative object (the concept of **geben** →) or away from the dative object (the concept of **nehmen** ←).[2] A large number of impersonal verbs and expressions also require a dative object:

> *Der Schüler antwortet → **dem Lehrer.***
> *Die Wanderer lauschen → **dem Gesang** der Vögel.*
> *Der Sohn folgt → **dem Rat** des Vaters.*
> *Ich helfe → **meinem Freund.***
>
> *Das Rauchen schadet ← **der Gesundheit.***
> *Der Hund entläuft ← **seinem Herrn.***
> *Ich weiche ← **der Gewalt.***
> *Er mißtraut ← **mir.***

---

[1] *Angehen* may also be considered in this category: *Das geht mich nichts an.*

[2] In English, dative objects are often paraphrased as prepositional objects, using the prepositions *to, for,* or *from* [→ H 356].

*Wie gefällt es **Ihnen** hier?*
__Mir__ ist eben etwas eingefallen.
*Es tat **ihm** leid, daß wir nicht kommen konnten.*
*Es ist **ihr** nicht geglückt, das Examen zu bestehen.*

The most common of these verbs are [cf. D 932]:[1]

absagen	entsagen	mißfallen
ähneln	entschlüpfen	mißlingen
antworten	entschwinden	mißtrauen
auffallen	entsprechen	(sich) nahen
ausweichen	entspringen	(nähern)
befehlen	entstammen	nutzen
begegnen	entströmen	(nützen)
behagen	entwachsen	passen
beikommen	entweichen	raten
beipflichten	entwischen	schaden
beistehen	fehlen	scheinen
beistimmen	fluchen	schmecken
beiwohnen	folgen	schmeicheln
belieben	gebühren	trauen
bevorstehen	gefallen	trotzen
bleiben	gehorchen	unterliegen
danken	gehören	vergeben
dienen	gelingen	vertrauen
drohen	genügen	verzeihen
einfallen	geschehen	vorgreifen
entfahren	glauben	vorkommen
entfallen	gleichen	weh tun
entfliehen	glücken	weichen
entgegnen	gratulieren	widersprechen
entgehen	grollen	widerstehen
entgleiten	helfen	widerstreben
entkommen	huldigen	winken
entlaufen	kondolieren	ziemen
entlocken	lauschen	zürnen
entrinnen	leid tun	

Separable verbs with the prefixes **entgegen-, nach-, vor-, (voran-, zuvor-)**

[1] Some of these verbs, like **befehlen, glauben, raten**, etc., may take an impersonal accusative object (**es, das**, etc.). Others, like **begegnen, gratulieren, schaden**, etc., are truly intransitive and never take a direct object [→ D 932 ff.].
    The impersonal expression **gut (schlecht) gehen** also requires a dative object.

527

in the sense of "ahead,"[1] and **zu-** in the sense of "toward,"[2] also require a dative object:

> *Er kam* **mir** *entgegen.*
> *Der Hund läuft* **seinem Herrn** *nach.*
> *Wir fuhren* **dem anderen Auto** *vor.*
> *Gehen Sie* **mir** *voran!*
> *Ich bin* **ihm** *zuvorgekommen.*
> *Er lächelte* **dem Mädchen** *zu.*

H 353   Many complements of manner [→ H 440] also require a dative object [→ D 936]:

> *Ich bin* **meinem Freund dankbar.**
> *Die Sache wird* **mir lästig.**
> *Der Sohn ist* **seinem Vater gehorsam.**
> *Ich bleibe* **Ihnen** *sehr* **verbunden.**

H 355   Most verbs which require an accusative object may also have a dative object which indicates the person with which the action is concerned (or, less frequently, a thing, place, or concept) [→ D 932]:

> *Der Schüler bringt* **dem Lehrer** *das Buch.*
> *Geben Sie* **mir** *das Heft!*
> *Der Räuber nimmt* **dem Mann** *das Geld.*
> *Sie zeigt* **ihm** *die Schule.*
> *Ich schreibe* **der Universität** *einen Brief.*

H 356   Often, a dative object may be replaced by a prepositional object in which a direction is indicated by the preposition:[3]

> *Ich schreibe* **meinem Vater** *einen Brief. — Ich schreibe einen Brief* **an meinen Vater.**
> *Er bringt* **seiner Frau** *Blumen. — Er bringt Blumen* **für seine Frau.**
> *Er entnahm* **seiner Brieftasche** *ein Stück Papier. — Er nahm ein Stück Papier* **aus seiner Brieftasche.**[3]

H 360   A dative object may also have a PREDICATE OBJECT (predicate infinitive), the subject of which is the object of the sentence [→ H 330 ff.]. The

---

[1] This would not include verbs like **vorhaben, vorschlagen,** etc.

[2] This would include verbs like **zueilen, zufliegen, zuhören, zustimmen,** etc., but not verbs like **zugeben, zumachen, zunehmen,** etc.

[3] In English, the paraphrase with *to* or *for* is possible, the paraphrase with *from* is necessary: *Er hat* **mir** *all mein Geld gestohlen.*

528

preposition **zu** establishes the connection between the dative object and the infinitive:

> *Ich erlaube **dir zu kommen**.*   (*Du darfst kommen.*)
> *Er befiehlt **mir zu arbeiten**.*   (*Ich muß arbeiten.*)
> *Er gestattet **ihr einzutreten**.*   (*Sie darf eintreten.*)

If the infinitive has modifiers of its own, they form an infinitive clause which is separated from the sentence field by a comma and occupies the postfield:

H 361

> *Ich erlaube **dir**, **mit uns zu dem Fest zu kommen**.*
> *Er will **mir** immer befehlen, **am Sonntag im Büro zu arbeiten**.*
> *Er hat **ihr** gern gestattet, **mit ihrem Bruder ins Zimmer einzutreten**.*

There are some verbs and expressions in which usage fluctuates between a dative or an accusative object:

H 362

> *Das lohnt **die Mühe** (or **der Mühe**) nicht.*
> *Es ekelt **mir** (or **mich**).*
> *Das Auto kommt **mich** (or **mir**) teuer.*
> *Das Studium kostet **ihn** (or **ihm**) viel Geld.*
> *Er trat **mir** (or **mich**) auf den Fuß.*
> *Der Hund biß **ihn** (or **ihm**) in das Bein.*
> *Du getraust **dich** (or **dir**) zu fragen.* But: *Du getraust **dir** diese Frage.*

The accusative, rather than the expected dative, appears in the following constructions:

H 363

> *Ich lasse **ihn** die Bilder sehen* [→ H 331].
> *Das geht **dich** nichts an.* [→ H 347 footnote]

In the following expressions, accusative and dative objects are used in different constructions, sometimes with a different meaning:

H 365

*Ich versichere **Sie** meiner Hochachtung.*	*Ich versichere **Ihnen**, daß ich das nicht weiß.*
*Sie hat **ihn** ins Gesicht geschlagen.*	*Ihre Worte schlagen **der Wahrheit** ins Gesicht* (i.e. flatly contradict the truth).
*Der Dorn stach **ihn** ins Auge.*	*Das Auto stach **ihm** ins Auge* (i.e. it appealed to him).
*Er zieht **mich** an den Füßen.*	*Es zieht **mir** an den Füßen* (i.e. there is a draft).

The Genitive Object

H 380   In modern German, only very few verbs require a GENITIVE object [→ D 955 ff.]. The genitive is often replaced by an accusative or by a prepositional phrase:[1]

*Er bedarf **des Trostes.***	*Er bedarf **den Trost.***
*Er entbehrt **der Hilfe.***	*Er entbehrt **die Hilfe.***
*Er harrt **der Dinge.***	*Er harrt **auf Antwort.***

H 381   The verbs **entraten** and **ermangeln**, both of which are rarely used, always require a genitive object:

*Das Gerücht ermangelt **der Wahrheit.***

H 382   In some verbs, genitive objects survive only in fixed idioms:

*Nach dem Essen pflegt er **der Ruhe.***
*Das spottet **jeder Beschreibung** !*
*Walte **deines Amtes** !*

H 383   Some verbs may take both a genitive and an accusative object. The accusative refers to a person and the genitive to a thing or concept. Many of these survive only in certain idiomatic constructions. The most important of these verbs are:

anklagen	entbinden[2]	überführen[4]
belehren	entheben	versichern
berauben	entledigen	würdigen
beschuldigen	entraten	zeihen
bezichtigen	entsetzen[3]	

*Man klagte **den Mann des Diebstahls** an.*
*Ich will **dich eines Besseren** belehren.*
*Ich entbinde **dich deiner Verpflichtungen.***
*Man enthob (entsetzte) **ihn seines Amtes.***
*Die Polizei überführte **ihn des Verbrechens.***
*Er würdigte **mich keines Blickes.***

---

[1] In some instances, minor differences in meaning exist between the two constructions. *Er entbehrt der Hilfe*, for instance, means that he never had any help, while *Er entbehrt die Hilfe* means that he used to have help but that he has to do without it now.

[2] = to release from (*not* to give birth).

[3] = to remove from (*not* to frighten).

[4] = to convict of (*not* to lead across).

Verbs with both an accusative and a genitive object also include a num- H 384
ber of reflexive verbs. With some of these, the genitive may refer to a
person. The most important of these verbs are:

sich annehmen	sich entäußern	sich (er)freuen
sich bedienen	sich enthalten	sich erinnern
sich befleißigen	sich entledigen	sich erwehren
sich bemächtigen	sich entsinnen	sich rühmen
sich besinnen	sich erbarmen	sich schämen
		sich vergewissern

> *Er bemächtigte sich **des Kindes**.*
> *Er schämt sich **seiner Dummheit**.*
> *Sie besann sich **eines Besseren**.*
> *Er rühmt sich **seines Mutes**.*
> *Erbarme dich **der Armen**!*
> *Freut euch **des Lebens**!*

Only two other verbs may take a person as a genitive object: **bedürfen** H 385
and **gedenken**:

> *Ich bedarf **deiner** nicht mehr.*
> *Gedenken wir **des Verstorbenen**!*

Many complements of manner [→ H 442] also require a genitive H 386
object [→ D 960]. The most important ones are:

bar[1]	geständig	(un)kundig	teilhaftig
bedürftig	gewärtig	ledig[2]	verdächtig
(un)bewußt	(un)gewiß	mächtig	verlustig
eingedenk	habhaft	(un)sicher	(un)würdig

> *Er ist **des Englischen** unkundig.*
> *Ich bin **meines Erfolges** gewiß (sicher).*
> *Die Polizei wurde **seiner** habhaft.*

Some other complements of manner, which used to require the genitive, H 387
are being more and more frequently replaced by the accusative or by a
prepositional construction. They are **(un)fähig, gewahr, müde, satt,
(un)schuldig, überdrüssig, voll,**[3] **(un)wert**:

> *Er ist **keiner schlechten Tat** fähig. — Er ist **zu keiner schlechten Tat**
> fähig.*

---

[1] "void of" — not "cash."
[2] "rid of" — not "unmarried."
[3] **Voll** is occasionally combined with the dative: *Er war voll **großen Erwartungen**.* It may
also be inflected itself: *Er war **voller Angst**.*

> *Wir wurden **unseres Irrtums** (**unseren Irrtum**) gewahr.*
> *Ich bin **dieser Arbeit** (**diese Arbeit**) müde.*
> *Ich bin **des trocknen Tones** satt. — Ich bin **den Streit** satt. — Ich habe **den Streit** satt.*
> *Er ist **des Diebstahls** schuldig. — Er ist **an dem Diebstahl** schuldig.*[1]
> *Wir sind **seiner** (**ihn**) überdrüssig.*
> *Das ist **keiner Antwort** (**keine Antwort**) wert.*
> *Ich hörte ihm **voll Mitleids** (**voll Mitleid**) zu.*

H 388   Similarly, genitive objects occur in a few idiomatic constructions:

> *Er machte mich **meines Lebens** froh.*
> *Ich halte ihn **dieses Verbrechens** für fähig.*
> *Er wurde **des Mordes** schuldig gesprochen.*

Prepositional Objects

H 390   Many verbs combine their OBJECT with a PREPOSITION. The case of the object is governed by the preposition involved [→ F 010 ff.]. It is impossible to list all the many combinations between verbs and prepositions which may be formed; for individual verbs, dictionaries must be consulted [→ F 061 and prepositions, F 100–798]:

> *Ich warte **auf** meinen Freund.*
> *Wir rechnen **mit** deinem Besuch.*
> *Er lebt **vom** Handel.*
> *Sie leidet **an** Asthma.*
> *Ihr lacht **über** mich.*

H 391   Often verbs require an additional object together with the prepositional object:

> *Ich bitte **dich um dein Fahrrad.***
> *Wir wollen **ihm auf seinen Brief** antworten.*
> *Habt ihr **ihn nach seinem Befinden** gefragt?*

---

[1] Do not confuse this construction with **schuldig** in the sense of "indebted": *Ich bin ihm großen Dank schuldig.*

Some verbs may change their meaning when they are used with different   H 392
prepositions:

> *Die Kinder freuen sich **über** das schöne Wetter* (i.e. they are happy
> about it).
> *Die Kinder freuen sich **auf** das schöne Wetter* (i.e. they look forward
> to it).

> *Das Buch besteht **aus** vier Teilen* (i.e. it consists of four parts).
> *Er besteht **auf** einer Antwort* (i.e. he insists on an answer).

Many complements of manner require a prepositional object [→ H 443   H 393
ff.]. These prepositional objects may sometimes appear in the postfield:

> *Ich bin **über den Erfolg** froh.*
> *Er ist **auf schwere Arbeit** gefaßt.*
> *Wir sind frei **von Sorgen.***
> *Sie ist stolz **auf ihre Schönheit.***

It is important to distinguish between verbs with prepositional objects   H 395
and separable verbs:

> *Die Betrüger wollten ihn **um** sein Geld **bringen.*** (Prepositional object)
> *Die Räuber wollten ihn **umbringen.*** (Separable verb)

> *Er **gewöhnt** sich **an** das Klima.* (Prepositional object)
> *Er **gewöhnt** sich das Rauchen **an.*** (Separable verb)

> *Die Kinder **hören auf** ihre Eltern.* (Prepositional object)
> *Der Regen **hört auf.*** (Separable verb)

> *Er **strebt nach** Reichtum.* (Prepositional object)
> *Er **strebt** seinem Meister **nach.*** (Separable verb)

It is also important to distinguish between verbs with prepositional   H 396
objects and adverbial modifiers [→ H 500 ff.]:

> *Ich bitte dich **um deine Uhr.***[1] (Prepositional object)
> *Ich komme **um ein Uhr.*** (Adverbial expression of time)

---

[1] It is possible to show this contrast even more sharply in the idiomatic expression **um
etwas kommen**: *Er ist **um eine Uhr** gekommen. — Er ist **um ein Uhr** gekommen.*

PREDICATE COMPLEMENTS

H 400   Predicate, subject, and object are the functional units of the sentence which together describe a situation in its entirety [→ H 200]:

> *Der Vater schläft.*
> *Die Sonne scheint.*
> *Der Schüler fragt den Lehrer.*
> *Mein Freund wartet auf mich.*
> *Der Lehrer gibt dem Schüler ein Buch.*

H 401   The verb by itself, however, often does not suffice to indicate the predicate function in its full extent. Therefore, the predicate frequently includes other parts of speech which take over a part of the predicate function. These sentence units are called PREDICATE COMPLEMENTS [→ H 220].

H 402   The predicate complement describes or defines the action or the state of being [→ H 003, 005], whereas the actual predicate itself often fulfills only a formal or partly formal, partly functional role within the sentence [→ H 020 ff.]:[1]

> *Wir haben ihn von der Sache **in Kenntnis** gesetzt.*
> *Die Polizei stellt dauernd **Nachforschungen** an.*
> *Er hat von einer Anzeige **Abstand** genommen.*
> *Sie hält mit ihm gut **Schritt**.*
> *Er setzte die Maschine **in Betrieb**.*

H 403   Often, the verb may be used to describe the type of event or the manner of the state of being:

> *Die Kinder begeben sich (gehen, fahren, laufen, rennen, schlendern) zur Schule.*
> *Er bringt (geleitet, befördert, transportiert, fährt) den Mann zum Bahnhof.*
> *Die Zigeuner sind (wohnen, hausen, zelten) im Wald,*

H 405   Predicate complements also expand the varieties of expression available to a language. The speaker has the possibility of stylistic variation and

---

[1] Note that in all these examples the verb without the predicate complement does not constitute a complete sentence. This feature distinguishes the predicate complement from the direct object or the predicate modifier [→ H 550 ff.].

534

of depicting a given situation in different ways, depending on the manner in which he views it or in which he wants to have it viewed:

> *Der Lehrer **fragt** die Schüler. — Der Lehrer **stellt** den Schülern **Fragen.***
>
> *Die Bäume **blühen**. — Die Bäume **stehen in Blüte**.*
>
> *Ich **freue mich** über das Geschenk. — Das Geschenk **macht** mir **Freude**.*
>
> *Mir **schmerzt der Kopf**. — Ich **habe Kopfschmerzen**.*
>
> *Sie **ängstigt sich** dauernd. — Sie **lebt in ständiger Angst**.*
>
> *Wir **räumen** das Zimmer **auf**. — Wir **bringen** das Zimmer **in Ordnung**.*

Forms of Predicate Complements

A predicate complement may contain various parts of speech or case forms, or subordinate clauses. The following possibilities exist:

ADVERBS: H 410

> *Das Auto fährt **schnell**.*
> *Er wohnt **hier**.*

ADJECTIVES: H 411

> *Bist du **krank**?*
> *Er stellt sich **dumm**.*

NOUNS in the NOMINATIVE [→ H 460 ff.]:   H 412

> *Mein Bruder ist **Soldat**.*
> *Es wird **Nacht**.*

NOUNS in the ACCUSATIVE:[1]   H 413

> *Er schenkte dem Redner **seine volle Aufmerksamkeit**.*
> *Er nahm von seiner Geliebten **Abschied**.*

NOUNS in the GENITIVE: H 414

> *Das Unglück geschah **eines Mittags**.*
> *Er ist **guten Mutes**.*

PREPOSITIONAL PHRASES: H 415

> *Er wohnt **in München**.*
> *Das Konzert findet **um 8 Uhr** statt.*

[1] These are not to be confused with direct objects [→ H 402 note].

H 416   INFINITIVES:

> *Wir gehen **tanzen.***
> *Ich gehe **schilaufen.***

H 417   PRESENT PARTICIPLES:[1]

> *Das Kleid deiner Tochter ist **entzückend.***
> *Der Film war **aufregend.***

H 418   PAST PARTICIPLES:[2]

> *Das Essen ist **angebrannt.***
> *Der Mann ist **betrunken.***

H 419   SUBORDINATE CLAUSES:

> *Ich wohne, **wo du auch wohnst.***
> *Wir gehen, **wann du willst.***
> *Meine Tochter bleibt, **was sie ist.***
> ***Als wir nach Europa kamen,** war Krieg.*

Types of Predicate Complements

Complements of Place

H 420   For events, COMPLEMENTS of PLACE either indicate the goal or destination towards which the subject is striving (question: **wohin?**), or the place from which the subject emanates or originates (question: **woher?**). For states of being, they describe the position at which the subject is located (question: **wo?**). Destination, origin, or location may of course also be used in a figurative sense, where questions of this type are not applicable. Complements of place are usually adverbs or prepositional phrases.

> *Ich wohne **in einem Hotel.***
> *Er fährt **nach München.***
> *Wir sind **hier.***
> *Er kommt **aus Berlin.***

> *Das Gesetz tritt am 1. Januar **in Kraft.***
> *Der Automat ist **in Betrieb.***

---

[1] These function like adjectives [→ B 807].

[2] These are either apparent passives [→ B 610] or function like adjectives [→ B 836].

536

If the sentence contains both a subject and an object [→ H 003], the complement of place indicates the position to which or from which the subject brings the object (question: **wohin?** or **woher?**) or the location at which the subject leaves the object (question: **wo?**). In figurative usages, these questions do not apply.

> *Ich stelle **den Teller auf den Tisch.***
> *Bringen Sie **das Essen ins Zimmer**!*
> *Wir haben **unsere Bücher zu Hause** gelassen.*
> *Er holt **seinen Wagen aus der Garage.***
>
> *Der Lehrer stellte **den Schüler zur Rede.***
> *Er nahm **sein Diplom in Empfang.***
> *Du hast **mich im Stich** gelassen.*

If the complement of place designates a part of the human body (both literally and figuratively), a personal modifier [→ H 558] names the person to whom the part of the body belongs. This modifier is in the dative [→ dative of possession D 941]:[1]

> *Sie schlug **ihm ins Gesicht.***
> *Er schaute **mir in die Augen.***
> *Der Ball flog **ihm an den Kopf.***
> *Sein Gerede fällt **mir auf die Nerven.***
> *Dein Wohl liegt **mir am Herzen.***

Besides the complement of place and the accusative object, such a dative construction may indicate the person to whom the action concerning the accusative object refers [→ H 556, dative of interest D 942]:

> *Ich warf **ihm den Ball an den Kopf.***
> *Er nahm **mir das Geld weg.***
> *Ich treibe **dir diese Idee aus dem Kopf.***
> *Er stellt **sich uns zur Verfügung.***

Complements of Time

COMPLEMENTS of TIME define or locate events and states of being with respect to time, specifying either a point or a space in time. The

---

[1] Although usually replaced by a possessive, the dative of possession also occurs in similar constructions in English: She hit him in the face. He looked me in the eye.

complement, which may be a noun, adverb, or prepositional phrase, answers various questions, such as **wann?, seit wann?, bis wann?, wie lange?, wie spät?,** etc.:

> *Friedrich der Große lebte **im 18. Jahrhundert.***
> *Der Unterricht dauerte **zwei Stunden.***
> *Es ist **neun Uhr.***
> *Sie blieben **drei Tage.***

H 431 They may also indicate the extent or duration of an event which appears in the sentence as an object (both literally and figuratively):

> *Man zog **die Verhandlungen in die Länge.***[1]
> *Er zog **die Bezahlung** seiner Schulden **auf drei Wochen** hinaus.*
> *Wir schoben **die Beantwortung** der Briefe **auf die lange Bank.***[1]

Complements of Manner

H 440 COMPLEMENTS of MANNER describe the state of being in which the subject finds itself; they are usually predicate adjectives or participles used adjectivally:

> *Peter ist **krank.***
> *Die Tür steht **offen.***
> *Der Saal wird **voll.***
> *Der Schüler benimmt sich **schlecht.***
> *Der Lehrer blieb **wütend.***
> *Du stellst dich **ungeschickt** an.*
> *Wir verhalten uns **ruhig.***

H 441 This state of being may also be placed into a relationship with another person [→ H 556 ff.; cf. dative of interest D 942]:

> *Die Tochter sieht **ihrer Mutter ähnlich.***
> *Der Mann ist **mir fremd.***
> *Regen ist **den Pflanzen nützlich.***
> *Das Auto war **ihm zu teuer.***
> *Ich stehe **dir zu Diensten.***

---

[1] In examples such as these, it is difficult to differentiate between figurative complements of place and time.

538

A genitive object together with a complement of manner indicates the concept, being, or thing which brings about the state of the subject [→ H 386]:[1]

> *Der Mann ist **des Diebstahls verdächtig**.*
> *Er war **dieser Auszeichnung** nicht **würdig**.*
> *Wir sind uns **unserer Schuld bewußt**.*
> *Die Polizei ist **des Diebes habhaft** geworden.*
> *Sind Sie **der englischen Sprache** mächtig?*

A complement of manner often requires a prepositional object to indicate the aim, the dependence, the being, concept, or thing, on which the state of the subject is based:[1]

> *Die Mutter ist **um ihr Kind besorgt**.*
> *Wir sind **mit dem Kauf einverstanden**.*
> *Ich bin **mit diesem Mann verwandt**.*
> *Er ist **wütend über euch**.*
> *Sei nicht so **hart gegen mich**!*
> *Wir sind **müde von der Arbeit**.*

A dative object may appear together with a prepositional object and a complement of manner, if the state or condition of the subject refers to a person [→ H 441]:

> *Der Sohn ist **seinem Vater im Charakter ähnlich**.*
> *Wir sind **ihnen in der Technik voraus**.*

A complement of place is added to the complement of manner if the condition or process referred to in the complement of manner requires clarification as to its location:

> *Ich bin **in Berlin beheimatet**.*
> *Sie ist **in München wohnhaft**.*

If a complement of manner requires an accusative object, especially after the verbs **wissen, wünschen, glauben, stellen, nennen, schimpfen,** etc., the

---

[1] As indicated in H 380 ff., prepositional objects are being used more and more frequently to replace genitive objects. The meaning may change slightly (e.g. *Wir sind müde von der Arbeit* instead of *Wir sind der Arbeit müde*).

complement describes the condition in which the object finds itself [→ H 338]:

*Ich nenne **ihn faul.***	(*Ich glaube, daß er faul ist.*)
*Ich wünsche **dich zufrieden.***	(*Du sollst zufrieden sein.*)
*Wir fühlen **uns müde.***	(*Wir sind müde.*)
*Er stellt **sich krank.***	(*Er tut, als sei er krank.*)
*Ich finde **sie entzückend.***[1]	(*Meiner Meinung nach ist sie entzückend.*)

H 447   A complement of manner may also describe the condition into which the accusative object is brought. Some complements of manner have been so firmly connected with some verbs, that they are written as one word with the infinitive and are considered as verb prefixes (e.g. **zu·knöpfen**):

*Er gibt **seine Verlobung bekannt.***	(*Die Verlobung wird bekannt.*)
*Sie brach **das Glas entzwei.***	(*Das Glas geht entzwei.*)
*Wir jagen **die Jungen davon** (**fort**).*	(*Die Jungen sind fort.*)
*Sie knöpft **ihren Mantel zu.***	(*Der Mantel ist zu.*)
*Wir essen **den Teller leer.***	(*Der Teller ist leer.*)

H 448   A complement of manner may sometimes appear to make an intransitive verb transitive by referring to an accusative object:

*Bei dem langen Marsch habe ich mir **die Füße wund** gelaufen.*
*Ich habe **mich** über den Komiker **krank** gelacht.*
*Das Mädchen weinte sich über den Verlust ihres Geldes **die Augen rot.***

H 449   When the action of the subject refers to a person, a dative object [→ H 441] may occur together with the complement of manner and the accusative object:

*Ich mache **dir die Regel klar.***
*Machen Sie **mir die Tür auf**!*
*Sie knöpfte **ihrem kleinen Kind den Mantel zu.***
*Er gab **seinen Freunden seine Verlobung bekannt.***

H 450   A genitive object together with a complement of manner and an accusative object indicates the being or thing which causes the condition in which the accusative object finds itself as a result of the action:

---

[1] Note the difference between *Ich fand sie entzückend* (I found, i.e. considered her to be, charming) and *Ich fand sie schlafend* (I found, i.e. discovered, her while she was asleep). **Entzückend** is used as an adjective, **schlafend** as a present participle.

*Das Gericht sprach **den Mann des Betrugs schuldig.***

With some verbs, the complement of manner is joined to the accusative   H 451
object by **als** or **für** [→ H 342]:

> *Ich betrachte diese Arbeit **als schwierig.***
> *Er hält die Angelegenheit **für gut.***

Complements of Cause

COMPLEMENTS of CAUSE indicate the reason or cause for an event; they   H 455
are prepositional phrases:

> *Er heiratete sie **aus Liebe.***
> *Er sieht den Wald **vor lauter Bäumen** nicht.*
> *Der Unfall geschah **aus Unachtsamkeit.***

Predicate Nominative

The PREDICATE NOMINATIVE serves as a complement of the verbs **sein,**   H 460
werden [but → H 467], **(ver)bleiben, sich dünken, heißen,** and **scheinen.**
It designates a person, concept, or thing which is to be equated with the
subject. The predicate nominative answers the questions **wer?** or **was?**
(sometimes **wie?**).

The predicate nominative may belong to the following parts of speech: H 461

1. NOUNS:

> *Dieses große Haus ist **eine Schule.***
> *Karl wurde **Ingenieur.***
> *Das gestrige Fußballspiel war **ein Ereignis.***
> *Jetzt wird es **Nacht.***
> *Herr Müller bleibt **Direktor** der Fabrik.*
> *Mein Freund heißt **Franz.***
> *Sie dünken sich **Helden.***
> *Ich verbleibe mit herzlichen Grüßen **Dein alter Freund Otto.***

2. INFLECTED ADJECTIVES[1] which have a classifying or demonstrative

---

[1] Uninflected adjectives are considered complements of manner [→ H 440]. After an
inflected adjective, there is always a noun to be understood; in English, this noun is usually
replaced by "one," except in such phrases as *Heute ist der dritte*: Today is the third (day
of the month). But: *Du bist heute der dritte, der mich das fragt*: You are the third one.

541

function and indicate the type or species to which the subject belongs. Declensional endings depend on the noun to which the adjective refers:

> *Sehen Sie die schönen Teppiche? Dieser hier ist **ein türkischer** und der dort ist **ein persischer.***
> *Dieses Auto ist grün, aber unseres ist **ein rotes.***
> *Die heutige Lage ist **eine kritische.***
> *Dein Kleid ist **kein billiges.***
> *Heute ist **der dritte.***
> *Die gestrige Konferenz war **die wichtigste.***
> *Der teuerste Stoff ist nicht immer **der beste.***
> *Seine Worte waren **folgende** (**die folgenden**).*

3. NUMERICAL ADJECTIVES:

> *Ihr seid **fünf.***
> *Wir sind **zehn.***

4. PRONOUNS, usually with strong (primary) inflection. If the pronoun, however, follows a definite article, it has weak (secondary) inflection:[1]

> *Wessen Haus ist das? Das ist **meins** (**meines**).*
> *Ist das nicht mein Füller? Ja, das ist **deiner.***
> *Wessen Haus ist das? Das ist **das meine.***
> *Was wir machen, ist immer **das gleiche** (**dasselbe**).*

5. INFINITIVES:

> *Wir stehen vor der Prüfung. Jetzt heißt es **arbeiten.***

6. PREPOSITIONAL INFINITIVES and infinitive clauses:

> *Er scheint **zu beten.***
> *Seine größte Freude ist, **Briefmarken zu sammeln.***

7. If a prepositional infinitive expresses a state of being, it refers to a passive process which depends on a modal verb. In English, this corresponds to something which is to be, can be, should be, or must be done:

> *Dieses Haus ist **zu verkaufen** (= **soll** verkauft werden).* This house is to be sold.
> *Der Gipfel des Berges ist von hier deutlich **zu sehen** (= **kann** gesehen werden).* The mountaintop can be seen clearly from here.

---

[1] In poetic usage, pronouns are undeclined: *Ich bin dein. — Mein ist die Rache.*

542

*Diese Sätze sind bis morgen **zu schreiben** (= **sollen, müssen** ge-schrieben werden).* These sentences are to be, should be, must be written by tomorrow.

*Das bleibt noch **zu entscheiden** (= ist noch nicht entschieden worden).* That is still to be decided.

8. SUBORDINATE CLAUSES:

*Der Wunsch des Vaters ist, **daß sein Sohn in Berlin Medizin studiert.***

*Das Wetter wird, **wie ich vorausgesagt habe.***

*Er ist geworden, **was er immer erstrebt hatte.***

*Die große Frage ist, **wie man schnell reich werden kann.***

9. RELATIVE clauses in the predicate nominative are preceded by an anticipatory **es**:

*Mein Freund war **es, der dich heute besuchen wollte.***

*Die Kinder sind **es, die den Eltern die größte Freude bereiten.***

*Graf Zeppelin war **es, der das nach ihm benannte Luftschiff erfunden hat.***

*Ich bin **es, der dir helfen will.***

Predicate nominatives may also occur after the conjunctions **als** and **wie** [but → H 472]:   H 465

*Ich komme **als guter Freund.***

*Er starb **als großer Held.***

*Er sprach **wie ein dummer Mensch.***

Notice the difference: H 466

*Er sprach **als** ein guter Freund der Familie* — as a good friend, i.e. in his capacity as friend.

*Er sprach **wie** ein guter Freund der Familie* — like a good friend, i.e. in the manner appropriate for a friend.

Werden may sometimes be followed by the preposition **zu** (with a noun in the DATIVE) in the sense of "to turn into, to be elected as," etc.:   H 467

*Er wurde **zum Verbrecher.***

*Er ist zum **Präsidenten** gewählt worden.*

Predicate Accusative

The predicate accusative is used to complement the verbs **glauben,**   H 470

543

heißen,[1] **nennen, schelten, schimpfen, schmähen, taufen,** and **titulieren** (archaic) [→ double accusative H 348] and a few reflexive verbs (e.g. **sich fühlen**). It designates a person, concept, or thing which is to be equated with the accusative object. It answers the questions **was?** or **wie?**

H 471   The following parts of speech occur as predicate accusatives:

1. NOUNS:

*Er nennt **mich seinen Freund.***	*(Ich bin sein Freund.)*
*Wir glaubten **ihn Herrn der Lage.***	*(Er war Herr der Lage.)*
*Er schreibt **sich Mueller.***	*(Sein Name wird „Mueller" geschrieben.)*
*Sie fühlt **sich Mutter.***	*(Sie ist Mutter.)*

2. INFLECTED ADJECTIVES:[2]

*Ich nenne eine solche Arbeit **eine ausgezeichnete.***

3. INFINITIVES with or without modifiers:

*Der Sportler hat für die hundert Meter knapp 10 Sekunden gebraucht. Das nenne ich **laufen.***

*Wenn jemand etwas Überflüssiges tut, nennt man das **Eulen nach Athen tragen.***

4. DEPENDENT CLAUSES:

*Nennen Sie es, **wie Sie wollen.***

H 472   Other verbs with similar denotations add a predicate accusative after the conjunctions **als** and **wie** [→ H 465] or the preposition **für**:

*Ich betrachte ihn **als einen ehrlichen Menschen.***
*Ich kenne Robert **als einen fleißigen Schüler.***
*Ich halte Robert **für einen fleißigen Schüler.***
*Er begrüßte mich **wie einen alten Freund.***

H 473   In a similar construction, the preposition **zu** may be used, with the noun following in the DATIVE [→ H 467]:[3]

*Man machte ihn **zum Direktor.***

---

[1] In the unusual sense of "to call": *Das heiße ich einen festen Schlaf!*

[2] An uninflected adjective is considered a complement of manner [→ H 446].

[3] Technically, this could be called a predicate dative. The term, however, is not used.

Subject as Predicate Complement

The subject itself may also be given the function of describing an event   H 475
or a state of being. It then becomes a predicate complement. Because of
its formal function within the sentence, it is called a PREDICATE SUBJECT.

Predicate subjects occur with predicates the verbs of which report of an   H 476
event or a state of being without mentioning it. Such verbs are **geschehen,
passieren, sich ereignen, vorkommen, stattfinden,** etc. Predicate subjects
differ from ordinary subjects by their position within the sentence field:
since they complete the predicate function, they occupy the first V_2
position at the end (posterior limit) of the sentence field [→ multiple
predicate parts, H 121; cf. H 734 ff.]:

> *Gestern ereignete sich um 5.30 Uhr am Stadtrand **ein Verkehrsunfall.***
>
> *Morgen findet in der Stadthalle **ein Konzert** statt.*
>
> *Heute ist unserer Köchin bei der Zubereitung des Essens in der Küche
> **ein Mißgeschick** passiert.*
>
> *Es wurde gemeldet, daß sich während der Atlantiküberquerung des
> Segelschiffes **ein schwerer Sturm** erhoben habe.*
>
> *Hans erzählte mir, daß den Schülern während des Geschichtsunter-
> richts bei dem neuen Lehrer **die Zeit** schnell vergangen sei.*
>
> *Gestern ist nach einer langen Regenperiode unerwartet schnell **eine
> plötzliche Wetterverbesserung** eingetreten.*
>
> *Während seines ganzen Lebens war diesem Mann **kein Erfolg**
> beschieden.*

Note the position of the subject if the verb in the predicate describes the   H 477
event by itself [→ H 711 ff.]:

> *Gestern verursachte **ein Autofahrer** um 5.30 Uhr am Stadtrand einen
> Verkehrsunfall.*
>
> *Morgen veranstaltet **unser Verein** ein Konzert in der Stadthalle.*
>
> *Im letzten Jahr erhob sich **das Volk** gegen die Militärdiktatur.*
>
> *Letztes Jahr ist **Peter** nach langem Zögern endlich in den Turnverein
> eingetreten.*

For expressions which describe feelings, sensations, or emotions, the   H 478
person to which these feelings refer is expressed by an accusative object;
the cause of these feelings is expressed by a subject nominative or a
subject clause. If the subject clause is in the postfield, the empty subject

545

position in the prefield is taken up by an anticipatory **es** [→ H 056]:[1]

Ganz besonders ärgert den Lehrer die Faulheit der Schüler.

Es   ärgert den Lehrer, daß die Schüler faul sind.

Mich schmerzt vor allem der Tod meines Freundes.

Es   schmerzt mich, daß mein Freund gestorben ist.

Dein Besuch freut uns.

Es   freut uns, daß du uns besuchst.

Object as Predicate Complement

H 480   Just like the subject, the object may also have the function of describing an event or a state of being as a predicate complement. Because of its function in the sentence, it is then called a PREDICATE OBJECT.

H 481   Among the verbs which may complete the predicate by having an accusative object as a predicate complement at the end of the sentence field are: **begehen, bieten, brechen, geben, gewinnen, haben, halten, leisten, machen, nehmen, schenken, schlagen, stiften, tragen, treiben, tun, werfen, wirken,** and others:[2]

*Er beging im Leben **viele Dummheiten.***

*Ein neuer Lehrer gibt heute in unserer Klasse **Unterricht.***

*Habt ihr an eurer neuen Arbeit schon **Geschmack** gewonnen?*

*Der Minister hält morgen im Kongreßsaal **eine Rede.***

*Der Professor hat im letzten Semester jeden Montag und Mittwoch um 2 Uhr **Vorlesungen** gehalten.*

*Wir wollen nächstes Jahr **eine Reise nach Deutschland** machen.*

*Leisten Sie dem Verletzten **Hilfe**!*

*Tun Sie mir bitte **den Gefallen** und tragen Sie sofort **Sorge,** daß die Kinder immer **Ruhe** halten.*

Summary of All Possible Predicate Complements

H 490   NOMINATIVE

as predicate nominative: *Mein Freund ist **Student.***
*Es wurde **Nacht.***

as predicate subject: *Gestern geschah in der Stadt **ein Unfall.***
*Morgen findet in der Stadthalle **ein Konzert** statt.*

---

[1] Occasionally, there may be no subject at all: *Es friert mich. Mich friert.*

[2] Speaking or understanding a language are also considered predicate objects: *Wir sprechen zu Hause immer **Deutsch.***

ACCUSATIVE OBJECT

as predicate object:	*Er beging im Leben **viele Dummheiten.***
	*Der Kaufmann will hier **Geschäfte** machen.*
+ dative object:	*Der Lehrer gibt **dem Schüler das Buch.***
	*Der Vater verbietet **seinem Sohn die Reise.***
+ genitive object:	*Man enthob **ihn seines Amtes.***
	*Er klagte **sie des Betrugs** an.*
+ prepositional object:	*Er schrieb **einen Brief an seine Mutter.***
	*Ich bat **ihn um Antwort.***
+ complement of place:	*Ich stelle **die Tasse auf den Tisch.***
	*Er bringt **das Auto in die Garage.***
+ complement of place and dative object:	*Er setzt sich **den Hut auf den Kopf.***
	*Sie brachte **mir die Zeitung ins Haus.***
+ complement of time:	*Man vertagte **die Sitzung bis Montag.***
	*Er verschob **die Reise auf nächstes Jahr.***
+ complement of manner:	*Sie ißt **den Teller leer.***
	*Ich halte **das Geschäft für gut.***
+ complement of manner and dative object:	*Wir tun **dir nichts zuleide.***
	*Ich mache **ihm das Leben sauer.***
+ complement of manner and genitive object:	*Ich halte **ihn dieses Amtes fähig.***
	*Das Gericht sprach **ihn des Mordes schuldig.***
+ complement of manner and prepositional object:	*Ich mache **Sie mit meiner Frau bekannt.***
	*Er machte **sich von seinen Eltern unabhängig.***
+ complement of cause:	*Sie heiratete **ihn aus Liebe.***
	*Er sieht **den Wald vor lauter Bäumen** nicht.*
+ predicate accusative:	*Der Pfarrer taufte **das Kind Peter.***
	*Er nannte **mich einen Dummkopf.***
+ accusative object:	*Er lehrt **mich die Grammatik.***
	*Die Reise kostete **ihn ein Vermögen.***
+ predicate infinitive:	*Wir sehen **die Kinder spielen.***
	*Ich bitte **dich zu kommen.***

DATIVE OBJECT

by itself:	*Das Rauchen schadet **der Gesundheit.**[1]*
	*Ich weiche **der Gewalt.***
+ infinitive object:	*Ich erlaube **dir zu kommen.***
	*Er befahl **ihr einzutreten.***

[1] Again, this could be (but is not) called a "predicate dative."

547

H 493   GENITIVE OBJECT

         by itself: *Er bedarf **der Hilfe**.*[1]

                                    *Das·spottet **jeder Beschreibung**.*

H 494   PREPOSITIONAL OBJECT

         by itself: *Sie leidet **an schwerem Asthma**.*

                                    *Ich rechne **mit deinem Besuch**.*

         + dative object: *Ich rate **dir von dieser Reise** ab.*

                                    *Sein Fleiß gereicht **ihm zur Ehre**.*

         + prepositional object: *Er sprach **zu seinen Freunden über seine Reise**.*

                                    *Er fuhr **auf drei Wochen** nach Deutschland.*

H 495   COMPLEMENT of PLACE

         by itself: *Ich, wohne **in einem Hotel**.*

                                    *Das Gesetz tritt morgen **in Kraft**.*

         + dative object: *Er schlug **dem Jungen ins Gesicht**.*

                                    *Wir eilten **dem Kind zu Hilfe**.*

H 496   COMPLEMENT of TIME

         by itself: *Sie blieben **drei Tage**.*

                                    *Es ist **neun Uhr**.*

H 497   COMPLEMENT of CAUSE

         by itself: *Der Unfall geschah **aus Unachtsamkeit**.*

                                    *Er tötete seine Frau **aus Eifersucht**.*

H 498   COMPLEMENT of MANNER

         by itself: *Die Tür steht **offen**.*

                                    *Der Lehrer ist **wütend**.*

         + dative object: *Das Kind sieht **seiner Mutter ähnlich**.*

                                    *Der Anzug steht **Ihnen gut**.*

         + genitive object: *Der Angeklagte ist **des Diebstahls verdächtig**.*

                                    *Die Polizei wurde **seiner habhaft**.*

         + prepositional object: *Mein Freund ist **bei allen Leuten beliebt**.*

                                    *Ich bin **über seine Frechheit empört**.*

---

[1] The term "predicate genitive" is not used.

548

+ prepositional object and dative object:	*Peter ist **seinem Freund im Sport über-legen.***
	*Das neue Auto ist **dem alten Modell im Äußeren gleich.***
+ complement of place:	*Richard ist **in England beheimatet.***
	*Ich bin **in Amerika wohnhaft.***

PREDICATE MODIFIERS

PREDICATE MODIFIERS are sentence units (words or phrases) which may be added to the description of a situation, in order to supplement the information contained in the statement [→ H 002, 004, 230]. They are not essential[1] for the description of the basic situation itself, but merely provide additional detail.

H 550

Modifiers may be recognized in a sentence by the test of omissibility. If we eliminate all sentence units which are not essential for the description of the situation (i.e. all units without which the remainder would still be a complete sentence), we have stripped the sentence down to the sentence core, i.e. the predicate and its complements, the subject, and the objects. The sentence units which were eliminated are predicate modifiers.

H 551

We must also distinguish between PREDICATE MODIFIERS, which are sentence units and therefore add information to the sentence as a whole,[2] and ATTRIBUTES [→ J 100 ff.], which are part of a sentence unit and provide additional information about a specific word. In the examples listed below, predicate modifiers appear in **bold print** between parentheses (to indicate their omissibility). Attributes, which are also nonessential additions, appear within brackets.[3]

H 552

> (*Am* [*gestrigen*] *Abend*) *sind wir* (***bei einem Spaziergang im Park zufällig***) [*unseren*] *Freunden begegnet.*
> *Peter fuhr* (***auf einige Tage mit seinen Eltern***) *an die See.*
> (***Wegen des*** [*schlechten*] ***Wetters***) *konnte* (***letzte Woche***) *der* [*seit langem geplante*] *Ausflug* (***nicht***) *stattfinden.*

---

[1] Note the contrast with predicate complements, which provide essential information.

[2] Essentially, they modify the verb, as an adjective modifies a noun.

[3] If a predicate modifier appears in the prefield, its omission requires rearrangement of word order, with the subject moving into the prefield position.

549

(*Trotz* [*hartnäckigen*] *Leugnens*) *konnte der Angeklagte* (*vom Gericht*) *des Diebstahls überführt werden.*

Ich habe (*meinem Freund*) *den Brief* [*, den er aus England bekam,*] (*mit Leichtigkeit*) *übersetzen können.*

Du bist (*doch eigentlich zum Sprachstudium*) *nach Deutschland gefahren.*

Types of Predicate Modifiers

H 555 According to their content, we distinguish the following three types of predicate modifiers:

1. Modifiers of Person
2. Circumstantial Modifiers (also called adverbial modifiers)
3. Particles (also called intensifiers)

Modifiers of Person

H 556 A modifier of person within a sentence indicates the person for (or against) whose benefit the situation occurs, or who is interested in the situation. This person, however, does not play an essential role in the situation itself [→ H 003, 210 ff., 230]. A modifier of person may follow the preposition **für** or it may occur in the dative [→ D 940 DATIVE of INTEREST]:

*Peter hat den Brief **für euch** zur Post gebracht* (*hat **euch** den Brief . . .*).

*Ich gehe **für meinen Kollegen** zum Direktor.*

*Die Arbeit ist zu schwer **für sie*** (*ist **ihnen** zu schwer*).

*Kinder sind eine Freude **für die Eltern*** (*sind **den Eltern** eine Freude*).

*Ich kann mit Hans nicht Schritt halten; er läuft zu schnell **für mich*** (*läuft **mir** zu schnell*).

*Er versteht eure Philosophie nicht; sie ist zu hoch **für ihn*** (*ist **ihm** zu hoch*).

*Helfen Sie der Dame und öffnen Sie **ihr** die Tür* (*öffnen Sie die Tür **für sie***)!

*Du warst **mir** immer ein treuer Freund.*

*Der letzte Sommer war **für die Landwirtschaft** katastrophal. **Den Bauern** ist die ganze Ernte verdorben.*

H 557 The difference between a dative object and a modifier of person in the dative (dative of interest) depends upon the verb in the predicate. If the

550

verb designates an event which must necessarily be directed towards a person, we are dealing with a dative object [→ H 350 ff.]; for example, verbs like **geben, helfen, schenken, schicken,** etc.:

> *Ich schenke **meinem Freund** das Buch.*
> *Er gab **mir** Geld.*
> *Er hilft **uns** immer.*
> *Sie schickte **ihren Eltern** eine Ansichtskarte.*

If, however, the event is not directed towards a person, but the subject performs an action in the interest or for the benefit of another person, we are dealing with a dative designating a modifier of person: [1]

> *Die Dame öffnet die Tür nicht selbst, sondern ich öffne **der Dame** die Tür.*
> *Nicht ich bezahle für den Anzug, sondern mein Vater kauft ihn **mir.***
> *Mein Freund ist beschäftigt, daher bringe ich **meinem Freund** den Brief zur Post.*

Occasionally, ambiguities may arise, since a sentence may sometimes have different meanings depending on whether the dative is interpreted as an indirect object or a modifier of person. If the context does not make the situation clear, misunderstandings may be avoided by replacing the dative modifier with the preposition **für**:

> *Ich kaufe **meinem Freund** Zigaretten* (i.e. I buy cigarettes which I intend to give to my friend as a present): DATIVE OBJECT.
> *Ich kaufe **meinem Freund** Zigaretten* (i.e. My friend gave me some money to buy cigarettes in his stead): MODIFIER of PERSON.
> Substitute: *Ich kaufe Zigaretten **für meinen Freund.***
> *Er schrieb **mir** einen Brief an die Universität* (i.e. I am at the University and he wrote a letter to me at that address): DATIVE OBJECT.
> *Er schrieb **mir** einen Brief an die Universität* (i.e. I needed a letter of recommendation to the University and he wrote one on my behalf): MODIFIER of PERSON.
> Substitute: *Er schrieb **für mich** einen Brief an die Universität.*

A modifier of person in the dative may also indicate a relationship of possession [→ D 941 DATIVE of POSSESSION], usually for parts of the body. The item mentioned in the sentence belongs to or is part of the person indicated in the dative.

H 558

---

[1] Again, the test of omissibility may be applied: the dative of interest does not provide essential information.

1. Subject:

>*Die Füße tun **mir** weh (**meine** Füße).*
>*__Ihm__ tränten die Augen vor Kälte (**seine** Augen).*
>*__Dem kranken Tier__ fallen die Haare aus (die Haare **des Tieres**).*

2. Object:

>*Ich putze **mir** die Zähne (**meine** Zähne).*
>*Die Mutter wäscht **dem Kind** den Kopf (den Kopf **des Kindes**).*
>*Sie hat **ihm** das Glas zerbrochen (**sein** Glas).*

3. Complement of place:

>*Der Hund sprang **ihm** an den Hals (an **seinen** Hals).*
>*Sie fielen **dem** Feind in den Rücken (in den Rücken **des Feindes**).*
>*Er ging **mir** aus dem Weg (aus **meinem** Weg).*

H 559   A dative modifier of person may also indicate a person who only indirectly takes an interest in the situation, but does not himself participate in it in any way [→ DATIVE of REFERENCE D 942]:

>*Fall **mir** nicht aus dem Fenster!*
>*Du gehst **mir** heute nicht ins Kino!*
>*Das war **dir** ein Kerl!*

H 560   Persons introduced by the preposition **von** in passive sentences are also considered as modifiers of person. Since the passive is a grammatical device of presenting an action as a process [→ H 006, B 590 ff.], the person causing the action (active voice) need not be mentioned in the process (passive voice) at all. This information is therefore non-essential to the sentence, and is classified as a predicate modifier:[1]

>*Der Angeklagte wurde (**vom Gericht**) zu drei Monaten Gefängnis verurteilt.*
>*Dort wird (**von der Baufirma Schweiger & Co.**) ein neues Hotel gebaut.*
>*Die Läden werden (**von den Besitzern**) abends um 7 Uhr geschlossen.*
>*Bei der Feier wurde (**von dem Redner**) der gefallenen Helden gedacht.*

H 561   The same also applies for persons introduced in passive sentences by the preposition **durch** [→ B 597]. This sentence unit is also a modifier of

---

[1] In some constructions, the person does constitute part of the essential information: *Diese Symphonie wurde **von Beethoven** geschrieben*. It would then be considered as a predicate complement.

person (i.e. provides additional information) and indicates the intermediary through whom the action is accomplished:

> *Der Brief wurde uns gestern (**durch einen Boten**) überbracht.*
> *Die Zimmer wurden uns (**durch ein Reisebüro**) vermittelt.*
> *Wir wurden (**durch einen Autofahrer**) auf das Unglück aufmerksam gemacht.*

Circumstantial Modifiers (Adverbial Modifiers)

CIRCUMSTANTIAL MODIFIERS describe the circumstances under which a   H 565
situation takes place. They thus modify the predicate as a whole. Since
their function is often performed by adverbs or other parts of speech
with adverbial meaning [→ H 568], they are also known as ADVERBIAL
MODIFIERS. According to their content, they can be divided into modifiers
of PLACE, TIME, MANNER, and CAUSE:

Wir gehen spazieren.

Wo gehen wir spazieren?   *Wir gehen **im Park** spazieren.*
(Place)

Wann gehen wir spazieren?   *Wir gehen **heute nachmittag***
(Time)   *spazieren.*

Wie gehen wir spazieren?   *Wir gehen **gemütlich** spazieren.*
(*Manner*)

Warum gehen wir spazieren?   *Wir gehen **wegen des schönen***
(Cause)   ***Wetters** spazieren.*

Normally, circumstantial modifiers follow one another in the sequence   H 566
Time — Cause — Manner — Place (T-C-M-P) [→ H 741]:

> ^{T} ^{P}
> *Wir gehen | **heute nachmittag** | **im Park** | spazieren.*
> ^{M} ^{P}
> *Wir gehen | **gemütlich** | **im Park** | spazieren.*
> ^{C} ^{M} ^{P}
> *Wir gehen | **wegen des schönen Wetters** | **gemütlich** | **im Park** | spazieren.*
> ^{T} ^{M}
> *Wir gehen | **heute nachmittag** | **gemütlich** | spazieren.*
> ^{T} ^{C}
> *Wir gehen | **heute nachmittag** | **wegen des schönen Wetters** |*
> ^{M} ^{P}
> ***gemütlich** | **im Park** | spazieren.*[1]

---

[1] Sentences with modifiers of all four types, to be sure, are rare.

553

H 567   When several modifiers of the same type appear in one sentence, the sequence is usually from the general to the specific:

> Wir gehen | *heute* | *nachmittag* | spazieren.
> Ich bin | *damals* | *wochenlang* | *jeden Abend* | *nach Mitternacht* | zu Bett gegangen.

Forms of the Circumstantial Modifiers

H 568   The following parts of speech may serve as circumstantial modifiers:

1. SIMPLE ADVERBS:

> Mein Freund besucht *heute* seinen Onkel.
> Wir gehen *hier oft* spazieren.
> Spielen Sie *gern* Schach?

2. ADJECTIVES USED ADVERBIALLY:

> Er fährt *schnell* zum Bahnhof.
> Er macht seine Sache *gut.*
> Die Schüler lernen in der Schule *fleißig.*

3. PRESENT PARTICIPLES USED ADVERBIALLY:

> Die Soldaten marschierten *singend* in die Stadt ein.
> *Lachend* antwortete er mir.

4. PAST PARTICIPLES USED ADVERBIALLY:

> Der Schatz lag *vergraben* unter einem Baum.
> Er lief *erschreckt* davon.
> Sie wurde *verletzt* ins Krankenhaus eingeliefert.

5. ACCUSATIVE NOUNS (adverbial accusative) [→ D 923]:

> Wir haben *drei Wochen* im Büro gearbeitet.
> Gestern hat es *den ganzen Tag* geregnet.
> Hier kommt *jede Stunde* ein Zug aus München an.

6. GENITIVE NOUNS (adverbial genitive) [→ D 965]:

> *Eines Tages* besuchte mich mein Onkel.
> *Des Mittags* ruht er immer ein wenig.
> *Eines Nachts* schlug ein Blitz in unser Haus ein.

7. Nouns with prepositions (prepositional phrase, used adverbially):

> *Er kam **aus der Schule** heim.*
> ***Wegen des schlechten Wetters** bleiben wir heute zu Hause.*
> ***Seit letztem Montag** liegt auf den Bergen Schnee.*

8. Adverbial clauses. A prepositional phrase may be replaced by a dependent clause which may occupy either the prefield or the postfield:

> ***Bei unserer Ankunft** in Salzburg regnete es.*
> ***Als wir in Salzburg ankamen,** regnete es.*
>
> ***Wegen des schlechten Wetters** blieben wir zu Hause.*
> *Wir blieben zu Hause, **weil das Wetter schlecht war.***

Present or past participles may be extended by means of modifiers of their own. In this case, they and all sentence units referring to them are set off by commas [→ B 840 ff.]. The participial clause may appear in the prefield, within the sentence field, or in the postfield: H 569

> ***Erstaunt über den plötzlichen Besuch seines Freundes,** trat er in das Zimmer ein.*
> *Die Frau lief, **laut um Hilfe schreiend,** durch die nächtlichen Straßen.*
> *Er starrte mich an, **die Augen weit aufgerissen.***

Types of Circumstantial Modifiers

As outlined in H 565, there are four types of adverbial modifiers: place, time, manner, and cause. H 570

Modifiers of Place

A modifier of place indicates the location at which the situation occurs. It answers the question **wo?**:[1] H 571

> ***In jener Schule** habe ich Deutsch gelernt.*
> *Die Wanderer kommen **des Weges.***
> *Das Buch liegt **auf dem Tisch unter der Lampe.***
> *Er arbeitet **draußen im Garten.***

---

[1] The questions **woher?** and **wohin?** refer to complements of place [→ H 420–3].

Modifiers of Time

H 575   A modifier of time may indicate the time span during which a situation occurs. It answers the question **wann?** or **wie lange?**

> *Heute gehen wir ins Theater.*
> *Man geht eine Stunde bis zum Gasthaus.*
> *Des Sommers wohnen wir auf dem Land.*
> *Im Herbst werden die Nächte kalt.*
> *In den frühen Morgenstunden hat sich ein Verkehrsunfall ereignet.*

H 576   It may indicate a point of time which coincides with the situation; it answers the question **wann?**

> *Am gleichen Tag erhielt ich einen Brief.*
> *Eines Tages besuchte uns ein Fremder.*
> *Damals war ich zehn Jahre alt.*
> *Bei meiner Ankunft in Köln (Als ich in Köln ankam,) regnete es sehr stark.*

H 577   It may indicate the time sequence after which several situations may occur. Question: **wann?**:

> *Zuerst will er seine Arbeit beenden und dann mit uns spazierengehen.*

H 578   It may indicate the repetition of a time span in which a situation occurs again and again. Question: **wann? wie oft?**:

> *Ich habe es dreimal versucht.*
> *Montags ist in der Schule kein Unterricht.*
> *Bei Ankunft eines Zuges (Sooft ein Zug ankommt,) gehen die Gepäckträger auf den Bahnsteig.*

H 579   It may indicate the point in time at which a situation begins or ends. Question: **ab wann?, seit wann?, bis wann?, wann?**:

> *Ab morgen arbeite ich in einer Fabrik.*
> *Seit letztem Montag ist Hans krank.*
> *Bis nächste Woche muß ich das Geld haben.*
> *Vor Ostern kann ich nicht zu dir kommen.*
> *Vor Beginn seines Studiums in Deutschland (Bevor er sein Studium in Deutschland beginnt,) muß Robert noch Deutsch lernen.*
> *Bis zur Abfahrt des Zuges wartete ich auf dem Bahnhof. (Ich wartete auf dem Bahnhof, bis der Zug abfuhr.)*

*Karl bleibt **bis zum Ende seiner Ferien** in München. (Karl bleibt in München, **bis seine Ferien beendet sind.**)*
***Seit dem Beginn des Semesters** haben die Schüler viel gelernt. (Die Schüler haben viel gelernt, **seit das Semester begann.**)*

Modifiers of Manner

A modifier of manner indicates the way in which a situation occurs. It   H 580
answers the question **wie?**:

*Wir gehen **schnell** in die Schule.*
*Der Schüler lernt **gut** Deutsch.*
*Er schläft **den Schlaf des Gerechten.***
***Erhobenen Hauptes** ging er aus dem Zimmer.*
***In aller Eile** beendete er seine Arbeit.*
*Er tötete die Schlange **mit einem Steinwurf** (, **indem er einen Stein nach ihr warf**).*
*Ich habe den Berg **ohne große Schwierigkeiten** bestiegen. (Ich habe den Berg bestiegen, **ohne daß ich große Schwierigkeiten hatte.**)*

It may indicate a real or imaginary comparison. Question: **wie?**:   H 581

*Die Soldaten kämpften **wie die Löwen.***
*Er benimmt sich einfältig **wie ein Kind.***
*Die Arbeiter bekommen ihren Lohn **je nach Leistung** (. . ., **wie er ihrer Leistung entspricht**).*

It may indicate a circumstance which accompanies a situation or one   H 582
which is missing. Question: **mit wem?, womit?, ohne wen?, ohne was?, wie?**:

*Ich gehe **mit meinem Bruder** ins Theater.*
*Sie geht **ohne mich** spazieren.*
*Treten Sie **ohne anzuklopfen** ein!*
*Er ging an mir vorbei, **ohne mich zu sehen.***
*Der Herr grüßte die Dame, **indem er den Hut zog.***

The modifier of manner also indicates a contrast [→ H 640]; no ques-   H 583
tion possible:

***Statt eines Motorrads** kaufte sich mein Freund nur ein Fahrrad.*
***Anstatt für die Schule zu arbeiten** (Anstatt daß du für die Schule arbeitest,) gehst du zum Tennisspielen.*

557

H 584   The modifier of manner may indicate a number of other circumstances
under which a situation occurs, such as extent, content, result, intensity,
motive, material, etc.:

> *Das Wasser hat sich **um 5 Grad** erwärmt.*
> *Er starb **den Heldentod** im Feindesland.*
> *Sie weinte **Krokodilstränen**.*
> *Er schwitzt **Blut**.*
> *Teer gewinnt man **aus Kohle**.*
> *Man stellt heute viele Dinge **aus Kunststoffen** her.*

H 585   The modifier of manner may indicate the result, consequence, or effect
of a situation. Question: **wie?**:

> ***Zur großen Freude** des Lehrers bestanden alle Schüler die schwierige
> Prüfung.*
> *Die Männer arbeiteten **zur Zufriedenheit** des Direktors.*
> *Er war über die Nachricht **zu Tode** erschrocken.*
> *Er sprach so schnell, **daß wir ihn nicht verstehen konnten**.*

H 586   It may also indicate that a result did not, can not, or should not occur:

> *Er ist zu müde, **als daß er noch weiterarbeiten könnte**.*

H 587   The modifier of manner may also indicate the means through which the
situation is accomplished, or the means which were not used:

> *Der Lehrer schreibt **mit Kreide** an die Tafel.*
> ***Durch Fleiß** erreicht man im Leben viel.*
> *Dort geht Hans; ich erkenne ihn **an seinem Gang**.*
> *Wir können heute **ohne Schirm** spazierengehen. (Wir können heute
> spazierengehen, **ohne einen Regenschirm zu benützen**. —, **ohne daß
> wir einen Regenschirm mitnehmen müssen**.)*
> *Der Arzt konnte das Leben des Patienten **durch eine sofortige
> Operation** retten. (Der Arzt konnte das Leben des Patienten
> **dadurch** retten, **daß er ihn sofort operierte**.)*
> ***Durch einen Druck auf diesen Knopf** wird die Maschine in Gang
> gesetzt. (Die Maschine wird in Gang gesetzt, **indem** man auf diesen
> Knopft drückt.)*

H 588   Sometimes a modifier of manner may indicate a combination of circumstance and cause:

> *Der arme Mann ist **Hungers** (**vor Hunger**) gestorben.*

558

Modifier of Cause

Modifiers of cause designate the reason or cause for a situation. We dis- H 590
tinguish the following types: insufficient cause, possible cause, and real
cause.

The modifier of cause indicates an INSUFFICIENT CAUSE if the circum- H 591
stance described did not or can not influence the situation sufficiently,
or does not cause the situation to occur:

> *Trotz seines Fleißes* konnte er die Prüfung nicht bestehen.
> *Bei allen Schwierigkeiten* hatte er doch Erfolg.
> *Trotz seines Reichtums (obwohl er reich ist,)* ist er nicht glücklich.

The modifier of cause indicates a POSSIBLE CAUSE if the circumstance H 592
states the conditions under which the situation may occur:

> *Bei gutem Wetter* wollen wir an die See fahren.
> *Im Falle einer Verschlechterung seines Zustands* muß der Kranke ins
> Krankenhaus.
> *Bei vorheriger Zahlung der Gebühren (Wenn Sie die Gebühren vorher
> bezahlen,)* können wir Ihnen einen Platz reservieren.

The modifier of cause indicates the REAL CAUSE if the circumstances H 593
mentioned are the logical reason or motive of the situation. Question:
warum?, weshalb?, weswegen?:

> Alle Leute lieben ihn **wegen seiner Freundlichkeit.**
> Sie konnte **vor Schmerzen** nicht schlafen.
> **Wegen des schlechten Wetters** (**Weil das Wetter schlecht war,**)
> blieben wir zu Hause.
> **Wegen der schlechten Straße** konnte ich nicht schnell fahren. (*Ich
> konnte nicht schnell fahren,* **da die Straße schlecht war.**)

The modifier of cause may indicate the purpose or goal of an action or H 594
the intention of the subject. Question: **wozu?**:

> Wir gehen heute **zum Tanzen** in ein Café.
> Das Orchester spielt **zur Unterhaltung der Gäste** (. . ., **um die Gäste
> zu unterhalten — damit die Gäste unterhalten werden**).
> Ich gebe dir Geld **zum Kauf eines neuen Anzugs** (. . ., **damit du dir
> einen neuen Anzug kaufen kannst**).

559

Particles (Intensifiers)

H 600   The so-called PARTICLES or INTENSIFIERS are sentence units which indicate the subjective attitude of the speaker toward the content of the utterance. They do not change the meaning of the statement, the question, the command, or the exclamation [→ H 002, 007]. They merely give the speaker the opportunity of expressing his surprise, admiration, impatience, skepticism, lack of interest, irony, etc.

H 601   Several conjunctions and a number of adverbs may occur as particles [cf. attributes of rank J 180 ff.]. Their precise meaning is very difficult to pin down, and their active use with all possible shades of emphasis demands a fine feeling for the language. They occur predominantly in colloquial language, but many of them are found in literary usage as well.

H 602   The following list does not lay any claim to completeness, neither in the listing of all possible particles, nor in all their conceivable different meanings.[1] The examples given are likewise intended to be merely illustrative, but by no means exhaustive. Any attempt to provide exact English equivalents would be futile.[2]

H 610   **aber**

ADMIRATION (often ironic):

> *Du bist **aber** ein kluges Kind!*
> *Das ist **aber** nett von dir!*
> *Sie haben **aber** eine schöne Reise gemacht!*

H 611   **also**

INTENSIFICATION, REASSURANCE:

> *Es ist **also** wahr!*
> *Sie wollen **also** nicht?*
> ***Also**, ich gehe!*
> *Machen Sie sich **also** keine Sorgen!*

---

[1] Except in a few special instances, the list does not include the various combinations and sequences which often occur: *Jetzt hab ich **ja doch schon wieder einmal** meinen Schirm vergessen!*

[2] Merely as an illustration, here are just a few of the many possible translations of the first example listed, *Du bist **aber** ein kluges Kind!*: Aren't you a clever child! (My,) what a clever child you are! You really are a clever child! You're a clever child indeed! (I must say), you *are* a clever child (aren't you?).

auch

GENERALIZATION:

> *Was er **auch** sagt, ist gelogen.*
> *Wie dem **auch** sei, er hat nicht recht gehandelt.*
> *So klug er **auch** sein mag, das wird er nicht wissen.*

ausgerechnet

SURPRISE or ANNOYANCE at inopportune situation:

> *Er kam **ausgerechnet**, als mein Vater da war.*
> ***Ausgerechnet** heute regnet es.*
> *Meine Frau hat sich **ausgerechnet** das teuerste Kleid gekauft.*

bloß

CONCERN:

> *Wenn es **bloß** nicht regnet!*
> *Was habe ich dir **bloß** getan, daß du so unfreundlich bist?*

denn

RESOLUTION

> *Wohlan **denn**, beginnen wir die Arbeit!*
> *Sei es **denn**!*

QUESTION showing personal INTEREST:

> *Wie ist **denn** das möglich?*
> *Wie geht es dir **denn**?*
> *Was ist **denn** los?*
> *Weshalb fragst du **denn** nicht den Lehrer?*
> *Muß **denn** das gleich gemacht werden?*

doch

EMPHASIS (unstressed):

> *Das ist **doch** allerhand!*
> *Warum gehen Sie denn schon? Es ist **doch** noch gar nicht spät!*
> *Frag **doch** den Lehrer, ich bin **doch** kein Auskunftsbüro!*

CONFIRMATION of FEAR (stressed):

> *Du warst also **doch** nicht in der Schule.*
> *Er ist **doch** hingegangen, obwohl ich ihn gewarnt hatte.*
> *Er hat also **doch** gestohlen!*

561

REALIZATION of UNEXPECTED result (stressed):

> Die Bank hat ihm denn **doch** Kredit gegeben.
> Dem Wissenschaftler ist das Experiment **doch** noch gelungen.
> Wir sind nun **doch** nach Wien gefahren.

INTENSE WISH (often with subjunctive II or imperative) (unstressed):

> Wenn er **doch** käme!
> Tue das **doch**!
> Nicht **doch**!
> Denk **doch** an die armen Leute!

IMPATIENCE (unstressed):

> Nun, komm **doch**!
> Gehen Sie **doch** schon!
> Frag nicht immer dasselbe, das weißt du **doch**!

CONCERNED QUESTION (grammatical form of a statement) (unstressed):

> Er kommt **doch** morgen?
> Sie ist **doch** nicht krank?
> Du wirst mir **doch** helfen?

H 617 **eben**

RESIGNATION:

> Das ist **eben** schwer.
> Man hätte ihm **eben** das Geld nicht geben sollen.
> Peter ist **eben** ein Dummkopf.

AGREEMENT:

> Das ist es **eben**.
> Das reicht **eben** aus.
> **Eben** das wollte ich auch sagen.

NEGATIVE STRESS (in postposition):

> Er ist nicht **eben** klug.
> Das war nicht **eben** nett von dir.

H 618 **eigentlich**

INCIDENTAL AFFIRMATION:

> Das ist **eigentlich** wahr.
> Er hat **eigentlich** recht.

562

INCIDENTAL QUESTION:

> *Was bringt dich **eigentlich** her?*
> *Wann kommt **eigentlich** dein Bruder?*

einmal (mal)   H 619

RESIGNED ACCEPTANCE:

> *Das ist (**ein**)**mal** nicht zu ändern.*
> *Ich bin **nun** (**ein**)**mal** so.*

EMPHATIC REQUEST:

> *Komm (**ein**)**mal** her!*
> *Hören Sie (**ein**)**mal**!*
> *Laßt mich (**ein**)**mal** in Ruhe!*

erst   H 620

EMPHASIS:

> *Jetzt wird es **erst** schwer.*
> *Ich habe eben **erst** angefangen.*
> *Lassen Sie mich **erst** nachdenken!*

STRESSED WISH (Subjunctive II):

> *Wäre ich doch **erst** zu Hause!*
> *Wenn ich **erst** die Prüfung hinter mir hätte!*

AWAITED RESULT:

> ***Erst** der Professor konnte mir die richtige Auskunft geben.*
> *Wenn du **erst** in Deutschland bist, lernst du schnell sprechen.*
> *Wir waren gestern abend beim Tanzen, aber es ging **erst** um 11 Uhr*
> *   richtig los.*

erst recht   H 621

STRESSED NEGATIVE:

> *Sie konnte nicht Französisch, und ich **erst recht** nicht.*
> *Das macht es **erst recht** schlimm.*

DEFIANCE:

> *Wir arbeiten jetzt **erst recht** langsam.*
> *Ich werde ihm **erst recht** nicht helfen.*
> *Nun **erst recht** nicht!*

H 622 **etwa**

CHANCE:

> *Er wird das doch nicht **etwa** glauben!*
> *Könnte das **etwa** wahr sein?*
> *Wenn Sie **etwa** hören, . . .*

QUESTION for which positive answer is feared:

> *Kommt heute **etwa** der Inspektor?*
> *Hast du **etwa** dein ganzes Geld ausgegeben?*
> *Er ist doch nicht **etwa** krank?*
> *Deine Schwiergermutter kommt doch nicht **etwa**?*

H 623 **ganz**

EMPHASIS:

> *Peter ist **ganz** sein Vater.*
> *Diese Arbeit ist **ganz** mein Fall.*
> *Er ist **ganz** der Mann dafür.*

INTENSIFICATION (usually of a negative adjective):

> *Das Wetter war **ganz** schlecht.*
> *Der Saal war **ganz** leer.*
> *Das ist **ganz** unmöglich.*
> *Das ist mir **ganz** gleich.*

LIMITATION (usually of a positive adjective, often ironic):

> *Das Wetter war **ganz** schön.*
> *Er kann **ganz** gut Deutsch.*
> *Er hat uns **ganz** schöne Schwierigkeiten gemacht.*
> *Wenn morgen der Inspektor kommt, kann das **ganz** lustig werden.*

H 624 **ganz und gar**

STRONG EMPHASIS, usually with negative meaning:

> *Er ist **ganz und gar** von Sinnen.*
> *Das ist **ganz und gar** unmöglich.*
> *Das habe ich **ganz und gar** nicht so gemeint.*

H 625 **gar**

INTENSIFICATION (usually negative):

> *Das kostet **gar** viel.*
> *Das glaubt dir **gar** keiner.*
> *Ich habe das **gar** nicht so gemeint.*

564

EXCESS (usually **gar so** or **gar zu**):

> *Sei nicht **gar so** wild!*
> *Du arbeitest **gar zuviel**.*

QUESTION showing SUPPOSITION or ASTONISHMENT, often ironic:

> *Wollen Sie **gar** Ihr Haus verkaufen?*
> *Er wird doch nicht **gar** verunglückt sein?*
> *Willst du **gar** mit dem Direktor selbst sprechen?*

gerade H 626
PRECISION or EMPHASIS:

> *Du kommst **gerade** recht.*
> ***Gerade** heute muß es regnen!*
> *Das ist doch **gerade** lächerlich!*

DEFIANCE: (negative)

> *Jetzt gehe ich **gerade** nicht.*
> *Nun nehmen wir **gerade** kein Geld!*

NEGATIVE STRESS (in postposition) [→ H 617 **eben**]:

> *Das war nicht **gerade** nett von dir!*

halt H 627
RESIGNATION:

> *So ist das Leben **halt**.*
> *Da kann man **halt** nichts machen.*
> *Er ist **halt** dumm.*

immer H 628
GENERALIZATION:

> *Laß ihn nur **immer** kommen!*
> *Iß, so viel du **immer** kannst.*
> *Wer **immer** den Arzt sprechen will, muß sich zuerst im Vorzimmer anmelden.*

ja H 629
EMPHASIS:

> ***Ja,** das wird kaum möglich sein.*
> *Ich schätze meinen Lehrer, **ja,** ich verehre ihn.*
> (stressed) *Es soll **ja** jeder hören, was ich zu sagen habe!*

SURPRISE:

> *Es schneit **ja** !*
> *Du siehst **ja** ganz blaß aus !*

CONFIRMATION of known fact:

> *Wir gehen zu Fuß, es ist **ja** nicht weit vom Bahnhof.*
> *Das brauche ich nicht zu betonen; das wissen Sie **ja** alle.*
> *Es kann **ja** nicht immer so weiter regnen.*

RESTRICTION:

> *Ich will dir **ja** das Buch leihen, aber gerne tue ich es nicht.*
> *Das wäre **ja** noch schöner, wenn er auf unsere Einladung nicht käme !*

URGENT REQUEST or WARNING (stressed):

> *Komm **ja** nicht zu spät nach Hause !*
> *Das soll er **ja** lassen !*
> *Sieh dir den Film **ja** an !*

H 630 **mal** → H 619 **einmal**

H 631 **nämlich**

EXPLANATION or REASON [→ G 400]:

> *Ich muß nach Hause gehen, es ist **nämlich** schon sehr spät.*
> *Karl konnte gestern nicht in die Schule kommen. Er war **nämlich** krank.*

H 632 **nicht**

NEGATIVE QUESTION expecting affirmative answer:

> *Ist unser Haus **nicht** schön?*
> *Habe ich **nicht** recht?*
> *Ist das **nicht** wunderbar?*

EMPHASIS (pleonastic negative):

> *Was man hier **nicht** alles zu essen bekommt !*
> *Wie oft habe ich dir das **nicht** gesagt !*
> *Verhüt' es Gott, daß du (**nicht**) krank wirst.*

H 633 **nicht (ein)mal**

SURPRISE about negative statement:

566

*Sie spricht über deutsche Literatur und hat **nicht einmal** Deutsch
gelernt!*

*Das will ein Kellner sein und kann **nicht mal** rechnen!*

nun

ACCEPTANCE of a situation:

> ***Nun** meinetwegen, ich habe nichts dagegen.*
> ***Nun** gut, ich gehe schon.*

IMPATIENCE (usually followed by **doch** or **schon**):

> ***Nun** sprich **doch**.*
> ***Nun,** gehen Sie doch **schon!***

nun (ein)mal

RESIGNATION:

> *Er will es nun **einmal** so haben, da kann man nichts machen.*
> *Unsere Lage ist **nun mal** nicht besser.*

nur

GENERALIZATION:

> *Du bekommst, was du dir **nur** wünschen kannst.*
> *Er erhält, soviel er **nur** braucht.*

EMPHASIS:

> *Er schlug die Tür zu, daß es **nur** knallte.*
> *Der Wagen fuhr **nur** so dahin.*
> *Das kenne ich **nur** zu gut!*

EMPHATIC WISH (subjunctive):

> *Wenn er **nur** käme!*
> *Wenn wir **nur** genug Geld hätten!*

INDIFFERENCE:

> *Laß ihn **nur** versuchen, er wird nichts erreichen.*
> *Er mag **nur** kommen, ich werde nicht mit ihm sprechen.*

ENCOURAGEMENT:

> *Komm **nur!***
> *Sei **nur** nicht so ängstlich!*
> ***Nur** Mut!*
> *Gehe **nur** nach Hause, dein Vater wird dich nicht strafen.*

567

WARNING:

> *Gehe **nur** nach Hause, du wirst schon sehen!*
> *Tue das **nur** nicht!*
> *Lassen Sie sich **nur** nicht betrügen.*

QUESTION indicating ANXIETY or CONCERN:

> *Wo ist er **nur**?*
> *Was ist **nur** los mit Ihnen?*
> *Was hat er **nur**?*
> *Weshalb hat er das **nur** gemacht?*

H 637 **schon**

CONCESSION:

> *Es wird **schon** gehen.*
> ***Schon** gut!*
> *Und wenn **schon**?!*

IMPATIENCE or ANNOYANCE:

> *Was ist denn **schon** wieder?*
> *Jetzt gehe ich **schon** gar nicht.*

LIMITATION or RESTRICTION:

> *Das Essen war **schon** gut, aber es hätte besser sein können.*
> *Wenn er es sagt, wird es **schon** stimmen, aber sicher bin ich nicht.*

EMPHASIZING a CONDITION:

> *Wenn ich **schon** in Deutschland bin, will ich auch München besuchen.*
> *Wenn du das Buch **schon** begonnen hast, lies es auch fertig!*

ENCOURAGING REQUEST:

> *Komm **schon** her!*
> *Fangen Sie **schon** an!*

SUFFICIENT DEGREE:

> ***Schon** für wenig Geld kann man einen Fotoapparat kaufen.*
> ***Schon** mit wenigen Wörtern kann man sich in einem fremden Land verständlich machen.*

568

so

INCIDENTAL QUESTION:

> *Wie geht es so mit deiner Arbeit?*
> *Was haben Sie so in Deutschland vor?*

APPROXIMATION:

> *Es war so um Mitternacht.*
> *Wie geht es Ihnen? Na, so, so.*
> *Er hat so seine Pläne.*

überhaupt

INCIDENTAL REMARK:

> *Kannst du mir 10 Mark leihen? Du bist mir überhaupt noch etwas*
> *Geld schuldig.*
> *Du kannst jetzt noch nicht gehen, überhaupt muß ich noch einiges mit*
> *dir besprechen.*

NEGATIVE STRESS:

> *Ich kann ihn überhaupt nicht leiden.*
> *Er hat überhaupt kein Geld.*

UNCERTAINTY:

> *Ich komme morgen, soweit ich es jetzt überhaupt schon sagen kann.*
> *Sie wollen Sekretärin bei mir werden? Können Sie überhaupt*
> *Fremdsprachen?*

vielleicht

ADMIRATION or ASTONISHMENT, often ironic:

> *Der Mann hat vielleicht gearbeitet!*
> *Sie haben vielleicht komische Ansichten!*

wohl

SUPPOSITION:

> *Er wird wohl heute noch kommen.*
> *Das ist wohl möglich.*
> *Es kann wohl nicht anders sein.*
> *Du bist wohl ärgerlich.*

APPROXIMATION:

> *Das ist **wohl** drei Jahre her.*
> *Es waren **wohl** dreihundert Leute da.*

WONDER:

> *Ob er mich **wohl** noch kennt?*
> *Wird er **wohl** kommen?*

QUESTION expecting an affirmative answer:

> *Hast du **wohl** morgen Zeit?*
> *Sie besuchen mich **wohl** später?*

CONCESSION:

> *Das ist **wohl** wahr, aber es hilft uns nicht viel.*
> *Heute nicht, **wohl** aber morgen.*

Negation

H 650   The adverb of negation **nicht** may be considered as a particle [→ H 631]. In general, however, when **nicht** negates the entire sentence (or, more specifically, the predicate), it usually functions like an adverbial modifier of manner [→ 580 ff.], and normally follows the same principle of position.[1] [For a fuller treatment of the position of **nicht**, → H 760 ff.] When **nicht** negates individual sentence units, however, it precedes the item which it negates [→ J 260]:

> *Mein Freund ist gestern abend **nicht** gekommen.*
> *Ich habe dem Kind die Schokolade **nicht** gegeben.*
> *Hast du die Tasse **nicht** auf den Tisch gestellt?*
> *Warum schreibst du den Brief **nicht** selbst?*
> *Wir fahren morgen nachmittag **nicht** nach Hamburg.*

H 651   If an indefinite noun is used as a predicate complement, the negation is made by means of the indefinite attribute **kein** [D 310–311], which follows the declension of the indefinite article:[2]

[1] **Nicht** normally follows subject, object, and expressions of time, and precedes other expressions of manner, modifiers of place, prepositional objects, and verb complements.

[2] **Kein** corresponds to English "not a," "not any," or "no" (as an adjective). **Nicht ein** is considered poor German style and is usually avoided (except when **ein** is stressed in the sense of "one": *nicht **einen** Pfennig*) [→ J 262].

570

*Trinken Sie Kaffee? Nein, ich trinke **keinen** Kaffee.*
*Der Zug hat hier **keinen** Aufenthalt.*
*Das ist doch **kein** Bleistift, das ist ein Kugelschreiber.*
*Heute findet **kein** Konzert statt.*

If, however, the negation refers to a definite noun, or if it is the action,   H 652
rather than the noun complement, which is being negated, the adverb
nicht is used:

*Ich trinke diesen starken Kaffee **nicht**.*
*Das Konzert findet heute **nicht** statt.*

The adverb **nicht** is also used for negation if a noun without article acting   H 653
as a predicate complement has become part of the verb itself:

Spielst du morgen mit uns Fußball? Nein, ich kann morgen leider
* **nicht** Fußball spielen.*
*Laufen Sie Ski? Nein, ich laufe **nicht** Ski.*
*Können Sie **nicht** Auto fahren?*

WORD ORDER

⤝ *Introduction*

The sequence of words or sentence units within the sentence field often   H 700
depends on the degree of significance, importance, or stress placed upon
a given unit. This results from the situation or the context.

If the meaning of each sentence unit is given its normal stress value   H 701
within the total utterance, then the various sentence units have a definite
position in the sentence field of the German sentence. This sequence of
sentence units is considered the NORMAL GERMAN WORD ORDER. The
stress value given to each sentence unit also determines the sentence
intonation pattern [→ K 035, K 045].

The following basic principle determines the sequence within the sen-   H 702
tence: The sentence unit which provides little or NO SIGNIFICANT new
INFORMATION occupies the BEGINNING (the anterior limit) of the sentence
field [→ H 020 ff.].[1] The more the stress value or informational value

---

[1] The beginning of the sentence field is not usually the beginning of the sentence itself,
since most German sentences have a PREFIELD [→ H 051 ff., H 705].

571

of a sentence unit increases, the closer it moves to the end of the sentence field. The sentence unit which provides the MOST IMPORTANT INFORMATION occupies the END (the posterior limit) of the sentence field.[1]

Increasing informational values

Main clause:[2] V_1 ⋯⋯⋯⋯⋯⋯⋯⋯⋯ V_2

Dependent clause:[2] C ⋯⋯⋯⋯⋯⋯⋯⋯⋯ V

H 703   If any sentence unit is to be given a greater stress value than it normally possesses within the sentence field, it moves out of its basic position to a place close to the end of the sentence field. This simultaneously produces a change in the sentence intonation pattern [→ K 075 ff.].[3]

H 704   The above sequence is characteristic for the German sentence. The sentence begins with the mention of a known element and introduces an element of suspense in the reader or listener. As additional new information is provided by subsequent sentence units, the suspense increases until it reaches its highest point at the end with the unit which contains the most significant information; thus, the suspense is resolved. Similarly, the sentence intonation pattern follows a parallel principle, culminating with the primary sentence stress on the sentence unit with the highest informational value [→ K 046].

The Contact Unit in the Prefield

H 705   In contrast to the other types of linguistic patterns (interrogative, imperative, exclamatory [→ H 001]), a declarative statement usually consists of more than one sentence. The sentences, the collective meaning of which makes up the content of the statement, together form a larger unit of speech, the utterance. Sentences are constituent parts of utterances.

In the same way in which the content of an utterance must have a logical connection with the situational context of the discourse, the

[1] The German sentence is sometimes described as a "target sentence" (**Zielsatz**), since it aims for the most significant item of information which is withheld until the end. This principle also accounts for the preference given in colloquial German to the present perfect over the past tense, since the informational verb unit then comes at the end.

[2] C designates a connecting unit, either a conjunction or a relative pronoun; V designates the verb or predicate [→ H 022, 040].

[3] In spoken utterances, it is possible to maintain normal word order and to impart a higher informational value to a given part of speech by a change in intonation and stress.

contents of the individual sentences must be in a meaningful relationship to one another. This relationship is manifest in the strict logical sequence of the sentences within the utterance, and in the form of the sentences, which are characterized by the existence of a PREFIELD. Almost all declarative statements have one sentence unit occupying the prefield [→ H 051 ff.].

The prefield of a declarative statement is occupied by a sentence unit which, in addition to its function within its own sentence, performs the role of a contact unit within the larger framework of the utterance. The contact unit relates the content of a given sentence to the overall situational context and connects it with the content of the preceding sentences.

It is within the nature of the contact unit that its content should always be a known or previously mentioned concept, rather than something new. Essentially, the following main functions of the contact unit may be defined:

In the FIRST SENTENCE of an UTTERANCE, the contact unit   H 706
1. establishes the connection with the overall context;
2. leads into the beginning of the utterance, establishes the relationship with the reader or listener, and initiates the suspense principle.

    This can be accomplished chiefly by **general statements** of **time, general statements** of **place** (or specific statements of place with which the listener or reader is familiar), **persons, things,** or **concepts** which the reader or listener knows or of which he has already heard, **conditions** on which the following situation depends, or **known reasons** which have caused the following situation [→ G 110, H 781]:

> *In unserem Haus*[1] *ist ein neuer Mieter eingezogen.*
>
> *Gestern abend bin ich mit meinem Freund ins Theater gegangen.*
>
> *Der Direktor unserer Schule ist auf Urlaub gefahren.*
>
> *Die Universität in München beginnt ihr Semester am 15. Oktober.*
>
> *Die Straße nach Salzburg wird neu asphaltiert.*
>
> *Wenn du mir Geld gibst, kann ich dir Zigaretten mitbringen.*
>
> *Da es im Winter oft sehr kalt wird, haben wir uns viele Kohlen gekauft.*

---

[1] Arrows → indicate the direction of contact.

573

H 707 In SUBSEQUENT SENTENCES of the utterance, the contact unit

3. establishes the connection with the content of the preceding sentence or sentences [→ G 011, coordinating conjunctions];

4. makes additional references to time or place which clarify the sequence of events;

5. introduces additional persons, concepts, or things which, however, must be placed into a relationship with the events previously described by appropriate attributes [→ J 100 ff.]:

Eines Tages machte ich mit meinem Freund einen Ausflug. Wir fuhren zuerst mit unseren Rädern in die Berge. Dort rasteten wir ein wenig in einem Gasthaus am Fuße eines steilen Berges. Nachdem wir uns gestärkt hatten, begannen wir mit dem Aufstieg. Unsere Räder hatten wir natürlich vorher im Gasthaus untergestellt. Der Aufstieg war sehr schön, aber schwierig. Zuerst kamen wir durch schöne Wälder, deren Bäume uns auf unserem Weg Schatten spendeten. Als wir aber dem Gipfel näher kamen, hörte der Wald auf. Die Sonne brannte auf uns hernieder, und der Pfad wurde immer steiler. Doch bald erreichten wir den Gipfel. Müde setzen wir uns in den Schatten eines Felsens und genossen die Aussicht. Sie hat unsere Mühe gelohnt. Wir sahen ein wunderschönes Tal unter uns liegen.

H 708 Note: The personal pronoun **es** as an accusative object can never occupy the prefield.

THE SENTENCE UNITS WITHIN THE SENTENCE FIELD

⋟ *Introduction*

H 710 The following principles of sequence for the various sentence units within the sentence field constitute REGULAR WORD ORDER [→ H 701]. They apply even if one of the sentence units mentioned leaves its regular position and moves into the prefield to act as a contact unit. The contact unit does not lose its claim to its normal position within the sentence, to which it reverts if the sentence assumes a different form [→ H 051]. As noted in H 702, variations from the normal sequence are possible for reasons of emphasis.

The following list explains the symbols and abbreviations contained in the schematic sentence diagrams:

V	Verbal unit (complete predicate)
V_1	First part of verbal unit (finite verb)
V_2	Second part of verbal unit (past participle, infinitive, verb complement)
C	Connecting link (conjunction, relative pronoun, etc.)
S	Noun subject
OA	Noun object, accusative
OD	Noun object, dative
OG	Noun object, genitive
OP	Noun object with preposition
s	Pronoun subject
oa	Pronoun object, accusative
od	Pronoun object, dative
og	Pronoun object, genitive
op	Pronoun object with preposition
PC	Predicate complement
PC_t	Predicate complement of time
PC_p	Predicate complement of place
PC_m	Predicate complement of manner
PC_c	Predicate complement of cause
PN	Predicate nominative
PA	Predicate accusative
PS	Predicate subject
PO	Predicate object
M	Modifier
M_t	Modifier of time
M_p	Modifier of place
M_m	Modifier of manner
M_c	Modifier of cause

The Subject-Object Group

Subject and object constitute the agents [→ H 003] within a sentence and perform the grammatical function of the sentence together with the

H 711

575

predicate (sentence core). The subject-object group thus constitutes the basic unit of word order.[1]

The following principles apply:[2]

H 712   Noun subject and noun objects follow the sequence **S** (subject) — **OD** (dative object) — **OA** (accusative object):[3]

$$V_1 - S - OD - OA - (V_2)$$
$$C \ - S - OD - OA - \ V \ (V_2 - V_1)$$

*Gestern gab **der Lehrer dem Schüler das Buch.***
(*Gestern hat **der Lehrer dem Schüler das Buch** gegeben.*)
. . .,   *daß **der Lehrer dem Schüler das Buch** gab.*
(. . .,   *daß **der Lehrer dem Schüler das Buch** gegeben hat.*)
. . .,   *um **dem Schüler das Buch** zu geben.*

H 713   When subject and objects are personal pronouns, they follow the sequence **s** (subject) — **oa** (accusative object) — **od** (dative object):

$$V_1 - s - oa - od - (V_2)$$
$$C \ - s - oa - od - \ V$$

*Gestern gab **er es ihm** (hat **er es ihm** gegeben).*
. . .,   *daß **er es ihm** gab (daß **er es ihm** gegeben hat).*
. . .,   *um **es ihm** zu geben.*

H 714   If nouns and pronouns appear together in the same sentence as subject and objects, the personal pronouns usually precede the nouns.[4] Within each group, however, the sequences established in H 712 and H 713 are maintained.

1. One personal pronoun:

$$V_1 - s - DO - AO - (V_2)$$
$$C \ - s - DO - AO - \ V$$

[1] Sentences without subjects are possible in German. They include impersonal passives (*Hier wird nicht geraucht*), dative passives (*Dem Mann kann geholfen werden*), impersonal dative constructions (*Mir ist kalt*), and occasionally impersonal accusative constructions (*Mich hungert*). Infinitive clauses also lack a subject, which is always understood to be the subject of the main clause: *Er versprach mir, **mich morgen zu besuchen.***

[2] Note that the subject may often appear in the prefield. Modifiers of person [→ H 556 ff.] are treated like dative or prepositional objects.

[3] The first pattern applies to main clauses, the second to dependent clauses, including infinitive clauses which have no subject. Parentheses indicate compound tenses.

[4] A noun subject may precede a pronoun object for the sake of emphasis.

576

*Gestern hat **er dem Schüler das Buch** gegeben.*
. . ., *daß **er dem Schüler das Buch** gab.*
. . ., *um **dem Schüler das Buch** zu geben.*

$$V_1 - od - S - OA - (V_2)$$
$$C - od - S - OA - V$$

*Gestern hat **ihm der Lehrer das Buch** gegeben.*
. . ., *daß **ihm der Lehrer das Buch** gab.*
. . ., *um **ihm das Buch** zu geben.*

$$V_1 - oa - S - OD - (V_2)$$
$$C - oa - S - OD - V$$

*Gestern hat **es der Lehrer dem Schüler** gegeben.*
. . ., *daß **es der Lehrer dem Schüler** gab.*
. . ., *um **es dem Schüler** zu geben.*

2. Two personal pronouns:

$$V_1 - s - od - OA - (V_2)$$
$$C - s - od - OA - V$$

*Gestern hat **er ihm das Buch** gegeben.*
. . ., *daß **er ihm das Buch** gab.*
. . ., *um **ihm das Buch** zu geben.*

$$V_1 - s - oa - OD - (V_2)$$
$$C - s - oa - OD - V$$

*Gestern hat **er es dem Schüler** gegeben.*
. . ., *daß **er es dem Schüler** gab.*
. . ., *um **es dem Schüler** zu geben.*

$$V_1 - oa - od - S - (V_2)$$
$$C - oa - od - S - V$$

*Gestern hat **es ihm der Lehrer** gegeben.*
. . ., *daß **es ihm der Lehrer** gab.*
. . ., *um **es ihm** zu geben.*

3. Three personal pronouns: → H 713.

If the function of the noun subject and the pronoun accusative object   H 715
can not be distinguished by their declensional endings (singular neuter,
singular feminine, and plural), the position within the sequence must

577

identify the subject-object relationship. In this case the subject always precedes the object:

$$V_1 — S — oa — (V_2)$$
$$C \ — S — oa — \ V$$

*Gestern fragte **die Mutter sie.**[1]*
*. . ., **daß die Mutter sie** fragte.*

H 716 If the entire sentence is to be negated, the adverb of negation **nicht** comes at the end of the sentence field, i.e. after subject and objects, but before the completion of the predicate:

*Gestern gab er dem Schüler das Buch **nicht.***
*Gestern hat er es ihm **nicht** gegeben.*
*. . ., daß ihm der Lehrer das Buch **nicht** gab.*
*. . ., daß es ihm der Lehrer **nicht** gegeben hat.*
*. . ., um es dem Schüler **nicht** zu geben.*

H 717 **Prepositional objects**[2] **(OP, op)** follow the subject and other objects:

$$V_1 — S — OD — OP — (V_2)$$
$$C \ — S — OD — OP — \ V$$

*Gestern dankte **der Sohn dem Vater für den Brief.***
*. . ., daß **der Sohn dem Vater für den Brief** dankte.*
*. . ., um **dem Vater für den Brief** zu danken.*

$$V_1 — s — od — op — (V_2)$$
$$C \ — s — od — op — \ V$$

*Gestern dankte **er ihm dafür.***
*. . ., daß **er ihm dafür** dankte.*
*. . ., um **ihm dafür** zu danken.*

$$V_1 — S — OD — op — (V_2)$$
$$C \ — S — OD — op — \ V$$

*Gestern dankte **der Sohn dem Vater dafür.***
*. . ., daß **der Sohn dem Vater dafür** dankte.*
*. . ., um **dem Vater dafür** zu danken.*

---

[1] *Gestern fragte sie die Mutter* would mean that she asked the mother.

[2] This includes compounds with **da(r)-** and a preposition; modifiers of person [→ H 556] may also be included.

578

$$V_1 - S - OA - OP - (V_2)$$
$$C \; - S - OA - OP - \; V$$

*Gestern hat **der Schüler den Lehrer um das Buch** gebeten.*
*. . ., daß **der Schüler den Lehrer um das Buch** bat.*
*. . ., um **den Lehrer um das Buch** zu bitten.*

$$V_1 - s - oa - op - (V_2)$$
$$C \; - s - oa - op - \; V$$

*Gestern hat **er ihn darum** gebeten.*
*. . ., daß **er ihn darum** gebeten hat.*
*. . ., um **ihn darum** zu bitten.*

$$V_1 - S - OA - op - (V_2)$$
$$C \; - S - OA - op - \; V$$

*Gestern hat **der Schüler den Lehrer darum** gebeten.*
*. . ., daß **der Schüler den Lehrer darum** bat.*
*. . ., um **den Lehrer darum** zu bitten.*
etc.

If the entire sentence is to be negated, the adverb of negation **nicht** H 718
precedes the prepositional object:

*Heute bat er seinen Freund **nicht** um Geld.*
*Heute hat er seinen Freund **nicht** um Geld gebeten.*
*. . ., daß er seinen Freund **nicht** um Geld gebeten hat.*
*Heute bat er seinen Freund **nicht** darum.*
*. . ., daß er seinen Freund **nicht** darum bat.*
*. . ., um ihn **nicht** darum zu bitten.*

Reflexive pronouns as objects follow the same rules as the personal H 719
pronouns:

*Heute rasierte **sich** der Vater nicht.*
*. . ., daß **sich** der Vater nicht rasierte.*
*. . ., um **sich** nicht zu rasieren.*

Deviations from the sequences may occur if one particular part is to be H 720
given a greater stress value, moving it towards the end of the sentence
field:

*Gestern gab der Lehrer das Buch **dem Schüler** (und nicht der Schülerin).*

579

H 721   SUMMARY: The subject-object group occupies the following sequence within the sentence field.[1]

$$V_1 - s - oa - od - S - OD - OA - op - OP - V_2$$
$$C \; - s - oa - od - S - OD - OA - op - OP - V$$

Predicate Complements

H 725   For simple verbs, predicate complements (**PC**) appear at the end of the sentence field after all sentence units.[2] For compound verbs, the predicate complement immediately precedes the nonfinite forms (past participle and infinitive) or the separable prefix. Complements of place in particular must always occupy a position at the end of the sentence field:

$$V_1 - S - O - PO - \mathbf{PC} - (V_2)$$
$$C \; - S - O - PO - \mathbf{PC} - V$$

H 726   **Complement** of **Place** (PC$_p$) [→ H 420 ff.]:

          SUBJECT   TIME   MANNER
Peter | *fährt* | *nächstes Jahr* | *mit seinen Eltern* | **nach München.**
..., *daß Peter nächstes Jahr mit seinen Eltern* **nach München** *fährt.*
..., *um nächstes Jahr mit seinen Eltern* **nach München** *zu fahren.*

          SUBJECT   OBJECT   MANNER
Stellen | *Sie* | *die Tasse* | *vorsichtig* | **auf den Tisch!**
..., *daß Sie die Tasse vorsichtig* **auf den Tisch** *stellen.*
..., *um die Tasse vorsichtig* **auf den Tisch** *zu stellen.*

H 727   **Complement** of **Time** (PC$_t$) [→ H 430 ff.]:

Er kam pünktlich **um 9 Uhr** *an.*
..., *daß er pünktlich* **um 9 Uhr** *ankam.*
..., *anstatt pünktlich* **um 9 Uhr** *anzukommen.*

H 728   **Complement** of **Manner** (PC$_m$) [→ H 440 ff.]:

          SUBJECT   OBJECT   PREP. OBJECT
Eigentlich ist | *der Sohn* | *seinem Vater* | *im Charakter* | **ähnlich.**
..., *daß der Sohn seinem Vater im Charakter* **ähnlich** *ist.*
..., *ohne seinem Vater im Charakter* **ähnlich** *zu sein.*

---

[1] No sentence, to be sure, can contain all these elements.

[2] See H 491 for table of combinations of various predicate complements.

580

Complement of **Cause** (PC$_o$) [→ H 455]:

> TIME   PLACE
> *Der Brand entstand | neulich | in der Fabrik |* **durch Unvorsichtigkeit.**
> *. . ., daß der Brand neulich in der Fabrik* **durch Unvorsichtigkeit**
> *entstand.*

If the entire sentence is to be negated, the adverb of negation **nicht**
precedes the predicate complement:

> *Peter ist letztes Jahr* **nicht** *nach München gefahren.*
> *Eigentlich ist der Sohn seinem Vater im Charakter* **nicht** *ähnlich.*

Predicate Nominative (PN) [→ H 460 ff.]:

> *Karl ist schon seit meiner Kindheit* **mein bester Freund.**
> *. . ., daß Karl schon seit meiner Kindheit* **mein bester Freund** *ist.*

Predicate Accusative (PA) [→ H 470 ff.]:

> *Er dünkt sich wegen seines Erfolges bei jungen Damen* **ein Don Juan.**
> *. . ., daß er sich wegen seines Erfolges bei jungen Damen* **ein Don Juan**
> *dünkt.*

The negation of sentences with a predicate nominative or a predicate
accusative uses **kein**, unless the noun appears with a definite article or a
possessive adjective (in which case **nicht** is used):

> *Er ist* **kein** *Arzt.*
> *Er dünkt sich* **kein** *Held.*
> *Er ist* **kein** *guter Arbeiter.*
>
> *Er ist* **nicht** *der Lehrer unserer Klasse.*
> *Er ist* **nicht** *mein Freund.*

Predicate Subject (PS) — Subject as Predicate Complement [→ H 475
ff.]:

The predicate subject differs from the usual subject by its position in the
sentence field [→ H 712]. Since it acts as a predicate complement, it
moves to the end of the sentence field:

> *Heute passierte unserer Köchin bei der Zubereitung des Essens in der*
> *Küche* **ein Mißgeschick.**
> *. . ., daß unserer Köchin heute bei der Zubereitung des Essens in der*
> *Küche* **ein Mißgeschick** *passierte.*

H 735   Sentences with predicate subjects are negated by **nicht**, if the predicate subject has a definite article, by **kein** if the predicate subject has an indefinite article (or no article at all):

> *Gestern ereignete sich in unserer Stadt trotz des starken Verkehrs **nicht** der kleinste Unfall (. . . **kein** einziger Unfall).*
>
> *Leider ist heute trotz der Wettervoraussage **keine** Witterungsänderung eingetreten (. . . die erhoffte Witterungsänderung **nicht** eingetreten).*
>
> *Bei der Arbeit sind den Leuten in der Fabrik **keine** Schwierigkeiten unterlaufen.*

H 736   **Predicate Object** (PO) — Object as Predicate Complement [→ H 480 f.]:

The predicate object differs from the direct object by its position:

> *Der Zug hatte in Köln am Hauptbahnhof nur drei Minuten **Aufenthalt**.*
>
> *. . ., daß der Zug in Köln am Hauptbahnhof nur drei Minuten **Aufenthalt** hatte.*

H 737   Sentences with predicate objects are negated in the following manner:

1. **Nicht** is used <u>before</u> the predicate object if there is a definite article (and in some predicate objects without an article):[1]

> *Die Soldaten haben **nicht** die Flucht ergriffen.*
> *Wir machen heute **nicht** den Anfang.*
> *Er hat sich **nicht** das Leben genommen.*
> *Er wollte **nicht** Wort halten.*
> *Wir haben **nicht** Abschied genommen.*

2. Most predicate objects without an article are negated by **kein**:

> *Sie haben ihm **keine** Hilfe geleistet.*
> *Wir können für Sie **keine** Ausnahmen machen.*

3. Some predicate objects without an article may be negated by either **kein** or **nicht**:

> *Ich wollte **nicht** (**keine**) Rücksicht nehmen.*
> *Er nahm **nicht** (**keine**) Rache.*
> *Sie leistete **nicht** (**keine**) Abbitte.*

---

[1] For direct objects **nicht** <u>follows</u> the object, for predicate objects it <u>precedes</u>: *Er gab mir das Buch **nicht**. — Er gab mir **nicht** die Hand.*

4. Predicate objects with an indefinite article are negated by **kein**:

> *Er stellte ihm **keine** Frage.*
> *Wir machen heute **keinen** Spaziergang.*

Predicate Modifiers

So-called CIRCUMSTANTIAL MODIFIERS, which may be adverbs or preposi- H 740
tional phrases [→ H 565 ff.], often appear in the PREFIELD, especially
modifiers of time or place:

> ***Gestern abend** hat mich mein Freund besucht.*
> ***In München** findet zur Zeit eine Kunstausstellung statt.*

When several modifiers appear within the sentence field, they usually H 741
follow the sequence Modifier of Time (M_t) — Modifier of Cause (M_c)
— Modifier of Manner (M_m) — Modifier of Place (M_p):[1] [→ H 566]

$$V_1 - M_t - M_c - M_m - M_p - (V_2)$$
$$C - M_t - M_c - M_m - M_p - V$$

$$\overset{M_t}{} \quad \overset{M_c}{}$$
*Die Schüler spielten | **gestern** | **wegen des schlechten Wetters** | **in der**
$\overset{M_p}{}$
Turnhalle.*

$$\overset{M_t}{} \qquad \overset{M_c}{}$$
*Der Zug kommt | **heute** | **wegen eines Maschinenschadens** | **mit**
$\overset{M_m}{}$ $\overset{M_p}{}$
Verspätung | **in München** | an.*

If there is more than one modifier of one type, the sequence is usually H 742
from the general to the specific [→ H 567]:

> *Das Flugzeug landete | **gestern** | **abend** | **um 7 Uhr**.*

If any one modifier is to be given special emphasis, it may be taken out H 745
of its normal sequence and moved to the end of a series of modifiers
[→ H 703]:

> *Der Student arbeitete wegen seiner bevorstehenden Prüfung jeden*
> *Tag **bis in die Nacht hinein** an seiner Doktorarbeit.*

[1] A quick and easy rule of thumb is the alphabetical order of the German interrogatives:
wann? warum? wie? wo?

Subject-Object and Modifiers within the Sentence Field

H 750 The various modifiers normally occur within the sentence field in a
position behind the noun subject and objects [→ H 712 ff.]. They thus
take the following place in the sentence diagram:

$$V_1 - s - oa - od - S - OD - OA - M - op - OP - PC - V_2$$
$$C \ - s - oa - od - S - OD - OA - M - op - OP - PC - V_2$$

> *Hat Peter seinen Freund **heute morgen** getroffen? Er hat mir **gestern
> in der Schule** gesagt, daß er ihn **seit langem nicht mehr** gesehen habe.*
>
> *Ich glaube, daß sich das Wetter **heute im Laufe des Tages** noch
> bessern wird.*
>
> *Ich habe meinen Eltern **letzte Woche** eine Postkarte geschickt.*

H 751 This sequence, however, is not rigid. Accusative noun objects frequently
follow after adverbial modifiers, and sometimes after prepositional
phrases. This applies especially to modifiers of time:

> *Hat Peter **heute morgen seinen Freund** getroffen?*
>
> *Ich werde **am Sonntag einen Brief** an meine Eltern schreiben.*

H 753 In general, the sequence of modifiers and objects depends on the emphasis which is to be placed on a specific item [→ H 703]. Thus, in
answers to informational questions [→ H 007], objects may appear
either before or after the modifier, depending on what is being asked for.
Modifiers, however, may not follow prepositional objects.

> ***Wann** hast du das Buch gelesen? Ich habe das Buch **gestern** gelesen.*
>
> ***Was** hast du gestern getan? Ich habe gestern **ein Buch** gelesen.*
>
> ***Wohin** gehst du nächste Woche? Ich werde nächste Woche **Peter**
> besuchen.*
>
> ***Wann** wirst du Peter besuchen? Ich werde Peter **nächste Woche**
> besuchen.*
>
> ***Wann** hast du ihn um Geld gebeten? Ich habe ihn **gestern** um Geld
> gebeten.*

H 758 Summary: The entire German sentence pattern may thus be diagrammed as follows:[1]

---

[1] Again, it should be pointed out that no single sentence can possibly contain all these
elements.

584

Main Clause

$$V_1 - s - oa - od - S - OD - (M_t) - OA - (M_t) - M_c - M_m$$
$$- M_p - op - OP - PC - V_2$$

Dependent Clause

$$C - s - oa - od - S - OD - (M_t) - OA - (M_t) - M_c - M_m$$
$$- M_p - op - OP - PC - V$$

The Position of *nicht* in the Sentence Field

The adverb of negation **nicht** may either negate the entire sentence (actually the predicate), or a single sentence unit. When it negates a specific unit, it precedes the word or phrase to which it refers [→ J 260 ff.].   H 760

Within the entire sentence field, **nicht** functions basically like an adverb of manner. It thus moves towards the end of the sentence field, but precedes other modifiers of manner (since it is a very general term), modifiers of place,[1] prepositional objects, predicate complements, and the second part of the predicate. The following examples will illustrate various positions of nicht: H 761

*Der Lehrer gab dem Schüler das Buch **nicht**.*
*Der Kranke hat die ganze Nacht **nicht** geschlafen.*
*Gestern fand das Symphoniekonzert **nicht** statt.*
*Faule Kinder werden **nicht** gelobt.*
*Der Junge will dem kleinen Mädchen seine Schokolade **nicht** schenken.*
*Die Kinder spielten gestern wegen des schlechten Wetters **nicht** im Park.*
*Er dankt seinem Vater **nicht** für das Geschenk.*
*Bist du **nicht** mit dem Autobus in die Schule gekommen?*
*Er hat meinen Brief **nicht** an die Universität weitergeschickt.*
*Er hat **nicht** auf mich gewartet.*
*Hans geht heute abend **nicht** ins Kino.*
*Die Mutter hängt die Wäsche heute wegen des Regens **nicht** auf die Leine.*
*Ich fahre nächsten Sommer **nicht** mit meinen Eltern nach Europa.*
*Ich bin im letzten Jahr **nicht** krank gewesen.*

[1] Adverbs of place sometimes precede **nicht**: *Man darf **hier** nicht rauchen.*

585

H 765   The combinations **auch nicht** (in the sense of "not either"), **auch noch nicht**, and **noch nicht** follow the same principles of word order.[1] The adverb **gern** is likewise a general adverb of manner which precedes other modifiers of manner; **gern**, however, follows **nicht**:

> *Ich habe diesen Film **auch noch nicht** gesehen.*
> *Sie hat mich **noch nicht** darum gebeten.*
> *Er war gestern **auch nicht** in der Schule.*
> *Wir gehen **gern** mit euch ins Kino.*
> *Meine Freundin spielt **gern** Klavier.*
> *Er geht **nicht gern** in die Schule.*

Prepositional Infinitive, Infinitive Clause

H 770   The prepositional infinitive (infinitive with **zu** without additional modifiers) occupies the end of the sentence field:

> *Wir fangen morgen um 7 Uhr **zu arbeiten** an.*
> *Gestern hat es während der Abendstunden **zu regnen** begonnen.*
> *Um wieviel Uhr wünschen Sie **zu frühstücken**?*

H 771   Often, the prepositional infinitive appears in the postfield:

> *Wir fangen morgen um 7 Uhr an **zu arbeiten**.*
> *Ich habe mich gestern angeboten **zu helfen**.*

H 772   If the prepositional infinitive has modifiers of its own and is thus expanded into an infinitive clause[2] with a sentence field of its own (but without a subject), it is separated by a comma and always occupies the postfield:

> *Ich habe mich angeboten, **deinem Bruder zu helfen**.*
> *Er wünschte, **morgens in seinem Zimmer zu frühstücken**.*
> *Die Kinder gehen in die Schule, **um dort lesen und schreiben zu lernen**.*

Dependent Clauses

H 780   Dependent clauses occupy the prefield, if their informational value is appropriate for this position [→ H 075, H 705 ff.], i.e. if they constitute

---

[1] This also applies to **auch schon**: *Wir sind **auch schon** in Berlin gewesen.*
[2] Considered an infinitive phrase in English.

586

an introductory unit or a contact unit. This applies especially to clauses of time and conditional clauses, since the situation in a clause of time establishes a temporal relationship with the following situation, and a conditional clause sets up the possibility of the main clause:

> **Als Robert nach Deutschland kam,** *sprach er noch kein Wort Deutsch.*
> **Als wir ins Zimmer traten,**   *stand meine Schwester vor dem Spiegel.*
> **Wenn ich ins Theater gehe,**   *ziehe ich immer einen dunklen Anzug an.*
> **Wenn du mir Geld gibst,**   *kann ich dir auch Zigaretten mitbringen.*

Causal clauses, which indicate the reason for the following situation, are also frequently in the prefield: H 781

> **Da Deutschland in Mitteleuropa liegt,** *ist es kulturell von Ost und West beeinflußt worden.*
> **Da wir die deutsche Sprache gründlich lernen wollen,** *müssen wir uns auch mit der deutschen Literatur beschäftigen.*

Other dependent clauses are usually in the postfield: H 785

> *Der Lehrer hat uns erzählt,*   **daß er eine lange Reise gemacht hat.**
> *In der Zeitung stand,*   **daß der Minister morgen in unsere Stadt kommt.**
> *Die Kinder gehen in die Schule,* **damit sie lesen und schreiben lernen.**
> *Wir gehen heute spazieren,*   **obwohl das Wetter nicht sehr gut ist.**

Sometimes a dependent clause may occur within the sentence field, especially if a sentence unit or another dependent clause occupies the prefield: H 787

> *Robert wollte in Berlin studieren; deshalb besuchte er,* **als er nach Deutschland kam,** *zuerst einen Deutschkurs.*

Attributive Clauses

Attributive or relative clauses do not represent sentence units, they are parts of a sentence unit [→ J 145 ff.]. Therefore they follow the sentence unit to which they refer: H 790

> *Der Schüler,* **den wir neulich gesprochen haben,** *hat gestern seine Prüfung bestanden.*
> *Meine Frage,* **wann er mir das Geld zurückgeben könne,** *beantwortete er nicht.*

H 791   If an attributive clause refers to the last sentence unit in the sentence field, it occupies the postfield [but → H 792]:

> *Hast du den **Brief** gelesen, **den ich heute bekommen habe?***
>
> *Er will mit dem **Mann** sprechen, **der unser Haus repariert hat.***

H 792   The attributive clause remains within the sentence field, if it does not refer to the unit core [→ J 100], but to some attribute, and if the form of the relative pronoun does not suffice to clarify the relationship:

> *Ich habe den Vater meines **Freundes, der lange Zeit krank war,** besucht.*[1]
>
> *Hast du den Garten am **See, der in der Nähe des Dorfes liegt,** verkauft?*[1]

[1] If the relative clause occurred in the postfield, it would refer to the father in the first sentence, to the garden in the second one.

J

⚘ Sentence Units and Attributes

SENTENCE UNITS

⚘ *Introduction*

A sentence unit may be a single word, a phrase (a word and its attributes),   J 001
or a clause, which fulfills a certain function in the sentence, such as
subject, object, etc.

The function of a sentence unit may be performed by a noun, pronoun,   J 002
adjective, adverb, participle, prepositional phrase, simple infinitive,
prepositional infinitive, or dependent clause.

In content and in function, the predicate is part of the sentence, but it   J 003
is not considered a sentence unit. Instead, the predicate acts as the
sentence core, forming the structure of the sentence and imparting the
character of sentence units to the other parts of speech in accordance
with their functional characteristics.

Nouns

Nouns may occur as SUBJECTS or OBJECTS; since declensional forms of   J 010
nouns are limited, words which accompany the noun as attributes

[→ C 201] take over the task of identifying the function which the noun performs as a sentence unit, by means of their declensional endings.

J 011   As SUBJECT, the noun appears in the nominative:

> *Die Kinder spielen.*
> *Alter Wein schmeckt gut.*
> *Peter ist jung.*

J 012   As OBJECT, the noun appears in whatever case the verb in the predicate demands [→ D 901]:

> ACCUSATIVE: *Der Lehrer fragt **den Schüler.***
> *Er schreibt **einen Brief.***
>
> DATIVE: *Der Arzt hilft **dem Kranken.***
> *Er antwortet **seinem Freund.***
>
> GENITIVE: *Die Trauernden gedenken **des Verstorbenen.***
> *Das entbehrt **jeder Grundlage.***

J 014   Since the declensional forms available in German often do not suffice to indicate unequivocally the manifold semantic and syntactic relationships, prepositions have taken over some of these functions. Sentence units introduced by prepositions follow the case governed by the preposition which precedes them (or, in the use of postpositions, which they precede) [→ F 010 ff.]:

> *Die Kinder denken **an ihre Eltern.***
> *Die Kinder sprechen **von ihren Eltern.***
> ***Dem Wetterbericht nach** soll es morgen regnen.*

J 015   If the verb determines the form of the object, the object is identified by its declensional form: ACCUSATIVE OBJECT, DATIVE OBJECT, GENITIVE OBJECT.[1] If, however, the declensional form is governed by the preposition dependent on the verb, the object is called a PREPOSITIONAL OBJECT.

J 017   The noun may also occur as PREDICATE NOMINATIVE or as PREDICATE

---

[1] The traditional equation of "direct" and accusative object is misleading, since (as is shown in the examples in J 012) dative and genitive objects also follow immediately after the verb and thus are, in a sense, "direct" objects from the German point of view. In addition, their English equivalents must also be considered direct objects [→ D 931, H 302].

590

ACCUSATIVE [→ H 731 f.]. The noun or its attributes then show the appropriate declensional ending:

> Peter ist **mein Freund.**
> Sie nennt ihn **einen Wohltäter.**

As a PREDICATE COMPLEMENT or MODIFIER, the noun may appear as a   J 018
sentence unit only in the accusative [→ H 413, H 470, H 568.5] or in
the genitive [→ H 414, H 568.6]. Otherwise, it can carry out this
function only together with a preposition or a conjunction:

> Wir glaubten ihn **Herrn der Lage.**
> Ich wartete **eine Stunde.**
>
> Der Wanderer kam **des Weges.**
> **Eines Tages** besuchten mich meine Freunde.
>
> Die Kinder wohnen **bei den Eltern.**
> Er brüllt **wie ein Löwe.**

Pronouns

Pronouns are substitutes for nouns and therefore also replace nouns as   J 020
sentence units. The functions of a pronoun as a sentence unit, however,
are not as extensive as those of the noun. Not every noun which functions as a sentence unit can therefore be replaced by a pronoun.

The pronoun may occur as SUBJECT or OBJECT, replacing the noun with   J 021
all its attributes. In contrast to the noun, the pronoun is capable of all
declensional forms by itself:

Subject: *Spielen **die Kinder**? Ja, **sie** spielen.*
          *Schmeckt **alter Wein** gut? Ja, **er** schmeckt gut.*
          Welches Buch** gefällt Ihnen? Mir gefällt **dieses.

Object: *Fragt der Lehrer **den Schüler**? Ja, er fragt **ihn.***
         *Schreibt er **einen Brief**? Ja, er schreibt **ihn.***
         *Hilft der Arzt **dem Kranken**? Ja, er hilft **ihm.***
         *Gedenken die Trauernden **des Verstorbenen**? Ja, sie gedenken*
           seiner.
         *Denken die Kinder **an ihre Eltern**? Ja, sie denken an **sie.***

If the noun designates a thing or a concept and functions as a preposi-   J 022
tional object, it can generally not be replaced by a pronoun. The noun

is then replaced in a compound by the adverb **da(r)-** in declarative statements, and by the interrogative **wo(r)-** in questions [→ D 040 ff.]:

> *Denkst du **an dein Versprechen**? Ja, ich denke **daran**.*
> *__Worüber__ freuen Sie sich? Ich freue mich **über das schöne Wetter**.*

J 025 As a PREDICATE COMPLEMENT or a MODIFIER, the pronoun may be used to replace a noun only if it designates a person:

> *Wohnst du **bei deinem Onkel**? Ja, ich wohne **bei ihm**.*
> *Gehst du **mit Karl**? Ja, ich gehe **mit ihm**.*

J 026 If a noun as a predicate complement or a modifier designates a thing, place, or concept, it is replaced by adverbs:

> *Gehst du heute **ins Theater**? Ja, ich gehe (**dort**) **hin**.*
> *Habt ihr **im Hotel Exzelsior** gewohnt? Nein, wir haben nicht **dort** gewohnt.*

J 027 Often, a prepositional predicate complement can not be replaced at all, but must be repeated:

> *Hat der Lehrer den faulen Schüler **zur Rede** gestellt? Ja, er hat ihn **zur Rede** gestellt.*

Adjectives

J 030 Adjectives occur as PREDICATE NOMINATIVE or PREDICATE ACCUSATIVE when they have an article and are declined [→ H 461.2, H 471.2]:

> *Hans ist **der älteste**.*
> *Inge ist **die klügste**.*
> *Meine Wahl nannte er **eine schlechte**.*

J 032 Most frequently, the adjective as a sentence unit is uninflected and acts as a COMPLEMENT of MANNER [→ H 411]:

> *Peter ist **krank**.*
> *Er stellt sich **dumm**.*

J 035 There are adjectives which are used exclusively as complements of manner or modifiers of manner. They include **abspenstig, allein, ausfindig, barfuß, eingedenk, gang und gäbe, gewahr, gewärtig, gram,**

592

habhaft, klipp und klar, leid, null und nichtig, quitt, recht und billig, schade, schuld, teilhaftig, untertan, zugetan, etc.:

> *Er war mir **gram**.*
> *Wir sind jetzt beide **quitt**.*
> *Sie wurden seiner **habhaft**.*
> *Wir machten ein billiges Geschäft **ausfindig**.*
> *Daß er die Belohnung erhalten hat, ist nur **recht und billig**.*

Adverbs

Adverbs as sentence units function as PREDICATE COMPLEMENTS [→ H 410] or MODIFIERS of MANNER [→ H 568.1]: — J 040

> *Wir kamen **glücklicherweise** rechtzeitig nach Hause.*[1]
> *Er wohnt **dort**.*
> *Mein Freund ist **schon** zwei Stunden **fort**.*
> *Die Tür ist **zu**.*
> *Der Unterricht ist **aus**.*

Uninflected adjectives used adverbially may also function as modifiers of manner: — J 042

> *Er ging **schnell** zum Bahnhof.*
> ***Traurig** erzählte er mir von dem Verlust seines Geldes.*

Notice that the modifier of manner refers to the subject if it is an adjective and to the predicate if it is an adverb: — J 045

> *Der Junge kam **traurig** nach Hause.*　(= der traurige Junge)[2]
> *Der Mann verließ **ärgerlich** das Zimmer.* (= der ärgerliche Mann)
> *Der Vogel fiel **tot** vom Baum.*　(= der tote Vogel)
>
> *Das Kind benimmt sich **gut**.*　(= das gute Benehmen)
> *Er lacht **laut**.*　(= das laute Lachen)
> *Wir liefen **schnell**.*　(= das schnelle Laufen)

Participles

Present and past participles [→ B 801 ff., B 821 ff.] as sentence units may fulfill the same functions as adjectives or adverbs: — J 050

[1] Note the difference between the sentences: *Die alte Frau is **glücklich** gestorben* (she died content) and *Die alte Frau ist **glücklicherweise** gestorben* (it was fortunate that she died).
[2] The boy came home *sad*, not *sadly*.

> *Er ging **betrübt** nach Hause.*
> *Dieses Mädchen ist **reizend.***
> *Ich muß **dringend** nach München.*
> *Der Unterricht ist **beendet.**[1]*
> *Die Straße ist **gepflastert.**[1]*
> *Er rief **verzweifelt** um Hilfe.*
> *Ich war **erstaunt.***
> *Ein Vogel kam **geflogen.***
> *Die Soldaten marschierten **singend** durch die Stadt.*

Infinitives

J 060   The infinitive of a verb may also act as a sentence unit. It may either appear as a simple infinitive or as a prepositional infinitive [→ B 925 ff.].

J 061   SUBJECT or OBJECT:

> ***Irren** ist menschlich.*
> ***Reisen** bildet.*
> *Die Kinder lernen in der Schule **lesen** und **schreiben.***
>
> ***Zu antworten** fiel ihm schwer.*
> *Ich empfehle Ihnen **abzureisen.***
> *Wir gedenken **zu bleiben.***

J 062   PREDICATE NOMINATIVE or PREDICATE ACCUSATIVE:

> *Arbeiten ist **verdienen.***
> *Sein Wunsch bleibt **zu studieren.***
>
> *Ich nenne das **faulenzen.***
> *Jetzt heißt es **anpacken.***

J 063   PREDICATE COMPLEMENT or MODIFIER:

> *Ich gehe jetzt **spazieren.***
> *Geht ihr heute **tanzen**?*
> *Wir bleiben hier **sitzen.***
>
> *Er geht in die Schule, **um zu lernen.***
> ***Statt zu schlafen**, arbeitet er bis spät in die Nacht hinein.*
> ***Ohne zu grüßen**, betrat er das Zimmer.*

---

[1] These describe states of being, not processes, and are therefore NOT passives (cf. *Der Unterricht **wird** beendet. Die Straße **wird** gepflastert.*) [→ B 610.]

594

Dependent Clauses

If a sentence unit indicates a person, place, thing, or concept, one of the above parts of speech is used. Often, however, the sentence unit describes an entire situation. Since a situation can normally be expressed only by means of a complete clause (i.e. by a predicate with all its necessary sentence units), a clause must be used as a sentence unit within a larger sentence. Such clauses are called DEPENDENT or SUBORDINATE CLAUSES.[1]   J 070

A dependent clause may act as SUBJECT, OBJECT, PREDICATE COMPLEMENT, or MODIFIER. The formal identification of a dependent clause may be made by means of its characteristic sentence field: the anterior (front) limit of the sentence field is formed by the connecting link C (conjunction, relative pronoun, relative adverb), and the posterior (rear) limit by the personal form of the verb V (V_2–V_1). [For exceptions, see J 072.2 and 072.3.]   J 071

> *Daß Peter nach England fahren will, war eine Überraschung für mich.*
> *Es ist noch nicht bestimmt, **ob sein Vater ihm das Geld für die Reise gibt.***
> *Gestern stand nicht in der Zeitung, **wie viele Personen bei dem gestrigen Autounfall verletzt wurden.***
> *Ihr werdet es später sicher einmal bereuen, **daß ihr in der Schule immer faul wart.***
> ***Als wir in München ankamen,** wurden wir von unseren Freunden am Bahnhof begrüßt.*

In a dependent clause, the various sentence units follow the same sequence within the sentence field as they do in a main clause. The only difference between the main clause and the dependent clause lies in the location of certain elements at the limits of the sentence field. According to these elements, it is possible to distinguish three types of dependent clauses: J 072

1. DEPENDENT CLAUSES WITH CONNECTING LINKS (conjunctions, relatives, interrogative adverbs, etc.). The connecting link indicates the

---

[1] The German functional term **Gliedsatz** (UNIT CLAUSE) is not used in English. It contrasts the dependent clause as a complete sentence unit with the attributive clause (relative clause) [→ J 100 ff.], which merely modifies a sentence unit.

595

formal and semantic relationship to the main clause. The dependent clause may occur in the prefield or in the postfield.

Anterior limit of sentence field: **connecting link.**

Posterior limit of sentence field: **personal** (inflected) **verb form.**

> *Bevor ich zur Arbeit gehe, lese ich die neueste Zeitung.*
> *Er fährt heute nach Berlin, weil nächste Woche das Semester beginnt.*

2. DEPENDENT CLAUSES WITHOUT CONNECTING LINK. These are dependent clauses which always occupy the prefield and in which the conjunction **wenn** [→ G 574 ff.] is omitted.[1] The main clause usually starts with **so** or **dann.**

Anterior limit of sentence field: **personal verb form.**

Posterior limit of sentence field: **second part of predicate.**

> *Wärest du nicht so spät nach Hause gekommen, so hättest du mich noch getroffen.*

3. DEPENDENT CLAUSES which have the FORM OF MAIN CLAUSES. They usually result from the omission of the conjunction **daß** in indirect discourse and occupy the postfield. With few exceptions, the subject of the dependent clause occupies the prefield of the clause itself.

Anterior limit of sentence field: **personal verb form.**

Posterior limit of sentence field: **second part of predicate.**

> *Du hast mir gesagt, du wolltest heute mit mir schwimmen gehen.*

J 073   The dependent clause may replace any of the following sentence units:

J 074   SUBJECT. Connecting links: **daß, ob, interrogative attributes, interrogative adverbs, interrogative pronouns.**

> *Daß Peter nach England fahren will, war eine Überraschung für uns.*
> *Es ist noch nicht bestimmt, ob ich morgen kommen kann.*
> *Um wieviel Uhr unser Ausflug stattfinden wird, ist noch nicht sicher.*
> *Wie viele Besucher in der Ausstellung waren, wurde von der Zeitung nicht berichtet.*
> *Wer morgen die Fabrik besichtigt, ist mir nicht bekannt.*

J 075   OBJECT. Connecting links: **daß, ob, interrogative attributes, interrogative adverbs, interrogative pronouns.**

---

[1] The same word order principle also applies if the conjunction **ob** is omitted in the double conjunction **als ob**: *Er tut, **als ob** er mich nicht gesehen hätte. Er tut, **als hätte** er mich nicht gesehen.*

596

*Peter schrieb mir, **daß er morgen kommen wolle.***
*Sie wollte mir nicht sagen, **ob ihr Vater zu Hause war.***
*Es ist mir unerklärlich, **auf welche Art er das getan hat.***
*Können Sie mir sagen, **wann der nächste Zug nach Hamburg abfährt?***
*Wißt ihr, **wer heute in der Schule war?***

PREDICATE NOMINATIVE. Connecting link: **daß.**   J 076

*Sein Wunsch ist, **daß sein Sohn Medizin studiert.***
*Meine Bedingung für den Kauf des Hauses bleibt, **daß das Haus***
zuerst renoviert wird.

PREDICATE COMPLEMENTS AND MODIFIERS. Connecting links: **subordinat-**   J 077
ing conjunctions and **conjunctive adverbs.**

The connecting link indicates whether the dependent clause replaces a predicate complement or modifier of place, time, manner, or
cause [→ conjunctions G 030 ff.]:

Place: *Wir fuhren, **bis wir ans Meer kamen.***[1]
         *Ich wohne, **wo mein Vater vor zehn Jahren gewohnt hat.***[2]

Time: ***Als wir am Hafen ankamen,** legte gerade ein Dampfer am*
         Kai an.
         *Du mußt noch viel Deutsch lernen, **bevor du nach Deutsch-***
         land fährst.

Manner: *Er verließ das Zimmer, **ohne daß wir es bemerkten.***
         *Er schaute uns an, **als ob er böse auf uns sei** (als sei er böse*
         auf uns).

Cause: *Robert lernt Deutsch, **weil er in Deutschland studieren will.***
         ***Da uns die Winterabende oft lang werden,** treffen wir uns*
         häufig mit unseren Freunden zu einem fröhlichen Bei-
         sammensein.

A special type of RELATIVE CLAUSES may also be considered in this con-   J 078
text, although relative clauses in general are attributive clauses, i.e.
clauses which replace or modify part of a sentence unit and do not
constitute a sentence unit in themselves [→ attributive clauses J 145].
There are some relative clauses, however, which refer to an indefinite
noun or pronoun, and which begin with a relative pronoun in the same

---

[1] In this sense, **bis** might be considered to have temporal meaning as well. Dependent
clauses introduced by conjunctions of place are rare.
[2] See J 079.

case as their antecedent (**ein Mensch, der; demjenigen, dem; das, was; alles, was**). As a result, the antecedent noun or pronoun is often omitted and replaced by the following relative pronouns: for persons **wer** (nominative), **wen** (accusative), **wem** (dative); for things or concepts **was** (nominative and accusative) [→ D 486].

Relative clauses introduced by these relative pronouns may function as subject or object clauses:

Subject: *Wer (derjenige, der)* **den Arzt sprechen will,** *muß sich im Vorzimmer anmelden.*

          Wer (jemand, der; derjenige, der; ein Mensch, der) **lügt,** *stiehlt auch.*

          Was (das, was; alles, was) **er geschenkt erhält,** *ist ihm immer willkommen.*[1]

Object: *Ich mache,* **was** *(das, was)* **ich will.**

          Ich frage, **wen** *(denjenigen, den)* **ich zuerst treffe.**

          Wem *(demjenigen, dem; denjenigen, denen)* **ich zu den Feiertagen gratulieren will,** *schicke ich eine Glückwunschkarte.*

J 079   Technically, relative clauses which are introduced by relative adverbs of place are also attributive clauses and not sentence units. They function like complements or modifiers of place, however, and have the form of a sentence unit, if the antecedent adverb of place is omitted. This may be done, whenever the local relationships in the main clause and in the dependent clause are identical [→ J 171]:

    Ich wohne (dort), **wo mein Vater vor zehn Jahren gewohnt hat.**

    (Dorthin,) **wo du hingehst,** *da will auch ich hingehen.*

    Wir kommen (dorther), **woher ihr auch kommt.**

J 080   Dependent clauses may contain sentence units which in their turn are replaced by subordinate clauses. These may again have dependent clauses of their own functioning as sentence units. It is thus possible to have complex sentences with multiple subordination. Accordingly, we differentiate among dependent clauses of various degrees.

J 081   A DEPENDENT CLAUSE of the FIRST DEGREE replaces a sentence unit in the main clause and is immediately subordinated to the main clause. A dependent clause of the SECOND DEGREE replaces a sentence unit in a

---

[1] Note that **was** is the OBJECT of its own clause; the entire clause, however, is the SUBJECT of the sentence as a whole. **Was** may, of course, also act as its own subject: **Was dir versprochen wurde,** *wird dir auch gegeben.*

598

dependent clause of the first degree, to which it is subordinated. There may also be subordinate clauses of the third degree, etc.

Dependent clauses of the first degree may appear in the prefield or in the postfield of the main clause. Only rarely do they occupy a position within the sentence field of the main clause itself. Dependent clauses of the second or third degree appear in the postfield of the clause to which they are immediately subordinated. Only rarely do they appear within the sentence field of the clause to which they refer.   J 082

The following sentences illustrate subordinate clauses of various degrees. In addition to the abbreviations explained in H 710 ff. to indicate various sentence units, the following symbols will be used: [1]   J 083

SC	subject clause
OC	object clause
RC	relative clause
IC	infinitive clause
DC	dependent clause
DC_t	dependent clause of time
DC_p	dependent clause of place
DC_m	dependent clause of manner
DC_c	dependent clause of cause
MC	main clause

The main clause will appear in CAPITAL LETTERS. Dependent clauses of the first degree are printed in **bold** face, dependent clauses of the second degree in ***bold italics,*** and those of the third degree in *italics*:

> **Wenn du mir versprichst,** ***daß du mir das Geld wiedergibst,*** *sobald dir dein Vater den Scheck geschickt hat,* KANN ICH DIR DIE 100 MARK GEBEN, **obwohl ich noch mindestens zwei Wochen warten muß,** ***bis ich mein nächstes Gehalt bekomme.***

Prefield	Dependent clauses	
	1st degree	**Wenn du mir versprichst,**
	2nd degree	***daß du mir das Geld wiedergibst,***
	3rd degree	*sobald dir dein Vater den Scheck geschickt hat,*

Sentence Field	KANN ICH DIR DIE 100 MARK GEBEN, (Main clause)

Postfield	Dependent clauses	
	1st degree	**obwohl ich noch mindestens zwei Wochen warten muß,**
	2nd degree	***bis ich mein nächstes Gehalt bekomme.***

---

[1] See appendix for complete list of symbols.

599

J 085   The entire sentence may be diagrammed as follows:

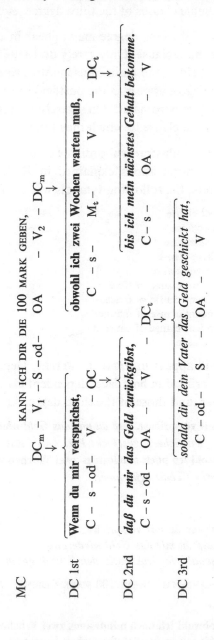

The following example for a complicated sentence with dependent   J 087
clauses of various degrees of subordination is taken from an anecdote
by Heinrich von Kleist (1777–1811), to illustrate extreme complexity of
style:

> DER ARME MANN WAR ABER GEWOHNT, **alles durch seine Frau**
> **besorgen zu lassen, dergestalt, *daß,*** *da ein alter Bedienter kam und ihm*
> *für den Trauerflor, den er einkaufen wollte, Geld abforderte,* **er unter**
> **stillen Tränen,** *den Kopf auf einen Tisch gestützt,* **antwortete:**
> *„Sagt's meiner Frau."*

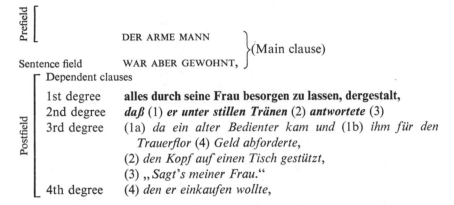

Prefield	
	DER ARME MANN ⎫
Sentence field	WAR ABER GEWOHNT, ⎬ (Main clause)
	⎰
	Dependent clauses
1st degree	**alles durch seine Frau besorgen zu lassen, dergestalt,**
2nd degree	***daß*** (1) **er unter stillen Tränen** (2) **antwortete** (3)
3rd degree	(1a) *da ein alter Bedienter kam und* (1b) *ihm für den*
	Trauerflor (4) *Geld abforderte,*
	(2) *den Kopf auf einen Tisch gestützt,*
	(3) *„Sagt's meiner Frau."*
4th degree	(4) *den er einkaufen wollte,*

Note: The dependent clause of the first degree is replaced by an in-   J 088
finitive clause [→ B 904]. One dependent clause of the third degree (1)
is really a double clause (1a, 1b), joined by the coordinating conjunction
und. Another dependent clause of the third degree (2) is replaced by a
participial clause [→ B 840]. The dependent clause of the 4th degree
does not constitute a sentence unit of its own, but is an attributive
clause [→ J 145] modifying a sentence unit within a dependent clause
of the third degree (1b).

J 089 The entire sentence may be diagrammed as follows:

MC DER ARME MANN WAR ABER GEWOHNT,
S – V₁ – C – V₂ – IC

DC 1st alles durch seine Frau besorgen zu lassen, dergestalt,
oa – M_m – V – M_m

DC 2nd daß, er unter Tränen, antwortete,
C – DC_t – s – M_m – DC_m – V – OC
(1)↓ (1b) (2)↓ (3)↓
(1a) +

DC 3rd da ein Bedienter kam und ihm für den Trauerflor, Geld abforderte, den Kopf auf einen Tisch gestützt, Sagt's meiner Frau.
C – S – V – C – od – M_c – OA – V OA – PC_p – V V_1 – oa – OD

DC 4th den er einkaufen wollte,
C – s – V

ATTRIBUTES

A sentence unit may consist of only one word; more often, however, it consists at least of one word plus a modifier (such as an article) which characterizes its function. Most frequently it consists of a group of words the content of which constitutes a semantic unit within the sentence. Such groups of words are called PHRASES.   J 100

A phrase constituting a sentence unit is divided into the UNIT CORE and the ATTRIBUTES. The unit core is that part of the phrase which is capable of carrying out the function of the sentence unit by itself; attributes are those parts of the phrase which describe the unit core in greater detail. The unit core is thus found by eliminating all those elements within the phrase which are not essential for the functional purpose of the sentence unit.   J 101

A sentence unit (that is, a unit core) may be modified by one or more attributes of the same type or of different types. For example, the sentence **Kinder essen hier Brot** contains sentence units each of which consists of only one word, the unit core. Each of these sentence units may now be described more specifically in various ways by means of attributes: J 102

> *Die Kinder **des Kaufmanns** essen hier Brot.*
> *Die **großen** Kinder essen hier Brot.*
> *Die Kinder essen hier **im Zimmer** Brot.*
> *Die Kinder essen hier **das Brot, das ihnen die Mutter gegeben hat.***
> *Alle **kleinen** Kinder essen hier **im Zimmer** das schwarze Brot, **das die Mutter selbst gebacken hat.***

It is important to realize that the distinction between the unit core and the attribute is strictly a formal one; while in a technical sense the sentence unit is grammatically complete without the attributes, in a semantic sense the attributes often contain the actual information which the phrase is intended to convey: J 104

> *Das Haus hat ein **rotes** Dach.*
> *In dieser Stadt gibt es **enge** Straßen.*
> *Siehst du dort im Wald **die hohen** Bäume?*

603

J 105 Sometimes, as a matter of fact, it is only the attributes which impart meaning to the entire sentence unit:

> *Er lernt **die deutsche** Sprache.*
> *Ich verkehre in **den besten gesellschaftlichen** Kreisen.*
> *Wir können aus **finanziellen** Gründen das Haus nicht kaufen.*

Noun Attributes

J 110 The following attributes are used BEFORE the noun:

1. Definite and indefinite ARTICLES:

> ***Der** Schüler schreibt **einen** Aufsatz.*
> ***Das** Kind liest **ein** Buch.*

2. DEMONSTRATIVE adjectives:

> ***Dieses** Haus gehört **jener** Familie.*
> *Geben Sie mir **das** Buch **da**! [→ D 423, E 831; cf. J 115.2]*

3. POSSESSIVE adjectives:

> ***Mein** Vater interessiert sich für **deine** Arbeit.*

4. INTERROGATIVE adjectives:

> ***Welches** Haus gefällt dir am besten?*
> *In **welcher** Straße wohnst du?*

5. INDEFINITE adjectives:

> ***Viele** Leute fahren jetzt in die Ferien.*
> *Ich habe heute **keine** Zeit.*

6. DESCRIPTIVE adjectives (including NUMERICAL adjectives):

> *Ein **fleißiger** Schüler wird immer eine **gute** Prüfung ablegen.*
> *Wir sind **dreißig** Schüler in der Klasse.*
> *Unser Klassenzimmer liegt im **zweiten** Stock.*

7. PARTICIPLES:

> *Springen Sie nicht aus dem **fahrenden** Zug!*
> *Das **geschlagene** Heer zog sich hinter die Grenzen zurück.*

604

8. POSSESSIVE GENITIVE attributes (mostly with proper names):

> **Deutschlands** *Klima ist relativ mild.*
> **Annas** *Kinder sind schon groß.*
> **Vaters** *Hut liegt auf dem Schrank.*

9. TITLES or descriptive NOUNS in the same case (APPOSITION):

> **Herr** *Müller wohnt in Frankfurt.*
> **Professor** *Sternheim liest schon seit Jahren an dieser Universität über*
> *antike Geschichte.*
> **Das Land** *Bayern liegt in Süddeutschland.*
> **Die Bundeshauptstadt** *Bonn ist der Sitz der westdeutschen Regierung.*

The following attributes are used AFTER the noun: J 115

1. DESCRIPTIVE ADJECTIVES:[1]

> *Hänschen* **klein** *ging allein in die weite Welt hinein.*
> *Ich sah ein Mädchen,* **jung** *und* **schön.**
> *Der Genitiv* **maskulin** *erhält die Endung -s oder -es.*

2. ADVERBS [→ J 110.2]:

> *Das Haus* **dort drüben** *gehört meinem Vater.*
> *In der Wohnung* **oben** *wohnt die Familie Mayer.*

3. PREPOSITIONAL PHRASES:

> *Die Wohnung* **im Erdgeschoß** *bewohne ich mit meiner Frau.*
> *Unsere Ferien* **an der See** *waren wunderschön.*
> *Ich habe den Brief* **von meinem Vater** *noch nicht beantwortet.*
> *Hier ist ein Ring* **aus Gold.**

4. CONJUNCTIONAL PHRASES in the same case (apposition):

> *Man kann auf Flugzeuge* **als Verkehrsmittel** *nicht mehr verzichten.*
> *Er war ein Mann* **wie ein Bär.**

5. GENITIVE attributes:

> *Die Hauptstadt* **Westdeutschlands** *ist Bonn.*
> *Das Haus* **meiner Eltern** *steht in der Kaiserstraße.*
> *Die Straßen* **unserer Stadt** *sind eng.*

---

[1] These conditions are rare.

6. EXPLANATORY NOUNS in the same case (APPOSITION):

> *Herr Müller,* **der Direktor der Maschinenfabrik,** *ist seit einer Woche verreist.*
>
> *Wir fahren im Sommer nach Bad Reichenhall,* **einem Kurort in Oberbayern.**

Use of Noun Attributes

J 120   Limiting adjectives (articles, demonstrative adjectives, possessive adjectives, interrogative adjectives, and indefinite adjectives) as noun attributes are used because of their declensional endings to indicate number, gender, and case of the noun which they modify. They are thus bearers of the function indicators for the noun. [For details, see the declensional patterns of the above parts of speech, D 300 ff., D 400 ff., D 600, D 240 ff., D 700 ff.]

J 121   Descriptive adjectives and participles as noun attributes serve to characterize, define, and describe the noun which they modify.

J 122   If the attributive adjective (or participle) precedes the noun, its declensional pattern depends on the noun which it modifies. If no other attribute precedes the descriptive adjective, its declensional endings indicate the number, gender, and case of the noun. These are called primary endings and are identical with those of the limiting adjectives listed above. If, however, the descriptive adjective is preceded by a limiting adjective with a functional ending, the declensional pattern of the descriptive adjective is limited to the so-called secondary endings. [For details, → E 100 ff.]

> *In* **dem großen** *Garten spielten* **viele kleine** *Kinder.*
>
> **Schöne** *Blumen stehen* **im** *Garten.*
>
> **Die hohen** *Häuser in* **dieser** *Stadt gefallen mir nicht.*
>
> **Der junge** *Mann sprang von* **der fahrenden** *Straßenbahn ab.*
>
> **Das verletzte** *Kind wurde in* **das nächste** *Krankenhaus gebracht.*

J 123   Attributive adjectives appearing after the noun are uninflected. In rare cases, descriptive adjectives may also appear before the noun without declensional endings. This use of the attributive adjective belongs to archaic or poetic style, or to some idiomatic phrases, in addition to a few adjectives which are always uninflected:

606

*Hänschen **klein** ging allein in die weite Welt hinein.*
*Meine Mutter hat **manch gülden** Gewand.*
***Schön** Rosmarin.*
*Ich bin auf **gut** Glück nach Köln gefahren.*
*Man muß **ruhig** Blut bewahren.*
*Sie kaufte sich ein **lila** Kleid.*

A GENITIVE ATTRIBUTE may express various relationships with the noun J 125
to which it refers [→ D 970].[1] They include, among other possibilities:

1. POSSESSION:

    *Das Haus **meines Vaters** ist schön.*

2. PROPERTY, FEATURE:

    *Die Farbe **der Wand** ist grau.*

3. EXPLANATION:

    *Die Furcht **des Todes** kennen alle Wesen.*

4. QUALITY:

    *Hier liegt ein Brief **neueren Datums.***

5. PARTITIVE:[2]

    *Eine Gruppe **junger Leute** wartete auf den Zug.*

6. SUBJECT of an ACTION expressed by the preceding noun (active
   genitive):

    *Die Erfindung **des Ingenieurs** hat alle Fachleute überrascht.*

7. SUBJECT of a PROCESS expressed by the preceding noun (passive
   genitive):

    *Die Erfindung **des Benzinmotors** war ein wichtiger technischer Fort-
    schritt.*

---

[1] A clear distinction must be made between the possessive ADJECTIVE, which will always
have the same case as the noun which it modifies, and the GENITIVE CASE, which may indicate many relationships other than possession (it is for that reason that the term "possessive
case" should be avoided). In general, a genitive expresses a relationship between two
nouns, which in English corresponds to the concept "the x of y."

[2] The partitive genitive is not used in such constructions as *die Stadt Berlin*, nor with
units of measurement: *ein Pfund Äpfel, ein Stück Papier, zwei Flaschen Wein, einige Tassen
Kaffee*, etc. Its use before nouns with descriptive adjectives is rare and stilted; in most
instances, parallel case structure is preferred: *Er trank ein Glas **roten Wein**. Sie kam mit
einem Glas **kaltem Wasser**.*

607

J 127 A genitive attribute is replaced by a prepositional attribute if the genitive of nouns or noun modifiers is not recognizable (usually in the plural). The preposition **von** is then used:

> *Herr Müller ist Vater **zweier Töchter*** (or: *Vater **von zwei Töchtern***).
> *Er ist Vater **von vier Kindern.***
> *Er ist Vater **vier kleiner Kinder*** (or: *Vater **von vier kleinen Kindern***).
> *Der Kauf **eines Hauses** ist sehr kostspielig. Der Kauf **von Häusern** ist sehr kostspielig.*

J 129 In an active genitive, the genitive noun is the SUBJECT of the ACTION which the verbal noun describes:

> *Die Erfindung **des Ingenieurs** hat alle Fachleute überrascht. (**Der Ingenieur** hat etwas erfunden.)*
> *Der Besuch **meines Freundes** hat mich sehr gefreut. (**Mein Freund** hat mich besucht.)*
> *Der Unterricht **des Lehrers** war heute sehr interessant. (**Der Lehrer** unterrichtet.)*

J 130 In a passive genitive, the genitive noun is the SUBJECT of the PROCESS described by the verbal noun (or the OBJECT of an IMPERSONAL ACTION):

> *Die Erfindung **des Benzinmotors** war ein wichtiger technischer Fortschritt. (**Der Benzinmotor** wurde erfunden — Man hat **den Benzinmotor** erfunden.)*
> *Das Betreten **dieser Baustelle** ist verboten. (**Diese Baustelle** wird nicht betreten. — Niemand darf **diese Baustelle** betreten.)*
> *Der Kauf **des Hauses** ist gestern abgeschlossen worden. (**Das Haus** ist gekauft worden. —Jemand hat **das Haus** gekauft.)*

J 131 The PREPOSITIONAL ATTRIBUTE has the same relationship to the noun which it modifies as a prepositional object or a prepositional predicate complement:

> *Seine Sehnsucht **nach der Heimat** ist groß.*   *Er sehnt sich **nach der Heimat**.*
>
> *Er hat keine Freude **an moderner Musik**.*   *Er erfreut sich nicht **an moderner Musik**.*
>
> *Wir wollen eine Reise **nach Italien** machen.*   *Wir wollen **nach Italien** reisen.*

608

Occasionally, however, a different prepositional construction is used for the noun attribute and for the predicate complement:

*Er hat kein Interesse **an** Musik.*   *Er interessiert sich nicht **für** Musik.*

An ADVERBIAL ATTRIBUTE places the noun which it modifies into a time or space relationship. Adverbial attributes either follow the noun directly, or are part of a prepositional phrase:[1]

*Der Junge **hier** geht noch nicht in die Schule.*
*Haben Sie schon die Zeitung **von heute** gelesen?*

Adjectives or participles used as nouns may be preceded by adverbs of manner or uninflected adjectives [→ E 410, E 840]:

*Das **kaum** Glaubliche ist doch eingetreten.*
*Der **lang** Erwartete kehrt nun endlich zurück.*

INFINITIVE ATTRIBUTES are used after nouns which indicate an ability, an inclination, a request, etc. The prepositional infinitive [→ B 985] is used:[2]

*Leider besitze ich nicht die Fähigkeit **zu zeichnen.***
*Wir haben alle den Wunsch **zu reisen.***
*Der Befehl **zu marscheren** wurde noch nicht gegeben.*

If the infinitive attribute contains sentence units of its own, it is considered an infinitive clause;[3] its sentence field is separated by a comma from the sentence field of the main clause:

*Ich habe heute keine Lust, **ins Kino zu gehen.***
*Er hatte die Absicht, **sich einen neuen Wagen zu kaufen.***
*Sein Wunsch, **in Berlin Medizin studieren zu können,** wurde ihm nicht erfüllt.*

---

[1] Occasionally, an attributive adverb may precede the noun and its other attributes: *Rechts die Tür führt in den Speisesaal.*

[2] Infinitive attributes also occur in some other phrases, such as *Gibt es etwas Gutes zu essen?* (The use of **zum** instead of **zu** should be avoided.)

[3] In English, there are no infinitive clauses; these would be considered infinitive phrases. In German, however, they are treated as clauses and follow the general rules of dependent clauses. Infinitive clauses, to be sure, do not have a subject. Their subject, by implication, is always the subject of the main clause.

J 137 The APPOSITION is a noun attribute which has the same case as the noun to which it refers. It may be found before or after the noun which it modifies. The most frequent types of apposition follow.

1. FIRST NAMES before family names, TITLES, PROFESSIONS, and family relationships precede the noun which they modify:

> *Klaus Schulz, Elli Bergmann*
> *Graf Bobby, Kaiser Franz Josef, Herzog Albrecht*
> *Bäckermeister Haeberlein, Inspektor Krause, Doktor Schwarz*
> *Onkel Otto, Tante Ida, meine Schwägerin Irmgard*

2. ORDINAL NUMBERS and DESCRIPTIVE ATTRIBUTES of rulers follow the noun:

> *Konrad der Erste, Wilhelm der Zweite, Karl der Kahle,*
> *Friedrich der Große*

3. Nouns descriptive of a TYPE, CLASS, or CATEGORY precede the noun to which they refer:

> *das Bundesland Bayern, die Stadt Berlin, die Provinz Schleswig-*
> *Holstein, das Jahr 1960, der Monat Oktober*

4. Units of MEASUREMENT precede the noun:[1]

> *fünf Glas Bier, ein Kilo Tomaten, zwei Sack Kartoffeln,*
> *drei Flaschen Wein*

5. Nouns which identify or NAME a preceding noun:

> *Der Zug München-Salzburg, die Universität Bonn, der Prozeß*
> *Müller gegen Schulz, das Drama „Die Räuber"*

J 140 Some nouns in apposition are linked to the noun to which they refer by the conjunctions **als** or **wie**:

> *Er war ein Mann wie ein Bär.*
> *Dr. Francke als Chefarzt des Krankenhauses wird bald eine Professur*
> *an einer Universität erhalten.*
> *In unserer Stadt finden viele Veranstaltungen, wie Konzerte, Theater-*
> *aufführungen, usw. statt.*

J 141 Some nouns or phrases in apposition, following the noun to which they refer, are inserted into the sentence as an explanatory comment. They are separated by a comma from the rest of the sentence. Like all

---

[1] Masculine and neuter units are always in the singular.

610

attributes in apposition, they must have the same case as the noun which they modify:[1]

> *Die beiden Mädchen,* **Inge und Gisela,** *fahren mit ihren Eltern in die Berge.*
>
> *Kennen Sie diese beiden Herren,* **den Direktor und den ersten Ingenieur der großen Maschinenfabrik?**
>
> *Ich habe mit Herrn Müller,* **dem Geschäftsführer der Firma,** *lange Jahre zusammengearbeitet.*
>
> *Die ganze Familie,* **Vater, Mutter und die drei Kinder,** *fährt nach Hamburg.*
>
> *Er kommt am Sonntag,* **dem 11. Mai.**

Note the difference:

> *Er kommt Sonntag,* **den 11. Mai.** *— Er kommt* **am** *Sonntag,* **dem** *11. Mai.*

A noun may have several attributes in apposition proceeding and following it: J 142

> **Der Chefarzt Dr.** *Müller,* **Direktor des städtischen Krankenhauses,** *hat einen Lehrstuhl an der Universität München erhalten.*
>
> *Maria Theresia,* **die Kaiserin des Heiligen Römischen Reiches Deutscher Nation,** *führte Krieg gegen Friedrich* **den Großen, den König von Preußen.**
>
> *Gestern verstarb* **Herr Otto** *Meier,* **Besitzer der Möbelfabrik Meier und Co., Ehrenbürger unserer Stadt, langjähriges Mitglied des Wohltätigkeitsvereins,** *im Alter von 82 Jahren.*

The following rules apply to the declension of proper names which are preceded by a title.   J 143

1. If the noun has no article, the title is not declined, but the name is:

> *Die Kriege König Friedrichs*
> *Das Vermögen Direktor Brauns*
> *Die Arbeiten Professor Müllers*

2. If the noun has an article, the article and the title are declined, but the name is not:

> *Die Kriege* **des** *Königs Friedrich*
> *Das Vermögen* **des** *Direktors Braun*
> *Die Arbeiten* **des** *Professors Müller*

---

[1] Note the difference: *Ein Freund seines Vaters,* **ein reicher Mann** ... refers to the friend. *Ein Freund seines Vaters,* **eines reichen Mannes** ... refers to the father.

3. The title **Herr** is always declined:

Der Besuch Herrn Krügers
Der Besuch des Herrn Krüger

4. A title following **Herr** is usually undeclined:

Der Besuch Herrn Professor Müllers
Der Besuch des Herrn Professor Müller

5. The title **Doktor** is never declined:

Der Sohn Doktor Müllers
Der Sohn des Doktor Müller

Attributive Clauses

J 145 When an entire situation is used to explain or identify a noun, the attribute becomes a clause of its own, which in form, function, and syntax is identical with all dependent clauses [→ J 070 ff.]. Attributive clauses, however, are not sentence units in themselves, but only attributes. The connection with the noun, to which the attributive clause refers, is established by a connecting link which simultaneously constitutes the anterior limit of the sentence field for the attributive clause. (The posterior limit is the personal form of the verb.) The connecting links may be relative pronouns or adverbs, interrogative pronouns or adverbs, or conjunctions.

J 146 We distinguish the following types of attributive clauses:

1. RELATIVE CLAUSES. Connecting links: **relative pronouns, relative adverbs** [→ D 500 ff.]:[1]

*Das Haus, **das ich gekauft habe,** liegt in einer schönen Landschaft.*
*Der Schüler, **den der Lehrer gelobt hat,** kommt aus einer armen Familie.*
*Mein Vater spricht gerade mit einem Herrn, **dessen Sohn ich seit langem kenne.***
*Die Kinder, **denen wir Schokolade geschenkt haben,** spielen dort im Garten.*

---

[1] Note that relative pronouns agree in number and in gender with their antecedent (the noun to which they refer), but that their case form depends on their use within their own clause.

612

*Siehst du dort die Schule, **in der wir zusammen Deutsch gelernt haben**?*

*Wir fahren morgen nach Berlin, **wo mein Freund schon mehrere Jahre Medizin studiert.***

2. INDIRECT INTERROGATIVE CLAUSES. Connecting links: **interrogative pronouns, interrogative adverbs** [→ E 870], **interrogative attributes with their nouns:**

*Er wollte mir die Frage, **wer ihn gestern besucht habe,** nicht beantworten.*

*Er konnte mir keine Auskunft geben, **um wieviel Uhr der Zug in Hamburg ankommen sollte.***

*Das Problem, **wie man diese Krankheit heilen kann,** ist noch nicht gelöst.*

3. CONJUNCTIONAL CLAUSES. Connecting links: **Subordinating conjunctions** [→ G 001 ff.]. These clauses usually act as attributes of action nouns:

*Ich mache dir den Vorwurf, **daß du immer die Unwahrheit sagst.***

*Sie hatten eine Freude, **als ob sie das große Los gezogen hätten.***

*Meine Frage, **ob er zufrieden sei,** hat er nicht beantwortet.*

*Deine Behauptung, **daß Peter heute nicht in die Schule gegangen sei,** ist falsch.*

4. INFINITIVE CLAUSES [→ B 985, J 135]:

*Wir haben keine Hoffnung, **ihn wiederzusehen.***

*Die Sorge, **ihr Kind zu verlieren,** machte die Mutter fast wahnsinnig.*

Attributive clauses usually follow immediately after the noun to which they refer. When the antecedent noun, however, occurs at the end of the sentence field, just before the second part of the predicate, the attributive clause moves into the postfield [→ H 792]: J 147

*Ich habe dem armen Mann das Geld gegeben, **das ich gestern gefunden habe.***

*Ich kann dir den Vorwurf nicht ersparen, **daß du zu oft die Unwahrheit sagst.***

Sometimes we find unconnected attributive clauses, which have the form of main clauses and are loosely attached to the noun to which they refer, usually separated by dashes. In appearance, they are similar to J 148 phrases in apposition. They are, however, complete clauses and do not have to agree in case with their antecedent:

> *Gestern besuchte ich Herrn Schulte — **er war früher Bürgermeister unserer Stadt** — im Krankenhaus.*
>
> *Ich will mit meinem Freund — **wir kennen uns schon seit zehn Jahren** — ein Geschäft eröffnen.*
>
> *Die Firma hat die Maschinenfabrik — **ich glaube, sie ist eine der angesehensten Fabriken auf diesem Gebiet** — an einen ausländischen Millionär verkauft.*

Attributes with Pronouns

J 150   Pronouns are capable of receiving only a limited number of attributes which always follow after the pronoun to which they refer.

J 151   The following attributes occur with pronouns.

1. NAMES, if a certain person within a group is addressed specifically:

> *Du, **Peter**, hilf mir bitte einmal!*
> *Haben Sie, **Herr Müller**, gestern bei mir angerufen?*

2. NOUNS after pronouns of the 1st and 2nd person. (The case agrees with the antecedent):

> *Du **Dummkopf** hast schon wieder einen Fehler gemacht.*
> *Ihr, **meine lieben Kinder**, seid sehr brav gewesen.*
> *Ich bitte Sie, **meine Herren**, Platz zu nehmen.*
> *Wir **Bedauernswerte** müssen bis spät abends im Büro arbeiten.*[1]
> *Ich helfe euch **Ungeschickten** nicht.*
> *Ich gratuliere Dir **Glücklichem** zu deinem bestandenen Examen.*

3. ADJECTIVES used as neuter nouns may appear as attributes after indefinite pronouns. These adjectives follow regular adjective inflection [→ E 100 ff.]:

> *Ich weiß nichts **Neues**.*
> *Ich habe auf der Reise viel **Interessantes** gesehen.*
> *Wir wünschen euch alles **Gute**.*
> *Er kam mit etwas **Schönem**.*

---

[1] Although correct application of grammatical rules calls for a primary ending here, secondary endings also occur (*Wir Deutsche — Wir Deutschen*).

614

4. ADVERBS:

> *Hast du **dort** schon deine Arbeit abgegeben?*
> *Wir **hier** haben in diesem Winter noch keinen Schnee gehabt.*
> *Sie **dort hinten**, kommen Sie einmal her!*

5. INFINITIVES (after indefinite pronouns):

> *Ich will meinem Freund etwas **zu rauchen** schenken.*[1]
> *Hier gibt es nichts **zu tun**.*

6. PREPOSITIONAL PHRASES:

> *Liebt ihr **in der Stadt** die Natur auch so sehr wie wir **auf dem Land**?*
> *Geben Sie mir etwas **von Ihrem Tabak**!*
> *Er erzählte uns alles **über seine Reise**.*

7. CONJUNCTIONAL PHRASES. (Case agrees with antecedent):

> *Du **als mein bester Freund** solltest mir eigentlich helfen.*
> *Du könnest mir **als deinem besten Freund** schon Vertrauen schenken.*
> *Sie **als Lehrer** verstehen sicher etwas von Psychologie.*

If the pronoun antecedent is the subject of the sentence and occurs in the prefield, the conjunctional attribute may be separated from the pronoun and appear in isolation within the sentence field. On the other hand, it is possible for the conjunctional attribute to appear in the prefield and thus precede the pronoun to which it refers:

> *Sie verstehen **als Lehrer** sicher etwas von Psychologie.*
> ***Als Lehrer** verstehen Sie sicher etwas von Psychologie.*

8. NUMERICAL ADJECTIVES after personal pronouns:

> *Was macht ihr **drei** hier?*
> *Sind Sie **beide** befreundet?*
> *Wir **vier** studieren schon lange in dieser Stadt.*

9. RELATIVE CLAUSES:

> *Alles, **was er mir erzählte**, war höchst interessant.*
> *Er, **der in der Schule immer so fleißig war**, hat bisher im Leben nur wenig Erfolg gehabt.*
> *Demjenigen, **der mir helfen hann**, verspreche ich eine Belohnung.*

---

[1] This may occur also as a prepositional phrase: *etwas **zum Rauchen**.*

J 152   If the relative clause has a pronoun of the 1st or 2nd person as an antecedent, the verb in the relative clause often appears in the third person [H 296]:

> *Ich, der den ganzen Tag arbeitet, wünsche abends meine Ruhe.*
> *Dir, der mir immer geholfen hat, bin ich ganz besonders dankbar.*

J 153   Often, however, the pronoun is repeated in the relative clause, and the verb then agrees with the pronoun [→ H 295]:

> *Dir, der du mir immer geholfen hast, bin ich ganz besonders dankbar.*
> *Ich, der ich den ganzen Tag arbeite, wünsche abends meine Ruhe.*
> *Wir, die wir gestern im Theater waren, müssen heute zu Hause bleiben.*
> *Ich habe euch, die ihr so reich seid, um etwas Geld gebeten.*

J 154   Note that gender of persons are distinguished by the relative pronoun; number can be distinguished only by the verb form:

> *Ich, der ich in diesem Haus wohne, . . .*
> *Ich, die ich in diesem Haus wohne, . . .*
>
> *Du, der du in diesem Haus wohnst, . . .*
> *Du, die du in diesem Haus wohnst, . . .*
>
> *Sie, der Sie in diesem Haus wohnen, . . .*
> *Sie, die Sie in diesem Haus wohnen, . . .*
>
> *. . . sie, die in diesem Haus wohnt, . . .*
> *. . . sie, die in diesem Haus wohnen, . . .*

J 155   If the pronoun antecedent occurs at the end of the sentence field, just before the second part of the predicate, the relative clause follows in the postfield [→ H 791]:

> *Wir haben euch gefragt, die ihr doch immer alles wißt.*

J 156   If the pronoun antecedent of the relative clause is **wir** in the nominative, the repetition of the pronoun in the relative clause may be avoided, since there is no formal need for the repetition of the subject:

> *Wir, die gestern im Theater waren, müssen heute zu Hause bleiben.*

J 157   If a relative clause depends on a pronoun in the 3rd person which refers to an indefinite person, thing, or concept, and if the pronoun and the

616

relative pronoun are in the same case, the pronoun itself is omitted and the relative pronouns **wer** and **was** are used instead [→ D 550 ff.]. Relative clauses of this type may be considered as sentence units [→ J 078]:

> *Wer (derjenige, der) dieses Gelände betritt, wird bestraft.*
> *Wen (jeden, den) ich auch immer auf dem Weg traf, grüßte ich höflich.*
> *Wähle dir aus, was (das, was; alles, was) dir gefällt.*

Relative clauses which are introduced by the pronouns **wer** or **was** may appear in the prefield of a sentence as attributive clauses for the following pronoun.   J 158

> *Wer mir bei meiner Arbeit hilft, dem zahle ich einen guten Lohn.*
> *Wem Gott gnädig ist, dem schenkt er ein langes Leben.*
> *Wer unangemeldet zu mir kommt, den lasse ich nicht in mein Haus eintreten.*

Notice the difference between indirect interrogative clauses and relative clauses: J 159

Interrogative Clauses: *Er erzählte mir, wer ihn gestern besucht hatte.*
Ich weiß nicht, wen ich fragen soll.
Frage ihn, wem du einen Brief schreiben sollst!
Er sagte uns nicht, was er eigentlich wolle.
Relative Clauses: *Wer lügt, der stiehlt auch.*
Ich frage, wen ich will.
Hilf, wem du helfen kannst!
Nehmen Sie, was Sie wollen.

Attributes with Adjectives and Participles

Adjectives and participles occurring in the predicate nominative may be followed by conjunctional attributes introduced by **wie** or **als** to form comparisons: J 160

> *Mein Bruder ist älter als ich.*
> *Es wurde später als ich gedacht hatte.*
> *Sie ist nicht so reizend wie ihre Freundin.*
> *Die Lage ist jetzt genau so ernst wie vor dem Kriege.*

617

J 161   Such adjectives or participles may also have adverbs preceding them as attributes:

> Dieses Buch ist *äußerst* (*höchst, sehr*) *interessant.*
> Er wurde **wirklich** *wütend.*
> Das Auto war **schwer** *beschädigt.*

J 162   Adjectives and participles which are in themselves noun attributes may be modified by attributes of their own, which always occur before the word to which they refer.

1. Adverbs:

> Er begrüßte mich mit **überaus** *freundlicher Miene.*
> Der Kaufmann machte uns ein **sehr** *preiswertes Angebot.*

2. Uninflected adjectives or participles used adverbially:

> Ein **eisig** *kalter Wind weht über die* **trostlos** *öde Ebene.*
> Die **modern** *eingerichteten Flugzeuge bringen einen in* **knapp** *fünf Stunden in* **entfernt** *gelegene Länder.*
> Die **laut** *singenden Soldaten marschierten durch das* **weit** *geöffnete Kasernentor.*

J 163   Adjectives and participles used attributively may be extended and further defined by additional sentence units (mostly prepositional phrases) which function like relative clauses without a relative pronoun and without a personal verb form. In contrast to relative clauses, which follow the noun or pronoun to which they refer, EXTENDED ATTRIBUTE constructions[1] precede the noun which they modify. The extended attribute may be preceded or followed by another descriptive adjective:

> Der **soeben auf Bahnsteig 2 einfahrende** *Schnellzug kommt aus Berlin.* (*Der Schnellzug, der soeben auf Bahnsteig 2 einfährt, kommt aus Berlin.*)
> Der Arzt hat den **alten, schon seit Jahren an Rheumatismus leidenden** *Mann* (*den* **schon seit Jahren an Rheumatismus leidenden alten** *Mann*) *endlich heilen können.* (*Der Arzt hat den alten Mann, der schon seit Jahren an Rheumatismus leidet, endlich heilen können.*)
> Diese **später für die Atomforschung so wichtige** *Entdeckung blieb zuerst unbeachtet.* (*Diese Entdeckung, die später für die Atomforschung so wichtig wurde, blieb zuerst unbeachtet.*)

---

[1] The term "participial modifier," which is often used, is misleading and should be avoided. Not all constructions of this type contain participles.

618

*Ich habe meine **mir durch langjährige Gewohnheit lieb gewordene** Arbeit aus Gesundheitsgründen aufgeben müssen. (Ich habe meine Arbeit, die mir durch langjährige Gewohnheit lieb geworden war, aus Gesundheitsgründen aufgeben müssen.)*

*Der **schnell aus in der Nähe liegenden Ortschaften herbeigeeilten** Feuerwehr gelang es nach einigen Stunden, den Brand zu löschen. (Der Feuerwehr, die schnell aus naheliegenden Ortschaften herbeigeeilt war, gelang es nach einigen Stunden, den Brand zu löschen.)*

Like all adjectives, the participle may be used as a noun [→ B 805, 830]; **J 164** form and meaning of the construction remain unchanged:

*Das **einmal in der Schule auswendig Gelernte** vergißt man oft sein ganzes Leben nicht. (Das, was man einmal in der Schule auswendig gelernt hat, vergißt man oft sein ganzes Leben nicht.)*

*Die **vor den feindlichen Soldaten Fliehenden** konnten sich endlich in Sicherheit bringen. (Die Menschen, die vor den feindlichen Soldaten flohen, konnten sich endlich in Sicherheit bringen.)*

Present participles preceded by **zu** lend a passive character to the ex- **J 165** tended attribute and indicate something which can be or should be done [→ B 625.7, B 815]:

*Diese Krankheit war ein **für die medizinische Wissenschaft jahrhundertelang nicht zu lösendes** Problem. (Diese Krankheit war ein Problem, das von der medizinischen Wissenschaft jahrhundertelang nicht gelöst werden konnte.)*

How far such extended attribute constructions should be carried and to **J 166** what extent adjectives and participles may be burdened with modifiers of their own is a question of style. Today, excessive extended attributes are considered clumsy and awkward by most Germans, and good style recommends giving preference to relative clauses. Nonetheless, constructions of this type still occur very frequently in journalistic and other expository prose, and especially in scientific articles and texts. When learning German, however, students should be urged to avoid using these constructions wherever possible.

From an English point of view, direct translations (and often even im- **J 167** mediate comprehension) are almost impossible in all but the shortest extended attribute constructions, since in English phrases like "the hitherto almost completely forgotten fact" are extremely rare indeed. The most striking feature which such constructions present is the

619

occurrence of a limiting (and sometimes a descriptive) adjective without a noun immediately following. The best practical method of unravelling these complex constructions is to find the noun which the adjective grammatically refers to, and then either express the intervening phrase as a relative clause or restate it as an attribute following the noun:

Der (**soeben auf Bahnsteig 2 einfahrende**) *Schnellzug kommt aus Berlin.*

The express train (which is) just arriving on track 2 comes from Berlin.

Diese (**für die Atomforschung so wichtige**) *Entdeckung blieb zuerst unbeachtet.*

This discovery, (which became) so important for atomic research, remained unnoticed at first.

Attributes with Adverbs

J 170   An adverb may have the following attributes:

1. Another ADVERB which precedes the adverb which it modifies:

*Wir gehen **sehr** gern ins Theater.*
*Warum kommst du **erst** jetzt?*
*Ich habe den Brief **noch** nicht geschrieben.*
*Wir haben **besonders** oft von dir gesprochen.*

2. Uninflected ADJECTIVES used ADVERBIALLY, also preceding the adverb to which they refer:

*Wir sitzen im Kino immer **ganz** hinten.*
***Hoch** oben auf dem Berg steht ein Haus.*
***Halb** rechts vor dir sitzt eine alte Dame.*

3. PREPOSITIONAL PHRASES following the adverb:

*Hinten **am Wald** endet der Weg.*
*Das Flugzeug flog hoch **über den Wolken.***
*Das Haus steht oben **auf dem Berg.***

620

4. CONJUNCTIONAL PHRASES with **als** or **wie**, following the adverb for comparisons:

> *Ich trinke Kaffee lieber **als Tee.***
> *Der Vogel flog so schnell **wie der Wind.***

5. RELATIVE CLAUSES: (Connecting link: relative adverbs of location.)

> *Er fährt dorthin, **wo ich im letzten Jahr war.***
> *Komm doch hierher, **wo ich jetzt stehe!***
> *Ich gehe dorthin, **wohin du auch gehst.***
> *Der Lärm kommt von dort her, **wo Fußball gespielt wird.***

If the spatial relationship indicated by the relative adverb coincides with that of the adverb of location to which it refers, this adverb may be omitted [→ E 861]. The relative clause then functions like a sentence unit [→ J 079]:   J 171

> *Ich wohne (**dort**), **wo** mein Vater vor zehn Jahren gewohnt hat.*
> *(**Dorthin**), **wo** du hingehst, will auch ich hingehen.*
> *Ich komme (**dorther**), **woher** er auch kommt.*

Attributes of Rank (Intensification)

Some adverbs, when placed in apposition before a sentence unit, act as attributes of intensification, which give special emphasis to that partic-   J 180
ular sentence unit. They are also called "attributes of rank" since they assign to the sentence unit a higher rank of significance or verbal stress than it would otherwise have within the sentence. They do not, however, affect the content of the sentence unit and are therefore not prop- erly speaking a part of this unit. Their use depends primarily on the SUBJECTIVE ATTITUDE of the speaker toward his utterance.

In most instances, attributes of intensification are identical with the so-called "particles" which act as predicate modifiers [→ H 600 ff.]. They give to the sentence unit which they precede the same shading of meaning which the particles or intensifiers give to the sentence as a whole.

The comments made in H 600 ff. therefore also apply here, and there is no need to repeat the entire list. In addition, there are a few

621

adverbs which function primarily as attributes of intensification, such as **allein, auch, besonders, nicht einmal, selbst, sogar,** etc.:

J 181 **allein:** EXCLUSIVITY. The following sentence unit is stressed.

> *Allein das vom Volk gewählte Parlament darf Gesetze verabschieden.*

J 182 **auch:** INCLUSION. The following sentence unit is stressed.

> *Auch ich habe schon in diesem Hotel gewohnt.*

J 183 **besonders:** EMPHASIS. The adverb is stressed.

> *Die Alpen sind besonders im Winter bei Touristen beliebt.*

J 184 **nicht einmal:** NEGATIVE STRESS.

> *In unserer Stadt haben wir nicht einmal ein Theater.*

J 185 **selbst, sogar:** UNEXPECTED STRESS or surprise (often negative) [→ D 483]:

> *Selbst ich kann Ihnen das nicht erklären.*
> *Er ist sogar mit diesem großen Gewinn nicht zufrieden.*
> *Selbst der Lehrer war erstaunt.*

J 190 Notice the differences between attributes of intensification in various positions, and predicate modifiers:

> *Allein das Parlament darf die Gesetze verabschieden.* (Attribute of intensification: Nobody else has this right.)
>
> *Das Parlament darf die Gesetze allein verabschieden.* (Modifier of manner: Parliament needs nobody else's help.)
>
> *Das Parlament darf allein die Gesetze verabschieden.* (Attribute of intensification: Parliament has no other duties or rights.)[1]
>
> *Gerade mit seinem besten Schüler hatte der Lehrer großen Ärger.* (Attribute of intensification: one would not expect the teacher to have trouble with his best student.)
>
> *Gerade hatte der Lehrer mit seinem besten Schüler großen Ärger.* (Modifier of time: a short while ago.)

Position of Attributes within the Sentence Unit: Summary

J 200 Attributes are grouped around the unit core. The unit core is that part of a sentence unit which, after all attributes have been eliminated, can

---

[1] This distinction is not always clearly made.

still fulfill the grammatical, syntactic, and semantic function of the sentence unit [→ J 100 ff.]. Nouns, pronouns, adjectives (including participles), and adverbs may act as unit cores. The following summary shows how the attribute may be distributed around the unit core:

NOUN AS UNIT CORE   J 210

Definite article:	*der*	Schüler	
Indefinite article:	*ein*	Kind	
Demonstrative adjective:	*dieser*	Mann	
Possessive adjective:	*mein*	Vater	
Interrogative adjective:	*welcher*	Berg?	
Indefinite adjective:	*viele*	Kinder	
Descriptive adjective:	*fleißige*	Schüler	
Numerical adjective:	*zehn*	Mädchen	
Present participle:	*lachende*	Kinder	
Past participle:	*verbotene*	Spiele	
Genitive:	{ *Karls*	Haus	
	{ *das*	Haus	*des Lehrers*
Apposition:	{ *Fräulein*	Breuer	
	{	Friedrich	*der Große*
Uninflected adjective:		Hänschen	*klein*
Adverb:	*dieses*	Haus	*hier*
Prepositional phrase:	*die*	Wohnung	*im Erdgeschoß*
Conjunctional phrase:	*das*	Auto	*als Verkehrsmittel*
Relative clause:	*das*	Haus,	*das ich gekauft habe,*
Interrogative clause:	*meine*	Frage,	*wo ich heute schlafen könne,*
Conjunctional clause:	*der*	Vorwurf,	*daß du zu faul warst,*
Infinitive clause:	*meine*	Bitte,	*mir zu helfen,*

If several attributes occur together before a noun, the following units   J 215
occupy the first place:

1. Articles and all other limiting adjectives which carry primary endings and thus act as function indicators of number, gender, and case;

2. Genitive attributes.

All other attributes (and, in the case of adjectives or participles,

623

extended attributes) occur between the first attribute and the unit core, the noun:

Der	*hier regelmäßig um 5 Uhr abfahrende* **Autobus** *fährt heute nicht.*		
Dieser	*seit gestern bei uns wohnende*	**Herr**	*kommt aus Berlin.*
Mein	*schönes, im Erdgeschoß liegendes*	**Zimmer** *gefällt ihm.*	
Welcher graue		**Mantel** *gehört dir?*	
Jeder	*wirklich freie*	**Mensch** *ist glücklich.*	
Vaters	*am Stadtrand gelegener kleiner*	**Garten** *ist schön.*	

J 216 Demonstrative attributes precede the possessive attribute:

> **Diese meine** *Arbeit gefällt mir sehr gut.*

J 217 The limiting attribute **all-** precedes the definite article, as well as possessives and demonstratives:

> *Ich habe* **all das** *Geld (***all mein** *Geld) verloren.*
> **Alle die** *fleißigen Schüler, die ihre Aufgabe gemacht haben, werden eine gute Note bekommen.*[1]
> **Alle meine** *Freunde warteten auf mich.*
> *Haben Sie* **alle diese** *Bücher gelesen?*

J 218 Other indefinite attributes follow articles, possessives, and demonstratives:[2]

> **Die vielen** *Blumen, die sie zum Geburtstag bekommen hatte, freuten sie sehr.*
> *Intelligenz ist eine von* **seinen wenigen** *guten Eigenschaften.*
> **Diese paar** *Minuten können Sie doch noch warten!*

J 220 PRONOUN as UNIT CORE

Proper Name:	*du,*	***Peter,***
Noun:	*du*	***Dummkopf***
Descriptive adjective:	*alles*	***Gute***

[1] In contrast to English, **alle** is normally not followed by a definite article (He knows all the pretty girls in town — *Er kennt alle hübschen Mädchen in der Stadt*) unless, as the above example illustrates, it is followed by a qualifying relative clause.

[2] This does not apply, of course, if the limiting adjective is part of a genitive construction: *Viele* **meiner** *Freunde wohnen in Berlin. Einige* **dieser** *Fragen sind sehr schwer. Wenige* **der** *Studenten waren je im Ausland.*

Adverb:		*wir*	**hier**
Infinitive:		*etwas*	**zu essen**
Prepositional phrase:		*ihr*	**in der Schule**
Conjunctional phrase:		*Sie*	**als Lehrer**
Numerical adjective:		*wir*	**drei**
Relative clause:	$\Big\{$	*ich,*	**der ich hier wohne,**
	wer mir hilft, *dem*		*helfe ich auch*

ADJECTIVE or PARTICIPLE as UNIT CORE   J 230

Adverb:	$\Big\{$**sehr**	*gut*	
	modern	*eingerichtet*	
Conjunctional phrase:		*schnell*	**wie der Wind**

ADVERB as UNIT CORE   J 240

Adverb:	**sehr**	*gern*	
Prepositional phrase:		*oben*	**auf dem Berg**
Conjunctional phrase:		*mehr*	**als gestern**
Relative clause:		*dort,*	**wo du wohnst,**

ATTRIBUTES of INTENSIFICATION precede the entire sentence unit to   J 250
which they refer:

> *Ich benutze meinen Wagen **nur** im Interesse der Firma.*
> ***Besonders** während der kalten Wintertage müssen die armen Vögel hungern.*

Only **eben** and **gerade** as attributes of intensification may appear before   J 251
or after pronouns:

> *Das **eben** wollte ich auch sagen. (**Eben** das wollte ich auch sagen.)*
> *Ihm **gerade** habe ich mein Vertrauen geschenkt. (**Gerade** ihm habe ich mein Vertrauen geschenkt.)*

Negation of Sentence Units

If the ENTIRE SENTENCE UNIT (but not the predicate or the sentence as a   J 260
whole) is to be NEGATED, the adverb of negation **nicht** appears before the
sentence unit. The conjunction **sondern**, introducing a correction of the

negated sentence unit, appears either immediately after the sentence unit or in the postfield:

> *Das Konzert hat **nicht** am Nachmittag, **sondern** erst am Abend stattgefunden. (Das Konzert hat **nicht** am Nachmittag stattge-funden, **sondern** erst am Abend.)*
>
> *Mein Freund kommt **nicht** morgen, **sondern** am Sonntag.*
>
> *Ich habe **nicht** mit deinem Bruder gesprochen, **sondern** mit deiner Schwester. (Ich habe **nicht** mit deinem Bruder, **sondern** mit deiner Schwester gesprochen.)*
>
> *Nicht **du** sollst die Arbeit machen, **sondern** Franz.[1]*

J 261   If a sentence unit is to be NEGATED ABSOLUTELY, the pronouns **niemand** and **kein-** [→ D 760, D 855] are used for persons and the pronoun **nichts** [→ D 775] for things. If a noun is mentioned, the negative indefinite attribute **kein-** [→ D 311] is used:

> *Ich habe **niemanden** gesehen.*
>
> *Es ist **keiner** gekommen.*
>
> *Warum habt ihr gestern **nichts** getan?*
>
> *Wir haben **kein** Geld.*
>
> *Er trinkt **keinen** Wein.*

J 262   The absolute negation can be EMPHASIZED by using **nicht** before a noun with an indefinite article.[2] Equally strong stress is placed on **nicht**, the indefinite article, and the noun:

> *Für meine Arbeit hat er mir **nicht einen** Pfennig gegeben.*
>
> *Ich habe **nicht ein** Wort zu ihm gesagt.*
>
> *Wir haben im letzten Jahr **nicht einen** Tag Urlaub bekommen.*

J 265   If a specific ATTRIBUTE is to be negated, **nicht** appears before the entire sentence unit, and the attribute to be negated receives special stress [→ K 037, 075]. A correction following the conjunction **sondern** usually appears in the postfield of the sentence:

---

[1] The correction can not occur immediately after the negated sentence unit (**nicht du**) in a sentence of this type, since it would pose a problem of agreement between verb and subject. Neither *Nicht du, sondern Franz **sollst** die Arbeit machen* nor *Nicht du, sondern Franz **soll** die Arbeit machen* sounds right.

[2] In English, the indefinite article would be expressed by "one" rather than by "a" or "an." In German, the emphasis is usually shown by spacing: *Er hat mir nicht e i n e n Pfennig gegeben.*

*Sie haben mir **nicht** den b l a u e n Bleistift gegeben, **sondern** den roten.*

*Wir haben **nicht** in d e m Haus hier gewohnt, **sondern** in dem anderen dort drüben.*

*Das Theater beginnt **nicht** heute n a c h m i t t a g, **sondern** erst heute abend.*

If the attribute is to be negated ABSOLUTELY, **kein-** is used before nouns.   J 266
Otherwise, **nicht** and special stress must be used as above.

*Habe ich Ihnen einen blauen Bleistift gegeben? Nein, Sie haben mir **keinen** blauen Bleistift gegeben.*

*Robert ist **nicht** in d i e s e m Zimmer, und im anderen ist er auch nicht.*

627

K

❧ Sentence Intonation

❧ Introduction

K 001   SPOKEN COMMUNICATION arises out of the immediate LINGUISTIC CONTEXT, which guides the speaker in the selection of his manner of expression and in the intonation and stress pattern of the sentence. This linguistic context provides the circumstances which cause a speaker to make a specific utterance in a specific way to a specific listener at a specific moment.

K 002   The kind and the extent of such an utterance depend on the following set of conditions:

1. What aspects of the situation to be communicated may be presupposed as being known or unknown?
2. How much information does the speaker wish to convey?
3. What is the attitude of the speaker towards the material to be communicated?
4. What is the relationship and attitude of the speaker to the person addressed?

5. What kind of factual impression, emotional reaction, response, or action does the speaker expect from the person addressed?

Basically, the same principles apply to a WRITTEN COMMUNICATION; K 003 however, the possibilities for determining the appropriate type of utterance and the desirable extent of the statement are incomparably more difficult, because the immediate speech contact is missing and, above all, because the written language is a rather inadequate instrument for recording linguistic utterances. To a large extent, it lacks the means of indicating intonation and stress, and thus lends itself to ambiguity.

Furthermore, the organization of a sentence into words, which is the K 004 result of an analytical approach to the written text, is often misleading. The basic conceptual units of a sentence are actually not words, but phrases. In its turn, the sentence which is composed of these phrases or sentence units is itself only a unit in a larger structure, the total utterance. Depending on the linguistic context, it is the total utterance which determines the sequence of the sentences and, within each sentence, the sequence of phrases or sentence units, and thus also the intonation of the sentence.

When a written text is reconstituted as a spoken utterance, that is in K 005 reading,[1] reading out loud, lecturing, declaiming, or acting, all the circumstances on which a spoken utterance depends [→ K 002] must be considered, or else the utterance runs the risk of being misunderstood.

The following remarks are a brief introduction to German intonation K 006 and stress patterns. They are not intended to be specific or complete.

INTONATION PATTERNS

The different types of linguistic utterances [→ H 002, 007 ff.] determine K 010 the sound pattern of a sentence. The basic sound pattern is either a RISING or a FALLING INFLECTION. A rising inflection creates anticipation and tension in the listener, which reaches its height simultaneously with

---

[1] Reading is to be considered in this context as silent speech.

629

the end of the inflectional rise, and is resolved in the rapidly falling inflection.

K 011 In a declarative statement [→ H 002], the inflection rises until it reaches the sentence unit which carries major stress [→ K 045] at the end of the sentence field, just before the posterior limit (if any). Thereafter (or in the last syllable of this word), inflection falls rapidly:

*Nächste Woche wollen wir **nach Berlin** fahren.*

*Peter hat sich gestern **ein neues Buch** gekauft.*

*Morgen soll das Wetter **besser** werden.*

*Nächste Woche fahren wir **nach Berlin.***

*Peter kaufte sich gestern **ein neues Buch.***

*Morgen wird das Wetter sicher **besser.***

Informational questions [→ H 007] have the same inflectional pattern:

*Wann wollt ihr **nach Berlin** fahren?*

*Wer hat sich gestern **ein neues Buch** gekauft?*

*Wann soll das Wetter endlich **besser** werden?*

K 012 For questions which can be answered by yes or no (alternative questions) [→ H 007], the intonation rises until the end of the sentence and thus continues the tension, which is only released by the answer:

*Wollt ihr nächste Woche **nach Berlin** fahren?*

*Hat sich Peter gestern **ein neues Buch** gekauft?*

*Soll das Wetter morgen **besser** werden?*

K 013 A command [→ H 008] follows the same inflectional pattern as the declarative statement [→ K 011]:

*Seid **ruhig!***

*Geht jetzt **ins Bett,** Kinder!*

*Laßt uns **ins Kino gehen!***

630

In an urgent command or request, however, the sentence may end with a rising inflection:

K 014

> *Geht doch endlich weg!*

> *Hinaus!*

> *Geben Sie das Geld her!*

An exclamation [→ H 009] ends with a rising inflection, if the listener is expected to agree:

K 015

> *Wie herrlich ist doch das Wetter heute!*

> *Peter ist doch ein Glückspilz!*

Otherwise, an exclamation has the same inflectional pattern as the declarative statement [→ K 011]:

> *Wie herrlich ist doch das Wetter heute!*

> *Peter ist doch ein Glückspilz!*

STRESS

In speaking, there are variations in the pronunciation of the sounds of words, phrases, and sentences which show marked differences in loudness. This accentuation of certain sounds is called stress.[1] The stress pattern determines the vocal character of the sentence. According to the unit which receives the accentuation, we distinguish the following types:

K 020

> 1. word stress [→ K 025]
> 2. sentence unit stress [→ K 035]
> 3. sentence stress [→ K 045]
> 4. series stress [→ K 060]
> 5. demonstrative stress [→ K 065]

Sentence stress and demonstrative stress dominate the sentence.

K 021

---

[1] The word "accent," which is sometimes used, is misleading, since it may refer to an accent mark, which does not exist in German.

K 022   Word stress, unit stress, and sentence stress are patterns which occur in all sentences; these patterns as well as series and demonstrative stress will occur even in isolated sentences (such as grammatical illustrations) which are without any relationship to a linguistic context [→ K 001].

K 023   Additional stress patterns which may occur in and dominate a sentence are

> 6. distinctive stress [→ K 075]
> 7. emotional stress [→ K 095]

These stresses can only acquire meaning in connected utterances or within a situational context.

Word Stress

K 025   The smallest sound unit which is capable of meaning by itself is called a word. A word consists of one or more syllables. In multisyllabic words, all syllables do not carry the same weight. We therefore distinguish between stressed and unstressed syllables. Depending on the number of syllables, various degrees of stress may be observed. One syllable, however — usually the stem syllable of the word — carries the major stress, the WORD STRESS.[1] A word is comprehensible to the listener only if the word stress falls on the right syllable. All other syllables are less strongly accentuated:

> *fáhren, lében, níemand, fértig, schȫn, beréit, verkaúfen, ántworten.*

K 028   Articles and prepositions as functional indicators act as an unstressed prefix for the word to which they refer and constitute a sound compound with it:

> *das‿Búch, ein‿Héft, der‿Wágen, der‿Verkäúfer, die‿Elektrizitǟt, im‿Zímmer, auf‿dem‿Báhnhof, ins‿Geschäft, von‿heúte, bis‿mórgen.*

K 030   In compound words, the modifier carries the major stress (´), with minor stress (`) on the stem word [→ A 095]:

[1] See A 080 ff.

die **Stráße**, die **Lámpe**:	die **Stráßenlàmpe**
das **Eísen**, die **Báhn**:	die **Eísenbàhn**
das **Signál**, der **Mást**:	der **Signálmàst**
kénnen, **lérnen**:	**kénnenlèrnen**
die **Kínder**, die **Erhólung**, das **Heím**:	das **Kíndererhòlungsheìm**

Personal pronouns and reflexive pronouns are combined with the finite   K 033
verb which they precede or follow, and together with it form a sound
compound, which is dominated by the major word stress of the verb.
The accusative pronoun carries the smallest amount of stress, so that
the vowel of the pronoun almost disappears:[1]

ich_gébe_ihn_ihr	*ich_hábe_ihn_ihr ... gegében*
du_gíbst_ihn_ihr	*du_hást_ihn_ihr ... gegében*
ich_gébe_ihn_ihm	*ich_hábe_ihn_ihm... gegében*
ich_gébe_es_dir	*ich_hábe_es_dir ... gegében*
gébe_ich_ihn_ihr?	*hábe_ich_ihn_ihr ... gegében?*
gíbst_du_ihn_ihr?	*hást_du_ihn_ihr ... gegében?*
gébe_ich_ihn_ihm?	*hábe_ich_ihn_ihm... gegében?*
gébe_ich_es_dir?	*hábe_ich_es_dir ... gegében?*

Sentence Unit Stress

The smallest conceptual component of a sentence is a sentence unit   K 035
[→ J 001 ff.]. A sentence unit may consist of a single word; more often
than not, however, it consists of a group of words which form a
semantic set. Such groups are called phrases. Their function as sentence
units (i.e. subject, object, etc.) can be recognized by a function indicator
(declensional ending, limiting adjective, preposition, etc.). If a sentence
unit consists of two or more words, one of these words carries the major
stress, the SENTENCE UNIT STRESS. A sentence unit stress is stronger than
that of any individual word, and therefore stronger than the normal
stress of that word would be if it were acting in a different capacity. The
word stress of all other words within the phrase is subordinated to the
sentence unit stress.

---

[1] The correct pronunciation of these compounds is very important for the sound pattern
of the entire sentence.

633

K 036   The sentence unit stress falls on the unit core [→ J 100 ff.] if the attribute merely explains or defines the unit core (explanatory attribute):[1]

K 037   The sentence unit stress falls on the attribute, if it serves the purpose of identification or differentiation (distinctive attribute):

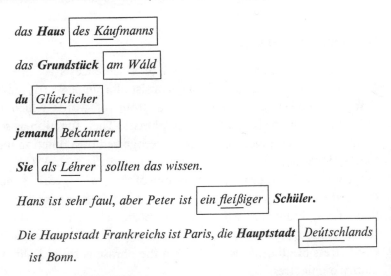

[1] The attribute appears in a box ; the unit core is in **bold print**. Unit stress is shown by an accent mark and by underlining.

634

Note the difference:

Hast du mit dem | *jungen* | **Mädchen** *gesprochen?* (Explanatory attribute)

Hast du mit dem | *júngen* | **Mädchen** *gesprochen?* (Distinctive attribute)

If it is possible to express the content of the attribute (in the same form   K 039
or in a different form) by placing it either before or after the unit core,
the explanatory attribute precedes the unit core and the distinctive
attribute follows it:[1]

Wir haben uns über | *Deutschlands* | **Haúptstadt** *unterhalten.* (Explanatory attribute)

Wir haben uns über die **Hauptstadt** | *Deútschlands* | *unterhalten.* (Distinctive attribute)

Hast du | *die heutige* | **Zéitung** *schon gelesen?* (Explanatory attribute)

Hast du die **Zeitung** | *von heúte* | *schon gelesen?* (Distinctive attribute)

Sentence Stress

Within a sentence, one sentence unit carries the strongest stress, the   K 045
SENTENCE STRESS. The sentence stress is stronger than the unit stress. The
unit stress of all other sentence units is subordinated to the sentence
stress.

Sentence stress can fall only on a sentence unit which is essential for the   K 046
description of the situation [→ H 003 ff.]. Above all, the agent (subject

[1] This is in line with the general word order principle of the German sentence, according
to which the item which carries the major informational value and thus the major stress
occurs at the end of its own syntactic unit [→ H 700 ff., K 046].

or object) in the last position within the sentence field will carry the sentence stress [→ H 700 ff., 711 ff.]:

> Gestern hat der Lehrer dem Schüler **das Búch** gegeben.
> Gestern hat es der Lehrer **dem Schüler** gegeben.
> Gestern hat es ihm **der Léhrer** gegeben.
>
> Heute hat Peter seinen Freund **um Géld** gebeten.
> Heute hat Peter **seinen Fréund** darum gebeten.
> Heute hat ihn **Péter** darum gebeten.

K 047 Personal pronouns, reflexive pronouns, and pronominal adverbs can not carry the sentence stress [→ K 033].[1] If all agents are replaced by personal pronouns or pronominal adverbs, the sentence stress falls on the part of the predicate which carries the meaning [→ H 020, 023]:

> Hat der Lehrer dem Schüler **das Búch** gegeben? Ja, er hat es ihm **gegében.**
> Gab der Lehrer dem Schüler **das Búch**? Ja, gestern **gáb** er es ihm.
> Gestern wollte er es ihm **gében.**

K 050 If the event or state of being is described by a predicate complement [→ H 220], the sentence stress always falls on the complement:

> Gestern sind meine Freunde **nach Berlín** gefahren.
> Herr Müller wollte schon seit seiner Jugend **Árzt** werden.
> Der Professor hat dem Studenten **schwere Frágen** gestellt.
> Wir haben unser Zimmer noch nicht **in Órdnung** gebracht.
> Bei den gestrigen Verhandlungen hat es **viele Mißverständnisse** gegeben.

K 055 Dependent clauses have their own sentence stress within their clausal structure. If the dependent clause appears in the prefield of the sentence, the sentence stress of the dependent clause is subordinate to the sentence stress of the main clause. If, however, the dependent clause occurs in the postfield, it carries the major sentence stress:[2]

> Als wir in München **ankamen,** begann es $\boxed{\text{zu }\underline{\text{ré}}\text{gnen.}}$
>
> Die Zeitungen **meldeten,** daß der Minister in unserer Stadt $\boxed{\text{eine Ré}\underline{\text{de}}}$
> halten wolle.

---

[1] Pronouns may, however, carry distinctive stress [→ K 075 ff.].

[2] Major sentence stress is $\boxed{\text{boxed}}$ and underlined.

*Wenn du mir **Geld** gibst, bringe ich dir* $\boxed{\text{**Zigarétten**}}$ *mit.*

*Ich bringe dir **Zigaretten** mit, wenn du mir* $\boxed{\text{**Géld**}}$ *gibst.*

The sentence stress never falls on any sentence unit in the prefield:[1]   K 058

*Herr **Breuer** wollte mich im letzten Jahr* $\boxed{\text{besúchen.}}$

*Der **Kranke** wurde gestern im Krankenhaus* $\boxed{\text{operíert.}}$

Adverbial or prepositional modifiers [→ H 550 ff.] can not carry the   K 059
sentence stress;[1] it then falls on the part of the predicate which carries
meaning:

*Sie hat **in der letzten Nacht schlecht*** $\boxed{\text{getráumt.}}$

*Dem Verletzten wurde **nach dem Unfall von einem Arzt*** $\boxed{\text{gehólfen.}}$

*Der Junge hat sich **bei dem Herrn wegen seiner Ungezogenheit***
$\boxed{\text{entschúldigt.}}$

Series Stress

If a sentence function is carried out by two or more words of the same   K 060
type (belonging to the same part of speech), a SERIES STRESS occurs which,
however, refers only to this group of words.

Within such a series, the last word carries the strongest stress, the series   K 061
stress. If the series contains three elements, the middle word carries the
weakest stress. The series stress, however, is not as strong as the sentence
unit stress or the sentence stress, unless, of course, it happens to fall on
this particular word:[2]

*Auf den **Stráßen und Plätzen** fanden sich* $\boxed{\text{viele junge Leute}}$ *ein.*

[1] Modifiers or sentence units in the prefield may, however, carry distinctive stress
[→ K 975 ff.].

[2] Sentence unit stress is $\boxed{\text{boxed}}$; the series is in **bold print**, with primary series stress
indicated by ´, secondary series stress by `. In addition, primary series stress is underlined.

> *Mittel und* <u>*Wége*</u> *müssen zur Lösung* | *der Schwierigkeit* | *gefunden werden.*

> *Wir schenkten* **dem Mädchen und dem Júngen** *ein Stück* | *Schokolade.*

> **Mein Vàter, meine Mutter und mein Brúder** *wollen mich morgen* | *besuchen.*

> *Viele* **blaùe, gelbe und <u>ró</u>te** *Blumen stehen* | *auf der Wiese.*

K 062 If the series is followed immediately by a word carrying a stronger stress (sentence unit or sentence stress), the series stress shifts to the first item in the series:

> *Er hat* **<u>Stein</u> und Bein** | *geschworen.*

> *Sie sind mit* **<u>Kind</u> und Kègel** | *abgereist.*

> *Ich habe* **<u>Hím</u>mel und Hòlle** | *in Bewegung* | *gesetzt.*

K 064 If a sentence contains several adverbial or prepositional modifiers [→ H 741], the last one carries the series stress:

> *Wir sind* **gèstern wegen des schlechten <u>Wét</u>ters** | *zu Hause* | *geblieben.*

> *Die Jungen warteten* **vor dem Ràdio mit <u>Spá</u>nnung** *auf die* | *Sportresultate.*

> *Der Zug kam* **hèute wegen eines Maschinenschadens mit Verspätung in <u>Mü</u>nchen** | *an.*

Demonstrative Stress

K 065 The DEMONSTRATIVE STRESS falls on demonstrative pronouns, demonstrative adverbs, etc., when they serve to anticipate a dependent clause or relative clause following in the postfield. The demonstrative stress is stronger than the normal sentence stress:

> *Der Mann hat den Jungen* **<u>dé</u>rart** *geschlagen, daß er* | *ins Krankenhaus* | *gebracht werden mußte.*

638

*Nur **dér** hat Erfolg im Leben, der fleißig* | *arbeitet.*

*Wir haben uns **só** darüber gefreut, daß wir es allen* | *erzählt* | *haben.*

Distinctive Stress

If a statement does not refer to the entire situation described in the sentence and all the circumstances accompanying it, but instead concerns the content of only one functional part of the sentence, this functional part carries DISTINCTIVE stress. Distinctive stress is stronger than normal sentence stress.

K 075

Any functional unit of a sentence (predicate, sentence unit, or attribute) may receive distinctive stress, if the speech situation or the linguistic context requires it. In reading, distinctive stress can be accurately placed only if all the circumstances which accompany the utterance are known [→ K 001 ff.].[1] The content and meaning of a statement change significantly if a distinctive stress occurs, and the change depends on the position of the distinctive stress.

K 076

The following examples will illustrate this shift in meaning:

K 077

NORMAL SENTENCE STRESS:

> *Gestern hat der Lehrer dem Schüler **das Búch** gegeben.*

DISTINCTIVE STRESS:

> *Gestern hat der Lehrer dem Schüler das **Búch** gegeben (nicht das Heft).*
>
> *Gestern hat der Lehrer dem **Schüler** das Buch gegeben (nicht der Schülerin).*
>
> *Gestern hat der **Léhrer** dem Schüler das Buch gegeben (nicht der Vater).*
>
> *Gestern hat der Lehrer **dém** Schüler das Buch gegeben (nicht einem anderen).*
>
> ***Géstern** hat der Lehrer dem Schüler das Buch gegeben (nicht heute).*
>
> *Der Lehrer hat dem Schüler das Buch **geschénkt** (nicht nur geliehen).*
>
> *Der Lehrer **hát** dem Schüler das Buch geschenkt (auch wenn du es nicht glaubst).*

[1] In print, distinctive stress is indicated in German not by *italics*, but by s p a c i n g.

K 078   In a spoken utterance, which arises directly out of the immediate linguistic context, the correct sentence intonation results automatically from the situation. Since in a spoken utterance the distinctive stress is stronger than the normal sentence stress, and thus lends a higher informational value to the unit which receives it, the position of the sentence units within the sentence field need not be changed. In a written statement, the situation is different, since spacing is relatively rarely used. Instead, a sentence unit which is to be given special informational emphasis is taken out of its normal position within the sentence and moves towards the end of the sentence field [→ H 702 ff.]. It thus follows that sentence units which do not occupy their normal syntactic position should be read with distinctive stress. Since, however, the possibilities of shifting sentence units out of their regular position are limited, the distinctive stress in many instances can be surmised only from the linguistic context:[1]

Sentence stress: *Ich habe in der Schule* **meine Aúfgaben** *gemacht.*

Distinctive stress: *Ich habe **in der Schúle** meine Aufgaben gemacht.*
    *Ich habe meine Aufgaben **in der Schúle** gemacht.*

Sentence stress: *Der Lehrer hat dem Schüler* **das Búch** *gegeben.*

Distinctive stress: *Der Lehrer hat **dem Schüler** das Buch gegeben.*
    *Der Lehrer hat das Buch **dem Schüler** gegeben.*

Sentence stress: *Wem hat der Lehrer* **das Búch** *geliehen? Er hat es* **dem Schüler** *geliehen.*

Distinctive stress: ***Wém** hat der Lehrer das Buch geliehen? Er hat es **dem Schüler** geliehen.*

Sentence stress: *An wen habt ihr gestern* **gedácht** *? Wir haben an* **deinen Brúder** *gedacht.*

---

[1] In the following examples, sentence stress is **boxed**, distinctive stress is in ***bold print***.

The second illustration for each distinctive stress, if any, shows a shift in word order, when it is possible.

640

Distinctive stress: *An **wén** habt ihr gestern gedacht? Wir haben an **deinen** Brúder gedacht.*

Sentence stress: *Habt ihr wirklich an ihn* ⎡gedácht⎤ *? Ja, wir haben an ihn* ⎣gedácht.⎦

Distinctive stress: *Habt ihr wirklich **an íhn** gedacht? Ja, wir haben **an íhn** gedacht.*

Distinctive stress: *Habt ihr **wírklich** an ihn gedacht? Ja, wir **háben** an ihn gedacht.*

Emotional Stress

The EMOTIONAL STRESS only occurs in excited speech, especially in ex- K 090
clamations. It may fall on any functional part of the sentence and is
stronger than the sentence stress or the distinctive stress:

> *Welch ein* SCHÓNER *Tag!*
> *Dieser* MISERÁBLE *Mensch!*
> DIÉSER *miserable Mensch?!*
> *Ich bin um mein* GÁNZES *Vermögen gekommen!*

641

APPENDIX I

List of Symbols and Abbreviations

C	Connecting link (conjunction, relative pronoun, etc.)	I_s	Infinitive of **sein**
		I_w	Infinitive of **werden**
DC	Dependent clause	IC	Infinitive clause
DC_c	Dependent clause of cause	M	Modifier
DC_m	Dependent clause of manner	M_c	Modifier of cause
DC_p	Dependent clause of place	M_m	Modifier of manner
DC_t	Dependent clause of time	M_p	Modifier of place
Dp I	Dependent infinitive	M_t	Modifier of time
F_a	Finite form of auxiliary (**haben** or **sein**)	MC	Main clause
		Neg	Negation
F_h	Finite form of **haben**	O	Object
F_m	Finite form of modal	OA	Accusative object, noun
F_s	Finite form of **sein**	oa	Accusative object, pronoun
F_v	Finite form of main verb	obj	Objective statement
F_w	Finite form of **werden**	OC	Object clause
Fut	Future	OD	Dative object, noun
I	Infinitive of main verb	od	Dative object, pronoun
I_a	Infinitive of auxiliary (**haben** or **sein**)	OG	Genitive object, noun
		og	Genitive object, pronoun
I_h	Infinitive of **haben**	OP	Prepositional object, noun
I_m	Infinitive of modal	op	Prepositional object, pronoun

645

PA	Predicate accusative	RC	Relative clause
PC	Predicate complement	S	Subject, noun
PC$_c$	Predicate complement of cause	s	Subject, pronoun
PC$_m$	Predicate complement of manner	SC	Subject clause
		SI	Substitute infinitive (**lassen, sehen,** etc.)
PC$_p$	Predicate complement of place		
PC$_t$	Predicate complement of time	sub	Subjective statement
Pft	Perfect tense	V	Verbal unit (complete predicate)
PN	Predicate nominative		
PO	Predicate object	V$_1$	First part of verbal unit (finite verb)
Pr	Prefix		
Pres	Present tense	V$_2$	Second part of verbal unit (non-finite verb form)
PP	Past participle		
PS	Predicate subject	wd	**worden**

APPENDIX II

The Gothic Alphabet and German Script

ROMAN TYPE	GOTHIC TYPE	GERMAN SCRIPT	APPROXIMATE ENGLISH PRONUNCIATION
A, a	𝔄, a		ah
Ä, ä	𝔄, ä		Umlaut ah
B, b	𝔅, b		beh
C, c	ℭ, c		tseh
D, d	𝔇, d		deh
E, e	𝔈, e		eh
F, f	𝔉, f		eff
G, g	𝔊, g		gay
H, h	ℌ, h		hah
I, i	ℑ, i		ee
J, j	ℑ, j		yot
K, k	𝔎, k		kah
L, l	𝔏, l		ell
M, m	𝔐, m		em
N, n	𝔑, n		en
O, o	𝔒, o		oh
Ö, ö	𝔒, ö		Umlaut oh
P, p	𝔓, p		peh

ROMAN TYPE	GOTHIC TYPE	GERMAN SCRIPT	APPROXIMATE ENGLISH PRONUNCIATION
Q, q	Ω, q		coo
R, r	ℜ, r		air
S, s	S, ß, ſ		ess
ß (No capital)	ß		ess-tset
T, t	T, t		teh
U, u	U, u		oo
Ü, ü	Ü, ü		Umlaut oo
V, v	B, v		fow
W, w	W, w		veh
X, x	X, x		iks
Y, y	Y, y		ippselon
Z, z	Z, z		tset

APPENDIX III

List of Strong and Irregular Verbs

Infinitive (3rd ps. sgl. pres.)	Past (Subj. II)	Past Participle	Reference
backen (bäckt)[1]	backte, buk (büke)	gebacken	B 290, 297
befehlen (befiehlt)	befahl (beföhle)	befohlen	B 973, D 933
beginnen	begann (begänne)	begonnen	B 252, 283
beißen	biß	gebissen	
bergen (birgt)	barg (bärge)	geborgen	
bersten (birst)	barst (bärste)	ist geborsten	
bewegen[1]	bewog (bewöge)	bewogen	B 212, 297
biegen	bog (böge)	gebogen	B 282
bieten	bot (böte)	geboten	B 222, 230, 260
binden	band (bände)	gebunden	
bitten	bat (bäte)	gebeten	B 285
blasen (bläst)	blies	geblasen	
bleiben	blieb	ist geblieben	B 246, 460.3
bleichen	blich	ist geblichen	B 296
braten (brät, bratet)	briet	gebraten	
brechen (bricht)	brach (bräche)	gebrochen	B 284, 462
brennen	brannte (brennte)	gebrannt	B 190, 195
bringen	brachte (brächte)	gebracht	B 190, 196
denken	dachte (dächte)	gedacht	B 190, 196, 940

[1] Weak conjugational forms also occur [→ B 290].

Infinitive (3rd ps. sgl. pres.)	Past (Subj. II)		Past Participle	Reference
dingen	dingte/dang (dänge)		gedungen/ gedingt	B 290
dreschen (drischt)	drosch (drösche)		gedroschen	
dringen	drang (dränge)	hat, ist	gedrungen	
dünken	dünkte/deuchte		gedünkt/ gedeucht	B 191, 290, D 911
dürfen (darf)	durfte (dürfte)		gedurft	B 421
empfehlen (empfiehlt)	empfahl (empfähle)		empfohlen	B 252, 973
erlöschen (erlischt)	erlosch (erlösche)	ist	erloschen	B 213, 296
essen (ißt)	aß (äße)		gegessen	B 222, 232, 276
fahren (fährt)	fuhr (führe)	ist, hat	gefahren	s. Index
fallen (fällt)	fiel	ist	gefallen	
fangen (fängt)	fing		gefangen	B 287
fechten (ficht)	focht (föchte)		gefochten	
finden	fand (fände)		gefunden	B 283, 619
flechten (flicht)	flocht (flöchte)		geflochten	
fliegen	flog (flöge)	ist, hat	geflogen	
fliehen	floh (flöhe)	ist	geflohen	
fließen	floß (flösse)	ist	geflossen	
fressen (frißt)	fraß (fräße)		gefressen	
frieren	fror (fröre)		gefroren	
gären	gor/gärte	ist	gegoren/gegärt	B 282, 290
gebären (gebiert/ gebärt)	gebar (gebäre)		geboren	B 284
geben (gibt)	gab (gäbe)		gegeben	B 285, B 922, D 921, 932
gedeihen	gedieh	ist	gediehen	
gehen	ging	ist	gegangen	B 212, 221, 286, 466, 950
gelingen	gelang (gelänge)	ist	gelungen	B 456
gelten (gilt)	galt (gälte)		gegolten	
genesen	genas (genäse)	ist	genesen	
genießen	genoß (genösse)		genossen	
geschehen (geschieht)	geschah (geschähe)	ist	geschehen	B 272, 456
gewinnen	gewann (gewönne)		gewonnen	H 481
gießen	goß (gösse)		gegossen	
gleichen	glich		geglichen	D 934
gleiten	glitt	ist	geglitten	
glimmen[1]	glomm/glimmte (glömme)		geglommen/ geglimmt	B 290
graben (gräbt)	grub (grübe)		gegraben	

[1] Weak conjugational forms also occur [→ B 290].

Infinitive (3rd ps. sgl. pres.)	Past (Subj. II)	Past Participle	Reference
greifen	griff	gegriffen	
haben (du hast, er hat)	hatte (hätte)	gehabt	B 410
halten (hält)	hielt	gehalten	
hängen[1]	hing	gehangen	B 295, 955
hauen[1]	hieb (haute)	gehauen	B 212, 221, 287, 290
heben	hob (höbe)	gehoben	B 212, 282
heißen	hieß	geheißen	B 287, 491, D 911
helfen (hilft)	half (hülfe)	geholfen	B 232
kennen	kannte (kennte)	gekannt	B 190, 195
klimmen[1]	klomm (klömme)	ist geklommen	B 290
klingen	klang (klänge)	geklungen	B 489
kneifen	kniff	gekniffen	
kommen	kam (käme)	ist gekommen	s. Index
können (kann)	konnte (könnte)	gekonnt	B 421
kriechen	kroch (kröche)	ist gekrochen	
laden (lädt)	lud (lüde)	geladen	B 210, 222
lassen (läßt)	ließ	gelassen	s. Index
laufen (läuft)	lief	ist gelaufen	B 211, 287
leiden	litt	gelitten	B 221, 280
leihen	lieh	geliehen	
lesen (liest)	las (läse)	gelesen	B 232, 285
liegen	lag (läge)	gelegen	B 285, 955
lügen	log (löge)	gelogen	B 282
mahlen	mahlte	gemahlen	B 197, 290
meiden	mied	gemieden	
melken (melkt)	melkte/molk (mölke)	gemolken/gemelkt	B 290
messen (mißt)	maß (mäße)	gemessen	B 285
mißlingen	mißlang (mißlänge)	ist mißlungen	
mögen (mag)	mochte (möchte)	gemocht	B 421
müssen (muß)	mußte (müßte)	gemußt	B 421
nehmen (nimmt)	nahm (nähme)	genommen	B 211, 230, 232, 284
nennen	nannte (nennte)	genannt	B 190, 195
pfeifen	pfiff	gepfiffen	B 281
pflegen[1]	pflog (pflöge)	gepflogen	B 212, 295, 920
preisen	pries	gepriesen	
quellen (quillt)[1]	quoll (quölle)	ist gequollen	
raten (rät)	riet	geraten	B 210, 973

[1] Weak conjugational forms also occur [→ B 290].

651

Infinitive (3rd ps. sgl. pres.)	Past (Subj. II)	Past Participle	Reference
reiben	rieb	gerieben	
reißen	riß	ist, hat gerissen	B 281
reiten	ritt	ist, hat geritten	B 210, 281
rennen	rannte (rennte)	ist gerannt	B 190, 195
riechen	roch (röche)	gerochen	
ringen	rang (ränge)	gerungen	
rinnen	rann (ränne)	ist geronnen	
rufen	rief	gerufen	B 287
salzen	salzte	gesalzen	B 197, 290
saufen (säuft)	soff (söffe)	gesoffen	B 282
saugen	sog/saugte	gesogen/gesaugt	B 282
schaffen[1]	schuf (schüfe)	geschaffen	B 212, 297
schallen	schallte/scholl	geschallt/ geschollen	B 290
scheiden	schied	ist, hat geschieden	
scheinen	schien	geschienen	B 920, D 911
schelten (schilt)	schalt (schälte)	gescholten	D 913, H 470
scheren[1]	schor (schöre)	geschoren	B 290
schieben	schob (schöbe)	geschoben	
schießen	schoß (schösse)	geschossen	B 282
schinden	schindete	geschunden	
schlafen (schläft)	schlief	geschlafen	B 287
schlagen (schlägt)	schlug (schlüge)	geschlagen	H 365, 481
schleichen	schlich	ist geschlichen	
schleifen[1]	schliff	geschliffen	B 297
schleißen[1]	schliß	geschlissen	
schließen	schloß (schlösse)	geschlossen	
schlingen	schlang (schlänge)	geschlungen	
schmeißen	schmiß	geschmissen	
schmelzen (schmilzt)	schmolz (schmölze)	ist, hat geschmolzen	B 282, 462
schnauben	schnob/schnaubte	geschnaubt	B 290
schneiden	schnitt	geschnitten	
(er)schrecken (erschrickt)	erschrak (erschräke)	ist erschrocken	B 295
schreiben	schrieb	geschrieben	B 270, 281
schreien	schrie	geschrien	B 223
schreiten	schritt	ist geschritten	
schweigen	schwieg	geschwiegen	
schwellen (schwillt)	schwoll (schwölle)	ist geschwollen	
schwimmen	schwamm (schwämme)	ist, hat geschwommen	B 283, 465
schwinden	schwand (schwände)	ist geschwunden	

[1] Weak conjugational forms also occur [→ B 290].

652

Infinitive (3rd ps. sgl. pres.)	Past (Subj. II)	Past Participle	Reference
schwingen	schwang (schwänge)	geschwungen	
schwören[1]	schwur, schwor (schwüre)	geschworen	B 282, 290
sehen (sieht)	sah (sähe)	gesehen	B 211, 468
sein (ist)	war (wäre)	ist gewesen	B 410
senden[1]	sandte (sendete)	gesandt	B 190 ff., 290
sieden[1]	sott (sötte)	hat, ist gesotten	B 290
singen	sang (sänge)	gesungen	B 270, 283
sinken	sank (sänke)	ist gesunken	
sinnen	sann (sänne)	gesonnen	B 940, B 252
sitzen	saß (säße)	gesessen	B 221, 285
sollen (soll)	sollte	gesollt	B 421
spalten	spaltete	gespalten	B 197, 290
speien	spie	gespien	
spinnen	spann (spänne)	gesponnen	
sprechen (spricht)	sprach (spräche)	gesprochen	
sprießen	sproß (sprösse)	ist gesprossen	
springen	sprang (spränge)	ist gesprungen	
stechen (sticht)	stach (stäche)	gestochen	
stecken[1]	stak (stäke)	hat, ist gesteckt	B 295, 955
stehen	stand (stünde)	gestanden	s. Index
stehlen (stiehlt)	stahl (stähle)	gestohlen	B 284
steigen	stieg	ist gestiegen	
sterben (stirbt)	starb (stürbe)	ist gestorben	B 250
stieben	stob (stöbe)	ist gestoben	
stinken	stank (stänke)	gestunken	B 283
stoßen (stößt)	stieß	gestoßen	B 287, 462
streichen	strich	ist, hat gestrichen	
streiten	stritt	gestritten	
tragen (trägt)	trug (trüge)	getragen	B 940
treffen (trifft)	traf (träfe)	getroffen	B 284
treiben	trieb	ist, hat getrieben	B 980
treten (tritt)	trat (träte)	ist, hat getreten	
triefen[1]	troff (tröffe)	getroffen	B 290
trinken	trank (tränke)	getrunken	
trügen	trog (tröge)	getrogen	
tun (tut)	tat (täte)	getan	s. Index
verderben[1] (verdirbt)	verdarb (verdürbe)	ist, hat verdorben	B 250, 290, 462
verdrießen	verdroß (verdrösse)	verdrossen	
vergessen (vergißt)	vergaß (vergäße)	vergessen	B 933
verlieren	verlor (verlöre)	verloren	
verlöschen[1] (verlischt)	verlosch (verlösche)	ist verloschen	B 213, 296

[1] Weak conjugational forms also occur [→ B 290].

653

Infinitive (3rd ps. sgl. pres.)	Past (Subj. II)	Past Participle	Reference
wachsen (wächst)	wuchs (wüchse)	ist gewachsen	B 222
wägen	wog (wöge)	gewogen	
waschen (wäscht)	wusch (wüsche)	gewaschen	
weben[1]	wob (wöbe)	gewoben	B 290
weichen	wich	ist gewichen	
weisen	wies	gewiesen	
wenden	wandte/wendete	gewandt/ gewendet	B 190 ff., 290
werben (wirbt)	warb (würbe)	geworben	B 250
werden (wird)	wurde, ward (würde)	ist geworden	B 410
werfen (wirft)	warf (würfe)	geworfen	B 250, 284
wiegen[1]	wog (wöge)	gewogen	B 297
winden	wand (wände)	gewunden	
wissen (weiß)	wußte (wüßte)	gewußt	B 134, 194–6
wollen (will)	wollte	gewollt	B 421
wringen	wrang (wränge)	gewrungen	
(ver)zeihen	verzieh	verziehen	D 933
ziehen	zog (zöge)	hat, ist gezogen	B 221, 282
zwingen	zwang (zwänge)	gezwungen	B 980

This table does not include compound verbs, since their conjugational forms are identical with those of the stem verb (e.g. *nehmen*, **benehmen**, **wegnehmen**, etc.). The auxiliary in the perfect tenses, however, may differ (**hat** *geschlafen*, **ist** *eingeschlafen;* **ist** *gekommen*, **hat** *bekommen;* etc.).

[1] Weak conjugational forms also occur [→ B 290].

GLOSSARY

Grammatical Terms

This glossary does not claim to be complete, either in the number of terms listed or in the definitions. It is an attempt to give brief and concise explanations of the most frequent technical terms of modern grammar, insofar as they apply to the analysis of German undertaken in this text. For the most part, recent German grammars have tended more and more to use internationally accepted Latin terminology; such words are not listed, if they are identical with the term used in English (e.g. *Verb, Konjunktion, Prädikat*, etc.). They are listed if German uses a different Latin term (*Rektion, Konjunktiv*, etc.). Moreover, where distinct German terminology exists (often there are several words used to describe the same phenomenon), they have been indicated in parentheses after the English term, and are also given in a separate alphabetical listing together with their English equivalent. On the other hand, in cases where English grammar has taken over German terms (e.g., *Umlaut*), these are included in the English alphabetical listing.

PART ONE: English

Ablaut Vowel gradation in past tense and past participle of strong verbs.

Absolute Accusative A noun in the accusative in an elliptic construction, where the subject-object relationship is no longer evident (e.g. *Guten Abend!*).

Absolute Comparative A comparative form of adjectives which expresses a general quantity, rather than a specific comparison.

655

Absolute Superlative A superlative form of adjectives and adverbs which denotes a very high degree of the quality indicated.

Accusative (*Wenfall, 4. Fall*) A declensional case form of nouns or pronouns and their modifiers, occurring either as the object of a verb or of a preposition. In the case of verbs, it indicates the person or thing with which the action is immediately concerned.

Action (*Handlung*) An event which is caused by the subject of the sentence.

Action Noun A noun derived from a verb, indicating an action or a process.

Active Voice (*tätige Form*) A verb form which indicates that the event is produced by the subject of the sentence.

Adjective (*Beiwort, Eigenschaftswort*) A part of speech which modifies nouns or acts as a predicate complement. Adjectives may be undeclined or have either primary or secondary endings. There are limiting and descriptive adjectives.

Adverb (*Umstandswort*) A part of speech which modifies or complements verbs, or acts as an attribute for adjectives and other adverbs. Adverbs are undeclined except for comparative and superlative endings on adjectival adverbs.

Adverb of Location An adverb indicating a position (*hier, da, dort*).

Adverb of Time An adverb indicating a relationship with regard to time (*jetzt, bald,* etc.).

Adverbial Accusative A noun in the accusative used as a modifier of time, place, or measurement (*Er blieb einen Tag*).

Adverbial Clause A dependent clause which replaces a predicate modifier and indicates the circumstances under which a situation occurs.

Adverbial Genitive The genitive of a noun used as an indicator of time, place, or manner (e.g. *eines Abends*).

Adverbial Modifier A predicate modifier (phrase or clause) indicating circumstances (time, manner, cause, place), which functions like an adverb.

Adversative Clause A clause which expresses the opposite of a previously stated concept.

Affix A morpheme (letter or syllable) added to a word initially, medially, or finally to change or modify its meaning or function.

Agent (*Rolle*) A person, thing, or object which participates in an event or a state of being as subject or object.

Agreement (*Kongruenz*) A formal relationship in number and person between subject and finite verb.

Alternative Question (*Entscheidungsfrage*) A question which inquires about an entire situation and which can be answered only by *ja, doch,* or *nein*; always begins with the finite verb.

Anterior Limit of Sentence Field (*vordere Satzfeldgrenze*) The finite (personal, conjugated) verb form in a main clause, or the connecting link (conjunction, relative) in a subordinate clause.

656

Anticipation (*Vorwegnahme*) An indefinite *es* or *da*(*r*) + preposition which refers to a noun, pronoun, or clause occurring later in the sentence.

Apparent Passive (*Zustandspassiv*) A construction with *sein* and the past participle of the main verb which, unlike the genuine passive, indicates a state of being, not a process. (*Die Tür ist geschlossen.*)

Apposition An attribute of a noun or pronoun which serves for further identification. It may precede or follow its referent and has the same case.

Article (*Geschlechtswort*) A limiting adjective modifying a noun and serving as a function indicator to show gender, number, and case. There are definite and indefinite articles.

Attribute (*Beifügung*) A word, phrase, or clause which serves to modify, describe or explain some other sentence unit.

Attribute of Rank (*Rangattribut*) An intensifier preceding and referring to a specific sentence unit, imparting to it special emphasis.

Attributive Clause A dependent clause (usually a relative clause) which serves as an attribute for a noun or pronoun.

Auxiliary Verb (*Hilfsverb*) A verb used in the formation of tense, mood, or voice, which the verb can not form by itself. The German auxiliaries are *haben*, *sein*, and *werden*. Modal verbs also have some auxiliary functions.

Base of a Compound (*Grundwort*) The stem of a compound which determines its basic meaning.

Bound Morpheme A syllabic affix which does not have independent meaning and can not exist by itself (inseparable prefix).

Cardinal Number (*Grundzahl*) The basic form of numerical adjectives used in counting.

Case (*Fall*) The form of a noun or pronoun (and its modifiers) which indicates its function in the sentence as subject, object of the verb, or object of a preposition. German has four cases: nominative, accusative, dative, genitive.

Causal Clause (*Umstandssatz des Grundes*) A dependent clause stating the cause, reason, or motive for an action.

Causative Verb (*veranlassendes Verb*) A verb which brings about (and is derived from) the action of another verb (e.g. *fällen: fallen machen*).

Circumstantial Modifier (*Umstandsangabe, freie Angabe*) A predicate modifier which indicates the circumstances (time, place, manner, cause) which accompany the event, or the person concerned. May be an adverb, a prepositional phrase, an accusative, dative, or genitive, or a dependent clause.

Clause (*. . . satz*) A sentence unit which in itself describes an event or state of being. There are main (independent) and subordinate (dependent) clauses. German also speaks of infinitive and participial clauses which are considered phrases in English.

657

Collective Noun (*Sammelname*) A singular noun referring to a group of persons, things, or concepts.

Command (*Befehl*) A form of linguistic utterance which requests a certain action or behavior. Usually in the imperative.

Common Noun A noun not used as a proper name.

Comparative (*Steigerung*) A form of adjectives and adjectival adverbs which shows a higher (or lower) degree of the quality indicated.

Complement of Cause (*Kausalergänzung*) A predicate complement which indicates the cause or reason for an event.

Complement of Manner (*Modalergänzung*) A predicate complement which indicates the manner in which an event takes place.

Complement of Place (*Lokalergänzung*) A predicate complement which indicates the location or direction of an event.

Complement of Time (*Temporalangabe*) A predicate complement which indicates the time at which an event takes place.

Complex Sentence A sentence consisting of a main clause and one or more dependent clauses.

Compound Predicate A predicate consisting of two or more parts.

Compound Sentence A sentence consisting of two or more main clauses.

Compound Tense A tense form requiring the use of an auxiliary verb and a nonfinite form of the main verb.

Compound Verb A verb consisting of a stem and a prefix or complement.

Compound Word A combination of two or more words, consisting of a base and one or more modifiers.

Concessive Clause (*Einräumungssatz*) A dependent clause indicating an effect or result other than that expected.

Conditional Clause (*Bedingungssatz*) A dependent clause stating the conditions or circumstances under which an event may occur.

Conditional Form The use of *würde* plus the infinitive of the main verb as a substitute for the subjunctive in contrary-to-fact conditions.

Conjugation (*Beugung des Verbs*) The inflectional changes of verb forms to indicate person, number, tense, and mood. There are weak and strong conjugations.

Conjunction (*Bindewort*) An uninflected part of speech which fulfills a connective function between words, phrases, and clauses. There are coordinating and subordinating conjunctions.

Connecting Link (*Verbindungsteil*) A conjunction, relative adverb, or relative pronoun which forms the front limit for the sentence field of a dependent clause and relates it to the main clause.

Consecutive Clause (*Folgesatz*) A clause indicating the result, effect, or consequence of an action.

Consonant (*Mitlaut*) A sound produced by some obstruction of the vocal passages (friction, stop, glide, etc.).

Contact Unit (*Aussageeinleitung*) A sentence unit in the prefield which establishes the overall context or connects a statement with previous utterances.

Contraction (*Zusammenziehung*) A word formed with parts of two other words (usually preposition plus ending of article, such as *ans, zum*, etc.).

Coordinating Conjunction (*Nebenordnende* or **beiordnende Konjunktion**) A conjunction which combines two sentence units or parallel clauses (i.e. main clause with main clause, dependent clause with dependent clause).

Copulative Verb A verb which establishes the connection between the subject and the predicate nominative (mainly *sein*, but also *werden, bleiben, scheinen*, etc.).

Correlate A pronoun in the prefield or in the sentence field which replaces, refers to, and anticipates a noun, pronoun, or concept occurring in the sentence field or in a dependent clause in the postfield.

Dative (*Wemfall, 3. Fall*) A declensional case form of nouns or pronouns and their modifiers, used as an object of verbs or prepositions. Often indicates the person towards whom the action is directed.

Dative of Interest (*Dativ des Interesses*) Indicates a person interested in or concerned with the action without being immediately involved in it (e.g. *Er öffnet mir die Tür*).

Dative of Person (*freier Dativ*) → dative of interest, dative of possession, dative of reference; modifier of person.

Dative of Possession (*Dativ des Zubehörs*) Indicates an object (usually part of the body) belonging to a person (e.g. *Die Sonne schien ihm ins Gesicht*).

Dative of Reference (*ethischer Dativ*) Indicates a person to whom the action has some kind of relevance (e.g. *Er arbeitet mir zu langsam. Das war dir ein Kerl!*).

Declarative Statement (*Aussage*) A form of linguistic utterance which describes a situation.

Declension (*Beugung der Nomen, Pronomen und Adjektive*) The inflectional endings of nouns, pronouns, and their attributes used to indicate number, gender, and case.

Defective Verb A verb which does not possess all tenses or conjugational forms.

Definite Article (*bestimmter Artikel*) An article used to indicate a specific noun or group of nouns. Occurs in masculine, neuter, and feminine gender, singular and plural, and all four cases.

Demonstrative Adverb (*hinweisendes Adverb*) An adverb of location (*hier, da, dort*) used to indicate or point to persons or objects. Usually combined with prepositions.

Demonstrative Attribute A limiting adjective such as *dieser* used to indicate or point to a certain person or thing.

Demonstrative Pronoun A pronoun pointing to a certain person or thing. Identical in form with demonstrative attribute.

Dependent Clause (*Nebensatz*) A clause which is subordinated to a main clause without which it does not constitute a full sentence. German differentiates between a clause which replaces a sentence unit (*Gliedsatz*) and one which modifies or replaces part of a sentence unit (*Attributsatz*).

Derivation (*Ableitung*) A modification of the form of a word in order to change it into a different part of speech or to change its meaning.

Descriptive Adjective (*beschreibendes Adjektiv*) An adjective describing a certain quality, feature, or characteristic of a noun or pronoun, in contrast to a limiting adjective.

Diphthong (*Doppellaut, Zwielaut*) A combination of two vowel sounds; in German *ai, ay, ei, ey; au; äu, eu; ui.* The combination *ie* is not a diphthong, except in words like *Familie*.

Direct Discourse (*direkte Rede*) A statement made to another person, reported verbatim and in quotation marks.

Direct Object The noun or pronoun which immediately receives the action. Usually, but not always, an accusative object. Also called primary object.

Directional Adverb (*Richtungsadverb*) Adverbs like *her* and *hin* (and their compounds) which indicate the direction of a motion.

Double Accusative Verbs capable of taking two accusative objects, usually one indicating a person, the other a thing or a concept (*jemanden etwas lehren*).

Double Infinitive The use of the infinitive of modals and a few other verbs together with the infinitive of the main verb in compound tenses.

Ellipsis The omission of certain elements within a statement which are considered to be understood, e.g. (*Ich wünsche Ihnen einen*) *Guten Morgen!*

Ethical Dative → dative of reference.

Event (*Geschehen*) An action or process described by a predicate. Opposite: State of Being.

Exclamation (*Ausruf*) A spontaneous utterance, intended to express a feeling.

Extended Attribute An adjective or, more frequently, a participle used adjectivally, which modifies a noun and is in turn modified by other sentence units.

Factitive Verb → causative verb.

Feminine (*weiblich*) A grammatical gender for nouns with the article *die*, replaced by the pronoun *sie*.

Final Clause (*Absichtssatz*) A dependent clause indicating purpose, aim, goal, or intention.

Finite Verb Form (*Personalform*) Conjugated form of the verb showing tense, person, number, and mood.

Fragmentary Sentence (*Satzfragment*) An incomplete sentence in which one or more essential elements are left out.

Free Morpheme A syllabic prefix which has meaning of its own and can exist by itself (separable prefix).

Front Limit of Sentence Field → anterior limit.

Future (*Zukunft*) A compound tense of verbs which indicates that the event described will happen at some later time. Formed with the present tense of *werden* and the infinitive of the main verb.

Future Perfect (*Vorzukunft, 2. Futur*) A compound tense of verbs which indicates that the event described will be completed by some later time. Formed with the present tense of *werden*, the past participle of the main verb, and the infinitive of *haben* or *sein*.

Gender (*Geschlecht*) A grammatical category of nouns and pronouns. German has three genders, masculine, feminine, and neuter, which do not necessarily coincide with natural gender (biological sex).

Genitive (*Wesfall, 2. Fall*) A declensional case form of nouns (or, less frequently, pronouns) and their modifiers, occurring as the object of a verb or preposition, and as predicate modifier. Sometimes (inaccurately) referred to as "possessive case."

Government (*Rektion*) The influence of one part of speech (verb, preposition) on the grammatical form of another (noun or pronoun). In English, the verb "to govern" is used more frequently than the noun.

Grammatical Interchange (*Grammatischer Wechsel*) A change in the consonantal structure of certain verbs in various persons and tenses (e.g. *ziehen, zog*).

Idiom A phrase or a single word used in a special meaning or form not necessarily identical with its usual lexical definition.

Imperative (*Befehlsform*) A verb form used to indicate a command or request directed to one or more persons.

Imperfect → past tense.

Impersonal Pronoun (*unpersönliches Fürwort*) The pronoun *es* used as the impersonal subject (*es regnet*), as the anticipator of the subject in the prefield (*es kamen viele Leute*), or anticipating a dependent clause (*Ich verstehe es nicht, warum er nicht kommt*).

Impersonal Verb A verb which can only have *es* or an indefinite pronoun as its subject.

Indefinite Adjective (*unbestimmtes Attribut*) An adjective denoting an undetermined number of persons or things (*einige, andere*, etc.).

661

Indefinite Article The numeral *ein* in its inflected forms used to indicate an undefined noun in the singular. Has no plural, except in its negative form (*kein*).

Indefinite Attribute → indefinite adjective.

Indefinite Pronoun A pronoun designating one or more undefined persons or things (*etwas, viele,* etc.).

Independent Clause (*Hauptsatz*) A clause capable of standing by itself as a complete sentence.

Indicative (*Wirklichkeitsform*) A verb form describing actual situations.

Indirect Discourse (*indirekte Rede*) The grammatical form of statements ascribed to another speaker, without use of quotation.

Indirect Object The person towards whom the action is directed. Often (inaccurately) equated with the dative object. Also called secondary object.

Infinitive (*Nennform, Grundform*) The form of a verb listed in the dictionary; used in the formation of future tenses, with modals, and in some other constructions. May occur by itself (simple infinitive) or with the preposition *zu* (prepositional infinitive).

Infinitive Clause (*Infinitivsatz*) An infinitive with modifying sentence units; always a dependent clause, has no subject of its own. Considered to be an infinitive phrase in English.

Infix An affix (letter or syllable) occurring in the middle of a word to change or modify its meaning or function.

Inflection (*Beugung*) A change in the form of a word to correspond to its function. Called conjugation for verbs, declension for nouns, pronouns, and adjectives.

Informational Question (*Ergänzungsfrage*) A question which inquires after some element in a situation. Begins with an interrogative adverb or pronoun in the prefield. Opposite: Alternative question.

Inseparable Prefix (*untrennbare Vorsilbe*) A verb prefix which has no independent meaning and can not exist by itself. Always attached to verb stem in all tenses and forms.

Instrumental Clause (*Umstandssatz des Mittels*) A dependent clause which indicates the means or method by which the situation in the main clause came to be.

Intensifier (*freies Modalglied*) Adverbs and conjunctions used to indicate subjective attitudes of the speaker towards the situation, and shades of meaning such as anger, impatience, surprise, etc. (*ja, doch, schon, wieder,* etc.). Also sometimes called particles.

Interest, Dative of → dative of interest.

Interjection (*Ausrufewort, Empfindungswort*) An exclamation used to indicate certain feelings or to bring about a certain action.

Interrogative (*Fragesatz*) A sentence form used to ask questions.

Interrogative Adverb An adverb used in informational questions to inquire after a certain circumstance in the sentence (*wann?, wie?, wo?,* etc.).

662

Interrogative Pronoun A pronoun used in informational questions to inquire after subject or object (*wer ?, was ?*, etc.).

Intransitive Verb (*nichtzielendes Verb*) A verb incapable of taking an accusative object.

Inversion (*Umkehrung*) The name given to the position of the subject following the verb, when the subject is not in the prefield. In actuality, however, the term is misleading, since this is not an inversion at all, but the most frequent (and therefore "normal") German word order.

Letter (*Buchstabe*) A unit of the alphabet.

Limits of Sentence Field (*Satzfeldgrenzen*) The parts of a multiple predicate. The anterior limit is replaced by a connecting link in dependent clauses. The posterior limit is missing for simple verbs in simple tenses.

Limiting Adjective (*begrenzendes Adjektiv*) An adjective which does not describe a noun, but defines or limits the category, such as numerical adjectives, articles, possessives, demonstratives, etc. Sometimes called pronominal adjective, since it can also function as a pronoun.

Linking Sound or Syllable (*Fugenlaut, -silbe*) A sound inserted between stem and affix or between parts of a compound to facilitate pronunciation.

Main Clause (*Hauptsatz*) A clause in a compound sentence capable of standing by itself; either combined with another main clause or with a dependent clause.

Main Verb (*Hauptverb*) The part of the predicate denoting the event or state of being which the sentence describes.

Masculine (*männlich*) The grammatical gender of nouns receiving the article *der* and replaced by the pronoun *er*.

Modal Verb A verb describing the circumstances of an action (compulsion, permission, ability) or the subjective attitude of the speaker (doubt, supposition, etc.). The modal verbs are *dürfen, können, mögen, müssen, sollen,* and *wollen*. Usually combined with the infinitive of another verb.

Modifier of Cause (*Kausalangabe*) A predicate modifier indicating the cause or reason for an event.

Modifier of Compound (*Bestimmungswort*) The first part of a compound word which serves to define the base or stem.

Modifier of Person (*Personenangabe*) A predicate modifier indicating a person concerned with the action but not participating in it. → Dative of interest, possession, or reference.

Modifier of Place (*Lokalangabe*) A predicate modifier indicating the location or the direction of an event or state of being.

Modifier of Time (*Zeitangabe*) A predicate modifier indicating the time at which the event takes place.

Mood (*Aussageweise*) The form of the verb which indicates the attitude of speaker towards the situation (indicative, subjunctive, imperative).

Morpheme The smallest unit of form capable of conveying meaning or function — stem, affix, or inflectional ending.

Morphemic Syllable (*Sprachsilbe*) A syllable based on separation of stem and affix, e.g. *Rechn-ung*. Opposite: phonetic syllable (*Sprechsilbe*), e.g. *Rech-nung*.

Multiple Infinitive (*mehrfacher Infinitiv*) The grouping together of several infinitives or substitute infinitives at the end of a clause.

Multiple Predicate A sentence core consisting of several verbs or verb forms.

Negation (*Verneinung*) The denying of an entire statement or any part of it.

Neuter (*sächlich*) A grammatical gender of nouns receiving the article *das* and replaced by the pronoun *es*.

Nominal Adjective An adjective used as a noun.

Nominative (*Werfall, 1. Fall*) A case form of nouns and pronouns used for the subject and as a predicate complement.

Nonfinite Verb Forms (*unpersönliche Verbalformen*) Parts of the verb incapable of conjugational changes (infinitive, participle, prefix). Sometimes called non-personal verb forms.

Noun (*Dingwort, Hauptwort, Nennwort, Nomen, Substantiv*) A part of speech designating people, places, things, or concepts. All other parts of speech may be used as nouns.

Number (*Numerus, Zahl*) A grammatical category distinguishing singular and plural.

Numerical Adjective (*Zahladjektiv*) A number used to modify a noun.

Object A sentence unit (noun, pronoun, or clause) indicating an agent participating in the situation, but not its subject. There are objects of verbs and of prepositions. They occur in the accusative, dative, or genitive. We distinguish between direct (primary) and indirect (secondary) objects.

Object Case (*Objektfall*) The case of a noun or pronoun (accusative, dative, genitive) when it functions as the object of a verb.

Object Clause (*Objektsatz*) A dependent clause functioning as an object.

Objective Statement (*Objektive Aussage*) A statement containing no expression of subjective attitude on the part of the speaker.

Onomatopoeia (*Lautmalerei*) An attempt to reproduce a natural sound by means of a word.

Ordinal Number (*Ordnungszahl*) A number indicating a position in a sequence (first, second, etc.).

Participial Clause (*Partizipialsatz*) A dependent clause without subject, consisting of a participle and its modifiers. Considered a phrase in English.

Participial Modifier → extended attribute.

Participle (*Mittelwort*) A nonfinite verb form which may be used as an adjective or adverb, or in the formation of compound verb forms. There are present and past participles.

Particle Sometimes used in German (*Partikel*) to describe all noninflected parts of speech, such as conjunctions, prepositions, etc. In English, usually refers to intensifiers (*freie Modalglieder*).

Partitive Genitive A genitive construction indicating a relationship of parts and whole within a group or quantity (*zwei meiner Freunde*).

Passive (*Leideform*) A grammatical device for expressing an action as a process, in which the subject is acted upon, rather than performing the action. Formed with the past participle of the main verb and a tense of *werden*. In passive sentences, the past participle of *werden* is *worden*.

Passive of Being (*Zustandspassiv*) → apparent passive.

Past Participle (*Partizip der Vergangenheit*) A participle indicating a completed action, used in the formation of perfect tenses and the passive voice, or as an adjective or adverb.

Past Perfect (*Plusquamperfektum, Vorvergangenheit, 3. Vergangenheit*) A compound tense form of verbs indicating that an event precedes another past event. Formed with the past participle of the main verb and the past tense of *haben* or *sein*. Also called pluperfect.

Past Tense (*Imperfektum, Präteritum, 1. Vergangenheit*) A simple tense form of verbs indicating that an event occurred prior to the present. Also called preterite, imperfect, or simple past.

Perfect A compound tense form of verbs indicating that an action refers to the past (present or past perfect) or to the future (future perfect).

Person A grammatical category indicating the speaker (1st person singular) or a group including the speaker (1st person plural); one or more people spoken to (2nd person); or one or more people, things, or concepts spoken of (3rd person).

Personal Pronoun (*persönliches Fürwort*) A pronoun designating a person, thing, or concept, and capable of replacing a noun with its modifiers. Always agrees with its antecedent in number and gender; its case depends on its use in the sentence.

Phoneme The smallest sound unit which may affect meaning.

Phonetic Syllable (*Sprechsilbe*) A syllable based on dividing a word into sound units (e.g. *Rech-nung*), as opposed to a morphemic syllable (*Sprachsilbe*, e.g. *Rechn-ung*).

Phrase (*Sinngruppe*) A part of speech with its modifiers which constitutes a complete sentence unit or an attribute.

Pluperfect → past perfect.

Plural (*Mehrzahl*) A grammatical category referring to two or more people, things, or concepts.

665

Positional Adverb → adverb of location.

Positive (*Grundform*) The basic stage of an adjective (or adverb) in its uncompared form.

Possession, Dative of → dative of possession.

Possessive Attribut (*besitzanzeigendes Attribut*) An adjective indicating ownership.

Possessive Pronoun A possessive attribute used pronominally. Unlike the attribute, which occurs without inflection in certain case forms, the possessive pronoun has a full range of primary endings.

Posterior Limit of Sentence Field (*Hintere Satzfeldgrenze*) The second part of a multiple predicate, consisting of nonfinite verb forms or complements. Its position is empty in the case of a simple predicate in a simple tense.

Postfield (*Nachfeld*) The part of the sentence following the second part of a multiple predicate. Frequently occupied by a dependent clause.

Postposition A preposition appearing after the noun or pronoun to which it refers and which it governs.

Predicate (*Satzaussage*) The verb or verbs defining the event or state of being which the sentence describes. The predicate forms the sentence core; its parts constitute the limits of the sentence field.

Predicate Accusative An accusative noun or pronoun in the predicate complement which is equated with the accusative object: *Er nennt mich seinen Freund.*

Predicate Complement (*Prädikatsergänzung*) A sentence unit which completes the concept of action if the verb itself is not sufficient to describe in its entirety.

Predicate Infinitive (*Objektsprädikat*) An infinitive used together with a direct object as a predicate complement of another verb, so that the accusative object of the finite verb is the subject of the infinitive action, e.g. *Ich sehe meinen Freund kommen: Ich sehe meinen Freund — Mein Freund kommt.*

Predicate Modifier (*Angabe*) A sentence unit describing a circumstance accompanying the situation (adverbial modifier) or a person interested in the action without participating in it (modifier of person). A predicate modifier may be omitted without rendering a sentence incomplete or unintelligible.

Predicate Nominative A noun or pronoun in the nominative acting as a predicate complement to a verb of being or becoming.

Predicate Object A noun or pronoun in the accusative which is not a direct object but a predicate complement, essential for the concept of verbal action (e.g. *Ich spreche Deutsch*).

Predicate Parts In a multiple predicate, the finite (conjugated) verb constitutes the first part; the nonfinite forms, i.e. the infinitive, past participle, separable prefix, predicate modifier, or any combination of these constitute the second part.

Predicate Subject A noun or pronoun in the nominative acting as a predicate complement to complete the concept of action together with the verb. It occupies the posterior limit of the sentence field.

666

Prefield (*Vorfeld*) The position before the anterior limit of the sentence field. May be occupied by the subject or by one other sentence unit acting as a contact unit.

Prefix (*Vorsilbe*) An affix occurring at the beginning of a word to change or modify its basic meaning or function.

Preposition (*Vorwort, Verhältniswort*) An uninflected part of speech showing various functional relationships. It determines the case of the noun or pronoun to which it refers. When it follows its referent, it is called a postposition.

Prepositional Case The case of a noun or pronoun when governed by a preposition rather than by its function in the sentence (i.e. objective case).

Prepositional Infinitive An infinitive preceded by *zu*.

Prepositional Modifier or **Phrase** A noun or pronoun preceded by a preposition which together act as an adverbial (circumstantial) modifier.

Present Participle (*Partizip der Gegenwart*) A participle indicating an action currently taking place. It may be used adjectivally as a noun attribute, as a complement of manner, or as a predicate modifier. Unlike English, it may not be used for progressive tense forms.

Present Perfect (*2. Vergangenheit, vollendete Gegenwart, Vorgegenwart*) A compound tense form of verbs indicating that an event took place in the past. Formed with the past participle of the main verb and the present tense of *haben* or *sein*.

Present Tense (*Gegenwart*) A tense form of verbs which indicates that the event described in the sentence takes place at the time the statement is made.

Preterite → past tense.

Primary Endings Inflectional endings on limiting and descriptive adjectives which correspond to pronominal endings in the respective case, number, and gender. Model: definite article or *dieser*. Often called "strong" endings.

Primary Object The noun or pronoun designating the person or thing which is the immediate recipient of the verbal action. Often called direct object.

Primary Stress (*Hauptbetonung*) The word or syllable which receives the strongest emphasis in a spoken utterance.

Process (*Vorgang*) A kind of event in the description of which the subject does not cause the event to happen. May occur in the active voice (*Das Wasser kocht*) or in the passive voice (*Der Brief wird geschrieben*).

Progressive Form A tense form of verbs using the auxiliary "to be" and the present participle of the main verb. Does not occur in German.

Pronominal Adjective → limiting adjective.

Pronominal Adverb An adverb or a combination of adverb and preposition which functions as a pronoun, i.e. replaces a specific noun or (more frequently) a concept.

Pronoun (*Fürwort*) A part of speech designating a person, place, thing, or concept, used to replace a noun with all its attributes.

Proper Name (*Eigenname*) A word designating a specific individual, place, etc.

667

Question (*Frage*) A request for information to be provided by another participant in the linguistic situation.

Quotation (*Zitat*) The citation of a statement made by some other person. There are direct and indirect quotations, using direct and indirect discourse, respectively.

Rank, Attitude of → attribute of rank.

Rear Limit of Sentence Field → posterior limit.

Reciprocal Pronoun A pronoun such as *einander*, indicating that the action mutually refers to two or more people.

Reference, Dative of → dative of reference.

Reflexive Pronoun (*rückbezügliches Fürwort*) A personal pronoun in the dative or accusative (3rd person *sich*) which indicates an identity between subject and object.

Reflexive Verb A verb of which the object is identical with the subject. Usually transitive, but occasionally with dative only (*Hilf dir selbst!*).

Relative Adverb An adverb which connects an attribute with the noun or pronoun to which it refers.

Relative Clause An attributive clause which modifies a noun or a pronoun and replaces a part of a sentence unit.

Relative Pronoun A pronoun which connects an attributive clause with the noun or pronoun to which it refers. Agrees with its antecedent in number and gender; the case depends on its use in its own clause.

Request (*Aufforderung*) → command.

Secondary Ending Ending on a descriptive adjective following a limiting adjective with a primary ending. Often called "weak" ending.

Secondary Object The person towards whom the action is directed. Often called indirect object and sometimes (but inaccurately) identified with the dative object.

Sentence (*Satz*) The smallest complete linguistic utterance for the expression of a statement, a question, a command, or an exclamation.

Sentence Core (*Satzkern*) The part of the sentence, exclusive of all modifiers, the content of which describes the event or state of being.

Sentence Field (*Satzfeld*) The part of the sentence enclosed (in the main clause) by the parts of the predicate, or (in the subordinate clause) by connecting link and predicate.

Sentence Unit (*Satzglied*) A word, phrase, or clause which constitutes a functional unit (subject, object, etc.) of the sentence.

Separable Prefix (*trennbare Vorsilbe*) A preposition or adverb which acts as a verb prefix in the infinitive and the past participle, but as a predicate complement in main clauses in simple tenses.

Simple Infinitive A single infinitive without the preposition *zu*.

Simple Past → past tense

Simple Predicate A predicate consisting of a single verb form.

Simple Tense (*einfache Zeitform*) A tense form which does not require any auxiliary verb, i.e. present and past indicative, subjunctive I and II, imperative.

Simple Verb A verb without prefix or complement.

Singular (*Einzahl*) A grammatical category referring to one person, thing, or concept.

Situation (*Sachverhalt*) The event or state of being expressed in the sentence.

Sound (*Laut*) The minimum phonetic unit of speech.

Split Predicate (*geteiltes Prädikat*) A predicate occurring partly at the beginning, partly at the end of the sentence field.

State of Being (*Sein*) A description of a condition or an unchanging situation, in contrast to an event (action or process).

Statement (*Mitteilung*) A form of linguistic expression describing a situation and providing information of a factual or assumed nature. May consist of one or more sentences.

Stem (*Stamm*) The basic form of a word when all affixes and inflectional endings are removed.

Stress (*Betonung*) The vocal emphasis given to a certain sound in a spoken utterance.

Strong Endings → primary endings.

Strong Verb (*starkes Verbum*) A verb which changes its vowel (and occasionally its consonantal stem) in the formation of past tenses and certain other conjugational forms.

Subject (*Satzgegenstand*) The sentence unit to which the verb refers, which agrees formally with the finite part of the predicate, and which indicates the originator of an action.

Subject Clause (*Subjektsatz*) A dependent clause which replaces the subject.

Subject Nominative The basic form of a noun or pronoun in which it occurs as the subject of a sentence or clause.

Subjective Statement (*subjektive Aussage*) A sentence which expresses the subjective attitude of the speaker towards the facts contained in his utterance. May use modals, subjunctive, or future tense.

Subjunctive (*Konjunktiv, Möglichkeitsform*) A verb form which expresses a subjective attitude of doubt, potentiality, or nonreality. Used primarily in wishes or conditions contrary to fact, and in indirect discourse. Subjunctive I is derived from the present tense, subjunctive II from the past tense of verbs. This does not, however, constitute a difference with regard to time.

Subordinate Clause (*Nebensatz*) → dependent clause.

Subordinating Conjunction (*unterordnende Konjunktion*) An uninflected part of speech introducing a dependent clause and indicating the relationship between that clause and the main clause of the sentence.

Substantive → noun.

Substitute Infinitive (*Ersatzinfinitiv*) The use of the infinitive for the past participle in perfect tenses of modals and a few other verbs.

Suffix (*Nachsilbe*) An affix occurring at the end of a word, changing or modifying its meaning or function.

Superlative (*Höchststufe, Meiststufe, 2. Steigerung*) A comparative form of adjectives and adverbs expressing the highest possible degree of the quality indicated.

Syllabication (*Silbentrennung*) The division of a word into syllables.

Syllable (*Silbe*) A group of sounds constituting a constituent part of a word. The number of syllables is usually determined by the number of vowel sounds.

Tense (*Tempus, Zeit*) The grammatical form of a verb used to indicate the relationship of the event or state of being to categories of time, such as present, past, and future.

Transitive Verb (*zielendes Verb*) A verb capable of taking an accusative object.

Umlaut A change of the vowels *a* (*au*), *o*, and *u* to *ä* (*äu*), *ö*, and *ü*. Occurs in the formation of noun plurals, comparative and superlative forms or adjectives, and certain conjugational forms of verbs.

Unit (*Satzglied*) → sentence unit.

Unit Clause (*Gliedsatz*) A dependent clause replacing a sentence unit.

Unit Core (*Gliedkern*) The central part of a sentence unit which carries its basic meaning, when all attributes have been removed.

Utterance (*Rede*) The linguistic form in which a concept is expressed. May consist of one or more sentences in a common context.

Verb (*Tätigkeitswort, Zeitwort*) A part of speech describing a state of being or an event (action or process). Conjugated according to person, number, tense, and mood. Performs the function of the predicate, and can also indicate subjective attitude of the speaker towards reality.

Verb Complement (*Verbzusatz*) A part of speech used as a separable verb prefix or functioning as the completion of the predicate concept.

Verner's Law A description of the principles underlying the phenomenon of grammatical interchange.

Voice (*Verhaltensrichtung*) The grammatical form by means of which the predicate indicates whether the subject performs the action (active) or is acted upon (passive).

Vowel (*Selbstlaut, Vokal*) A sound produced without obstruction of the vocal passages. In German *a, e, i* (*ie*)*, o, u, y; ä, ö, ü.* Diphthongs are also vowel sounds.

Weak Endings → secondary endings.

Weak Verb (*schwaches Verb*) A verb which does not change its stem vowel in the formation of past tenses, but instead adds an ending.

Word (*Wort*) The smallest linguistic unit which expresses independent meaning.

Word Stem → stem.

PART TWO: German

abhängige Rede indirect discourse
Ablaut vowel gradation
Ableitung derivation
Anführungszeichen quotation mark
Angabe (predicate) modifier
Anlaut initial sound
Art und Weise manner
Aufforderung request
Auslaut final sound
Ausruf exclamation
Ausrufewort interjection
Ausrufezeichen exclamation point
Aussage declarative statement
Aussageeinleitung contact unit
Aussageweise mood

Bedingung condition
Befehl command
Befehlsform imperative
begrenzend limiting
Beifügung attribute
beiordnend coordinating
Beistrich comma
Beiwort adjective
beschreibend descriptive
Besitz possession

bestimmter Artikel definite article
Bestimmungswort modifier
Betonung stress
Beugung inflection; declension (nouns, pronouns, adj.); conjugation (verbs)
bezüglich relative
Bindestrich hyphen
Bindewort conjunction
Bruchzahl fraction
Buchstabe letter of the alphabet

Dingwort noun
Doppel- double
Doppellaut diphthong
Doppelpunkt colon

Eigenname proper name
Eigenschaftswort adjective
einfach simple
Einzahl singular
Empfindungswort interjection
Entscheidungsfrage alternative question
Ergänzung complement
Ergänzungsfrage informational question
Ersatzinfinitiv substitute infinitive
ethischer Dativ dative of reference

671

Fall case
  1. **Fall** nominative
  2. **Fall** genitive
  3. **Fall** dative
  4. **Fall** accusative
Flexion inflection
Frage question, interrogative
Fragezeichen question mark
freie Angabe circumstantial modifier
freier Dativ dative of person
freies Modalglied intensifier
Fugenlaut linking sound
Fürwort pronoun

Gedankenstrich hyphen
Gegenstand subject (sometimes object)
Gegenwart present tense
Geschehen event
Geschlecht gender
Geschlechtswort article
geteilt divided, split
gleichordnend coordinating
Glied unit
Gliedkern unit core
Gliedsatz dependent clause, unit clause
grammatischer Wechsel grammatical interchange (Verner's Law)
Grund cause
Grundform infinitive (verb)
Grundstufe positive (adj. or adv.)
Grundwort base
Grundzahl cardinal number

Handlung action
Haupt- main, primary
Hauptsatz main clause, independent clause
Hauptwort noun
Hilfsverb auxiliary verb
hinweisend demonstrative
Höchststufe superlative

Inlaut medial sound

Kongruenz agreement
Konjunktiv subjunctive

Laut sound
Lautmalerei onomatopoeia
Leideform passive
Lokaladverb adverb of place

männlich masculine
mehrfach multiple
Mehrstufe comparative
Mehrzahl plural
Meiststufe superlative
Mitlaut consonant
Mitteilung statement
Mittel means
Mittelwort participle
Modaladverb adverb of manner
Möglichkeitsform subjunctive

Nachfeld postfield
Nachsilbe suffix
nebenordnend coordinating
Nebensatz dependent clause
Nennform infinitive
Nennwort noun
nichtzielend intransitive
Nomen noun
Numerus number

Objektsprädikat predicate infinitive
Ordnungszahl ordinal number
Ort place

Personalform conjugated (finite) verb form
Personenangabe modifier of person
Plusquamperfektum past perfect
Punkt period

Rank rang
Rede discourse, utterance
Reibelaut fricative
Rektion government
Richtung direction
Rolle agent
rückbezüglich reflexive

672

sächlich neuter
Sachverhalt situation
Sammelwort collective noun
Satz sentence, clause
Satzaussage predicate
Satzfeld(grenze) (limit of) sentence field
Satzgegenstand subject
Satzglied sentence unit
Satzkern sentence core
Satzzeichen punctuation mark
Sein state of being
Selbstlaut vowel
Silbe syllable
Silbentrennung syllabication
Sinngruppe phrase
Sprachsilbe morphemic syllable
Sprechsilbe phonetic syllable
Stamm stem
Steigerung comparison
   1. Steigerung comparative
   2. Steigerung superlative
Stellung position
stimmhaft voiced
stimmlos voiceless
Strichpunkt semicolon
Substantiv noun

tätige Form active voice
Tätigkeitswort verb
Tempus tense
trennbar separable

Umkehrung inversion
Umlaut vowel variation
Umstandsangabe circumstantial (adverbial) modifier
Umstandssatz adverbial clause
Umstandswort adverb
unbestimmt indefinite
unpersönlich impersonal, nonpersonal
unterordnend subordinating
untrennbar inseparable

Verbindungsteil connecting link

Vergangenheit past tense
   1. Vergangenheit past tense
   2. Vergangenheit present perfect
   3. Vergangenheit past perfect
Vergleich comparison
Verhaltensrichtung voice
Verhältniswort preposition
Verneinung negation
Verschlußlaut stop
Vokal vowel
vollendete Gegenwart present perfect
Vorfeld prefield
Vorgang process
Vorgegenwart present perfect
Vorsilbe prefix
Vorvergangenheit past perfect
Vorwegnahme anticipation
Vorwort preposition
Vorzukunft future perfect

weiblich feminine
Weise manner
Wemfall dative
Wenfall accusative
Werfall nominative
Wesfall genitive
Wirklichkeitsform indicative
Wortart part of speech

Zahl number
Zeichensetzung punctuation
Zeit time, tense
Zeitwort verb
zielend transitive
Zitat quotation
Zubehör possession
Zukunft future
   1. Zukunft future
   2. Zukunft future perfect
Zusammensetzung compound
Zusammenziehung contraction
Zustandspassiv apparent passive, passive of being
Zwielaut diphthong

INDEX

The following index not only contains all grammatical concepts and categories treated in this book, but also all German words, syllables, and sounds dealt with or listed as examples for a point of grammar. It does not include words which occur only in illustrative sentences, nor does it include the introduction. All references are to chapter and paragraph; **bold-faced** entries indicate more extensive treatment.

A

a- A 284, A 336.2
-a C 160
ab D 361, F 010–1, **F 105–6**
  von . . . ab F 683, F 687
ab- B 310, B 335
Abbreviations A 090.4, C 060, H 155, H 710, J 083
abbrechen B 462
-abel A 195
aber G 001, G 003, G 009, **G 030–8**
  intensifier **H 610**
  aber doch G 033, G 037
aber- A 284, **A 300**
sich abgeben mit B 940
der Abgeordnete E 515
abgesehen davon, daß G 160, G 186
abhalten B 980
abhängen von B 940
ablassen von B 941
Ablaut Series B 221, **B 280–7**
absagen H 351
abscheulich A 090.1
absehen auf B 940

abseits F 040, F 110
in der Absicht G 158
Absolute Accusative D 926
Absolute Comparative E 380 ff.
abspenstig machen E 250, J 035
abzielen auf B 940
Accusative C 202, D 903–8, **D 915–29**
  adverbial D 923, H 568.5
  as predicate complement H 413
  with dative D 932
  with reflexive verbs D 140
  prepositions with acc. D 927, F 010 ff.
  prepositions with dative or accus. D 928, F 030 ff.
  See also accusative object, predicate accusative
Accusative Object H 215, H 302, H 325, J 012, J 015
  position H 711 ff.
  infinitive clause H 312
  object clause H 320
  with complement of manner H 446–51
  with complement of time H 430
ach G 810
sich in acht nehmen B 982

675

achten auf F 061
Achtung F 065
Action B 010, B 590 ff., H 005–6
Active Voice B 502, B 590
→ Passive, B 480–96, B 590–628
ad- A 285
Address, Form of A 111.4, **D 020–025**, D 357
→ *du, ihr, Sie*
Adjective **E 001–796**
  attributive E 100 ff., J 110.6, J 115.1, J 121–3, J 210, J 220
  capitalization E 220
  comparative E 300 ff.
  formation E 251, E 260–8
  indefinite adj. D 780–897, **E 150–55**
  participle as adj. B 801 ff., B 829, H 417–8, J 110.7
  nominal adj. C 176–7, D 740, D 742, E 160, **E 500–30**, E 690–95, H 259.1, J 151.3
  numerical adj. **E 600–796**
  predicate adj. E 250
  as sentence unit J 030
  in compounds A 205, A 240
  in predicate accusative H 471.2
  in predicate complement E 420, H 411
  in predicate nominative E 010, E 422, H 461.2
  in sequence **E 140–4**
  uninflected E 012–3, E 050, E 220, E 230, E 240, E 250, E 405, E 420, J 115.1, J 123
  with accus. object D 924.3, E 440–50
  with dat. obj. D 938, E 440–50
  with gen. obj. D 960, D 971, E 440–50
  with prepositional obj. E 440–50, F 070
Adverb **E 800–911**
  comparison E 820 ff.
  formation E 807–9
  forms E 805–9
  position E 800
  types of adverbs E 830–45
  adv. of cause E 845
  adv. of manner E 840 ff.
  adv. of negation H 650, H 760, J 260
  adv. of place E 830 ff.; with relative adverb E 860–2; as adjective E 268, E 810; as noun attribute J 133; as pronoun attribute J 151.4
  adv. of time E 835–7; as adject. E 260–1; with verbs B 512–3, B 542; with *her* and *hin* E 884–5
  → directional adverb E 880 ff.
  → interrogative adverb D 230–36, E 870 ff.
  relative adv. D 527–8, D 555, D 565–6

use E 810 ff.
  as attribute J 115.2, J 133, J 151.4, J 162, J 170, J 210, J 215, J 220, J 230, J 240, J 250
  as attribute of rank J 180 ff.
  as circumstantial modifier H 565 ff.
  as conjunction E 850–1
  as intensifier (particle) **H 600 ff.**
  as modifier in compounds A 205, A 240
  as modifier of rank J 180 ff.
  as noun H 259.5
  as predicate complement H 410
  as sentence unit J 040
  as stem word in compounds A 206
  as substitute for noun J 026
  with attributes J 170–1, J 240
  with prepositional infinitive B 987
Adverbial Accusative D 923, H 568.5
Adverbial Case D 904
  accusative D 923, H 568.5
  genitive D 369, D 965, H 568.6
Adverbial Clause H 568.8
Adverbial Genitive D 965, H 568.6
Adverbial Modifier B 965 ff., H 230 ff., H 565 ff., H 740 ff.
-after **A 300**
-age A 192, C 040.6, C 134
Agent H 003.2, H 202–3
  in passive voice B 595, B 600.2, B 612
  no agent H 268
  object H 300
  subject H 210
Agreement subject/predicate B 012, **H 275** ff., H 280 ff.
ah, aha G 810
ähneln D 934, H 351
Ahnen C 186
ähnlich D 938, E 150, E 440
Ahorn C 040.4
Airplanes, names of C 040.3
-al A 195, C 160
Album A 193
all, all- D 721, D 733, D 746, **D 780–95**
  with adj. D 740, D 788, E 121, E 530
  with attributes J 217
  personal pronouns with *all* D 061
  all das D 432
  bei all F 197
alledem D 432
allein
  pronunciation A 090.1
  as adj. E 250, J 035
  as attribute of rank J 181
  as conjunction G 008, G 023, **G 040**
  as intensifier J 190
aller- E 387
allerdings G 011, G 023

677

B

679

Posaune A 090.1
Positional Adverbs **E 895–9**
Positive (adj.) E 300
Posse, -n C 078
Possession, Dative of → dative
   Genitive of D 970.1, J 125.1
Possessive Attribute D 071–4, **D 600–65**,
   J 110.3, J 210, J 215–18
   capitalized D 024, D 608, D 650
   relationship with antecedent D 608,
   D 610–11, D 645
   replaced by dative D 660, D 941–2
   replaced by definite article D 333, D 665
   replaced by *dessen, deren* D 435, D 522,
   D 645
Possessive Pronoun D 604, D 620–5,
   D 630–1, D 640
Posterior Limit → sentence field
Postfield H 050, **H 070–8**, H 272, H 393
Postpositions D 929, D 946, D 976, F 005,
   F 013–15, F 021, F 024, F 043–7
   → individual entries F 100 ff.
prahlen B 941
pre- A 285
Precipitation C 020.4, D 080
Predicate H 005, H 020 ff., **H 100–65**
   agreement with subject H 275–97
   as sentence unit J 003
   form H 112–13
   in dependent clause **H 040**, H 126 ff.
   position H 120–65
   simple predicate H 023, H 125
   split predicate H 020–036
   with dependent infin. H 130 ff.
Predicate Accusative **H 470–2**
   adj. as H 446, H 471.2, J 030
   dependent clause as H 471.4
   infin. as B 960, H 471.3, J 062
   noun as H 471.1
   position H 732
Predicate Complement H 005, H 126,
   H 128, H 220–3, **H 400–98**
   adj. as E 420, H 411, J 032, J 035
   adverb as H 410, J 040–5
   dependent clause as H 419, J 071, J 077
   infin. as H 416, J 063
   noun as D 911–12, H 412–14, J 018
   participle as B 807–8, H 417–18, J 050
   prepos. phrase as D 361, H 415, J 018
   pronoun as J 022–7
   position **H 725–37**, H 758
   → complement of cause, manner, place,
   time; predicate accus., nom., object,
   subject
Predicate Infinitive **B 970–82**, **H 330–5**,
   H 360–1
   with accus. object H 491

Predicate Modifier H 230 ff., H 396,
   H 550–653
   position **H 740–65**
   adj. as J 030–5
   adverbs as E 830–45, J 040
   dependent clause as J 077
   genitive as D 965
   infin. as B 965 ff., J 063
   particles (intensifiers) as H 600 ff.
   past participle as H 568.4
   prep. phrase as D 361
   pres. participle as B 801.3, B 841,
   H 568.3
   modifier of cause B 841, E 845, H 590 ff.,
   H 741
   modifier of manner B 801.3, B 841,
   D 965.3, E 840, H 340–43, H 565-6,
   H 580 ff., J 032 ff.
   modifier of person H 556–61
   modifier of place E 830, H 571
   modifier of time E 835, H 575 ff.
Predicate Nominative D 911–13, H 222,
   H 460–6, H 490
   adj. as E 420, E 422, H 461.2, J 030
   dependent clause as H 461.8–.9, J 076
   infin. as B 960, H 461.5–.7, J 062
   possessive pronoun as D 640, H 461.4
   position H 731
   as part of predicate H 034
Predicate Object **H 480–1**, H 491
   position H 736
Predicate Parts
   definition H 020 ff.
   position H 120 ff.
   → predicate
Predicate Subject **H 475–8**, H 490
   position H 734
Prefield H 050, **H 051–62**, **H 705–8**
   dependent clause in prefield H 075
   es in prefield H 053 ff.
   second predicate part in prefield H 123–5
   sentences w/o prefield H 025
Prefix A 081, A 085, **A 280–350**
   for verbs B 300–45
   → inseparable, separable prefix
preisgekrönt B 362
Preposition **F 001–901**
   as modifiers in compounds A 205, A 240
   as nouns C 030.5, H 259.6
   as stems A 206
   as verb prefixes A 253, A 255, A 260,
   B 300 ff., H 113.7, H 120 ff. (position)
   contractions with article D 307, D 335–40
   da(r)- plus preposition D 040–50, E 900–
   911
   governing accus. D 927, D 929, F 010 ff.
   governing dative D 945–6, F 020 ff.

700

702